Modern Internal Auditing

MODERN INTERNAL AUDITING

Appraising Operations and Controls

VICTOR Z. BRINK
Graduate School of Business
Columbia University

HERBERT WITT
Office of Inspector General
Department of Health
and Human Services

Fourth Edition

175 YEARS OF PUBLISHING

1807 1982

A Ronald Press Publication
JOHN WILEY & SONS
New York   Chichester   Brisbane   Toronto   Singapore

Copyright © 1982 by John Wiley & Sons, Inc.

All rights reserved. Published simultaneously in Canada.

Reproduction or translation of any part of this work
beyond that permitted by Section 107 or 108 of the
1976 United States Copyright Act without the permission
of the copyright owner is unlawful. Requests for
permission or further information should be addressed to
the Permissions Department, John Wiley & Sons, Inc.

Library of Congress Cataloging in Publication Data:

Brink, Victor Zinn, 1906-
   Modern internal auditing.

   Includes index.
   1. Auditing, Internal.   I. Witt, Herbert.
II. Title.

HF5668.25.B74   1982   657'.458   82-571
ISBN 0-471-08097-7   AACR2

Printed in the United States of America

10   9   8

To Brad Cadmus
for pioneer professional leadership
and to our wives,
Dorothy and Hiala,
for loyal support

Preface

Since 1973, when the third edition of *Modern Internal Auditing* was released, the role of the internal auditor in all organizations has continued to expand. This has been due in part to the acceleration of social expectations for higher standards of professional conduct and for greater protection against inefficiency, misconduct, illegality, and fraud. One response to the greater needs for protection was the Foreign Corrupt Practices Act of 1977 and the related implementation of that act by the Securities and Exchange Commission. There has also been a more realistic recognition of the fact that the internal auditor can contribute importantly to satisfying the expanded protective needs.

At the same time there is the continuing truth that organizations must be productive and achieve the best possible utilization of their resources. The welfare of society is directly dependent on that productivity. Moreover, unless organizations are productive, they cannot survive and be the focus for protective concerns. There is also greater recognition that internal auditors can make major contributions in helping organizations achieve the needed productivity.

Together, therefore, these basic needs for protection and productivity define the dual role of the modern internal auditor. Being exposed as he[1] is to the day-to-day operations of the organization, the internal auditor is uniquely able to service the total needs on an integrated basis.

It follows, therefore, that this fourth edition of *Modern Internal Auditing* retains the previously established operational approach as its primary thrust, but has been further focused on effective protective controls. There is a combined concern for the broader system of internal control, which covers both productivity and the narrower portions of that control, which deal with internal accounting controls.

Although the book is couched for the most part in terms of the business organization, this is only for convenience. In truth, all organizations—business, governmental, or other—have protection and productivity needs that provide the common basis for the needed services of the internal auditor. It follows,

---

[1]The use of the personal pronouns he or him—here and throughout this book—is for convenience only. Excellence in internal auditing is not limited by sex, color, race, or nationality.

therefore, that all portions of the book have general application for all types of organizations.

This edition includes coverage of a number of new developments of special contemporary significance, of which the following are especially noteworthy:

The interpretation of the new "Standards for the Professional Practice of Internal Auditing" released by The Institute of Internal Auditors in 1978.

More emphasis on the expanded protective needs relating to the system of internal accounting control stemming from the Foreign Corrupt Practices Act of 1977.

Expanded coverage of the internal auditor's relations with people.

Expanded coverage of social responsibilities and new coverage of business ethics.

A new chapter on internal auditing for governmental and other nonprofit organizations.

A new chapter on fraud and investigative audits.

New material about serving the audit committee of the board of directors.

Expanded coverage of maintenance activities.

We have, however, eliminated the three chapters dealing with the review of financial statements. There is an increasingly large number of standard auditing books available which provide the needed coverage of that area of auditing practice—an area where the internal auditor usually has less direct responsibilities.

We continue to follow the approach of emphasizing principles and concepts that can provide a sound basis for the actual practice that must unavoidably be tailored to individual audit situations. In that sense the book is a useful *guide* and not a finalized audit program. Such actual audit programs must necessarily be developed to cover the specific needs of the individual audit assignment.

The book is addressed primarily to practicing internal auditors in all levels of organizations. It should, however, be of major value to a number of other major groups. One group is the external auditors, who are concerned with many of the same problems as the internal auditors, and who must also work closely with them. For similar reasons the book should be useful to financial executives, management personnel, audit committees, legislators, and others who are concerned about internal auditing. We also believe that the book is directly usable by educators at all college levels for the increasingly needed courses in internal auditing.

In developing this edition we are again indebted to a host of practitioners, educators, writers, and others who have both provided comments and suggestions and leadership in all areas. The increasing interest in internal auditing has substantially expanded the range and substance of such contributions. As always, we continue to learn from our experience and through our relationships with each other.

Finally, we reaffirm our faith in the expanding service role of the internal auditor, and our personal satisfaction in participating in the effort to broaden and improve the quality of that service to organizations and to society in general for a span of over four decades.

VICTOR Z. BRINK
HERBERT WITT

New York, New York
Mill Valley, California
March 1982

Contents

Part Four Special Relationships and Evaluation

Appendices

Index

Modern Internal Auditing

PART ONE

Foundations for Internal Auditing

CHAPTER ONE

The Nature of
Internal Auditing

WHAT IS INTERNAL AUDITING?

There is no better way to begin this book about modern internal auditing than to turn to The Institute of Internal Auditors, the professional association of internal auditors. In the Standards for the Professional Practice of Internal Auditing, released in May 1978, there is the following definition:

> Internal auditing is an independent appraisal function established within an organization to examine and evaluate its activities as a service to the organization.

We can, perhaps, make this statement more meaningful by focusing more directly on the key terms that have been used. The term "auditing" itself suggests a variety of ideas. On the one hand, it can be viewed very narrowly as the checking of arithmetic accuracy or existence of assets, and on the other as thoughtful review and appraisal at the highest organizational level. In this book we use the term to include the total range of levels of service.

The term "internal" is to make clear that this is auditing work carried on by the organization and by its own employees. In this way the auditing work here is distinguished from such auditing work as may be carried on by outside public accountants or any other parties not directly a part of the particular organization.

The remainder of the statement covers a number of important key dimensions of the internal auditing work, as follows:

1. The term "independent" characterizes the audit work as being free of restrictions that could significantly limit the scope and effectiveness of the review or the later reporting of findings and conclusions.
2. The term "appraisal" confirms the evaluation thrust of internal auditors as they develop their conclusions.
3. The term "established" confirms the fact of definitive creation by the organization of the internal auditing role.
4. The terms "examine and evaluate" describe the action role of internal auditors first as fact-finding inquiry, and second, as judgmental evaluation.

3

5. The words "its activities" confirm the broad jurisdictional scope of the internal auditing work as applying to all of the activities of the organization.

6. The term "service" identifies help and assistance as the end product of all internal auditing.

7. The term "to the organization" confirms the total service scope as pertaining to the entire organization—which includes all corporate personnel, boards of directors (including their audit committees), and stockholders.

Focus on Control

A better understanding of internal auditing can be obtained by recognizing that it is a kind of organizational control which functions by measuring and evaluating the effectiveness of other controls. When an organization establishes its planning at all levels and then proceeds to implement those plans in terms of operations, it must do something to monitor the operations to assure the achievement of established objectives. These further efforts can be thought of as "controls." The internal auditing function is itself one of the types of control used. However, there is a wide range of other controls, and it is the special role of the internal auditing work to help measure and evaluate those other controls. Thus internal auditors must understand both their own role as a control and the nature and scope of other types of controls.

All this means that internal auditors who do their job effectively become experts in what makes for the best possible design and implementation of all types of control. This expertise includes understanding the interrelationships of the various controls and their best possible integration in various ways in the total system of internal control. It is thus through the "control" door that internal auditors come to "examine and evaluate" all organizational activities and to provide maximum service to the organization. Internal auditors cannot be expected to equal—let alone exceed—the technical and operational expertise pertaining to the various activities of the organization. But internal auditors *can* help the responsible individuals achieve more effective results by appraising existing controls and providing a basis for helping to improve those controls.

Historical Background of Internal Auditing

It is normal for any activity—including a control activity such as internal auditing—to come into being as a result of emerging needs. We can also understand better the nature of the activity which currently exists if we know something about the changing conditions in the past which created the needs for that activity. What is the simplest form of internal auditing and how does it come into existence? How has internal auditing responded to changing needs?

In strict theory the internal auditing function can exist when any single person sits back and surveys something that he has done. At that point the individual asks himself how well he has done the particular thing and, perhaps, how he might do it better if he were to do it again. When a second person is involved, the function is expanded to include the review of the second person's activities. In a small business, the owner or manager will be doing this to some extent with all of his employees. In all of these situations the internal auditing function is being carried out directly as a part of the basic management role.

However, as the operations of the business become more voluminous and complex, it is no longer practicable for the owner or top manager to have enough contact with the various operations so that he can review satisfactorily the effectiveness of performance. Although he can build a supervisory system and try to keep an overview through that supervisory system, it becomes increasingly difficult for him to know whether the interests of the business are being properly serviced. Are established procedures being complied with? Are assets being properly safeguarded? Are the various employees functioning efficiently? Are the current approaches still effective in the light of changing conditions? The ultimate response to these needs is that he must have further help. This help is provided by assigning one or more individuals to be directly responsible for reviewing activities and reporting on the above-mentioned types of questions. It is here that the internal auditing activity comes into being in a formal and explicit sense.

The first internal auditing assignments usually originated to satisfy very basic and sharply defined operational needs. The earliest special concern of management was whether the assets of the organization were being properly protected, whether company procedures and policies were being complied with, and whether the financial records were being accurately maintained. There was also considerable emphasis on fraud detection and maintenance of the status quo. To a great extent also the internal auditing was viewed as a closely related extension of the work of the external auditor. The result of all of these factors was that the internal auditor was viewed as playing a relatively narrow role. At the same time the internal auditor himself was viewed as a person of relatively limited responsibility in the total managerial spectrum. He was the financially oriented checker and more of a policeman than a co-worker. Understanding this situation is important because it is an image which to some extent still exists for modern internal auditors, even when the character of the internal auditing function is now actually very much different.

Over a period of time, however, this situation has changed a great deal. The operations of the various organizations were increasing steadily in volume and complexity. The managerial problems thus created have resulted in new pressure on higher-level management. The managerial executive has therefore sought new ways of responding to these pressures. It was quite natural, then, that management would recognize the possibilities of better utilization of the services of the internal auditor. Here were individuals moving through the organization—in various departments and in various geographical areas—and there seemed to be every good reason for getting greater value from these individuals with relatively little increase in cost. At the same time, the internal auditors themselves were perceiving the existing opportunities and were more and more initiating new types of service. Thus internal auditors took on a broader and more management-oriented character. Because the earlier internal auditing was very much accounting oriented, this upward trend was felt first in the accounting and financial control areas. Subsequently, however, it was extended to also include the nonfinancial areas.

The Situation Today

Internal auditing today, like any other evolving function, reflects a broad spectrum of types of operational activity and levels of coverage. In many organizations internal auditing—as a formal staff activity—is quite new and its more permanent role is still being defined. In other situations—for various reasons—the internal auditing is still functioning to a major extent at the more routine compliance level. In some other situations it still suffers from being integrated with regular accounting or other operating activities. In certain situations the internal auditing is carried out entirely or substantially only in the strictly financial areas. In other situations the focus has shifted to a varying extent to the more general nonfinancial operational areas. In most situations the internal auditing group has moved to very high levels in all operational areas and has established itself as a valued and respected part of the top management effort. To an increasing extent also the internal auditor is serving the board of directors—usually via the audit committee of that board. The overall situation, however, reflects major progress in the scope of coverage and the level of service in the individual areas. The internal auditing profession itself, through its own self development and dedication, has contributed to this progress and has set the stage for a continuing upward trend.

Composite Nature of Operational and Financial Auditing

In recent years there has been a strong tendency on the part of many internal auditors to adopt the label of "operational auditing" in place of the traditional "internal auditing." The rationale appears to be that "internal auditing" as a term is tied too closely with the more basic financial auditing—including both basic financial control activities and the review of financial statements. There is a desire to focus more on the other operational activities that provide the greater opportunities for increased profit and overall management service. In its most extreme form the so-called operational auditor would like to disassociate himself entirely from the so-called financial areas. However, such a separation involves matters of both substance and self-interest for the internal auditor.

Traditionally, the internal auditor has been concerned with accounting and financial matters, and some expertise in these areas has generally been considered to be essential. The coverage of these matters has also served to provide the opportunity of expanding the range of service into the broader operational areas. Since the accounting record directly or indirectly reflects *all* operational activities, the financial review has served to open the door to the other activities.

This type of extension has been most advantageous and there are major doubts as to whether this advantage should be abandoned. There would seem to be no good reason why the level of the operational outreach should be limited because of the route taken.

Finally, in terms of strategy, the abandonment of the accounting–financial areas could well be to create a vacuum that would invite the emergence of other competitive groups. The organization certainly needs to have someone covering the accounting and financial areas, and whoever does that will inevitably spill over into the broader operational areas. Therefore, the internal auditor needs to cover the accounting and financial areas in his own long-run self-interest. It is recognized that there are some internal auditors who feel that a continuing connection with financial auditing hinders the effort to exhibit adequately the potentials of operational auditing. Still other internal auditors favor having the internal auditor do work in both areas but to deal with them separately. On balance it is reasonable to conclude that there is an important linkage between the so-called financial and nonfinancial areas and that it is desirable to recognize and to take advantage of that linkage. At the same time there is no reason why all of the internal auditing efforts cannot be shaped, with various types of emphasis, to serve organizational needs in the total operational area in the most effective manner possible. It is believed, therefore, that both modern operational auditing and financial auditing can find full expression within the framework of modern internal auditing. In a very real sense there no longer is operational and/or financial auditing but only good modern internal auditing.[1]

Increasing Recognition of Internal Auditing

Over recent years there has been a continuing expansion of business and non-business activities. This in itself would have caused a continuing increase in the need for the services of internal auditors. But in addition there have been some new environmental forces that have created still further needs. These environmental forces are a part of the generally accelerated rate of social expectations in such areas as protection of natural resources, pollution, minority groups, higher levels of business responsibility, and moral standards. In the latter area we can include higher standards for corporate management, greater involvement of boards of directors (including the greater use of audit committees), a more active role for stockholders, and greater independence of the outside public accountant. On the legislative side one specific development in the United States has been the Foreign Corrupt Practices Act of 1977 and the supportive regulation on the part of the Securities and Exchange Commission. A second important legislative development has been the Inspector General Act. As a result of these new pressures, the services of the internal auditor have become more important to all parties of interest. This has been reflected

[1]This integration of financial and operational auditing is more fully discussed in Chapter 6.

in more and better qualified internal auditing personnel and higher-level organization status. During this period The Institute of Internal Auditors has
grown from its charter chapter in 1941 with 25 members to an international
association of about 25,000 members and 150 chapters. At the same time a new
and impressive literature has also been developed. It can well be said that the
internal auditing profession has reached major maturity and is well positioned
for continuing dynamic growth.

FUNCTIONAL ROLE OF INTERNAL AUDITING

Relationship of Internal Auditing to Other Company Activities

An essential basis for understanding the nature of internal auditing is to examine
the relationship between internal auditing and other company activities. In the
first place the work of the internal auditor needs to be detached from the
regular day-to-day operations of the company. A good practical test is that if
the internal auditing activity—partially or completely—was temporarily inac-
tive, the regular company operations would go on for the time being in the
normal manner. The reasons for this detachment are very practical. To the
extent that the internal auditing group is charged with day-to-day activities—as,
for example, validating disbursements, reconciling bank accounts, approving
movements of assets, and the like—the separate and supplementary review has
ceased to exist. Instead, the internal auditing activity has simply taken the
place of regular accounting or other operational responsibility. At times there
is a temptation on the part of management to assign such operational responsibilities to the internal auditor, but when this is done, it is based on a misunderstanding of the loss of the independent review.

A second important aspect of the relationship of internal auditing to other
company activities is that the internal auditor is a staff man and that, therefore,
he should not usurp the role and responsibility of other individuals. Thus the
line manager or supervisor has the basic responsibility for his own particular
sphere of the operations and he cannot shift the responsibility to the internal
auditor. This does not mean that the internal auditor is without responsibility.
The internal auditor has his responsibility to do a job that is competent in a
professional sense. But if he were to relieve line personnel of their responsibilities it would indeed weaken the motivation of the line managers and to a
considerable extent lessen the value of their roles. Thus the findings and recommendations of the internal auditor are always informative and advisory, and
in no way carry any direct authority to command specific action. The latter
must be determined by the line personnel based on the soundness and persuasiveness of the particular information and recommendations.

A final point concerns the unavoidable overlap of the internal auditing role
with many other company activities. In principle, all personnel in an organization are committed to doing their particular jobs effectively and in helping

to achieve maximum company welfare in an overall sense. This commitment increases as one goes up the organizational ladder, including the various staff areas. Thus a financial analysis group, an operations research group, or some other staff group might be very much concerned with operational analysis and assistance. Frequently also, special task forces will be created to study designated organizational problems. What then is so unique about the role of the internal auditor in providing analysis and service? The answer here is that the internal auditing group is the one that is completely detached from both the operational components and the functional staff groups (finance, marketing, production, and the like) and which can look at the various problems independently in terms of overall control. Here also competence in the design and implementation of the control gives it a needed credential to round out its overall professional capability. No other group in the company so well combines the fact of detachment, the objectives of organizational service to the organization, and the major competence in the field of control. In the federal government this independence is further provided by the Inspectors General and the General Accounting Office.

Relationship of Internal Auditing to Board of Directors

As a result of the previously mentioned environmental pressures, the board of directors is playing a more active role and assuming increased responsibilities in its relationships with both corporate management and the stockholders. One of the ways in which the board has coped with these increased responsibilities is through the formation or expansion of the role of its audit committee. Although the proper role of the audit committee is still emerging, it normally includes an overview of the completeness and integrity of the financial statements, the effectiveness of the system of internal accounting control, and the adequacy of the total audit effort. The latter includes relations with both the outside independent auditor and the internal auditor. Although the more usual arrangement is for the internal auditor to report administratively to either the chief executive officer or chief financial officer, the need also exists for both defined reporting and assistance to the audit committee. As will be discussed in more detail in subsequent chapters, the internal auditor customarily has a dual relationship to corporate management and to the audit committee, and in both connections appropriately coordinates his work with that of the independent public accountant—the external auditor.

Relationship of Internal Auditing to the External Auditor

Mention has been previously made of the earlier view that the internal auditing activity was in a major sense an extension of the external auditor effort. In fact, in many cases the internal auditing program was designed by the external auditor and utilized directly to serve the needs of the outside audit. Frequently also, the internal auditing personnel were recruited from the outside auditing profession and their internal assignments were all the more attuned to public auditing standards and interests. It is now, however, more clearly recognized that despite certain common interests, their priorities are quite different. The external auditor has a primary responsibility to parties outside the client organization, while the internal auditor is primarily responsible to the organization. The external auditor is interested more specifically in the soundness of the financial statements, whereas the internal auditor is concerned predominantly with the overall effectivess of company operations and resulting profitability. But, although both audit groups have different primary missions, there are many common interests that provide the basis for an extensive coordination effort—an area discussed in more detail in Chapter 29. Primarily, however, the common interest stems from the fact that the soundness of the system of internal accounting control is an important basis for each group achieving its primary mission. This common interest has also become especially important because of the requirement in the Foreign Corrupt Practices Act of 1977 that corporations maintain a system of sound internal accounting control, and by the interest of the Securities and Exchange Commission in pressing for a report from management covering the adequacy of the system of internal control.

SOME PRELIMINARY CONSIDERATIONS

Universal Applicability of Internal Auditing

The development of internal auditing has to a major extent been centered in business organizations. This tie continues in the existing literature of the profession and the convenient treatment of problems within the framework of business organizations. These ties, however, unduly deny the universal applicability of internal auditing to all types of organizations. Moreover, they fail to recognize that some of the most progressive internal auditing is now being done by nonbusiness types of organizations. A related fact also is that many organizations are a blend of business and nonbusiness activities—as for example, where a governmental authority like the Port Authority in the New York area is created and charged with the responsibility for operating public service facilities.

All of these developments confirm the truth that the need for internal auditing exists in all types of organizations where the complexity of the activities, the volume of transactions, and the dependence on large numbers of people exist in some combination to create operational problems. Organizations can exist for a variety of purposes, but the very reason for their creation is that there are objectives to be achieved. It is then the common role of all organizations to utilize the available resources in the most productive manner possible to achieve the organizational objectives. In that endeavor all responsible managers require effective control and in all cases can utilize the assistance of the internal auditing group. Thus there is a need for internal auditing in all types of organizations and there is a common body of professional knowledge that applies to all of these varied internal auditing activities.

A second aspect of the universal applicability is that there is potentially a need for the services of the internal auditor at any organizational level in any particular company or organization. This means that there can be legitimate needs for internal auditing services by the stockholders, the board of directors, and by the responsible management at the corporate headquarters level, the subsidiary or divisional level, and other lower levels. The controlling principle here is that whenever given organizational responsibilities are established there are potential needs for internal auditing services which should be served in some way. It is possible that all of these needs might be served by a central internal auditing group, provided that the central group can structure and administer the total operation in a sufficiently competent manner. In other cases the lower-level organizational components may believe that their own needs are best served by an internal auditing group of their own—even though indirectly responsible to the central group. What is important, however, for our present purposes is to recognize that internal auditing needs are directly linked to all organizational components.

Problems of Terminology

There is always the problem of how different terms shall be used and whether individual terms are viewed narrowly or broadly. This is especially a problem when the activities associated with the terms are undergoing major change, and when new terms are being introduced. At the time of the first edition in 1941 the term "internal auditing" had just begun to emerge fully as describing the independent review activity of the type described above. Prior thereto the more commonly used term was "internal audit" and here the term was frequently used as a part of the term "internal audit and control," encompassing a combination of true internal auditing activities, internal accounting, and other regular operational procedures. Today, the term "internal auditing" is believed by many to be unduly restrictive in describing the broad operational scope of the internal auditing effort. These individuals would prefer some broader term such as "management auditing," "management analysis," "operations analysis," and the like. Thus far, however, it has been concluded that there is more to be lost than gained by changing the name and we are left, therefore, with the need to develop a new understanding of the broader scope of the internal auditing effort.

A similar problem of terminology exists in the case of the terms "internal check" and "internal control." At the time of the first edition in 1941 the term "internal check" was viewed as having reasonably broad coverage. By the time of the second edition in 1957, this particular term had come to have a fairly narrow application to lower-level types of cross check. "Internal control" had then become the broader term. There were also other new terms, such as "managerial control," "organizational control," and just plain "control." Different people, of course, use these terms in different ways.

More recently also, a new term has been introduced by the American Institute of Certified Public Accountants, "internal accounting control." This particular term is intended to apply to that portion of the total internal control that pertains to the data in the financial reports about which the outside public accountant is expressing an opinion. The internal accounting controls, then, when coupled with internal administrative controls, are viewed as constituting the entire system of internal control. The term "internal accounting control" has also been used in the new Foreign Corrupt Practices Act of 1977 and by the Securities and Exchange Commission in its regulatory pronouncements.

Our own treatment will be somewhat along the following lines. Internal audit is viewed more as the individual audit review within the total field of internal auditing. When we come to the area of control we start with the recognition that the term "control" is the general term which covers all types of control and which needs further identification as to the particular type of control. "Managerial control" is then viewed as the broadest type of control, of which internal auditing is one part. "Organizational control" is then viewed as the part of managerial control that pertains to the assignment and direct coordination of organizational responsibilities. "Internal control" is used to describe internal procedures and practices that pertain to achieving organizational objectives better. "Internal check" will be hardly used at all, but where used, will apply to the lower-level cross checks between procedures, within the broader types of internal control. Finally, we will use "internal accounting control" in the same way as the American Institute of Certified Public Accountants and as used in the Foreign Corrupt Practices Act of 1977.

Plan of the Book

Our overall plan in this edition will be to deal first with foundation concepts and other considerations that apply to all internal auditing assignments. The foundations include an analysis of "Standards for the Professional Practice of Internal Auditing," issued by The Institute of Internal Auditors in 1978, an examination of the nature and scope of control, and other approaches and skills. We then deal with the closely related problem of administering the total internal auditing effort in an organization.

The stage is thus set for the coverage of the various operational areas covered by internal auditing assignments. In each of these operational areas the objective is to identify the individual controls and combinations of controls that are important in achieving results in the particular operational areas. The understanding of these controls then provides the basis for developing specific audit programs. In addition, however, audit guides are provided to assist further in the development of those specific audit programs.

The remainder of the book deals with certain aspects that need to build on the actual audit work. Included here are the increasingly important relationships with the audit committee of the board of directors and the external auditor. Included also is a consideration of the problem of self-evaluation and external reviews. Finally, we look at the future prospects of internal auditing and express certain general conclusions.

Objectives of the Book

This book has been designed to serve a wide range of needs of internal auditors. There is on the one hand the objective of providing practical assistance to internal auditors as they carry out individual parts of their internal auditing assignments. Whether the particular need is for report writing, the review of computer operations, service to audit committees, the coordination effort with external auditors, or whatever, the book should serve as a helpful reference in taking particular action. Even at this level, however, the approach of the book is to provide basic information and guides rather than detailed instructions. At all levels the work of the internal auditor must be tailored to the particular operational or other type of organizational situation. At the same time there is the very serious intention to develop a theory and philosophy of internal auditing that will generate depth thinking and professional development. Here too the objective is to provide a better understanding of the total environment of which the internal auditing effort is a part. To a considerable extent, therefore, the book requires thoughtful study. Hopefully, together the basis may thus be laid for an expanded range of service by professional internal auditors. Hopefully also, it will help provide all other interested parties with a better understanding of what they may properly expect from internal auditors, and how to relate to internal auditors more effectively.

CHAPTER TWO

Professional Standards for Internal Auditing

The most authoritative statement about the nature and scope of internal auditing exists in the form of the "Standards for the Professional Practice of Internal Auditing."[1] These Standards were approved by The Institute of Internal Auditors in June 1978. They are described in the foreword to those Standards as being "the criteria by which the operations of an internal auditing department are evaluated and measured. They are intended to represent the practice of internal auditing as it should be, as judged and adopted by the Board of Directors of The Institute." In that foreword, it is stated that "Organizations which have already established an internal audit function or are planning to establish one, are urged to adopt and support the Standards for the Professional Practice of Internal Auditing as a basis for guiding and measuring the function."

It is appropriate therefore that we use these Standards to expand our review of the foundation concepts of modern internal auditing beyond the brief coverage in Chapter 1.

Why Standards?

To qualify properly as a profession there are a number of requirements. These requirements include a recognized and well-defined area of service to society,

---

[1]Prior to the approval of these Standards the most authoritative statement was the Statement of Responsibilities of the Internal Auditor, originally issued by The Institute of Internal Auditors in 1947, and subsequently revised in 1957, 1971, 1976, and 1981. That Statement of Responsibilities was believed to have continuing informational value as a summary of what internal auditing is all about, and was therefore revised in 1981 to eliminate inconsistencies with the new Standards.

Quite clearly it was important that the Statement be consistent with the Standards. It does mean, however, that the Statement is now subject to some of the same limitations as the Standards—to be described later in this chapter. One important loss is the elimination of language in the older Statement pertaining to the internal auditor's interest in *improving* all types of operational performance. On the positive side, however, the Statement expands the service role of internal auditing from operational management to the entire organization. Another gain is that in the first paragraph the revised Statement retains an earlier sentence "It [internal auditing] is a control which functions by examining and evaluating the adequacy and effectivess of other controls"—a sentence unfortunately omitted from the Standards. The revised Statement is attached as Appendix A.

special knowledge and skills for providing that service, standards of performance, a code of ethics, and a procedure by which the members can be disciplined. Because of the key role of standards it was therefore both appropriate and essential that The Institute of Internal Auditors develop and validate a set of standards for the professional practice of internal auditing.

The standards serve both the members of The Institute and the larger society served by internal auditors. Through properly developed standards the internal auditors—as individual members, as internal auditing departments, and as a professional body—can have a benchmark against which to measure the level and quality of their internal auditing activities. At the same time the standards become a basis for education and training to achieve the desired levels of excellence. For those outside the internal auditing profession—management, boards of directors, stockholders, investors, regulatory bodies, and all other interested parties—the standards serve as a useful measure of what they all should expect to receive in the way of internal auditing services.

Structure of Standards and Our Plan of Treatment

The Standards consist of (1) a foreword, (2) an introduction, (3) a summary of general and specific standards, and (4) five chapters covering five sectors of concerns—in each case with the applicable general and specific standards, plus supporting guidelines. In the foreword, two points of special interest have already been quoted—in the definition at the beginning of Chapter 1 and in the opening of this chapter. A third important point of interest is the indication of the intent to modify the standards from time to time in response to the continuing change in business and society. The introduction in total appears to serve a dual purpose. On the one hand, it is useful background for the standards and guidelines that follow. On the other hand, some statements are anticipatory of the standards themselves. Although such anticipatory statements are not officially part of the standards, they do to a considerable extent take on the role of the standards, especially when they go beyond the coverage in the official standards and the supporting guidelines.

In discussing the above-mentioned standards and guidelines we need to recognize that they were developed by committee members based on their individual thinking and comments received from many other interested members, both inside and outside the internal auditing profession. In such a group of participants there was quite obviously a varying range of expertise, experience, and values. It was unavoidable therefore that the final language has some overlap, compromise, and incompleteness. As a result, individual standards and guidelines may be subject to varying interpretations. Our own approach will be to quote the text of each Standard, and then endeavor to develop an informed interpretation as to the particular issue involved. At the same time we will identify what we believe to be further needs and indicate our own views as to how those needs should be dealt with. Our overall objective will be to develop the best possible conceptual foundation for the more detailed treatment of modern internal auditing in the various chapters of this book.

THE INTRODUCTION

Opening Paragraph:[2] Definition

Internal auditing is an independent appraisal function established within an organization to examine and evaluate its activities as a service to the organization. The objective of internal auditing is to assist members of the organization in the effective discharge of their responsibilities. To this end, internal auditing furnishes them with analyses, appraisals, recommendations, counsel, and information concerning the activities reviewed.

The first sentence will be recognized as the definition of internal auditing quoted and interpreted at the beginning of Chapter 1. Reference should therefore be made to that discussion.

The second sentence can be viewed as a further elaboration of the definition. In this connection there is the recognition of the fact that the way for the internal auditor to serve the organization is to *assist* the members. There is also the recognition of the fact that such assistance has as its end objective the *effective* discharge of their responsibilities by the members. We also believe that it should be more clearly stated that the objective should be for *maximum* effectiveness. This more fully recognizes that the organization should continuously seek the *best* possible utilization of its resources under the existing conditions. To help the organization achieve that "best possible" utilization of those resources is in our view the central core of the role of the modern internal auditor.

The third sentence is a further useful elaboration of the definition because it defines more specifically how the internal auditor actually renders the service previously mentioned. Quite clearly many ways exist in which information relative to the internal auditor's examination and evaluation of the activities of the organization is made available to the properly designated members of the organization. But these various ways do, of course, include the means thus identified.

Second Paragraph: Groups Served and How

The members of the organization assisted by internal auditing include those in management and the board of directors. Internal auditors owe a responsibility to both, providing them with information about the adequacy and effectiveness of the organization's system of internal control and the quality of performance. The information furnished to each may differ in format and detail, depending upon the requirements and requests of management and the board.

The paragraph is an introductory statement about issues with which we will deal in greater detail at various points. Especially important, however, is the

---

[2]Individual sections of the Standards will be quoted verbatim in this chapter. However, the complete Standards will be found in Appendix C.

clear statement that the organization served by the internal auditor includes both management *and* the board of directors.

Third Paragraph: The Charter as a Source of Authority

The internal auditing department is an integral part of the organization and functions under the policies established by management and the board. The statement of purpose, authority, and responsibility (charter) for the internal auditing department, approved by management and accepted by the board, should be consistent with these *Standards for the Professional Practice of Internal Auditing*.

These sentences are also introductory statements about issues that will be dealt with in greater detail at a later point in the Standards and in our own analysis. However, a point made here, and not repeated later, is that the charter should be consistent with the Standards—a situation definitely desirable and necessary.

Fourth Paragraph: Content of the Charter

The charter should make clear the purposes of the internal auditing department, specify the unrestricted scope of its work, and declare that auditors are to have no authority or responsibility for the activities they audit.

This paragraph again covers an area to be dealt with at a later point. There is, however, some especially useful language, as follows:

1. "That the charter should make clear the *purposes* of the internal auditing department." Presumably such "purposes" should be based on the language used in the opening paragraph.
2. To "specify the unrestricted scope of its work" parallels a later standard (110-.01-.4) but is especially definite and hence very useful.
3. The last requirement—that auditors have no authority or responsibility for the activities they audit—parallels a later standard (350-.01) but is an especially clear and useful statement covering the primary responsibility for the organizational activities reviewed by internal auditors.

Fifth Paragraph: Impact of Environment

Throughout the world internal auditing is performed in diverse environments and within organizations which vary in purpose, size, and structure. In addition, the laws and customs within various countries differ from one another. These differences may affect the practice of internal auditing in each environment. The implementation of these *Standards*, therefore, will be governed by the environment in which the internal auditing department carries out its assigned responsibilities. But compliance with the concepts enunciated by these *Standards* is essential before the responsibilites of internal auditors can be met.

These sentences are important because they recognize the wide range of situations and environmental influences encountered by individual internal auditing departments. Hence it is very properly concluded that the implementation of the Standards must also necessarily vary. But there is also the important conclusion that there must be compliance with the *concepts* enunciated in the Standards before the responsibilities of internal auditors are met. Just what that exactly means is not entirely clear. Presumably it is recognized that there will necessarily be differences in practice in differing organizational situations, but that these differences must not extend to concepts. But there is the question as to just what the concept is that must not be violated, and as to where that concept starts and stops as applied to practice. Quite clearly identifying that line will require considerable judgment.

Sixth Paragraph: Independence

"Independence," as used in these *Standards*, requires clarification. Internal auditors must be independent of the activities they audit. Such independence permits internal auditors to perform their work freely and objectively. Without independence, the desired results of internal auditing cannot be realized.

These sentences are anticipatory of the further coverage in the standards pertaining to Independence—which we will discuss in more detail at that point. However, the last sentence is especially useful in linking independence to the realization of "the desired results of internal auditing."

Seventh Paragraph: Pertinent Developments

In setting these *Standards*, the following developments were considered:

1. Boards of directors are being held increasingly accountable for the adequacy and effectiveness of their organizations' systems of internal control and quality of performance.
2. Members of management are demonstrating increased acceptance of internal auditing as a means of supplying objective analyses, appraisals, recommendations, counsel, and information on the organization's controls and performance.
3. External auditors are using the results of internal audits to complement their own work where the internal auditors have provided suitable evidence of independence and adequate, professional audit work.

These three important developments were discussed in Chapter 1. They are indeed very important and will be continuously recognized throughout this book.

Eighth Paragraph: Purposes of the Standards

In the light of such developments, the purposes of these *Standards* are to:

1. Impart an understanding of the role and responsibilities of internal auditing to all levels of management, boards of directors, public bodies, external auditors, and related professional organizations

2. Establish the basis for the guidance and measurement of internal auditing performance
3. Improve the practice of internal auditing

The *Standards* differentiate among the varied responsibilities of the organization, the internal auditing department, the director of internal auditing, and internal auditors.

This listing of the purposes of the Standards parallels our own interpretations at the beginning of this chapter and differs only in the manner of classifying the several aspects involved. The last sentence is an especially useful recognition of the fact that the Standards have unique impacts on the several entities affected. It needs, however, to be also recognized that the "internal auditors" group covers a wide range of practitioners at various levels in an individual internal auditing department. As a consequence, the responsibilities of individual internal auditors will also vary greatly.

Ninth Paragraph: Format of the Standards

The five general *Standards* are expressed in italicized statements in upper case. Following each of these general *Standards* are specific standards expressed in italicized statements in lower case. Accompanying each specific standard are guidelines describing suitable means of meeting that standard. The *Standards* encompass:

1. The independence of the internal auditing department from the activities audited and the objectivity of internal auditors
2. The proficiency of internal auditors and the professional care they should exercise
3. The scope of internal auditing work
4. The performance of internal auditing assignments
5. The management of the internal auditing department

This outline of the format to be followed is self-explanatory. Our own analysis and interpretations will follow that same outline.

Tenth Paragraph: Three Terms with Specific Meanings

The *Standards* and the accompanying guidelines employ three terms which have been given specific meanings. These are as follows:

The term *board* includes boards of directors, audit committees of such boards, heads of agencies or legislative bodies to whom internal auditors report, boards of governors or trustees of nonprofit organizations, and any other designated governing bodies of organizations.

The terms *director of internal auditing* and *director* identify the top position in an internal auditing department.

The term *internal auditing department* includes any unit of activity within an organization which performs internal auditing functions.

The explanations here are also self-explanatory. The extensions of the terms to cover both profit and nonprofit-type organization is also very important.

The designation "director of internal auditing" is somewhat cumbersome in repetitive use, while the single term "director" alone is sometimes not sufficiently precise. In actual practice the term "general auditor" is very frequently used to identify the head of the internal auditing departments, and in this book we will more often do the same.

The Introduction in Perspective

As previously noted, the introduction to the more formal standards deserves careful consideration. In part it provides new concepts—as, for example, the definition of internal auditing in the opening paragraph, background in the form of developments considered and the purposes of the standards, basic definitions, and other substantive statements which in a very real sense overlap with, and further extend, the formal standards themselves. Whether or not the Introduction has the same authority as the formal standards can be subject to differing views. But the fact that substantive issues have to some extent been dealt with leads unavoidably to the conclusion that we need to give the Introduction serious attention.

SUMMARY OF STANDARDS

This summary, as shown on pages 21 and 22, contains the general and specific standards. The standards are then repeated in the five following sections and serve as a foundation for the supporting guidelines. These standards and guidelines are discussed individually in the remainder of this chapter.

100   INDEPENDENCE

INTERNAL AUDITORS SHOULD BE INDEPENDENT OF THE ACTIVITIES THEY AUDIT

   .01 Internal auditors are independent when they can carry out their work freely and objectively. Independence permits internal auditors to render the impartial and unbiased judgments essential to the proper conduct of audits. It is achieved through organizational status and objectivity.

In this summary standard the desired independence for the professional practice of internal auditing is defined as being independent of the activities audited. This general requirement is basic to all other specific standards and supporting guidelines.

The first sentence of the guideline (.01) parallels the second and third sentences in the sixth paragraph of the Introduction but more clearly links the existence of independence for internal auditors to whether they can carry out their work *freely and objectively*. The second sentence also parallels the last

SUMMARY OF GENERAL AND SPECIFIC STANDARDS
FOR THE PROFESSIONAL PRACTICE OF INTERNAL AUDITING

100 **INDEPENDENCE** — *INTERNAL AUDITORS SHOULD BE INDEPENDENT OF THE ACTIVITIES THEY AUDIT.*

    110 **Organizational Status** — *The organizational status of the internal auditing department should be sufficient to permit the accomplishment of its audit responsibilities.*

    120 **Objectivity** — *Internal auditors should be objective in performing audits.*

200 **PROFESSIONAL PROFICIENCY** — *INTERNAL AUDITS SHOULD BE PERFORMED WITH PROFICIENCY AND DUE PROFESSIONAL CARE.*

    The Internal Auditing Department

    210 **Staffing** — *The internal auditing department should provide assurance that the technical proficiency and educational background of internal auditors are appropriate for the audits to be performed.*

    220 **Knowledge, Skills, and Disciplines** — *The internal auditing department should possess or should obtain the knowledge, skills, and disciplines needed to carry out its audit responsibilities.*

    230 **Supervision** — *The internal auditing department should provide assurance that internal audits are properly supervised.*

    The Internal Auditor

    240 **Compliance with Standards of Conduct** — *Internal auditors should comply with professional standards of conduct.*

    250 **Knowledge, Skills, and Disciplines** — *Internal auditors should possess the knowledge, skills, and disciplines essential to the performance of internal audits.*

    260 **Human Relations and Communications** — *Internal auditors should be skilled in dealing with people and in communicating effectively.*

    270 **Continuing Education** — *Internal auditors should maintain their technical competence through continuing education.*

    280 **Due Professional Care** — *Internal auditors should exercise due professional care in performing internal audits.*

300 **SCOPE OF WORK** — *THE SCOPE OF THE INTERNAL AUDIT SHOULD ENCOMPASS THE EXAMINATION AND EVALUATION OF THE ADEQUACY AND EFFECTIVENESS OF THE ORGANIZATION'S SYSTEM OF INTERNAL CONTROL AND THE QUALITY OF PERFORMANCE IN CARRYING OUT ASSIGNED RESPONSIBILITIES.*

    310 **Reliability and Integrity of Information** — *Internal auditors should review the reliability and integrity of financial and operating information and the means used to identify, measure, classify, and report such information.*

3

320 **Compliance with Policies, Plans, Procedures, Laws, and Regulations** — *Internal auditors should review the systems established to ensure compliance with those policies, plans, procedures, laws, and regulations which could have a significant impact on operations and reports and should determine whether the organization is in compliance.*

330 **Safeguarding of Assets** — *Internal auditors should review the means of safeguarding assets and, as appropriate, verify the existence of such assets.*

340 **Economical and Efficient Use of Resources** — *Internal auditors should appraise the economy and efficiency with which resources are employed.*

350 **Accomplishment of Established Objectives and Goals for Operations or Programs** — *Internal auditors should review operations or programs to ascertain whether results are consistent with established objectives and goals and whether the operations or programs are being carried out as planned.*

400 **PERFORMANCE OF AUDIT WORK** — *AUDIT WORK SHOULD INCLUDE PLANNING THE AUDIT, EXAMINING AND EVALUATING INFORMATION, COMMUNICATING RESULTS, AND FOLLOWING UP.*

410 **Planning the Audit** — *Internal auditors should plan each audit.*

420 **Examining and Evaluating Information** — *Internal auditors should collect, analyze, interpret, and document information to support audit results.*

430 **Communicating Results** — *Internal auditors should report the results of their audit work.*

440 **Following Up** — *Internal auditors should follow up to ascertain that appropriate action is taken on reported audit findings.*

500 **MANAGEMENT OF THE INTERNAL AUDITING DEPARTMENT** — *THE DIRECTOR OF INTERNAL AUDITING SHOULD PROPERLY MANAGE THE INTERNAL AUDITING DEPARTMENT.*

510 **Purpose, Authority, and Responsibility** — *The director of internal auditing should have a statement of purpose, authority, and responsibility for the internal auditing department.*

520 **Planning** — *The director of internal auditing should establish plans to carry out the responsibilities of the internal auditing department.*

530 **Policies and Procedures** — *The director of internal auditing should provide written policies and procedures to guide the audit staff.*

540 **Personnel Management and Development** — *The director of internal auditing should establish a program for selecting and developing the human resources of the internal auditing department.*

550 **External Auditors** — *The director of internal auditing should coordinate internal and external audit efforts.*

560 **Quality Assurance** — *The director of internal auditing should establish and maintain a quality assurance program to evaluate the operations of the internal auditing department.*

4

sentence of that same sixth paragraph of the Introduction but now more specifically establishes independence as essential to the proper conduct of audits. The third sentence identifies the two means by which independence is achieved—organizational status and objectivity.

110   Organizational Status

The organizational status of the internal auditing department should be sufficient to permit the accomplishment of its audit responsibilities.

.01   Internal auditors should have the support of management and of the board of directors so that they can gain the cooperation of auditees and perform their work free from interference.

.1   The director of the internal auditing department should be responsible to an individual in the organization with sufficient authority to promote independence and to ensure broad audit coverage, adequate consideration of audit reports, and appropriate action on audit recommendations.

.2   The director should have direct communication with the board. Regular communication with the board helps assure independence and provides a means for the board and the director to keep each other informed on matters of mutual interest.

.3   Independence is enhanced when the board concurs in the appointment or removal of the director of the internal auditing department.

.4   The purpose, authority, and responsibility of the internal auditing department should be defined in a formal written document (charter). The director should seek approval of the charter by management as well as acceptance by the board. The charter should (a) establish the department's position within the organization; (b) authorize access to records, personnel, and physical properties relevant to the performance of audits; and (c) define the scope of internal auditing activities.

.5   The director of internal auditing should submit annually to management for approval and to the board for its information a summary of the department's audit work schedule, staffing plan, and financial budget. The director should also submit all significant interim changes for approval and information. Audit work schedules, staffing plans, and financial budgets should inform management and the board of the scope of internal auditing work and of any limitations placed on that scope.

.6   The director of internal auditing should submit activity reports to management and to the board annually or more frequently as necessary. Activity reports should highlight significant audit findings and recommendations and should inform management and the board of any significant deviations from approved audit work schedules, staffing plans, and financial budgets, and the reasons for them.

The specific standard deals with the first of the two types of requirements —organizational status. It provides the general test that the organizational status "should be sufficient to permit the accomplishment of its audit responsibilities." This presumably means sufficient to permit accomplishment of proper audit objectives and to discharge the related responsibilities assigned by appropriate organizational authority.

The guideline (.01) identifies the support of management and the board of directors as a necessary basis for gaining the cooperation of auditees and performing internal auditing work free from interference. The six supporting subguidelines then interpret that more general guideline.

In the first paragraph (.1) we have a listing of the criteria by which we evaluate the adequacy of the authority of the individual to whom the director of internal auditing reports. The first of these deals with the individual's capability in promoting independence. The criterion is presumably that the director reports to someone who is sufficiently powerful to assure such backing for the director of internal auditing as may be necessary.

In the second paragraph (.2) the requirement of "direct" communication of the director of the internal auditing department with the board is first established. Coupled then with the second sentence there is the further indirect requirement that the communication also be *regular*. The rationale —presumably intended to apply to both of those requirements—is that this helps assure independence and provides a means of keeping both parties informed as to matters of mutual interest. Both the requirements and the underlying rationale are quite clearly sound. These issues are dealt with in Chapter 28.

In the next paragraph (.3) the point is made that when the board concurs in the appointment or removal of the director there is an enhancement of independence for the director. The standard thus clearly encourages the concurrence practice. Also, the term "concurs" is used instead of "approves." This treatment appears to recognize the related fact that the primary reporting responsibility is more likely to be to management rather than to the board. The requirement of concurrence is very important because it gives the board an opportunity to question the appointment or removal action and thus have a better basis for evaluating the judgment of the management pertaining to the action. There is the further advantage that the board is alerted to the need to establish a proper working relationship with a new director of internal auditing. Thus, on balance, it is believed that the arrangement for concurrence is extremely important and should definitely be *required* practice.

The next recognized support action (.4) covers the very important need that the total role of the internal auditing department be defined in a formal written document (the charter). It parallels, but importantly extends, the coverage in the fourth paragraph of the Introduction. That charter should be *approved* by management and *accepted* by the board. It is also important what level of management does the approving. We believe that the approving officer should be the chief executive officer, so that all company officers are then clearly bound by the terms of that charter. The term "acceptance" used to define the board's involvement again suggests much the same logic as was previously discussed for the "concurrence" action. However, because the charter covers responsibilities to both management and the audit committee, we believe the approvals by both parties should be equally important. In the final sentence we then have some of the requirements for the content of the charter. We also discuss these problems in Chapter 28.

In the next part (.5) the range of the reporting of the director of internal auditing is more specifically outlined—an area we cover in Chapter 12. The language "to management for approval and to the board for its information" again suggests a primary reporting responsibility to management. The final sentence in this part covers the very important need of keeping both management and the board properly informed as to the activities of the department, although presumably the information provded to the audit committee would be in less detail. This provides needed understanding and an opportunity to raise questions and shape the program to cover the needs of all recipients. The inclusion in this sentence, however, of possible "limitations" is a much more complex matter. Actually, the coverage in the charter—as discussed in .4 above and in the Introduction—should have properly established the freedom from limitations. If there is a denial of that freedom later by members of management, it would usually lead to some kind of a confrontation. Then, if any problems cannot be effectively dealt with, the audit committee would need to become involved.

The final paragraph (.06) also deals with current reporting to management and the board—in this case audit results and conformance to established plans. Although the standard again does not say whether the volume and detail of such reports should vary as between management and the board, we would reasonably expect that the reporting to the board would be in more summary form. These matters are dealt with later in the chapters dealing with the administration of the internal auditing department.

Broader Aspects of Support

The six paragraphs just discussed are all presumably directed to showing the manner in which management and the board of directors provide sufficient support to the internal auditing department. It needs to be recognized, however, that support can also be provided in other ways. These other ways go beyond official organizational status, as shown in organization charts, charters, reports, and other formal stipulations. We refer here to the extent to which higher-level management and the board demonstrate their interest in internal auditing activities and the manner in which they interpret the various formal arrangements. It is a fact of life that individuals at all levels in the organization directly or indirectly continue to test whether formally stated arrangements have real higher-level support, and hence whether they should be taken seriously. It is therefore necessary that higher-level management and the board are continuously alert to this danger and that they continuously reaffirm their support for the internal auditing department. This support is especially critical when—as so often happens—a particular high-level officer resists evaluation by internal auditors and tries to convince higher-level management that internal auditing activitiies are having a detrimental impact on the achievement of his own organizational objectives. Such problems need to be promptly resolved through depth review by still-higher-level management, so that obstacles to effective internal auditing are properly eliminated.

What Is Sufficient Authority to Assure Effective Internal Auditing?

In the standards quoted above it is stated that the director of the internal auditing department should be responsible to an individual in the organization with sufficient authority to assure effective internal auditing. This wording asserts a proper principle but it does not specify the organizational status of that individual. Some further discussion of this problem therefore is appropriate.

A good starting point is to review the results of several surveys of actual practice reported in *Research Report 24*, "Evaluating Internal/External Audit Services and Relationships," of The Institute of Internal Auditors (see Exhibit 2.1). These comparisons show very clearly the continuing trend toward a higher-level reporting responsibility for the internal auditing department. However, the greater number still report to a vice president. Typically, in actual practice, that vice president is the chief financial officer.

Opinions relative to the merits of alternative reporting arrangemments will vary as between the different parties of interest and particular individuals. On the one hand, there is the very logical view that the higher the reporting authority, the greater the independence of the internal auditor as a basis for effective internal auditing. On the other hand, reporting to the higher level may deprive the internal auditor of important day-to-day support. Moreover, the merits are quite different in companies of different size and maturity. Because of the pressure of the Foreign Corrupt Practices Act and other considerations we can foresee in most organizations a vice president status for the

EXHIBIT 2.1. Comparing Reporting Responsibilities with Previous Studies[a]

	Year-End Percentages				
	1957[b]	1968[c]	1975[d]	This Study[e]	1979[f]
Board of directors	7	6	7	8	10
President	7	10	11	18	13
Vice president	16	31	32	41	46
Controller	42	32	20	23	11
Other	28	21	30	10	20

[a]The classifications were regrouped to facilitate comparisons.
[b]The Institute of Internal Auditors, Inc., *1957 Survey of Internal Auditing* (New York: The Institute of Internal Auditors, Inc., 1958), p. 17.
[c]The Institute of Internal Auditors, Inc., *1968 Survey of Internal Auditing* (New York: The Institute of Internal Auditors, Inc., 1969), p. 13.
[d]The Institute of Internal Auditors, Inc., *1975 Survey of Internal Auditing* (Altamonte Springs, Fla.: The Institute of Internal Auditors, Inc., 1976), p. 23.
[e]Survey questionnaire data used in this research effort was collected in 1977.
[f]The Institute of Internal Auditors, Inc., *1979 Survey of Internal Auditing* (Altamonte Springs, Fla.: The Institute of Internal Auditors, Inc., 1980), p. 20.
Source: The Institute of Internal Auditors, *Research Report 24* (Altamonte Springs, Fla.: The Institute of Internal Auditors, Inc., 1980), Table 21, p. 31.

director of the internal auditing department and a primary reporting responsibility to the chief executive officer, but this does not mean that a reporting to a chief financial officer needs to be ruled out. Additionally, there must always be defined secondary responsibilities to the board of directors, the content of which we also discuss further in Chapter 28. The typical and future versions of the reporting responsibility are shown in Exhibits 2.2 and 2.3, respectively.

120   Objectivity

Internal auditors should be objective in performing audits.

.01   Objectivity is an independent mental attitude which internal auditors should maintain in performing audits. Internal auditors are not to subordinate their judgment on audit matters to that of others.

.02   Objectivity requires internal auditors to perform audits in such a manner that they have an honest belief in their work product and that no significant quality compromises are made. Internal auditors are not to be placed in situations in which they feel unable to make objective professional judgments.

   .1   Staff assignments should be made so that potential and actual conflicts of interest and bias are avoided. The director should periodically obtain from the audit staff information concerning potential conflicts of interest and bias.

   .2   Internal auditors should report to the director any situations in which a conflict of interest or bias is present or may reasonably be inferred. The director should then reassign such auditors.

   .3   Staff assignments of internal auditors should be rotated periodically whenever it is practicable to do so.

EXHIBIT 2.2.   Typical Organizational Placement of Internal Auditing Department

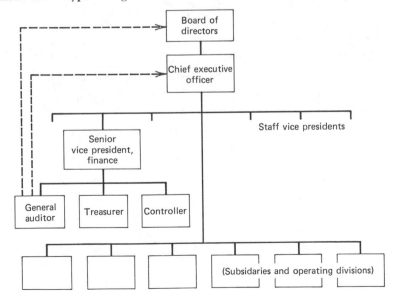

.4   Internal auditors should not assume operating responsibilities. But if on occasion management directs internal auditors to perform nonaudit work, it should be understood that they are not functioning as internal auditors. Moreover, objectivity is presumed to be impaired when internal auditors audit any activity for which they had authority or responsibility. This impairment should be considered when reporting audit results.

.5   Persons transferred to or temporarily engaged by the internal auditing department should not be assigned to audit those activities they previously performed until a reasonable period of time has elapsed. Such assignments are presumed to impair objectivity and should be considered when supervising the audit work and reporting audit results.

.6   The results of internal auditing work should be reviewed before the related audit report is released to provide reasonable assurance that the work was performed objectively.

.03   The internal auditor's objectivity is not adversely affected when the auditor recommends standards of control for systems or reviews procedures before they are implemented. Designing, installing, and operating systems are not audit functions. Also, the drafting of procedures for systems is not an audit function. Performing such activities is presumed to impair audit objectivity.

This specific standard establishes the requirement that internal auditors "should be objective in performing audits." Although recognizing the need for objectivity in performing audits, we believe that the quality of objectivity is also important in every other phase of the internal auditor's activities.

EXHIBIT 2.3. Future Organizational Placement of the Internal Auditing Department

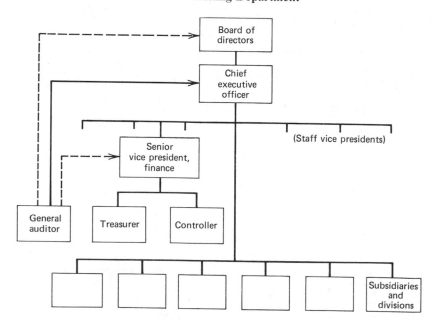

In the first sentence of the first guideline (.01) the truth is recognized that there must be an independent mental attitude on the part of the internal auditors. This independent mental attitude is something that is directly up to the individual internal auditor, irrespective of organizational status. The second sentence then goes on to stipulate that the internal auditor, having reached conclusions through an independent mental attitude, must not compromise by yielding to the pressures of other affected parties. These pressures can come from people at all levels who either have strong contrary views about the judgment of the internal auditor, or who see possible embarrassment from the visibility that will result from the internal auditor's findings and conclusions. This does not mean that the internal auditor will not consider these other views. But it does mean that the internal auditor must do what he thinks is necessary and proper.

The special focus of guideline (.02) is on the way internal auditors carry out their various audit assignments. It stipulates that the audit must be made in a manner that makes possible honest belief in the work product on the part of the internal auditor. Hence the internal auditor must avoid shortcuts and compromises that block or dilute the adequate basis needed for the sought-after "honest belief." In the second sentence the related important point is then made that internal auditors should avoid being placed in situations where objective professional judgments are not possible. Six lower-level guidelines then identify specific requirements bearing on objective professional judgments.

The first of these requirements (.1) is that the staff assignments should be made in such a way that conflicts of interest and/or bias are avoided. It might well be that the particular internal auditor has enough character and objectivity that conflict of interest or bias would not be any problem. However, this is not enough. In addition, all staff assignments should be avoided where the possibility *could* exist that conflicts of interest or bias might affect audit judgments. In the second sentence the director is also directly charged with the responsibility of obtaining information about existing conflicts or potential bias on the part of individual staff members. Such information can then be given appropriate consideration when actual staff assignments are made.

In the first sentence of the second requirement (.2) the same problem is then attacked via the internal auditor himself. Here the internal auditor is specifically charged with the responsibility to take the initiative and report any situation involving either actual or reasonably inferrable conflict of interest or bias. In the second sentence the director of internal auditing is directed in such a situation to reassign that internal auditor. Thus there is the joint responsibility of the two individuals to prevent the existence of conflict or bias.

In the third requirement (.3) the director is charged with the further responsibility of periodically rotating the staff assignments of internal auditors. However, it is recognized indirectly that factors may exist which limit the practicability of such rotation. It is generally believed that the rotation of audit assignments is beneficial solely on the ground of providing fresh and often more effective approaches to particular audit assignments. However, the special significance in achieving objectivity is that a continuation of assignment to the same audit task may result in personal relationships that may somehow dilute the independence and related objectivity of the particular internal auditor. Auditees very often prefer the relative comfort of dealing with the same internal auditor, and in some cases will exert pressure for the continuation of that arrangement. However, on balance, rotation appears to be a very desirable practice in the total interest of the organization.

The fourth requirement (.4) covers a number of different important aspects of the total effort to generate and sustain needed objectivity. In the first sentence there is the basic truth that internal auditors should not assume operating responsibilities. The reasons for this, as previously discussed in Chapter 1, are that the internal auditor then becomes a line individual and no longer functions as an independent internal auditor. In the second sentence, however, the possibility very realistically is recognized that the internal auditor may be *directed* by proper organizational authority to take on a particular operating responsibility. However, it is soundly recognized that all interested persons should understand that the internal auditor is then not functioning as an internal auditor. Under those conditions, therefore, the director of the internal auditing department should also assign other staff personnel to provide the regular internal auditing service.[3] All of the foregoing should of course be properly explained to management. The third sentence is concerned with a related but somewhat different problem. The threat to objectivity in this instance arises when an auditor goes back as an internal auditor to a particular organizational component for which he previously had authority or responsibility. Here there is the very real possibility that the internal auditor will be biased, based on his prior involvement. The final sentence then seems to presume that such an audit assignment has in fact been made and then goes on to caution the internal auditor to be especially careful of the possibility of loss of objectivity when he is developing his report.

The fifth requirement (.5) builds on the threat to objectivity just discussed under (.4) and states that audit assignments covering activities previously performed should not be made until after a reasonable time has elapsed. Whether the activity involves previously held responsibilities or operational participation, the key factor is of course the amount of intervening time that has elapsed. A too strict interpretation here can unduly limit the availability of the particular auditor for various audit assignments. Moreover, there can also be some very real benefits in using such individuals because of their better understanding of the activity now being covered as an audit assignment. Nevertheless, the last sentence quite properly sounds the warning to the internal auditor to be aware of the potential danger of loss of objectivity, and to do all possible to guard against loss of objectivity.

---

[3]See also the discussion in Chapter 9.

The final requirement in this group (.6) is that the results of internal auditing work need to be reviewed before the release of the audit report. This entire problem is discussed in more detail in the section of the Standards pertaining to the performance and supervision of audit work.

Guideline (.03) has to do with a special problem that exists when major systems or procedures are developed in the organization and when the internal auditor needs to avoid any involvement that would undermine his independence when he later makes a regular internal audit of the completed project. The problem is that once a typical system or major procedure is operative it usually becomes very costly—in terms of time, cost, and impact upon the organization—to correct deficiencies identified by the internal auditor in his later internal audit of that system or procedure. It makes far greater sense in terms of total company welfare for the internal auditors to make available his expertise regarding controls, so that his counsel can be utilized in the design of that system or procedure. This guideline therefore recognizes the propriety of internal auditors providing such counsel as pertaining to *standards of control*. At the same time, however, internal auditors are cautioned not to get involved in designing, installing, operating those systems, or in drafting procedures— thus impairing their objectivity. Moreover, such involvement is time consuming and could be such a drain on the internal auditing resources that the regular internal auditing function would suffer. However, what is difficult is how and where the internal auditor draws the line in interfacing with the individuals directly charged with the development of the various policies and procedures. Here too good sense and sound judgment are essential. This problem is discussed further in Chapter 22.

Objectivity in Perspective

There is general agreement as to the desirability of objectivity by internal auditors and the utilization of all means practicable to protect such objectivity. To a considerable extent the means of achieving needed objectivity is in the hands of internal auditors themselves. In other instances, however, the arrangements that assure needed objectivity are in the hands of other individuals and groups in the organization. What is important in the latter situations is that internal auditors utilize every possible means to inform and guide the other parties in the organization about their impact on objectivity. By so doing, internal auditors can best assure the needed setting for achieving the proper levels of objectivity. In the last analysis objectivity is a state of mind on the part of the internal auditor, and the ability to develop that needed state of mind is one of the greatest challenges to the truly professional internal auditor.

Independence in Perspective

We have seen how independence is an essential basis for effective modern internal auditing. We have seen also that independence is achieved both by the conditions imposed upon the internal auditing department by the organization and through the objectivity of the individual internal auditors. Therefore, a necessary continuing effort must be made to maintain and improve both kinds of the basic conditions that affect the achievement of the needed independence. We must, however, be fully aware of the truth that complete independence can never be achieved. This is true because there are always conditions that to some extent limit independence. For example, a board of directors is subject to the constraints of its accountability to government and society. A chief executive officer has the same constraints plus the constraint of the board itself. The outside public accountant can never fully forget that the client pays his fees and that these fees are necessary to maintain a viable public accounting firm. The internal auditor reports to someone in the organization and is dependent on that organization to a major extent for his own livelihood. It is also always something of a problem to resist pressures from organizational colleagues with whom the internal auditor wishes to maintain good working relationships. What all this means is that no person is an island unto himself and that independence is always a relative term—that is greater or less, but never absolute. This in no sense depreciates the value of independence or detracts from the various efforts to upgrade the extent and quality of the desired independence. In the case of internal auditors our continuing effort must always be to strengthen the needed independence even though there are, and always will be, substantive limitations to that independence. The internal auditor himself does this first, by doing effective work and having the courage to stand up for his convictions, and second, by exerting every effort practicable to induce and obtain the organizational arrangements that will best assure his independence. In both cases the worth of the effort lies in the contribution of that greater independence to providing effective internal auditing services, which can ther make for maximum organizational welfare.

200   PROFESSIONAL PROFICIENCY

INTERNAL AUDITS SHOULD BE PERFORMED WITH PROFICIENCY AND DUE PROFESSIONAL CARE

.01 Professional proficiency is the responsibility of the internal auditing department and each internal auditor. The department should assign to each audit those persons who collectively possess the necessary knowledge, skills, and disciplines to conduct the audit properly.

The second section of the Standards deals with the very necessary professional proficiency of the practice of internal auditing. The general standard properly establishes the requirement that proficiency and due professional care are essential qualities in the performance of internal audits.

In the first sentence of the supporting guideline (.01) the responsibility for professional proficiency is made the responsibility of *both* the internal auditing department and each internal auditor. This dual assignment is important because the department and the individual each has its own roles to play and each has differing opportunities to further professional proficiency. In the second sentence there is a specific supporting requirement pertaining to the role of the internal auditing department—to assign persons to each audit who possess the necessary knowledge, skills, and disciplines to conduct the audit properly. The further component requirements are covered in the specific standards and their supporting guidelines.

The Internal Auditing Department

210   Staffing

The internal auditing department should provide assurance that the technical proficiency and educational background of internal auditors are appropriate for the audits to be performed.

.01   The director of internal auditing should establish suitable criteria of education and experience for filling internal auditing positions, giving due consideration to scope of work and level of responsibility.

.02   Reasonable assurance should be obtained as to each prospective auditor's qualifications and proficiency.

This subsection deals in more detail with the responsibilities attributable to the internal auditing department—the first of which pertains to staffing. In the specific standard those overall responsibilities are described as providing assurance that internal auditors have the technical proficiency and educational background appropriate for audits performed. This is the normal managerial responsibility that staff personnel assigned to individual audits are capable of doing the required job.

In the supporting guidelines two ways to satisfy the above-mentioned responsibility are indicated. The first (.01) pertains to the director of the internal auditing department. This action establishes the criteria needed for filling the various staff positions presumably after giving consideration to the scope of work and level of responsibilites pertaining to those positions. The second way (.02) comes at the problem through procedures that identify the capabilities of individual applicants. These two ways together provide needed assurance that individual audit assignments will be carried out by properly qualified internal auditors.

We must recognize the fact that the nature and scope of particular audits carried on are always changing and that staff personnel previously having adequate qualifications may no longer satisfy the new needs. Hence the effort to assure the proper fit is never ending. But the internal auditing department must, according to the previously mentioned specific standard, provide assurance that the qualifications are appropriate for the audits to be performed. What "provide assurance" actually means is not entirely clear, but in addition to the actions just discussed it is reasonable to conclude that there should be adequate documentation covering both prescribed actions in .01 and .02 and the manner in which the matching is actually made in terms of individual capabilities and work assignments.

220   Knowledge, Skills, and Disciplines

The internal auditing department should possess or should obtain the knowledge, skills, and disciplines needed to carry out its audit responsibililies.

.01   The internal auditing staff should collectively possess the knowledge and skills essential to the practice of the profession within the organization. These attributes include proficiency in applying internal auditing standards, procedures, and techniques.

.02   The internal auditing department should have employees or use consultants who are qualified in such disciplines as accounting, economics, finance, statistics, electronic data processing, engineering, taxation, and law as needed to meet audit responsibilities. Each member of the department, however, need not be qualified in all of these disciplines

The second type of responsibility of the internal auditing department deals with knowledge, skills, and disciplines. The related specific standard establishes the requirement that the department should possess *or obtain* staff personnel with those particular capabilities as necessary to carry out its audit responsibilities. In the first interpretative guideline (.1) the focus is on knowledge and skills. One further clarification is, however, the use of the word "collectively"—which presumably means that the particular needed knowledge or skill is *somewhere* among the staff members. The second qualification is that the knowledge and skills include proficiency in *applying* internal audit standards, procedures, and techniques—thus stressing the importance of effective managerial implementation.

In the second interpretative guideline (.02) the focus is on the kinds of disciplines required. The examples cited include accounting, economics, finance, statistics, electronic data processing, engineering, taxation, and law; but presumably the listing is intended to be open ended and must be reappraised in the light of the particular audit need. A further interpretation here is that consultants may be used if the needed capabilities are not available from staff personnel actually in the department. And a second related interpretation is that any one member does not need to be qualified in *all* the relevant disciplines.

230   Supervision

The internal auditing department should provide assurance that internal audits are properly supervised.

.01   The director of internal auditing is responsible for providing appropriate audit supervision. Supervision is a continuing process, beginning with planning and ending with the conclusion of the audit assignment.

.02   Supervision includes:

.1   Providing suitable instructions to subordinates at the outset of the audit and approving the audit program

.2   Seeing that the approved audit program is carried out unless deviations are both justified and authorized

.3   Determining that audit working papers adequately support the audit findings, conclusions, and reports

    .4   Making sure that audit reports are accurate, objective, clear, concise, constructive, and timely

    .5   Determining that audit objectives are being met

    .03   Appropriate evidence of supervision should be documented and retained.

    .04   The extent of supervision required will depend on the proficiency of the internal auditors and the difficulty of the audit assignment.

    .05   All internal auditing assignments, whether performed by or for the internal auditing department, remain the responsiblity of its director.

This third type of responsibility of the internal auditing department deals with supervision. The related specific standard covers the responsibility for the proper supervision of internal audits. Again also, there is the requirement to provide assurance—presumably including adequate documentation. In the first supporting guideline (.01) the same requirement for proper supervision is repeated. The second sentence, however, is an important clarification of the total span of the supervising responsibility—that is, from the initial planning to the conclusion of the audit assignment. We should also recognize the need for prior planning by the director himself.

In the second guideline (.02) five aspects of the supervisory process are identified. It is interesting to note that now there is no specific identification of the planning phase, even though planning personnel would also need to be supervised. All of this supervisory phase is discussed further in Chapter 11.

The third guideline (.03) very properly emphasizes the need for adequate documentation, and for the retention of that documentation, to provide evidence of proper supervision.

The fourth guideline (.04) is a useful recognition of the truth that the need for supervision is directly dependent on two key variables: (1) the proficiency of the particular audit personnel involved in varying audit assignments and (2) the difficulty of the particular assignments. Relevant also would be the significance of the activity being reviewed in terms of impact on organizational welfare.

The fifth and final guideline is a useful recognition of the truth that the man at the head of any group can never escape ultimate responsiblity, irrespective of delegations to subordinates. This ultimate responsibility also extends properly to work which that group head may get done by obtaining audit assistance from persons outside his own departmental staff.

The Internal Auditor

240   Compliance with Standards of Conduct

    Internal auditors should comply with professional standards of conduct.

    .01   The *Code of Ethics* of The Institute of Internal Auditors sets forth standards of conduct and provides a basis for enforcement among its members. The *Code* calls for high standards of honesty, objectivity, diligence, and loyalty to which internal auditors should conform.

This next subsection deals with the responsibilities for professional proficiency that are attributable to the internal auditor as an individual staff person. Attention is also directed to the first type of responsibility—that of compliance with professional standards of conduct.

The supporting guideline (.01) is self-explanatory in its reference to the Code of Ethics of The Institute as the standards of conduct to which the internal auditor is required to conform.

250   Knowledge, Skills, and Disciplines

Internal auditors should possess the knowledge, skills, and disciplines essential to the performance of internal audits.

.01   Each internal auditor should possess certain knowledge and skills as follows:

    .1   Proficiency in applying internal auditing standards, procedures, and techniques is required in performing internal audits. Proficiency means the ability to apply knowledge to situations likely to be encountered and to deal with them without extensive recourse to technical research and assistance.

    .2   Proficiency in accounting principles and techniques is required of auditors who work extensively with financial records and reports.

    .3   An understanding of management principles is required to recognize and evaluate the materiality and significance of deviations from good business practice. An understanding means the ability to apply broad knowledge to situations likely to be encountered, to recognize significant deviations, and to be able to carry out the research necessary to arrive at reasonable solutions.

    .4   An appreciation is required of the fundamentals of such subjects as accounting, economics, commercial law, taxation, finance, quantitative methods, and computerized information systems. An appreciation means the ability to recognize the existence of problems or potential problems and to determine the further research to be undertaken or the assistance to be obtained.

The specific standard (250) reasserts the previously stipulated matching of professional efficiency (knowledge, skills, and disciplines) with audit assignment needs, but now focuses on the responsibilities in that respect of the *individual* internal auditor. The supporting guideline then outlines the specific dimensions of the needed proficiency in terms of knowledge and skills.

In the first specification (.1) there is the requirement that there be proficiency in applying internal auditing standards, procedures, and techniques. That proficiency is then interpreted as the ability to apply that knowledge to the individual audit situation likely to be encountered and to deal with those situations without extensive technical research and assistance. Needed also is the further ability to recognize just *when* further technical research and assistance may be needed.

The second specification (.2) covers the requirement for proficiency in accounting principles and techniques when the internal auditor works extensively with financial records and reports. There is the related truth, however, that all internal auditing work at some point usually relates to financial records and reports. It follows therefore that all internal auditors should have at least some understanding of that discipline.

In the third specification (.3) there is a major recognition of the truth that internal auditors need to understand management theory and to know how that theory applies to varying operational situations. Quite clearly, that understanding is a basic foundation for carrying out internal auditing assignments in a manner that best contributes to management needs. In Chapter 3 we deal in greater depth with that type of knowledge.

Finally, in the fourth specification (.4) the broad knowledge requirements of 220-.02 are outlined in terms of the individual internal auditor.[4] It also follows that each internal auditor need not have expertise in all categories. However, what is important is again the level of expertise in each, which enables the internal auditor to know when actual or potential problems may exist in the various areas. Put in other words, it is the capability to know when the point is reached when further information or special assistance is needed.

260   Human Relations and Communications

Internal auditors should be skilled in dealing with people and in communicating effectively.

.01   Internal auditors should understand human relations and maintain satisfactory relationships with auditees.

.02   Internal auditors should be skilled in oral and written communications so that they can clearly and effectively convey such matters as audit objectives, evaluations, conclusions, and recommendations.

In this specific standard the necessity for understanding people and communicating effectively is properly recognized. Clearly, this need exists for the internal auditor in *all* of his audit activities.

The first guideline (.01) addresses itself to the first of these two areas by the requirement that internal auditors should understand human relations and maintain satisfactory relationships with auditees. With respect to the first part of the requirement—understanding human relations—it needs to be recognized that this is something exceedingly complex and never fully achieved. In Chapter 7 we deal with this problem in greater depth.

The reference to maintaining satisfactory relations with auditees is also sound but again should also include *all* other persons with whom the internal auditor has contact during his internal audit activities. The need for understanding human relations also applies to all of those contacts.

The second guideline (.02) now focuses on the importance of being skilled in both oral and written communications. The need for this expertise also

---

[4]The areas specified here are similar but vary slightly from those specified for the internal auditing department, but again will depend on the specific work assignments.

applies to *all* individuals and groups which are either involved in or affected by the total internal audit effort. We also deal in greater depth with this problem in Chapter 7. There are also particular situations when the internal auditor will need to seek special assistance from communications specialists.

270   Continuing Education

Internal auditors should maintain their technical competence through continuing education.

.01   Internal auditors are responsible for continuing their education in order to maintain their proficiency. They should keep informed about improvements and current developments in internal auditing standards, procedures, and techniques. Continuing education may be obtained through membership and participation in professional societies; attendance of conferences, seminars, college courses, and in-house training programs; and participation in research projects.

This specific standard (270) clearly states the need to maintain technical competence through continuing education. In our dynamic and changing world it is self-evident that this is the only way for the professional internal auditor to avoid becoming obsolete and ineffective.

The supporting guideline (.01) in its first sentence reaffirms the need for continuing education but now for "proficiency"— a somewhat broader term than the previously used "technical competence" and one that we believe is more appropriate. The second sentence then focuses on the content of the continuing education. Again the question can be properly raised as to whether continuing education should not also extend to many nontechnical but related areas in terms of impact on the effectiveness of internal auditors. In the final sentence the various means are identified by which the continuing education can be obtained. Presumably, other ways would also be acceptable if proper relevance was established.

280   Due Professional Care

Internal Auditors should exercise due professional care in performing internal audits.

.01   Due professional care calls for the application of the care and skill expected of a reasonably prudent and competent internal auditor in the same or similar circumstances. Professional care should, therefore, be appropriate to the complexities of the audit being performed. In exercising due professional care, internal auditors should be alert to the possibility of intentional wrongdoing, errors and omissions, inefficiency, waste, ineffectiveness, and conflicts of interest. They should also be alert to those conditions and activities where irregularities are most likely to occur. In addition, they should identify inadequate controls and recommend improvements to promote compliance with acceptable procedures and practices.

.02   Due care implies reasonable care and competence, not infallibility or extraordinary performance. Due care requires the auditor to conduct examinations and verifications to a reasonable extent, but does not require detailed audits of all transactions. Accordingly, the internal auditor cannot give absolute assurance that noncompliance or irregularities do not exist. Nevertheless, the possibility of material irregularities or noncompliance should be considered whenever the internal auditor undertakes an internal auditing assignment.

.03 When an internal auditor suspects wrongdoing, the appropriate authorities within the organization should be informed. The internal auditor may recommend whatever investigation is considered necessary in the circumstances. Thereafter, the auditor should follow up to see that the internal auditing department's responsibilities have been met.

.04 Exercising due professional care means using reasonable audit skill and judgment in performing the audit. To this end, the internal auditor should consider:

.1 The extent of audit work needed to achieve audit objectives

.2 The relative materiality or significance of matters to which audit procedures are applied

.3 The adequacy and effectiveness of internal controls

.4 The cost of auditing in relation to potential benefits

.05 Due professional care includes evaluating established operating standards and determining whether those standards are acceptable and are being met. When such standards are vague, authoritative interpretations should be sought. If internal auditors are required to interpret or select operating standards, they should seek agreement with auditees as to the standards needed to measure operating performance.

This specific standard asserts the need for due professional care in performing internal audits. Certainly, "due professional care" is one of the basic foundation components of the sought-after "professional effectiveness." At the same time the definition, measurement, and final evaluation of that professional care becomes extremely difficult. The five guidelines endeavor to come at that problem in different ways.

In the first guideline (.01) the first two sentences deal with basic substance. This substance is first, the concept of "a reasonably prudent and competent" internal auditor. The key problem here is how one should measure and evaluate "reasonably." Second, there is the recognition of dependence on the complexities of the particular circumstances—certainly a very necessary qualification. In the second sentence "complexities of the audit" is recognized as one type of variation between individual situations. However, one should also take into consideration the economic or operational significance of the activity subject to audit.

The remainder of this first guideline shifts from the basic concept of professional care to a number of somewhat different—although related—issues. In the third sentence the focus is on particular types of problems to which the internal auditor should be alert—specifically the possibility of intentional wrongdoing, errors and omissions, inefficency, waste, ineffectiveness, and conflicts of interest. In the next sentence there is the further caution to be alert to those conditions and activities where irregularities are most likely to occur.

Again, in all these situations we would add that the extent of the alertness depends on the economic or operational significance of the activity being audited. The fifth and final sentence is a direct statement pertaining more appropriately to the scope of audit work, to be discussed later.

The first three sentences of second guideline (.02) together cover the unavoidable fact that all internal audits have limitations and cannot provide complete assurance that all noncompliance and irregularities have been disclosed. There are a number of reasons for these limitations, but they include the fact that the extent of audit work must be guided by costs and potential benefits, that audits of expanded scope will not always detect all regularities, and that internal auditing work is, like any other activity, subject to the limitations of human beings. But in the final sentence there is a more positive consolation prize for the audit recipients by requiring the internal auditor for each audit assignment to keep in mind the possibilities of material irregularities or noncompliance. Clearly, the internal auditor has *some* responsibilities in this area, and we discuss that in more detail in Chapter 26.

The third guideline (.03) deals with a somewhat different matter—the procedure for the internal auditor when wrongdoing is suspected. In the first sentence there is the requirement of informing the appropriate authorities. Quite clearly, some judgments will have to be made, including how significant the suspected wrongdoing, the extent of the belief that such a wrongdoing in fact exists, and the identification of the appropriate authority to advise. The second sentence then makes it permissive that there also be a recommendation for an investigation covering the situation, where wrongdoing is suspected. This involves still more judgment on the part of the internal auditor. Finally, in the third sentence there is the requirement that the internal auditor follow up to see that the internal auditing department's responsibilities have been met. What those responsibilities actually are, and when those responsibilities have been met then involves still further judgments.

The fourth guideline (.0) focuses on the meaning of "exercising due professional care," and again comes back to the test of "reasonable" audit skill and judgment in performing the audit. However, the internal auditor is instructed to consider the four factors detailed in .1 to .4 inclusive. In this connection items .1, .2, and .4 appear to be the key considerations. The inclusion of item .3, "The adequacy and effectiveness of internal controls," is less clear because, as further confirmed in the next section of the standards, adequacy and effectiveness of the internal controls involved is itself the key objective of the audit work rather than being a determinant of due professional care.

The fifth guideline (.05) again deals with a problem that probably pertains more directly to scope of work. There is first, confirmation as to the internal auditor's concern with evaluating operating standards for acceptability and then as to whether those standards are being met. The second sentence then goes on to require the internal auditor to seek authoritative interpretations if the standards being used are vague. In the third sentence there is the further requirement that the internal auditor seek agreement with auditees when new interpretations or selections of standards are required. All of this raises some interesting questions. Since the internal auditor is typically always interpreting standards there is the question as to whether seeking agreement as to those interpretations is always required. A second question is the extent to which selection by internal auditors of operating standards for use by operating personnel is appropriate—since such selection is usually considered to be a responsibility of operational management. However, management will typically welcome assistance in setting operating standards.

Professional Proficiency in Perspective

"Professional proficiency" is one of those interesting terms that can be viewed at varying levels. At its highest level the term encompasses the achievement of total effectiveness of the entire internal auditing effect. But as used in this section, the term relates more to how the audit work is carried out for particular audit assignments. As such, professional efficiency becomes, on the one hand, the responsibility of the internal auditing department and, on the other hand, the responsibility of the individual internal auditor. This is true despite the fact that some responsibilities can be dealt with more effectively by either the department or the individual. But in total there is the common objective of matching staff personnel with audit assignments in a manner that best assures the desired high level of internal auditing service to the organization. To achieve this common objective there must somehow be adequate capabilities. But in addition to capabilities there must be due professional care. Here, however, the measurement and evaluation become very difficult and resort must ultimately be made to concepts of reasonableness depending on the significance of the activities being audited, the costs of audit work, and the benefits thought to be derived. Judgment thus becomes the final determinant, the soundness of which must be demonstrated over an adequate period of time.

The guidelines relating to due professional care for the most part focus on protective type concerns in such areas as fraud, compliance, and conservation of assets. This protective orientation should not, however, let us forget the equal relevance of professional care of internal auditors in carrying out the broader management improvement types of audit services. That is, the needs for proper professional care are just as compelling for identifying and properly recommending opportunities for potentially greater management effectiveness and profitablity. We are again reminded that the dual protective and improvement objectives of the internal auditor are what distinguishes him so importantly from the external public auditor.

A final point that also needs to be made is that internal auditors as a group will be in varying stages of their professional career development. They will therefore have different levels of capabilities in terms of knowledge, skills, and disciplines, depending directly both on their different personal capabilities and the extent of their experience. All of these factors must be considered when individual internal auditors are assigned to particular audit tasks.

300   SCOPE OF WORK

*THE SCOPE OF THE INTERNAL AUDIT SHOULD ENCOMPASS THE
EXAMINATION AND EVALUATION OF THE ADEQUACY AND
EFFECTIVENESS OF THE ORGANIZATION'S SYSTEM OF INTERNAL
CONTROL AND THE QUALITY OF PERFORMANCE IN CARRYING OUT
ASSIGNED RESPONSIBILITES*

  .01   The scope of internal auditing work, as specified in this standard, encompasses what audit work should be performed. It is recognized, however, that
management and the board of directors provide general direction as to the scope
of work and the activities to be audited.
  .02   The purpose of the review for adequacy of the system of internal
control is to ascertain whether the system established provides reasonable
assurance that the organization's objectives and goals will be met efficiently
and economically.
  .03   The purpose of the review for effectiveness of the system of internal
control is to ascertain whether the system is functioning as intended.
  .04   The purpose of the review for quality of performance is to ascertain
whether the organization's objectives and goals have been achieved.
  .05   The primary objectives of internal control are to ensure:

  .1   The reliability and integrity of information
  .2   Compliance with policies, plans, procedures, laws, and regulations
  .3   The safeguarding of assets
  .4   The economical and efficient use of resources
  .5   The accomplishment of established objectives and goals for operations
        or programs

The general standard (300) covers the total scope of the internal audit and
identifies its two key aspects—"the examination and evaluation of the adequacy
and effectiveness of the organization's system of internal control" and "the
quality of performance in carrying out assigned responsibilities." The first of
these aspects thus deals with the kind of work to be performed and the second
the quality of the performance pursuant to that established range. The two
aspects have distinctive characters but are obviously closely interrelated.

    In the first guideline (.01) we have a matter of major significance. In the
first sentence the scope of work is tied to the coverage of the aforementioned
general standard. In the second sentence, however, there is the qualification
that the scope of the audit work and activities to be audited are subject to the
general direction of management and the board of directors. This qualification
might be interpreted as endorsing a situation where the internal auditing department was restricted in exercising its own judgment as to what kind of an
internal audit program was appropriate—even if based on the Standards. The
use of the word "general" avoids to some extent a possible contradiction between the two sentences, and hopefully provides an adequate basis for such
management direction as is not inconsistent with the Standards. We must make
that assumption because otherwise there would be a potential threat to the
independence of the internal auditor.

In the second guideline (.02) the accomplishment of the organization's objectives and goals in an efficient and economical manner are tied directly to the adequacy of the system of internal control. This is indeed an important tie. It might suggest, however, that the system of internal control is the only means of assuring the accomplishment of the objectives and goals of the organization efficiently and economically. We do need to recognize, however, that other approaches can also be utilized.

The third guideline (.03) now defines the purpose of the review of the system of internal control as ascertaining whether the system is functioning as intended. This guideline may be too narrowly structured. Certainly, the internal auditor is also concerned with identifying any additional means by which the system can be improved. That is, internal auditors should always search for betterment as well as protection.

The fourth guideline (.04) now defines the purpose of the review of performance as ascertaining whether the objectives and goals of the organization have been achieved. However, further elaboration is appropriate. Quite clearly the quality of performance pertains to the level of contribution being made to the ultimate achievement of the objectives and goals, but in addition management utilizes many means to achieve those objectives and goals, and does itself have the final responsibility for that achievement. Moreover, in a very practical sense, goals and objectives are ongoing and never fully achieved.

In the fifth guideline the primary objectives of internal control are defined as assuring the five types of results. We can first note that the first three of these desired results pertain to the more protective services of the internal auditor and the final two to the higher-level constructive services. All are sound objectives. Although we are substantially in agreement with this guideline, a somewhat better approach might be to recognize that the five results sought are more directly the objectives of the internal auditor, and that the internal auditor utilizes his review of internal control as the major means by which he achieves those desired objectives. At the same time the internal auditor is endeavoring to assist management to achieve *maximum effectiveness* in the use of resources as well as economy, efficiency, and established objectives—a somewhat broader audit mission.

Basic Role of the System of Internal Control

The preceding comments may perhaps be better understood by a more integrated overview. What we believe should be avoided is a view that the organization approaches its achievement of goals and objectives exclusively through the system of internal control. Instead, we favor the view that management and the board establish sound goals and objectives for the organization and then seek to achieve those goals and objectives in a variety of ways—a process we examine in more detail in Chapter 3. The system of internal control then becomes only one of the means—even though a very important one—by which that total achievement process is both protected and improved. The internal auditor at the same time endeavors to contribute directly to the total effectiveness of the management process. In this connection he utilizes his review and appraisal of the system of internal control as a major means by which he can assist management. What we then have is a major role for the system of internal control but without it constituting the total channel by which the organization effectively achieves its goals and objectives.

310   Reliability and Integrity of Information

Internal auditors should review the reliability and integrity of financial and operating information and the means used to identify, measure, classify, and report such information.
.01   Information systems provide data for decision making, control, and compliance with external requirements. Therefore, internal auditors should examine information systems and, as appropriate, ascertain whether:

.1   Financial and operating records and reports contain accurate, reliable, timely, complete, and useful information.
.2   Controls over record keeping and reporting are adequate and effective.

In the specific standard above the internal auditors concern for the reliability and integrity of financial and operating information—plus the means used to identify, measure, classify, and report such information—is confirmed. Now also this mandate is made *directly* to the internal auditor, rather than as an objective of internal control—an approach that more closely agrees with our own views.

In the supporting guideline the implementation of this internal auditing objective is usefully described. The first sentence expands on the importance of the data provided by information systems. The second sentence goes on to identify two key approaches of the internal auditor—first to focus on the records and reports produced by the system and second, to focus on the adequacy and effectiveness of the underlying controls.

The separate identification of "financial" and "operating" records and reports presents no problems, even though in practice both types of records are closely interrelated and very frequently either overlap or are integrated. Also any operational record or report eventually affects or becomes a part of other financial records.

320   Compliance with Policies, Plans, Procedures, Laws and Regulations

Internal auditors should review the systems established to ensure compliance with those policies, plans, procedures, laws, and regulations which could have a significant impact on operations and reports, and should determine whether the organization is in compliance.
.01   Management is responsible for establishing the systems designed to ensure compliance with such requirements as policies, plans, procedures, and applicable laws and regulations. Internal auditors are responsible for determining whether the systems are adequate and effective and whether the activities audited are complying with the appropriate requirements.

This specific standard deals with the second primary objective outlined above—that of the organization's compliance with existing policies, plans, procedures, laws, and regulations. The two means again utilized are through established systems and directly via the confirmation of compliance. Over the years compliance has always been one of the foundation concerns of the internal auditor. The concern expressed is protective—that is to avoid the various costs of noncompliance—but it should also include the search for improved controls and higher levels of compliance.

In the supporting guideline (.01) the first sentence reaffirms the basic responsibility of management for establishing the systems designed to ensure the various types of compliance. The second sentence focuses on the determinations by the internal auditor of both (1) the adequacy and effectiveness of the systems and (2) the ultimate compliance action. In total the compliance actions involve policies, plans, procedures, laws, and regulations, plus other specified actions authorized by management—formally or implicitly. These compliance actions apply to any level of organizational activity and again involve both protective and improvement aspects.

330 Safeguarding of Assets

Internal auditors review the means of safeguarding assets and, as appropriate, verify the existence of such assets.

.01 Internal auditors should review the means used to safeguard assets from various types of losses such as those resulting from theft, fire, improper or illegal activites, and exposure to the elements.

.02 Internal auditors, when verifying the existence of assets, should use appropriate audit procedures.

This specific guideline focuses on the third objective stated above and recognizes the two types of audit approaches. The first of these approaches is through reviewing the means employed and the second through the direct verification of the existence of the assets involved. The safeguarding of asset activities of the internal auditor has again always been a foundation-type responsibility of internal auditors. As noted in Chapter 1, this and the two previous objectives of the internal auditor in the areas of reliability and compliance have combined to first generate the initial establishment of the internal auditing function in the typical organization.

The first supporting guideline (.01) then focuses on the evaluation of the means employed by the organization to safeguard assets. The wide range of the safeguarding activities is, of course, directly dependent on the particular type of asset involved. Some of the various threats that need to be considered are also illustrated. The importance of safeguarding assets is also, of course, directly dependent on the extent and significance of the risk of loss to the organization. For example, cash is especially vulnerable and requires safeguarding actions that are very detailed and intensive. On the other hand, the risk may be very low for another type of asset that is bulky and relatively immobile. Obviously, considerable judgment is required to determine the extent of risk and how best to deal with the related problems.

The second guideline (.02) focuses on the direct verification of the existence of the particular assets. The additional coverage, however, has to do with the requirement that appropriate procedures are used in carrying out that verification. The significance of the term "appropriate" is that verifying the existence of some assets involves important types of total verification control such as for the previously mentioned vulnerability and possibilities of cross substitution.

340   Economical and Efficient Use of Resources

Internal auditors should appraise the economy and efficiency with which resources are employed.

.01   Management is responsible for setting operating standards to measure an activity's economical and efficient use of resources. Internal auditors are responsible for determining whether:

.1   Operating standards have been established for measuring economy and efficiency.

.2   Established operating standards are understood and are being met.

.3   Deviations from operating standards are identified, analyzed, and communicated to those responsible for corrective action.

.4   Corrective action has been taken.

.02   Audits related to the economical and efficient use of resources should identify such conditions as:

.1   Underutilized facilities

.2   Nonproductive work

.3   Procedures which are not cost justified

.4   Overstaffing or understaffing

This specific standard has to do with the predominantly constructive role and responsibility of the internal auditor in helping to achieve the economical and efficient use of the resources of the organization. The key word here is "appraisal" by the internal auditor as he seeks to assist the organization in this very important aspect of total organizational welfare.

The first guideline (.01) has to do with clarifying the respective responsibilities of management as compared to the internal auditor. It is first recognized that management has the responsibility to set the various operating standards. The responsibilities of the internal auditor are then indicated to be the determination of the four specifically enumerated implementing-type actions. These four aspects are essentially the range of the control cycle as applied in a variety of situations, and will be dealt with in greater depth in Chapter 4. However, at this point some further clarification of the respective management and internal auditing roles may be useful.

What needs to be more strongly recognized is that the total control cycle is basically the responsibility of management. The internal auditor's role then is to assist by providing further information as to how economically and efficiently the various parts of the control cycle are actually being carried out—and including also how those various parts can be improved. The interpretation of this guideline should therefore be subject to the aforementioned truth and at no point give the impression that the internal auditor is being given some special responsibility which either conflicts with or dilutes the basic management responsibility.

In the second guideline (.02) there is some further elaboration of the kinds of specific conditions which need to be identified—and presumably also appraised—by the internal auditor. All of the types of conditions indicated are definitely potential causes of the organization falling short of the proper level of accomplishing the economical[5] and efficient use of its various resources. However, there can also be other causes. In total the internal auditor is challenged to use his various skills to identify and establish priorities by which he can best assist management to achieve the ever important objectives and goals of *best possible utilization* of resources. As dealt with further in Chapter 3, the most effective utilization of resources is the basic central thrust of all management efforts. That central thrust then in turn sets the thrust of modern internal auditing.

350   Accomplishment of Established Objectives and Goals for Operations or Programs

> *Internal auditors should review operations or programs to ascertain whether results are consistent with established objectives and goals and whether the operations or programs are being carried out as planned.*
>
> .01   Management is responsible for establishing operating or program objectives and goals, developing and implementing control procedures, and accomplishing desired operating or program results. Internal auditors should ascertain whether such objectives and goals conform with those of the organization and whether they are being met.
>
> .02   Internal auditors can provide assistance to managers who are developing objectives, goals, and systems by determining whether the underlying assumptions are appropriate; whether accurate, current, and relevant information is being used; and whether suitable controls have been incorporated into the operations or programs.

This specific standard deals with the accomplishment of established objectives and goals for operations or programs. There is the specific concern that results are consistent with established objectives and goals and whether the operations or program are being carried out as planned. It is closely related to the preceding standard covering the economical and efficient use of resources and to a considerable extent overlaps with it. Indeed, the accomplishment of objectives and goals unavoidably involves the economical and efficient use of resources.

As in the preceding case, the first guideline (.01) distinguishes between the responsibilities of management and the internal auditor. To management is attributed the responsibility for establishing operating or program objectives

---

[5]We prefer the term "effective" to "economical" because of its higher-level coverage of improvement.

and goals, developing and implementing control procedures, and accomplishing desired operating or program results. To the internal auditor is attributed the responsibility of ascertaining whether such objectives and goals conform with those of the organization and whether they are being met. Here again it needs to be recognized that internal auditors should also assist management in its continuous search for better and improved policies and procedures, and in turn higher objectives.

The second guideline (.02) goes still farther in supporting a participative role of the internal auditor—this time to provide assistance to managers developing objectives, goals, and systems. The areas of assistance include whether the underlying assumptions are appropriate; whether accurate, current, and relevant information is being used; and whether suitable controls have been incorporated into the operations or programs. The first two types of assistance must again not go so far as to undermine basic management responsibilities. The third type of assistance—relating to the suitability of controls again involves the question discussed in connection with guideline 120-.03.

Scope of Work in Perspective

The central truth relating to scope of work is that the internal auditor accomplishes his objectives of assisting management through his reviewing and evaluating the various internal controls, both individually and collectively—even though that is not necessarily his only approach. Admittedly, management can alter that scope, but such alteration should not prevent the aforementioned basic concentration ōn the system of internal control. The higher-level objectives thus accomplished are the protective services of sound compliance, and safeguarding of assets; and the constructive role of contribution to the improvement of resource utilization in terms of economy, efficiency, *and effectiveness* in terms of properly established and properly achieved objectives and goals. In all of these connēctions the role of the internal auditor is always advisory and never to relieve management of its basic responsibility for utilizing the resources for maximum organizational welfare.

400   PERFORMANCE OF AUDIT WORK

AUDIT WORK SHOULD INCLUDE PLANNING THE AUDIT,
EXAMINING AND EVALUATING INFORMATION,
COMMUNICATING RESULTS, AND FOLLOWING UP.

.01   The internal auditor is responsible for planning and conducting the audit assignment, subject to supervisory review and approval.

The fourth section of the standards deals with the actual performance of audit work. That performance is viewed as including the planning of the audit, examining and evaluating information, communicating results, and following up. These phases are the component work segments of the individual internal audit. The supporting guideline (.01) then goes on to stipulate that it is the responsibility of the internal auditor to plan and conduct the audit, presumably at all levels of audit responsibility and utilizing proper supervisory review and approval. This classification of the individual phases and the related concept of responsibility comes off as logical and acceptable. All of these aspects are also discussed in much greater depth in the chapters covering the administration of internal auditing activities.

410 Planning the Audit

Internal auditors should plan each audit
.01 Planning should be documented and should include:

.1 Establishing audit objectives and scope of work
.2 Obtaining background information about the activities to be audited
.3 Determining the resources necessary to perform the audit
.4 Communicating with all who need to know about the audit
.5 Performing, as appropriate, an on-site survey to become familiar with the activities and controls to be audited, to identify areas for audit emphasis, and to invite auditee comments and suggestions
.6 Writing the audit program
.7 Determining how, when, and to whom audit results will be communicated
.8 Obtaining approval of the audit work plan

The specific standard properly confirms the necessity of planning each audit. The supporting guideline then provides in more detail the scope of that planning. The first item (.1)—establishing audit objectives and scope of work—is clearly the essential first step. Items .2, .3, and .4—as listed—cover important preparatory activities. Item .5—the on-site review, as appropriate—can be viewed as further preliminary work, but probably more as an integral phase of the audit itself. At this point the audit work has really begun and as a result definitive judgments will be made as to the more formal audit program. Item .7—determining how, when, and to whom audit results will be communicated—are interesting questions for preliminary consideration. It needs to be recognized, however, that these questions must be continually reappraised based on what the audit results actually turn out to be.

420 Examining and Evaluating Information

Internal auditors should collect, analyze, interpret, and document information to support audit results.
.01 The process of examining and evaluating information is as follows:

.1 Information should be collected on all matters related to the audit objectives and scope of work.
.2 Information should be sufficient, competent, relevant, and useful to provide a sound basis for audit findings and recommendations.

Sufficient information is factual, adequate, and convincing so that a prudent, informed person would reach the same conclusions as the auditor.

Competent information is reliable and the best attainable through the use of appropriate audit techniques.

Relevant information supports audit findings and recommendations and is consistent with the objectives for the audit.

Useful information helps the organization meet its goals

.3   Audit procedures, including the testing and sampling techniques employed, should be selected in advance, where practicable, and expanded or altered if circumstances warrant.

.4   The process of collecting, analyzing, interpreting, and documenting information should be supervised to provide reasonable assurance that the auditor's objectivity is maintained and that audit goals are met.

.5   Working papers that document the audit should be prepared by the auditor and reviewed by management of the internal auditing department. These papers should record the information obtained and the analyses made and should support the bases for the findings and recommendations to be reported.

The specific standard here deals with the collection, analysis, interpretation, and documentation of information to support audit results. Support here necessarily pertains to the development of audit conclusions a well as the backup of those conclusions. That is, information must be first analyzed and interpreted as a basis of developing audit findings and related conclusions. Then, as definitive conclusions and recommendations are developed, there is the further special need to be sure that there is adequate backup documentation to support those conclusions. Such backup is especially important when later those conclusions are studied and possibly challenged. This is made more clear in the supporting five components of the process for examining and evaluating information.

The first of these five components prescribes the nature of the desired information relating to audit objectives and scope of work. The second component is an important statement as to the adequacy of the basis for findings and conclusions. The qualities specifically enumerated are sufficiency, competence, relevance, and usefulness, and each of these qualities is then further defined. Again here we fall back on our previously introduced concepts of due care and reasonableness of content. The coverage of "useful" overlaps with the other three more definitive qualities and is really not a separate point. The third component is an important recognition of the need to expand or alter audit procedures in the light of the evolving circumstances. The fourth component reaffirms the importance of supervision as a basis for needed objectivity and accomplishment of audit goals. Finally, the fifth component covers the importance of properly prepared and reviewed working papers. In total these five components constitute the basis for an effective examination and evaluation of information, the development of appropriate conclusions, and the supporting documentation for work done and conclusions reached.

430 **Communicating Results**

Internal auditors should report the results of their audit work.

.1 A signed, written report should be issued after the audit examination is completed. Interim reports may be written or oral and may be transmitted formally or informally.

.2 The internal auditor should discuss conclusions and recommendations at appropriate levels of management before issuing final written reports.

.3 Reports should be objective, clear, concise, constructive, and timely.

.4 Reports should present the purpose, scope, and results of the audit; and, where appropriate, reports should contain an expression of the auditor's opinion.

.5 Reports may include recommendations for potential improvements and acknowledge satisfactory performance and corrective action.

.6 The auditee's views about audit conclusions or recommendations may be included in the audit report.

.7 The director of internal auditing or designee should review and approve the final audit report before issuance and should decide to whom the report will be distributed.

The specific standard confirms the internal auditor's responsibility to report the results of his audit. Quite obviously, findings and conclusions are of very little value unless reported to those members of management who have the authority to take the actions that make possible the benefits potentially available to the organization.

The supporting guidelines pertain to the form and content of the aforementioned reports pus the manner of their preparation and distribution. The first of these guidelines (.1) confirms the need for a signed written report plus possible interim reports that can be written or oral, formal or informal, depending on the significance of the contents and the degree of urgency.

The second guideline (.2) mandates the preliminary discussion of conclusions and recommendations with appropriate levels of management, thus both assuring input which may be relevant and for building proper relations with auditees.

The third guideline (.3) properly describes the desired quality of reports—to be objective, clear, concise, and timely.

The fourth guideline specifies the coverage of purpose, scope, and results of the audit and, *where appropriate,* an opinion. The latter action is usually associated with financial statements but can apply also to some operational situations. In many cases, however, there is no formal opinion, even though any conclusion is to some extent an opinion.

The fifth guideline makes recommendations for potential improvement permissive. It would be better, we believe, to recognize that internal auditors should always seek to identify potential improvements. This same sentence also makes permissive the acknowledgment of satisfactory performance and corrective action. In most cases such acknowledgments are clearly desirable for the record and also because they help build a good relationship with the auditees.

The sixth guideline deals with a more complicated question—whether the auditee's views about audit conclusions or recommendations should be included in the audit report. Ideally, the internal auditor reaches agreement with the auditee on all matters, and any still existing disagreement suggests that the several parties of interest may not have adequately reviewed the facts. However, there may be good reasons why the auditee has different views than the internal auditor and why those different views should be reported. In any event, the application of this guideline needs to be handled with extreme care and objectivity.

Finally, the seventh guideline mandates appropriate supervisory review of the report before issuance and again comes back to the earlier point of now reappraising what the distribution of the report should be. Normally, there is a standard distribution, but the unique findings and recommendations from a particular audit may justify a special distribution of all or part of the particular report.

440   Following Up

Internal auditors should follow up to ascertain that appropriate action is taken on reported audit findings.

.01   Internal auditing should determine that corrective action was taken and is achieving the desired results, or that management or the board has assumed the risk of not taking corrective action on reported findings.

This specific standard provides that the internal auditor should follow up to ascertain that appropriate action is taken on reported audit findings. The supporting guideline (.01) restates that requirement as a determination but does go on to recognize more definitely the possibility that management may decide not to take the recommended corrective action, instead assuming the related risk. Again we have a similar issue to the one discussed under standard 340. Certainly, the internal auditor has an interest in the utilization of his findings and recommendations, and he will wish to assist in assuring that utilization in every practicable manner. That assistance must not, however, become so structured, or administered in such a way, that it impinges on or undermines the basic responsibility of management to give consideration to the audit results and to take appropriate action. It needs to be recognized that appropriate action may in management's judgment be no action at all.

Typically, management uses one of its regular line or staff components to administer a formal program of monitoring responses, action, and ultimate clearance of all audit recommendations—including both the recommendations of the internal and external auditor. The internal auditor then periodically reappraises the effectiveness of that procedural program. As a part of the next audit he will also review action on previously made audit recommendations —again of both his own making and those of the external auditor—and incorporate noncompliance findings in the current audit evaluations. This procedure is we believe more consistent with proper roles and responsibilities of the internal auditor and other organizational components. It also avoids having the internal auditor take on a police image and thus endanger his own partnership relationship with the auditee.

Performance of Audit Work in Perspective

The section on performing audit work focuses more directly on the four sequential phases: planning the audit, examining and evaluating information, communicating results, and following up. It does, of course, build on the standards of independence, and it does unavoidably overlap with the sections on professional efficiency and scope of work. It is not surprising, therefore, that there is occasionally repetition of the same basic point, as well as situations where the coverage of a particular point could logically be in either of the other sections. This is not a serious problem, but it does mean that the various sections must be viewed as an integrated whole. Together the proper base is then established for the final section of the standards dealing with management of the internal auditing department.

500 MANAGEMENT OF THE INTERNAL AUDITING DEPARTMENT

THE DIRECTOR OF INTERNAL AUDITING SHOULD PROPERLY MANAGE THE INTERNAL AUDITING DEPARTMENT

.01 The director of internal auditing is responsible for properly managing the department so that:

.1 Audit work fulfills the general purposes and responsibilities approved by management and accepted by the board.

.2 Resources of the internal auditing department are efficiently and effectively employed.

.3 Audit work conforms to the *Standards for the Professional Practice of Internal Auditing*.

The final major section of the Standards has to do with the management of the internal auditing department. The mandate here is that the director of internal auditing should properly manage that internal auditing department. All the specific standards and supporting guidelines are about the manner in which the director should accomplish that management mission.

The supporting guideline (.01) to the specific standard deals first with the end objectives of the internal auditor's management mission. The first of these objectives (.1) is to satisfy the established expectations of management and the board as officially approved and accepted by them. This assumes, of course, that such established expectations properly reflect the professional services of the range and level for which internal auditors have proven their capabilities. Quite obviously, the particular director of internal auditing is bound by the currently established general purposes and responsibilities, but there is also a professional responsibility of the director to somehow activate the forces that will result in sufficiently high level purposes and responsibilities.

The second objective (.2) then goes on to recognize for the director of internal auditing the same responsibilities that exist for all managers, that is, to make effective use of assigned resources. In best practice also the internal auditor should seek the *most effective* utilization of those resources that is practicable. All of this recognizes the fact that the director is himself a manager as he administers his own department.

Finally, the third objective (.3) properly confirms the need of audit work in the department to be consistent with the Standards for the Professional Practice of Internal Auditing—thus tieing in the earlier statement in the foreword that the standards are intended to represent the practice of internal auditing as it should be, as judged and adopted by the Board of Directors of the Institute.

510 Purpose, Authority, and Responsibility

> *The director of internal auditing should have a statement of purpose, authority, and responsibility for the internal auditing department.*
>
> *.01*   The director of internal auditing is responsible for seeking the approval of management and the acceptance by the board of a formal written document (charter) for the internal auditing department.

This specific standard deals directly with the responsibility of the director to have a statement of purpose, authority, and responsibility for the internal auditing department. In the supporting guideline (.01) there is also the further mandate of the director's responsibility for *seeking* a statement that is both approved by management and accepted by the board. Presumably also, the content of that statement (the charter) should be consistent with the Standards in total, as stated in the third paragraph of the Introduction. Presumably, that statement should also specify the unrestricted scope of the internal auditor's work, as stated in the fourth paragraph of the introduction. Presumably also, that statement should incorporate the high-level objectives of internal auditors—as stated in 300-.05 of Scope of Work—which include services to the organization in the areas of the economical and efficient use of resources and the accomplishment of established objectives and goals for operations or programs. What perhaps needs to be more specifically covered by the current specific standard and guideline is that the charter should be of sufficiently high level in terms of purpose, authority, and responsibility. It is also part of the internal auditor's responsibility to help make that desired situation come to pass when it does not already exist.

520 Planning

> *The director of internal auditing should establish plans to carry out the responsibilities of the internal auditing department.*
>
> *.01*   These plans should be consistent with the internal auditing department's charter and with the goals of the organization.
>
> *.02*   The planning process involves establishing:

.1   Goals
.2   Audit work schedules
.3   Staffing plans and financial budgets
.4   Activity reports

.03   The goals of the internal auditing department should be capable of being accomplished within specified operating plans and budgets and, to the extent possible, should be measurable. They should be accompanied by measurement criteria and targeted dates of accomplishment.

.04   *Audit work schedules* should include (a) what activities are to be audited; (b) when they will be audited; and (c) the estimated time required, taking into account the scope of the audit work planned and the nature and extent of audit work performed by others. Matters to be considered in establishing audit work schedule priorities should include (a) the date and results of the last audit; (b) financial exposure; (c) potential loss and risk; (d) requests by management; (e) major changes in operations, programs, systems, and controls; (f) opportunities to achieve operating benefits; and (g) changes to and capabilities of the audit staff. The work schedules should be sufficiently flexible to cover unanticipated demands on the internal auditing department.

.05   *Staffing plans and financial budgets*, including the number of auditors and the knowledge, skills, and disciplines required to perform their work, should be determined from audit work schedules, administrative activities, education and training requirements, and audit research and development efforts.

.06   *Activity reports* should be submitted periodically to management and to the board. These reports should compare (a) performance with the department's goals and audit work schedules and (b) expenditures with financial budgets. They should explain the reasons for major variances and indicate any action taken or needed.`

Planning is the basis for achieving effective results in every organization. It is therefore to be expected that this specific standard should require the director of internal auditing to establish plans to carry out the responsibilities of the internal auditing department. It also follows, as covered in the first supporting guideline (.01), that those plans should be consistent with the internal auditing department's charter and with the goals of the organization. Again, however, it becomes important, as previously discussed, that the charter provide for sufficiently high-level professional internal auditing service. It is also important that the goals of the organization be at a sufficiently high level and be properly defined.

In the second guideline (.02) the span of the planning process is outlined. That planning process covers the planning of both the goals, covered by the first subguide (.1), and the framework for the implementation, as covered by the other three subguidelines. All of these aspects are dealt with in greater detail in Chapters 9 to 12, covering the administration of the internal auditing department. Our purpose in this chapter is only to recognize fully the critical nature of the planning process as a basis for later sound implementation, and in turn for best possible utilization of internal auditing resources for maximum organizational welfare.

530   Policies and Procedures

> *The director of internal auditing should provide written policies and proce-*
> *dures to guide the audit staff.*

   .01   The form and content of written policies and procedures should be appropriate to the size and structure of the internal auditing department and the
complexity of its work. Formal administrative and technical audit manuals may
not be needed by all internal auditing departments. A small internal auditing
department may be managed informally. Its audit staff may be directed and
controlled through daily, close supervision and written memoranda. In a large
internal auditing department, more formal and comprehensive policies and procedures are essential to guide the audit staff in the consistent compliance with
the department's standards of performance.

The specific standard properly recognizes the importance of written policies
and procedures for guidance to the audit staff. Actually, policies and procedures
can be at either of the two levels—for planning or for implementation. At the
planning level the policies and procedures become the basis for more detailed
elaboration and execution as part of the following implementation. This means
that such higher-level policies and procdures usually need to be formally
developed.

   The foregoing is important for the interpretation of the supporting guideline
(.01). This guideline properly recognizes that the need for formal administrative
and technical audit manuals will vary, depending on the size and complexity
of the organization. This is due to the fact that in smaller organizations enough
can be accomplished through closer supervision. It is important to recognize,
however, that this greater informality is applicable predominantly to the implementation phase. That is, formal definition is usually always desirable in the
higher-level planning phase.

540   Personnel Management and Development

> *The director of internal auditing should establish a program for selecting and*
> *developing the human resources of the internal auditing department.*

   .01   The program should provide for:

   .1   Developing written job descriptions for each level of the audit staff
   .2   Selecting qualified and competent individuals
   .3   Training and providing continuing educational opportunities for each
          internal auditor
   .4   Appraising each internal auditor's performance at least annually
   .5   Providing counsel to internal auditors on their performance and profes-
          sional development

Managerial results are accomplished through people. The director of internal
auditing, like any other manager, must accomplish his managerial objectives
through people. This specific guideline therefore very properly mandates the
director to establish a program for selecting and developing the human resources of the internal auditing department.

   The five supporting guidelines then go on to cover in more detail the significant components of such an adequate program. This entire area is covered in much greater detail in Chapters 9 to 12, on the administration of an effective internal auditing department. Several broad observations are, however, appropriate at this point. One of these observations is that the personnel management process actually begins with the determination of personnel needs for the internal auditing department, based on the total needs of the organization, and then extends to the time when the individuals actually leave the internal auditing department. It follows that all intermediate aspects of the employment of the individual involve personnel management. In some cases these intermediate aspects are covered by definitive and special subprograms, and in other cases they are handled as a part of the regular managerial processes—as for example in the case of regular supervision.

Finally, there is also the need that the personnel management activities be related properly to those of the larger organization of which the internal auditing department is a part. In some cases personnel activities for the internal auditing department are handled by another organizational group, in other cases separately by the internal auditing department, and in still other cases together. Moreover, the policies of the larger organization are normally controlling. What this means is that the director of internal auditing must determine what he needs to be doing to supplement the policies and procedures of the organization to achieve his own proper objectives. But at the same time his own activities must properly conform to the established organization's activities.

550 External Auditors

The director of internal auditing should coordinate internal and external audit efforts.

.01 The internal and external audit work should be coordinated to ensure adequate audit coverage and to minimize duplicate efforts.

.02 Coordination of audit efforts involves:

.1 Periodic meetings to discuss matters of mutual interest
.2 Access to each other's audit programs and working papers
.3 Exchange of audit reports and management letters
.4 Common understanding of audit techniques, methods, and terminology

This specific standard deals with the responsibility of the director of internal auditing to coordinate his internal auditing efforts with those of the external auditor. This is an area that is becoming increasingly important and it is dealt with in greater detail in Chapter 29.[6] While the coordination of the two audit efforts is becoming increasingly the role of the audit committee of the board of directors, it should be noted at this time that the internal auditor should do his part to assuring the best possible two way coordination of the two audit efforts. A similar responsibility exists on the part of the external auditor.

[6]Reference should also be made to *Research Report No. 24,* "Evaluating Internal/External Audit Services and Relationships," released in December 1980 by The Institute of Internal Auditors.

The first supporting guideline (.01) goes on to confirm the need for coordination and then to define the objectives of that coordination as ensuring adequate audit coverage and minimizing duplicate efforts. Both of these stated objectives perhaps suggest unduly a nice quantitative fit of the two audit efforts. A better overall objective would be "to best ensure maximum effectiveness of the total audit effort "

The second guideline (.02) then goes on to specify the major components of the aforementioned coordination effort. All of the components mentioned are certainly important to an effective coordination effort. However, it needs to be recognized more precisely that effective coordination begins with advance planning between the two audit groups. Such joint planning is also facilitated by (1) understanding and recognition by each audit group of the other's primary roles and responsibilities, (2) a more definite acceptance of their major common interest in the effectiveness of the system of internal accounting control, (3) a demonstration of adequate professional competence on the part of the internal audit staff, and (4) the acceptance of an environment in which two mutually respected partners work together to exploit best total common interests. The total scope of this coordination effort is so far reaching that overall coordination by the audit committee of the board is all the more desirable—a matter dealt with in greater detail in Chapter 28.

560   Quality Assurance

The director of internal auditing should establish and maintain a quality assurance program to evaluate the operations of the internal auditing department.

.01   The purpose of this program is to provide reasonable assurance that audit work conforms with these *Standards*, the internal auditing department's charter, and other applicable standards. A quality assurance program should include the following elements:

.1   Supervision
.2   Internal reviews
.3   External reviews

.02   *Supervision* of the work of the internal auditors should be carried out continually to assure conformance with internal auditing standards, departmental policies, and audit programs.

.03   *Internal reviews* should be performed periodically by members of the internal auditing staff to appraise the quality of the audit work performed. These reviews should be performed in the same manner as any other internal audit.

.04   *External reviews* of the internal auditing department should be performed to appraise the quality of the department's operations. These reviews should be performed by qualified persons who are independent of the organization and who do not have either a real or an apparent conflict of interest. Such reviews should be conducted at least once every three years. On completion of the review, a formal, written report should be issued. The report should express an opinion as to the department's compliance with the *Standards for the Professional Practice of Internal Auditing* and, as appropriate, should include recommendations for improvement.

This final specific standard deals with an aspect that has increasingly become an important dimension of the internal auditor's standards for professional practice—that of establishing and maintaining a quality assurance program to evaluate the effectiveness of the operations of the individual internal auditing department. Although quality as an objective is always in the mind of any manager, what is important is the recognition of the need for a definite supplementary effort to measure, protect, and generate the desired high levels of quality.

The first supporting guideline (.01) goes on to outline three levels or components of such a quality assurance program. These components are supervision, internal reviews, and external reviews—each of which is then further described in the subsequent three guidelines. The first of these components is the further recognition of the supervisory responsibility covered in the earlier specific standard (230). The specific recognition in the second guideline (.02), however, properly identifies that supervision as a definitive component of the total quality assurance program.

The third guideline (.03) then deals with internal reviews. In actual practice the supervision at the various levels in the internal auditing department provides various types of internal reviews. The new kind intended, however, is a separate audit review conducted under the same procedures and standards as any other audit assignment.

Finally, in the fourth supporting guideline (.04) the nature and scope of the external review is outlined. The conditions enumerated include the adequacy of the qualifications of the external reviewer, independence from the organization, and freedom from any real or apparent conflict of interest. The alternatives for these external reviews and their relative merits are discussed in detail in Chapter 30.

Standards for the Professional Practice of Internal Auditing in Perspective

In this chapter we have endeavored to provide a better understanding of internal auditing as a total professional activity. In accomplishing this objective we have utilized the "Standards for the Professional Practice of Internal Auditing" as approved by The Institute of Internal Auditors. In using these Standards we have gone beyond them to develop related principles, concepts, and approaches. In so doing we have unavoidably identified areas where the coverage in the standards appears to be incomplete and where therefore further interpretation and elaboration appear to be needed. The recognition of such conditions is not unexpected when one considers the fact that the Standards were a joint effort of many practitioners and necessarily involved compromise and adjustment. This in no way detracts from the monumental significance of the Standards and the level of achievement on the part of those who produced them. Hopefully, however, the further interpretations and views expressed in this book can be useful in the further evaluation of the existing Standards.

CHAPTER THREE

Understanding
Management Needs

Importance of Management Focus

In the three previous editions of this book, service to management was regarded as the controlling mission of the internal auditor. Initially, the concerns were also with the narrower and more protective needs of management. There has, however, been a continuous upward trend over the years, both as pertaining to the level of those protective needs and now the more effective use of resources. At the same time the internal auditors mission has been expanded to cover the board of directors and through that board the stockholders, government, and the total society. We therefore now properly refer to the controlling mission of the modern internal auditor as service to the organization.

Quite clearly, many recipients of the more expanded internal auditing services have certain special needs—the exact nature of which are still evolving. The truth remains, however, that management effectiveness is still a major concern of *all* parties of interest. If organizations are not well managed, all members of society suffer. At the same time the management role is becoming more complex because of the rapidly changing external environment and the new tools available to managers. All of these factors combine to make it all the more important that the internal auditor assist managers in every way practicable.

But if the internal auditor is going to assist management properly, he must continuously strive to understand management needs. We need to understand management objectives and how managers go about it to identify and solve problems, as they seek to achieve those objectives. We need to learn to think like managers so that we can truly achieve a partnership relationship with them in their managerial endeavors.

There is still another important reason why internal auditors need to understand good management theory and practice. This is because internal auditors themselves—as directors and supervisors—are managers of their own professional activities. Such individuals must develop objectives and apply managerial practice to achieve those objectives. working through people and with other resources, just as do all other managers. One can really not be a qualified counselor to managers if he himself cannot effectively manage his own operations. There is the need in fact to provide a model that can be observed and followed by all others.

In this chapter we look briefly at some of the more general concepts of management. In Chapters 4 and 5, we then probe more deeply into control and the other types of organizational control utilized by all managers. In Chapter 28 we also examine in more detail the services rendered to the audit committee of the board of directors. At the same time all the other chapters involve important management areas. Effective internal auditing in all respects involves understanding management needs and working with management to best serve those needs. That understanding is directly necessary to make possible the *capability* to serve management. But it is also an essential ingredient in providing *credibility* for the internal auditor. Recipients will then respect the internal auditor and listen to his counsel. Only then also will managers and internal auditors achieve effectiveness in all operational areas and thus best promote maximum organizational welfare.

What Is Management?

The mention of the words "mangement" or "manager" will suggest a variety of thoughts to different people. In its most simplistic form there will be an image of someone getting a job done and doing it in an effective manner. In other cases, it may suggest an individual or a group of individuals dealing with large and complicated problems. Typically, however, there is the common thread of a more enlightened and more systematic accomplishment of some defined objective.

When we come to developing formal definitions of management—the actions of managers—we can again have a wide range of ideas in terms of nature and scope. Our own most compact definition is: "*Management is the process of achieving the effective utilization of resources.*" This definition recognizes that management is an active *process*, that it deals with *resources* (including both human and nonhuman resources), and that the end objective is *utilization* of those resources in the *most effective* manner practicable. This maximizing the effective utilization of total resources is indeed the most basic aspect of what management is all about. Managers get the best possible results, and they do it in the best possible manner. In business this normally means maximum profitability, based on long-run standards and giving fair consideration to the rights of all parties of interest.

Expanding the Definition. If we go on to expand the basic definition of management above, we would need to recognize that the resources exist in an environment and that managers seek to relate the strengths and weaknesses of the particular resources in terms of existing environmental restrictions and opportunities. Out of that analytical study, the managers develop the highest goals and objectives to be accomplished that are practicable. Those determinations include consideration of the major strategy to be employed and this leads into the development of lower-level strategy policies, and plans for implementation.[1] Finally, there is the actual implementation of all the preceding plans, by and through people, leading to the maximum achievement of established goals and objectives. This is an interrelated continuing process as we move through time. We will come back to this more defined process later in the chapter. We then develop in greater depth the management process as a model for application in all managerial situations through continuing reiteration and refinement. But first we need to recognize several other ways in which we can look at management, and to identify more precisely some of the key attributes that need always be given serious consideration.

Management as a Series of Subprocesses. Another very popular way to look at the management process is through breaking it down into a number of related subprocesses. Different students of management do this in different ways. Our own preferred approach is, as follows:

1. *Planning.* This subprocess involves the studies and decisions pertaining to where we want the organization[2] to be at stated times in the future. It includes the total range of planning, from the highest-level determination of major goals and objectives, to the lower-level strategies and supporting policies, to the still lower procedures and methods for actual operational implementation. It is the foundation for all the other subprocesses.

2. *Organizing.* This subprocess has to do with breaking down the work of the organization into pieces and then bringing those pieces back together so that the total work of the organization can be accomplished. This also enables each individual in the organization to know what he is supposed to do, and to whom he can go for direction and help. Developing all of these relationships is itself a kind of planning but more properly builds upon the previous planning.

3. *Providing Resources.* Overlapping into the planning and organizing is the particular subprocess of providing other needed resources. It includes the procurement of material resources—plant, equipment, and all types of materials and supplies—and the recruitment and development of people. The latter activities are to a major extent part of the modern personnel function, although all managers must be deeply involved.

---

[1]Our usage of terms is that *goals* are the highest level ends we try to achieve, and that *strategies* are the means by which those goals are achieved. We then use the term *objective* as lower-ranking goals, and the term *policies* as lower-level strategies, and finally the term *procedures* to describe the still lower means by which policies are made operative. In actual practice, different people use the terms in a variety of ways. Also, individual terms unavoidably take on different meanings, depending on the organizational level of the user.

[2]The principles in all of these subprocesses can also be applied to any component of the organization.

4. *Administering*. This is the subprocess when work is actually done. It includes three different types of supportive action which are basic to the execution of work assignments. The first of these is "directing"—which has to do primarily with how instructions are communicated to subordinates, the second is "coordinating"—which has to do primarily with providing needed information between all workers; and the third is "leading"—which is essentially the motivation of workers through the example set by the leaders, and the way those leaders work with the individuals who have subordinate responsibilities.

5. *Controlling*. Current work accomplishment is unavoidably affected by changing conditions and varying human capabilities. We must therefore identify deviations from plans and deal with such deviations effectively. This controlling is the necessary subprocess to help us to achieve best the established objectives. It is also the area in which the internal auditor has special expertise. We deal with this important subprocess in greater depth in Chapter 4.

Management in Functional Areas.   We can also view management in terms of the functional areas of a typical organization. These functional areas refer to the various groups of work activity that are similar in character. The classification in this case will vary depending on the importance of the particular functional area in a given organization. Typical areas so recognized include research, engineering, production, marketing, administration, personnel, and finance. The management process in each area is subject to the same subprocesses previously discussed but the focus now is on achieving the performance of the designated function in the most effective manner practicable. When combined with general management, they comprise the total management of the organization. Because each of these functional areas also has its own relatively unique problems, the coverage of the internal auditor's concerns with controls have been similarly structured in the third section of this book.

Nature of the Environment

The individual organization with its resources operates in a very complicated environment, requiring some elaboration as to the features contributing to that complexity. Part of this complexity arises because of the various types of environmental factors which are operative. A possible classification of these types of factors would include the economic, the competitive, the technological, the political, and the social. Each of these deserves some brief comment.

Economic Aspects.   A major portion of the environment has to do with the various economic factors. There are first of all the dimensions of the state of the economy in terms of the world situation, the nation, and the specific regional areas affected. Within this framework we are concerned with the more specific factors which relate to the products and services of the particular company.

Who uses the products and why? How strong is that demand in terms of other needs? Where are the users of the product? How able are they to afford the use of the product? There are then, on the other hand, the factors relating to the supply of the product or service. Where do the materials and services come from that are needed to produce the aforementioned products, and what is their availability? What kinds of facilities are needed to produce the products, and what kind of production processes are involved? What are the requirements in terms of capital, know how, and costs? Finally, these factors relating to both demand and supply have to be equated in terms of whether there are acceptable profit potentials.

Competitive Aspects.   Coupled also with the economic aspects just described is the existing competitive situation. Who are the competitors? How many are there? How large are they in relation to our own company? What are their particular competitive strengths? And how easily do competitors enter the field and withdraw from it? All of these factors combine to determine the character of the competitive environment which bears on the industry in a broad sense, and on the particular firm in a more direct sense. Very often the competitive relationship has a number of dimensions. A can maker, for example, is subject to the competition first, of other can makers, and second, to makers of other types of containers—glass, plastic, paper, and the like. At a still broader level there is the competition for the consumer dollar from other products that do not require the use of any kind of a package.

Technological Aspects.   All organizations, by the nature of the kind of business they are in and the industry in which they operate, are subject to the technological factor in their own special way. A company in the aerospace industry is illustrative of a situation where there is a major technological impact. On the other hand, a company in the restaurant business is illustrative of where the impact is relatively low. In the former situation changes in the technology can constitute both major risk and major opportunity. In the second case there may also be risk and opportunity, but not so much from the changes in the existing technology. The varying impact will be on the kind of people required, the extent of research, the time span of planning, and the like.

Political Aspects.   The political side of the environment refers to the extent to which there are laws or other kinds of governmental regulation that have important bearing on the operation of the particular organization. In the case of a public utility, the regulatory aspect is very significant. In the automobile industry the new regulations covering safety and emissions represent a more recent type of regulatory development. In the steel industry the political factor may take the form of pressure on pricing or wage levels. All organizations, however, to some extent are subject to legal controls and restrictions of various types.

Social Aspects. Back of existing law is the force of the society, which is expressed ultimately through the political process, and then in some cases in the enactment of various types of laws. Present also are the attitudes and views of the society, which themselves constitute important environmental forces. Here there is a wide spectrum of developments, including such important matters as decaying urban areas, minority rights explosions, attitudes toward pollution, and overall rising social expectations as to various types of conduct relating to the operations of both business and nonbusiness organizations. These social aspects represent some of the most difficult problems every company faces if it is to survive and prosper. This is especilly true when there is an increasing demand for business organizations to assume a greater degree of social responsibility.

Nature of the Environment at Lower Organizational Levels

Our discussion of environmental factors has been from the standpoint of the entire company or other independent organizational entity. But management entities also exist at lower organizational levels—subsidiaries, divisions, departments, and the like. In these cases the environmental factors previously discussed include additionally the authority and controls of the higher organizational levels to which the lower-level management entity is accountable. On the positive side, there are the resources of the higher-level management organization which may be available to augment the already assigned resources. On the other side are the constraints of various kinds which may be imposed by the higher-level management authority.

Some Important Attributes of Management

As stated previously, we need also to understand certain key attributes and truths about the management process before reviewing the major model of the total process. Those that we regard as being especially important are described next.

Dependence on People. We have seen that people are one part of the resources for which the effective manager is seeking the best possible utilization. Thus people can be resources in terms of their knowledge, skills, and experience. But people have a unique importance that goes far beyong those considerations. This importance stems from the basic truth that all management action is carried out by and through people. An effective manager, therefore, is directly dependent on people to make plans and to implement those plans through definitive actions. This means that we need to understand people so that we can relate to them in an effective manner and obtain their maximum contribution toward the achievement of managerial goals and objectives.

But understanding people is not a simple accomplishment. People as individuals are human in that they have feelings and emotions and they must be properly motivated. Put in other words, there is a continuing challenge to find the best possible fit and integration of individual and organizational goals. That integration can never be perfectly achieved because individuals are human and are always subject to continuously changing conditions. It is something, therefore, that we must always keep working at. The area is so important that we devote a complete chapter (Chapter 7) to providing background understanding that will be useful in all areas of management.

Focus on Decision Making.   If we go back far enough, all managerial action is based on a decision of some kind. Some of these decisions are at a very high level—as in the case of a major strategic policy decision involving entry into a new kind of business. Other decisions are at relatively low levels—as in the case of the decision to purchase a piece of small equipment. There is, however, a commonality among all of such decisions as respects principles and methodology. The problem must be identified, alternatives explored, the use of all information available or reasonably attainable, and a judgment as to the selected type of action.

What differs in decision making is the magnitude of the problem, the extent to which information is available, the criteria that are most appropriate, and the extent to which judgment be exercised. Thus there is a continuous effort to make decisions in a more effective manner. In addition, there are the factors of time available, risk levels that are acceptable, and the costs of improving the basis for the actual final decision. The quality of the implementation is also extremely important. But the necessary first requisite is always to identify the right problem and then to make the best possible decision covering its solution.

Effect of Risk Level.   The above-mentioned varying acceptability of the level of risk requires some further elaboration. To a considerable extent risk can be reduced, or in some cases substantially eliminated, by better information about operational and environmental factors. The limitations here are the costs of obtaining the various types and levels of information desired. But increasingly one is confronted with the fact that there are uncontrollable factors that affect our desired results. To some extent again we can reduce the aforementioned risk by statistical calculations of probabilities. However, here also, there are increasingly substantive limitations. The overall result is that the total certainty is impossible because of both practical and absolute limitations. This means that decisions pertaining to management actions reflect the levels of risk deemed to be acceptable to the particular responsible manager. Usually, there is a correlation between the potentially available profitability and the extent of risk but there is also the varying capacity to survive failure and operational losses. There are also varying inclinations to take risk. Each manager must therefore make his own evaluations within the parameters of his own authority and preferences.

Management Is Judged by Results.   This attribute is important in the first place because it is the truth that everything a manager does in the way of action is judged by how it furthers the achievement of his established goals and objectives. Managers are always primarily interested in results as opposed to letting an intermediate phase be an end in itself. But the significance of this attribute goes much deeper. Often, there are different ways to achieve managerial objectives. And often, different approaches in individual situations can achieve the same desired results. At the same time, what appear to be similar approaches to management problems can end up with completely different measures of success.

What this means is that there are always variables that cannot be fully predicted or adequately dealt with. These variables then often become of such force that they are controlling. Additionally, personnel effectiveness varies in dealing with similar obstacles. As a result, the merits of particular managerial decisions or approaches are often extremely controversial. In the last analysis, therefore, we must judge management competence mostly by the results achieved. It is quite possible that the good results actually achieved in a particular situation might have been better with what we think is a more enlightened management approach. On balance, however, we tend to equate managerial excellence with the quality of the results.

Time Span for Appraising Results. The judgment of management by results as a general concept is quite clear. It does, however, raise a related question of the time frame in which the particular results are evaluated. In the typical situation a manager can show short-term profitability, but buy that profitability by undermining the longer-run profits of the organizational component for which he is responsible. For example, quality can be temporarily sacrificed with resulting short-term profits, but be so damaging to customer satisfaction that future products are no longer purchased by consumers. Good managers therefore think in terms of long-term factors and resist tempting shortcuts that endanger longer term potentials.

When all of the foregoing is understood by all parties of interest, the correct judgments are quite clear. More often, however, there are complicated factors involved. One of these factors is how long the time span should be for the decisions made today. How long will higher-level managers or stockholders wait for longer-run rewards? A second complicating factor is the difficulty of measuring the long-run effect. Managers often innocently make bad estimates in these areas and often also are victims of "wishful" thinking. In still other cases lower-level managers ignore long-run consequences because of the probability that they will not be around when the final outcome becomes evident. Moreover, even then the evaluation is usually controversial. In total this means that the evaluation of results must be made with great care and with all possible judgment.

Continuing Reconciliation of Change and Regularity. One of the central truths of management is that conditions are always changing. A valued employee is lost to the organization, a new invention obsoletes existing practice, consumer preferences shift, or something else unforeseen develops. As a result, all dimensions of the management process must be reappraised and redirected. An organization's capacity to foresee such possibilities and to adapt to them once they come to pass is a measure of their ability to survive and prosper. But at the same time, there are benefits of standardization and regularity that include lower cost and a more effective supervisory effort. We constantly seek to exploit the benefits and economies of regularity through mass production, standardizing services, and comprehensive policies and procedures. The benefits are the reduced cost of facilities, labor, and managerial involvement. But herein lies a conflict in that change may be needed for growth or even survival. Hence there is a continuing challenge to management to find the proper balance between the two types of pressure.

An example here is the extent to which capital investment should be made in a single-purpose machine when a change in product design will make that machine obsolete. It was also a problem faced by Henry Ford when he thought all motor cars should be black. It is a problem that is never properly solved at any one point of time and the reconciliation continues to be complex as conditions continue to change. It is, however, the ability to cope with this kind of challenge that identifies and measures managerial competence.

General Applicability of Management Concepts. All of the theoretical and practical concepts of management need to be applied to individual managerial situations in a manner that recognizes the unique factors operative in the particular situation—an area we discuss in greater detail later in the chapter. But at the same time, the basic principles and concepts of management are generally applicable to all managerial situations. These managerial situations exist whenever there are resources for which a particular individual is directly or indirectly responsible. The situation may be in any business organization or in government or any nonbusiness type of organization. Moreover, the situation may be at the top of the organization—which may be as large as the General Motors Corporation—or it can be a very low operational unit far down in the organization. In all of these situations, however, the problems in principle are the same to the extent that all managerial concepts and practices are of use in evaluating resources and considering how to best achieve managerial objectives. This is true despite the fact that the character of the individual situation requires a different application of the concepts. All this is true even for a single individual as he or she seeks to maximize individual resources and have the most successful career possible.

Reconciliation of Economic, Personal, and Social Goals

In the typical business organization, the success of that organization is measured to a major extent by its ability to grow and be profitable. In our free enterprise system, a business organization that cannot be profitable over a reasonable period of time is either viewed as an organization no longer providing a needed product or service, or as an organization not being effectively managed. Although this profit measure does not exist in the governmental or other nonbusiness organization, there is a comparable yardstick available. This is the achievement of various types of service or impact objectives, in terms of quantity or quality, at minimal cost.

The determination and evaluation of these economic or other measurable goals can also, at the same time, be affected by personal goals. These are the very real—even though often denied—desires of managers to do something personally satisfying to themselves. Having the most impressive office facilities, being number one in unit or dollar volume, or favoring relatives for staff appointments over better qualified people are all common examples. Sometimes managers have the power to make such personal goals prevail, but in any event their cost should be known in terms of its effect on fully economic or other more rational goals.

The more significant conflict, however, exists in relation to socially oriented goals. Increasingly, there is the pressure from society on the business organization to act in a manner that achieves so-called social objectives. Examples are conservation of natural resources, improving the physical environment, special assistance for minority groups, and pressuring a country that violates human rights—all involving actions that may often go beyond existing legal requirements. The rationale here is that these are major responsibilities of a business organization in this modern world. As a result, the manager in a business organization is subject to conflicting pressures. Somehow he must assure the survival of the growth and profitability of the organization. At the same time, he must satisfy the society which, through government, has legalized its organizational existence. The problem is how to reconcile these pressures and to thus assure continuing healthy survival. Here a balance must be found of what can be appropriately called "enlightened self-interest."[3] That is an intermediate point where there can be needed levels of profitability with concurrently adequate recognition of, and adjustment to, the social demands.

Is Management an Art or a Science or a Profession?

All the variables we have discussed lead to the question of whether management is an art or a science. The correct answer to this question is "probably both." To the extent that scientific surveys, analyses, and methodology can be developed—as, for example, with the tools of management science and electronic data processing—the practice of management moves in the direction of being a science. However, information can never be complete and there are always variables that are too complicated, diverse, and uncontrollable to be assessed adequately. At some point, therefore, management must depend on judgment and personal effectiveness. To that extent management remains an art. Quite obviously, we are continually trying to expand the scientific dimensions, and thereby to reduce the impact of the variables with their related risks. But the world continues to become increasingly complex and we are usually hard pressed just to keep even.

A related question is whether management is a profession. By the standards outlined in the two preceding chapters, we can say that we are moving in that

[3]This problem is discussed in greater detail in Chapter 24.

direction. Also, managers increasingly develop the kinds of capabilities that enable them to move relatively freely from one organization to another and from industry to industry. That freedom of involement is also being increasingly demonstrated. Increasingly, professional managers exhibit a breadth of responsibility for the needs of the larger society. We can therefore be proud of the high professionalism of modern managers even though few would claim that we have reached a fully satisfactory level. However, we are certainly moving more and more in the "professional" direction.

Model for Management in Action

Thus far we have talked about management in terms of concepts and major characteristics. We now propose to discuss the management process as a defined sequence of various types of action. In doing this we again need to recognize that all management action covers a great span of levels and scope. We think, however, that the most useful way to look at management action is at the highest level—that is, from the viewpoint of the top manager of a large business organization. We do this because the principles involved are more clearly identifiable at that level, and lower-level situations differ only in that there is a degree of contraction of factors for which the manager has significant control. Moreover, it is always easier to understand one's managerial situation more clearly when that situation is viewed as a component of a larger situation for which we do have understanding.

The basic setting of our management situation is the existence of identified resources which are to be utilized over a future period of time to achieve established goals. This utilization takes place within an environment that is changing as we move through time. In graphic form the foregoing situation would look something like this:

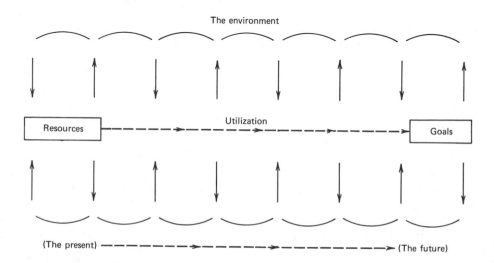

The two-way directions of the arrows between the environment and the goal achievement process is deliberate. Although for the most part the process is responding to the environment, the arrows directed outward recognize that to some extent the environment can be influenced by proper managerial action.

Resources as a Starting Point.   In most cases, the starting point for management action is the existence of specific resources. It is quite possible, however, that the recognition of a market or end product need can come first and that *then* we acquire the necessary resources. But in any event, resources include both those we already have, plus those we can obtain, once we provide appropriate justification for the need. For our purposes it is satisfactory to start with the resources we have—their size, value, and service capabilities. At this point we seek to understand these resources in terms of both current and potential utilization.

Understanding the Environment.   A second logical necessity is to understand the environment in which we presently or potentially will use our resources. Here we seek to understand the environmental factors outlined earlier in this chapter as they are, how they are changing, how future changes can be influenced, and how the changing environmental factors involve risk with its various degrees of magnitude. Obviously, such an achievement is never fully possible. Moreover, the extent of achievement depends on how broadly we view the environment and how much time and money we are willing to devote to the effort of identification and measurement. But there can never be total certainty.

We know that the general aspects of the total or larger environment cannot be ignored. However, we are especially concerned with the portion of the environment that relates more directly to our own resources. Here we seek to identify and evaluate the problems and opportunities which appear to exist in that more narrowly defined part of the total environment, and to appraise the strengths and weaknesses of our particular resources. At this stage we are concerned with relationships between our resources and the particular part of the environment that has potential for productivity and profitability in the face of competition and other types of risk.

Identification and Evaluation of Alternative Product/Market Missions.   From the general overview given previously we now move to a more defined identification of alternative combined product and market choices. We seek the particular niches or sectors which indicate the greatest promise. We are at the same time evaluating those alternatives at the aggregate levels (as to quantification) of goals and supporting strategy. We are dealing at the aggregate level to facilitate the necessary breadth of the search, without the expenditure of time and money that is necessary for more precise quantitative evaluation. But we are still using our knowledge and experience to weigh the merits and problems of the various alternatives. Basic to this evaluation is the fact that, as we consider alternatives that involve new skills and new geographical areas, the degree of risk increases proportionately. It follows that with equal profit opportunities we give priority consideration to products and markets where we have knowledge and experience—thus achieving effective utilization of resources with lowest possible risk.

Choice of Major Product/Market Mission.   Out of the preceding evaluation now should come the tentative choice of the combined product and market combination that appears to promise the maximum rewards at acceptable levels of risks. At this point we are more precisely defining our goals, the supporting strategy, and the planned implementation. At this time we are also reconciling personal, economic, and socially oriented goals and objectives—a conflict previously discussed—especially as to impact on the goals and strategy. The further definition of planned implementation also becomes important both for setting the stage for later to come actual implementation, and for further validating the soundness of goals and strategy.

Development of Supporting Strategy and Policies.   Management is now ready to move to the next lower level of developing the many needed supporting strategies and policies. These supporting plans are now developed in the various functional areas of finance, production, personnel, distribution, sales, promotion, procurement, and the like. They pertain also at the same time to the subprocess areas, such as organizing, providing resources, administering, and controlling—and go on to include the various types of procedural systems for information and control.

Continuing Planning Blended with Implementation.   At this stage, various types of procurement, training, construction, testing, initial production, market testing, preliminary promotion, and the like, are involving actual implementation. At this stage also, plans are developed for defined time periods—typically at something like a five-year span and then in more detail for the first year as an annual budget. These plans are quantified—at the five-year level on a more aggregate basis but with reasonable precision for the budget year—for operations and profit goals.

Full-Scale Implementation.   At this point, the organization is in full-scale operation applying planned policies and procedures and utilizing the previously acquired resources. During this actual implementation we are directly dependent on our administrative skills in the areas of directing, coordinating, and leading. At the same time the results accomplished are appropriately reported and compared to planned objectives at all operational levels. As a result of these comparisons, gaps and variances are identified and appraised, and such actions taken as appear best to assure the achievement of established goals.

Goal Achievement and Reappraisal. The preceding stages have now achieved, to the maximum extent practicable, the desired goals of the total management process. However, there are normally deviations both up and down. These deviations may be due to various aspects of the planning and implementation which have been faulty in some respect. These deviations should of course be dealt with on their merits. Other deviations are due to new factors in the changing environment. The challenge here is to identify the causal factors and to take the new approaches that will best enable us to deal with the particular problems.

The Graphic Model in Expanded Form

As originally shown, the graphic management model emphasized the managerial action flow from resources to goals and objectives. The revised graphic goal shown below is now in more detail and also stresses the circular action, which exists in two important ways:

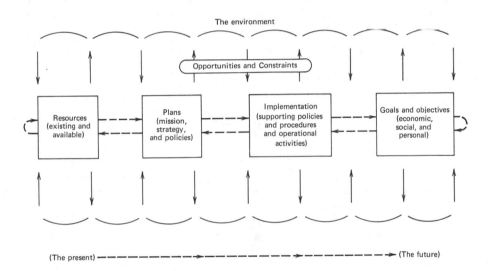

The first of these circular actions comes in the planning phase covered by the forward steps previously outlined. The circular action is the several cycles by which plans are studied and restudied at various lower levels of precision. Thus planning at the product/market mission level is in terms of broad aggregates, whereas planning in terms of the annual budget is at the level of operational precision. The second aspect of the circular action is in terms of repetitive planning as we move from one time period to the next. Thus this year we have our five-year plan and annual budget, but at least a year later we repeat the same planning process, based on the then-existing conditions, and establish new budgets and five-year plans.

Adapting the Model to Situations at All Levels

In accordance with our earlier stated election, we have developed our model of the management process in terms of the top-level executive who is responsible for a large completely integrated organization. But management analysis and action takes place at all organizational levels. How, then, do we use our model to be helpful in all of these other situations? The variables in these different situations are twofold: the resources and the environment. In the case of resources the nature and scope can, as we have seen, be very much restricted at lower organizational level. Also to a greater extent, resources are provided by high-level authority subject to established organizational policies and procedures. The manager must therefore deal with those resource facts as they are. In the case of environment there is again a wide range of controls and restrictions with which the manager must contend. The restrictions become more and more substantial as we move to lower and lower organizational levels. Nevertheless, the *process* of relating the particular resources to the existing environmental factors to determine goals is the same in principle as it is for the top executive himself. It follows also that strategy and policy determination must be subject to the planning actions of the higher-level organizational managers. Finally also, the actual implementation will be subject to higher-level procedures and controls. At the same time, managers at all levels have an opportunity to reappraise the effectiveness of those higher-level organizational determinations and to make all efforts practicable to press for needed change.

Solving Management Problems

The graphic model just discussed shows the way the key components of resources, environment, plans, implementation, and goals relate to each other as an ongoing process over time. These same components can also be rearranged to better illustrate and facilitate specific management decisions:

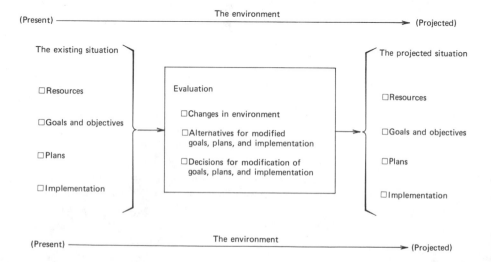

The approach is to start with the existing situation of all components and then to make the judgment of alternative modification actions as related to estimated projected outcomes. Again, this management decision model can be applied in any organization, at any organizational level, and to any management problem of any magnitude and substance.

Understanding Our Own Business

What we have covered thus far in this chapter have been principles and concepts of a very general nature which apply for the most part to every managerial situation in all kinds of business and nonbusiness activities. These principles and concepts are basic and need to be the first foundation for all managerial activities. How they are applied, however, depends on the kind of business or nonbusiness activity in the particular managerial situation. Varying physical factors, technology used, nature and scope of processes to produce the product or service offered, capital investment, types of facilities, distribution, sales, maintenance, conditions of product usage, extent of risk, social visibility, and a host of other factors combine to make managing different in individual situations. As a result, the various aspects of the management process need different kinds of attention with differing priorities and pertinent considerations. Effective managers must therefore be informed about these practical factors, and indeed the more they know the better, provided that the various factors are kept in proper balance.

Granted the importance of adequately understanding these pertinent factors, how do the manager and those who would serve management acquire the needed knowledge and understanding? There are also the related questions of how much one needs to know versus depending on others, and when the pursuit of such expertise is unduly costly as judged by other alternative utilization of available time. The resolution of these questions is obviously something that needs continuing judgment in the light of changing conditions. This resolution is also different for each manager in terms of his own ongoing career aspirations and utilization of his own resources in the most effective manner over future years.

Alternative Approaches for Developing Special Expertise. At the top of the alternative approaches for understanding the nature and scope of particular types of operations is certainly actual experience as a worker on the job. To the extent that an individual can have direct responsibility for particular types of operational activities, the more likely that individual is to become familiar with the types of problems that arise. The drawbacks are the amount of time required and the fact that much experience can become unduly repetitive—thus having diminishing value as a setting for desired levels of earning. A second alternative approach is through observation. Such observations may take the form of deliberately planned learning, but can also exist as a by-product of other responsibilities. The observations afforded by the conduct of internal auditing activities are illustrative. Finally, there is the alternative approach of actual study of the various areas pertaining to the production and use of the particular products. This, too, can take many forms and can involve a varying range of focus. In addition, in the case of all the alternative approaches just indicated, there is usually the further opportunity to combine the learning of unique aspects with the principles and concepts discussed in the earlier part of this chapter.

Partnership Role of the Internal Auditor

The accomplishment of the basic service role of the internal auditor to management starts with understanding management problems and needs, but then goes on to involve a partnership role between the manager and the internal auditor at all operational levels—a partnership role that extends to helping management achieve its managerial goals and objectives to the maximum extent possible. Such an effective partnership role can be achieved in many ways. We believe, however, that the following are essential ingredients of a sound program to achieve the desired results:

1. The ability to provide basic protective services but, at the same time, to help management achieve desired improvement. Moreover, the protective contributions often provide an important foundation for making the constructive contribution.
2. Being continuously alert to use the point of detachment from actual operational responsibilities as a special capability to identify, evaluate, and support issues of significant management interest.
3. The capacity to interface in a persuasive manner with managers at all levels. This is a combination of operational understanding plus a manner of personal appearance and conduct.
4. Avoidance of the inherent temptation of auditors to use unduly available power with management and other operational auditees. Such actions generate auditee resistance that then blocks ongoing constructive relationships.
5. The strategic focus on control as the credential for the analysis and review of operational areas. Since the technical expertise of the auditee is typically always superior, the focus on control provides a more acceptable justification of the audit assistance offered.
6. The respect at all times during the process of assistance for the responsibility that managers have for operational results. Hence staff recommendations must stand on their own merits, as judged by those who have operational responsibility.
7. The continuing blending of the objectives of assistance at auditee levels with the necessity for upward disclosure within the framework of total organizational welfare. It is indeed the latter focus which neutralizes all lower-level conflict for the upward exposure.

Understanding Management in Perspective

The potential of service to the organization through assistance to management at all levels is a major goal for professional internal auditors. It is these potentials that justify every possible effort on the part of the internal auditor to see the management job through the eyes of management and to render all possible assistance for maximum goal achievement of all managers. The problems of management are very complex and are continually changing in the light of both internal and external environmental factors. This means that management increasingly needs the assistance of internal auditors and will, in most cases, welcome it when the ability and credibility of the internal auditor are established. It is a continuing challenge to internal auditors to render assistance which is in fact made productive through management acceptance and application.

Applying Management Concepts to Internal Auditing

The discussion of management concepts in this chapter has been in terms of any business or nonbusiness organization. It is also appropriate to recognize that these management concepts can also be used directly by individual internal auditing departments and by the total profession. The latter type of application is dealt with in the final chapter of this book, "Conclusions and Future Prospects." In that chapter we examine in some depth the resources, environmental factors, goals and objectives, strategy, and implementation of the total internal auditing profession.

CHAPTER FOUR

Fundamentals of Control

NATURE OF CONTROL

Internal Auditor's Major Focus on Control

In Chapter 1 we saw that internal auditing is a type of organization control that functions by measuring and evaluating the effectiveness of other controls. In Chapter 2 we considered in greater depth the internal auditor's concern with the system of internal control. In Chapter 3 we recognized the importance of control in the total management process. The importance of the control function comes from the fact that the examination and appraisal of control are normally a part—directly or indirectly—of every type of internal auditing assignment. Moreover, the internal auditor's special competence in the control area is what justifies his review of a wide range of operational activities, even though he does not possess special knowledge about the substance of those activities. We need, therefore, to examine more closely the basic fundamentals of control so that we can apply the concepts and principles more effectively in all operational situations. It is the purpose of this chapter to probe these underlying concepts and principles. We hope to identify a common framework and philosophy of the control process which is at the heart of the internal auditor's professional expertise.

Basic Nature of Control

Control as a process is needed in all areas of human activity, both inside the organization and for the total society. In most respects the concepts and principles used are the same. However, because the internal auditor's primary mission is to serve the organization, our own approach will be to focus on control as it applies to the activities of the organization. This more focused application is most often referred to as "internal control." It is the area of concern we intend even though we may often use the broader term "control."

Control as an organizational activity—or as a component of any organizational activity—exists at all organizational levels and is the concern of many different individuals in the organization. Its basic nature can best be understood in terms of the major phases of the total management process. That total process begins with planning and the related establishment of objectives. The planning is then

78

supported by organizing and the necessary further providing of resources—including people. Managers then take the definitive operational actions to achieve the previously established objectives. But these operational actions will normally by themselves not be enough. Things seldom work out exactly as planned. Our underlying knowledge and estimates are never that good. Moreover, people are human and errors are made. Also environmental conditions change. We, therefore, need *supplementary measures and action to provide appropriate readings on our progress and to provide the basis for further actions which will better assure the achievement of our objectives*. We also need *procedures that assure desired types of action and prevent those that are not desired*. The control function in concerned with providing these supplementary measures, actions, and procedures.

It is, of course, apparent that the control function cannot exist unless we have objectives. If we do not know where we want to go, we can hardly know what kind of measures and actions should be taken to get us there. It is also apparent that the taking of the supplementary actions brings us back again into the actual management process as further managerial actions are taken. Thus control exists as an independent phase of the management process but at the same time an essential part of it.

A very simple illustration of the control function is a boat setting sail for a given port with a planned arrival date. At interim points the progress is determined. Because of the prevailing winds, or engine problems, the boat may be off course. As a result, changes in direction are made necessary, and possibly speeds may have to be modified. If necessary, there will be a revision of the scheduled arrival. The control function here is to consider and evaluate the impact of the new developments in actual progress, and to provide a proper basis for needed supplementary action. It thus contributes to reaching our destination on a timely basis and in the most efficient manner practicable.

Range of Interest in Internal Control

The broad scope of the interest in control can be better understood by recognizing the range of control applications and relating that range to the varying levels of users. In terms of applications we can start at the highest level of organizational activity. Here, for example, there is the application of monitoring the various key factors that determine rates of profitability and growth. Another example is monitoring the factors that pertain to maintaining dividend policies and to attracting needed investment. At still lower operational levels is, for example, the monitoring of divisional profitability or the market acceptance of individual products. At still lower operational levels, for example, are applications to ensure the proper billing of sales to customers or the collection of accounts receivable. At the lowest level is the monitoring by each individual of his own daily work activities. Other low-level controls exist as specific procedural requirements.

To a considerable extent these varying levels of control applications parallel the interests of different types of users, although often in a varying range of combinations. For example, we have the high-level interests of a regulatory body such as the Securities and Exchange Commission, the special interests of the independent auditor, and the increasingly narrow interests of different individuals, as determined by their declining levels of organizational responsibility. These levels of organizational or other user interest interface with the range of control applications to provide and define the total universe of control activities. In all cases, however, there are objectives for which controls are needed to measure performance and to help guide us toward the objectives we have established. The control function is thus a multidimensional tapestry covering the entire range of organizational activities.

Types of Control[1]

While control is always tied directly or indirectly to objectives, and while the nature and scope of objectives can vary widely, the manner in which control is exercised can also vary. In general, there are three different types of controls.

1. *Steering Controls.* One major type of controls is through the identification of events which prompt us to take interim actions that will be contributory to the achievement of larger objectives. These interim events can be very precise or very broad. However, the common characteristic is that they alert us to the need to take some type of managerial action on a timely basis. In the case of the driver of the boat previously mentioned, the drift of the boat to one side first indicates the need for definitive steering action. Various types of gauges in a manufacturing process indicate the fact of developing conditions that require particular processing actions. A drop in dealer orders triggers the carmaker's problem of declining market acceptance of his product and the related need to adjust production schedules. In still other cases a broad index of economic trends can alert us to changing conditions that spark protective or other opportunity-oriented actions.

2. *Yes–No Controls.* Controls of this type are those designed to function more automatically to protect us or to otherwise help assure the accomplishment of desired results. In its simplest form it could be a quality control gauge through which only a product part of the exact specifications can pass. In another illustrative situation the control could be a required approval on a business form—thus ensuring that a particular individual had made a necessary review of the action involved. The design of organizational responsibilities also properly exploits opportunities to assure needed cross evaluation of major business decisions and implementing action. The common element is that there is a preestablished control device or arrangement that under normal conditions will more or less

[1]This classification and discussion is based in part on one developed by William H. Newman in his book *Constructive Control* (Englewood Cliffs, N.J.: Prentice-Hall, 1975).

automatically help assure the desired protective, or improvement action.

3. *Post-Action Controls.* A third type of control overlaps with the two types just discussed but is distinctive in that the managerial action comes about some time later and takes the form of doing the best thing possible under the circumstances existing then. The action taken may be to repair a product that has been damaged or the action may be to change a policy or procedure. Or the action may be to dismiss or reassign an employee. That after-the-fact action may be immediately feasible or require extended study and development. The analyses done by internal auditors are typically directed to determining the nature and scope of the most effective type of after-the-fact action, even though that action be very much future oriented. Control needs here are thus identified by looking at the past but always to the extent possible are oriented to improving future activities.

Internal Control as Viewed by Certified Public Accountants

The definitions in the United States by the American Institute of Certified Public Accountants (AICPA) pertaining to internal control are of special interest because of their relationship to the work of the Certified Public Accountant (CPA)[2] which underlies his expression of an opinion as to the fairness of the financial statements of his client company. As further discussed below, these definitions have also been used as a guide by the Securities Exchange Act in developing regulations covering the enforcement of the Securities Exchange Act of 1934 and the Foreign Corrupt Practices Act of 1977. In the AICPA's codified standards covering auditing practice (320.09) there is the following definition:

> Internal control comprises the plan of organization and all of the coordinate methods and measures adopted within a business to safeguard its assets, check the accuracy and reliability of its accounting data, promote operational efficiency, and encourage adherence to prescribed managerial policies.

Other definitions in paragraphs 320.27 and 320.28 then further define the two sectors of that internal control as follows:

> **.27** *Administrative control* includes, but is not limited to, the plan of organization and the procedures and records that are concerned with the decision processes leading to management's authorization of transactions. Such authorization is a management function directly associated with the responsibility for achieving the objectives of the organization and is the starting point for establishing accounting control of transactions.

> **.28** *Accounting control* comprises the plan of organization and the procedures and records that are concerned with the safeguarding of assets and the reliability

---

[2]Although the focus here is on public accounting practice in the United States, the principles are generally applicable to the Chartered Accountant and other independent public accountants.

of financial records and consequently are designed to provide reasonable assurance that:

a. Transactions are executed in accordance with management's general or specific authorization.

b. Transactions are recorded as necessary (1) to permit preparation of financial statements in conformity with generally accepted accounting principles or any other criteria applicable to such statements and (2) to maintain accountability for assets.

c. Access to assets is permitted only in accordance with management's authorization.

d. The recorded accountability for assets is compared with the existing assets at reasonable intervals and appropriate action is taken with respect to any differences.

The overlapping relationship of these two types of internal control is then further clarified in paragraph 320.29:

.29 The foregoing definitions are not necessarily mutually exclusive because some of the procedures and records comprehended in accounting control may also be involved in administrative control. For example, sales and cost records classified by products may be used for accounting control purposes and also in making management decisions concerning unit prices or other aspects of operations. Such multiple uses of procedures or records, however, are not critical for the purposes of this section because it is concerned primarily with clarifying the outer boundary of accounting control. Examples of records used solely for administrative control are those pertaining to customers contacted by salesmen and to defective work by production employees maintained only for evaluating personnel performance.

In both paragraphs 320.09 and 320.49 it is also made clear that the system of internal control extends beyond those matters which relate directly to the accounting and financial statements, but that the CPA's primary interest for purposes of the review of financial statements is with the internal accounting control. In paragraph 320.49 there is the specific statement that

accounting control is within the scope of the study and evaluation of internal control contemplated by generally accepted auditing standards, while administrative control is not.

Although the interests of the internal auditor extend beyond internal accounting control to the effectiveness of the total system of internal control, the internal accounting control is part of the larger system, Moreover, the line of demarcation from the part to the larger whole is never exactly clear. Hence interpretations by both the Securities and Exchange Commission and AICPA relating to the system of internal accounting control are extremely important. Similarly, the voluminous interpretations and guidelines developed by leading CPA firms are of great value to the practicing internal auditor. These materials are discussed further in Chapter 6.

Impact of the Foreign Corrupt Practices Act of 1977

In 1977, responding to an increasing public concern with reported practices of U.S. business corporations, Congress enacted the Foreign Corrupt Practices Act. In this act the following requirements, based directly on the statements by the AICPA, were established:

> (2) Every issuer which has a class of securities registered pursuant to section 12 of this title and every issuer which is required to file reports pursuant to section 15(d) of this title shall—
>
> (A) make and keep books, records, and accounts, which, in reasonable detail, accurately and fairly reflect the transactions and dispositions of the assets of the issuer; and
> (B) devise and maintain a system of internal accounting controls sufficient to provide reasonable assurances that—
>> (i) transactions are executed in accordance with management's general or specific authorization;
>> (ii) transactions are recorded as necessary (I) to permit preparation of financial statements in conformity with generally accepted accounting principles or any other criteria applicable to such statements, and (II) to maintain accountability for assets;
>> (iii) access to assets is permitted only in accordance with management's general or specific authorization; and
>> (iv) the recorded accountability for assets is compared with the existing assets at reasonable intervals and appropriate action is taken with respect to any differences.

The special significance of these new requirements is that they establish more clearly the responsibility of management for an adequate system of internal accounting control. This responsibility overlaps with, but goes beyond, the CPA's concern with the internal accounting control to the extent that he relies on that internal accounting control for purposes of supporting his opinion as to the fairness of the financial statements of his client company. However, it is significant that the FCPA requirements use word for word the previously quoted definition by the AICPA.

Control Process

Another way to better understand controls and to be better able to apply them to all types of organizational activities is to focus on the control process. This control process, which to some extent underlies every individual operational application in the organization, has been broken down by various authorities in differing ways. However, our own interpretation is as follows:

1. *Development of Objectives*. The first step is the determination of what it is we wish to achieve—some kind of an objective. This objective can be one which is at a very high level or it can be a very detailed and definitive sort of thing. In the latter instance it is commonly referred to as a standard. Thus the allowance of a given amount of time to carry out

a particular operation on an automobile assembly line is thought of as a work standard. Low-level objectives also include specific procedural requirements—as, for example, an approval by a certain officer. The common characteristic in all cases is, however, that there is a determined objective. What is of greatest importance from the standpoint of the control process is the validity of the objective. This total quality includes how carefully the objective was determined, how specific it is, whether there is agreement as to its legitimacy, and the extent to which its achievement can be measured. Thus the effectiveness of the control process is linked directly to how well the underlying objectives have been established.

A further way to utilize objectives is to use available interim guidelines to provide faster response to problems that can significantly affect future results. Sometimes these interim guidelines are already available—as, for example, when initial sales at a new model car show can be used to appraise total customer response. In other cases, through controlled field tests we can make more scientific preliminary estimates of product acceptability. In still other cases the varying rate of accomplishment can be recognized in a series of programmed interim objectives—as, for example, to reflect cyclical patterns—to recognize more realistically changing interim conditions.

2. *Measurement of Results.* Assuming that the objective has been stated in the terms by which it can be measured, the second step of the control process is to provide the actual measures of current performance. We need to know what we are actually accomplishing in the way of progress toward the established objectives. Also, this information as to performance needs to be available in the right places, at the right time, and to the right people. Thus while we need to know where we want to go, we must also know what we are doing through actual performance toward the achievement of those goals. Only in this way can we have the proper basis for the comparisons and analysis of what corrective or other managerial action may be needed on an interim basis.

3. *Comparison of Actual Performance Against Objectives.* We are now ready to match the data of actual performance against the previously established objectives. This makes possible the identification of the differences, frequently referred to as variances. This comparison can be both for current time periods and for longer cumulative periods. Although the comparison is a specific step in the control process, it is in practice often combined with the reporting of actual results. Quite clearly, the making of these comparisons depends on actual performance and objectives being stated in the same manner—a need that must be anticipated when the objectives are established.

4. *Analysis of the Causes of Differences.* The next step is to determine what the causes were for the differences reported. This is the probing to identify the various causal factors, plus the efforts to measure the effect of each.

The approach in part is to push backward for more detailed information about the various operational activities. There is also an effort to determine both immediate and more basic causes. At the same time there is a judgmental evaluation of how important individual factors actually are as causes. This is the essential step in utilizing the results portrayed in the three preceding steps. It is the responsibility of every manager, whether done by himself or by another party. It is also the typical work of the internal auditor, whether done directly from basic data or superimposed on previously accomplished analysis.

5. *Determination of Appropriate Managerial Action.* The analysis of the causes of differences unavoidably blends to some extent with the determination of appropriate managerial action. In some cases the responsible manager will himself be making part or all of the analysis. In most cases, however, this will be done by a separate analyst, and this analyst may also make recommendations for management action. The actual determination of management action in any event belongs to the person who has the line responsibility for the particular operational activities involved. Here the available alternatives must be evaluated and the very important judgment reached as to what, if any, specific action should be taken.

It is useful to note also that the responsibility for the proper analysis and determination of appropriate managerial action *is* the responsibility of the manager in charge and in turn of higher-level managers, irrespective of the extent to which those activities are delegated to subordinates or other staff groups. This is consistent with the fact of every manager's overall responsibility for final acceptance and utilization of all actions pertinent to the achievement of his own goals and objectives.

6. *Taking Action.* The judgment just reached as to appropriate managerial action must now actually be implemented. The needed instructions are now issued in a manner that gives consideration to the required urgency, the level of personnel being dealt with, and the complexity of the actions to be taken. The action to be taken may be something that can be accomplished quickly—like correcting an error—or it may extend over a long period—as, for example, modifying a complex system. In all cases, however, there is a further control problem as to what followup there should be to satisfy the responsible manager that action has been completed as desired.

In some situations the proper action determined to be taken may be to do nothing at all. Perhaps the cost of correction outweighs the risk. Or, perhaps, there is knowledge of future developments that will be adequate to cure the presently existing problem. It needs to be recognized, however, that taking no action is itself a decision, and hence a kind of responsive action.

7. *Continuing Reappraisal.* A final step in the control process is the appraisal of results after the aforementioned actions have been carried out. This in effect is a further check on the soundness of the earlier deter-

minations of needed action and the manner in which the actions were actually taken. This final step now provides the necessary linkage of the original control cycle to the next cycle. This continuing appraisal thus blends into the next measurement of progress analysis, and determination of further managerial action. Indeed, post appraisal is a continuing action reflecting the input of changing conditions, more experience, and greater knowledge of all factors.

Thus the total control process can be conveniently reviewed in terms of the seven key steps. We will deal with some of the major problems that relate more specifically to the individual steps. First, however, we look briefly at some more general aspects of the control function in the total management process.

Relation of Control to Total Management Process

In our discussion of the nature of the control process we saw that the control function begins with the defining of objectives and ends with the achievement of those objectives. As applied to the conceptual framework outlined in Chapter 3, this control function has mostly to do with the effectiveness of the implementing actions whereby strategies are translated into action to achieve established goals and objectives. It is also useful to see in more depth how the control function interrelates with the major stages of the conventional management process—planning, organizing, providing resources, and administering.

Tie to Planning.   As we know, planning is concerned with determining sound objectives for the company, both as a whole and for each operational component. These objectives in total, and in the case of each operational component, provide the points of reference for the supporting control activities. Complete and comprehensive planning thus provides the foundation for the control function. We know that management recognizes the need for good planning. But it needs to be emphasized also that anyone interested in developing or improving effective control must necessarily be concerned with both the adequacy of the design for planning and the effectiveness with which the planning is actually done. Our first interest, therefore, is to have sufficiently good planning throughout the total company.

Tie to Organizing.   The importance of organizing to the control function is that it is through organizing that work assignments are made, authority delegated, and accountabilities determined. In this way organizing provides the framework for control. More specifically, the organizational responsibilities of individuals and groups of individuals (including organizational components) make possible the more systematic identification of objectives and the measurement of operational results. Again this means that if we want effective control we must be concerned with improving the soundness of organizational design and related organizational arrangements.[3] Good organizing thus becomes a major building block for effective control.

Tie to Providing Resources. The acquisition, handling, and disposition of all resources involve problems of control. But in the case of human resources the problems are all the more critical because control—like the total management process of which the control process is a part—is done by people who are supposedly properly selected, trained, and administered. Also, where there are capable managers, the administration of control functions will be done in a more effective manner. Thus the achievement of effective control must involve all of the key aspects of the staffing and personnel function.[4]

Tie to Administering. We know that administering has to do with the issuing of instructions, supervising people, working with people, coordinating, and leading. At this stage managers also administer the control system and take the actions determined to be necessary as a result of the variations fom planned performance. The manner in which this total directing role is carried out can either support the control system or hinder it. This means then that achieving effective control requires a close partnership with responsible managers so that actions in that area are supportive of control needs.

Design and Implementation

Another useful way to approach the control function is in terms of the dimensions of design and implementation. *Design* has to do with the selection of the particular operational aspects to be controlled, the determination of the extent to which these aspects are to be controlled, and the choice of the way that control actions are to be carried out. Such a design effort of course takes into consideration the later implementation of the system, but it tends to focus more directly on the more basic dimensions of managerial needs. A particular type of standard is determined, a procedure for measuring results is developed, and a program is laid out for review and possible action. All of this involves a considered judgment as to benefits expected and costs to be incurred. The second part of the control system then has to do with the actual *implementation*, that is, the installation of the system and the subsequent administration of it. At this point we focus directly on actual performance and the people who are involved. At this point the need is for administrative skill and judgment to deal with the many unforeseen developments and the unavoidable human problems. What is important here is that we recognize that there are two interrelated but still fairly separate problems areas. In both cases we must learn how to deal with them effectively.

[3]See Chapter 5.
[4]See Chapter 20.

Need to Blend with Management System

A closely related problem to the aforementioned design and implementation is the extent to which the control measures can be blended with normal managerial procedures and actions. What we are trying to do is to avoid as much as possible having the control measure as a supplementary and separate type of activity. Instead, we seek to achieve our control objective as much as possible through the regular operational procedures. The reason for this is twofold. There is, first, the benefit of avoiding the extra cost which is otherwise necessary. Second, there is a lesser irritation to the persons who are directly or indirectly being controlled. For example, if the acceptance of a particular part by a using department from the producing department can be automatically determined by whether it fits into the larger assembly, then we may not have to set up an intermediate inspection group. Similarly, we seek to cover the administration of control as a part of normal management relationships rather than to deal with it as a separate type of problem. Every control specialist is always looking for these opportunities for achieving control as a part of regular operating procedures.

Protective and Constructive Dimensions

Another important way to look at control systems is to recognize their protective and constructive dimensions, and then to try to maximize the latter, as much as possible. To a major extent controls do serve to protect higher-level managers from what may go wrong at the lower levels. Some controls have as at least one of their major purposes the prevention of particular kinds of action not desired by higher-level management. Illustrative of such undesirable actions would be the improper use of company property, the making of commitments beyond an authorized level, or improperly preparing a particular form. Other controls are protective in the sense that higher-level management wants to know of particular types of developments so that they can take corrective or defensive action on a timely basis.

In other cases, however, the controls emphasize more the constructive possibilities. Here the control is viewed as a guide as to where we might improve some aspects of our operation. For example, a control in the form of consumer preference testing would enable us to develop new products or differently present existing ones to exploit new consumer trends. Part of this constructive approach can be achieved by emphasizing the positive benefits which normally follow control actions that are protective in the first instance. Illustrative would be the emphasis on customer satisfaction and company reputation which is a result of protective-type inspection measures. Frequently also, the control can be defined in a broader manner which will better motivate the persons subject to the control. Illustrative would be the use of profit performance controls over a subsidiary instead of detailed operational controls. In still other cases the constructive emphasis can come through a more understanding and sensitive administration of controls. In all of these situations the objective of the control specialist is to cover the protective needs in a manner which avoids the emphasis in that direction, and instead to stress the constructive potentials.

Risk Analysis for Protective Objectives

As we have just seen, the evaluation of effective internal control involves both protective and constructive types of objectives. The fact of that dual interest is especially important for corporate managers, and in turn for internal auditors who seek to serve the total range of management interests. Moreover, the evaluation of controls in relation to constructive and broader improvement objectives are a higher level and more sophisticated type of evaluation—especially when improvement objectives involve increased corporate profitability. However, protective objectives are basically very important and need to be covered properly. As it happens also, the evaluation of internal control for protective objectives lends itself especially to more scientific and structured risk analysis.

Evaluation of risk for protective objectives focuses directly on (1) the nature and scope of the impact of the particular types of potential deficiencies, and (2) the feasibility and cost of the actual controls. This kind of evaluation must of course be made individually for each company and its various operational situations. But when so done it can be a useful guide as to what kind of controls, and the extent of their use, actually make good business sense. What does further complicate the evaluation, however, are the often existing conflicts between the reduction of potential direct losses with broader management needs and operational objectives. An example in a retail store would be the extent that merchandise for sale should be immediately available to the customer for examination. In this situation we can keep the merchandise locked up—and thus minimize theft—but we may thereby discourage examination of that merchandise and unduly restrict sales. What all this means is that risk analysis can be sound or unsound in management terms depending on the extent to which all related management objectives are properly recognized and evaluated.

Problem of Human Responses to Control

We have at various points noted the fact that people are involved in the control process and that this calls for special kinds of skills in dealing with them. We will also in Chapter 7 discuss in greater detail the problems of effective human relationships. At this point, however, we need to recognize the special problems that are raised on the human side in developing an effective control system. The basic source of the problems comes from the fact that most individuals instinctively like independence and freedom of action. The very fact that people are required to do something makes them tend to view such a control with aversion, and even with hostility. The extent of the tolerance for controls depends to a considerable extent upon the individual himself—his intelligence, experience, cultural background, emotional stability, and the like. But we can say that there is a normal tendency to resent controls and to resist them to some extent. Much also depends on the way controls are developed, and how they are presented and administered. Therefore, in our endeavor to achieve effective control we need to understand this normal human response and to try to do everything possible to minimize the existing problems.

How can we deal with these human barriers to effective control? We suggest the following types of action:

1. *Augmenting Total Company Image*. Undoubtedly the most basic approach to achieving effective control is to establish an overall company reputation for competence and integrity. This reputation must first be established at the top and then disseminated down through the entire organization. A greater general receptivity for control measures is thus established.

2. *Providing Adequate Rationale*. People especially resent any kind of control which they do not understand. Indeed, they are then tempted to interpret the control actions as arbitrary and unfair. This means that it is necessary to go out of one's way to explain the reasons for particular types of control. The rationale behind a "keep off the grass" sign may be sufficiently obvious, but in other cases the reasons for the particular restriction need to be understood to be acceptable to the people affected. Budgetary controls are, for example, better received if there is some understanding of the objectives of the budgetary process and how it needs to operate.

3. *Manner of Presentation*. In addition to adequate rationale there is much that can be done in the way the particular control is initiated. People respond to courtesy and to evidence of reasonable consideration. There is also the need for proper explanations of how the controls are to work and a reasonable opportunity for people to adjust to them.

4. *Legitimacy of Source*. People especially resent controls that are imposed by persons not believed to have the authority to impose them. The solution here is that the particular control be sponsored by a sufficiently high level of authority, where there is no question as to its being proper. Supporting details can then be supplied, where necessary, by a lower level of authority.

5. *Participation*. In many cases it is not practicable for all parties who are to be subject to the control to be able to participate in the formulation of the control itself. We do know, however, that the further we can go in that direction, the greater will be the acceptance of the control. Thus the acceptance of budgetary controls requires a participation of the responsible manager with his superiors. Even in the case of work standards, the joint consideration between representatives of management and labor achieve important participation benefits.

6. *Manner of Administration*. Finally, much can be done in the way controls are administered. The need here is to avoid being arbitrary, to the extent

possible, and to demonstrate understanding of the problems involved. For example, budgetary controls, which are applied in a mechanical manner not only destroy current motivation, but in addition lead to built-in protection when the next budget is developed. People being controlled need to know that there is an interest in operational problems and that there is a willingness to listen to subordinates. This important quality of the administration emphasizes flexibility rather than rigidity.

It is not claimed that the problems of human responses to controls can be completely eliminated by these approaches. But we can do much in these ways to make controls more acceptable to most people. Since controls do have a necessary role to play, our next best type of action is to learn to deal with them in the way that is most acceptable to the people being controlled.

PROBLEMS OF THE CONTROL CYCLE

We have thus far dealt with control in its entirety. We now go back to the seven steps in the control cycle and examine in greater detail some of the major operational problems which relate more specifically to each phase of the cycle.

Problems of Objectives

We have already discussed the fundamental role of objectives in the total control process. Our further interests now are the following individual features of process through which objectives are developed.

What Should Be Controlled?   In developing meaningful control we must first ask ourselves what it is we wish to control. This is a question that needs to be asked for the company as a whole and at each level of operational activity. Even though we may be dealing with a specific level of operational activity, we need to relate the particular needs there to other operational activities, and to the larger company activities as a whole. In making this determination it will be helpful to think in terms such as the following:

1. *What are the key resources?* At each level of operational activity, and as required by the nature of the particular operational activity, there will be resources of people, machines, money, materials, customer loyalty, and the like. What resources are the most valuable in relation to the others, and what are the risks in each case of waste, misappropriation, or failure to be used productively? Where also are the most potential possibilities of effective utilization? What are the values of these resources in relationship to each other and to other company resources, both in terms of dollar value and operational impact?
2. *What are the key costs?* A related way to look at the particular situation is in terms of key costs. What are the largest types of expenditures?

Which of these types of expenditure are the most controllable? Which offer the greatest potentials for saving, and which the greatest opportunities for other types of effective utilization? The solution here involves careful analysis and good judgment so that we can direct our control efforts where the results will be most rewarding.

3. *What are the critical issues?* Still another way to look at a particular operating activity (or group of activities) is in terms of their impact on the other company activities. What happens to other specific operational groups if this particular group does not do its job effectively? What is the impact upon total company welfare? Perhaps, for example, the later failure of a small part being produced can endanger the performance of the completed assembly, and even involve the lives of people.

4. *What combinations of control needs?* It is especially important to relate specific control needs to each other in proper combinations. There is the danger that particular controls will unduly overlap and be at odds with each other. For example, a control in the form of maintenance labor cost per mile of pipeline might overlap with additional controls over hours worked or rates paid. The overlap could easily restrict the manager's effort to use available types of labor most effectively. A second illustration is where controls over the level of bad-debt losses might conflict with efforts to increase profits through increased sales.

5. *Are control objectives consistent with decentralization policy?* A useful way to look at the problem of properly combining control needs is to ask ourselves whether the level of control objectives at each operational level is consistent with the intended decentralization of responsibility to the next-lower management level. This is especially important if the decentralization policy has been implemented by hiring managers of the higher-level capabilities. In such cases, too detailed objectives will waste the money expended as salaries to those capable managers.

How Can the Objectives Be Defined?   The determination of what should be controlled leads us to the question of how we should define the particular objectives. Our concern at this point is with the specific characteristics of such definition. These essential characteristics include:

1. *Need to Be Specific.* Our first need is to go beyond the level of generality and to be specific about our control objectives. At a high level, for example, it is not enough to say we want a company to be profitable. In addition, we need to specify the exact terms by which that profitability shall be measured. At a lower level it is not enough to say that we want a worker to be productive. We need also to specify the terms in which that productivity will be measured—units produced, hours per unit produced, sales achieved, costs incurred, and the like.

2. *Maximum Quantification Practicable.* In addition to the need to be spe-

cific, there is the related need to express the objectives to the extent practicable in quantitative terms. If the objective is increased profits per share, how much of an increase? If the objective is increased sales, we need to specify the amount of that desired sales increase. In many situations the quantification is difficult and there is a reluctance to come to grips with it. We need to remember, however, that quantification provides a necessary degree of precision to the control effort.

3. *Fixing of Time Dimensions.* The specification of objectives in quantitative terms also involves a proper determination of the time dimension. If the objective is increased earnings per share, we need to specify the periods to be covered. In other cases the time dimension becomes the key quantitative dimension. Illustrative is the fixing of target dates for the various stages of the installation of a new system. Again these time dimensions are essential to provide an adequate framework for control.

4. *Anticipation of Measurement Phase.* Finally, the specification of objectives must anticipate the later need to measure performance against those objectives. At this point consideration must be given to the scope of the existing accounting system and other related operational reports. If new types of measurement are to be involved, consideration must also be given to the feasibility and cost of such supplemental procedures.

How Will the Objective Actually Be Established? The determination of what is to be controlled, and how the objective will be defined, now sets the stage for the actual determination of the objective. The concern at this stage is with the adequacy of the study effort upon which that determination will be based. Is the determination in effect pulled out of the air, and hence more wishful thinking than cold reality? Or is the objective based on a reasonable examination of the pertinent factors involved. It is quite evident that, unless the objectives are properly determined, there can be no meaningful ongoing control effort. In making this determination there are certain types of input which need to be provided and given proper consideration. These inputs include the following:

1. *Historical Data.* One useful type of guide is what has happened in the past. From that experience we know how successful certain efforts have been, what problems have been encountered, and what costs have been incurred.

2. *New Factors in the Current Situation.* Historical data are, however, based on previously existing conditions. The situation now may involve different people capabilities, new types of equipment, and better techniques. Hence adjustments must be made to give considerations to all things that are different from the previously existing situation.

3. *Future Projections.* We need also to give consideration to further changes which may be expected in the future. Perhaps new types of equipment

will be available. Or, perhaps, there is an environmental development that can reasonably be predicted. We need, therefore, to project these expected changes and build them into our future objectives.

4. *Extent of Task.* Finally, there is the factor of improvement which should be built into the objective. This is a highly judgmental question and is directly dependent on the relations of the higher and lower levels of supervision. The task factor can, on the one hand, be set so low that it fails to induce the full potential. On the other hand, however, it can be so high that it unduly discourages and alienates the parties whose performance is to be measured. The challenge here is to find the proper intermediate balance.

Rule of Reason. The discussion of the particular features of developing objectives has emphasized the need to select the right things to be controlled, to define them in specific terms, and to have an adequate basis for their actual determination. It is, indeed, right and proper that we should push in those directions. However, it is also important to apply a rule of reason in each case. We can, for example, extend the scope of our control to detailed activities which result both directly in excessive cost and conflict with other important management needs. We can also push the quantification effort to a point where important qualitative dimensions are ignored. Illustrative here would be measuring the effectiveness of a public relations program by the *number* of accepted news releases, without consideration of the size of the individual news stories or the substance of them. Such undue reliance on quantification provides an appearance of effective control that is both fallacious and full of risk. Finally, in the area of actual determination, tbere can be an excessive concentration on underlying facts and details which is both too costly and too time consuming. The establishment of objectives, therefore, requires at all times a great deal of judgment add good sense.

Challenge of Establishing Objectives. We have endeavored in our discussion of objectives to show the needs and potential possibilities, and at the same time to point out the problems and pitfalls. The challenge that exists in all operational situations, at all levels, is to find the right kind of balance. The job of the control specialist is to push the control function into new areas by a more capable analysis of the pertinent factors, and by a more perceptive determination of proper objectives. At the same time adequate consideration must be given to the feasibility of subsequent implementation, the costs involved—both in terms of direct operational costs and in its other types of operational impact such as the human responses discussed earlier. To a considerable extent this is a part of the basic responsibility of every manager at each operational level. But it is the role of the control specialist to provide direct assistance in this area. What is increasingly clear is that the proper identification and development of meaningful control objectives is at the heart of the effectiveness of the total control effort. The challenge is to carry out this part of the total process in a way that will best provide a sound foundation for productive operational activities.

Problems of Measurement

The objectives that have been established now set the stage for the measurement of performance in terms of those objectives. The establishment of those objectives has, as we have seen, necessarily considered the supporting need for measurement. Presumably, then, the practicability of measuring the particular kind of performance involved has already been anticipated. However, it will still be necessary to provide for any special procedures that go beyond the regular reporting program. At this stage also there are certain features of the reporting which need to be given proper recognition. These include:

1. *Consistency with Structure of Objectives.* Performance data need to be reported in exactly the same terms as the objectives. This means that the structure of the objectives should be followed also in the reporting of performance data. This requirement has special application in relation to a budget or profit plan.

2. *Accuracy.* A second basic requirement is that performance data be accurately stated. Errors can never be completely avoided, but excessive errors destroy the credibility of the data, and to that extent undermine the effectiveness of the remainder of the control system. This does not preclude the use of sampling as a basis for the development of certain kinds of performance data, since this method frequently provides the basis for more effective management action. However, the manner in which the samples are used needs to be clearly disclosed.

3. *Timing.* Effective control depends directly on performance data being made available promptly. Every possible means should, therefore, be taken to streamline the processing and reporting of performance data. The importance of the managerial needs in many situations makes it desirable to use estimates.

4. *Use of Preliminary Measures.* In many situations, as previously discussed, it is possible to develop preliminary measures that serve as warning signals. Illustrative would be the case where a periodic check of stocks of independent dealers can provide a basis for anticipating the volume of sales by a manufacturer to those dealers. The trend of incoming applications can similarly provide a good basis of judging how registrations for colleges will subsequently become actuality.

5. *Distribution.* In an effective control system performance data flow first to the supervisory level which has direct responsibility. The data are then summarized in an appropriate manner and made available to the next supervisory level. The sequence is important because normally the lower supervisory level needs to be alerted first as a basis for promptness in taking needed action. Also, that supervisory level can then prepare itself

for questions and discussions with the next-level supervisors. The further summarization at each operational level is important because higher-level supervisors have a range of larger responsibilities and must keep their work loads within the limits of effective use of time.

Problems of Comparing Performance with Objectives

The problems that arise in the comparison of actual performance with objectives involve all the problems previously cited in connection with measurement. This is because the two stages overlap and are normally combined in some way. However, several additional problems need to be properly dealt with:

1. *Presentation*. If control reports are to be used in an effective manner, it is first necessary that they be presented in a clear and understandable manner. Actual data and objectives are usually best put in separate columns and favorable and unfavorable variances clearly identified. In the case of interim reporting—as, for example, in the case of budgets—the comparisons are usually made both for the current period and the cumulative performance to date.

2. *Adjustments in Standards*. When conditions have changed and standards previously developed are to that extent obsolete, there is always the question of whether the basic standards should be adjusted for the known changes, or whether the fact of the change should continue to be a part of the later analysis of causes of deviations. There is no single answer to ths question, but if standards are changed, the adjustment of the standards should be clearly disclosed.

3. *Use of Future Projections*. In many situations, especially in the case of budgets and profit plans, the best control is made possible by currently translating current experience into revised future projections. As we move through the total period, new developments take place. The revised future projections then can be made to reflect the impact of these new developments. The revised projections then better alert management to the need to take all possible action to deal with new problems so that future results can be as close as possible to wanted objectives.

Problems of Analysis

At this stage we are probing for the explanations of why the actual performance is what it is when compared to the established objectives. What are the causal factors and what is their individual impact? The special problems here will include:

1. *Extent of the Analysis Effort*. The analytical effort is carried on in part by the responsible supervisor since he is the person best informed about the operations involved. To some extent, however, use is normally made of staff personnel. In all cases there is the judgmental question of how much effort is justified. Involved in this question is also how far one

should go backward in examining causes of causes. We have here again the necessity for the rule of reason.

2. *Timing of the Analysis.* Since management action depends on identification of causes, the timing of the analysis again becomes a critical dimension of a good control effort. The extent of the analysis must, therefore, be balanced against the loss of value of the findings when unduly delayed.

3. *Identification of Controllable Causes.* The heart of the analysis effort is the extent to which controllable causes are identified and evaluated in relation to noncontrollable causes. We need to know which causes are those that we can do something about. The problems of separation is, however, often very difficult and there is need both for good techniques and good judgment. It is also necessary to recognize that the degree of controllability varies over time. For example, investment in equipment is fixed for the short run but *is* controllable in the longer run. But something like political action is always relatively uncontrollable.

Problems of Determining Constructive Action

Analysis provides the explanation of causes, but there still must be the determination of appropriate action which will best serve the company's interest. It is clearly crucial that this determination be made efficiently. The special problems at this stage will include:

1. *Supplementing the Analysis.* The determination of what should be done requires to a considerable extent the further and more definitive testing of the adequacy of the analysis. This further testing is especially important if the analytical effort has been delegated to staff personnel. It includes direct contacts and discussions with the people who have been involved in the actual performance, and with other people who either have provided various types of input or who have particular types of expertise. All of this supplementary analysis is directed to finding answers that are sufficiently reliable to become a sound basis for action.

2. *Timing.* When decisions for action are being made there is always the human tendency to stop short of the final determination. Although decisions should not be made hastily in relation to the seriousness of the issue involved, there is a time when decisions are necessary. We need, therefore, to discipline ourselves to do what on balance is needed.

3. *Evaluating Conflicting Factors.* Determining appropriate action, like all decision making, involves a balancing of conflicting factors. Short-run considerations need, for example, to be weighed against long-run impacts. In other cases the gains in one operational feature have to be weighed against the restrictions which are generated for another operational feature. Relative risks also need to be considered in the light of the capacity and willingness to assume risk. And the impact on people and people relationships must always be carefully evaluated. All of these conflicting

factors, therefore, have to be evaluated and viewed incrementally as to their net addition to company interests.

4. *Need for Flexibility*. Finally, the determination of appropriate action requires a flexible approach. Stereotyped determinations lose touch with the real world of change and frequently lead to undesirable types of actions. In addition, they undermine effective human relationships. Hence there must be a sensitive and flexible approach to these important determinations.

Problems of Taking Action

The decision to take particular types of action now having been made, the next step is to actually take that action. The concern now is with how effectively that action phase is carried out. The special problems here include:

1. *Who should take the action?* It would seem to be obvious that the best person to take the action is the responsible supervisor, and, therefore, every possible effort should be made to see that the matter is handled in just that way. However, there may be cases where the action must actually be taken in some other way. In such a situation the responsible supervisor will normally alert the lower-level supervisor of what is to be done. In other cases, the pressures of time and managerial responsibilities will make it necessary to work through staff personnel. The need in this type of situation is that the staff person carry out his role as the *agent* of the responsible supervisor. What needs to be avoided is that actions are taken by persons who are not viewed as legitimate sources of authority.

2. *How should the action be taken?* What is even more important, perhaps, is how the action is taken. First, it is necessary that recipients are given proper understanding of why the action is being taken, thus avoiding the undesirable interpretation that the action is arbitrary in nature. Second, the action needs to be free of emotional characteristics or personal indictments that will generate hostility and resistance. Wherever possible, the facts should speak for themselves and action instructions presented in a purely objective and professional manner. We have here again the earlier mentioned problem of human responses to control and the need to deal with them in a capable manner. It is useful to remember that good managers are interested in results rather than proving they were right or demonstraing personal power.

Problems of Continuing Appraisal

We know that the operations of a business continue on into the future. The problems of control are, therefore, also never ending. The previously taken control actions, therefore, blend into the subsequent recurring control cycles. The further appraisal of the actions taken provides another important input for the effectiveness of the next control cycle. The special problems at this stage include:

1. *Need for a Learning Attitude*. The starting point for effective continuing appraisal is that the various responsible personnel have an attitude of wanting to improve operations and to learn how improvement can best be achieved. This approach emphasizes the fact that control actions are never perfect and can always be subject to further improvement.

2. *Providing for Feedback*. Coupled with the right attitude for learning and improvement is the importance of providing adequate means for feedback. This feedback provides information as to how effective the control action was and what we might have done to improve it. The feedback is made possible in part by establishing the proper climate for free expression. It is also made more effective by specific programs of inquiry and evaluation. In some cases, also, special types of reporting need to be utilized.

Impact of Computers

Any discussion of the control process must necessarily recognize the major impact that computers have had on all parts of that process. We will look at computer developments in more detail in Chapters 8 and 22. We should, however, at this point briefly identify the special types of impact on the control process.

1. *Better Availability of Information*. An important contribution that computers make to the control process is in providing more complete information at all stages of the control process. This has a number of important features—more complete information, better analysis and dissemination of that information, and availability on a more timely basis. In all cases a better basis for effective control action can thus be provided.

2. *Programmed Controls*. The computer has a special capability to program the handling of sequences of transactions and operations so that they can be executed in a prescribed manner. It is also possible to build into those programs various types of controls. Thus to a considerable extent the objectives of control can be accomplished in a planned manner, and with intervention by individuals only in accordance with previously established rules and criteria. Control objectives are thus again more efficiently achieved.

3. *Direct-Access Capability Dangers*. A particular capability of computers is that they can establish memory banks of operational data which can be tapped by available technical means. In many respects this provides greater assistance to all persons charged with control responsibilities. It does, however, pose some special problems. These problems are that higher-level supervisors can have access to operational data relating to lower organizational levels before data flow up to them in accordance with the regular system. This availability does not necessarily mean that the data should be or will be utilized in violation of normal organizational sequences, but it does provide a new possibility that it can and might be

done. These possibilities can have a significant impact on the total control system and need to be covered carefully.

4. *Types of Risks.* The use of EDP by its very nature involves a concentration of data and processing that, on the one hand, eliminates segregation of duties and related safeguards that are part of manually operated systems. This concentration then brings with it increased security risks pertaining both to improper entry of data and the later protection of it from physical loss. These risks in part pertain to individual programs and need to be dealt with through individual application controls. Other risks pertain to the facilities as a whole and to all applications. The potentials of computer-based crime have become of major magnitude—as discussed further in Chapters 22 and 26.

5. *Built-In Controls.* A final aspect of the control problem generated by EDP usage is that needed system controls should to a major extent to be built into the system during the design and development stage—as also discussed in Chapter 22. If this is not done, it may be too costly or even impossible in any reasonable sense to remedy the deficiencies. The unique nature of this problem indeed poses special problems to internal auditors who typically review operational developments on an "after-the-fact" basis.

EVALUATION OF THE CONTROL PROCESS

Control System In Perspective

In concluding our discussion of the control process it may be useful to view the control system in summary perspective. Building on the total discussion of the chapter, five key aspects seem to stand out:

1. *Importance of Achieving Effective Control.* Before there can be control there must be operational activities to control. Hence we cannot say that control is the most important management need. We can say, however, that wanted results are not achieved unless operations are subjected to proper control. Operational progress must be measured and evaluated, and determinations made as to the best supplementary action to take to achieve objectives. Control, therefore, becomes a critical part of the total management effort. The challenge here is to provide the needed control in a manner that is most compatible with the total management effort.

2. *Recognition of the Interrelated Scope.* In devising effective control we need to understand the manner in which the control system represents a wide range of interrelationships. These interrelationships are, on the one hand, the inevitable result of the interrelationships of managerial objectives and subobjectives at all operational levels. All controls necessarily relate to other operational controls at higher levels, at lower levels, and in related operational areas. The interrelationships in a second

important way also involve all other dimensions of the management effort—planning, organizing, providing resources, and administering.

3. *Need to Achieve Balance under Changing Conditions.* The problem of determining how much and what kind of control is needed requires a sensitive evaluation of different kinds of operational objectives and needs, and the application of controls must take cognizance of the existing differences. What this means is that we must provide control in a manner that appropriately balances conflicting operational objectives both as between the individual objectives themselves and with the control system itself. Moreover, conditions are continuously changing over time, and hence that balance must be continuously reappraised and adjusted.

4. *Eternal Problem of Cost.* This problem of balance between operational objectives and the control system unavoidably presents the problem of cost. There is, first, the necessity to understand all of the costs that are involved when controls are established so that we can endeavor to minimize them. Costs here include both the direct costs of providing the control and the costs in the form of undesirable operational responses. The second requirement is then to evaluate these costs in relation to the benefits actually expected to be achieved—better protection and utilization of resources in various ways. All aspects of the control system here must meet the important profitability test.

5. *Control as a Means to an End.* Finally, it is important to remember that control is a means to an end, not an end in itself. This in effect is restating the profitability test in another form, but it serves to help us avoid the temptation to become so enamoured with the trappings of control that we overlook the greater effectiveness of achieving control through the other types of management effort. To a major extent good control is good management and we take supplementary measures only as justified to achieve the central objectives.

Summary Control Specifications

While effective control involves many substantive dimensions that are closely interrelated, it may be useful to have a summary checklist of the desirable specifications, to be achieved to the extent practicable, with unavoidable overlapping.

1. As to soundness of design:
   a. Maximum integration with regular operational procedures.
   b. Objectives soundly established and quantitatively based.
   c. Consistency with regular reporting system.
   d. Maximum simplicity for ease of understanding.
   e. Consistency of control procedures with legitimacy of authority.
   f. Consideration of normal human resistance.
   g. Reasonable balance of cost and potential benefit.
   h. Consideration of conflict with other managerial objectives.

     i. Participation by affected individuals in design.
     j. Use of early warning signals.
     k. Involvement and understanding at all management levels.
     l. Adequacy of development effort for total control plan.

2. As to effectiveness of implementation:

     a. Timely reporting and analysis.
     b. Maximum consistency with recognized authority.
     c. Minimization of emotional and personal involvement.
     d. Fairness of administration.
     e. Understanding of noncontrollable problems.
     f. Continuing managerial interest and support.
     g. Timely corrective action.
     h. Continuing reevaluation of soundness of objectives.
     i. Maximum integration with regular operational actions.
     j. Sound reconciliation of consistency with needed flexibility.
     k. Continuing reevaluation of all control procedures.
     l. Reasonable sensibility to human impact.

Internal Auditor's Role in Control

In the earlier chapters we recognized the major concern of the internal auditor with the control process. The logical basis of that interest now becomes all the more apparent, and can be summarized as follows:

1. As we have seen, a major part of the management process has to do with control. Thus every manager has an important responsibility to develop a program of control that will most effectively contribute to the kinds of performance of which he is in charge. This control program consists of the overall control effort covering the activities for which he is responsible, and the individual control efforts which together comprise the total control effort.

2. The internal auditor is committed to organizational service and in turn to management service. Therefore, he is interested in the control effort as an essential part of his objective of management service.

3. The internal auditor is especially able to provide the board and management with assistance in the control area. The basis for this special capability to a major extent comes from the fact that he is independent of all operational activities but at the same time exposed to them. This provides both the necessary objectivity and the overview of all operational activities, their interrelationships, and the related controls. The internal auditor also possesses the capabilities for analysis and good business sense which are necessary in order to appraise the effectiveness of control.

4. The internal auditor additionally has the distinct advantage of being able to approach the various problems through the basic financial records. From those financial records it is possible to move effectively first to

financial activities (with their related financial controls) to other operating activities with their related financial and operational controls. This does not mean that the control problems cannot be focused on directly and independently of financial records. However, most control problems to some extent involve financial records, all of which adds to the internal auditor's capabilities.

5. The special capability in the control area provides an essential entry to the various operational activities, which then in turn opens up the opportunity to observe and appraise all aspects of those operational activities. The foundation is thus laid for a range of greater service at all management levels.

The concern with the control process on the part of the internal auditor is thus both of major immediate and long-run interest. He should respond to that interest by focusing his efforts on a greater understanding of the control process and the means by which control can be made most effective in every type of operational situation.

Achieving Control in Operational Areas

In actual practice controls are developed and administered in terms of individual operational situations. In Part III these individual operational areas are reviewed and appropriate controls identified and evaluated. In all cases, however, the general principles and basic processes discussed in this chapter are applicable. Indeed, the foundations dealt with in this chapter should be continuously reexamined as individual operational areas are dealt with in more specific terms.

CHAPTER FIVE

Organizational Control

NATURE OF ORGANIZATIONAL CONTROL

The problem of control has been dealt with on an overall basis in the preceding chapter and has been continuously identified as a major concern of the internal auditor. Organizing has also been dealt with in Chapter 3 as a major part of the total management function which the internal auditor seeks to support. Organizational control is a part of the larger control process and has to do with the more detailed coverage of the organizing activity. It will be the purpose of this chapter to develop a better understanding of the nature and scope of this important type of control and to determine how the internal auditor can contribute more effectively in this very important area.

A discussion of organizational control should most logically begin with a consideration of what is meant by the term "organization." This term is used interchangeably with the term "organizing" and to most people means about the same thing, that is, that organizing is the action process which results in organization. There is, however, a tendency for some individuals, both educators and practitioners, to use organization as a broader term. In some instances, indeed, the term "organization" is used so broadly that it includes all of the problems of management, and the latter two terms then become interchangeable. The situation is further confused by the fact that almost everyone uses "organization" as a general term to refer to an organizational entity, like a company, a corporation, or any organized group. We use "organization" in this chapter as the set of *organizational arrangements* which is developed as a result of the organizing process.

The concept of organization can be described as the way individual work efforts in any company or other organizational entity are both assigned and subsequently integrated for achievement of the larger organizational goals. In a sense this is a concept that could be applied to the way in which a single individual organizes his own individual effort. But in a more meaningful sense it becomes applicable when a number of people are involved in a group effort. In the case of the large modern business corporation it becomes increasingly a major problem. The organization of the total is clearly a necessity if the individual persons and subgroups of persons are to know what to do. Employees must have direction in terms of meaningful relationships to the total goals and objectives of the group or entity of which they are a part. Without such organization there could only be confusion and waste.

As we have also seen previously, the need for an effective organizational effort exists for every type of entity. There is an organizational problem in every kind of enterprise, whether the enterprise be business, governmental, philanthropic, or of any other type. It is a problem that exists at every organizational level in an enterprise as any subgroup looks at its own organizational needs within the framework of its own organizational setting. This situation is, of course, to be expected in view of the similar applicability of the total management problem.

Breakdown and Integration Aspects

Since the concept of organization has to do with both the assignment and integration of the total work effort, it will be useful to look at these two aspects of the organizing process more closely. The first aspect is essentially the way responsibilities are defined in terms of job descriptions and then structured in terms of organization charts. Although such assignments can never fully escape some overlapping or joint responsibilities, the more definitely and precisely these responsibilities can be stated, the better it will be. The decisions as to how the responsiblities will be assigned are primarily concerned with avoiding confusion and conflict as between individual and group work efforts, but they must also be concerned with the later feasibility of relating these efforts in the subsequent integration stage. The second aspect of the organizational process is now to bring back together the previously designed job responsibilities into an integrated total work effort. This integration also has its own special problems. Here there will normally be the need for specific organizational arrangements to best assure the needed integration. Illustrative of this would be the creation of various types of coordinating committees, requirements for review and approval, and specific assignments of the responsibility for relating and integrating the results of different types of activities.

Design and Implementation Aspects

Another useful way to look at organizational arrangements, for a better understanding of them, is in terms of the design and implementation aspects. In the design phase the primary concern is with laying out the organizational arrangements as we think they should be carried out. At this point there should be, and there normally is, consideration given to the problems of implementation. But the primary focus is on the design of what *ought* to be. Now the stage is set for the implementation itself—how people actually operate under the previously designed organizational arrangements and under the actuality of the particular operational conditions. Here, then, is the testing of how sound the organizational design turns out to be and what unforeseen problems may now have to be contended with. The effectiveness of the organizational arrangements will be judged in large part on the basis of whether results are being achieved in terms of organizational goals and objectives. The difficulty is always to determine the extent to which the organizational arrangements are a causal factor. But if and when that determination is made, the stage is set for either different approaches to the various kinds of implementation or the modification of the underlying design of the organizational arrangements.

Tie Between People and Organizational Arrangements

The development of effective organizational arrangements will very properly utilize the contributions which result from rational thought and analysis. This rational contribution consists of the logical expectations which come as a result of factual analysis, nonhuman forces, and views as to the way things ought to be. But at the same time, and even more important, is the basic dependence at all stages on people. The dependence exists in a number of ways. The design of the organizational arrangements first identifies the needs for people—what kinds, how many, and of what quality. The design must also necessarily take into consideration the people who are available within the company and the recognition of the fact that in most cases we will, for various reasons, have those same people with us for some time. What normally happens here is that we organize differently at this time because of the people who are available to be assigned the particular responsibilities—keeping in mind changes in those organizational arrangements which we can make later with new people. Also, the design phase, to the extent that it deals with the later feasibility of implementation, must take into consideration how people will actually operate during that implementation phase.

In the implementation phase itself there is a still more important link to people. Here it is the people that make the organizational arrangements work. Are we recruiting the right kind of people? Have we too many or too few of the right type? Are we fully utilizing the people we have? These are problems that must be solved if the organizational arrangements are to be administered effectively. It is also these people relationships which generate the need for modification of the design of those arrangements. We deal with some of the more detailed problems of people utilization later in the chapter.

Approach to an Understanding of Effective Organization

Competence in the area of organizational control assumes a general familiarity with a number of basic organizational concepts. These concepts are sometimes referred to as organizational principles. At times also this approach is extended to take the form of a listing of do's and don't's. Such an approach does, however, have distinct limitations because of the extent to which individual operational situations vary, and that approach may actually be harmful. We prefer, therefore, to think of there being certain basic concepts with which anyone dealing with management and organizational problems needs to be familiar. It is also necessary to recognize that the important objective is to apply the various concepts to a variety of operational situations in a manner which will be most supportive to management. The applications to these varying situations to a major extent almost always involves controversial factors for which there must be a trade-off. This trade-off is a highly judgmental process. All this means that the greatest need for internal auditors is to understand the kinds of problems that are related to the various organizational concepts as they are applied in actual situations.

The individual organizational concepts can be identified and grouped in various ways. There is no really satisfactory solution to that problem because of the high degree of interrelationship between the various concepts. There is also an ever-present design and implementation aspect. For the present purpose we deal first with the concepts relating primarily to design, and then move to the concepts that relate more to implementation.

Alternative Ways to Group Activities

Perhaps the most far-reaching decision which must first be made in developing organizational arrangements is to which way and to what extent the activities shall be grouped. The major approaches normally utilized in practice are functional, product, and geographical. In the functional approach the company organizes along the lines of the major functions such as production, marketing, personnel, and finance. The control over these individual functions is centralized at the vice president or divisional level, and while there may be some lateral coordination between the functions at lower levels, the major coordination comes at the highest level. The benefits exist in the specialized concentration of authority which flows down through the various organizational levels. For example, production people report upward from the lowest operational level to other production people, and finally to the vice-president— production. The major disadvantages are that key decisions must be coordinated and made at the top, all of which is a very long and time-consuming process—restricting the possibility of more urgently needed response at field levels.

The product approach comes at the problem in terms of grouping the various functional responsibilities which pertain to a given product or group of products and fixing the responsibility for the results, normally the profit results, in terms of that product. Illustrative of this would be the Chevrolet Division of General Motors. The advantages here lie in the possibilities of more effective coordination of the activities pertaining to a major product or product line.

The geographical approach in turn is the grouping of activities in terms of geographical areas. The managerial responsibility will now be for all products, and all functions relating to those products, in a given geographical area. Illustrative of this would be the regional operations of a national grocery chain. The benefits here lie in the better coordination of all operations in the specified geographical area.

The choice of approaches depends, of course, on the kind of operational activities involved and what particular types of activities require or appear to need centrally controlled direction. In this respect the geographical approach would not fit General Motors, but it does fit the Great Atlantic and Pacific Tea Company. In all situations, however, there is bound to be some special adaptation. That is, some functions will be organized on one basis and some on another. Also, there will normally be variations in the approach at different organizational levels. The sales effort, for example, may be set up at the top on a functional basis, but at the field level it may be organized on a geographical basis (with district and regional offices), and perhaps even on a customer basis at some level (retail users, industrial users, etc). The organizational problem in practice is to find what seems to be the best combination of approaches.

Decentralization

Common to all of the previously considered approaches to the grouping of activities is the issue of the extent to which the authority and responsibility for various types of operations shall be decentralized downward in the organizational hierarchy. The scope of this decentralization will normally be greatest under the product approach but even in the functional approach—and again using the production example—the responsibility for the operation of a particular plant can be either narrowly or liberally construed. In some situations this decentralization becomes a practical necessity, as in the case of foreign operations. In other situations the benefits versus the risks will be harder to evaluate. The controlling factors include the importance of coordinating various operational factors at the field level, the urgency of decisions in response to changing conditions, the qualifications of the people who will make the lower-level decisions, and the significance of the particular decisions in terms of overall company welfare.

Profit decentralization is one of the more advanced types of decentralization. Here the responsibility for operational activities is defined in terms of profit results and all management activities can be coordinated and administered in terms of those profit results. Whether this is the best approach again depends on a number of factors. It may not be feasible to decentralize enough of the activities to make the profit responsibility meaningful—as where, for example, the design and production of products may need to be centralized. Or there may be certain interdivisional relationships which cannot be measured with sufficient accuracy. In addition, there are unavoidable extra costs for needed staff assistance. There may also be possible costs from dividing up operations which could otherwise be handled centrally with more efficiency. To offset these costs must be the better coordination of lower-level operational factors, greater managerial motivation, and perhaps management development. The net evaluation of all these factors has always been controversial and dependent to a major extent on managerial judgment.

Line and Staff

Traditionally, particular assignments of managerial responsibility have been viewed as either line or staff in basic character. The former type of assignment is considered to fix the responsibility for the final achievement of the company's goals and objectives. The staff group, on the other hand, is viewed as helping the line group to do its job. It provides this help through advice and counsel at various levels, through providing service, or by providing needed control for line executives at higher levels over both line and staff operations at lower levels. In more recent times the distinction between the two types of activities has become somewhat blurred, and many students of organization feel that the two types of activity are now so closely interrelated as to make the distinctions relatively meaningless. The development of modern computerized systems has been one important development which leads to this particular conclusion. Nevertheless, in most situations the line responsibiity continues to exist in a meaningful sense as identifying the persons who must ultimately integrate all dimensions of operational activities and take the responsibility for the final results. It is also usually desirable that the responsibility for the success or failure of particular managerial policies and actions can be reasonably identified.

A major type of design problem in connection with line and staff is how much staff support needs to be provided, and where in the organizational hierarchy it should be placed. In the area of advice and counsel, for example, it is never easy to know how much of that counsel is justified. Staff personnel in all the various areas can usually build a good case for the extent of their potential service to management. Also, in many cases staffs can become empires in themselves and in addition to being unduly costly may dilute basic line responsibilities. It is also always difficult to know whether it is best to concentrate these staff efforts at particular organizational levels, or to diffuse them to line managers at other organizational levels. The latter type of problem is also present in the area of manufacturing service activities. The establishment of one service group at the headquarters level may appear to be very desirable because of the economy of scale resulting from the greater volume of activity, but it may not serve the current operational needs of lower-level managers as effectively. If the staff operations are essentially for control purposes over lower-level operations, we also again have our eternal question of whether the benefits outweigh the costs.

Scope of Assignment of Responsibility

In developing organizational design a number of problems revolve around the matter of the scope of the defined responsibility. There is first, the general desirability of matching properly the two dimensions of authority and responsibility. Authority without responsibility is certainly undesirable. Similarly, responsibility without authority is not realistic. A second desirable feature is that the lines of responsibility be as clear as possible. This is important both for the person directly involved to know to whom he is responsible and also to the superior who needs to know how much he can utilize the subordinate. At the same time, other individuals need to know this to best get their own jobs done. A related consideration is that the responsibility should not be dual—that is, run to two superiors—again, as far as it is possible to avoid such a situation. If for necessary reasons there is a dual reporting responsibility, the nature of the individual responsibilities needs to be defined, including the designation of which one has the central or controlling responsibility. All of this also needs to be supported by proper documentation, usually in the form of published job descriptions.

Relation to Internal Control. The assignments of responsibility are especially important to the internal auditor because it is here that responsibilities for different types of activities can be so arranged that adequate internal control can be achieved. At lower levels this often takes the form of separating the responsibility for performing the actual activity from the record covering that performance. Illustrative of this would be the separation of the responsibility for the accounts receivable ledgers from the creation of paper affecting the individual accounts. At higher levels one type of responsibility can serve as a control against another type of responsibility, as, for example, where customer complaints serve as a control against other groups who design, produce, or service the product. The merging of responsibilities must, of course, take place at some organizational level, as for example, in the case of a profit center, but the objective is that responsibilities at some lower-level point become as clear as possible and that to the maximum extent practicable we reap the benefits of the cross controls that these assignments can make possible.

Overlapping and Joint Responsibilities. Having described the benefits of clearly defined organizational responsibilities it is necessary to recognize at the same time that there are definite limitations to how far one can go in this direction, especially at higher organizational levels. There is in many cases the very real problem of properly defining the scope of the individual responsibility. There is here on the one hand the danger of making it so limited that the recipient will not be sufficiently motivated to extend his role in ways that might be very beneficial to the company. But there is also the danger that the as-signment may be so broad that it becomes both unrealistic and unduly im-pinging on other responsibilities. A good illustration of this type of problem is where a vice president–finance has a given assignment of corporate-wide responsibility in the finance area, and the vice president and general manager of an operating division has a line responsibility for profits for his division. The vice president–finance responsibility for accounting procedures may be clear enough, but in the area of operational questions which also have major financial implications, the balance of authority and responsibility may not be that clear. The president, on the other hand, does not want the vice president–finance to overrule directly the operational vice president. Nor does he want the operational vice president to ignore unduly the expertise of the vice presi-dent–finance. The result is that there are unavoidable areas of overlap which the president hopes will be resolved on a mutually agreed-upon basis between the two officers. If necessary, the president can and will arbitrate a difference between the two officers, but this approach has its own longer-run problems and will normally be avoided as much as possible by all the parties.

Span of Control and Levels of Organization

A frequently occurring problem concerns the number of persons any manager should have who report directly to him. This is referred to as the span of control. The problem also involves the number of organizational levels because action, for example, to reduce the span of control normally leads to the injection of additional managers, which thereby adds another level of organization. Although attempts have been made to fix limits as to what the span of control should be, such efforts have not been very productive. The best answer seems to be that it all depends on the particular situation. Pertinent are such factors as the type of work effort involved, the related need for interaction, the competence of the incumbents at both organizational levels, and the overall climate of the company. However, a span of control with only one subordinate has very real problems. If it does exist at all it will probably be best justified on the basis of the need for two persons who would then function in a co-partnership role, although even in that case there can still be problems. We can also say that the adding of too many organizational levels may solve a span of control problem, but may at the same time result in undesirable delay as decisions move up and down the organizational hierarchy. As a normal objective it is desirable to keep the number of organizational levels to a minimum, thus making it important to justify carefully any increases.

Design of Coordinative Efforts

The design of all organizational arrangements must necessarily give consideration to how the various work assignments and related possibilities will subsequently be coordinated and integrated. The concept of organizational structure as a kind of a pyramid implicitly recognizes that individual responsibilities are merged increasingly at each higher organizational level, coming in the last stage to the overall responsibility of the chief executive officer. In addition, there may be other types of organizational arrangements which focus directly on this integrative need. One of these efforts is illustrated by the stated requirements for various types of review and approval and/or concurrence by parties not directly in the line of primary responsibility.

Committees. Another common approach is to provide for creation of various types of committees which will meet periodically to coordinate activities in which there is a wider range of interest. Illustrative of this would be scheduling committees, product planning committees, and capital projects committees. The use of committees is viewed more favorably by some managers than others. In some instances there can be undue reliance on committees, to the extent that basic managerial responsibilities are undermined. Moreover, committees may be unduly time consuming. There is no doubt that in many situations the committee approach is not used in an effective manner. However, such instances should not deny the fact that there is a proper and productive use of this particular organizational arrangement. The correct answer is to use this device, but to use it with care and judgment.

Project Teams. Another commonly used coordinative effort is that of the project team. This is an approach that is used to study a particular type of problem, or to carry out a special nonrecurring type of operational venture. Through this project team approach the representatives of all of the organizational components which have an important interest are brought together. It is usually not a permanent part of the organizational design in the usual sense, but is brought into being in response to special temporary needs. A good example is a project group that would be formed to study a proposed computerized system which cuts across a number of operational areas and which also usually involves a number of staff interests. This type of approach has demonstrated its usefulness in many situations and is increasingly used.

Implementation of Assignments of Responsibility

As we turn more to the phase of the organizational problem that involves the implementational arrangements, we need to understand a number of important concepts. The first group of these implementation concepts has to do with the earlier discussed assignments of organizational responsibilities.

Delegation. As previously noted, the design of the organizational arrangements necessarily involves the delegation of authority in combination with a resulting responsibility. Now at the implementation stage there is a further delegation process which goes on between every manager and his subordinate. This is when the particular person-to-person relationship is actually established. On the one hand, the manager can go to the extreme of giving such freedom of action to his subordinate that he will improperly abdicate hs own responsibility, something that he has no right to do. At the other extreme, the delegation can be so restrictive that the subordinate is unable to do his job effectively. For effective implementation we seek the proper intermediate balance, recognizing that this must vary as between individual situations and over time in the same situation.

Supervision. Closely related to the delegation problem is the nature and scope of the related supervision. Again there can be an extreme where the subordinate is not given adequate guidance and is left too vulnerable to operational problems. The result is then more often a less than required level of performance both in terms of quality and direction. The other extreme is where the manager is monitoring the performance so closely that both parties suffer—the manager because he is diverting his available time from other important matters, and the subordinate because he can neither make his own possible contribution or experience the management development which is possible. Again there is need for the more intermediate type of approach.

Accountability. We speak generally of accountability as an automatic expectation of assignment of responsibility. Actually, the achievement of this desired end is somewhat more complicated. In more precise terms there are three necessary types of action:

1. An assignment of duties to be performed.
2. A grant of authority to carry out those assigned duties.
3. An acceptance of the obligation by the person involved.

In this way responsibility in the very real sense of accountability is established. The important point here is that the relationship is bilateral, rather than being just unilateral, and that achieving the relationship requires both an understanding of what needs to be done and a certain managerial skill in carrying it out.

Participation. Another important apect of the implementation of assignments of responsibility is the extent to which the benefits of the participative process are fully exploited. Participation means that the recipient of responsibility participates both in the assignment of the responsibility and in the subsequent major decision making which comes along pursuant to that responsibility. Participation has two major benefits. The first is that the extra input on the part of the subordinate can usually be an important contribution to what is being decided. An area is frequently involved where the subordinate has knowledge and experience over and above that possessed by the higher-level manager. The second benefit is that the subordinate will as a result of the participation more likely feel a sense of commitment—the very opposite of hostility which might otherwise be the case. Again there is the need for special managerial skill if the participative process is to achieve its proper potential. It is also important that it not be carried to such extremes as to either be an undue delaying factor or to create unrealistic expectations.

Coordination. Finally, the effective implementation of the assignment of responsibility depends on adequate coordination. This desirable coordination needs to be generated both at the subordinate and higher managerial level. In the case of the subordinate it means keeping in touch with other organizational counterparts to be informed of developments which might in some way bear on the assigned responsibility. The subordinate should also keep his superior properly iformed of progress and any new developments bearing on the assigned responsibility. In the case of the higher-level manager it means a similar type of alertness in counterpart areas to which he has access and then passing on what is appropriate to the subordinate.

Implementation of Line and Staff Relationships

In our discussion of the design phase the difficulties of the assignment of line and staff responsibilities were described. Now at the implementation stage more needs to be said of how this latter phase can be made most effective. We have here one of the most delicate of relationships and one that requires both a proper attitude and special skill on the part of both the staff advisor and the line operator.

Perhaps the greatest burden is with the staff advisor because that role can so easily be misunderstood and the potential power misused. The staff advisor in the first place is frequently younger, more aggressive, intellectually better equipped than the line manager, and usually possesses special expertise. Normally also, he is in closer touch with top-management echelons and has a certain standing with them. Under these circumstances he is tempted to feel over-zealous and over-confident in the rightness of his recommendations, and impatient with any obstacles to putting them to work. Finally, he may be tempted to look good in the eyes of the superiors on which his advancement and level of compensation so much depend. The problem, therefore, is for him to recognize that the line manager has both the final responsibility for results and normally both ability and valuable experience. The need, then, is to see the total problem objectively and to accept a partnership relationship with the line manager from which the line manager will normally and properly receive the major credit.

The line manager at the same time has his responsibilities. He must recognize that he needs all possible help in doing his job and that the staffman can have important contributions to make to the solution of the operational problems. He needs, therefore, to have an open and receptive attitude toward the studies and recommendations of the staff counselor. This does not mean that he is bound to accept those recommendations. But it does mean that he ought to have good reasons for rejecting them. In all cases he must be looking for the best possible answers and then it is his right and responsibility to make the final choice. He has that right because he and only he has final responsibility for the results.

Problem of Organizational Rigidity

The design of organizational arrangements normally includes the development of a structure of organizational responsibilities of the type portrayed in an organization chart. In the implementation phase the problem then becomes one of how rigid that structure should be. It may at the one extreme be a straight jacket by being interpreted as a requirement that all flows of information be only through the channels as formally reflected in the organization chart. Critics of formal organization have at times condemned this possible state of affairs as oppressive, and at other times have taken the view that it is both unrealistic and counterproductive. In any event the effective implementation of organizational design needs to recognize that there must be a great deal of interaction not directly in line with formal organizational design. Under these circumstances the organization chart becomes only a guide to basic organizational responsibilities and not as a requirement for burdensome intraorganizational interaction. It needs to be recognized also that organizational relationships evolve over time through informal relationships, and that these informal relationships set the stage for changes which ultimately need to be recognized and confirmed in formal organizational structure.

How do we avoid organizational rigidity? One major way is to disseminate information in a manner in which it can be immediately available and useful for the discharge of individual organizational responsibilities. Modern information systems are in fact contributing more and more to that need. A second major way to provide organizational flexibility is to create the right kind of managerial climate. The responsibility for this latter kind of climate is directly with the top management of the enterprise. It starts with the encouragement of a free interchange of information and organizational freedom. It also encourages creative thinking without premature judgment of the worth of that creative thinking. It also has a high tolerance for error. On balance it can produce a dynamic and creative organization with excellent motivation and a high degree of cohesiveness.

People Utilization

The design of organizational arrangements should be and is concerned with people needs. In fact, unduly elaborate organizational design will automatically generate excessive manpower. But over and above this aspect is the fact that the implementation of organizational arrangements is the phase when an enterprise does or does not properly utilize people. This is to say that as the current operations go forward, judgments are continuously made about people utilization, and these judgments can have a varying quality level in terms of the total company interest. People utilization covers a wide range of managerial actions. How are the organizational requirements interpreted as to numbers of people? Similarly, how is the determination made as to the kinds of people required and as to what their particular qualifications should be? Is talent that is either very costly or very scarce wasted through assignment to jobs that do not fully utilize those talents, and are the people involved being supported and coordinated in a manner that makes possible the full utilization of their potentials? People as people are clearly both the most expensive and the most volatile resource. The proper utilization of people, therefore, becomes a major dimension of the effectiveness of organizational arrangements.

Leadership

All of the foregoing leads to a final conclusion that the effective implementation of organizational arrangements depends to a major extent on the quality of leadership at all managerial levels, beginning at the top management level. Especially, it is true that the chief executive officer sets the tone for both the development and implementation for effective organizational arrangements. Admittedly at this point, we are in danger of taking over another previously assigned part of the total management process. At each level, however, it depends on recognized competence, basic integrity, and a clearly demonstrated consideration of other people. In all situations, leadership is the lubricating force that makes even poor organizational arrangements work satisfactorily and makes *all* organizational arrangements work more effectively.

Concluding Observations as to Organization

As we look at the various factors that have played a part in the design and implementation of effective organizational arrangements we come to certain overall conclusions as to the nature and scope of the organizational process. These conclusions can be briefly outlined, as follows:

1. Organizational arrangements are and must always be viewed as supportive to management in the larger effort to achieve the stated goals and objectives of management. There is no one general answer as to what are good organizational arrangements. Rather, good organizational arrangements are those which in the particular situation enable the particular management to best do its job. They are a means and not an end.

2. Organizational arrangements need to be flexible and responsive to changing management needs. These changing needs are a result of changing internal and external factors. There is, therefore, a necessary dynamic and evolving character to all organizational arrangements. These dynamic requirements overshadow the stability that is normally sought through the development of organizational arrangements.

3. Organizational judgments require a consideration and evaluation of a variety of complex and conflicting considerations. The decisions regarding organizational arrangements are, therefore, often necessarily inexact and always highly judgmental in character. This is especially true because the organizational arrangements combine rational analysis with the unavoidable problems of human behavior. In all cases the major component is good sense.

The Nature and Scope of Organizational Control

We have devoted the greater part of this chapter to a consideration of the nature and scope of the organizational process. This can be defended only by the fact that the basis of organizational control depends primarily on an adequate understanding of what we are trying to control. This is all the more true when we describe organizational control as the means by which we best provide assurance of the most effective possible use of organizational arrangements. Put in other words, *organizational control is what we do to best achieve effective organizational arrangements*.

In Chapter 4 we also discussed in some detail the nature of the control process. All of this is generally applicable since organizational control is part of the total control process. The special character of organizational arrangements, however, as compared to the normal type of operational activity, suggests a special structure for our approach to the control of organizatonal arrangements. This modified approach is as follows:

1. There needs first to be the careful development and establishment of a program of organizational arrangements. This problem should be a best effort to apply the kinds of considerations previously outlined to the needs of the particular enterprise. It is the equivalent of objectives which are basic to any type of control.

2. The second need is that there be policies and procedures for monitoring significant changes in the established organizational arrangements. The types of changes and the organizational levels to which they apply must be identified. The procedures should be clear as to how those changes are to be proposed and approved. At the same time an official organization manual would normally be maintained.

3. Finally, there is the need for a continuing program of reappraisal of all organizational arrangements. The study of the various aspects of those arrangements can originate through proposals under the procedures outlined above, or they might be initiated by the staff group that administers those procedures. In all cases there is the recognition that further experience, new developments, and new knowledge can set the need for improvements of various kinds in the organizational arrangements.

Thus we see that with an initial starting point the organizational control activity is administered in an orderly manner and that there is provision for its continuous self-renewal.

ACHIEVING ORGANIZATIONAL CONTROL

Assuring Reappraisal of Organizational Control[1]

As we have seen, the continuing reappraisal of the effectiveness of all organizational arrangements is a basic part of the organizational control process. The question then becomes one of how we best assure that continuing reappraisal at the proper level of professional competence. We will look first at what the company should be doing, apart from the internal auditing effort, and then consider what the role of the internal auditor should be.

Basic Managerial Responsibility for Organizational Control. The clear responsibility of all managers for both the organizing and the control functions has previously been emphasized. It logically follows that each manager has a basic responsibility for organizational control as it pertains to his particular area

---

[1]Additional material relating to the way individual companies and their internal auditors are responding to the need for organizational control is contained in *Research Report No. 18*, "The Internal Auditor's Review of Organizational Control," issued by The Institute of Internal Auditors.

of operational responsibility. He, therefore, should be continuously initiating such actions as he deems appropriate, putting them into effect insofar as he has the authority, or channeling his proposals to those individuals who have been charged with the responsibility of monitoring changes in the organizational arrangements. The initial ideas may originate from his own independent thinking. They can develop out of interactions with subordinates and superiors, or they may come from other managers in the company who frequently have an opportunity to see the problems with greater perspective and objectivity. In all cases the individual manager gives such consideration to the various ideas as he thinks appropriate.

In many situations the approach to organizational control is along these lines of primary dependence on the managers themselves. At the same time, however, there are certain paper and procedural problems which have to be handled by someone. Employees have to get on payrolls, raises have to be processed somehow, titles must be designated, and the like. There procedural matters are necessarily handled in some way by individuals in the personnel department and the accounting department. As an enterprise expands, the consistent and desired handling of these matters presents increasing difficulties. As gaps or problems develop, there is more and more likely to be confusion and an excessive diversion of valuable managerial time.

Special Staff for Organizational Control.   The kinds of problems just outlined tend gradually to move the enterprise toward a greater centralization of control over these various matters, which are on the fringe of basic organizational control. Combined with this pressure is one that comes out of the greater trend for forward planning at all levels. As a part of such planning there is the related need to project organizational changes and to consider further management personnel needs. All of the foregoing leads more and more to the creation of posts or units which are charged with the overall role of both coordinating current organizational changes and in studying ongoing organizational needs. In the first instance these new staff units have most often been set up within the personnel function, thus recognizing the important tie to people and to the related personnel services. In its more advanced stage, however, the organizational group is removed from the personnel function and made directly responsible to a more senior officer, in some cases to the chief executive officer himself. Under any of these arrangements there is no denial of the basic responsibility for organization control on the part of individual managers. Rather, the organizational department is set up to assist managers at all levels. There is also the need of providing necessary control company-wide over all organizational arrangements. This is necessary to provide assurance that all changes in organization arrangements are sound in terms of company interests and that they conform to established company policies. Also, job ratings, titles, and levels of compensation need to be applied uniformly. The special staff group thus works in a close partnership relationship with the managers, at times initiating studies, but in the last analysis responding to management needs in the most effective fashion possible.

Role of Internal Auditor in Organizational Control

The interest of the internal auditor in organizational control is a logical extension of his concern for the total control process as part of his overall objective of service to management. The practical question then becomes one of how he can best make his contribution in this very important special control area.

Interest in an Effective Setup for Organizational Control.   The point needs to be emphasized that the internal auditor's first interest is that the company have an adequate program for organizational control, as detailed in the previous discussion of the nature and scope of organizational control. This is to say that the internal auditor's role is the same as with any part of the control system—to assist in, but not to take direct responsibility for, providing organizational control. This is to say also that the internal auditor welcomes and supports the creation of a properly qualified organization department which will monitor current organizational changes and provide assistance to managers in the study of the changing needs for all types of organizational arrangements. When that organizational department is set up, the internal auditor will want to work with that group in every practical way possible.

Direct Focus on Organizational Control.   It follows also that there should be no more restrictions on the internal auditor's authority and responsibility to review the program of organizational control at any level than there would be with any other type of operational activity. The practical restrictions here would, of course, be the same as in any operational area, that is, the level of competence and the extent of genuine backing from top management. Admittedly, organizational arrangements involve some of the most sensitive management issues because they have to do with people—especially when those people are at high management levels. But there is, nevertheless, an even stronger basis here for concern on the part of the internal auditor. This stronger basis is that organizational arrangements are the key building blocks of effective management performance.

Familiarization with Organizational Arrangements of Operations Audited. The interest of the internal auditor in the field of organizational control can also be expressed in an important way through his regular internal audit reviews of all operational activities. The first application here comes when the internal auditor is doing his preparatory work for any one of his audit reviews. At that time the internal auditor will want to review the scope of the existing organizational arrangements. This review can take place in part at the headquarters office, and would properly include discussions with the organization department. It would take place also at the field level. The major purpose at this stage is to understand the nature of the particular operations to be reviewed, together with the related organizational arrangements, and at the same time to have a reference point to be used as he later determines how the organizational arrangements are operating in actual practice.

Relating Organizational Arrangements to Operational Deficiencies. It is possible that the audit review will lead directly to a deficiency in the organizational
arrangements. Illustrative of this would be the case where the internal auditor
found in his preparation phase that there was no up-to-date organization chart.
Or the review could lead directly to an identification of a significant difference
between the organizational arrangement in practice and those originally represented to be in force. Such deficiencies should, of course, be handled on
their merits in the customary manner.

There is, however, another type of development that can yield very important results. This is the situation when a significant deficiency of any kind is
found to exist and when the internal auditor is then probing for the causal
factors which relate to that deficiency. At that time the internal auditor is in
an excellent position to consider the extent to which existing organizational
arrangements in some way may be a cause of the problem. It is here that an
understanding of basic organizational concepts provides the foundation for appraising the soundness of the particular organizational arrangements that have
been developed. The identification of such problems, and such appraisal and
recommendations reasonably warranted can, indeed, be one of the most valuable types of contribution made by the internal auditor.

*Application of Organizational Control to the Internal Auditing Depart-
ment.* Finally, there is the concern for organizational control which the internal auditor should have as it pertains to his own internal auditing group.
The head of the internal auditing department is himself a manager of his own
operations and he, too, must recognize his basic organizational responsibilities.
As always, the internal auditor also has a special responsibility to provide a kind
of showcase example of what he is recommending to other operational units.
Like any other manager, the internal auditor has the problem of balancing
conflicting considerations and making judgments as to particular organizational
arrangements. He must also be sure that he is alert to changing developments
which may suggest the desirability of modifications in the existing organizational
arrangements. We deal more with some of these problems in Chapter 9, where
we discuss the planning and organizing of the internal auditing function.

CHAPTER SIX

The Operational Approach of
the Internal Auditor

NATURE OF THE OPERATIONAL APPROACH

In the preceding chapters we have considered at some length the nature and scope of the internal auditing function. In this chapter we focus on the internal auditor as an individual and how he views his internal auditing job. Our consideration of the operational approach of the internal auditor will include his attitude toward his work, how he defines the scope of his review, the needed qualifications, the key phases of his review, and certain problems he encounters which are common to all of his reviews. We also discuss the needs for satisfying the requirements of the Federal Corrupt Practices Act of 1977, including the related regulations of the Securities and Echange Commission. These new requirements pertain to the now clearly established responsibilities of management for the adequacy of the system of internal accounting control. Although, as previously stated the internal auditor's interests go beyond the system of internal accounting control, the internal auditor recognizes the expanded nature and scope of the greater concerns of the organization in that area. Additionally, the internal accounting control is an integral part of the total internal control, and the evaluation of the part is therefore a major portion of the evaluation of the whole.

Comparison with the Approach of the External Auditor

One way to help understand the operational approach of the internal auditor is to compare it with the way the external auditor views his work. It has often been said that the external auditor starts with the end result and works backward, whereas the internal auditor starts with the basic activities and works forward to his organizational service objectives. Although such a statement is an oversimplification of the comparative types of approach, it does have a certain amount of substance. In the case of the external auditor, his primary interest is to be able to express an opinion as to whether the financial statements fairly present the current financial condition and the results of the operations over the preceding year. He is, therefore, more concerned with final financial statement balances, and he works backward from them for the evidence to support the validity of those balances. The internal auditor, on the other hand, is more concerned with the effectiveness of basic operational activities, and how those operational activities contribute to the total company profitability and economic welfare of the company. All of this means that the two auditing groups will approach information sources with different priorities, in somewhat different sequences, and with quite different end objectives.

Operational-Financial Linkage

The work of the external auditor has sometimes been described as financial auditing, and this tie has perhaps partially contributed to the movement of the modern internal auditor away from so-called financial auditing toward operational or management auditing. As indicated in Chapter 1, however, the separation of the two types of auditing is not that simple. There is, in fact, some linkage at several different levels and in certain situations. The first of these is where the internal auditor is asked by management to make a standard financial audit of a division subsidiary or other operational entity. In this situation the internal auditor is doing regular financial auditing and at the same time extending his work into promising operational areas. At another level the internal auditor may be reviewing operating activities that relate primarily to the financial or accounting function. But in such situations the internal auditor may also extend his review into other operational activities which go beyond the normal financial or accounting jurisdiction. Finally, there is the situation where the review focuses directly upon a regular operating activity as, for example, the receiving operations, or perhaps the custody and control of mobile equipment. Here the review activities may properly extend into matters of expense and revenue control which become more financial in character. Although in some cases the operational auditing may deal almost entirely with nonaccounting activities, in most situations there are many important linkages which argue against the sometimes asserted noninvolvement in so-called financial auditing.

Going Behind Financial Statements. The foregoing comments can now become a basis for a further statement of the integration of so-called financial and operational auditing into totally effective modern internal auditing. Financial auditing in its most fundamental sense focuses on the reliability of financial statement balances—including such aspects as accuracy, reliability, and compliance with authoritative rules and standards. But these financial auditing objectives are only a component and starting point for covering other objectives of organizational concern. Now we can go behind those financial results to examine all aspects of the processes whereby those balances were created, sustained, and reduced—with full recognition of the ever-present overlapping relationships between various assets and liabilities in the balance sheet and the different types of income and expense that comprise the income statement. In all cases we are concerned with the policies, decisions, procedures, and performance that affect those changing financial statement balances. In this sense financial auditing can be, to some extent, unavoidably a component of the total internal auditing mission—but a limited component only—that is expanded through operational auditing to cover the total objective of maximizing organizational welfare. Admittedly, the degree of emphasis on final balances and related operational issues can vary significantly in individual audit assignments, but the fact remains that so-called financial and operational auditing can be fully integrated in good internal auditing. The audit programs and audit activities must continuously focus on the broader total internal auditing mission.

Organizational Service Approach

As we saw in Chapters 1 and 2, the mission of the internal auditor is to serve the organization. The range of this service extends from the board of directors (including the audit committee of that board) to the various levels of management in the corporation itself. The practical effect of the foregoing extended range is that the different recipients of the services have needs that have major similarities but at the same time with varying degrees of emphasis. All recipients have some interest in operational effectiveness (including profitability) but in differing degrees of intensity and detail. All recipients also have need for protective service but in varying degrees and emphasis, depending on the nature of their particular responsibilities. For example, boards of directors are relatively more concerned with legality, public relations, and personal liability. Because of these varying needs, the approach of the internal auditor must be broad enough to properly serve *all* recipients. Our approach in this book, however, is to emphasize the operational needs. This does not mean that protective needs can or will be neglected. It does, however, reflect the belief that the organization's highest-level need is for operational effectiveness and that at the same time protective needs can be adequately provided. Thus we are concerned with internal accounting controls but not as the end or highest-level objective of the internal auditor. We thus focus first on the management service objectives of the internal auditor.

Management Service Focus

The wide range of management service that can be provided by the internal auditor was outlined in some detail in the preceding chapters. The tie to the operational approach of the internal auditor is that all aspects of the internal auditor's initial direction, the actual execution of his review effort, and the subsequent reporting of conclusions and recommendations are conditioned by the overall objective of helping management at all levels to do the managerial job most effectively. A good way to describe this management-oriented approach is that the internal auditor tries to look at things as if he were the owner himself, and thus directly seeks to get the needed facts for the solution of managerial problems. The focus here is on maximum company welfare. The internal auditor is trying to represent the owners in situations where the limitations of time and energy preclude both owners and the responsible managers from being directly exposed to particular aspects of the operations. The internal auditor in such a role has often properly been called the "eyes and ears" of management.

Profitability Focus

Still another good way to understand the operational approach of the internal auditor is to recognize the primary focus on profitability. This has sometimes been called the business approach, to emphasize the continuing emphasis on doing what is good business: that is, finding the ways and sponsoring the types of action that enhance the long-run profitability of a particular enterprise. Long-run profitability here merges into the total management objective of achieving the most productive utilization of organizational resources, thus providing a focus that is equally applicable to all types of organizations, whether of a business or nonbusiness character.

Profitability as a term itself is much more complicated than it first appears and needs further clarification. There is, first the fact that profitability is the net result of cost and revenue factors which in some cases are independent, but more often very closely interrelated. We know, for example, that reducing costs will increase profitability, but we also need to recognize that additional costs might be the basis of generating revenue greater in amount than the amount of the additional costs. Illustrative of this could be increased advertising expenditures. Conversely, reduced costs could in some cases lead to a still greater reduction in revenue. Illustrative of this could be an excessive cutback in service, which would generate customer complaints and ultimately reduce sales. Because of this major interrelationship we more properly speak of effective cost performance, that is, of the level of costs (whether higher or lower) which, after taking into consideration the impact on revenue, yields the greatest profit.

Profitability also has the complication of encompassing a time dimension which must be evaluated over a sufficiently long-term period. This is to say that management action does not usually have its major impact until some time in the future. As a result, we have two types of problems. One of these is that we must extend our time dimensions far enough into the future so that the cost and revenue effects are properly matched for sound evaluation. The second problem is that the longer the period necessary for that type of evaluation, the more speculative becomes the estimate of the longer-run benefit. All in all it is difficult, therefore, to evaluate properly the effectiveness of cost–revenue relationships, and to determine whether present actions are really in the long-term interests of the enterprise. But this is just what the business manager and owner must do, and in turn what the internal auditor must do if he is to provide useful help and counsel.

Coverage of the Review

An examination of the operational approach leads us directly to the problem of the various ways in which the internal auditor can define the coverage of his review. The major issue here is whether the review should deal with a given function or with the total operational responsibilities of a given organizational entity. The function being reviewed will be something like purchasing or receiving, and can involve a single operational entity or extend through all or particular organization levels, as desired. In the entity approach the review covers all of the activities carried on by a particular entity, regardless of how many functions are involved. The entity involved can be an entire company, division, or other operational unit. If a particular operational entity is responsible only for a single function, the two approaches, of course, become the same thing. Both functional- and organizational-type reviews can vary greatly in complexity, depending on the volume of operations and the number of people involved.

Although most internal auditing reviews have the character of either a functional or organizational type, many reviews will also have a defined scope which is determined by the specific request of management. Such requests can have to do with the verification of a particular fact or set of facts, the determination of the cause for a particular development, the correction of a specific deficiency, or for further information about any managerial question. Thus operational activities can be broken down in any way desired as a basis for establishing what is wanted in the way of the work of the internal auditor. In the last analysis the scope of a particular review is determined by a combination of what management wants and what the internal auditor sees professionally as being the needs of management.

IIA Standards Approach

In Chapter 2 we discussed the "Standards for the Professional Practice of Internal Auditing." We refer to them again at this point because the treatment of scope of work also provides an excellent framework for the operational approach of the internal auditor. That framework is: (1) Reliability and Integrity of Information; (2) Compliance with Policies, Plans, Procedures, Laws, and Regulations; (3) Safeguarding of Assets; (4) Economical and Efficient Use of Resources; and (5) Accomplishment of Established Objectives and Goals for Operations or Programs. Our own analysis was also stated in some detail in Chapter 2. That analysis, together with the earlier comments in the chapter, of the operational approach of the internal auditor are in most respects very similar to the aforementioned framework in the Standards. What is most significant, however, is our own greater emphasis on helping management *better utilize* its resources in terms of profitability and related management welfare. That better utilization also includes possibly still higher goals and objectives. Assistance to management in maximizing the achievement of managerial effectiveness is indeed the central core of modern internal auditing. It is in every respect the most rewarding level of service to the organization by the internal auditor.

TECHNICAL APPROACH OF THE INTERNAL AUDITOR

Up to this point we have dealt with the various kinds of attitudes which the internal auditor should possess and the problems of determining the scope of the review. We turn now to the way in which the internal auditor proceeds to carry out his internal auditing activities. Again, we are concerned here with the particular technical approaches which have general application to all types of internal auditing reviews. They will, however, provide a framework into which he can inject the audit programs that apply to the individual activities.[1]

Familiarization

The first and perhaps the most basic activity on the part of the internal auditor is to inform himself about the operational activity that is to be reviewed, a phase commonly referred to as *familiarization*. There are two broad levels of familiarization. One includes everything that is done prior to arriving at the field or departmental location and the other includes what is done "on location". Before going to the field location the following types of activities would typically be carried out:

1. *Definition of the Overall Purpose of the Review*. This definition might come from the head of the internal auditing group or one of the senior auditors. Or the review might have been defined through a request from some level of interested management. In either case the scope of the assignment should normally be agreed upon between the internal auditing group and the management at an appropriate level.

2. *Discussion with Other Interested Personnel*. Discussions with other company personnel should include any levels of responsibility between the level previously referred to under definition and the level of management at the field location. It should also include other staff managers and key personnel to the extent that they are involved through the definition of the assignment. These discussions serve a number of purposes, but are primarily to alert these individuals to the fact that a review is to be made and to get from them either questions for attention or information that may be useful in connection with the review.

3. *Accumulation of All Pertinent Data*. The internal auditor will wish to obtain and review any kind of information which he thinks could be applicable to the field review. He will wish to review the working papers

---

[1]The discussion here of concepts covering the individual internal auditor is anticipatory of the broader and more detailed coverage in Part II on administering internal auditing activities.

and reports from the last review. He will also wish to obtain and review any other types of reports or materials from other sources that may be relevant.

4. *Advance Arrangements with Field Location.* Unless for proper reasons the review is to be on a surprise basis, the internal auditor will normally communicate with the field location and advise the responsible head of the planned review. At the same time necessary preparatory and administrative arrangements can be handled.

Familiarization at the Field Location

The internal auditor is now ready to move to the field location. The field location, of course, can be a distant location or an activity group of some kind at the home office where the internal auditing group is located. The familiarization phase here includes such types of activity as the following:

1. *Discussion with the Responsible Manager.* This will be the manager to whom the final report will ultimately and normally be directed. The discussion would normally include the overall purpose of the review, timing plans, and other special arrangements. The internal auditor will get first hand that manager's description of the operational activities, organizational relationships, problem areas, and other points of interest.

2. *Discussion with Other Key Personnel.* The discussions with the responsible managers will then be supplemented with discussions with other key personnel. These discussions will normally provide additional detail about the various subactivities and at the same time serve as a cross check against the information previously obtained.

3. *Review of Policies and Procedures.* Discussions with personnel at all levels will necessarily be supplemented by a review of written policies and procedures of all kinds which bear on the adminstration and control of the various types of operational activities carried on by the total organizational group.

4. *Continuing Familiarization.* The familiarization phase now extends into the actual internal auditing review. This is to say that the carrying out of the regular review program involves a further familiarization with detailed activities not completely covered by other key personnel in the earlier phase. Included here would be further discussions with personnel, actual observations, and the preparation in many cases of flow charts.

The objectives of all of the familiarization activity is that the internal auditor needs to know what the operational activity involves and how it is supposed to be managed.

Verification

From the base of familiarization the internal auditor moves to his verification phase. Here we need always to recognize that the two types of activity are interwoven as one moves downward through the organizational levels. But, conceptually, verification is the independent determination of the extent to which actuality conforms to what was asserted to be, as per the familiarization phase. This verification is achieved in a number of ways, but the essence of that achievement is that there is evidence of some kind which is sufficiently credible. This evidence can come through oral inquiries, observations, written confirmations, the tracing of the processing of data, tests, and in other ways. The quality of the evidence will vary, not only with the type of evidence, but also with the manner in which the individual effort is carried out. All of these aspects have a highly judgmental character, both as to the quality of the particular evidence and as to how much effort should be expended in obtaining additional evidence. The application of the necessary judgment in turns depends on the particular level of professional competence possessed by the internal auditor.

Analysis

A related phase of the internal auditor's approach concerns analysis. This is the more detailed examination of information in terms of its component elements. It is very frequently carried out as part of the verification process, as where, for example, the detailed analysis of an account balance might also serve to help verify the correctness of the account. On the other hand, in an operational situation the detailed breakdown of performance under different types of operating conditions can provide the basis for determining better ways to control the particular type of performance. In all types of analysis there is a highly judgmental aspect both in making the decision as to *how* a particular type of information or operational activity shall be analyzed and subsequently in obtaining the potential benefits as the analysis is carried out. In the latter case there is an especially fine opportunity to observe the evolving elements and to perceive relationships or other matters of managerial interest. Analysis is, indeed, the major route to effective internal auditing service.

Evaluation

Familiarization, verification, and analysis have now set the stage for evaluation. This is the critical phase of the internal auditor's work when he seeks to draw conclusions that may provide a basis for definitive management service. Its scope can best be understood by viewing it as being carried out at three levels:

1. *How good is the result presently being achieved?* This may be a fairly narrow question like how well a particular procedure has been complied with, or it may be a more serious question as to how efficiently a given operational activity is being carried out. Or it may be the overall judgment of how effective is the total performance of the operational activity under review.

2. *Why is the result what it is?* At the next higher level, and interwoven

with the first evaluation, is the evaluation of why the results are as they are. Why is the performance as good or bad as it is? Why it is not better? This now involves the evaluation of causal factors, especially, the evaluation of the extent to which those causal factors might have been more effectively controlled.

3. *What could be done better?* And now at the highest level, and again unavoidably interwoven with the former types of evaluation, are the judgments as to what could be done to achieve better results in the future. Can the procedures be made more effective? Should a particular policy be changed in some respect, or even abandoned? Are the people involved of the right type, and are they properly trained and administered? Some of these conclusions may be reasonably clear and can become the basis for specific recommendations. In other cases more information may be needed. In the latter cases it may be feasible for the internal auditor to develop the further information. Or in other cases this may not be practicable and the recommendation may simply be that further study be made. These determinations as to the scope of the recommendation are, of course, highly dependent on the situation and the capability of the internal auditor.

Continuing Search for Effectiveness

During all phases of the internal auditor's work there is the always the continuing need for maximum effectiveness. Nothing the internal auditor does can ever be done in a routine or mechanical manner. Whether the internal auditor is examining documents, talking with individuals, or observing various operational activities he is always thinking of the underlying conditions pertaining to that part of the review. What is right? How responsible was the particular action carried out? How valid are the results? What else could be done? These are typical questions that are always in the internal auditor's mind. The internal auditor does not have a distorted belief that everything is wrong or that disaster is imminent. But on the other hand, he is not a naive optimist. In short, he has an inquiring and challenging approach and a relatively greater need than an ordinary person to be convinced. Hopefully, the internal auditor is always open-minded and fair. But there is more natural skepticism and a need that there be a reasonable showing of relevant facts. All of these qualities come together in the continuing alertness of the internal auditor as he continuously seeks to utilize all relevant information bearing on the objectives of his review and related conclusions. It is an alertness that helps to provide protective service. But also, it always goes further in the continuing search for improvement.

Maximizing Completed Action

The work of the internal auditor has now come to the stage of the conclusion and recommendation. There is now a range of possibilities as to what might be done in the way of completed action. At the one extreme there will be no action now and we will proceed directly to the reporting phase, leaving the determination of exactly what action will be taken, and when, to a later time. At the other extreme is the completion of the recommended action in the field while the internal auditor is still there. The real issue is the extent to which it is possible to move individual matters toward completed action. In many cases the particular matter will clearly be something that should be handled immediately. This could be the correction of an error, or perhaps a more informed interpretation of a company policy. Other cases may be more con- troversial and may require decision review at higher organizational levels. The important thing, however, is that all parties are committed to the concept of maximum completed action. The reasons for this approach quite obviously reflect the truth that the earlier action accelerates the timing of the achievement of the expected benefits. A further important reason is that the partnership relationship of the internal auditor and the responsible management is thus more effectively implemented. Now the internal auditor and the management work more closely together and agree together as what needs to be done. It can also be more realistically demonstrated that the internal auditor is there to *help* local management—and not to police them—and that they can work together in the overall company interest.

Reporting

The reporting phase is now the means by which the internal auditor summarizes what has been accomplished and makes this information available to higher- level management and other interested parties. The content of the reports will, of course, be determined directly by the extent of the completed action and what matters still require further consideration and possible action. In Chapter 12 we deal in greater detail with the various ways in which reports can be developed. But it can be said at this point that it is a major means by which the internal auditor relates to all interested company personnel, especially to the officers to whom he is directly responsible. Reporting, therefore, needs to be handled with special care. On the other hand, however, it needs to be said that the modern internal auditor is more and more concentrating on what can be accomplished at the field level and less on what goes into reports. This is to say that the internal auditor is serving company interests better in most situations by helping responsible management at the field level. Under these circumstances the reporting of completed action does not need to be as elaborate as when the basis for a recommended action is being presented. At the same time the higher-level management needs to understand this newer approach and to be supportive of it.

Internal Auditor's Credentials

A continuing issue is the extent to which the other members of the organization understand and accept the role of the internal auditor. The range here extends from the lowest-level employee in the operational area being reviewed to the highest-level responsible managerial executive. Especially important is the manager who is responsible for the operational area to be reviewed. The question can arise in such circumstances as to whether the effort required to accommodate to an internal audit is justified in relation to the benefits to be received. That is, the manager may resent the making of the internal audit activity as counterproductive to the achievement of his own operational objectives. The human factors that contribute to that attitude and that are involved in dealing with such an attitude are dealt with in greater depth in Chapter 7. Our interest at this point is to identify more clearly the fact that this problem often does exist and what the rationale is for overcoming the obstacles. We assume, of course, that the manager wants to maximize his own interests in terms of greater achievement of his objectives but that he does not see the internal auditor as being able to contribute to that end in a worthwhile manner.

The reconciliation of the dilemma described above is that the internal auditor must make it clear that he does not claim to have the technical knowledge or experience to tell the manager what his operational objectives should be or how those objectives should be achieved in an operational sense. Instead, the truth that needs to be conveyed is that all operational activities have common needs in the *manner* in which they establish objectives and the *manner* in which implementing actions are planned and controlled. The internal auditor's major competence is in understanding how the planning and operational activities can utilize the best possible controls as proven to be effective in other operational situations. These approaches include both underlying management concepts and more detailed procedures that assure desired levels of performance and final results. Once the internal auditor has been given the opportunity to demonstrate what he can do in providing such assistance, the credentials and related acceptability of the internal auditor rise steadily. Hopefully, however, better communication to such a manager of the rationale of potential service can help to provide the initial acceptance. If, additionally, the particular internal audit review is mandated by higher-level management, the same kind of communication can help break down otherwise existing barriers.

QUALIFICATIONS OF THE INTERNAL AUDITOR

Technical Qualifications

If the internal auditor is to be effective in carrying out the technical approaches just described, he must necessarily have a certain professional competence. This leads us to a consideration of the various technical and personal qualifications which are important. In the technical group a number of questions are involved which deserve consideration.

1. *What basic technical qualifications are needed?* We know that the individual internal auditor must be prepared to deal with a wide range of

operational situations. For that reason he will need to have technical qualifications of the broadest possible application. These technical qualifications pertain to both education and experience. For education the current trend is for a college degree in an established school of business. For experience there needs to be previous involvement in operational activities or at least reasonable exposure to them. The activities most useful would vary with the individual company but they will preferably have been in situations where a number of people were involved and where there were problems of administrative direction and control. Second, a general useful qualification would be some experience in or understanding of the accounting and financial control processes. This type of qualification does not necessarily involve direct work of an accounting nature but it does at least involve the kind of exposure that provides a reasonable understanding of this area. This is consistent with the view that the financial control dimension can be an effective starting point for the examination of the broader types of operational control.

2. *To what extent are special types of technical qualifications needed?* In reviewing many operational activities it will be helpful to have some special expertise with respect to those particular operational areas. Illustrative of this would be computer activities, various kinds of engineering activities, and different kinds of production processes. Again depending on the company, the need for this special expertise may be of different degrees. The answer here would then seem to be to look for this special skills as staff members are recruited and developed. At the same time, however, it must be recognized that there are some very real practical limitations. In the first place it will clearly be impossible and impracticable for all personnel to have all of the types of technical skill that might be needed at one time or the other. At best we should seek to have a balanced staff with some personnel having certain skills and others having different ones. In the second place, at some level of excellence in the particular skill, the question might be raised as to whether a particular individual could not be more useful to the company if he were assigned directly to those operations.

3. *When are the skills needed?* In addition to the problem of agreeing on what kinds of general and special technical skills are needed, there is the question of when they need to be available. The answer here is, of course, that everything is relative. To some extent we need to have personnel who do already meet certain standards with respect to these skills. In other cases we can acquire individuals who fall below those standards but who have the potential to acquire them. We might, for example, start with a college graduate, or perhaps with an employee who has been working in some part of the company operations. Through experience and perhaps some special training we can then expand the area of competence. What is important is that the personnel capabilities in total meet the needs of actual internal audit assignments. In addition, there is always

the possibility of going outside the department to obtain special expertise. The latter may be available in the company, but it may at times be necessary to go outside the organization.

Personal Qualifications

While the technical qualifications just discussed are an important foundation for the internal auditor's level of effectiveness, the personal qualifications of each individual also play a major role. Here we are confronted with a long list of personal qualifications which are normally deemed to be desirable. The problem is further complicated by the fact that the identification and evaluation of these individual qualifications is at best very subjective. Yet the area is important and we must try to cope with it. Perhaps the most useful approach is to look at these personal qualifications in terms of the major end objectives. Under this approach we can identify three types of end objectives:

1. To achieve a good first impression.
2. To develop a more enduring relationship over a longer period of time.
3. To provide an additional basis for sound professional results.

These three end objectives are, of course, closely related, but they do emphasize particular types of personal qualifications.

Achieving a Good First Impression. First impressions can be, as we know, both good and bad. When there is to be a longer relationship the importance of the first impression may not be so great, although even then it may help to get things off to a good start and avoid handicaps which later have to be eliminated. But in many situations the contact is by its very nature a limited one. Illustrative of this would be a particular inquiry made in connection with any audit review, especially when that inquiry involves an outside party or where there are limitations as to being able to go back again. Also illustrative of this would be the case of conferences where matters are going to be discussed with new people, and decisions of one kind or another reached. Under these circumstances the emphasis must necessarily be on making a good impression in a very short time. It leads us to the question of what can be done to contribute to a successful first impression. The answer is: a combination of personal appearance and the ability to capitalize quickly on limited opportunities. With respect to personal appearance, standards of dress and grooming should be in the middle range between extreme conservatism and high style. With respect to the capitalizing of opportunities, one should be able to respond effectively to questions, and be able to inject himself in the discussion in a manner that demonstrates courtesy and professional competence. In total the objective sought is to engender respect and confidence as a basis for a proper degree of receptivity for the technical contribution that the internal auditor is prepared to make.

Building Longer-Run Relationships. In the longer run, there is the greater opportunity to develop effective personal relationships. The major difference here is that there is a more ample period for the demonstration of good qualities through ongoing actions and the testing of those actions. The relationships here can be with personnel in the operational activities being reviewed, and with managerial personnel at all levels. In these kinds of situations what are the types of personal qualifications that become especially important? In other words, what personal qualifications most contribute to achieving a relationship in which the internal auditor will earn respect and cooperation? We suggest that the following are especially important:

1. *Basic Fairness and Integrity.* The kind of response that anyone will make to the internal auditor is first conditioned by a judgment as to whether he can reasonably expect fair treatment. At lower levels the concern will be whether the internal auditor will take advantage of his position in any manner, and whether he can be trusted to deal fairly with information made available to him. At higher levels there will be a similar judgment—even though in a more sophisticated manner—which then determines how candid that higher-level manager will be in his relations with the internal auditor.

2. *Dedication to Company Interest.* Closely related is the concern as to whether the internal auditor is primarily motivated by what is good for the company. The internal auditor must demonstrate that he will not be putting special or personal interests ahead of the company welfare.

3. *Reasonable Humility.* All of us tend to react in a hostile manner to someone who gives the impression of being too egotistical. More often, no one individual can be that sure of having all of the right answers, and a reasonable recognition of those limitations is both more realistic and more likely to impress the people one is coming into contact with.

4. *Professional Poise.* People respect a person who appears to be competent and who conducts himself in a professional manner. This also combines a lack of aloofness with the avoidance of being too forward or excessively friendly.

5. *Empathy.* This is the ability to project oneself to an understanding of how the other person feels. It involves courtesy and consideration for how what one is saying or doing is affecting the other person. It reflects a proper degree of general interest in people, to which all of us respond favorably. On the other hand, it can stop short of being overly solicitous or insincere.

6. *Role Consistency.* The persons with whom the internal auditor has contact have a set of expectations as to what the role of the internal auditor should be. To the extent that those expectations are appropriate, they need to be confirmed, and to the extent that they are inappropriate, they have to be modified carefully by the actions of the internal auditor. In all cases, however, the role played by the internal auditor must be stable

and consistent. We need to build a feeling of confidence in the eyes of the people with whom we associate.

Building a Basis for Professional Results. All of the foregoing are important in establishing an effective relationship with the people with whom the internal auditor associates. There are in addition, however, a group of personal qualifications that bear more directly on his competence in a strictly professional sense. These personal qualifications relate particularly to the way he goes about his actual internal auditing activities. We suggest the following:

1. *Curiosity.* The internal auditor should have a natural curiosity to probe for possible underlying explanations. He should not be satisfied with generalizations or types of explanations that ignore important considerations.

2. *Critical Attitude.* The quality here is not to be critical in the sense of giving criticism, but critical in the sense of making careful judgments about the various matters with which the internal auditor is involved. It is an extension of the above-mentioned curiosity with a high standard for the adequacy of information.

3. *Alertness.* The internal auditor needs to be alert to all possible sources of information that may in some way bear on the issues under consideration. He utilizes the innumerable interrelationships which always come with individual types of developments.

4. *Persistence.* The internal auditor does not give up easily when he is blocked in some way in his pursuit of needed information or for possible solutions of problems that need answers. He needs to have a genuine motivation to get good answers.

5. *Energy.* Energy is in a sense the backup quality for persistence. It is the force that keeps us going when others would give up and settle for whatever has already been found. It is a combination of temperament, dedication, and good health.

6. *Self-Confidence.* Self-confidence generates confidence in others. It is the inward conviction that one knows what one is doing and that it is the right thing to do. It is backed up both by knowledge and the belief that one is doing the best thing possible.

7. *Courage.* Closely related to self-confidence is courage. The quality of courage, however, goes further and involves the willingness to stand one's ground in the face of pressures and risks. It is a personal qualification that indeed adds status to the internal auditor and to his effectiveness, especially when that courage has been demonstrated. All internal auditors will face this problem at one time or another.

8. *Ability to Make Sound Judgments.* All of us are beset with conflicting factors of all types as we deal with individual questions. Judgment is the ability to weigh these conflicting factors calmly, including the impact of the varying time dimensions, and to come out with sound judgments.

Here the requirement is not for a perfect record but rather how many more correct judgments there are versus the ones that were in error.

9. *Integrity*. We repeat integrity here because of its basic importance. It is the quality that leads others to rely on the findings and conclusions of the internal auditor. This reliance includes the belief in the professional competence and fairness and honesty with which the material has been presented. It is, indeed, a major basis for any continuing good professional relationship.

10. *Independence*. Closely interrelated with all of the foregoing is the capacity to be independent and not to compromise unduly in the face of pressures of various kinds. It builds especially upon courage and integrity.

Professional Standards

The desire on the part of the internal auditing profession to maximize its effectiveness in serving management leads naturally to the desire to develop standards by which there can be some better measure as to how well the internal auditor is carrying out his function. Moreover, the basic interest of the internal auditor in achieving effective control and the customary use of standards in that effort would logically suggest that he can better control his own internal auditing activity through the development of standards. In response to these needs The Institute of Internal Auditors authorized a major study effort and in 1978 published its new "Standards for the Professional Practice of Internal Auditing." These Standards were reviewed in considerable detail in Chapter 2.

The new Standards have been accepted with real enthusiasm by all interested parties. For internal auditors they have provided an important base of reference in their practice of modern internal auditing. For all others—including management, boards of directors, public accountants, government, businessmen, and educators—it has provided more definitive information about what they should expect from internal auditors. Admittedly, the Standards have limitations—as discussed in more detail in Chapter 2—but they do constitute a major step forward. It is also to be expected that in due time there will be further refinements and elaboration as necessary based on experience and changing conditions.

Certification Program of The Institute of Internal Auditors

Another important accomplishment of The Institute of Internal Auditors has been the development of a certification program in 1972 utilizing the designation Certified Internal Auditor (CIA). The foundation for this program was a major study of what constituted a needed "common body of knowledge for the internal auditor." Subsequently, an examination program was established that has been administered by The Institute on a regular basis. While a large number of qualified practicing internal auditors were given certificates on the basis of previous experience—the so-called grandfather clause—the number of persons sitting for the examination has steadily increased. In combination, an increasingly large number of internal auditors now have the certificate.

A continuing problem of the certification program is the difficulty of defining and evaluating the knowledge that internal auditors should have. This is because the operational activities covered by internal auditors in actual practice are so broad. However, that problem has been dealt with in a most commendable manner and the major benefits of the total certification program have been amply demonstrated.

One unfortunate coincidence of the CIA designation has been the possible confusion of the letters CIA with an existing governmental organization—especially in worldwide usage. In retrospect, a word such as "Registered" or "Approved" would have eliminated that problem, but thus far it has been considered even less desirable at this later time to change the name of the program.

Still another problem pertaining to the certification program is the fact that the greater number of Institute members are still not certified. This is in contrast to the approach taken by the American Institute of Certified Public Accountants, where the holding of a CPA certificate is a requirement of membership. One contributing factor to the existing problem is that movement of individuals in and out of internal auditing practice is often very great—thus reducing the incentive to make the effort needed to achieve certification. Although we strongly support the increased professionalism of the internal auditor, the related greater career commitment and the resulting longer tenure in internal auditing practice, we do at the same time recognize that management's interests can often be best served by moving individuals in and out of the internal auditing department. We therefore see no presently foreseeable basis for changing the now existing restrictions. However, we should at the same time encourage all internal auditors to qualify for the CIA certificate.

Relationships with People

In carrying out his internal auditing activities, the internal auditor interfaces with other individuals in and outside the organization. These relationships extend from the level of the board of directors to all levels of management and other organizational personnel. There are also the relationships within the internal auditing department itself. The relations with auditees present a special challenge to induce their cooperation in achieving the audit objectives to which internal auditors aspire. In addition, there are the critical relationships with higher-level management personnel whose support for the internal audit effort is so essential. In total the relations with people are so important that all of Chapter 7 is devoted to the many human problems always involved. At this point we say only that these relations with all individuals are critical to any successful internal auditing effort.

REVIEW OF INTERNAL ACCOUNTING CONTROL

Internal Control and Internal Accounting Control

We have previously defined the major mission of the internal auditor as assisting the organization in achieving the most effective use of its resources. We have also recognized that this mission is achieved primarily through the review of all types of internal control. We further recognized that this broader range of internal control included the narrower internal accounting controls that focuses more directly on protection, reliable financial statements, and compliance with the Foreign Corrupt Practices Act of 1977. The latter statutory development has also sparked a major effort on the part of the larger public accounting firms to propose systematic approaches to the review and evaluation of internal accounting control. This new material is clearly helpful to corporate financial and accounting personnel directly responsible and to internal auditors discharging their own related review responsibilities. However, the question is how the internal auditor can use that material and at the same time carry out his previously described broader objectives. Put in other words, how can the internal auditor best shape his own review in terms of blending the narrower interests of internal accounting control with his broader interests in the entire system of internal control? Also, how can internal auditors best utilize the total review as a means of achieving the full range of service to the organization?

Extent of Responsibility for Internal Accounting Control

In Chapter 4 we recognized that the Foreign Corrupt Practices Act of 1977 had directly confirmed the responsibility of management for maintaining an adequate system of internal accounting control. In actual practice the chief executive officer usually delegates this responsibility to the chief financial officer, but the overriding responsibilities of top management and the board are still there. The external auditor's responsibility in this area has also become more visible; although the external auditor (CPA) has quite clearly asserted that his concern for internal accounting control, as a basis for his independent opinion, is narrower than the concerns of management. All of the foregoing have in turn tended to involve the internal auditor to a major extent. This involvement is appropriate both because of the fact that internal accounting control is part of the total internal control and because all concerns of management are directly or indirectly the concerns of the internal auditor. The form of the involvement by the internal auditor has varied but as always is subject to the truth that the internal auditor's role is to assist management but to stop short of assuming direct responsibilities that belong to other organizational personnel. The result, therefore, is typically that the internal auditor works in a *cooperative* fashion with the chief financial officer and the external auditor and with all of their personnel. Because of this cooperative relationship it also follows that the internal auditor is very much interested in the new material that has been developed by the CPA firms, even though that material focuses directly on internal accounting control.

CPA Approaches to Review of Internal Accounting Control

The new focus on management's responsibility for adequate internal accounting control has, as previously noted, sparked the release of a number of proposals for assistance. This has been a natural development both because of the desire of CPAs to assist their client companies, and because of their own direct concern with the internal accounting control on which—at least to some extent—they rely when expressing their independent opinion regarding the fairness of the financial statements. The CPA firms at the same time have not been unmindful of the special opportunities to expand their own public image in a competitive professional environment. In any event we need to utilize this new professional input. We will do this by first briefly comparing the new guidance material released by the so-called Big Eight public accounting firms. We will then go on to identify the major issues and approaches that appear to us to be especially relevant for all organizations as each organization reviews and evaluates its own systems of internal accounting control.

The eight publications were all generally inspired by the Foreign Corrupt Practices Act of 1977. In other respects also they draw on a common professional literature. In addition, all of these public accounting firms have had extensive experience with large client companies of the kind that have complicated internal accounting control problems. There was, therefore, as one might expect, considerable similarity in the identification and coverage of the various pertinent issues. Especially noteworthy is that they all use as their starting point the previously quoted definition of internal accounting control. To a major extent, also, they follow the approach outlined in the Statement of Auditing Standards (SAS) 30, "Reporting on Internal Accounting Control," issued in 1980 by The Institute of Certified Public Accountants (AICPA). Under that approach the accountant (1) plans the scope of the engagement, (2) reviews the design of the system, (3) tests compliance with prescribed procedures, and (4) evaluates the results of his review and tests. SAS 30 also views the design of the system of internal accounting control in terms of (1) the flow of transactions through the accounting system, (2) the specific control objectives that relate to points in the flow of transactions and handling of assets where errors or irregularities could occur, and (3) the specific control procedures or techniques that the entity has established to achieve the specific control objectives.

But having noted the aforementioned common directions, the individual efforts of the eight public accounting firms vary greatly in the interpretation and implementation of the established guidelines. The variations include:

1. Overall magnitude of the effort.
2. Depth of coverage of key concepts.
3. Extent of emphasis on transaction analysis.
4. Manner of classifying transaction cycles.
5. Sequencing of the review and evaluation efforts.
6. Understanding and utilizing the related internal auditing activity.
7. Emphasis on environmental factors.

8. Use and guidance for risk analysis.
9. Extent of illustrative review procedures.
10. Key evaluation concepts.
11. Guidance for documentation.
12. Clearness of identification of organizational responsibilities of interested parties.
13. Manner of identifying and evaluating deficiencies.
14. Guidance as to reporting of deficiencies.
15. Style of presentation.

Several of the proposals are massive and very detailed, whereas several are quite brief and general. All, however, provide helpful guidance to the organizations charged with the actual responsibilities for internal accounting control. All of the proposals should therefore be carefully reviewed by internal auditors.

Recommended Framework for the Review of Internal Accounting Control

It is neither feasible nor appropriate in this book to develop still another set of guidance material reflecting our own views for developing and completing an effective review of internal accounting control. We do think, however, that it would be useful to suggest an overall framework for the review of the adequacy of individual systems and then to supplement that framework through further brief comments. We therefore propose the following overall framework:

1. *Review and Evaluate the Background Environment.* This includes an understanding of the kind of business (or businesses) carried on by the particular organization, the goals and objectives, and the current status of the operations. It includes also a reasonable understanding of the major internal activities, policies, and organizational arrangements. The focus is consistently on the extent of risk thereby generated.

2. *Acquire an Understanding of the Existing System of Internal Accounting Control.* This includes whatever is required in the way of observations, inquiries, and transaction analysis. It also includes proper documentation of those findings. The focus continues to be on the extent of risk.

3. *Undertake a Preliminary Evaluation of the Adequacy of Design of the Existing System.* This includes the extent to which the organization has defined its internal accounting control objectives and the manner in which it perceives the achievement of those objectives. Cost/benefit analysis is utilized in a preliminary manner based on professional judgment and experience.

4. *Test Compliance with the Aforementioned Existing System.* This is the more precise determination of whether the system is functioning in the manner intended. This includes both observation, interregation, and scientific sampling. The focus is on the nature and scope of errors being made.

5. *Reevaluate the Entire System in Depth in Terms of Both Current Design and Actual Implementation.* This includes more definitive evaluation of all significant controls—both individually and in combination. It uses extensively the use of cost/benefit analysis. The evaluation covers both the goodness of the design and the quality of implementation singly and in all combinations.

6. *Summarize and Report on Deficiencies and Present Appropriate Recommendations.* In this final phase judgments are made as to significance and materiality. These conclusions and recommendations do recognize the prerogatives of management to make final decisions as to the extent they wish to incur costs to control risk. However, management should have the views and recommendations of the reviewer.

Collateral Considerations

The framework just outlined is subject to certain important collateral considerations, as follows:

1. *Recognition of Direct and Indirect Factors.* All evaluations involve a range of factors from those very direct and immediate to those that are more indirect—and hence more difficult to perceive. For example, in evaluating the environmental factors it is as much what responsible people do, and how they do it, as what it is that those people assert. Thus top management can assert the desire for control but not respond vigorously or decisively to disclosed deficiencies. A further example involves the causes of faulty compliance with a procedural control. Is the deficiency caused by such direct factors as inadequate design of the control, unusual operating conditions, or inadequate training of personnel? Or is the deficiency due more indirectly to the more basic environmental factors?

2. *Documentation of Findings.* The impact of the Foreign Corrupt Practices Act has been to put increased emphasis on adequate documentation. Such documentation is desirable both to assure a more systematic and thorough review and to provide backup evidence if the adequacy of the review is later challenged. However, documentation can become too elaborate and become too costly to prepare. There is also continuing cost to maintain such documentation to reflect changing conditions accurately. An example here could be overly elaborate transaction analysis and related flowcharts. Clearly, good judgment is very much needed as to where to strike a practical balance.

3. *Choice of Transactions.* The fact that the different review guides prepared by the various CPA firms have used different transaction groupings, with varying degrees of overlap, demonstrates that there is no single best grouping. Moreover, the varying operational practices in different kinds of organizations require different types of classifications. The more important thing quite clearly is to define properly the terms actually used

and to provide enough flexibility so that they can be adjusted to the needs of the particular organization.

4. *Structuring of Review Approach*. The different approaches by the CPA firms to the sequencing and combining of the review steps again demonstrates that there is no single best approach. The problems stem from the fact that evaluation proceeds at various levels and that it is unavoidably interwoven to some extent with the checking of compliance. Our own recommendations are of course subject to these same limitations, but we believe that our proposal presents a sound and practical approach.

5. *Need to Distinguish Between Design and Implementation*. It is inevitable that design considerations overlap with considerations of implementation. It is important, however, to try to draw the line between design and implementation in the several review steps as a basis for focusing more sharply on the source of existing significant strengths and weaknesses. In most situations the remedial action is significantly different for correcting design as compared to implementation.

6. *Need to Adapt to Established Responsibilities*. Responsibilities for the environmental conditions, the design of controls, and the implementation of those controls exist at various levels in the organization. At the same time the basic responsibility varies—as for example among the accounting department, operational personnel, the internal auditor, and the external auditor. It is important at all times therefore that the review and evaluation procedures be compatible with the underlying responsibilities as defined for particular individuals and groups of individuals.

7. *Continuing Focus on Risk*. In all phases of the review and in evaluating each activity level the central focus of the review and evaluation of internal accounting control must necessarily be on risk and related cost benefit. This is simply to say that risk is what we are trying to minimize but that the desired minimization must be in balance with the costs thereby incurred. Here we must also recognize that all kinds of costs must be considered to the extent significant. There is also always the question of how accurately we can measure the current and future impact of alternative procedural approaches on risk. There is also the question of the level of risk acceptable to management.

We outline these related considerations, not to emphasize the inherent limitations of every review of internal accounting control, but rather to help reviewers better understand the problems and thus induce the level of competence and care that is necessary. Certainly, all participants in the total review process—including the internal auditor—can make important contributions in helping to generate the needed capabilities.

Operational Approach in Perspective

Having the proper operational approach is a necessary basis for effective internal auditing. As we have seen, the starting point is the development of professional

competence. Here the important ingredients are personal and technical qualifications, combined with a reasonable understanding of human relations issues
and problems. The major thrust of the operational approach of the internal
auditor is to see the operations of the company through the eyes of management,
and to seek to appraise all operational situations as the responsible manager
would do it if he himself were actually there. In doing this the internal auditor
does not take the place of management or relieve individual managers of their
own responsibilities. But he does everything possible to provide the means by
which management can have both the backup it desires, and the basis for
ongoing management determinations. This is the management service focus of
the internal auditor, which properly envelops and conditions his total internal
auditing effort. It is the hallmark of the operational approach of the internal
auditor.

Historically, the narrower internal accounting control has also always been
part of the internal auditor's concern but in many cases being increasingly a
smaller proportion of the total internal auditing effort. This changing proportion
was a natural result of the expanded operational auditing role in terms of both
scope and management level. At the present time the special concern for the
more protective internal accounting control, as reinforced by the Foreign Corrupt Practices Act, has reversed to some extent the aforementioned trend. In
the light of the presently perceived needs of management this is a needed and
proper special concern by internal auditors for internal accounting control. At
the same time, however, it is important that the special current interests in
internal accounting control do not limit the broader service role. Ideally, internal auditing staffs will be increased to take care of the special current needs
for achieving sound internal accounting control, so that there will be no dim-
inution of broader management services. This is consistent with our own belief
that the greater service potential of the higher-level contribution is achieved
through modern operational auditing. Our continuing structure of the areas of
operational auditing in Part III are again also consistent with that view.

CHAPTER SEVEN

Relations with People

Importance of People

We have emphasized the importance of people in every kind of operational activity that directly or indirectly concerns management and in turn the internal auditor. In a true management sense people are resources that need to be properly utilized. But in this case there is the further truth that all managerial activities are carried out by and through people. Whether those managerial activities involve planning, organizing, providing resources, administering, or controlling, we do things through people. It is therefore quite clear that we need to do everything practical to understand people and thus to be better able to deal with the especially difficult problems of utilizing them. In this way we can obtain the very rewarding benefits and better achieve maximum organizational welfare.

The importance of people in internal auditing practice can be identified in three major areas:

1. All operational activities reveiwed by internal auditors involve people. Therefore, every major issue dealt with and every conclusion reached require consideration of the impact of people. In most operational judgments the way people are used and the way the perform becomes a critical element.

2. As the internal auditor carries out his audit work at all levels, he is interfacing with people. His effectiveness therefore directly depends on how successful he is in influencing all of those people and in receiving the information and other assistance from them that he so very much needs. Here an understanding of people enables internal auditors to get the responses and support that help them best achieve their professional objectives.

3. The internal auditor is also the manager of an internal auditing department. As such, like every operational manager, the internal auditor selects and supervises people. Here an understanding of people enables the internal auditor to work with his staff personnel effectively and to best promote the professional interests of the internal aditing group.

Ethical Aspects of the Effective Utilization of People

A question might be raised at the outset as to whether the effective utilization of people involves pressures or other types of excessive influence that border on unacceptable manipulation. At some point admittedly the focus on the end result can conceivably lead to an undue justification of the means. Although there are ethical and moral standards that must be respected, the line of demarcation between acceptable and unacceptable means is often very difficult to draw. The truth remains, however, that there is a legitimate area of influencing people to serve proper organizational goals that is good for both the organization and the individual. When there is that mutual benefit, the process is especially proper and acceptable. Our own treatment of the relations with people and our effort to achieve a better understanding of people therefore combine to seek the the best possible utilization of people in a proper professional sense. We believe that this approach is basic to the effectiveness of managers and internal auditors alike.

Problems of People Relations

What is it that makes the relations with people so unique and often so complicated? How can we approach the study of these relations so that the interface with individual persons in real life can be better understood and handled? We believe that the following major sources of problems can give us a useful overview and at the same time enable us to deal better with the lower-level details effectively relating to people.

1. *Major Variations in Basic Capabilities and Traits of Individuals.* People are not like nonhuman materials in the sense of uniformly complying with given specifications and characteristics. On the contrary, they vary greatly in many respects. Although we defend the principle that all individuals have the same common rights, we do know that they are not equal in terms of basic capabilities and traits. There are also the related considerations of the particular kinds of aspirations that different individuals have and how vigorously and steadfastly different individuals pursue those aspirations. The identification and measurement of these other factors have major limitations, but we do need to know that these differences exist and to be able to do everything practicable to measure such varying capabilities, traits, and aspirations.

    Sometimes we can get useful indicators of these factors by knowing the lineage of individuals, but here too there are unexpected deviations. Other helpful indicators are the environment to which individuals have been exposed and the accomplishments to date. We always have our own impressions of persons as we see and work with them face to face. All of these sources and judgments are important to guide us in our determinations of what now exists and how much we can change or influence individual persons over time.

2. *Major Impact of Feelings and Emotion.* Granted that individuals vary greatly as between their basic capabilities and traits, they also vary greatly in their own performance over given time periods. Conditions of life continuously change, and people respond to these changing conditions in many different ways. To some extent the responses are traceable to basic capabilities and traits, but they are also due to a major extent to the truth that people are both emotional and rational. The term "rational" as used here refers to the analysis and evaluation of all types of data and related input in a logical fashion. On the other hand, the term "emotional" goes beyond that logic and includes personal feelings and sensitivity. These rational and emotional approaches are combined in differing ways in changing situations.

   The challenge is, of course, to identify the particular composition of the emotion/logic mix and to try to understand the nature and scope of the combined responses—thus enabling us to deal with them in a more effective manner. What is important, however, is that we recognize the reality of the feelings and emotional side and the resulting further fact of the major variability of how individuals then respond to the different, changing conditions.

3. *Related Varying Perceptions.* The way people are in terms of capabilities and traits, and the combination of the rational and emotional in a changing environment, also mean that they have varying perceptions of all things in the external environment. To a major extent all individuals live in their own private world and see the external world in terms of their own needs and desires. In addition, our perceptions are limited and greatly controlled by our own background and experience. A given comment of a superior can, for example, be interpreted as complimentary or critical depending on the recipient's desires and/or apprehensions.

   We thus too often hear what we want to hear and tune out that which we do not want to hear. Conversely, the individual sending the message may appraise the force of that message in terms of *his* own needs and desires. For example, the superior can delude himself into thinking that he has forcefully communicated a serious performance deficiency to his subordinate when in fact the subordinate has interpreted the comment as being neutral or at the most only mild criticism. Too often all of us perceive things in a manner that suits our own needs, and it is always difficult to be completely objective.

4. *Impact of Group Size on Behavior.* A fourth major source of problems is to understand better the influence of the size of the group. Individuals tend to behave one way as individuals and differently as they interface on a person-to-person basis, in small groups, or in larger groups. We deal further with those differences and try to understand better the resulting impact on people. In these situations there are both problems to be avoided and opportunities to be legitimately exploited.

5. *Impact of Various Operational Situations.* A fifth source of special problems and opportunities in achieving effective people relations is to focus

on those relations in particular types of operational situations. Each particular operational situation has its particular types of impact of how participating individuals feel and act. Some of these situations are those pertaining to all managers, and others involve more specifically the activities of the internal auditor. We deal further with some of those operational situations later in the chapter.

In total the substantial variabilities and the greater unpredictability of people in varying circumstances combine to make relations with people a most difficult but, at the same time, a most rewarding area for those who would effectively achieve managerial goals.

Understanding the Individual

We move now to the detailed review of the behavior of the individual. At many times in both the managerial and internal auditing activities we are dealing with a single individual. Hence we need to understand that individual in all ways possible. In addition, individuals may be functioning in larger groups and, even though subject to additional influences, we are still dealing with individuals as the basic components.

Common Needs of Individuals.　All individuals have a different combination of needs, with a varying level of intensity of particular types of each. An understanding of human behavior clearly starts with an understanding of the nature and scope of those needs. These types of needs have been classified in numerous ways by students of human relations. Our own approach is as follows:

1. *Basic Physical Needs.* The most basic or lower-level type of need of all individuals has to do with their physical well-being. Even though the intensity may vary greatly, all individuals have primary needs for food, water, temperature, health, rest, avoiding pain, and the like. The satisfaction of these basic needs is essential up to a certain point and has first priority as against higher-level needs of mind and spirit. At the same time the absence of satisfaction of these needs can so disturb individuals as to prevent directing their attention to higher-level needs. This means that we must see to it that these basic needs are reasonably well taken care of if we are to use people effectively for other management purposes. In this connection the situation is also complicated by the fact that more intensive concern for physical needs may overlap with and be a component of other higher-level needs—as, for example, when clothes both keep people warm and satisfy needs of vanity and status.

2. *Security Needs.* Closely allied to the above-mentioned physical needs are those for security. At their lower level these security needs overlap with physical needs, but they extend to include desired freedom from the fear of war, crime, poverty, and ill health. These security needs are also potential distractions to individuals and therefore also require priority coverage to a certain extent if we are to utilize our people resources

effectively. Again, excessive security needs overlap with and become components of other higher-level needs of mind and spirit.

3. *Social Needs.* The satisfaction of physical and security needs is normally not enough. The typical individual is not an island unto himself. Instead, that individual wants companionship, fellowship, and friends. At a still higher level he[1] wants love, admiration, and respect from others. The failure to have such needs satisfied can make an individual emotional, turn inward, and in a variety of ways undermine his otherwise existing effectiveness. Again, therefore, it is important that we do all that is practicable to see that those social needs are satisfied, if we are to obtain the best possible utilization of individuals for managerial purposes.

4. *Self-Fulfillment Needs.* At the highest level we find the needs of self-expression and personal fulfillment. The need may apply to something that is more a hobby than his business—as, for example, playing a fine game of golf—or it may pertain to something more associated with his livelihood—as, for example, to produce a good technical book, to be a leader in his profession, or to demonstrate his ability to make a corporation successful. In other cases these self-expression needs take the form of dedication to a religious, political, or social cause. These are the needs that have maximum intensity and hence the greatest potential. It follows, therefore, that to be able to identify with such needs and to be supportive of them is typically the way to achieve the best total utilization of people. This is especially true when self-fulfillment needs can be identified and integrated with organizational needs and interests.

Common Characteristics of Individuals. We have previously spoken of the wide variations that exist among individuals as to type, capability and traits, and intensity of feelings. There are, however, also certain common characteristics that normally exist to some extent in every individual. A review of these common characteristics can also be useful. A recognition of their existence can often enable us to induce the kind of human relationships that can become the foundation for the most effective utilization of people. The following types of common resources exist in a wide range of levels of intensity:

1. *To Be Productive.* The truth of this common characteristic is not fully accepted by all observers. We believe, however, that the normal individual wants to be busy rather than idle. We also believe that the normal individual wants to do something that is meaningful rather than something that is wasteful or without purpose. We believe that this is the more enduring characteristic and is especially true after a period of exposure to the opposite kind of experience.

2. *Urge for Dedication.* The typical person tends to respond to a cause and derives real satisfaction in expending his efforts in the active support

[1]The reader is again reminded that "he" and "his" are used for convenience and are intended to cover all individuals.

of that cause. Strong leaders have utilized this human characteristic even when the cause itself was not really valid.

3. *Desire to Serve*. The urge here is closely allied to productive work and to the urge for dedication, but it goes beyond these to include the urge to provide genuine assistance to another individual. The source of the motivation can be the need of the other individual, the natural love of humankind, or a basic quality of kindness.

4. *To Be Free to Choose*. The normal individual resents conditions that restrict his independence and freedom of choice. Although that individual may not later elect a paritcular alternative, he resists being deprived of the right to make that choice. Americans especially take pride in their relatively high freedom of choice. Typically also, individuals will make great personal sacrifices in other ways to achieve that freedom —especially when the freedom involves such highly emotional issues as religion and nationalism.

5. *Fairness and Honesty*. The normal individual wishes everyone to be dealt with fairly, and will be resentful of any action that he thinks is at odds with that fairness. Although this need applies mostly to how other people treat *us*, it does to some extent carry over to our concern about actions affecting other individuals. This fairness then blends into the need for related honesty. Normally also, as individuals we ourselves respond to fairness and honesty from others with similar attitudes.

6. *Bias Toward Self*. Some individuals are said to be their own worst critics. More often, however, we are not fully objective in evaluating our own qualifications or performance. Also, most of us tend to expect more in the way of praise than criticism, and typically are defensive against criticism from others. Although typically we are reasonably objective regarding matters involving others, that objectivity does not extend to ourselves in the same manner. We also tend to blame others for deficiencies for which we are partially or fully responsible. Somehow we must defend our own image and self-respect.

7. *Satisfaction of Ego*. A closely related characteristic is that typically all individuals like to be complimented and praised, especially if that praise is visible to other persons. We are hungry for legitimate self-respect, and hence we seek all possible reinforcement of that self-respect through the evaluation of others. Even when we know that praise is not fully warranted, we still respond favorably to those from whom we receive it.

8. *Desire to Get Value*. Most of us want very much to get our money's worth. This judgment is of course different for different people and in each case takes into consideration the elements that are of special worth for the individual evaluator. Conversely, we resent not getting our money's worth, especially if we are somehow tricked or otherwise unduly influenced to take the action we now appraise more realistically. Our emotional response in these circumstances often exceeds the significance

of the amounts actually involved and may approach the level of very real indignation.

9. *Habit*. To a major extent we are all creatures of habit. In the first place we tend to welcome familiar situations to which we can respond in the same manner and with minimal effort. Then having enjoyed that repetitive response we resent all the more any developments that disturb or threaten that habit. Although some variety is also needed, we tend in balance to value higher the things we have become accustomed to—and often even more so after experiencing variety.

10. *To Be Part of a Team*. This characteristic overlaps to some extent some of the previously mentioned characteristics. It is, however, such a powerful motivator that it deserves special emphasis. Typically, an individual who is part of a team derives direct satisfaction in sharing in the team effort. The fact of his membership in a team—especially when that team is successful—also reinforces his own ego image. It is commonly existent in sports, but it has a similar application in business and other operations.

11. *To Have Compassion*. Some people appear totally to lack compassion. More often, however, individuals are compassionate and respond to the distress of others. This is especially true when the compassionate action is visible to others. We believe that most people want to help those in distress once they are sufficiently conscious of that distress. This willingness is, of course, subject to conflicting considerations, as, for example, being ones self exposed to danger through the compassionate action.

12. *Self-Interest*. Although people tend to give of themselves, there is still the basic truth that the typical individual is guided by self-interest. In its most extreme form, self-interest becomes selfishness and greed, but at its normal level stops short of that. In part this is a by-product of the need to survive in the face of a hostile environment. In part there is also the desire to avoid being judged not sufficiently tough and realistic. It is, of course, true that many individuals are very generous, but more often that generosity is operative only after certain levels of self-interest have been achieved, or where there are other overriding needs.

13. *Sensitivity*. Most individuals take pride in their ability to keep their calm in the face of developments of various kinds that are displeasing and distressing. But whether or not the responsive feelings are visible to others, most of us do often have feelings of dissatisfaction and resentment. These feelings may be well controlled or they may be volatile in nature. In all forms, however, they usually impede rational thought and tend to induce actions that may later be regretted. This sensitivity of feeling is perhaps the most dynamic ingredient of human behavior.

Individuals in Perspective

Understanding individuals and relating to them effectively constitutes a continuing challenge. As we have seen, there are major variations in basic capabilities and in the response to all types of developments. Because of the mix of reason and emotion, the understanding of every individual represents a unique challenge. This requires knowledge, patience, care, and alertness for anyone who seeks to work effectively with other individuals. At the same time, every individual seeks to understand himself better and thus be a more productive recipient of and responder to the actions of others. The entire problem is complicated also because as all individuals know more about all aspects of human relations, they become more sophisticated in their evaluations and responses. Thus effective relations with individuals are always changing and are consequently a never-ending challenge. What makes this all the more important is that all individuals have wide ranges of emotional receptivity, a range that is not necessarily diminished by either greater knowledge or higher-level organizational status. Hence there are major opportunities for achieving more effective human relations at all organizational levels that well justify the efforts required.

Person-to-Person Relationships

When we move from the individual as a single person, we come first to the situation where one individual is interfacing with one other individual. Here we start with the already existing complexities of the two different individuals which then combine to magnify further the nature and scope of previously discussed problems. There is also the special difficulty of relating these two individuals to each other. Especially important is the status relationship that exists. Is the interface between two friends on a completely relaxed friendship basis, or are there elements of power possessed by either individual that will affect the relationship? Of special interest to us also is the type of interface when one individual is seeking to achieve a given objective—such as information, influence, or definitive action. To be effective in such interface we also need to know more about the process of interpersonal communications—an area that is discussed below as an operational application. At this point we emphasize only the greatly magnified complexity of the human relations problems when two indviduals are brought together in a face-to-face relationship.

People in Small Groups

The next higher level of human relations exists when more than two persons are directly interfacing with each other. Now we have the increased complexity of an even greater number of already complex individuals. We also now have the fact of a number of two-way conversations woven together in a larger framework. But now also there are further complexities that are unique.

One of the new complexities has to do with the now greater visibility of each individual to other members of the group. Each individual is now conscious of the fact that his actions are being observed and evaluated by all other members of the group. The importance of that expanded visibility relates to the immediate work of the group, but it goes beyond that to include actions that the other individuals may take at a later time. The overall result is a constraint that typically makes each individual continuously evaluate the impact of his own actions on the evaluation and actions of all the other members of the group. This consciousness can have a two-way effect. One effect may be to motivate extreme caution—that is to make one very careful what he says or does. There is now the concern about how one's actions will be interpreted by other individuals. The other effect is to motivate an individual to take advantage of the opportunity to be heard by the others. To some extent we now have a captive audience for our ideas and views.

A second, related complexity is that the group tends to exert pressures for conformance. This happens after relatively open discussions have taken place and when the group begins to move toward some kind of consensus or conclusion. Now it becomes more difficult to oppose the gathering majority conclusion and to defend a conflicting view. Now also the pressures mount to have the agreement and/or support of the person who is still dissenting. On the one hand, the holdout individual would like to be in tune with the group. On the other hand, that individual may have deep conviction as to the merits and consequences of the alternative conclusions and may therefore wish to stand his ground. In other cases the individual may be only seeking attention and self-gratification. What we need to understand here is the fact of the group pressure and thus to have a better foundation for what further actions we may take as one of the concerned individuals. How can we control the impact of this group pressure when that becomes necessary, and how can we use group pressure as a positive force when that outcome is more consistent with the higher-level goals we seek to achieve?

People in Large Organizations

The range of the size of groups can move us to larger and larger groups, one of which is the large organization of which managers and internal auditors are a part. Now we have all of the previously mentioned problems but with still greater complexities because of the greater number of people involved and the many new obstacles to effective interface. These new obstacles are strongly interrelated, but for convenience of coverage can be grouped and described as follows:

1. *Problems of Communication.* We know that large organizations can involve hundreds and thousands of people. As we also saw in Chapters 3 and 5, these individuals must have assigned job responsibilities so that the total work of the organization can be done. These job assignments can also extend over major geographical areas. But those more narrowly focused and widely dispersed job assignments bring with them the necessity of properly coordinating the individual and group work efforts for total organizational achievement. This coordination depends directly on good communication between the individuals involved. However, communication becomes all the more difficult because of the large numbers of people and the specialization of their more narrowly assigned job

responsibilities. In some cases there can be simultaneous communication through a speech or a published policy. More often, however, the communication must move in a more laborious manner down, upward, and sideways through the organization in a maze of direct and indirect channels. It is inevitable under such circumstances that there are stoppages, errors, and faulty interpretations. We need to be aware continuously of such possibilities and to be able to protect ourselves.

2. *Impersonal Character*. The magnitude of the large organization, with its more difficult communication and less direct personal contacts, unavoidably generates an impersonal character to organizational activities. Now the individual finds that his own personal needs are being less satisfied. There is then less motivation to contribute effectively toward established higher-level organizational goals. As a result, there is a widening gap between the personal and organizational goals. The individual tends more to see himself as a cog in the big machine and not as a working partner. The lesser involvement then deprives the organization of the better contribution and the individual of the satisfaction of self-fulfillment. All of this means that managers in large organizations face increasingly difficult problems to combat this relatively destructive impersonal feeling.

3. *Expansion of Threats to Organizational Welfare*. The increased difficulties of size and organizational complexity clearly tend to undermine the more positive cohesion that more often is associated with a smaller organization. But the problem goes still deeper in that there is the greater possibility of hostility and negative actions that can more easily be threats to organizational welfare. These negative actions can range from the individual troublemaker to the more organized clique or power group. It can involve a level of substance ranging from waste of company resources to theft and deliberate sabotage. Everything of a negative nature can be more easily generated and enlarged in the more strained operational environment of a large corporation.

OPERATIONAL SITUATIONS INVOLVING PEOPLE RELATIONS

With the previously established background of the nature and scope of human characteristics of people relations, we can now look more closely at a number of operational situations that especially involve those relations with people. We start by reemphasizing that people and human relations are a basic ingredient of every organizational component at all levels, in every type of operational situation, and in every phase of the total management process. In the latter case we have the people relations aspects of planning, organizing, providing resources, administering (via the subprocesses of directing, coordinating, and leading), and control. It will be useful, therefore, to examine more directly the people aspect of a number of especially important managerial approaches and operational situations. All of these applications directly involve the internal auditor as he carries out his audit reviews and as he evaluates operational activities to develop appropriate recommendations. We will also more directly examine the people aspect of the internal auditor's own responsibilities. In dealing with these individual approaches and types of operational situations, some overlap is unavoidable because of the built-in interrelationships. However, in total they should add to our capabilities to properly blend people considerations with our larger managerial and internal auditing interests.

Maximizing Job Satisfaction

Job satisfaction is of two kinds. One kind consists of the expected things that are essentially what other good employers are doing. Included here would be reasonably pleasant working conditions, fair compensation (including reasonable fringe benefits), and qualified supervision. Because these satisfactions are *expected*, they are not major motivating factors to employees. But on the other hand, if they are *not* provided, as judged by reasonable competitive standards, they can be a major source of irritation and dissatisfaction. The other kind of job satisfactions are those at the higher levels of self-expression and self-fulfillment. Included here would be the assignment of greater job responsibilities, more authority, the opportunity to learn and develop, broader career opportunities, and more freedom in achieving results without burdensome controls or other restrictions. This kind of job satisfaction is also achieved by the organization providing above-average managerial competence in the way of planning, organizing, providing resources, administering, and controlling. Employees typically take pleasure in being part of an organization that is well managed, as evidenced by above-average reputation, profitability, and growth. They also associate such companies with expanded opportunities for qualified people.

Job Enrichment.   At lower organization levels the effort to provide maximum job satisfaction is called job enrichment. The worker in an automotive assembly line who attaches a small part as the partially assembled motor car moves down the line provides a classic example of a job that can be boring and potentially disturbing. Truly, the worker is like a cog in a large machine. Job enrichment comes when a worker is given other duties that provide some variety and that expand the nature and scope of his responsibilities. Unfortunately, there are limitations to that job enrichment because of the fact that cost savings are more often directly dependent on automated production processes. However, every possible effort should be made to provide as much job enrichment as possible without unduly sacrificing needed cost savings.

Participative Management

When there is participative management the worker joins to some extent in the planning of his work and in the development of policies and procedures by which that work is actually accomplished and administered. The potential benefits can affect both employer and employee. Higher-level management can benefit through the input that comes from experience and firsthand exposure to actual operations. Higher-level management can also benefit from the greater commitment of employees that usually results from their part in reaching decisions or setting standards. However, the employee also benefits both because of greater job satisfaction and because of his better basis for claiming the rewards of any resulting greater productivity.

Participative management can be practiced successfully in connection with all phases of the management process—planning, organizing, providing resources, administering, or controlling—especially in connection with making key decisions about goals, policies, and procedures. At the same time there must be a continuing awareness of the problems. If the participative effort is not a genuine one and is perceived by the lower-level subordinates as being superficial—as, for example, when views submitted are not fairly or adequately considered—then the entire managerial approach can do more harm than if never attempted. Other limitations include a possible lack of available time and the need for withholding certain vital information. In total, however, participative management has major potentials and is especially contributory to effective relations with people. It should therefore be sought after by all managers to the extent practicable.

Management by Objectives

Closely related to participative management is the practice of management by objectives (MBO). The similarity is that the higher-level manager and his subordinate together establish the objectives by which the subordinate will be judged. MBO goes further, however, typically by letting the subordinate then operate more independently and be more fully judged and evaluated by his performance (in terms of those mutually agreed on objectives). MBO can, of course, vary greatly depending on the nature of the operations and the extent to which freedom of action is really provided. Quite obviously, there can never be complete independence of the subordinate. The higher-level manager still has some very real responsibility to know what is going on and to provide needed assistance. At the same time the subordinate not only needs some help but also must protect himself from failure by keeping his superior informed to some extent of progress and problems encountered. There is thus a combination of benefits and risks that need to be equated with judgment. However, on balance, MBO has major potentials both in terms of effective relations with people and for higher-level achievement of organizational goals. Every reasonable effort should therefore be made to practice this approach.

Performance Evaluation: Rewards and Penalties

An essential part of the management of people is to establish proper standards for the rewards and related penalties. The rules governing those rewards and penalties then must be defined, properly interpreted, and administered throughout the organization. Related also are the performance reviews that need to be made at regular intervals and in a manner that properly serves the mutual interests of both the organization and the employees. These matters will be dealt with as appropriate in other parts of this book. What is important here is to recognize their importance in people relations and the need that they be done in a manner that demonstrates genuine concern and fairness to all participants.

Because of the sensitive nature of these matters and the varying objectivity of individuals in evaluating fairness there are bound to be differences of opinion and some resulting dissatisfaction. On balance, however, as judged over time by the parties of interest, administration of these matters will usually find its deserved level of acceptance. In this connection each individual will judge the system both in terms of the impact on him and on other individuals. The criteria will also be the fairness of the system as designed and as administered. Because all aspects so directly involve sensitive relations with people, the challenge is to administer all those aspects in a manner that will best demonstrate the desired fairness.

Communication

Earlier in this chapter we recognized the importance of good communication both on a person-to-person basis and in the larger groups and organizations. Our present objective is to examine more closely both the problems involved and how we can then better cope with those problems.

Effective Two-Way Communication. Situations continuously arise in the operations of an organization when two individuals need to communicate with each other. Illustrative would be giving an oral instruction, discussing an operational problem, counseling a subordinate, interviewing a prospective employee, or conducting a performance review. In all of these situations there are differing personal relationships but there is a continuing two-way flow of messages that follows a definable technical model. That model can be portrayed as follows:

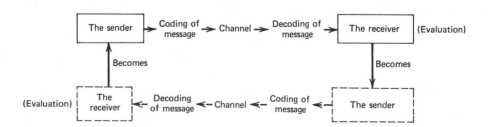

The sender is the first speaker. He has a message but must put it into some kind of a code or symbols (in this case words) that can then be transmitted by a channel (in this case his voice). The symbols as transmitted are then decoded by the receiver. When the receiver replies, a similar process is involved as the message flows back to the first speaker.

Our interest in the model is first, to know the process involved. Our interests go further, however, to identify the kinds of problems that can distort or actually prevent an effective communication process. These problems, which affect all steps in the technical model, include:

1. Not giving proper consideration to the power relationship of sender and receiver.
2. Ignoring temporary emotional stress by either sender or receiver.
3. Not properly evaluating capacity of recipient to receive and understand the message.
4. Use of words that can have multiple meanings and which therefore can convey unintended meanings.
5. Undue haste in transmission of message that undermines clarity and/or credibility.
6. Temptations of sender to unduly satisfy his own needs, thus inducing emotional resistance and blocks.
7. Failure to build needed foundations for the core message and related bad timing.
8. Lack of clarity or conviction because of reluctance to cause dissatisfaction to receiver.
9. Impact of nonverbal actions such as tone of voice, facial expressions, and manner of communication.
10. Not giving consideration to the perceptions and related feelings of the recipient.

All of these problems are part of the larger need for the sender to project himself and to try to give proper consideration as to how he would himself receive the message if he were the particular receiver. This capacity on the part of the sender is sometimes referred to as "empathy." When this projecting is done with sensitivity and judgment, we have the foundation for effective two-way conversation. This means that the communicator must do everything practicable to understand how the receiver thinks and feels and then to discipline himself to communicate in a manner that gives all possible consideration to that knowledge. Needless to say, the communicator often has conflicting higher-priority needs that prevent him from fully satisfying the receiver. However, it is still important that we have the best possible understanding of the total situation so that we can make the choices that are most consistent with overall organizational welfare.

Continuing Two-Way Communication. The continuing process of two-way communication builds on the principles just discussed and becomes a combination of individual messages back and forth between the two individuals. Now, however, the knowledge gained from individual messages becomes a further

foundation for the new messages. Now both parties—especially the main activator—learns from the questions and comments made by the receiver in
response to a series of messages. This is called "feedback." Part of effective
continuing two-way communication is also the capacity to induce that feedback
to the maximum extent so that the main activator has the best possible basis
for determining whether he is achieving his managerial objective—or if not,
to take different approaches in the continuing messages.

The capacity to induce and utilize good feedback is something that needs
to be developed carefully. To achieve that capacity requires concentration and
patience—at least to the extent practicable in the face of other needs for greater
urgency. A related component of the needed capacity is also to be able to
"listen." The listening is important for at least two reasons, the first of which
is to utilize the feedback better. The second and equally important reason is
to demonstrate better to the other party that one is genuinely interested in the
other person and his views. Otherwise, the result is to create an emotional
response that can significantly block the receiver's acceptance and understanding of the sender's intended message.

Broader Organizational Communication.   Earlier in this chapter we discussed
the problems of people in large organizations and the obstacles that exist for
effective communication. Our objective now is to provide overall guidance as
to how we can achieve the desired effective communication. The available
approaches are typically oral and written. What can be done in each area?

Oral communication quite clearly depends on good management and related
interaction as practiced at each organizational level and in each organizational
component. At each of those levels and in each of the organizational components
certain information is needed to carry out assigned job responsibilities. Basically, there is the need on the part of each individual—depending on his
particular job responsibilities—to provide proper information to his subordinates, to other responsible individuals in related operational areas, and upward
to the person to whom he reports. In this total effort he can communicate
directly on a "face-to-face" basis or by available technological means (for example, telephone, telegraph, cable, computer, and the like) or he can provide
reports or other written memoranda. In the oral area he is utilizing the capabilities previously discussed in this chapter. Other available means include
meetings and more extensive conferences in which the interested groups can
be brought together for needed group communication. Such situations are, of
course, a means not only of providing needed information but also for key
people to get better acquainted with each other, and thus augment morale and
work motivation.

Written communication, on the other hand, builds first on the regularly
established reporting system. This involves such questions as: (1) What information is needed for the overall operations of the particular enterprise? (2)
Who should get this information? (3) When should the information be provided?
and (4) What will all of this cost? The determinations here go beyond the

rational needs of the people in the organization and also involve questions of status and related ego. When needed information is received at the right time, it can be effectively utilized and job satisfaction is maximized. Also, people then usually feel that they are important in the total organizational effort. However, when people are embarrassed because of lack of information, or if they receive important information after managerial actions have already been taken, they are resentful. The total managerial information system must therefore be appropriately designed and then carefully maintained in terms of both rational and human considerations.

Managing Small Groups

The understanding of people as individuals and in small groups is closely linked to achieving desired levels of managerial productivity for such groups. Two types of small groups are frequently involved—one being a regular production or service group, and the other a decision group. In the first type we seek to establish some kind of a group objective that will generate loyalty and cooperative effort to the extent practicable. Under such conditions a majority of the members properly motivated will normally exert pressure on the nonproductive member and even assist him in various ways to do his work more efficiently. Contrariwise, however, if the majority are not properly motivated, they can bring pressure to restrain an individual who wishes to exert proper effort. In such situations there is also the opportunity for the strong leader to emerge and to exert major influence on other members of the group. The group members also tend to develop great loyalties to each other, and it is therefore desirable not to change the membership any more than is necessary.

In the other type of small group the objective is to reach some kind of a conclusion or decision that provides the best possible basis for effective managerial action. This means that we first need to obtain the input from each member of the group that bears on the particular concern, and in a manner that is demonstrably fair to all participants. This is usually achieved by a clear definition of the issue involved and then giving each member an opportunity to state his views and other pertinent ideas. The second phase is then appropriate cross discussion in which the merits and limitations of the alternative courses of action are tested and evaluated. During this stage the best conclusion may emerge or the controversial areas may be more sharply defined. This process must, of course, be monitored by the person in charge in a manner that will be sufficiently open that no one feels unduly constrained or ignored. At the same time the discussion cannot be allowed to either wander or become unduly personal. Then when consensus or the best possible conclusion seems to have been identified, the person in charge can summarize the discussion and state what appears to be the best conclusion. Or the person in charge may conclude that the gap is too great and defer a real conclusion. What is involved here is a very sensitive and skilled leadership role for the person in charge, relating always to the logic and emotional responses of the individual members, and always using judgment.

Climate and Creativity

Organizations vary as to the extent to which the individuals in it feel free to express themselves and to contribute in their own way to organizational welfare. An organization that is too conservative and too rigid in its operations typically tends to restrict innovative thinking and related productive action. Conversely, an organization that is more open and flexible, and that encourages its people to be imaginative, usually induces the most innovative thinking and welds together an organization that has good morale and higher productivity. The courage to provide a good climate and the ability to administer it is indeed one of the most critical managerial applications of relating to people and utilizing them to further organizational welfare. The ability to provide such a climate combines knowledge about people with the willingness to take the attendant risks. It tends to combine the following specific types of managerial action:

1. Greater delegations of authority and responsibility.
2. More management by objectives.
3. Greater freedom from supervision in achieving agreed-upon objectives.
4. Wide use of the principles of participative management.
5. More tolerance for individual opinions, criticism, and dissent.
6. Greater willingness to let individuals go ahead with their own ideas under conditions of greater risk and with less fear of what will happen in the event of failure.
7. Good backup of subordinates when needed by them.
8. Generous credit for contributions of individuals for individual and group results.
9. Genuine commitment of higher-level managers to excellence and high standards.

In all of these circumstances, management needs are satisfied to a greater extent and they combine to assure more effective operations.

Conflict and Its Utilization

People have varying needs that relate alternatively to competition (that can lead to conflict) and cooperation (that focuses on common goals). Traditionally, conflict has been viewed as destructive and hence undesirable. Indeed, managers were thought to have a primary responsibility to eliminate conflict somehow. Now, however, it is believed that conflict, when properly administered, can be useful in achieving organizational welfare. The more enlightened approach now, therefore, is to perceive the constructive aspects and to utilize those constructive elements to the extent practicable. This does not mean that conflict cannot get out of control. What it does mean is that we need to utilize conflict to the point where it is constructive and to control it when it threatens to get out of hand. To do this effectively quite clearly depends on a good understanding of people and a great deal of practical judgment.

Constructive Organizational Conflict.   Assigned job and group responsibilities, as required to get work done, unavoidably generate differing goals that set the stage for competition and potential conflict. Individuals continuously compete in terms of job performance for the rewards of personal recognition, better jobs, and higher compensation. Organizational units similarly compete for recognition and the associated rewards for the individuals involved. Normally also, organizational units are competing for resources, common services, and other management support. To a major extent, that competition then induces imaginative and sound thinking and high-level work performance. It is indeed quite natural that we do better when we have something against which we can evaluate our performance and where we can have the challenge of competing for the prizes that go to the winner. At the same time the forces generated can be so intensive that the competitors seek any means to win, irrespective of the questionable propriety and legitimacy of those means. At that point the organizational welfare ceases to be furthered and appropriate corrective action is needed. The managerial challenge is therefore to exploit the benefits of competition and healthy conflict in a legitimate professional sense but to control the process to avoid excesses.

Controlling Conflict.   How can managers deal with conflict so that they can derive the benefits but still be able to control it? The following approaches are considered by most authorities to be useful.

1. *Capability in Establishing Organizational Arrangements.* Although it is quite desirable to establish organizational responsibilities in a manner that induces a competitive effort, the ground rules need to be fairly defined and properly communicated. These ground rules should have the tone and coverage that emphasizes acceptable types of action to be taken by each of the parties of interest. Especially there is the need to emphasize desired cooperation and high-level organizational goals. At the same time, the established rewards must be sufficiently realistic that they do not induce the destructive actions that then seem necessary to win the designated rewards.

2. *Continuous Supervisory Focus on Higher-Level Goals.* Although the achievement of the immediate goal—that is, to win—is an important and desirable motivation, it is the responsibility of every manager to make subordinates understand that there are other things more important to the larger organizational welfare than that particular winning. Put in other terms, people need to understand that it is more important how one wins than the fact of winning. These principles also need to be continuously reinforced by the rejection of approaches that are not in the common interest. This means that management must be both continuously involved and alert.

3. *Effective Use of Umpires.* In many cases the parties of conflict adjust their own differences themselves. In other cases the conflicts are settled

by regularly established higher-level organization officials. When that problem is dealt with by higher-level authority, it is of course necessary that the basis for the settlement be well justified by the manner in which it is done. In extreme cases, also, it may be desirable to designate a qualified third party, or perhaps create a new special committee to resolve the conflict.

4. *Other Direct Resolutions.* In other cases still more decisive action may become necessary. Rules may be amended, particular individuals disciplined, personnel assignments readjusted, and the like. Ideally, conflict will not be allowed to develop to the point where these more dramatic direct actions are necessary. But when they are, it is important that the problem be dealt with in a decisive manner.

In summary, there is the managerial challenge to utilize conflict but not to let it get out of control to such an extent that it is counterproductive. This requires good leadership qualities coupled with good judgment based on a proper understanding of people.

Use of Power

Still another important operational application of utilizing our understanding of people has to do with the use of power. Power means different things to different people in terms of what it is, the extent to which it is good, and how it should be dealt with. In general, power denotes a higher level of capacity to influence or control the activities of someone else. In an organization it can come about directly or indirectly in a variety of ways—and always with considerable overlap. The following sources are illustrative:

1. As specifically associated with a delegated authority—as, for example, the authority to approve an expenditure of a given amount.
2. As linked to the various types of job responsibilities supporting an organization chart.
3. The ability to effect rewards of various kinds, including related punishment.
4. Based on expertise, special knowledge, or anything else especially needed or desired by the other person.
5. Human attributes that are especially respected or valued by others.

In all these situations there is usually great difficulty in defining precisely the extent of actual power. Moreover, the way the recipient views the existence of the power of another will vary widely and often lacks clarity.

Perhaps the most significant result of the foregoing mixed dimensions of power is the limitation that typically exists in its use. This limitation is essentially that no one really knows the extent of power until it is actually tested. This is a truth that is usually recognized by both the user and the recipient of power. At the same time, neither party welcomes the risk of being embarrassed by having made an incorrect judgment about the extent of that power. Thus the user fears to some extent that his power will not stand up when tested and perhaps lead to an unwanted personal confrontation. He also risks being over-ruled by his superiors if there is an appeal. On the other hand, the recipient fears that the power challenged *will* really stand up. In addition, the recipient knows that he may suffer to some extent by challenging the power, irrespective of whether or not the power actually does stand up. Finally, there is the further complication that both the user and the recipient are human beings and thus guided to some extent by emotion. All of this makes the power relationship most sensitive and potentially volatile.

What do we learn from all of this? Probably the major lesson is that power should be used, by he who has it, in a most careful and cautious manner. Very often, the definitive use of power will induce the very emotional response the user would like to avoid. What also emerges is the truth that the underlying threat of power is most effective when it is not used in a definitive manner. The effective use of power is therefore to tread softly and to stop short of crossing the line where there is likely to be a direct confrontation and an unwanted emotional response. In total the effective use of power is a continuing challenge, involving again good understanding of people and judgment as to how far one can go in the actual use of it.

Effecting Organizational Change

In the typical organizational situation there is a continuing need for properly relating stabilization and change. On the one hand, we seek stabilization through developing policies and procedures whereby operations are standard-ized to save managerial time and to assure the best handling of recurring similar types of events. On the other hand, changing conditions call for amended policies and procedures. The problem then becomes one of finding the proper balance between stabilization and needed change.

The above-mentioned problem is complicated by several related matters. The first of these is that the perception and resolution of needed changes is often very difficult and controversial. That is, the factors involved are usually hard to analyze and measure. As a result, the change effort must be effected by people with the required expertise, adequate funds, and strong managerial direction. An existing obstacle is that we become used to the existing policies and procedures and tend to become biased in their favor—thus making us often unaware and unresponsive to needs for change. Additionally, people typically do not like to accept change even when the need for it begins to be reasonably clear. Somehow convenience tends to triumph over objectivity. This means that we face a great deal of resistance to introducing change, irrespective of the real merits.

Sources of Needed Change. At the highest level the need for change may involve new strategies, new business ventures, changes in products, or new supporting policies. Related changes may involve new organizational structure, relocation of plants, new production processes, or changes in people. At a still lower level the changes needed may involve a new system—as, for example, a new computerized system that involves drastic changes in the way operations are controlled, and information processed, and in job assignments of individual persons. At the lowest level the change may involve the minor modifications in an individual's work assignment, a changed coffee break, or a service previously available. In some cases these changes involve only established habit or convenience. In others they may require more substantial personal adjustments. In still others there may be the threat to work security or a career. From our understanding of people it naturally follows that there would be a kind of built-in resistance to change ranging from minor attitudes to deliberate defensive action—including sabotage in its most extreme form. The managerial challenge is that when a decision involving change has been properly made, we then find the ways in which resistance—whatever it may be—is minimized, eliminated, or at least reasonably controlled.

Dealing with Change. How can we deal with change? How can we achieve needed change in a manner that will best serve higher-level organizational welfare? Our actions along this line are both preparatory and during the change process. In all cases the nature and scope of the different types of action of course depend on the significance of the particular change. We suggest the following:

1. The decision as to the making of the particular change should be carefully made, and should include the proper evaluation of the effect on people.
2. Reasonable notice of the change should be given, in combination with an adequate explanation of why the change is being made.
3. Plans for effecting the change should be carefully made. The planning process should also involve those individuals who will be affected—at least to the extent practicable.
4. Individuals with new roles and responsibilities should be adequately trained.
5. Plans should be developed and publicized covering all affected individuals, especially those whose job security is threatened or actually affected. There must also be every reasonable effort that those plans are fair.
6. Other people affected indirectly by the change should be advised as to how both their actual and perceived needs will be affected.
7. Sufficient time should be allowed for effecting the change, including reserves for unexpected developments.
8. Providing adequate information as to progress while the change is being carried out.
9. Conscientious follow-through of all promises and commitments made that pertain to the affected individuals.

In total it is again clear that handling organizational change, in addition to other aspects, involves very sensitive relations with people. We are again reminded of the importance of understanding people and then applying good managerial judgment.

Dealing with Professionals

The greater number of professionals in all types of organizations and the special characteristics of professional personnel deserves attention from managers and internal auditors alike. "Professional" as used here goes beyond the desire of all managers to think of themselves as professionals with increasingly professional standards. The focus now is more on long-established groups, such as scientists, engineers, lawyers, and accountants, that traditionally have had a body of special knowledge and relative unique patterns of performance. When managers—and in turn internal auditors—deal with such professional groups, the unique characteristics present some new problems and in turn require more in the way of special handling.

The problems of dealing with professionals come from the relatively unique characteristics typically associated with professionals. These include:

1. Goals and work characteristics built more around the standards and customs of their particular profession.
2. A greater concern for recognition by their professional peers as compared to that coming from the organization.
3. A relatively greater loyalty to their profession than to the organization and a related greater job mobility.
4. A relatively higher disdain for rules and procedures that apply to other organizational personnel and their activities.

An illustrative application of the problems associated with professionals is a research group. Here work habits are typically more informal and often less structured in terms of timing and manner of work. Also, the results achieved are usually more difficult to measure and appraise. At the same time, however, the ultimate results achieved are usually very critical to the welfare of the organization. What this means, then, is that managers must make a special effort to understand these individuals and must make more adjustment to them than is ordinarily required. More patience and flexibility are needed. There is the special challenge to deal with the problems involved in a manner that best serves overall organizational interests. The related "greater than normal" resistance to controls creates an especially substantive challenge to both managers and internal auditors.

Effective Control Systems

In Chapter 4 we discussed the problems of developing effective control. At that time we also discussed the existing human problems and how those problems could be best dealt with. Because an individual places such a high priority on his freedom of action, the design and implementation of controls are an area where human considerations become especially important. Since all managers to some extent are responsible for controls and at the same time subject to controls, it is also important that the impact on people be carefully considered in all ways. Perhaps in no phase of the management process is an understanding and consideration of people so critical. The coverage in Chapter 4 should therefore be reviewed for integration with the present chapter.

Effective Leadership

As we saw in Chapter 3, effective leadership is an essential part of the total management process. That effective leadership is the motivation of people to contribute as much as is feasible to established organizational goals. It is a two-way process. The first of these processes is understanding people so that the leader can induce all possible motivation of other people to the maximum achievement of organizational goals—matters with which this entire chapter have been concerned. The second of these processes builds on the understanding of people but relates more directly to the personal performance of the leader. We see that personal performance as involving three major dimensions:

1. *Professional Competence.* This includes the depth of knowledge about management principles, concepts, and procedures. It includes also the leader's competence in managing effectively in terms of demonstrated results. In combination they build respect for the leader as a competent professional.

2. *Ability to Balance Personal and Organizational Needs Properly.* This includes understanding human needs but being able to balance fairly the extent to which they can be provided in terms of larger organizational needs. Inevitably, there are conflicts between the needs of particular individuals and between groups of individuals versus the needs of the people as a whole and broader organizational goals. The needed utility is then to be able to strike the proper balance.

3. *Nature and Quality of the Leader Himself as a Person.* This includes the demonstrated character that the leader himself conforms to the same rules and high standards that he seeks to apply to his subordinates. This is where the leader's actions—when even under the greatest pressure—conform to the words asserted. This generates respect for the leader as a person of character and integrity—the kind of person to whom we all like to give our allegiance.

In total the achievement of effective leadership is linked to a proper understanding of people and then actually relating to individuals in a manner that commands their respect. As a result, people are individually and collectively motivated to be productive in terms of the maximum achievement of organizational goals.

UNDERSTANDING PEOPLE IN INTERNAL AUDITING

The discussions thus far in this chapter have focused on the interests of all managers in connection with their relations to each other, including both their higher-level managers and their subordinates. All of that is of interest to internal auditors as a component part of their review and analysis of operational situations. It is also of interest to internal auditors as they manage their own subordinates. It will be useful, however, to supplement those discussions by looking more closely at some of the more unique problems that confront the internal auditor in his work activities.

Overall Image Problem of the Internal Auditor

An overall burden of the internal auditor is that he has an image problem. To some extent this image problem is due to the fact that the term "auditor" is part of his title and that the term "auditor" is often thought of as focusing excessively on detail and compliance and being threatening. In many situations the image has been earned because of the manner in which internal auditors were first used in organizations. To some extent also the image is caused because internal auditors today do not do enough themselves through their audit work and mode of personal relations to build a better image. But in fairness to the internal auditor we must recognize that there are also some serious problems in changing the existing image. This is because the internal auditor typically is charged with certain protective-type responsibilities that tend to make other personnel see him in the role of an antagonist. But the internal auditor's total role—as we have seen in preceding chapters—goes far beyond the narrow protective service. The modern internal auditor is no longer the "policeman" as such or the person with the green eyeshade who buries himself in detail. Instead, the internal auditor is concerned with total organizational welfare at all levels and in relation to all organizational activities. The internal auditor is at the same time a specialist in the effectiveness of controls. The challenge is to broaden the image of the internal auditor as a broad professional serving total organizational welfare.

With this background we propose to focus more directly on the typical relationships of the internal auditor with people outside his own department and try to identify the best available opportunities to work with people to achieve his broader organizational objectives. We will sequence our coverage to follow the announcement, conduct, and completion of an internal audit and then to certain higher-level relationships.

Early Contacts Relating to the Audit

The decision that an internal audit of some type is to be made can come about in a variety of ways. It can be requested by the person who has the responsibility for the operational area to be reviewed, it can be requested by a still-higher-level officer, or it may be initiated by the director of internal auditing himself as a part of his own broader program of needed audit coverage. The significance here is that in the first instance the receptivity for the audit has been at least partially established. However, there is still the further necessity of trying to provide the responsible officer with the proper professional intentions. Of first importance is the need for a face-to-face discussion, if at all practicable, although frequently this must be by telephone. In any event there is the need to demonstrate to the extent needed that:

1. The internal audit is part of an overall program mandated by higher-level authority to meet higher-level organizational needs for *both* protection and maximum constructive benefit.
2. The objective of the review is to provide maximum service in *all* feasible managerial dimensions.
3. The review will be conducted with minimum interference with regular operations and demands on operating personnel.
4. The responsible officer will be kept fully informed and have an opportunity to review findings and recommendations before any audit report is formally released.

These dimensions will be dealt with more fully in Chapters 9 through 12. Our focus on them at this point is to emphasize their importance in terms of people relationships. At this point major benefits can be achieved, or contrariwise a hostile image can be established. The principles expressed apply also to any other individuals who need to be informed prior to the time that the review work of the audit actually begins. The benefits derived include the better understanding of the internal auditor's role, avoiding the undesirable reactions of those individuals who might otherwise be caught by surprise, and the personal gratification given such individuals that the internal auditor is concerned about their feelings. What is basic is that these people have apprehensions about the impact of an audit and they therefore need, as far as is possible, to be put at ease. The internal auditor needs to go out of his way to establish a good person-to-person relationship.

Relations with Auditees

Assuming at this point that the audit is actually under way, the next group of people relationships has to do with all the personnel whose work and records are being examined or to whom inquiries of various types are made. In these cases also, the principles detailed above are also generally applicable. Now, however, there is the more definitive problem of obtaining the desired cooperation of the individuals directly involved in the particular operations being reviewed. The problem can be substantial because a number of possible factors may generate resistance. Such factors include:

1. A previous bad experience with an internal auditor.

2. The general image of the internal auditor as a policeman against whom all manner of resistance is appropriate.

3. The related fear that errors or faulty performance will be discovered and used against them.

4. The fear that the internal auditor will go out of his way to find things that can be used for personal advancement of the auditor.

5. A resentment against the presence of the auditor with its related potential of siphoning off the workers' time and effort, and generally interfering with necessary work performance.

6. Some lack of confidence in the quality of their own work, and the fear that it will not stand up under close scrutiny.

The problem the internal auditor faces is to try to alleviate those fears but at the same time not to provide assurances that cannot fully be delivered. Put in other words, the internal auditor does wish to help the auditee in every way practicable, but he does have a responsibility to his own higher-level personnel. At this point the internal auditor does not know what problems he may find. All he can really do is to try to convince the auditee that he is fully motivated by total organizational welfare and that the total welfare includes the welfare of the auditee and his particular segment of the operations. The auditor also needs to communicate the fact that he intends to be honest and fair. Typically, the internal auditor can only be partially successful in achieving these objectives at the outset of the particular part of the audit (unless his relationship has already been established through a previous audit) and further time will be required before the auditee will have depth confidence. The internal auditor must therefore be patient, making as much progress as possible during the current audit but also looking ahead to audits in the future.

Finding the Best Balance. In more summary form the internal auditor's problem of having effective relationships with auditees comes down to finding the best possible balance between two inherently conflicting forces. On the one hand there is the unavoidable truth that the auditee to some extent feels threatened by the internal auditor, and on the other hand the unavoidable truth that the internal auditor has a responsibility to determine and report on the existing facts. There is therefore some unavoidable conflict. Under such circumstances the internal auditor can go to the one extreme and give the first priority to appeasing the auditee—the so-called "be nice" approach. Or the internal auditor can go to the other extreme and focus only on his need to get the facts and to report them to his superiors. The higher-level truth, however, is that organizational welfare is ultimately best served by everyone working together to get the operational job done better. The internal auditor therefore needs to find the proper balance between the two extremes and to find the composite approach that will minimize existing conflict and best assure long-term benefits. This is an approach that requires understanding, continuing education, patience, sincerity, and always sound judgment. As with everything one does, this is the eternal problem of finding the best possible balance between a number of divergent forces.

Partnership Approach.   In its most successful form the internal auditor induces a *partnership* relationship with the auditee. The essence of that partnership relationship was especially well stated in Research Report No. 17, "Behaviour Patterns in Internal Auditing Relationships," published in 1972 by The Institute of Internal Auditors, as follows:

> The participative approach—the teamwork approach—the problem solving part-nership may well be the light at the end of a dreary tunnel. Our goals should be the auditor and auditee working together to improve conditions; and not the critic telling the doer how to do his job better.

This partnership approach at its most effective level is a cooperative work effort between two mutually respected persons with full understanding of their respective responsibilities, but with clear recognition of their very real long-term common interests. It is the internal auditor's special challenge to generate that type of constructive relationship.

Closing Conferences

To a considerable extent the closing conference is an extension of the human relationships described previously and hence is guided by the same previously stated principles. It is, however, a key stage in the finalization of an internal audit because it is a more systematic exposure of the audit findings and draft conclusions, a confirmatory check on the content of the findings and the soundness of the conclusions, and a means of generating commitment for appropriate managerial action. The size of the conference will vary depending on the nature and scope of the particular internal audit. Typically, however, the group will include (1) higher-level staff and line operational personnel not previously directly involved in the audit, (2) key operational personnel already involved in the audit work, (3) all or key audit personnel that have made the particular audit, and (4) sometimes a higher-level internal audit official who has come to the location especially for that closing conference. Typically, this closing conference is the final and most decisive event just before the departure of the internal audit staff from the field location.

Preceding the closing conference there have already been a usually considerable number of interfaces between members of the audit staff and other concerned operational personnel. However, from a human relations standpoint the closing conference now takes on a new higher level of sensitivity. This is because the large number of people involved are to a major extent reviewing each other—both as between the internal auditors themselves and between operational personnel as individuals and as groups directly or indirectly involved. Now there is the normal desire on the part of each person to "look good" to the others present. There is also the deeper knowledge that individual and group interests can be significantly affected by what actually goes into the final audit report.

What can be done by the internal auditor to assure the success of the closing conference in terms of effective human relationships? We suggest the following:

1. A careful preparation for the actual conference with advance dissemination of the draft material best projects fairness to the recipients and at the same time assures the adequacy of the internal auditor's preparation.

2. The courteous but firm direction of the conference by the internal auditor chairing the meeting minimizes disruptive diversion of the discussions. At all times, however, openmindedness and company welfare interest must be continuously demonstrated.

3. The internal auditor must press for conclusions that are as definitive as possible. However, the internal auditor needs to retain the right for such later editing as may be required to comply with standards of good presentation and higher-level views. Continuing good human relations require, however, that the auditees later receive no unreasonable surprises when the final report is released.

4. The internal auditor should build goodwill by expressing his appreciation for the cooperation extended by all of the operational personnel who have been involved in the particular audit. The objective is to retain so far as is possible the continuing cooperation and support of all company personnel.

Follow-Up Activities

A final important group of relations with people involves follow-up activities after an audit report is released. These activities may pertain to the further explanation of findings and related recommendations or to the adequacy of operational actions being taken as a result of the audit recommendations. Their importance in terms of people relations is that the extent of the internal auditor's competence and his overall assistance to management is being tested continuously. These follow-up contacts are also important in that they provide a major setting out of which further internal audits can be made more responsive to managerial needs. It is therefore most important that these follow-up contacts be carefully nurtured and effectively serviced. It may very well be, for example, that it will be desirable to have audit personnel actively involved in the particular review travel to the central locations to participate in the follow-up discussions.

Follow-up activities in a broad sense also include other contacts with managerial personnel that apply to other possible internal audits. In those circumstances the nature of the people relationships is very similar to those discussed above in connection with early contacts.

Relations with Audit Committees

In some cases the significance of particular internal audits will lead to the involvement of the audit committee of the board of directors, usually via the chairman of that committee. In other cases internal audit action of various kinds will be directly mandated by the audit committee. In still other cases the contacts with the audit committee will be in connection with required summary reports. These relations are discussed in more depth in Chapter 28. Our present interest is to emphasize the significant people relationships that are involved. The greater legal and public concerns are generating expanded responsibilities for audit committees and a related more active participation in the activities of the organization—including a more active interface with the internal auditing department. This interface is especially important to the internal auditor because of the authority of the audit committee and the related effect on the nature and scope of the internal auditor's work. Audit committee members are also typically people of considerable stature and ability. All of this means that the internal auditor needs to handle his relations with them with special care.

What can the internal auditor do to make these relationships effective? We suggest the following:

1. Although the internal auditor cannot by himself establish his reporting arrangements with the audit committee, he should be alert to every opportunity to do so. He should then also respond promptly and fully to needs thus initiated.

2. The internal auditor should thoroughly study the nature and scope of audit committee needs and do all possible to demonstrate an understanding of those needs—thus enabling the internal auditor to respond properly to all needs expressed to him by the audit committee and at the same time to help guide that committee.

3. The internal auditor needs to be aware on a continuing basis of the possible apprehension of top management about the impact of direct relationships with the audit committee. The internal auditor thus needs to keep top management fully informed about those direct relationships. At the same time the internal auditor needs to avoid being put into an adversary posture toward management by the audit committee. Again, the demonstration of total company welfare is the greatest strength of the internal auditor in preserving good relationships with both management and the audit committee.

Relations with the External Auditor

As we have seen in previous chapters, the internal auditor and external auditor have different primary missions but at the same time certain common interests. In Chapter 29 we discuss the various relationships in greater detail. Again, however, we need at this point to emphasize the people relations involved that build on the expertise previously described in this chapter. That coverage can be supplemented as follows:

1. Because the external auditors have a great deal in common with internal auditors, there is a better basis of understanding each other and thus relating to each other effectively. However, there is at the same time a

certain amount of professional pride and different self-interest that often makes the relationships very sensitive.

2. Both audit groups have certain power capabilities that generate caution in the various face-to-face relationships. The internal auditor is in a position to press for greater company welfare through more effective coordination (usually resulting in lesser external audit costs) while the external auditor usually has special access and influence with the audit committee and top management, and hence can importantly influence those parties in their attitudes toward the internal auditor.

3. Joint appearances of the internal and external auditors before both management and the audit committee involve especially sensitive considerations and therefore need to be carefully planned and executed.

4. The internal auditor again needs to demonstrate his dedication to total organizational welfare, and his interest in the partnership efforts of the two audit groups to further that organizational welfare.

Relations within the Internal Auditing Department

The people relationships of internal auditors within the internal auditing department itself are dealt with in more detail in Chapters 9 through 12. Again, however, we need to emphasize in this chapter that those internal relations need to apply the same concepts covered earlier in this chapter. As we know, internal auditors are managers like all other managers and must therefore manage their people resources in an effective manner. At the same time each member of the internal auditing staff has the common human needs previously discussed. That coverage can, therefore, be supplemented as follows:

1. Internal auditors are professionals and there is therefore the special need to relate to them as professionals. This means less direct supervision and more coaching and dependence upon established objectives.

2. Internal auditors have above-average visibility in the organization and therefore need to recognize that they have special responsibilities to serve as a model and standard in their people relationships.

3. Internal auditors in their own departmental relationships need to develop the kind of high-level image that builds a better foundation for projecting that same image to other organizational personnel.

4. Staff personnel need continuously to be indoctrinated as to their opportunities to help build the proper internal auditor image with all organizational personnel with which they are involved. At the same time they need to be fully assured that they have proper backing when they take needed positions with auditees.

Relations with People in Perspective

Because organizational resources include people, and because all organizational activities are typically carried out by people, the overall importance of developing effective relations with people cannot be overemphasized. We believe, therefore that it will be useful to summarize the key elements of a proper approach to effective people relations:

1. There must first be an initial acceptance of the truth that people as individuals are important and that they need to be continuously considered as key factors in all organizational activities.

2. All managers need to have a reasonable understanding of people as individuals and in larger groups. Moreover, we need to recognize that human capabilities are continuously changing and that we therefore need to update continuously that understanding of people.

3. All managers need to have a reasonable understanding of the types of operational applications for people as treated briefly in this chapter. In this connection our own coverage needs to be augmented by further study and observation.

4. All managers need continuously to strive to find the best possible balance between accommodating to human needs and broader organizational welfare. In this connection the needs of the larger group (including the organization as a whole) must be balanced against the needs of the smaller group and/or the individual.

5. The internal auditor needs to recognize that he has a built-in image problem. His continuing objective must therefore be to change that image within the limits of discharging the responsibilities with which he has been directly assigned.

6. In all aspects, relations with people are a continuing challenge that involves a kind of a target that is always moving forward. But at the same time the success in meeting that challenge provides one of the greatest available opportunities to serve the organization and to achieve its maximum welfare.

CHAPTER EIGHT

Using Computers and Statistical Sampling

The continuous expansion of the range of internal auditing services, together with the limited resources available, have created increased interest in finding new ways in which the internal auditor can achieve his audit objectives more efficiently. At the same time the major developments in electronic data processing have provided new capabilities. All of these factors have led internal auditors to make greater use of computers in their audit work. That use is especially advantageous when there are voluminous data and processing involved. Computers also make possible to a greater extent the use of the many types of statistical sampling. It is appropriate, therefore, that we examine in more depth how internal auditors can utilize computers in achieving their audit objectives in all operational areas.

COMPUTER-ASSISTED AUDIT TECHNIQUES

The extended use of computers by companies of all sizes has stimulated changes in the auditor's approach. The auditor can no longer be satisfied with only manual audit procedures to fulfill audit objectives. The whole internal control environment may change from those in a manual setting. The nature of the audit evidence changes when information is readable only by electronic means. The use of computer-assisted audit techniques may result in the performance of audit tests by the computer which were previously done manually. In addition, these techniques may enable the auditor to carry out audit procedures that were hitherto impracticable. As new systems are acquired or developed, he can determine whether data can be accumulated and stored in a manner that will facilitate later audit. Through maximum utilization of computer-assisted audit techniques, the internal auditor may not only improve the quality of audits, but also sharpen his capabilities to perform special reviews for management and thus provide better service.

Requirements for a Computer Audit Program System

Prior to selecting a computer audit package, a review should be made of the generalized computer audit program systems that have been developed by other organizations. No single software package may satisfy all the requirements of every audit group or assignment. The following are some characteristics of an effective system.

1. *Simplicity*. The system should be simple to use and eliminate the need for remembering countless details normally required in writing or revising computer programs.

2. *Understandability*. The system should be readily understandable by members of the audit staff, even those with little computer expertise. The capabilities of the system should be known, and it should be easy to use. Coding forms provided should not be difficult to understand.

3. *Adaptability*. The system should be capable of writing computer audit programs for the various types of computers used in the company or expected to be acquired. Thus the package will be usable if equipment is changed in the future.

4. *Vendor Technical Support*. In considering the types of package to be acquired, it is important that the vendor provide adequate support. This includes assisting in the initial installation and providing adequate documentation. In addition, training provided for the audit staff is important. Also, maintenance service should be furnished, and provision made for future revisions in the programs.

5. *Statistical Sampling Capability*. Since statistical sampling is an important application in auditing, the package should be able to perform the various statistical routines. This should include the selection of items on a random basis, determination of sample size, and evaluation of results at different confidence levels. In addition to simple random sampling and stratified sampling, it should have routines for more complex sampling such as cluster and multistage sampling. The subject of statistical sampling and computer applications is discussed in more detail later in the chapter.

6. *Acceptability*. The system should be acceptable to both the auditors and to computer centers. For the auditors the programs should be easily carried to the site and practical to use. For the computer center the programs should be compatible with the system and be capable of minimum interference with normal routines.

7. *Processing Capabilities*. The package should be able to process many different types of applications. For example, it should accept all common file media and process multiple file input. It should have the capability for extended data selection and stratification. It should have the ability to operate under multiprogramming situations. It should have powerful, generalized audit commands.

8. *Report Writing*. The package should have a strong report writing func-

tion. This should include the ability to prepare multiple reports in a single program run and to generate flexible output report formats. Exhibit 8.1 shows some commonly used programs and sources where they are available.

Using the Computer in Audits

If data of audit interest are processed on a computer, the auditor should be on the lookout for methods of using the computer to audit such data. The capabilities of most computer audit packages open up new opportunities to use the

EXHIBIT 8.1.   Generalized Computer Audit Packages

Package	Equipment that Can Be Used to Process Packages	Developer
AUDIT	Any computer with COBOL compiler	U.S. Army Audit Agency Research Division Washington, D.C. 20201
AUDITAPE	IBM 360/370, Honeywell 200, Spectra 70	Deloitte Haskins & Sells 1114 Avenue of the Americas New York, N.Y. 10036
AUDITRONIC	IBM 360/370	Ernst & Whinney 1300 Union Commerce Building Cleveland, Ohio 44115
CARS	Any computer with COBOL Compiler	Computer Audit System, Inc. 725 Park Avenue East Orange, N.J. 07017
DYL 260	IBM 360/370	DYLAKOR Software Systems, Inc. 16255 Ventura Boulevard Encino, Calif. 91436
HEWCAS	Any computer with COBOL compiler	Dept. of Health and Human Services OIG Audit Agency Room 5700, North Building 330 Independence Avenue S.W. Washington, D.C. 20201
MARK IV	IBM 360/370	Informatica, Inc. 21050 Vanowen Street Canoga Park, Calif. 91303
SAMPLER	IBM 360/370	U.S. Army Audit Agency Research Division Washington, D.C. 20201
SCORE	IBM 360/370, Honeywell 200, Spectra 70	Programming Methods, Inc. 51 Madison Avenue New York, N.Y. 10019
STRATA	IBM 360/370	Touche Ross & Company 1633 Broadway New York, N.Y. 10010

computer to fulfill audit responsibilities. The use of the computer is especially desirable when there is a large volume of data and the data are readily available from the computer files. The auditor determines the identity and content of all potentially useful files early in his audit, and obtains a copy of the data layout for each record written on those files.

Mechanics of Use.   Once the auditor has recognized the availability of computer files of interest in the audit, he considers methods for using a computer audit package. It is important to understand how the computer audit package works. Basically, the package has the capability of listing those records which match other records in the same file or in different files. One or more data fields designated by the auditor are compared. Record layouts of the two files can be different, except for the fields to be matched. The computer audit package can also print account details and totals for records defined by the auditor.

In addition, the audit package is capable of performing various calculations and solution of formulas. Special programs can be used for any computational task required. Sampling plans can be developed, and the results of sampling tests evaluated and projected. In addition, the computer, using its comparison capability, can select all or a sample of records having the characteristics stated by the auditor. Multiple sets of characteristics can be designated for a single application. For each stratum, statistics are provided on the number of records on the input file, the number of records selected, and the sum of designated fields. Each stratum may be sampled or printed in its entirety.

Applications.   There are various areas in internal auditing for use of audit software packages. Once the techniques are mastered, the applications to computer files are limited only by the auditor's imagination. One approach is to review prior audit procedures performed manually and determine the feasibility of applying computer techniques. Another approach is to include special computer routines in the normal, everyday processing. An example is in the review of check disbursements. As transactions are processed, the computer can automatically select a sample, or print out expenditures in excess of a specified dollar amount by classification. The following are some applications for potential use by internal auditors.

1. *Inventories.* The use of computer software packages in reviews of inventories results in significant savings of audit staff time and elimination of detailed checking of voluminous data manually. In testing a perpetual inventory, a statistical sample can be taken by the computer of inventory parts, stratified as to high and low dollar amounts. Counts made by the auditor are compared with the inventory record on tapes, and the differences summarized and tabulated by quantity, dollars, and percentages. In addition, tests of pricing can be made by comparison of perpetual inventory records with a master cost tape showing the costs of all parts.

Other applications include tests for meeting standards for filling requisitions, printouts of stocks with recurring shortages or overages, and summaries of trends in losses through pilferage.

2. *Payrolls*. There are various operational as well as financial areas relating to payrolls that lend themselves to the use of audit software packages. Printouts can be made to review labor utilization—amount of overtime, labor charged to jobs in excess of standards, and downtime. Comparisons can be made with prior performance as well as with standards to indicate performance needing improvement. In addition, the programs can identify new and terminated employees, as well as changes, for checking against payroll authorization files in the personnel department.

3. *Maintenance*. Overruns in excess of specified percentages can be pinpointed for analysis of causes. Backlogs of maintenance requests can be aged and printed out for review.

4. *Energy*. Plants or departments with excessive use of gas and electricity are identified for monitoring under the energy program.

5. *Travel and Telephone*. Excessive charges by employee or departments can be identified for follow-up and possible reductions.

6. *Sales*. Data can be accumulated as to sales by salesperson, territory, or product in relation to quotas and performance by others.

Use in Audit Management.   In addition to use in auditing, the special software systems can be adapted to perform certain record-keeping and reporting functions for the internal audit department. This may include audit planning and budgeting, maintaining records of time spent on audits, and preparing various reports. An example is the training record and reporting function. As internal audit staffs grow in size it becomes increasingly difficult to keep track of the training of individual auditors. This is important in order to encourage personal development and to provide a basis for enrolling staff members in specific classes. The following are some key elements in one company's development of a training reporting system.

1. *Language*. It was decided that BASIC was the preferred language to provide flexibility and reduced on-line storage when compared with data base languages.

2. *File Structures*. It was decided to use a variable record format. In this format the data for each training entry are appended to the existing employee record. To keep each record manageable in terms of size, a maximum number of entries per record is established.

3. *Employee Information*. Employee name, geographical location, and title were considered essential.

4. *Training Information*. Because of the inconsistent length of course names, it was decided to use a coding scheme to reduce storage requirements. Identifying over 300 different course titles of interest, a three-

digit number was assigned to each course. Using the same method for sponsoring organizations, a two-digit coding method was developed. Since different course names are sometimes used for the same subject material, a type code was developed for each course. This allows a search to be made using the type code. The month and year of attendance are also recorded. Another piece of information recorded is the employee's evaluation of the course on a scale from 1 to 10.

5. *System Input.* To ensure that proper training information is entered, a form is completed by the employee after attending each training session. The form is used as an input document and as a hard-copy backup for the master file. When new data are entered, a binary search is made of a file of course titles to ensure that such a title exists and obtain its three-digit code from the course file. If the course is new, it can be entered on the course file. The program performs a numeric edit of the month and year of the course, the number of hours, and the evaluation code.

6. *Reports.* These include a printout of courses taken by each employee, a listing of individuals who have taken a specific course, a listing of individuals who have not taken a specific course, and a quarterly or annual training report. The reports may be modified or deleted and new reports added as needed.

STATISTICAL SAMPLING

The responsibilities of the modern internal auditor are often extensive, and require the use of many different audit approaches. In a particular assignment the internal auditor may review policies and procedures of the company to determine if they are adequate. He may perform surveys and overall comparisons of information to determine trends. He may perform a study and evaluation of the existing internal control system of the company to determine its reliability.

When the internal auditor finds the internal control system satisfactory in principle, he still must determine whether the system is operative. He thus must examine documents and other records to determine the effectiveness of the system in practice. For example, the review of a purchasing system may indicate that effective controls exist on paper to assure that the company's interests are protected. It is only by testing actual purchase documents, however, that the internal auditor has assurance that the system is working and employees are not evading the restrictions of the system.

It is when the auditor decides to test (invoices, reports, inventory items, etc.) that he considers using statistical sampling as an audit tool. Statistical sampling is basically a method of learning about many items by looking at a selected few. In the early stages of internal audit it was not uncommon to perform a 100% examination of entries or documents. As companies grew larger it was no longer feasible to examine items on a 100% basis. Thus the internal auditor examined a portion of the entries, using what was called the test approach. As illustrated in Exhibit 8-11, statistical sampling developed as one method that could be used in testing.

The auditor faced with performing a variety of tests in a review must answer the question: "Should I use statistical sampling?" The decision may be complicated because of such factors as small population size, lack of technical expertise or computer availability in the field, nonacceptance by management, and shortage of audit resources available for reviewing any areas other than known problem conditions. Since the decision as to what audit procedures are to be used is a matter for judgment, the auditor must carefully weigh the advantages of the various procedures in a particular situation, with statistical sampling as one option.

Why Use Statistical Sampling?

We are all familiar with the use of statistical sampling, whether in polls or in quality control testing in a plant. The transition to an approach of considering the use of statistical sampling in each test an auditor performs, however, may be difficult. The following are some reasons for using statistical sampling.

1. *Conclusions about Entire Field.* If a statistical sampling method is used, information can be obtained about the entire field, within certain statistical limits as explained later. The auditor can thus arrive at conclusions about the field without performing a 100% check, thereby obtaining savings.

2. *Sample Result Objective and Defensible.* Since items in a field are randomly selected, each has an equal opportunity of being selected. The audit test is thus objective, and is defensible in a court of law. A judgment sample, however, may be distorted (for example, only large or sensitive items may be examined).

3. *Less Sampling May Be Required.* Since the amount of testing does not increase in proportion to the increase in the size of the field tested, savings in time and money may be obtained. Frequently, large fields are oversampled because of the belief that larger fields require proportionately larger samples. By using statistical sampling, less testing may be required than might be used by judgment sampling.

4. *May Provide Greater Accuracy than 100% Test.* When voluminous data are counted in their entirety, there is often the chance of clerical errors. However, when a small sample is taken, there may be fewer errors made. The sample would be subject only to sampling error resulting from the statistical projection.

5. *Coverage of Different Locations.* Since under statistical sampling auditors can work independently and their work combined, audits can be performed at different locations. Small samples may thus be possible at individual sites under an overall sampling plan. Also, an audit started by one auditor may be continued by another.

6. *Simple to Apply*. With the availability of computer software packages, the application of statistical sampling has become simplified. Recently, professional books and manuals have become available that show how to apply statistical sampling.[1] Also, training courses have been increased by professional organizations to facilitate learning sampling techniques.

The auditor must keep in mind, however, that exact information cannot be obtained about a population of items based in a sample, whether it be judgmental or statistical. It is only through making a 100% test that the auditor can obtain the exact information. If the auditor uses judgmental sampling, however, he obtains information only about those items he examines. If he uses statistical sampling, he obtains positive information about all of the items in the population (a range at a given confidence level). Regardless of the number of items examined, if the auditor makes a random selection, he can project the results of the sample to the entire account or transactions.

Judgment Sampling

Although the merits of statistical sampling are generally accepted, auditors frequently use judgment, or nonstatistical, sampling to perform tests. Statistical sampling is not mandatory in the profession, as borne out by the American Institute of Certified Public Accountants Statement on Auditing Standards I, paragraph 320A.04, which states that the use of statistical sampling "is permissive rather than mandatory under generally accepted auditing standards."

Auditors generally justify the use of judgment sampling by the following:

Auditing is a matter of judgment rather than mathematical analyses.

Judgment sampling is easier to apply.

The auditor's general reviews and analyses identify the sensitive items that need to be examined.

Management is interested in information as to specific deficiencies found, not projections based on statistical sampling.

There is thus a tendency on the part of some auditors to use judgmental sampling despite its disadvantages. Judgment sampling may take many forms: (1) examination of fixed percentage, such as 10%, of the items or dollars, often selected haphazardly; (2) selection of all or part of items in a period, such as a month, or of a particular letter of the alphabet; (3) selection of items for audit with a large dollar amount; (4) examination of items readily available, as in a particular file drawer; (5) review of sensitive items only; and (6) selection of

---

[1]Especially recommended are the *Handbook of Sampling for Auditing and Accounting* by Herbert Arkin (New York: McGraw-Hill, 1974), *Sampling in Auditing* by Henry P. Hill, Joseph L. Roth, and Herbert Arkin (New York: The Ronald Press, 1962), *The Sampling Manual for Internal Auditors* (Altamonte Springs, Fla. Institute of Internal Auditors, 1967), and the *Supplement to the Manual for Internal Auditors* (Altamonte Springs, Fla. Institute of Internal Auditors, 1970). These references provide more detailed material covering the various statistical concepts and methods, examples of statistical applications, and useful statistical tables.

one or a few transactions for audit to determine if a system is working. Although useful data may be obtained by these samples, the results may be misleading and cannot be used to arrive at conclusions about the whole.

In using a judgment sample, the auditor is making a threefold judgment: size of sample, method of selection, and interpretation of results. Without the use of statistical sampling, there can be no scientific way of measuring the effect of errors or determining other information about the whole based on a test check. The auditor's reliance on judgment may thus often be the use of intuition. As knowledge of statistical sampling in auditing expands and auditors become more proficient in the techniques, it is expected that the use of statistical sampling will grow.

Exhibit 8.2 illustrates statistical sampling applications used in one company. Applications were selected based on review of prior tests performed, errors found, and volume and accessibility of data.

Statistical Probability

When a sample is selected on a random basis from a group of transactions, it is one of many samples that can be selected. The characteristics of the sample drawn by one auditor may be different from the characteristics of the sample drawn by another auditor, and both may be different from the results of an examination of all the transactions. To determine how far a sample result differs

---

EXHIBIT 8.2.   Selected Statistical Sampling Applications

Maintenance orders (cost overruns, warranties)

Customer accounts (circularization, write-offs)

Consultants (need, effectiveness)

Equipment rentals (lease versus buy, options exercised)

Purchase orders (need, competition, timeliness)

Inventories (physical observation, pricing, quantities, obsolescence)

Payroll (rates, hours, classification, utilization)

Expenditures per voucher register (need, discounts, distribution, double endorsements)

Research projects (cost transfers, overruns)

Travel (entertainment, need, personal)

Reports (need, accuracy, use)

Service centers (billing rates, surpluses or deficits)

Fixed assets (need, acquisition, utilization, disposal)

Depreciation (accuracy, life, capitalization)

Sales (prices, discounts, warranties)

Quality control (tolerances, corrective action, timeliness of reports)

Investment portfolio (rate of return, safety)

Bills of materials (quantities, prices)

Production orders (timeliness, overruns, validity of costs)

---

from that of a 100% test, the auditor must have knowledge of the behavior of all possible results of samples that might be drawn from the population.

If the sample means of all possible samples were determined and plotted, the distribution would approximate the normal curve, or normal distribution. The properties of this normal distribution have been scientifically determined, and are that 68% of the individual members of the distribution lie within plus or minus 1 standard deviation of the arithmetic mean of the total distribution, and 95.5% lie within plus or minus 2 standard deviations. Expressed another way, 90% of the members lie within plus or minus 1.65 standard deviations and 95% within plus or minus 1.96 standard deviations. Based on this, if one sample were drawn at random, the auditor can calculate the probability that the sample mean would fall within a certain range. For example, with a mean of $100 and a standard deviation of $10, 95% of the observations would fall within plus or minus 1.96 standard deviations, or plus or minus $19.60. Thus there is a 95% probability that the mean of a sample drawn at random would be within the range $80.40 to $119.60. If there are 1,000 items in the population, the point estimate (or estimated parameter of the population) would be $100,000, and the range at the 95% probability would be between $80,400 and $119,600.

The term "confidence level" is used to express the probability that the value obtained from the sample will not depart from the true value of the population by more than the confidence interval, or precision. The term "precision" refers to the range within which the population characteristic will lie at a stated confidence level.

SAMPLING PLANS

Statistical sampling activities of internal auditors are carried out under a number of different types of sampling plans. These sampling plans are applicable to special types of conditions and reflect the different audit objectives that exist in each case. We discuss three of these plans that are most often used by internal auditors. These are attribute sampling, variables sampling, and discovery sampling.

Attributes Sampling

A type of sampling plan commonly used by internal auditors has to do with the measurement and evaluation of attributes. This is a qualitative evaluation of a particular group of items or transactions based on how many times a particular attribute is occurring. Normally, the attribute being measured is an error or other type of deficiency. The extent of the existence of the particular deficiency determines the seriousness of the situation and what the internal auditor will report in terms of conclusions and recommendations. The attributes or characteristics can have to do with any physical item, any financial record, any internal procedure, or operational activity. Its focus normally will be on compliance with a designated policy, procedure, or established standard.

The use of the attributes sampling plan can be illustrated by the concern that might exist for the correct coding of accounts payable disbursement vouchers. The starting point will be the determination of an expected error rate. At the same time a judgment must be made as to the acceptable precision limits and the degree of wanted confidence. It is now possible to determine the size of the sample that will provide the basis for a reliable conclusion as to the total condition of the population of the size being dealt with. This determination is made for us through statistical methods and can be obtained from available tables or by computer runs. This provides the *initial* basis to the internal auditor for the size of the sample to be reviewed. The internal auditor now selects his sample in a proper manner and examines it to determine the number of errors that exist in the sample. As can be expected, that error rate in the sample will normally be higher or lower than the previously designated acceptable error rate. If it is lower, the internal auditor has, of course, established that he is safely within the limits he selected. If, on the other hand, the sample shows a higher error rate, tables are available to tell him what degree of reliability he now has. The internal auditor will now have to determine whether the results are satisfactory and what further he should do. Conceivably, the sample can be expanded or the internal auditor may feel that he has an adequate basis for arriving at a conclusion.

Variables Sampling

A second type of sampling plan, referred to as variables sampling, has to do with the size of a specified population. Here the focus is on "how much" as opposed to the "how many" of attribute sampling. The objective served is to be able to project aggregate quantities on the basis of a sample. Illustrative would be the desire to estimate the total value of an inventory, or perhaps to estimate the amount of obsolescence in that inventory. Still another practical application would be the determination of the estimated aggregate dollar amount of excessive items in a group of expense reports. Variables sampling is thus concerned with absolute amounts as opposed to the number of a particular type of error. There are various types of variables samples: (1) single stage, (2) stratified, (3) multistage, and (4) stratified multistage.

The statistical problems involved in this type of sampling are closely related to attributes sampling, but include certain additional concepts and calculations. One of these additional complexities is the necessity to compute the standard deviation of the sample as a measure of the range of variability of the sample. Because of the more complicated nature of this approach, a step-by-step analysis of the method of application is given below for single-stage variables sampling. The example is based on a simplified manual method for estimating the standard deviation when computer-developed or other information on the standard deviation is not available.

Steps in Application. The total application of variables sampling can be understood best by listing and discussing the sequential steps that must be carried out. These are:

1. *Determination of Audit Objective*. Assuming that the internal auditor has an assignment to determine the validity of a given population—as, for example, an inventory—the first step is to decide the desired level of confidence and the desired degree of precision. The latter is normally first expressed as a percentage, but is then converted into a dollar amount. This dollar amount can then be translated into the average amount per inventory item. This degree of precision can be called the sampling error.

2. *Selection of Preliminary Sample*. Through a proper selection process, discussed later in the chapter, a preliminary sample of about 50 items is selected.

3. *Arrangement of Preliminary Sample*. The preliminary sample is now arranged in groups of six, seven, or eight items, but subject to the requirement that the number of groups as a multiple of the item content equals the total of the items in the preliminary sample. For example, a preliminary sample of 48 items would be composed of eight groups of six each.

4. *Determine the Average Range*. In each group the difference between the highest and lowest item constitutes the range. The ranges of all groups are then added and an average computed.

5. *Calculate Estimated Standard Deviation of Population*. The estimated standard deviation of the total population can now be calculated through a simplified method by dividing the average range, just computed, by an amount which is known in statistics as the d_2 factor. For a group content of 6, 7, and 8, the d_2 factor is respectively, 2.534, 2.704, and 2.847.

6. *Computation of Stipulated Sampling Error*. The sampling error per average inventory item, as expressed in dollars, is now divided by the previously calculated estimated standard deviation. This will yield a new ratio called the *stipulated sampling error*.

7. *Determination of Complete Sample*. Using the previously established level of confidence and the just computed ratio of sampling error, tables are available to show the size of the complete sample to be used.

8. *Evaluation of Sample Size*. At this point the internal auditor has an opportunity to reevaluate his audit objective. It may be that the sample indicated is so large that he may wish to reevaluate the confidence level and level of precision (the amount of the sampling error). It is possible by decreasing the former and/or increasing the latter to decrease the size of the needed sample.

9. *Examination of Sample*. The indicated sample, based on the criteria just discussed, will now be examined in complete detail and the sampling error determined for this now more complete sample.

10. *Reevaluation of Sampling Error*. The reliability of the complete sample

can be further established by recomputing the stipulated sampling error for the complete sample in the same manner as was done for the preliminary sample. Again tables are available to measure the significance of the variance from the error shown by the preliminary sample, and a reevaluation of the audit objectives may be necessary.

11. *Projection to Total Population.* The results obtained from the complete sample can now be projected to the total population. In some cases the conclusion or recommendation developed may be of a general nature. In other cases the final action may be a definitive adjustment of the inventory.

Difference Estimates. The preceding application has been based upon the amounts of the individual inventory items. Frequently, it is practicable instead to deal with the differences between the book and actual (as determined by the auditor). Under this approach a similar procedure is followed but all of the samples and computations pertain to the differences data. The advantage to be achieved is that the auditor is dealing with smaller amounts (and thus smaller standard deviations) and that, therefore, normally a smaller sample will be required to achieve the same levels of confidence and precision. It is, of course, possible that the differences will be as great or almost as great as the absolute values and, therefore, the advantages may disappear. However, the use of differences is a good technique for use in the appropriate situations, and can often be used as a first approach.

Ratio Estimates. A similar type of special efficiency is often achieved through working with ratios instead of absolute values. Computations of the standard deviations under this method are more complicated. But where these computations can be made by computers there can be significant time savings. The ratio estimates method is preferable to the use of the difference estimates method when the errors found are related in size to the value of individual items being tested.

Discovery Sampling

In certain situations the concern of the internal auditor may be as to whether a particular type of deficiency exists. The deficiency involved is normally a very serious one and would be expected to have a very low occurrence rate. Illustrative of this kind of situation would be the possibility that there are fictitious employees on the payroll, or perhaps the failure to obtain collateral for loans which, under company policy, are supposed to be secured. In this case we are concerned with a type of occurrence, and to that extent it is like attribute sampling. However, in this situation we know the size of the population, and we are endeavoring on the basis of a given sample to determine the probabilities that the particular kind of deficiency does or does not exist. Discovery sampling is used for a more limited or special purpose, but again is part of the kit provided by the statistical approach.

Application of Discovery Sampling.   In applying the discovery sampling plan we would first determine the population, decide what is an acceptable occurrence rate, establish the desired confidence level, determine the sample size required, examine the sample, and evaluate the results. Tables are available that will provide the size of the appropriate sample when the population is known and the confidence level established. If in the examination of this indicated sample no instances of the deficiency are found, the internal auditor can safely conclude that he is within the boundaries of the previously established confidence level and occurrence rate. If one or more deficiencies are discovered, the procedure can be reversed to determine the probabilities that the ocurrence rate in the sample applies to the total population. At the same time, of course, the internal auditor would focus on the causes of the deficiency or deficiencies actually encountered and appraise the scope and timing of various types of corrective action.

Dollar-Unit Sampling

Another method of obtaining a probability sample is to select the sampling units with probabilities proportional to size. Dollar-unit sampling is an example of this, in which the size is the recorded amounts. Those transactions with large recorded amounts will have a greater opportunity to be selected since they contain more dollars. This type of sampling is discussed in more detail later in the chapter.

Nonnormal Distribution

The question is sometimes raised as to the feasibility of use of statistical sampling with populations that do not have normal distribution. There are, however, methods of handling this problem, as discussed below.

The basis of the question is that the method of computation of the sampling error assumes that the sampling distribution is in the form of a normal distribution. If it is not, the computation of the confidence interval will not be correct. If the population is positively skewed (right), the lower and the upper confidence limits would be understated if the normal approximation is used to establish the confidence limits. On the other hand, if the population is negatively skewed (left), the lower and the upper confidence limits would be overstated. Populations of accounting data are almost always right skewed. With respect to differences found in audited amounts, the distribution of the difference is often positive because many items either have no errors or have positive errors (overstatements). There are various methods for dealing with this problem.

1. *Increasing Sample Size.* One method of assuring more accurate results when a sample is drawn from a badly skewed population is to increase the sample size. The Central Limit Theorem says that as the sample size gets larger, the shape of the sampling distribution of the mean becomes that of the normal distribution. If the skewness is not known and large sample sizes are impracticable, other approaches may be needed.

2. *Use of Lower Limit*. The lower limit is sometimes used in auditing claims when disallowances are taken. When the differences found are right skewed, a statistical projection understates the error or disallowance. It is thus a fair method of requesting refunds, although benefiting the auditee.

    This method is sometimes criticized when used for government auditing purposes on the basis that more money could be refunded with a larger sample. However, each sampling plan must be designed on an individual basis, with consideration of cost and problems in auditing additional items, availability of staff, alternative uses of scarce resources, and nature of item being questioned.

3. *Calculating Precise Limits*. The precise confidence limits can be calculated using tables based on measures of skewness and kurtosis from either the population or the sample.[2] This calculation will enable the auditor to project from skewed populations with greater accuracy.

Minimum Sample Sizes

In practice there are various sample sizes used by internal auditors as minimum samples in an audit. On the one hand, an auditor may conservatively select a large sample, say 1,000, on the basis that he will get better results and management will be more apt to accept the results if a large sample is selected. On the other hand, an auditor may choose a sample size of 50 on the basis that he may be able to arrive at adequate conclusions based on a limited amount of work. These decisions are sometimes made without regard to scientific statistical analysis as to required sample size.

    The objectives of the audit, of course, determine the extent of sampling. If survey work is being performed, tests to determine acceptability of the system may be minimal. If significant weaknesses are found, however, and the test is to determine the extent and magnitude of the deficiency, then the auditor should perform appropriate statistical analysis to determine the number to be tested. Under conditions such as this, some audit organizations have adopted a minimum size for sampling, such as 200, with the use of a larger sample as considered necessary. This provides auditors and management with a minimum assurance that conclusions reached are valid.

Reporting a Specific Amount

In variables sampling the auditor must decide how he will report the projection of dollar amounts, whether it be for adjustments or for estimates of the effect of a particular deficiency. Under statistical sampling the projection would normally be stated at a range of values for a given confidence level. From the viewpoint of management, however, the use of a specific dollar amount may be preferable.

[2]Herbert Arkin, *Sampling Methods for the Auditor—An Advanced Treatment* (New York: McGraw-Hill Book Company, 1982, p.71.).

Point Estimate or Midpoint.   The point estimate is the best single estimate of the value of a universe, being the point of maximum likelihood. It is calculated by multiplying the sample mean times the number of items in the universe. This estimate is generally used when the range of values, or confidence interval, around the point estimate is small. For example, the point estimate based on a statistical projection of the results of audit was $100,000. The precision at the 95% confidence level was ±$4000, for a range between $96,000 and $104,000. Under these circumstances the use of the point estimate would generally be warranted. However, if the range were between $60,000 and $140,000, the auditor would have to either increase the sample size or use a different method of reporting. One method of reporting is to state: "We estimate with a probability of 95% that the recorded inventory value of $2.5 million is overstated between $60,000 and $140,000, and is most likely $100,000."

Upper Limit.   By stating the projection in terms of the upper limit, the auditor can determine the assurance that the amount of error or deficiency is not greater than this amount. For example, in a statistical review of equipment on hand the auditor projected at the 95% confidence level that the maximum overstatement of the equipment was $30,000. Since this amount was not material in relation to the $5 million of equipment owned by the company, the auditor concluded that the amount of error was not significant. He also analyzed, however, the causes of errors found in his sample to determine procedural weaknesses that required correction.

   The upper limit is frequently used by the internal auditor to determine the validity of account balances for financial statement purposes. A tolerable error rate is first determined for the population. If the projected error rate using the upper limit does not exceed the tolerable error rate, the account is considered reasonably stated for financial statement purposes.

Lower Limit.   A one-sided confidence limit can be used to demonstrate that the total universe value is not less than some amount at a given confidence level. For example, in a statistical sample of fixed asset acquisitions it was found that equipment costing over $1,000 was being expensed rather than capitalized. The auditor's projection showed that there was 95% confidence that the amount expensed in error was at least $150,000. The lower limit is used sometimes in government auditing for recommending refunds, as discussed previously, especially when the precision is not sufficiently tight. Appendix D shows this treatment in the policy statement of the Internal Revenue Service.

Use of Standard Confidence Level

Some audit organizations have adopted a fixed confidence level, such as 95%, for performing and evaluating statistical tests. This is justified on the basis that the confidence level should be sufficiently high in all instances, and should be a consistent reference for projections. See Appendix D for the use of a fixed confidence level by the Internal Revenue Service.

   Other audit organizations use flexible confidence levels based on individual circumstances. For a particular audit test an 80 or 90% confidence limit may be used; in another test a 95 or 99.9% confidence level might be preferred. In some cases the auditor will restate the precision at two or more confidence levels as a basis for making judgments.

SELECTION TECHNIQUES

To obtain the advantages of statistical sampling, a probability sample must be drawn. This involves a more precise approach than is used in judgment sampling in order to be able to evaluate the results scientifically. The auditor must remove bias in his selection once the sampling plan has been developed. Through this method a sample can be obtained that is representative of the population, and the results become defensible. Exhibit 8.3 is a listing from a form for outlining the sampling plan as well as a method of selection and evaluation. These more precise requirements can be stated, as follows:

1. The population (or universe or field) that is to be sampled must be clearly defined. The population is made up of sampling units, which are the individual items from which the sample is drawn. This definition must include scope (for example, the accounts payable vouchers for a year) and the specific characteristic of audit interest (for example, the fact of a specific type of approval).

2. The population should not cover such a range of characteristics (for example, such very large and small amounts) that the statistical conclusions will not be sufficiently precise.

EXHIBIT 8.3. Statistical Sampling Plan

1. Statement of objectives
2. List of characteristics to be tested
3. Sampling unit
4. Type of sampling plan used (attributes, variables, etc.) (If stratified sampling not used, explain why.)
5. Size of universe and strata
6. Expected error rate
7. Desired precision
8. Desired confidence level
9. Selection of sample size (Indicate if probe sample.)
10. Random number table used—include start and ending point (If computer was used, attach documentation.)
11. If using systematic sampling—starting point and method of selecting random start and interval between sample units
12. Evaluation of results and conclusions

Prepared by: Date   Approval   Date

_____   _____   Supervisor: _____   _____

3. Every item in the particular population must have an equal chance of being selected in the sample. Thus there must be no bias created through the poorer availability (or even lack of availability) of particular items.

4. The person selecting the sample should have no bias in that selection. This includes also the avoiding of any method of selection that could involve such a bias.

Four common types or techniques involved in the selection process are: random number selection, interval selection, stratified selection, and cluster selection. The latter two techniques are also often referred to as kinds of sampling, but they are more properly identified as selection techniques. Next, we discuss very briefly each of these techniques.

Random Number Selection

The random number technique by its name emphasizes the basic requirement of the sample that it should be selected at random, with each item in the particular population having an equal chance to be selected as a part of the sample. If it were practicable, we would place all the items (or numbers that would identify particular items) in a container, mix the items thoroughly, and then draw the individual items for the sample from the container in a blindfolded manner. Since this may not be feasible, we must seek other means. One of these means is the use of random number tables. This type of table is illustrated by Exhibit 8.4. Random number tables can be utilized as a basis for determining the sample of items actually to be reviewed by the internal auditor. Random numbers can also be generated by computers, but our discussion will at this point pertain to the way in which the tables are used in typical audit situations. The problems here center chiefly around the way in which items in the population are related to numbers in the tables, the starting point in using the tables, and then the route to take after the determination of the starting point.

Relating Audit Items. Where the audit items in the population to be evaluated are already numbered, the numbers provide a ready basis for use of the table. It will be necessary, however, to work with the table in a way that will provide random numbers with the same number of digits. The columnar data can be used in any manner desired, provided that the particular approach is used consistently. Numbers encountered that are outside the limits of the audit sequence must be ignored. If the audit items are in a broken series, the auditor will have to ignore the random numbers encountered that do not apply to the actual audit sequences. Where the audit items are lettered, the letters need to be converted to a number equivalent before the random number tables can be used. Similarly, audit items lacking any formal sequencing designation must be provided with some kind of a numerical equivalent. If by chance the same random number comes up again, thus repeating the identification of a particular audit item, the duplicate number should be ignored, and the next applicable number used. There is clearly no point in auditing the same item twice.

Starting Point. The objective is that all starting points be established on a random basis. One danger here is that many of us tend to start at the top left

EXHIBIT 8.4.   Table of Random Numbers

10480	15011	01536	02011	81647	91646	69179	14194	62590
22368	46573	25595	85393	30995	89198	27982	53402	93965
24130	48360	22527	97265	76393	64809	15179	24830	49340
42167	93093	06243	61680	07856	16376	39440	53537	71341
37570	39975	81837	16656	06121	91782	60468	81305	49684
77921	06907	11008	42751	27756	53498	18602	70659	90655
99562	72905	56420	69994	98872	31016	71194	18738	44013
96301	91977	05463	07972	18876	20922	94595	56869	69014
89579	14342	63661	10281	17453	18103	57740	84378	25331
85475	36857	53342	53988	53060	59533	38867	62300	08158
28918	69578	88231	33276	70997	79936	56865	05859	90106
63553	40961	48235	03427	49626	69445	18663	72695	52180
09429	93969	52636	92737	88974	33488	36320	17617	30015
10365	61129	87529	85689	48237	52267	67689	93394	01511
07119	97336	71048	08178	77233	13916	47564	81056	97735
51085	12765	51821	51259	77452	16308	60756	92144	49442
02368	21382	52404	60268	89368	19885	55322	44819	01188
01011	54092	33362	94904	31273	04146	18594	29852	71585
52162	53916	46369	58586	23216	14513	83149	98736	23495
07056	97628	33787	09998	42698	06691	76988	13602	51851
48663	91245	85828	14346	09172	30168	90229	04734	59193
54164	58492	22421	74103	47070	25306	76468	26384	58151
32639	32363	05597	24200	13363	38005	94342	28728	35806
29334	27001	87637	87308	58731	00256	45834	15398	46557
02488	33062	28834	07351	19731	92420	60952	61280	50001
81525	72295	04839	96423	24878	82651	66566	14778	76797
29676	20591	68086	26432	46901	20849	89768	81536	86645
00742	57392	39064	66432	84673	40027	32832	61362	98947
05366	04213	25669	26422	44407	44048	37937	63904	45766
91921	26418	64117	94305	26766	25940	39972	22209	71500
00582	04711	87917	77341	42206	35126	74087	99547	81817
00725	69884	62797	56170	86324	88072	76222	36086	84637
69011	65795	95876	55293	18988	27354	26575	08625	40801
25976	57948	29888	88604	67917	48708	18912	82271	65424
09763	83473	73577	12908	30883	18317	28290	35797	05998
91567	42595	27958	30134	04024	86385	29880	99730	55536
17955	56349	90999	49127	20044	59931	06115	20542	18059
46503	18584	18845	49618	02304	51038	20655	58727	28168
92157	89634	94824	78171	84610	82834	09922	25417	44137
14577	62765	35605	81263	39667	47358	56873	56307	61607
98427	07523	33362	64270	01638	92477	66969	98420	04880
34914	63976	88720	82765	34476	17032	87589	40836	32427
70060	28277	39475	46473	23219	53416	94970	25832	69975
53976	54914	06990	67245	68350	82948	11398	42878	80287
76072	29515	40980	07391	58745	25774	22987	80059	39911
90725	52210	83974	29992	65831	38857	50490	83765	55657
64364	67412	33339	31926	14883	24413	59744	92351	97473
08962	00358	31662	25388	61642	34072	81249	35648	56891
95012	68379	93526	70765	10592	04542	76463	54328	02349
15664	10493	20492	38391	91132	21999	59516	81652	27195

position. However, this will technically introduce bias in the results. A practical method is not to look at the table and simply let one's finger find a starting point on a blind-thrust basis.

Route. Once the starting point has been established and the number of digits related to the table in some way, the identification of the random numbers to be used can proceed in any direction. The only condition is that the use of the columns and the selected direction be maintained on a consistent basis.

Other Problems. Frequently, the size of the sample as originally selected may have to be increased or decreased. In the first situation the auditor should go back to his previous stopping point and then again continue. If the sample needs to be reduced, the random numbers last selected should be eliminated in reverse sequence. Normally, it is more convenient to err on the overselection side.

A second problem has to do with putting the random numbers in a sequence that will make it convenient to proceed sequentially to locate the actual audit items. In some cases the simplest solution is to rearrange the random numbers sequentially after they have been selected. In other cases it may be easier to use a work schedule to line up the selected numbers on a sequential basis during the actual process of selection. Random numbers may be arranged sequentially by use of a special program, if a computer is available.

Finally, it is important to document the manner in which the random selection process was actually carried out. This documentation then serves to confirm the scientific basis for the sample selection, and can in fact be auditable, if such proof is ever necessary.

Interval Selection

Another way to select the items in the sample and still to provide a statistically sound sample is through interval selection (sometimes called systematic sampling). This approach consists of selecting the individual items of the sample based on a uniform interval in the series of items comprising the total population to be sampled. This technique is especially useful when the particular population does not have assigned numbers that make it practicable to work from the items selected on the basis of random table numbers. For example, we would be able to develop our sample by selecting every *n*th item in an inventory listing. It is, of course, necessary that we are dealing with a reasonably homogeneous population, in terms of type of item, and that there is no bias in the arrangement that would result in the interval approach coming up with a sample that is not statistically representative of the population.

Application of Interval Selection. The special requirements in the application of interval selection is that the interval to be used is properly related to the size of the sample (as determined in the usual manner) and the size of the total population. Where necessary the population can be estimated. The sample size divided into the population size then establishes the proper interval. Thus a population of 5000 and a needed sample of 200 would yield an interval requirement of 25. We would then examine every twenty-fifth item in the population series. The starting point in the first interval group must now be established on a random basis, preferably from a random numbers table. In the event that the actual population turns out to be larger than was estimated, a practical solution is to increase the sample by extending the interval selection on the same basis. If, on the other hand, the actual population is less than estimated, it will be necessary to complete the sample through a new interval selection based on the number of short items in relation to the total population size. The latter more complicated problem can be avoided by having a safety margin through selecting a larger sample.

Stratified Selection

The nature of stratified selection is that the particular population is divided into two or more subgroups or classes (referred to as strata) and that each subgroup is dealt with independently in the statistical sampling processes. In its simplest terms two or more separate populations are established within the framework of a larger population of which they are a part. It is a supplement to the random and interval selection techniques because either of those selection techniques can be applied to the smaller population. In some cases one of the new populations may be examined in complete detail. The basic need for this stratification or subdivision is that the larger population combines a number of significantly different characteristics, and that the auditor wishes to evaluate the subgroup on a more individual and precise basis. Through reducing variability, stratification can decrease the standard deviation, and thus help to reduce sample sizes.

Use of Stratified Selection. One of the most common situations requiring stratification is one in which the particular population—such as inventories, accounts receivable, or invoices—has some items of very high value. Since these high-value items have much greater significance, the auditor may properly wish to subject them to higher standards of scrutiny. This may take the form of higher sampling standards or detailed examination. In other cases the need for stratification may arise from the fact that individual subgroups are processed in different ways, or by different groups. In other cases the nature of the items may call for different standards of audit scrutiny, as, for example, where some types of inventory are more subject to theft. Under these kinds of conditions the larger variability in the total population makes a single type of testing and evaluation inapplicable. Needless to say, these principles have long been recognized and applied by good internal auditors. The special importance in statistical sampling is, however, the contribution of stratification to more meaningful statistical measures (higher levels of confidence and lower precision limits), together with the possibility of using smaller samples.

Once the stratification selection technique has been adopted and the subgroups subjected to different standards of audit scrutiny, the results of each evaluation can be used in several ways. In some cases the results are used quite independently, based on the sampling of the separate populations. In other cases they may be brought back together to support a consolidated finding and conclusion relative to the total operational population, using a stratified sampling projection.

Cluster Selection

Another approach used by auditors is known as cluster selection. Under this approach the sample is made up of systematically selecting given subgroups or clusters from the particular total population. It is used when items are filed in shelves or in drawers and it is physically more convenient to select subgroups based on shelf area or individual drawers. The rationale is that the items on particular portions of the shelf areas (or in designated drawers) are substantially similar, and that a sample thus selected will be representative of the total population. However, the reported experience is that the variability *within* the individual samples is frequently less than the variability *among* the samples. Hence it is customary to use a larger sample when using the cluster selection approach to offset this lesser reliability. A variation of the aforementioned approach, called multistage sampling, is to *sample* the individual clusters instead of examining the sample as a whole.

Use of Cluster Selection. Assuming a population of 60,000 items filed in shelves that have a linear coverage of 2,000 feet, and that a sample of 600 will provide the desired level of confidence and limits of precision, we might, perhaps, plan on 20 clusters. Then each cluster would need to have 30 items. Since the average number of items is 30 per linear foot (60,000 ÷ 2,000), each cluster will cover an area of 1 foot (30 ÷ 30). These individual clusters would then be selected at intervals of 100 feet (2000 ÷ 20) and with a random start. It should be recognized that the scientific basis of the total sample is more dependent on a consistency of the population. That is, random number selection or regular interval selection would presumably assure a better representative sample. Hence cluster sampling must be used with special care.

STRATIFIED SAMPLING APPLICATIONS

The trend in statistical sampling is to use stratified sampling in most auditing applications of variable methods.[3] Although in some cases it may not be practicable to stratify the population, or it may be not be possible to identify the items for which differences will occur, these situations are rare.

[3]Donald M. Roberts, *Statistical Auditing* (New York: American Institute of Certified Public Accountants, 1978), p. 65.

Changes in Approach

When judgment sampling was the method primarily used in testing, the auditor often performed preliminary analysis before deciding which items to select. This analysis was based on review of correspondence in the files, discussions with auditee's staff to obtain explanations and leads, review of prior audit findings, comparison of operations and data, and study of the universe to determine the larger or sensitive items for test.

When statistical sampling was first introduced into auditing, simple random sampling was generally used. This method was relatively easy to learn and apply, especially under manual methods. Thus, when there was an area to test, the auditor immediately took a random sample of the universe. In some cases this was justified as a probe sample, or test of the universe, to find out more about the items before developing a sampling plan. The results of the probe sample, however, were often used to arrive at final conclusions as to the acceptability of the area being tested. Thus, in the process of switching to the new statistical sampling technique, the auditor may have used relatively simple statistical approaches.

With the advent of the computer to simplify sample selection and projection of results, the use of stratified sampling has grown. Often, the only practical method for selecting a stratified sample is by use of a computer. Also, as auditors gained in sophistication in applying statistical sampling, they experimented with more advanced techniques to get better precision.

Advantages of Stratified Sampling

Stratified sampling provides greater representation of the larger recorded amounts if they are included as separate strata. In this respect the method resembles dollar-unit sampling, in which each dollar is the sampling unit.

A major advantage of stratification is that it improves the efficiency of the testing. When the population variability (standard deviation) is high, sample sizes may be reduced for the desired levels of precision and reliability by using stratified random sampling. If a sufficient number of strata is selected, often the sampling error can be reduced substantially. With the use of computers, this becomes more feasible as an approach to be used by auditors.

Another advantage is that emphasis can be given to sensitive areas that require audit. Often, the auditor's preliminary analysis will disclose areas with potential errors or problems. These can be classified in separate strata and audited 100% or on a sampling basis, as warranted.

Methods of Stratification

As described above, the use of stratification provides the auditor with a tool for reviewing sensitive areas on a scientific basis. He must, however, use the utmost judgment in selecting strata for audit. The information available on computer tapes will, of course, be important in selecting a method. The following are some factors to consider in determining methods of stratifying.

Type of item.

Dollar amount.

Storage location.

Volume of activity.

Prior problems or deficiencies.

Items handled by certain employees.

Items involving weak controls.

Post-Stratification

An auditor may take a random sample of units, expecting to project using difference estimates. In some instances where the results are imprecise, the auditor can stratify after the simple random sample is selected. This is referred to as post-stratification.

If the auditor knows the number of units in the population for each strata, he can take the results of the original sample, eliminate the sensitive (or special strata) units, and put them in a separate stratum. If the auditor does not know the total number of items for the separate strata, he can assign a zero value to the sensitive (or separate strata) items without decreasing the sample size. He then examines the separate strata, with an estimate made of the strata universe based on the incidence in the original sample.

DOLLAR-UNIT-SAMPLING APPLICATIONS

Method of Application

Dollar-unit sampling is a method of statistical sampling in which every dollar, or other monetary unit, in a population has an equal chance of selection. The sampling unit is thus each dollar rather than a physical unit such as an invoice or payroll check. For example, if purchases are being tested for a year, the population consists of the total dollar value of purchases made, and the sampling unit is each dollar of purchases.

When errors are found in the invoice, they are related to individual dollars in the invoice by various methods. One method, called tainting, determines the ratio of dollar errors to the amount of the invoice. This ratio is then applied to the dollar sampling unit. Another approach is the use of a fixed decision rule. Under this method, as one option, if there is an error the last dollar units within the physical unit, to the extent of the errors, may be considered wrong.

As a relatively new method used by auditors, dollar-unit sampling is currently being experimented with by various groups. Public accountants have been especially interested in this method for estimating the amount of overstatement of accounts. In evaluating the merits of the method, comparisons are often made with the more conventional probability methods, commonly described as the *classical approach*. The following are some advantages and disadvantages of dollar-unit sampling in relation to the classical approach.

Advantages of Dollar-Unit Sampling

Detection of Material Errors.   Dollar-unit sampling provides a probability of including a unit in the sample proportional to its dollar value. Thus there is less risk under this method of failing to detect a material error. Although stratification reduces the risk under usual probability sampling methods, there is less risk under dollar-unit sampling since all the large dollar units are divided into individual dollars.

Smaller Sample Size.   When no errors are found in the initial sample, relatively small sample sizes may be used. The auditor can readily determine the maximum possible overstatements and restrict his auditing in some circumstances. In addition, the auditor obtains the benefits of unlimited stratification by use of a dollar sampling unit.

Normal Sampling Distribution.   The sampling distribution involved is the binomial distribution, for which exact confidence limits can be established. Thus normal approximations are not necessary as in the use of variables sampling.

Low Error Rates.   When few errors are found in classical sampling the confidence level may not be reliable.[4] Under these circumstances a larger sample may have to be drawn. A major advantage of dollar-unit sampling also is that it eliminates the problems of nonnormal distribution discussed earlier in this chapter.

Disadvantages of Dollar-Unit Sampling

Overstatements.   The dollar-unit method can be applied only to overstatements. Since the method results in the selection of dollars reported, any understatement of dollars results in units missing from the population. They thus cannot be sampled. Accordingly, the auditor cannot project a value of the population using dollar-unit sampling.

Zero or Negative Values.   Under this method, zero or negative values would have to be sampled using a physical unit approach. Since there are no dollar values included in these, there is no chance that zero or negative values would be sampled.

Total Population Value.   Since the projection is made to a universe of dollars, a total book value must be known. The method cannot provide estimates of unknown population values. Also, under dollar-unit sampling it is necessary to accumulate the dollars progressively in drawing the sample.

[4]John Neter and James K. Loebbecke, *Behavior of Major Statistical Estimators in Sampling Accounting Populations* (New York: American Institute of Certified Public Accountants, Inc., 1975), p. 5.

Training Availability.   As a relatively new concept for use by auditors, there is currently little training provided in dollar-unit sampling. The method is now being subject to rigorous proof to determine its acceptability. The literature in the field is related primarily to classical sampling, and professional certification examinations are based on the classical approach. As the use of dollar-unit sampling becomes more widespread, and its benefits and limitations better understood, it is expected that additional training will be developed.[5]

COMPANY USE OF STATISTICAL ANALYSIS

Most company operational activities make use of statistical methods and concepts to some extent. The key questions are first, whether they are being as fully utilized as they should be, and second, whether the uses actually being made are carried out in an effective fashion. The internal auditor will, of course, be very much interested in both of these questions. The answers to these questions may require special counsel from persons with adequate professional expertise, but much can be done in the way of a preliminary screening. Also, much can be done in the way of evaluating how operational managers are developing orderly procedures and good administration over these more technical activities. For our present purposes it will be useful to identify some of the more common applications of statistical methods in the various operational activities.

1. *Production Activities.* Production has always been one of the major areas for statistical applications. One of the most common of these is the use of statistical tests by quality control groups as to the extent to which individual manufacturing units are completing particular parts or processing operations in accordance with desired specifications. The same problem exists also in connection with purchased parts, materials, and partial assemblies. Other applications will include the forecasting of machine capacity needs and the continuing maintenance needs.

2. *Inventory Management.* A related important statistical application is in connection with the determination of needed inventory levels by individual types of items. This will involve production and other operational areas as well.

3. *Marketing.* In recent times statistical testing has come to be widely used to measure and evaluate consumer preferences. A related application has to do with the testing of new products before commitments are made to large-volume production. Other major applications relate to the evaluation of advertising approaches, promotional activities, sales techniques, and the like.

---

[5]See Donald Leslie, Albert Teitlebaum, and Rodney Anderson, *Dollar-Unit Sampling* (Toronto: Copp Clark Pittman, 1979), for further discussion of theory and applications.

4. *Personnel*. Common statistical applications in the personnel area include the analysis and evaluation of staff needs, recruitment policies, training methods, employee turnover, compensation schemes, and so on.

5. *Finance*. At a high level the statistical applications in the finance area will include pricing policy, capital project evaluation, and all types of cost and revenue projections. At the lower level they will be the testing of accuracy and compliance in connection with the various types of internal processing.

6. *General*. The ready availability of computer capabilities has provided a major impetus to the statistical measurement and evaluation of many new types of activities. Illustrative of the newer applications are leadership styles, organizational arrangements, types of work assignments, group incentives, and communication patterns.

USE OF COMPUTERS IN SAMPLING

The computer has proved to be an invaluable tool to auditors in applying statistical sampling. It simplifies the calculations necessary, eliminating the need for reference to formulas or tables. In addition, it facilitates the use of sophisticated techniques, thus enabling the auditor to obtain more precise and unbiased results. The auditor can, of course, use calculations in some instances to solve formulas when a computer is not available, but this is more time consuming. Auditors can sometimes take a portable terminal to the site when needed for statistical applications. The auditee may have a computer available. In other cases the data may be telephoned or mailed to a central location for input to the computer.

Use of Software Packages

Exhibit 8.5, based on the *1979 Survey of Internal Auditing* by The Institute of Internal Auditors, illustrates that various software packages are used by internal auditors.

Programs Available

There are various statistical sampling programs available in the software packages. Some commonly used ones are as follows:

1. *Random Number Generators*. Numbers can be obtained in generated order or arranged in sequence. Single numbers or numbers in pairs can be obtained, such as for selecting a random page number and item on the page. Also, random numbers can be developed for more than one strata using different frames, or numbering sequences.

2. *Determining Sample Size*. These programs give the sample size required

EXHIBIT 8.5. Use of Software Packages[a,b]

Audit software systems used by organizations?

	U.S.–Canada				Other International				1979 Total	1975 Total
	Small	Medium	Large	Total	Small	Medium	Large	Total		
[None] We don't use audit software	63.2	41.0	19.5	37.4	25.0	58.3	40.0	47.6	39	45
Ask 360	0.0	0.6	1.1	0.7	0.0	0.0	20.0	4.8	1	—
[Audassist]	—	—	—	—	—	—	—	—	—	—
Audex	0.0	1.2	2.2	1.3	—	—	—	—	1	1
Cinfex	0.0	0.0	1.1	0.4	—	—	—	—	0.4	—
Audit	0.9	0.0	1.6	0.9	—	—	—	—	1	—
Audit Analyzer	0.9	2.5	3.8	2.7	—	—	—	—	2	—
Auditape	4.7	5.6	8.1	6.4	25.0	25.0	0.0	19.0	7	5
Auditpak	0.9	0.6	3.2	1.8	25.0	8.3	0.0	9.5	2	4
Auditronic 32	1.9	3.1	1.1	2.0	—	—	—	—	2	2
Audit Reporter	0.9	0.0	1.1	0.7	—	—	—	—	1	—
[CFA]	—	—	—	—	—	—	—	—	—	1
[AY Audit/Mgt. System]	—	—	—	—	—	—	—	—	—	1
DYL 260	0.0	5.6	14.1	7.7	0.0	8.3	0.0	4.8	7	—
DYL-Audit	0.0	0.0	2.2	0.9	—	—	—	—	1	—
CARS	0.9	3.7	6.5	4.2	0.0	8.3	0.0	4.8	4	2
Easy Audit	0.9	3.7	3.2	2.9	0.0	0.0	20.0	4.8	3	—
[Easytrieve]	—	—	—	—	—	—	—	—	—	—
EDP Auditor	1.9	3.1	9.2	5.3	—	—	—	—	5	3
HEWCAS	0.0	0.6	2.2	1.1	—	—	—	—	1	6
[MARK IV] Auditor	2.8	1.9	14.6	7.3	0.0	8.3	20.0	9.5	7	5
PROBE 5	0.9	0.6	0.5	0.7	—	—	—	—	1	—
[SCORE]	—	—	—	—	—	—	—	—	—	—
STRATA	1.9	2.5	6.5	4.0	—	—	—	—	4	2
SYSTEM 2170	3.8	6.2	7.0	6.0	—	—	—	—	5	4
Sample size (number)	106	161	185	452	4	12	5	21	497	343

[a]Percentages (all entries except sample size) are the percent of respondents checking the indicated item.

[b]As can be seen, various software systems are utilized by the audit managers who responded. Still of particular note is the result that 39% indicated that they did not use any audit software systems, with two-thirds of small U.S. and Canadian firms not using any audit software. However, a slight increase can be seen in the use of the software systems listed above and on the following pages.

Based on: The Institute of Internal Auditors, Inc., 1979 Survey of Internal Auditing (Altamonte Springs, Fla.: Institute of Internal Auditors, Inc., 1980), p. 76.

for various types of statistical samples, such as attributes, variables, and stratified.

3. *Appraisal of Results.* These programs give appraisals of various types of samples: unstratified, stratified, multistage, and dollar unit. Included in these are special programs for mean unit estimates, difference estimates, and ratio estimates.

Exhibits 8.6 to 8.9 are examples of two programs available and the corresponding runs. Exhibit 8.10 is an example of a computer printout used for evaluating the results of a statistical sample using difference estimates. Additional data are stated for confidence levels at 90% and 95%. In addition, the sample sizes are given which are required to attain precision at stated percentages from the point estimate. Estimates of skewness and kurtosis are made.

EXHIBIT 8.6.   Sampling Programs—Random Numbers

Filename:	*SAMPLE (SMPFRA)
Title:	Random Numbers: Sampling Frame
Language:	BASIC
Application:	Executable program
Purpose:	Provides unduplicated random numbers which fall within the boundaries of two or more strata (series of numbers). The boundaries of each stratum are specified by the user. The user also specifies the quantity of random numbers to be sorted for printing in sequential order, and the quantity of additional "spare" numbers to be printed in the order generated by the program.
Instructions:	The user inputs data in the following sequence:

		Series Boundaries	
Stratum	Line	Low	High
1	1 DATA	1001	11000[a]
2	2 DATA	35000	36008[b]
3	3 DATA	37000	38050

Quantity of Numbers		Random
Sequential Order	Generated Order	Two-Digit Number
10	2	29

[a]Not necessary to use a separate DATA line for each stratum. Commas must be placed between entries, but not at the end of a line.
[b]The strata boundaries may overlap, although they do not in the example.

EXHIBIT 8.7. Computer-Run Random Numbers

SMPFRA—Example of Run
*Sample   13:03   07/24/79

ENTER '1' FOR RAND NOS; '2' FOR APPRAISAL OF RESULTS 1
ENTER DIGIT FOR TYPE RAND NOS. NEEDED
1 - SINGLE STAGE NOS; 2 - PAIRS OF NOS; 3 - SETS OF 3 NOS EACH
4 - SETS OF 4 NOS EACH; 5 - SMPLG FRAME; 6 - SMPLG FRAME W/PAIRS OF
NOS. 5

ENTER THE STARTING AND ENDING SERIAL NOS. OF EACH STRATUM
(SERIES) OF THE SAMPLING FRAME, STARTING ON LINE 1, AS BELOW:
    1 DATA 7530,7987,3453,8813
    2 DATA 10140,10719,15283,15824
CONTINUE W/SUBSEQUENT LINES AS NEEDED.
AFTER INPUT OF DATA, ENTER 'RUN' AND PRESS 'RETURN' KEY.
NOW AT 3500
SRU'S:1.2
READY
    1 DATA 1001,11000,35000,36008
    2 DATA37000,38050
    RUN

*SMPFRA   13:12   07/24/79

SAMPLING FRAME
DO YOU WISH A PERIODIC PAUSE FOR ADJUSTING PAPER; 1 = YES;2 =
NO? 2
DO YOU WISH BLANK LINES BETWEEN PAGES; 1 = YES;2 = NO? 2
QTY WANTED OF (W) RANDOM SMPLG FRAME NOS. (S) SPARE RANDOM
SAMPLING FRAME NOS. AND (R) A RANDOM 2-DIGIT INTEGER ARE:
QTY REG,SPARE NOS; INTEGER (W,S,R)? 10.2.29
THE RANDOM SAMPLING FRAME NOS ARE UNDUPLICATED

NO OF STRATA = 3
SIZE OF POPN = 12060

STRAT NO.	RAND NO.	SMP FRAME NO.
10 SETS IN SEQUENTIAL ORDER		
1	1173	2173
1	3884	4884
1	4105	5105
1	4317	5317
1	4776	5776
1	7526	8526
1	8107	9107
3	11494	37484
3	11859	37849
3	12029	38019

204

EXHIBIT 8.7. *(Continued)*

2 SPARE SETS IN GENERATED ORDER

1	9503	10503
2	10539	35538

END
NOW AT 3500
SRU'S:0.5
READY

EXHIBIT 8.8. Sampling Programs—Appraisal of Stratified Sample

Filename:	*Sample (STRTV)
Title:	Variables Appraisal: Stratified Single-Stage Sample
Language:	BASIC
Application:	Executable program
Purpose:	Compute difference estimates found during audit of a stratified single-stage sample. Specifically, provides the mean (average) value for the observations, the projected point estimate for the population, and the lower and upper estimates at either the 90% or the 95% confidence level. The precision, mean and population projection for each stratum are presented individually, followed by the composite measurements for the overall population.
Instructions:	Because reruns of an appraisal are common due to adjustments or increases in sample size, input data for samples with a large number of observations should be saved on a disk file on the time-sharing system prior to running *SAMPLE. The file must begin with line 200. It is a good practice to make line 200 a REMARKS line describing the contents of the file. The following presentation identifies the values placed into the file TEST1 used in the example run shown on the next page. Commas must be placed between entries, but not at the end of a line.

Note that it is not necessary to place the values for each stratum on a separate DATA line, and that multiple DATA lines can be used for a single stratum. It is the "3E33" sentinel that signals the end of a stratum.

Stratum	Population Size	Number of Zero Observations	Observation Values	Sentinel
1	20000	23	34, 45, 56, 67, 78	3E33
2	30000	43	65, 87, 90, 56	3E33

EXHIBIT 8.9. Sampling Programs

STRTV—Example of Run

*SAMPLE   13:51   07/24/79

ENTER '1' FOR RAND NOS; '2' FOR APPRAISAL OF RESULTS? 2
ENTER '1' FOR ATTRIBUTES APPRAISAL; '2' FOR VARIABLES? 2
ENTER DIGIT FOR VARIABLES APPRAISAL NEEDED
1 - SINGLE STAGE VARIABLES; 2 - STRATIFIED VARIABLES SMPL
3 - MULTISTAGE VARIAB SMPL; 4 - STRATIFIED MULTISTAGE
VARIAB SMPL; 5 - DOLLAR-UNIT SMPL? 2

STRATIFIED SMPLG FOR VARIABLES.
IF INSTRUCTIONS DESIRED, ENTER '1', ELSE '2'? 1
ENTER SUBPOPN SIZE, NO. OF ZERO VALUE OBSERVATIONS IN THE STRA-
TUM SMPL AND THE VALUE OF EACH NON-ZERO VALUE OBSERVATION
IN THE STRATUM, STARTING WITH LINE 200 PER BELOW.
ENTER '3E33' AT THE END OF THE ENTRIES FOR EACH STRATUM.
    200 DATA 6298,208,179.54,592.35,654.05,554.40,573.18,3E33
    201 DATA 1863,415,445.20,365.20,556.15,217.95,3E33
CONTINUE W/SUBSEQUENT LINE NOS. AS NEEDED.
AFTER DATA HAVE BEEN INPUT, ENTER 'RUN' & PRESS 'RETURN' KEY.

NOW AT 2830
SRU'S:0.9
READY
MERGE TEST1
READY
LIST TEST1

TEST1   18:26   01/09/80

200 REMARKS THIS IS TEST DATA USED TO DEMONSTRATE
202 REMARKS VARIABLE SAMPLE APPRAISAL PREPARATION
206 DATA 20000,23,34,45,56,67,78,3E33
206 DATA 30000,43,65,87,90,56,3E33
READY
RUN
*STRTV   13:53   07/24/79

ENTER '1' FOR 90% CONF LEVEL; '2' FOR 95% CONF LEVEL? 2
STRATIFIED-VARIABLES- 95 PCT CONF LEVEL

POPN	SMP SIZE	PRECISION	MEAN	POPN X MEAN
20000	28 + −	8.85	10.00	200000
30000	47 + −	6.29	6.34	190213

TOTAL FOR POPN OF 2 STRATA

50000	75 + −	5.18	7.80	390213

STATISTICS FOR POPN OF 2 STRATA
SIZE OF POPULATION   50000

EXHIBIT 8.9. *(Continued)*

SIZE OF STATISTICAL SAMPLE	75
SAMPLE MEAN VALUE	7.80426
POINT ESTIMATE FOR POPULATION	390213.
SAMPLING PRECISION	+ − 5.17501
SUM-(POPNSQ X SMPLG ERRORSQ)	6.69519E + 10

95 PCT CONF LIMITS

LOWER LIM	UPPER LIM	LOWER LIM EST	UPPER LIM EST
2.62924	12.9793	131462.	548963.

NOW AT 2830
SRU'S:0.2
READY

EXHIBIT 8.10.   **Evaluation of a Statistical Sample Using Difference Estimates**

THIS PROGRAM COMPUTES CONFIDENCE LIMITS OF POPN MEAN FOR 90 AND 95 PCT CONFIDENCE LEVELS BASED ON STATISTICAL SAMPLING DATA. TO USE, ENTER THE DATA STARTING W/LINE 200, PER BELOW:

200 DATA $x(1), x(2), x(3), x(4)$...............$x(N)$
(CONTINUE W/SUBSEQUENT LINE NOS. AS NEEDED)

WHERE THE X(1) ARE VALUES, OTHER THAN ZERO, OF SAMPLE OBSER-VATIONS.

AFTER ALL SAMPLE OBSERVATIONS HAVE BEEN INPUT, ENTER 'RUN' AND PRESS THE 'RETURN' KEY.
NOW AT 3810
SRU'S:0.8
READY
200 DATA 120,65,57,121,235,146,67,82,51,74,25,70,5,240,196
RUN

*VARIAB   15:42   10/03/80

ENTER '1' FOR ADDITIONAL ANALYSIS, ELSE '2'?1

SIZE OF POPULATION	?1297
SIZE OF STATISTICAL SAMPLE	?200
NO. OF ZERO VALUE OBSERVATIONS	?185

VARIABLES

VALUES OF SAMPLE STATISTICS

SIZE OF POPULATION	1297
SIZE OF STATISTICAL SAMPLE	200
MEAN VALUE-SAMPLING UNIT	7.77
EST OF STD DEVIATION	33.3752
EST OF STD ERROR OF MEAN	2.17125

EXHIBIT 8.10. *(Continued)*

PRECISION OF MEAN VALUE,
AT CONFIDENCE

LEVELS	90%	95%
LOWER LIMIT	4.18093	3.4883
UPPER LIMIT	11.3591	12.0517

POINT ESTIMATE
FOR POPN   10077.7

PRECISION OF POINT ESTIMATE,
AT CONFIDENCE

LEVELS	90%	95%
LOWER LIMIT	5422.67	4524.33
UPPER LIMIT	14732.7	15631.1

THE DIFFERENCE BETWEEN THE POINT ESTIMATE AND THE UPPER OR LOWER LIMIT AT THE 95 PERCENT CONFIDENCE LEVEL EQUALS 5553.36 WHICH IS + − 55.1055 PERCENT OF POINT ESTIMATE:
TABLE OF SMPL SIZES FOR THIS POPN DESIRED? '1' = YES; '2' = NO?1

THE TABLE BELOW SHOWS THE SAMPLE SIZES NEEDED TO ACHIEVE OTHER CONFIDENCE LIMITS.

SAMPLE SIZE NEEDED	90 PERCENT CONF LEVEL		95 PERCENT CONF LEVEL	
	FOR PRECISION EXPRESSED AS A			
	+ − PCT	+ − VALUE	+ − PCT	+ − VALUE
1295	+ − .83 %	+ − 84	+ − 1 %	+ − 101
1288	+ − 1.68 %	+ − 169	+ − 2 %	+ − 202
1276	+ − 2.51 %	+ − 253	+ − 3 %	+ − 302
1261	+ − 3.35 %	+ − 338	+ − 4 %	+ − 403
1241	+ − 4.19 %	+ − 422	+ − 5 %	+ − 504
1218	+ − 5.03 %	+ − 507	+ − 6 %	+ − 605
1192	+ − 5.86 %	+ − 591	+ − 7 %	+ − 705
1163	+ − 6.71 %	+ − 676	+ − 8 %	+ − 806
1131	+ − 7.54 %	+ − 760	+ − 9 %	+ − 907
1099	+ − 8.38 %	+ − 845	+ − 10 %	+ − 1008
1064	+ − 9.22 %	+ − 929	+ − 11 %	+ − 1109
1029	+ − 10.06 %	+ − 1014	+ − 12 %	+ − 1209
994	+ − 10.90 %	+ − 1098	+ − 13 %	+ − 1310
958	+ − 11.74 %	+ − 1183	+ − 14 %	+ − 1411
922	+ − 12.57 %	+ − 1267	+ − 15 %	+ − 1512
887	+ − 13.42 %	+ − 1352	+ − 16 %	+ − 1612
852	+ − 14.25 %	+ − 1436	+ − 17 %	+ − 1713
818	+ − 15.09 %	+ − 1521	+ − 18 %	+ − 1814
785	+ − 15.93 %	+ − 1605	+ − 19 %	+ − 1915
753	+ − 16.76 %	+ − 1689	+ − 20 %	+ − 2016
494	+ − 25.14 %	+ − 2534	+ − 30 %	+ − 3023
333	+ − 33.53 %	+ − 3379	+ − 40 %	+ − 4031
235	+ − 41.91 %	+ − 4224	+ − 50 %	+ − 5039

EXHIBIT 8.10. (Continued)

ADDITIONAL ANALYSIS OF SAMPLE RESULTS

PRECISION OF MEAN VALUE-90 PCT CONF LEVEL	+ − 3.58907
PRECISION OF MEAN VALUE-95 PCT CONF LEVEL	+ -- 4.2817
COEFFICIENT OF VARIATION (SD/MEAN)	4.29539
RATIO OF ONE STANDARD ERROR TO MEAN (SE/MEAN)	.27944
ESTIMATE OF STANDARD SKEWNESS	5.12804
ESTIMATE OF KURTOSIS	30.9509
STANDARD EXCESS KURTOSIS (KURTOSIS MINUS 3)	27.9509

GUIDELINES FOR APPLICATION

Audit Decisions

The auditor may or may not decide to test transactions in performing an audit. He may, for example, decide on the basis of overall comparisons and other auditing procedures that a test of transactions is unnecessary. Also, the amounts involved may not be sufficiently material to warrant testing.

However, in reviewing internal controls the auditor is often faced with situations that require sampling of transactions. The best of control systems cannot eliminate errors resulting from system breakdowns. Overall reviews or tests of a few transactions may not be sufficient to disclose whether internal controls are operating effectively. The company's procedures may appear to be adequate, but the auditor generally must test actual transactions to determine whether the procedures have been followed in practice. If tests are made, statistical sampling should be considered as a basis for arriving at more valid conclusions.

If the test of transactions indicates that the operations are acceptable, no further work is required. Where errors are found, however, the auditor is faced with the decisions described below in arriving at a conclusion.

Isolating Errors.   Through review of the types of errors and their causes, the auditor may be able to isolate the total amount of errors. For example, one vendor may be submitting erroneous invoices, and a review of all of the vendor's invoices may pinpoint all the errors. As another example, one accounting clerk may be causing the errors, and a special review of his work may be required. This type of analysis may enable the auditor to determine the amount of deficiency as well as the basic cause.

Reporting on Items Examined.   When the auditor encounters significant errors, it may only be necessary to report the results of the tests to operating personnel. The nature of the errors may be such that it is the responsibility of operational managers to strengthen procedures and determine the magnitude of errors. As part of his review the auditor may determine the causes for the condition and make specific recommendations for corrective action. Unless the auditor projects the results of his statistical sample, however, management is provided only with errors or amounts pertaining to the items examined.

Performing 100% Audit.   Although the auditor is not expected to perform a detailed examination, in some instances he is called upon to do so when significant errors are found. An example is where recoveries are due from vendors, and the specific vendors and amounts have to be identified. In other instances, the necessity to have exact information as to the extent and amount of errors may not be justified in terms of cost involved. Under such circumstances, a projection of a statistical sample may suffice.

Projecting Results of Sample.   If the selection of items for the test is made on a random basis, the results can be evaluated using statistical tables. The number and dollar amount of errors can be projected to determine the range of errors in the entire field at a given confidence level. The projection can be used to make an adjustment, or as a basis for decisions of the kind described in the preceding paragraphs.

Audit Sampling Decision Model.   A decision model for assisting the auditor in the use of statistical sampling in audits is shown in Exhibit 8.11.

Extending the Use of Statistical Sampling

Internal auditors are continuously experimenting with the use of statistical sampling in operating areas. Examples are in the review of equipment to assure effective utilization, and in tests of purchase requisitions to determine the timeliness of filling requests.

EXHIBIT 8.11.   Audit Sampling Decision Model

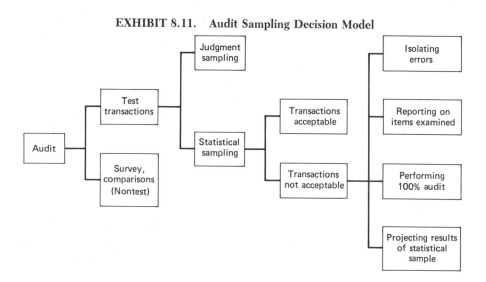

There are many other areas in which the auditor performs tests of transactions or items in connection with various auditing techniques or procedures. These procedures include inquiry, observation, vouching, confirmation, computation, and analysis. In performing these tests, statistical sampling should be considered as a useful method for improving audit results.

As a basis for extending the use of statistical sampling, the auditor can review areas in which testing was performed on prior audits. An analysis is then made of the objective of each test, period covered, use of judgment or statistical sampling, number of items in both the field and sample, results of test, and feasibility of using statistical sampling in subsequent audits. A review of this nature has the following benefits:

1. Pinpoints areas where auditors have been overauditing on the basis of judgment sampling.
2. Indicates examples where testing has been performed for short periods (for example, one month, although the auditor reports for the entire year).
3. Indicates areas where auditors have not been testing other than sensitive or high-dollar items.
4. Discloses areas where statistical sampling is practicable in light of objectives of the test, number of items in the field, and prior testing performed.

Techniques for Efficient Use

The following techniques will facilitate the use of statistical sampling by auditors:

1. *Combining Audit Steps*. Savings in audit time can be achieved if various audit steps are performed as part of the same statistical sample. This can be done by testing for as many attributes or characteristics as possible in the sample. For instance, in a review of purchases the primary audit objective may be to determine whether there is adequate documentary support. In addition, the auditor may decide to include tests, as part of the statistical sample, to determine whether excess materials are being acquired.
2. *Using Preliminary Sample*. Auditors often devote considerable effort to developing a sampling plan based on a certain confidence level, precision, and expected error rate or standard deviation. However, in many cases there is insufficient information on which to develop the sampling plan, as, for example, in a first audit. By taking a preliminary sample of from 50 to 100 items, the auditor is in a better position to make decisions on the extent of sampling required. The preliminary sample can then be included as part of the final sample. Also, the results of the preliminary sample may lead the auditor to conclude that no additional testing is required.
3. *Performing Interim Audits*. When a sampling plan is prepared in advance for a year, the items can be examined on a monthly or other interim basis without waiting until the end of the year. Thus staff auditors can be

utilized when available to perform the statistical sampling on an interim basis. For example, if the sample calls for examination of every hundredth voucher, these can be selected for examination as the transaction is processed.

4. *Enlarging the Field.* A basic consideration in statistical sampling is that the sample size does not vary to a great extent with an increase in field size. Thus savings can be obtained by sampling for longer periods of time, or from a field composed of more than one department or division. In some cases the auditor may decide to test a particular account for a two-year period, with selection of items during the first year on an interim basis as part of the two-year test.

5. *Using Attributes and Variables Sampling.* In some cases the auditor does not know in advance whether variables sampling is required. Since variables sampling is more complex to apply, he may pick a random sample for attributes, evaluate the results, and decide at that point, on the basis of dollar errors, whether variables sampling is required. If it is, the sample can be projected at that point or incorporated in an extended sample selected for variables. The important point is that once a sample is taken on a random basis, it can be evaluated using different sampling methods.

6. *Applying Simple Methods.* Some auditors believe that they must use complex methods of sampling and spend considerable effort and study in arriving at the method to use. In most instances, a simple estimation sample will provide adequate results, without the need for techniques that are difficult to understand, apply, and explain.

    This does not mean that the auditor can overlook judgment in his tests. Sensitive items should be examined in addition to a random selection of items, if required. These can be examined on a 100% basis or sampled as part of a separate stratum.

7. *Determining Costs versus Benefits.* The auditor should consider the costs of examining each sampling unit when considering extending his sample. The costs of additional work should be compared with benefits from obtaining increased confidence or precision in the final results.

The manner in which statistical sampling techniques can be used in everyday practice can be illustrated by the following typical examples.

Computer Selection of Sample of Disbursements

The company's yearly disbursements, made on a centralized basis, are approximately $650 million. The number of checks written is about 420,000 per year, or 35,000 a month. All accounting records are maintained on a large-scale, third-generation computer.

Objectives. The internal auditor was interested in determining that disbursements were properly supported, reasonable, justified, and economical. In order to see that controls over disbursements are operative on a continuing basis, he performs interim checks of disbursements during the year. In addition to the review of high-dollar, sensitive items, he makes selective tests of low-dollar items (items under $5,000). Although stratified sampling could have been used, the following illustrates the use of statistical sampling with the computer in testing the low-dollar items only.

Statistical Sampling Plan. With a universe to test of about 350,000 items under $5000, the auditor reviewed prior experience in the audit of disbursements and found that the maximum error in tests of any of the attributes examined was 5%. With an expected error rate of 5% and a desired precision of ±2% at the 90% confidence level, the sample size required was 321.[6] Using systematic sampling, every 1,090th item would be selected (350,000 ÷ 321).

Computer Selection. A flowchart was prepared and given to the programmers for developing a program to select the items during normal processing of vouchers. The program was prepared at the time the system was being developed for the computer, thus minimizing changes required. An interval of 545 was used in order to select twice the number of items (642, or 2 × 321) in the sampling plan. This was done to provide additional items in case the auditor wished to increase his sample. By looking at every other item selected by the computer, he would be examining 321 and could extend his sample if required without an additional computer run. A printout of the items selected was furnished to the auditor.

Coordination with Other Auditors. The selection of the first items in January was made at random jointly with the outside public accountants and government auditors in residence. The purpose of the joint selection was to assure objectivity. The results of the internal auditor's review of the vouchers were made available to both the public accountants and the government auditors, thus limiting the cash auditing required. Since printouts were made available monthly, the auditors could review disbursements on a continuing basis, thus pinpointing weaknesses in controls as soon as they occurred.

Statistical Sample of Personnel Management

The internal auditor in a large research and development organization was interested in expanding the audit of payroll to include attributes related to personnel management. Once the statistical sample was selected, these attributes could be incorporated in the audit program applied to each payroll check (sampling unit) selected.

Objective. The objective of the statistical sample was first, to determine the accuracy of the total company payroll for the year, and second, to determine whether controls over personnel administration were adequate for the period.

---

[6]See Arkin, *Handbook of Sampling for Auditing and Accounting*, p. 297.

Attributes.   In accordance with the objectives, each item on the payroll selected for test was verified by checking hours and rates, as well as payroll
deductions, to underlying documents and records. In addition, factors relating
to the individual throughout the personnel program cycle were evaluated, such
as the basis for hiring, assignment, training and advancement, and utilization.

Statistical Sampling Plan.   Based on the prior year's experience and staff projections for the coming year, it was estimated that there would be approximately
104,000 annual payroll payments made for the 4,000 average number of employees. With an expected error rate of 2% and a desired precision of ±1.25%
at the 90% confidence level, a sample of 339 was selected.[7]

Selection.   Since all payroll checks are serially numbered, random numbers
were selected between 1 and 104,000. The selection of the random numbers
and the rearrangement of the numbers in sequence were done by use of a
computer. As the payroll checks with the preselected numbers were written,
they were automatically selected for interim audit work (about 28 per month).

Evaluation.   The error rates for attributes related to payroll accuracy were
minimal, resulting in general acceptability of payroll amounts. Review of attributes related to general personnel management also disclosed the effectiveness of controls, except in the area of utilization. It was found that 10% of the
employees paid in the sample had excessive idle time. At the 90% confidence
level this represents 7.3 to 13.3% of the total number of payments for the year.[8]
Analysis indicated that the employees with excessive idle time were charging
the idle time to various indirect cost categories. Because sample results showed
that the idle time was extensive, the results could be disclosed to management
without the need for further sampling.

Analysis as to Cause.   Review of the sample results indicated that management
was not separately identifying idle time. Analysis indicated that certain types
of research work had decreased during the year, and researchers who ordinarily
charged their time direct were idle for long periods and were charging time
to various indirect categories. Summary information was not provided management as to the extent of this type of idle time. Based on recommendations
of the internal auditor, a special computer report was prepared, showing direct
project workers by department who were idle for more than one month. This
report was then used to facilitate certain management decisions, such as action
required on work-load scheduling, hiring and termination policies, and pricing
under changing conditions.

[7]Ibid., p. 296.
[8]Ibid., p. 400, noninterpolated table.

Statistical Sample of Facilities Management

As part of the audit of facilities in a manufacturing company, the internal auditor wished to test selectively internal controls over fixed assets. There were 5,470 items of fixed assets on hand according to the property records, with a book value of $22.5 million. Previous audits had covered only specific segments, such as accuracy of depreciation, accuracy of property records, and verification of acquisitions and disposals.

Objective.   The purpose of the statistical procedure was to test management decisions, review internal controls, and verify the accuracy of fixed-asset records.

Attributes.   For each item selected in the statistical sample, the approach was to:

1. Review controls over the determination of need, acquisition, utilization, maintenance, and disposal. When items were acquired in prior years, reliance is placed on previous audit work, with current emphasis on savings through buying equipment now leased, or examining present use of the equipment.
2. Verify the accuracy of recording purchase, depreciation, transfer, and disposal.
3. Make physical examination of items, determining that they are on hand, and observe or test that they are properly maintained and in use.

Sampling Plan.   Based on an expected error rate of not over 5%, with a precision of ±2.5% at the 90% confidence level, a sample size of 199 was drawn.[9] The expected error rate was based on the results of previous audits as well as potential deficiencies in areas not audited before.

Selection.   The sampling unit was each item of equipment on hand during the year, both owned and leased. Each item of equipment was recorded on a separate IBM card. Using systematic sampling, each twenty-seventh card was selected for testing (total universe of 5,470 divided by sample size of 199). Since there are approximately 145 IBM cards to the inch, a card would be selected every 0.19 inch by measuring off with a ruler.

Results.   Minor deficiencies were noted in recording fixed asset transactions and in calculating depreciation. In addition, there were 12 deficiencies in providing adequate documentation to support lease versus buy decisions. These represented a 6% error rate and, when projected to the universe at the 90%

[9]Ibid., p. 297.

confidence level, an error rate between 3.6 and 9.5%.[10] A recommendation was made to improve documentation in support of these decisions.

Further analysis indicated that there were four examples of office equipment being leased when the period of the lease justified purchase. These represented a 2% error rate and, when projected at the 90% confidence level, an error rate between 0.7 and 4.5%.

The annual savings per year through purchase were $1,000. These savings were projected using variables sampling to provide an estimate of the total annual savings on leased equipment. With a confidence of 90% it was estimated that the annual savings through purchasing rather than leasing equipment were between $19,309 and $35,719, and were most likely to be $27,514.[11] Based on the potential dollar savings a review was made of all lease agreements. Annual savings of $25,500 were obtained in equipment costs by changing from lease to purchase agreements. This amount was within the confidence limits disclosed by the sample.

Conclusions. The review included tests of controls in management areas, as well as in accounting, for items selected in the statistical sample. The auditor was thus able to obtain information about the facilities as a whole (universe), for the use of both management and the public accountant.

CONCLUDING STATEMENT TO PART I

With this chapter we complete our discussion of the basic foundation aspects of internal auditing. These eight chapters are applicable to the actual operating work of the internal auditor to be discussed in the chapters that follow. These foundation concepts are directly applicable to all of the remaining material—the managing of the internal auditing activity in Part II, the internal auditing problems and opportunities of the various operational areas in Part III, and the special relationships and conclusions in Part IV. The sections in this Part I should therefore be reviewed from time to time in connection with the consideration of the new material.

[10]Ibid., p. 388.

[11]Ibid., p. 456. Calculated by multiplying the standard deviation of $13.16 by the multiple in the table of 0.1140 and then projecting it to determine the range.

PART TWO

Administering Internal Auditing Activities

CHAPTER NINE

Planning and Organizing
Internal Auditing Activities

PLANNING

Administering for Results

In this section we describe how to bring our efforts together to obtain meaningful results. Previous chapters dealt with the foundations and standards of internal auditing, the nature of controls, and the operational approach of the internal auditor. Here we are concerned with the manner in which the work of the internal auditor is administered. In running his department the internal auditor performs the management role of utilizing existing resources best to accomplish established objectives.

The administrative effort is necessarily a practical type of activity that must be adapted to the individual company situation. We can, however, identify the major types of administrative problems and consider the merits of alternative ways of dealing with them. In this connection it will be useful to use the conventional framework of the management process—planning, organizing, providing resources, administering (directing, coordinating, and leading), and controlling—a framework that was discussed in Chapter 3. We are now interested, however, in the specific application by the internal auditor as he directs his activities to provide maximum service.

With the publication of standards by The Institute of Internal Auditors, there is new emphasis on the quality of work. In performing the various administrative functions the internal auditor must reexamine audit techniques and approaches to determine conformance with standards of the profession. There is thus increased concern as to how the audit is performed.

Dynamic Approach to Planning

The internal auditor's role should be a dynamic one, continually changing to meet the needs of the organization. A posture of habitual reviews of selected areas may provide certain assurance, but there is the need for changes as circumstances warrant. These changes may include coverage of new areas, assistance to management in solving problems, and development of new techniques for audit.

Planning is especially important in the face of uncertainty. The demands of modern business life make it important that the internal auditor change his plans as the needs arise. When management's needs change, he must analyze trends and develop the flexibility to adjust to the new conditions.

Nature of Planning

Planning is concerned with the formulation of goals and objectives which provide the matching of environmental opportunities and available resources to achieve the most effective utilization of those resources.[1] To the internal auditor the resources are his staff, his budget, and the reputation he has earned with company personnel. These resources include both what he actually has in hand, and what he can reasonably expect to get as a result of further management support. The environment includes the company of which he is a part, and in a broader sense also the world of which the company is a part. Within the company it includes his boss, his boss's bosses, and other personnel at all levels. There are the executives responsible for the various operational components audited, the intermediate managers, and the rank and file personnel. Some of these individuals will be supportive, some hostile, and some relatively indifferent. Some individuals will be in such a position that their attitudes are very important, while in other cases, the relationship is more detached. It is this environment that the internal auditor seeks to appraise—again as it currently exists and as it might be changed over time. It is then through the study and evaluation of the resources and the environment that goals and objectives can be formulated in an intelligent manner. But while planning is vitally concerned with this process of formulating objectives, it goes still further. Planning has to do with developing the supporting strategies, policies, procedures, and programs that will best assure that actions carried out currently will move the internal auditing department toward the achievement of the future objectives. Thus to the internal auditor, planning means projecting where he wants to go in the future, and then devising the means that will help him best to get there. Like every other manager, the internal auditor must be concerned about his present and future role.

Agreement on Objectives

In operating an internal auditing department there must be a clear understanding of objectives. What does management expect of the internal auditor? What types of coverage and findings are desired? These and other questions must be answered in formulating objectives.

---

[1]See also Chapter 3.

In prior chapters of this book we considered the kind of role that internal auditors could and should play in the organizations of which they are a part. These professional concepts must now be defined in specific terms by each individual internal auditor who is responsible for the internal auditing activities in his own company. This is to say that one must determine where it is he wants to go, before he can intelligently shape and direct current operational actions. This is not an easy task and hence it is frequently not done adequately. However, the more carefully and sharply it is done, the more likely it is that the supporting activities will be carried out effectively. Additionally, it is important to note that goals and objectives thus established are not for all time. As conditions change goals and objectives should be reappraised, with such modification of them as is appropriate.

What kinds of questions does the establishment of goals and objectives actually involve? We suggest that the following aspects should be included:

1. *Type of Managerial Assistance.* A determination needs to be made as to the specific types of managerial assistance which the internal auditing group will seek to render. This will include the question of whether that service will be limited to ascertaining compliance, and the extent to which a definitive effort will be made to search out and report possibilities for improvement. In the latter case the question needs to be faced as to whether improvement means operational efficiency of existing policies and procedures, or, additionally, the reappraisal of underlying policies and decisions. This latter approach, of course, holds the greatest potential for meaningful management service.

2. *Level of Managerial Assistance.* The related question that also needs to be faced is the extent to which the reappraisal role will involve specific organizational levels. How far up in the organization should the internal auditor go in carrying out his review role? Reference here is to what the internal auditor seeks in this respect, even if not now existing. In this case access to the chief executive officer level holds the greatest promise for management service.

3. *Degree of Independence.* An important part of the established goals and objectives is the extent to which the internal auditor seeks independence, both in terms of access to various parts of the company's operations, and authority to report on all matters pertaining to the company's welfare. As we have previously seen, such independence is vital to full management service.

4. *Resources to Be Provided.* Goals and objectives should also properly include the identification of the kind of internal auditing department that is sought after. What is meant here is the size of the department, the composition of it in terms of people and their qualifications, and the level of budgetary support. These determinations will necessarily be linked to projections of the growth of the company.

5. *Excellence of Service.* An important aspect of setting goals and objectives is the quality of service to be provided management. The internal auditor is interested in fulfilling the needs of management, and thus strives to improve the contribution of audits. Compliance with the standards of the profession will help to achieve this. In addition, the internal auditor will wish to achieve excellence through experimentation with new techniques and reexamination of product to determine how best to satisfy management expectations.

6. *Excellence of Staff.* The selection and training of staff are extremely important in internal auditing. It is the quality of staff that determines whether a particular audit, and audits in general, will be productive. It is thus important that goals and objectives properly consider the desired level of staff development.

Formulating Strategy

Strategy in managerial terms represents the major operational approaches by which the goals and objectives are achieved, over time. They are closely related to the goals and objectives and are in fact very much taken into consideration when formulating the goals and objectives. Also strategies and goals and objectives are sometimes reviewed as identical. Conceptually, however, they are different. Goals and objectives are where one wants to go, and what is to be achieved, whereas strategies are a means of accomplishing the desired results. Strategies are sometimes also called major policies, the term "major" distinguishing these higher-level determinations from the more routine supporting policies pertaining to the implementation actions. Strategy to the internal auditor will include such considerations as the following:

1. *Manner of Organizing.* A major means by which the internal auditor will seek to achieve the established goals and objectives is through the manner in which he organizes his own internal auditing staff. This is essentially the question of how much decentralization and physical dispersion there should be. These matters are discussed later in further detail.

2. *Staffing Policies.* Closely related to the organizational question is the matter of staffing policy. At the highest level this has to do with the kinds of qualifications that will be established for staff personnel, and with the required numbers of the various kinds of people. These problems are discussed in more detail in Chapter 10.

3. *Manner of Administering.* The administering of the actual internal auditing activities is a combination of issuing instructions, coordinating the efforts of the individual persons, and providing effective leadership. The major strategy or policy issue here is the extent and manner in which the directing aspect of the administering is delegated, within the framework of the selected organizational approach. Related also is the extent to which the directing will be participative. The trend here is definitely toward greater delegation and more of a democratic approach.

4. *Extent of Formal Auditing Procedures*. Related closely to the broader issue of directing is the extent to which auditing procedures should be developed in writing, the form of those written procedures, and the degree of latitude allowed in their use.

5. *Manner of Reporting*. A further aspect of the current administration is the question of how findings resulting from the audit work shall be disseminated to the various interested parties. This includes the subsidiary questions of timing and substance. These questions are discussed in more detail in Chapter 12.

6. *Flexible Programming*. Often changes need to be made in programs because of unforeseen audit requirements and management requests. Although these cannot be predicted with any accuracy, a flexible approach will enable the maximum service with existing resources.

7. *Level of Aggressiveness*. An overall strategy issue is the level of aggressiveness that the internal auditor and his staff should adopt as they carry out their total internal auditing activity. What is meant here is the extent to which the internal auditors will base their actions on high standards, how imaginative and innovative they will be, and how strongly they will press for new and higher levels of management service. Assuming that there is the proper foundation of competence, there is still the question of the level of courage to be adopted in the face of greater risk. While clearly the realization of greater internal auditing potentials is linked to a high level of courage, the level of that courage is a policy question that must be worked out by each internal auditing group.

8. *Action on Recommendations*. The internal auditor is interested in the action taken on recommendations as well as reporting the conditions leading to the recommendations. The strategy would be to obtain management acceptance of the findings, agreement to take constructive action—whether to correct deficiencies or to make new improvements—and actual implementation of the recommendations. A well-written report serves no useful purpose unless it is read by management and used as a framework for appropriate action.

9. *Identification of Time Periods*. All of the previous aspects of the goals and objectives need to be related to specific time periods, normally in years. In certain cases also the accomplishment of the individual goals and objectives will be sought after in specific phases—so much in one year, so much in two years, and the like.

The process here raises the further question of whether these goals and objectives should be based on the internal auditor's private desires, or whether there must also be management agreement. Quite clearly it is the latter that is desired, and ultimately needed. In any event, that agreement is more likely to be achieved if the internal auditor first thinks through the issues carefully and presents his version in the proper manner. To the extent, however, that the management will not accept the internal auditor's views, two sets of goals and objectives then emerge—those accepted by management (which are, therefore, available for general company knowledge) and those which are temporarily held in abeyance by the internal auditor. In such a situation the latter set serves as a useful base point for subsequent negotiation with management, as conditions become more favorable.

Objective measures should be determined whenever possible for goals and accomplishments in the stated periods. These will enable the internal auditor to measure performance and evaluate progress to date. Specific projects should be developed, where feasible, to accomplish each of the objectives. Exhibit 9.1 is an example of projects under one objective.

Development of Supporting Policies and Procedures

The higher-level strategies and major policies must now be backed up by a great number of supporting policies and operational procedures. Many of these will relate to the previously mentioned areas of organizing, staffing, manuals, and reports, all of which will be discussed in our later more detailed coverage of those areas. Some will relate to the current day-to-day administration of current work matters, to be discussed in more detail in Chapter 11. Others will have to do with the more formal planning activities to be discussed next. We pause at this point only to recognize several important general aspects of these supporting policies and procedures.

One of these general aspects is the way in which these policies and procedures come into existence. Where no formal policy or procedure exists, the basis of action is an independent determination of what shall be done each time the particular problem arises. The advantage of this approach is a fresh appraisal of the problem based on the specific situation. The disadvantages are first, that a great deal of valuable time is consumed over and over again while wrestling with the same kind of problem. Second, there is the lack of consistency which is bound to result when different people are dealing with the same type of problem, or even by the same individual over a period of time. The practical needs, therefore, at some point lead to the development of written policies and procedures.

A second significant aspect of all policies and procedures is the extent to which they rigidly provide for particular types of action or, on the contrary, leave some flexibility in their application. A related factor here is the extent to which the policy or procedure is detailed. More detailed statements generally tend to be more restrictive. The determinations here, of course, need to be made with care, with appropriate consideration of the importance of exact compliance of the matter being covered, the stage of development of the particular problem, and the effect on the motivation and overall effectiveness of the users.

Finally, it must be recognized that the development of policies and procedures by the internal auditor covering his own activities is closely linked to what exists in the way of company policies and procedures. In many instances company policy covers the matter—as, for example, in the case of allowed

EXHIBIT 9.1. Objective 5: Excellence of Service

Project	Area	Target	Project Coordinator	Dates Beginning	Dates Ending
1	Improve timeliness of audit reports	Decrease by 30% the number of reports taking more than 3 months to complete	Smith	3/1	11/30
2	Experiment with new techniques—audit software package	Use software package in audit of three new areas: purchasing, cost transfers, and payroll	Brown	1/15	10/15

vacations. In other cases the company policy or procedure needs something of a supplementary nature, as would normally be the case, for example, in the development of job descriptions. In still other cases the problems are completely in the hands of the internal auditor. Illustrative would be policies and procedures covering the actual audit reviews and the reporting of results.

The basic policy statement under which the internal auditor functions is the charter, or formal written document for the internal auditing department. The Standards issued by The Institute of Internal Auditors state: "The director of internal auditing shall have a statement of purpose, authority, and responsibility for the internal auditing department." The director is responsible for seeking a statement that is approved by management and accepted by the board. As official company policy, this statement serves not only as a guide to the internal auditing function but as a clarifying document for various levels of managers as to the role of internal auditing. Exhibit 9.2 is an example of an internal auditing charter.

Annual Budget

While the use of longer-range profit plans will vary quite widely as between different companies, it is normal practice in any well-run organization that an annual budget be developed. In its final form this budget represents the agreement with top management as to the spending and performance levels for each operational component, subject to later change only in accordance with specified procedures. The budget thus becomes an important means by which

---

EXHIBIT 9.2.   Internal Auditing Charter

Statement of Responsibilities

Authority: By recommendation of the President and with approval of the Audit Committee of the Board of Directors, this Statement of Responsibilities of the Internal Audit Department has been developed.

Standards: It is expected that the Internal Audit Department will maintain the highest professional standards commensurate with standards issued by The Institute of Internal Auditors. To provide consistently high quality work, it is expected that managerial policies of the Department will include a means to audit the auditors.

Scope: The Internal Audit Department should examine and evaluate the adequacy and effectiveness of the company's system of internal control. This includes the review of compliance with policies, procedures, and laws, the safeguarding of assets, the economic and efficient use of resources, and the accomplishment of stated objectives and goals.

Access to Records: The Department will have access to all records, property and personnel of the parent company and controlled affiliated companies.

Independence: By organizational structures, relationships, and assignments, it is required that internal audit personnel maintain objectivity with respect to the areas reviewed. The annual budget of the Internal Audit Department, the annual audit plan, and the organization structures are to be reviewed with the Audit Committee to ensure the adequacy and effectiveness of this function.

---

management controls the various parts of the company operations, and in turn the total operations. But the even greater significance of the budget is the planning effort that must be carried out to develop and support the budgetary proposals.

In the case of the internal auditor the budgetary process means that he must plan the total auditing program to be carried out over the year ahead. This will include how he is going to implement that program in terms of number of personnel, travel, and supporting services. Here he must justify both the overall validity of his proposed audit plan, and the efficiency with which he is going to carry out the program. What locations are to be covered? What kind of audit work is to be done? How long will it take to do the job? What staff will be required? What will be the travel costs? What supporting services need to be provided? The answers to these questions require a depth analysis of the major factors pertaining to the operations of the internal auditing department.

The plans as finally approved and supported by financial budgets then provide a major basis for administering and controlling the day-to-day operations during the budget year. How tight that control will be depends on how much flexibility has been approved in the finalization of the budget, and on the overall policies of the company as to budgetary compliance. Under best practice the budget is viewed as a major guideline, but one that is subject to change when it is agreed that new developments warrant such change.

Developing Work Programs

Work programs play an important role in a successful internal audit operation. Without a program, efforts may drift and be overly subject to pressures from without.

Periods Covered.   Basically, the program is a planning document, in which areas are selected for audit coverage for a period, generally a year. In some instances, a longer period is used, such as two to five years. However, it is frequently difficult to plan more than a year in advance because of special requests by management, changes in business operations, losses of personnel, and delays in completing audits. Sometimes scheduled areas are preempted by special audits with higher priority. One alternative is to prepare annual programs and to develop a priority list of backlogged audits to be performed at a later date. Because of changes during the year, it is often desirable to schedule programming meetings monthly to revise the program for the ensuing three-month period.

Coordination.   Prior to developing the program the auditor should request suggestions from management for areas of emphasis. This should include selected middle management as well as top management because of their familiarity with operations. Audit managers who have the responsibility for individual operational areas should also be requested to submit their proposals for audit coverage. In addition, other key members of the audit staff should also be contacted, and innovative ideas obtained for audits. The preparation of the program thus stimulates the staff to reexamine objectives and select those audits of most importance.

Benefits are also derived from coordinating with other audit groups. In addition to the public accountants, government auditors may perform reviews of operational and financial matters, and information should be obtained as to their reported areas of concern and planned future audits. After preparation of the plan, it should be distributed to various management and audit groups. An excerpt from an organization's annual work plan is shown in Exhibit 9.3.

Priorities. In selecting audits for the annual work program, many factors have to be considered. The following are some criteria to be applied in reviewing potential audits for coverage.

1. *Prior Findings.* Deficiencies may have been reported in the prior audit, indicating the need for follow-up review. This is especially important where significant findings were reported in more than one prior audit.

2. *Management Requests.* The chief executive officer or other high official may request specific audits. In addition, the Audit Committee may ask for coverage of various areas. These requests must, of course, be given priority. Also, various levels of management may ask for audits, such as department heads or branch managers.

3. *Prior Coverage.* Significant delays may have occurred in auditing or reauditing an area because of higher priorities. As the time between audits increases, additional weight has to be assigned this area for audit coverage.

4. *Required Internal Audits.* Compliance with certain legislative or other governmental requirements may have been assigned to the internal auditing department. Also, the department may have a fixed role to play in providing assistance to the outside public accounting firm in its annual audit.[2] Thus some assignments represent fixed requirements that have to be budgeted.

5. *Sensitive Areas.* There may be sensitive areas within a company that require audits. An example is the review of conflicts of interest in purchasing in the aftermath of unfavorable publicity. These sensitive areas

EXHIBIT 9.3.   Annual Work-Load Plan, 198–

Description of Assignment	Date of Prior Audit	Date Guide to Be Prepared	Issue Date	Location					Total Hours
				A	B	C	D	E	
Maintenance	None	2/15	6/15	300		400			700
Computer utilization	6/10/–	N/A	9/15		40	30	70		140

[2]See Chapter 29.

may change in view of revised conditions, or may be inherent in the nature of the company's operation.

In selecting areas for inclusion in the program the internal auditor often has to use his best judgment. Some organizations have experimented with applying weighting factors to stated criteria to provide a basis for decision making. This may be especially worthwhile when there is a large backlog of audits for which resources are not available.

ORGANIZING THE INTERNAL AUDITING EFFORT

As previously noted, the actions taken in organizing the internal auditing activities at their highest level become one of the major strategies for achieving the goals and objectives of the internal auditing effort. At the same time a great number of supporting policies and procedures revolve around organizing approaches. Moreover, the organization of the internal auditing department has much to do with the current administrative direction and control of the group. This is bound to be true since organizing has to do with the way the responsibilities are assigned to specific individuals and groups, and resulting accountabilities established. We need to focus more sharply then on the merits of alternative organization approaches and to understand better some of the major problems involved in effective organization.[3]

Turning first to organizational structure, we can identify at least four commonly used approaches. These are on the basis of types of audits, conformance to the organizational structure of the company, by geographical area, and by combining the aforementioned approaches with a headquarters staff. Needless to say, these approaches can be used independently or combined to any extent desired.

Organization by Type of Audit

The approach of organizing by type of audit rests on the very practical logic that individual internal auditors will be most effective if they are assigned the review responsibility for a particular type of company operation. This is the recognition of the efficiency that is achieved through specialization. The problems pertaining to the particular company operation can be studied closely and special expertise developed in dealing with them. In one large company there are a great number of district and regional sales offices having the same kinds of operational activity. That company has responded by developing a special internal auditing group that does nothing but audit these sales offices. The practical benefits here are believed to be substantial.

At the same time, however, it is necessary to recognize that there are certain disadvantages to using the "type of audit" approach. One of these disadvantages

[3]See also Chapter 5.

is that there is unavoidably some duplication of travel costs and a related loss of time. Where several types of audits exist at a given field location, it is necessary that each specialist journey to that location. This extra cost in time and money must then be clearly offset by the great efficiency of the several experts. A second disadvantage—and probably the more important one—is that carrying out different types of audits to a considerable extent makes for a more effective audit. This is because a variety of assignments keeps an internal auditor from getting in a rut and performing his audit review in too mechanical a fashion. As we know, variety is the spice of life and keeps us all alert and well motivated. In this connection also the new auditor brings a fresh approach to old problems, something that frequently pays good dividends. Finally also, it is important to note that mixed assignments for individual internal auditors lend themselves best to growth and professional development.

On balance, therefore, there is the danger that the gains through specialization may be more than offset by the offsetting factors just outlined. There is even perhaps the danger that the gains will appear to be more substantial than they actually are. The conclusion is that this approach should be used very cautiously. In borderline cases it is more likely that the use of the "type of audit" approach to organizational structure is at odds with achieving maximum quality of the internal auditing effort. Especially will this be true as the concern of the internal auditor moves further away from reviewing lower-level procedures, and in the direction of broader managerial issues.

Organizing a Parallel Company Organization

When a company is very large there is the very practical alternative that the assignment of internal auditing responsibilities should be along the same lines as the company organization. Thus there would be individual internal auditors, or groups of internal auditors, assigned to specific line and staff company components. When these components are specialized there is again the previously mentioned benefit of greater depth understanding of the particular type of operational activity, and the related development of greater expertise. Another advantage in this approach is that company executives in charge of the various operations, and other operating personnel as well, can develop more effective working relationships with the responsible internal auditing personnel. The internal auditing people come to speak the language of the particular type of operation and can, it is believed, become more useful to the individual managements. The internal auditors can also develop more effective working relationships with responsible managers at all levels.

But again also there are certain disadvantages. Some of these disadvantages are the same as existed in connection with the "type of audit" approach—duplication of field travel, the lesser motivation of the internal auditor, and reduced management development. There is also another major disadvantage here in that the more definitive alliance with particular divisional or staff personnel can sometimes undermine the independence and objectivity of the individual internal auditors. To a greater extent there may come to be the atmosphere of being an employee of that organizational component. The internal auditor can also very easily develop a more personal attachment to the particular organizational component and its managerial personnel. It is possible, of course, for a strong central management of the internal auditing department to offset this pull on the internal auditor, but there is the question of whether that counter-pull can be fully effective, or even whether it is really something a central internal auditing headquarters ought to have to worry about. Again we conclude that this type of auditing approach is more controversial than it first appears, and that is should be used very cautiously.

Area Approach to Organizing

Under the area approach, all the company's operations in a given geographical area are assigned to a particular internal auditor or group of internal auditors. This type of approach frequently includes the setting up of regional offices in those individual areas, but the latter action is really a separate problem and will be discussed later. In some cases this geographical approach can automatically, to some extent, become a "type of audit" or "company organization" approach when particular types of company operations are concentrated in particular geographic areas, but usually there will be some diversity of audit assignments in the individual areas. The advantages and disadvantages of this kind of an organizational approach are reasonably well indicated by the evaluation of the first two types. On balance, this is the approach that more often seems to be best, and it is indeed the type of approach most commonly used in practice. The choice of the areas to be used will depend on the scope of the company's operations. In some cases there may be a number of areas within the United States. In other cases the international company operations may constitute a separate area. In still other cases, there may be a number of international areas.

Use of Headquarters Staff

The three approaches to the organization of field activities just discussed will always be supplemented by some kind of headquarters organization. At its minimum this headquarters will consist of the head of the internal auditing department, commonly carrying the title of General Auditor or Director of Internal Auditing, and his secretary. Its expansion above this minimum depends on what work is delegated to the line components and what types of services are provided by the central unit. In the typical situation all or most all audit reports will be reviewed and processed at the central headquarters. Typically also, manuals will be developed there, or at least finalized, and distributed by the central headquarters. There is also some planning and administrative work that either must be done, or is preferably done, at the company headquarters. Most of these activities will require secretarial and staff personnel. Other activities will be done in part by the general auditor but will usually require additional assistance. This additional assistance can be provided by one or more assistant general auditors or by other planning and administrative personnel. Normally, the general auditor will want one of these individuals to have the authority to act for him in his absence, thus ensuring a needed continuity of operations.

Special Functional Staff. A somewhat different kind of problem exists when a special type of expertise is needed but where it is not practicable or efficient to provide each of the line components with this particular skill. A good illustration of this problem is the case of needed computer expertise. There is first of all the question of whether each auditor, or perhaps each auditor of a given level, should have enough computer expertise to handle existing problems. The alternative is to have one or more computer experts at the central headquarters who will have special expertise and will be available to assist the other personnel. Usually, the latter is the more practical solution, if not absolutely necessary. In addition, this central expert, or group of experts, can cover the necessary liaison with the company group that is handling computer operations and computer systems development. Other illustrations of situations where special expertise is needed can include training, statistical sampling, report writing, and the like. In each case there is the problem of the extent to which the central headquarters should include personnel who have the particular type of expertise either for the direct assistance of the general auditor, or for assistance to field personnel as they carry out their various field audits.

Illustrative Organization Chart

A typical organization chart of the internal auditing department, using the area-type approach, would appear as shown in Exhibit 9.4.

EXHIBIT 9.4.   Organization of Internal Auditing Department

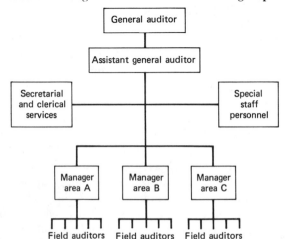

Personnel Complement

The number of staff needed for each assignment is directly related to the types of jobs. Normally, more responsible job assignments and more capable people can be translated into smaller numbers of total personnel. But again much depends on the kind of auditing that is contemplated. Much also depends on the opportunities for service and company benefit that are perceived. In the usual situation the general auditor and his associates are convinced that they could use better people and more of them than company management is willing to approve. In most companies there is a relentless pressure for cost reduction on the part of all company components. What this means is that the performance of existing personnel must clearly demonstrate the sufficiency of profitable return to the company to win the approval of further increases in staff. At the same time this level of profitable performance, that is, the value that is obtained over and above the cost of the individual auditor, must be maintained adequately as a basis for resisting pressures for staff reduction. The general auditor's concern should be to determine fairly what numbers are most optimum, irrespective of whether such numbers are larger or smaller than the present complement. Additionally, this evaluation needs to be made in terms of dollar cost to equate for the varying cost of personnel with different qualifications. In this connection the continuing shift toward higher-level internal auditing should mean a more than proportional reduction of less qualified personnel. Thus costs as a whole may go up while the total numbers rise slowly, stand still, or actually decline.

Extent of Decentralization of Authority

The alternative ways of developing organizational structure may to a varying extent suggest the decentralization of authority. However, the problem here is technically independent, as any type of structural approach can be administered on a very centralized or decentralized basis. The central question here is the extent to which individual decisions should be made and actions taken at lower organizational levels, as opposed to requiring clearance or approval by the central headquarters (or in other cases by intermediary organizational levels). The kinds of decisions and actions involved will include modification of required audit procedures, need to report given types of deficiencies, negotiation of actions on findings, manner of reporting findings, finalization of reports, signing reports, and follow-up of corrective action covering reported deficiencies.

The arguments, or claimed benefits, that support decentralization generally are:

1. Relief of higher level personnel so that they can deal with other important matters.
2. Lower-level personnel have better facts and understanding of the problem and can act in a more intelligent manner.

3. Delays are avoided that would be necessary if higher-level personnel must be contacted.

4. Lower-level personnel are better motivated and will have the opportunity to develop to a greater extent.

5. Lower-level personnel will then be viewed with more respect by other company personnel, thus increasing their overall effectiveness.

6. Such delegations are more consistent with the effort to develop a partnership relationship between the auditor and the auditee.

The counter-arguments generally include the following:

1. Lower-level personnel may not know the full implications of particular types of judgments and decisions.

2. It is then much more difficult to maintain uniform company-wide standards.

3. The company image of the internal auditing effort may be improperly presented.

4. The higher-level person runs the risk of being charged with abdicating his responsibility for important parts of the internal auditing effort, especially when something goes wrong.

5. The higher-level person can get out of touch with current developments.

6. A valuable communications link is lost for coordination and personnel administration purposes.

There are, of course, in-between positions possible where some matters are delegated and others are not. There is also the possibility of adopting a procedure for automatic ratification after a given period of time. Still another approach is to carry out a post-review of actions taken pursuant to the delegation. It is not practicable to lay down a single solution to all these alternatives. What we can say is that the general auditor at the top has a final responsibility for all actions of his staff. Similarly, the persons at each organizational level have a responsibility for the actions of their subordinates. Granted that there must be delegations, the basic necessity is that the higher-level personnel, starting with the general auditor himself, must weigh carefully the merits of the scope of each type of delegation, and the effectiveness of the related supplementary controls, and be satisfied that on balance his particular mode of handling is in the total company interests. The delegator must also be prepared to amend that delegation when developments indicate that the existing delegation is not working out satisfactorily.

Decentralization on a Functional Basis.   A special kind of decentralization of responsibility exists when internal auditing groups exist in the company which are not part of the regular company internal auditing group, but which instead report directly to the management of individual subsidiaries and divisions. The responsibility of the central group in this kind of situation is to serve in an advisory capacity, and, therefore, the administrative considerations being dealt with in this chapter are not directly involved. There is, however, a special professional concern as to the effectiveness of the local auditing groups that goes beyond the normal interest in the effectiveness of all company operations. The special relationship to the local auditing groups will normally be indicated on a complete company organization chart by the showing of dotted lines. In these situations it should be clear that the existence of the lower-level groups responsible to local management does not preclude the regular internal auditing department from making such supplementary reviews of the subsidiaries and divisions as is deemed necessary. There cannot be a responsibility for company-wide internal auditing results except where there is both access and line control over all supplementary internal auditing work.

Use of Field Offices

In the greater number of cases all members of the internal auditing staff are based at the central headquarters location, and travel from that home base to the various places where the company operations need to be reviewed. One type of deviation that frequently develops first, however, is that an individual auditor's travel time will be substantially reduced if he is based somewhere nearer his major audit work. The pressure here is the extra cost of travel, as well as the time lost because of that travel. In many cases also the pressure for the new arrangement comes from the field auditor's family. For these reasons an individual auditor is sometimes based away from the headquarters area. The next step, which then often follows, is that the person now based at a different location needs office facilities and supporting office services. At this point a field office may be established, and perhaps other personnel assigned to that office. The administrative question here is to weigh the relative merits and advantages of such an arrangement. On the side of the claimed advanatages are the following:

1. Reduction of travel time and expense.
2. Making it more practicable to use married persons or others who would often not accept the travel required.
3. Better service to the company operations in the geographical area served by the field office.
4. Greater motivation to the internal auditor who is administering his own activities to a greater extent.

The disadvantages include the following:

1. The extra cost of maintaining the field office.
2. The greater possibility that the personnel at the field office may lose objectivity through the closer relationship with personnel of audited locations.

3. Less direct contact with the personnel assigned to the field office, thus leading to a lack of adequate control.

4. The greater difficulty of maintaining uniform company-wide standards.

On balance, the advantages of field offices can be exaggerated and, accordingly, great care should be exercised in moving in this direction. This is especially to be emphasized because it is much harder to reverse the approach once it has been adopted. There is also often a temptation to judge the move on the basis of the persons first sent out by the central headquarters. When, however, new personnel are recruited for the field office, and often from the area adjacent to the field office (as is frequently done at foreign field offices) the closeness of the link with the central headquarters may deteriorate. If the move to the field offices is made, it is all the more important then to shift personnel back and forth periodically, so that the staffing at any point of time includes personnel who are familiar with headquarters needs. It is also important that these individuals are persons in whom the central headquarters can have adequate confidence.

Organizing to Handle Nonauditing Assignments

We know that the possibility exists of the internal auditing group being asked to carry out operational activities of a protective nature for management, even though those operational activities are so much a part of the regular day-to-day company activities that they do not satisfactorily meet the test of true internal auditing. Illustrative would be the responsibility for reviewing and approving current cash disbursements before those disbursements are actually made. Assuming that the internal auditing group has no alternative than to accept such an assignment, the recommended organizational approach is to segregate these additional activities from the normal internal auditing activities, and to subject those special activities to the periodic review of the regular internal auditing group. The organization chart of the internal auditing department would then be as shown in Exhibit 9.5.

Wherever possible, however, this kind of a situation should be avoided. The basic problem is that the dual responsibilities will tend to infringe on the time needed by the general auditor for his higher-level internal auditing activities. In addition, there is the very real danger that the dual responsibilities will weaken the image that the general auditor projects to the other company personnel.

Informal Organizational Arrangements

Our consideration of organizational arrangements has dealt chiefly with so-called formal types of structure. Such formal arrangements are essential guidelines for efficient operations. In addition, there are various kinds of interrelationships in the internal auditing department that cut across the established organizational lines. Such interrelationships are informal and take place as

EXHIBIT 9.5.   Organization of Dual-Function Internal Auditing Department

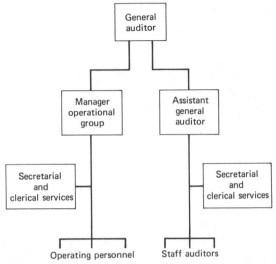

necessary to meet current operational needs. They will exist under all types of formal arrangements. Within reasonable limits the informal organizational arrangements serve a useful operational purpose. In addition, they often point the way to needed formal modifications. If carried too far, however, they can undermine the effectiveness of the basic organizational approach. The important thing, therefore, is to recognize their necessity, but to keep them within sensible bounds.

Periodic Review of Organizational Arrangements

In closing the discussion of organizational arrangements it is important to emphasize the changing nature of organizational needs as they apply to the internal auditing group. These organizational needs are a reflection of the changing company situation. As the company operations change, both in terms of size and basic nature, the organizational approach being followed by the internal auditing group also needs to be reappraised. Organizational arrangements in the last analysis are a means to an end, never an end in themselves. Although this reappraisal can and should be made on a rather continuous basis, the preparation of the annual budget provides an especially good opportunity to carry out a more complete reevaluation. At the same time, consideration can be given to the matters of staff administration and control that are discussed in Chapter 11. The latter activities have an important bearing on organizational arrangements.

CHAPTER TEN

Staffing, Training, and Preparatory Activities

STAFFING

Providing resources in the management of an internal auditing department starts with obtaining adequate funds so that needed material and human resources can be procured. On the material side there is the need for office facilities and equipment, proper maintenance, supplies, travel, and the like. The major problem of providing resources, however, has to do with the staffing. We therefore devote this chapter to that major resource need of the internal auditing department.

Nature of Staffing

The staffing of the internal auditing department has to do with providing the personnel to carry on the activities of the department, and thus to achieve the established objectives. This part of the administrative function depends directly on the organization plan discussed in Chapter 9. The decisions made there have determined the types of organizational responsibility, the level of qualifications needed, and the number of people required. The staffing needs also go beyond the current situation and look to the future. These future needs are determined by the plans of the company and the related plans of the internal auditing department. The future staffing needs must also be properly projected and programs developed by which the additional personnel can be provided.

The staffing functions of the internal auditing department, with its central focus on providing needed personnel, cover a spectrum that runs from the recruitment of internal auditing personnel, through the training and development of them, to policies relating to their ongoing employment, and ending when the individual voluntarily or involuntarily leaves the department. The activities carried out in these areas supplement and are interrelated with the personnel services provided by the company.[1] The staffing activities merge into the directing and controlling aspects of the total administrative effort. Since

---

[1]Personnel activities of the company as a whole are discussed in Chapter 20.

everything the internal auditing department does is through and by people, the staffing activities are of major importance. Basically, the nature and quality of services that can be performed are dependent on the capabilities of staff.

Recruitment

The initial step in the staffing process of the internal auditing department is the recruitment of personnel. Recruitment policy is, of course, closely related both to what kind of people are wanted and to what extent the present staff is being trained and developed.

Within the Company. Some General Auditors prefer to fill vacancies from personnel in the company. Company personnel are considered to have familiarity with operations and procedures of the organization, and are given the opportunity to apply for positions that become vacant.

1. *Promotion of Internal Auditors.* A heavy emphasis on internal development will mean that most higher-level openings will be filled from the ranks. Under a strong training program staff personnel are continually given more challenging assignments to prepare them for higher-level work. When openings arise, they are given the opportunity to fill them. Managers have previously had the opportunity to observe their work and know their capabilities firsthand. In addition, promotion from within makes higher jobs available for other personnel. This makes for good morale. Also, recruitment is often easier if an internal auditing department has a record of progressive advancement from within. This, of course, requires a program of extensive training and development of staff to be successful.

2. *Transfers of Experienced Personnel.* One of the widely used sources of recruitment is from other company components. One advantage of this approach is that the candidate is normally much better known in terms of character, personality, degree of industry, and other personal qualifications. A second advantage is that his experience and work qualifications can be more precisely evaluated. In this connection the candidate's familiarity with a specific phase of the company's activities can be exactly what is wanted. Since that experience is in the company, it therefore also includes a familiartiy with company policies and practices. This approach can be especially advantageous from an overall company point of view. The movement of company personnel into the internal auditing group can provide both special training and a broader perspective of company operations. It needs to be recognized, of course, that this is a two-way street, in that people will then also be leaving the internal auditing department to go back into various company assignments. But this outward flow can also be useful in establishing a better understanding of the internal auditing role with other company people. It also builds good staff morale because of the greater number of career opportunities which are

provided to internal auditors, not only within the department but in higher management positions in the company.

3. *Use of Management Trainees.* In some companies assistants are hired directly from colleges and universities and enrolled in a management training program. Under this program they are given an opportunity to rotate through various departments of the company before permanent assignment. A short tour of duty in internal auditing not only provides them with excellent training in analyzing and evaluating controls, but also provides the department with a valuable resource.

Outside Recruitment. In many areas the recruitment must extend to areas outside the company. The internal auditing department must weigh carefully the advantages and disadvantages of this type of recruitment in filling vacancies.

1. *Public Accountants.* Since the early history of internal auditing public accountants have been a fertile source for recruitment. Their experience in carrying out audit procedures and gathering evidence in accordance with professional standards has been a useful asset in making the transition to internal auditing. Often there is close coordination between the public accountant and internal auditors, and each becomes familiar with the other's work and capabilities. When vacancies occur in the internal audit department, many companies look to public accountants for able candidates.

2. *Universities and Colleges.* The employment of new graduates of educational institutions depends in part on the related programs for training and development. There is, however, an increasing tendency to hire some graduates of both undergraduate colleges and graduate-level business schools. As previously noted, this may also be done as a part of a larger company program. From the standpoint of the internal auditing department there is the advantage of getting a person who has up-to-date competence in new skills; for example, operations research, computer operations, human behavior, and the like. From the standpoint of the candidate, there is the opportunity to learn about all the company's operations, with the option at a future time of deciding what direction he may then want his career to take, either in that company or elsewhere.

   In order to hire outstanding candidates, it is often necessary to interview students at college, establish strong relations with faculty, give speeches before accounting and student groups, and attend employer –student functions. This provides the faculty and students with an opportunity to become familiar with the company, and gives company internal auditors an opportunity to know the students. Through contacts of this nature the internal auditing department may be able to hire students with excellent potential.

3. *Internal Auditors.* In some cases the General Auditor may wish to hire applicants with previous internal auditing experience. The applicant may

be required to have the Certified Internal Auditor certificate. This certificate has become the badge of the profession, and is evidence that the applicant has a better understanding of internal audit concepts and procedures. Suitable candidates can be found at meetings and conferences of The Institute of Internal Auditors and through advertisements in The Institute's Journal, *The Internal Auditor*.

4. *Non-Accountants*. The broader scope of the internal auditing activities has very naturally increased the need for persons who have other types of qualifications than accounting. Individuals with various combinations of education and experience may very often be needed in such operational areas as computer operations, production, construction, quality control, legal, and the like. Such additions can add strength to the capabilities of the internal auditing group and enable it to expand its range of management service. These special capabilities can be especially advantageous when they are combined with some financial orientation. It is also useful to recognize that the accountant designation is no longer restricted to the so-called "bookkeeper" type but instead covers a wide range of other operational capabilities. The important point is that an increasing wide range of skills is needed for internal auditing, and that the recruitment effort should focus on those needed skills irrespective of standard designations. At the same time it must be recognized that the internal auditing group can never be expected to have special expertise in every type of operational activity. What is sought is a reasonable balance.

Job Descriptions

To be useful, job descriptions must be specific as to the requirements for performing work. If stated in general terms, they serve only as a description of functions rather than a statement of job responsibilities. Critical elements of the job should be pinpointed and performance standards separately stated so that the employee can be rated realistically.

Job descriptions are usually prepared for the General Auditor, Audit Managers, Audit Supervisors, Senior Auditors, and Assistant Auditors. Examples of job descriptions for the various levels of auditors and for a specialist are given in Exhibits 10.1 to 10.6.

TRAINING AND DEVELOPMENT

Training activities of the internal auditing department build on the qualifications of personnel recruited. These activities are one of the major means by which the internal auditing bridges the gap between present and needed staff resources. In addition, an effective training program enables staff to assume additional responsibilities and advance in the organization. Thus the program

EXHIBIT 10.1.   **Job Description: General Auditor, Internal Auditing Department**

I. *Introduction*

The internal auditing department is responsible for the performance of audits of all departments, offices, and functions of the company. Audits are made in conformance with Standards for the Professional Practice of Internal Auditing issued by The Institute of Internal Auditors.

II. *Major Duties and Responsibilities*

A. Directs his subordinates in carrying out the functions of an internal auditing department, which includes planning, coordinating, and directing the conduct of all audits of the company and subsidiaries.

B. Develops policies and procedures for carrying out the audit activity.

C. Prepares long-range and annual work plans after consultation with department heads and other company officials.

D. Initiates special audits and performs studies to provide assistance to management in solving problems.

E. Reviews the effectiveness of internal controls in safeguarding company assets, achieving efficiency and economy in operations, obtaining compliance with company and government regulations, and achieving results.

F. Develops an effective staff management program which includes recruitment, training, performance appraisal, and promotion of internal auditors.

G. Provides management with reports of individual audits and periodic summaries of findings.

H. Maintains a follow-up system on deficiencies noted in audits and determines the adequacy of responsive action taken.

I. Monitors the preparation of the budget for the internal audit department and is responsible for expenditures made within the budget.

J. Performs special reviews for fraud, following up on allegations and coordinating closely with law officials.

K. Coordinates his audit planning and findings with the audit committee of the board of directors in accordance with the charter.

L. Coordinates his audit planning and other internal auditing activities with the outside public accountant.

III. *Supervision and Guidance Received*

Reports directly to the president of the company. Works independently in performing audits, subject to approval by the president of the annual work plan.

---

acts as an incentive for drawing capable people into the department and keeping them.

Each internal audit department, however, needs to reexamine continuously the quality of its training program. Sometimes training activities fall into a fixed pattern which is not sufficiently responsive to changing conditions. Other times, training is relegated to a minor role so as not to interfere with current demand

EXHIBIT 10.2.   Job Description: Audit Manager, Internal Auditing Department

I. *Introduction*

The internal auditing department is responsible for the performance of audits of all activities of the company. Audits are made in accordance with Standards for the Professional Practice of Internal Auditing issued by The Institute of Internal Auditors.

II. *Major Duties and Responsibilities*

A. Assists the general auditor in the performance of his duties, serving on a rotating basis as the general auditor in his absence.

B. Develops long-range and annual work-load requirements for the areas to which he is assigned.

C. Determines staffing requirements for his assignments, assuring that capable personnel are available to perform the work.

D. Plans, develops, and reviews the performance of the segment of the work plan under his responsibility.

E. Provides technical assistance in resolving complex problems arising during the audit.

F. Develops final audit report, assuring that standards are met as to required quality.

G. Evaluates and recommends appropriate action in regard to special requests for audit and allegations of fraud.

H. Initiates suggestions for innovative audits and revised methods of conducting audits.

I. Assures that audit work meets performance standards and is done within budgets for worker-days and elapsed time.

III. *Supervision and Guidance Received*

Works directly under the supervision of the general auditor, receiving general guidance and assurance as needed. Keeps the general auditor informed as to progress on audits and major problems encountered.

for audit service. To be meaningful, however, on-job and off-job training need to be continually updated to meet the current and expected needs of staff.

Individual Training Objectives

The importance of setting individual training objectives cannot be overemphasized. There appears to be no substitute for the first step in training—the supervisor must determine clear objectives for his subordinates. He must know exactly what he would like to have changed, after examining each one's work. He also must plan as clearly as possible the kind of performance toward which he is aiming after the change.

In setting training objectives, individual differences must necessarily be recognized. Employees generally have varied educational and experience back-

EXHIBIT 10.3.   Job Description: Audit Supervisor, Internal Auditing Department

I. *Introduction*

The internal auditing department is responsible for the performance of audits of all activities of the company. Audits are made in conformance with Standards for the Professional Practice of Internal Auditing issued by The Institute of Internal Auditors.

II. *Major Duties and Responsibilities*

A. Supervises the accomplishment of two or more concurrent audits.
B. Plans work to be accomplished by audits and sets priorities.
C. Selects and assigns staff as needed to conduct planned audits.
D. Provides guidance to audit staff on areas of emphasis and allocations of time.
E. Coordinates with other supervisors on scheduling audits and assigning and releasing staff.
F. Provides technical guidance in developing the audit plan and performing the field work.
G. Assures that standards of planning, field work, and reporting are met by subordinate auditors.
H. Monitors the conduct of audits to assure that time budgets are met.
I. Approves changes in scope of audit and resulting adjustments in budgets.
J. Participates in recruitment, selection, training, and evaluation of staff.
K. Identifies areas requiring special attention by management, including patterns of deficiencies and sensitive matters.

III. *Supervision and Guidance Received*

Works under an audit manager, providing information to the audit manager and general auditor as to results of audits performed. Is responsible for the independent accomplishment of work assignments. Receives guidance as needed on significant problems encountered in the audit.

---

grounds, and different capacities, or learning curves, in their ability to benefit from specific experience. Training objectives should thus be set for each auditor based on individual needs, as well as the needs of the company. These objectives should not be static but should be changed in accordance with progress made by the employee during the course of his various assignments. Exhibit 10.7 is an example of an individual training plan prepared for a staff member based on specific developmental needs.

Because of their importance, training objectives become part of the audit objectives in planning assignments. It may thus be necessary that time be made available for a staff member to leave a job to attend a specific training course. Also, sufficient time should be budgeted on assignments to provide developmental opportunities. Short-run considerations thus have to give way to long-run improvements in individual performance.

EXHIBIT 10.4.   Job Description: Senior Auditor, Internal Auditing Department

I. *Introduction*

The internal auditing department is responsible for the performance of audits of all departments, offices, and functions of the company. Audits are made in conformance with Standards for the Professional Practice of Internal Auditing issued by The Institute of Internal Auditors.

II. *Major Duties and Responsibilities*

   A. Plans and conducts complete audits of company activities and serves as a team leader over other auditors. Exercises a high degree of responsibility and personal judgment. Evaluates the effectiveness of internal controls reflected in policies, procedures, and practices. Determines the reliability of accounting and other records. Evaluates the degree to which management practices are conducted in an efficient and economic manner, the extent to which operations conform with policies and regulations, and the degree to which program results have been achieved.

   B. Assists the supervisor in planning the audit schedule, and develops the individual audit steps of the assignment. Instructs individual team members on their responsibilities.

   C. Conducts entrance and closing conferences with audited officials. Is responsible for informing them of findings and obtaining their responses.

   D. Reviews working papers and findings prepared by subordinates and prepares draft report.

   E. Prepares internal reports such as audit plans, progress reports, and reports of significant findings being developed.

III. *Supervision and Guidance Received*

Is under the administrative and technical supervision of a supervisory auditor. Receives assignments with general instruction as to purpose and problems. Works independently in developing the audit program, which is reviewed by supervisors to assure consistency among audits and professional competence.

On-Job Training

In addition to the need for extensive education and training classes in modern internal auditing practice, on-job training is also of utmost importance. Although classrooms try to simulate reality, they cannot take the place of day-to-day experience. It is on the job that the auditor has the opportunity to solve problems under time pressures, supervise a staff, and work with management to arrive at conclusions and gain acceptance of findings.

In considering on-job training, the problems of making a qualitative appraisal of experience come to mind. What are the standards for satisfactory experience for internal auditors? How well do the practices of my department meet these standards? What can the profession do to improve the experience and training which are given staff members?

**EXHIBIT 10.5.   Job Description: Assistant Auditor, Internal Auditing
Department**

I. *Introduction*

The internal auditing department is responsible for the performance of audits
of all departments, offices, and functions of the company. Audits are made in
accordance with Standards for the Professional Practice of Internal Auditing
issued by The Institute of Internal Auditors.

II. *Major Duties and Responsibilities*

A. Assists in planning work and developing approach to audit.
B. Performs assigned audit or segment of audit under the direction of a senior
auditor.
C. Develops or assists in the development of audit programs.
D. Evaluates the adequacy and effectiveness of operating controls.
E. Assists in selecting audit procedures and performing audit program.
F. Prepares working papers summarizing evidentiary data obtained and con-
clusions reached.
G. Discusses results of work with management, including deficiencies found
and recommended corrective action.
H. Participates in writing findings developed in the audit, including making
revisions as needed.

III. *Supervision and Guidance Received*

Is under the administrative and technical direction of a senior auditor. Receives
assignments with specific instruction as to purpose and how to perform work.
Receives continuing direction, with work monitored closely by his supervisors.

Planning Developmental Assignments.   Whenever practicable, assignments
should not be made on a piecemeal basis, but in accordance with a plan that
results in the continuing development of the auditor as well as in timely completion of audits. Often, this cannot be done because of the exigencies of work
load; we are all familiar with rush assignments and the problem of obtaining
personnel to perform them. However, much can be accomplished by a deliberate intent on the part of supervisors to make assignments purposeful.

The assignment of an auditor to different supervisors is recognized as a
valuable learning tool. However, unless each supervisor becomes familiar with
the manner in which the auditor has performed in the past and the areas in
which he needs improvement, the benefits from an assignment may be less-
ened. A review of prior performance appraisals and discussion with other staff
members will provide the supervisor with information that will assist in carrying
out both the audit assignment and the desired training.

Diversification.   The development of a staff member into a top-flight senior
or manager requires training in the ability to handle increasingly more complex

EXHIBIT 10.6. Job Description: Coordinator, Advanced Audit Techniques, Internal Auditing Department

I. *Introduction*

The internal auditing department is responsible for the performance of audits of all departments, offices, and functions of the company. Audits are made in accordance with Standards for the Professional Practice of Internal Auditing issued by The Institute of Internal Auditors.

II. *Major Duties and Responsibilities*

A. Assists in the selection and development of the most cost-effective audit approaches and techniques used.

B. Provides technical guidance to staff on the use of advanced audit techniques, such as statistical sampling and computer auditing.

C. Develops and modifies audit software packages for application to specific audit assignments.

D. Participants in auditing computer systems, including the adequacy of controls in systems under development.

E. Monitors and provides technical assistance to auditors in the development and application of statistical sampling plans.

F. Obtains knowledge of various computer programming languages to meet the variety of computer needs in internal auditing.

G. Performs cost/benefit studies on the feasibility of purchasing computers for use by the internal auditing department compared with using a time-sharing system.

H. Meets with staff members, representatives of other companies, and professional and business organizations to discuss complex problems in the use of advanced techniques.

I. Develops instructions and procedures for the use of advanced techniques by the staff.

J. Provides training courses in advanced audit techniques for various levels of personnel.

III. *Supervision and Guidance Received*

Works under the general supervision of the general auditor. Because of the technical nature of the position, the coordinator has wide latitude in the exercise of professional judgment.

---

problems. It is through diversification of audit assignments that the staff member becomes familiar with problems in the audit of various parts of a business whole. The auditor who has worked for a year on the audit of inventory and supply, for example, is going to obtain a specialized knowledge of these areas only. On the other hand, the staff member who has been assigned to the audit of various operational areas on a planned basis over a period of time will have a better opportunity to obtain the wide experience needed to advance. Under

EXHIBIT 10.7. Individual Training Plan

Name: Robert Jackson

Date: December 31, 198–

Developmental Needs (from Appraisals)

 Needs to develop findings more fully, providing additional analysis of cause and effect

 Needs to give more direction to staff members and monitor their work

 Needs to use statistical sampling in audits, as well as computer software packages

 Needs to develop himself professionally by studying for the CIA or CPA examination

Training Received since Last Training Plan

 Accelerated Reading Course

 Introduction to Computer Auditing

Types of Assignments and Training for Reaching Goals

 1. Immediate Goal: Promotion to Supervisor

  Additional writing experience, including rewrite of findings

  Course in Supervision and Management

  Hands-on experience in using computer software packages

 2. Long-Range Goal: Promotion to Manager

  Enrollment in certification study course

Discussion with Employee

 Employee participated in selecting the training and stated that he will complete the course in Supervision and Management and the course in Statistical Sampling within the next year. He also asked for larger audits with more subordinates assigned, since he has been working primarily by himself during the last year on special reviews.

          Signed:

          Supervisor: Kelly White

          Employee: Robert Jackson

best practice a record is kept of types of assignments by staff as a basis for planning.

Supervision and Job Instruction. There are many opportunities for the supervising auditor to aid in on-job training in the course of planning, organizing, and controlling the performance of audit assignments. The supervisor must always keep in mind that he is responsible for the field training of staff assigned. This responsibility is easily overlooked with the pressures of the job. He should, however, realize that his own position is strengthened by his ability to develop subordinates. This training may take several forms, such as instruction, demonstration, encouragement, criticism, and advice. The subordinate should be made to feel that criticism is given in a constructive manner with the object of helping him improve.

In general, the method of giving instruction to subordinates plays an important part in on-job training. Communication of objectives down through the organization is very important, such as by explaining the meaning and purpose of the work to be undertaken. Specific assignments should be related to the overall audit program. The subordinate should thoroughly understand instructions given. Supervised study of prior years' reports and working papers, or working papers prepared on similar audits, will assist the auditor in his development.

Counseling. The importance of counseling must be emphasized as a device for augmenting and strengthening the learning process in on-job training. An effective counseling program helps to point out an individual's weaknesses and suggest ways to correct them. Counseling serves to obtain the staff member's viewpoint, and thus furthers his participation in shaping his own training program. It may also assist in the staff member's personal adjustment to the firm's work practices and personnel. Through use of effective counseling techniques the staff member can thus be motivated to accelerate his learning and ability to advance.

Leadership Development. The personal development of the auditor is an important element of on-job training. The ability to get along well with others should be emphasized. The ability to talk intelligently and sell ideas is important. Effective leadership of subordinates is also an integral part of his development.

There are many opportunities for the supervisor to develop these traits on the job. The staff member should be encouraged to express himself in various job situations. He should be encouraged to participate in discussions with department heads and with his superiors. He should be stimulated to arrive at independent decisions and gather sufficient evidence to support his position. His ability to plan, organize, and control the work of subordinates should be emphasized, including the ability to get along with his staff.

Delegation of Responsibilities. It is primarily through the assumption of additional responsibilities that the auditor develops. Supervisors must be alert to the strengths and weaknesses of staff, and continually try to assign them more difficult work. This work must be challenging to the auditor so that he will benefit from the assignment. The supervisor must then give the auditor freedom to do the work, providing him assistance and guidance as needed. The final product, however, should be that of the auditor. In turn, the auditor should delegate as much as possible to his subordinates to develop their capabilities.

Periodic Appraisal of Performance

Performance appraisals serve to inform various levels of management and supervisors as to the abilities of staff members and what they are accomplishing. Appraisals thus provide important input in connection with the consideration of promotion, compensation, transfer, and removal. They also serve as a useful tool in staff training through:

  Requirement for periodic appraisal and documentation of strengths and weaknesses.

  Aid to determining basic training needs and planning methods of improving performance.

  Basis for assignment of staff to individual jobs.

  Aid to counseling employee as to his ability in meeting performance standards.

  Permanent record of individual trends (for example, reaching a plateau).

Performance appraisals are usually completed at the end of each job assignment. In addition, composite ratings are prepared, usually on an annual basis, to provide an overall evaluation of work under various supervisors. The value of the appraisals can be significantly increased, with proper instruction given to supervisors on how to fill them out, including the importance of full disclosure as a guiding principle. This involves, on the one hand, the understanding by supervisors that criticism on the appraisal is meant to help the subordinate. On the other hand, there should be an understanding by staff that criticisms shown in appraisals are constructive in nature and are used as a basis for helping him progress and advance. An example of a performance appraisal form is given in Exhibit 10.8

Performance Standards

To have an effective performance appraisal system it is necessary that performance standards be established. These permit the accurate evaluation of job performance on an objective rather than a subjective basis. When possible the standards should be stated in quantifiable terms that can be easily interpreted. Although this may not be readily possible for all internal auditing positions, an attempt should be made to quantify the standards as far as practicable. Employees should be encouraged to participate in establishing these quantified standards, both to gain support for the system and to assure fair and equitable treatment.

In developing performance standards the job description should first be reviewed and a list made of major responsibilities. One or more objectives for each responsibility are then identified. Then one or more standards of performance are established for each objective, either in quantitative or qualitative terms. Finally, points can be assigned to each objective if desired.

Because of the many responsibilities reported on in appraisals it may not be practicable to develop standards for each rating element. Exhibit 10.9 is an example of standards for planning and directing an audit, stated in qualitative terms for a supervisor.

Formal Training

Although the training provided in the course of audits is ongoing and contributes the most in shaping individual progress, there is also the need for classroom instruction. Attendance at training classes is arranged for staff members to meet recurring needs, such as in strengthening report writing. New technology and changes in the profession must be studied for application in day-to-day assignments. Successful approaches for performing audits have to be disseminated to the entire staff. For these and other reasons, each internal auditing department should have a program of formal training.

Larger departments have found it desirable to sponsor some training classes within the company. In addition to being cost effective, the training can be tailored to meet the specific needs of the company. In some cases, internal auditors in the department are used as instructors, and training material is standardized. In other instances, outside instructors are hired to provide training classes in selected subjects (e.g., statistical sampling). In-house capability can then be developed for teaching subsequent courses.

Professional courses available in the community should be periodically screened. In some instances local colleges schedule courses which are applicable to internal auditing. Professional organizations also publish training schedules of interest to auditors. Some of the organizations are:

The Institute of Internal Auditors

American Institute of Certified Public Accountants

EDP Auditors Association

American Management Association

Association of Government Accountants

National Association of Accountants

Orientation. The purpose of orientation is to provide the new employee with information to enable him to do his job. Through off-job instruction, generally two to three days, he gains familiartiy with procedures and methods of work. When employees are hired at the same time, such as recent college graduates,

EXHIBIT 10.8. Staff Performance Appraisal

Employee's
Soc. Sec. No.

Name

Rating Period
From   To

Rater's
Signature

Position

Reviewer's
Signature

Appraisal Section

Explanation of Appraisal Categories:
N, Irrelevant or no opportunity to observe employee's performance
A, Did not meet requirements
B, Usually met, but rarely exceeded minimum requirements
C, Met and sometimes exceeded requirements
D, Exceeded requirements, but not to an exceptional degree
E, Exceeded requirements to an exceptional degree

Part A: For All Employees

Part B: Supervisors

1. Quantity and timeliness   A B C D E   10. Oral communications   N A B C D E   1. Delegating   A B C D E

2. Quality of work products   A B C D E   11. Writing skills   N A B C D E   2. Administrative responsibilities   A B C D E

3. Job knowledge   N A B C D E   12. Informing/consulting N A B C D E   3. Training, development, and counseling   A B C D E

	N	A	B	C	D	E
4. Initiative	☐	☐	☐	☐	☐	☐
5. Persistence	☐	☐	☐	☐	☐	☐
6. Adaptability/flexibility	☐	☐	☐	☐	☐	☐
7. Functioning in interpersonal situations	☐	☐	☐	☐	☐	☐
8. Resourcefulness	☐	☐	☐	☐	☐	☐
9. Planning, organizing, and setting priorities	☐	☐	☐	☐	☐	☐

	N	A	B	C	D	E
13. Negotiating	☐	☐	☐	☐	☐	☐
14. Analytical reasoning	☐	☐	☐	☐	☐	☐
15. Decision making	☐	☐	☐	☐	☐	☐

	A	B	C	D	E
4. Motivating subordinates	☐	☐	☐	☐	☐
5. Establishing performance requirements	☐	☐	☐	☐	☐
6. Evaluating subordinates	☐	☐	☐	☐	☐
7. Enforcing rules and regulations	☐	☐	☐	☐	☐
8. Equal employment opportunity	☐	☐	☐	☐	☐

For comments and supporting statements required for item ratings of A or E:

Employee's Signature, Date

EXHIBIT 10.8. *(Continued)*

Item Definition Section

Part A: For All Employees

1. *Quantity and timeliness of work products:* Amount of work accomplished. Extent to which goals, objectives, and time limits were met.

2. *Quality of work products:* Extent to which output, products, or services were free from substantive errors, deficiencies, or omissions.

3. *Job knowledge:* Amount of technical and procedural knowledge.

4. *Initiative:* Capacity for self-starting. Self-reliance as demonstrated by degree to which employee began working promptly on assignments.

5. *Persistence:* Degree to which employee followed through to conclusion whatever was started, and took the lead in getting things done.

6. *Adaptability/flexibility:* Effectiveness in working under unusual conditions or pressures, and in responding to procedural changes. Degree of responsiveness to constructive criticism.

14. *Analytical reasoning:* Effectiveness in thinking logically and arriving at plausible interpretations (e.g., in evaluating reports and documents).

15. *Decision making:* Effectiveness in perceiving existence of problems; recognizing, choosing, and implementing sound, effective, timely solutions.

Part B: Supervisors

1. *Delegating:* Effectiveness in assigning the proper person to each job. Willingness to allow sufficient latitude to employee to effectively complete assignments.

2. *Administrative responsibilities:* Effectiveness in assuring that the organization's staff, material, and service needs are met. Effectiveness in operating within organizational, budget and staffing constraints. Effectiveness in position management and classification.

3. *Training, development, and counseling:* Effectiveness in recognizing subordinates' technical training and career development needs and seeing that they are appropriately met. Providing information, advice, and guidance on career planning.

4. *Motivating subordinates:* Maintenance of a work environment in which employees are encouraged to perform at the highest level. Recognition of work well done (awards, commendations). Empathy with employee's personal needs.

5. *Establishing performance requirements:* Effectiveness in developing, maintaining, and communicating realistic performance requirements, and helping employees set and meet appropriate job goals and objectives.

6. *Evaluating subordinates:* Accuracy and fairness of evaluation of performance.

7. *Enforcing rules and regulations:* Effectiveness in obtaining willing conformance with personnel, safety, and health rules, regulations, and instructions. Appropriateness of response when infractions occur.

8. *Equal employment opportunity:* Extent to which supervisor displayed positive support for EEO program by assuring fair treatment for all employees in making selections, by recognizing employee accomplishments and by displaying sensitivity to developmental needs.

7. *Functioning in interpersonal situations:* Effectiveness in working as a team member, dealing tactfully and sensitively with the feelings and ideas of coworkers, establishing and maintaining rapport with those outside the work group.

8. *Resourcefulness:* Effectiveness in utilizing available materials, methods, services, etc., and in devising better methods and approaches to work situations.

9. *Planning, organizing, and setting priorities:* Effectiveness in handling work load through proper time scheduling, orderly arrangement of procedures, and systematic planning.

10. *Oral communications:* Appropriateness of organization of material; clarity, conciseness, and impact of presentation.

11. *Writing skills:* Degree of completeness, clarity, conciseness, and organization of material; appropriateness of style and language level to intended audience.

12. *Informing/consulting:* Perceptiveness in recognizing, and appropriateness in responding to the need for providing information and for consultation.

13. *Negotiating:* Effectiveness in obtaining voluntary agreement and cooperation from parties with differing viewpoints.

EXHIBIT 10.9. Standards for Planning and Directing an Audit

Responsibility

Planning, organizing, directing, and controlling the audit process for two or more concurrent audits.

Objectives

Develop or assist in the development of an audit program.

Review the survey plan and results and recommend to supervisor areas for further review.

Determine appropriateness of audit coverage and staffing needs.

Review milestones, target dates, and estimates of time requirements for the selected audit objectives.

Standards

1. *Exceeded Requirements*
   - Considers all professional standards and company procedures.
   - Includes sufficient work in the planning, survey, and execution phases to demonstrate that audit objectives are met.
   - Assigns priorities based on significance to assure that available resources are used effectively.
   - Provides guidance in the development of findings and special reports and discussion of results with management.
   - Sets forth realistic milestones and staff requirements, including methods of monitoring so that delays and problems may be anticipated and action taken to finish the audit in a timely manner.
   - Attempts new approaches to audit and applies advanced audit techniques to accomplish the work in a minimum of time.
   - Provides strong leadership to staff, including delegation of responsibility and close monitoring of their work.

2. *Satisfactory Performance*
   - Considers significant professional standards and company procedures.
   - Includes planning, survey, and execution phases, which address audit objectives and identify areas of priority.
   - Specifies basic reporting requirements, such as report format.
   - Sets forth milestones and staff requirements
   - Specifies use of new approaches and advanced audit techniques.
   - Provides instructions to staff that are understandable and usable.

3. *Less-than-Satisfactory Performance*
   - Reflects inconsistent or partial application of professional standards and company procedures.
   - Omits one of planning, survey, or execution phases of the audit without justification or does not address all audit objectives and priorities.
   - Does not provide adequate reporting under the circumstances.
   - Does not meet milestones for performance and exceeds worker-days budgeted.
   - Does not consider new approaches to audit, although survey results show that they are feasible.
   - Does not provide clear instructions to members of staff.

the orientation can be provided to them as a group. The following are some subjects covered:

Auditing Standards
Company Charter for Internal Audit
Organization Charts
Administrative Matters
Policies and Procedure Manuals
Overview of Training
Specialized Techniques—Statistical Sampling
EDP Technology and Practice
Interviewing Techniques
Audit Life Cycle
Planning the Audit
Survey
Audit Programs
Use of Computer Software Programs
Obtaining Evidence
Preparation of Working Papers
Writing Findings
Review of Set of Working Papers

Staff Advancement. For staff members who have been with the department for six months to a year it is advantageous to have an off-job training class to synthesize learning to date. This class will cover such matters as audit objectives and procedures, methods of analyzing evidence, clearing open items in working papers, and report writing. The class provides staff members the opportunity to digest what has been learned to date, discuss mutual areas of concern, and learn how to solve problems in the field.

Statistical Sampling. With the widespread use of statistical sampling by internal auditors, it is especially important that staff members become familiar with the concepts at an early date. The course should enable the staff to know when to apply statistical sampling, how to select the best method, and how to apply it. The auditor is also instructed in evaluating and reporting sample results.

Computer Auditing. A course should be provided to staff members in the use of audit software packages as a tool. Recently, there has been a proliferation of various software methods available to the auditor. He should become familiar with the recommended method for the department and examples of its application. Hands-on experience should be provided on computer terminals. In addition, the staff member should become familiar with computer controls and techniques for auditing through the computer. He should also know when he needs to obtain assistance from other persons who have special expertise in electronic data processing technology.

Report Writing.   To alleviate the problems in learning how to prepare internal audit reports, auditors should be given experience in writing as soon as they develop their first findings. In addition to on-job experience, case studies should be developed for use in off-job training. These case studies help the auditor to understand basic attributes of a finding—condition, criteria, cause, effect, and recommendation. He also obtains practice in writing complete findings and having them evaluated.

Supervision and Management.   As the auditor advances in the organization, he should be provided with training in supervision. It is often difficult to progress from the technical aspects of audit to supervising a staff of subordinates. As an aid to making the transition, a course can be provided to cover such areas as motivating subordinates, management styles, methods of delegating and controlling, and human relations problems.

Staff Meetings.   Periodic staff meetings are an important off-job training device for staff members. The meetings serve as a basis for discussing changes in audit plans and new techniques and procedures. Formal lectures may be given or intensive staff participation invited. Staff members are selected to handle certain subjects, and examples of field problems are often presented with their solution. The staff meetings are especially useful in exchanging ideas and providing information on current developments.

Annual Conferences.   A more extended version of the staff meeting is the annual conference. When a departmental staff is geographically dispersed to a number of field offices, this is an especially important way to bring everyone together face to face. On the technical side there is the opportunity to achieve broader technical understanding of existing policies, procedures, and problems. In this connection it is possible to use various qualified educators, practitioners, specialists, and other authorities. These individuals can come both from within the company and from the outside. At the same time the use of company officials—especially those at high levels—can provide an important opportunity to develop better understanding of common interests and to make those company officials more receptive to future internal auditing services. All of these inputs combine with the personal contacts thus provided to help build better departmental morale on the part of the entire internal auditing staff. Existing barriers are broken down and the stage is set for later contacts that can contribute importantly to overall effectiveness.

Self-Improvement

It is not only through training activities that the staff member develops, but also through his self-improvement endeavors. These may take the following forms:

1. *Passing the Certified Internal Auditor (CIA) Examination.* This examination, prepared by The Institute of Internal Auditors, tests the candidate on such subjects as internal auditing concepts, standards, and procedures. It has become accepted in many companies as a requirement for advancement to higher levels.

2. *Self-Reading Program.* Current developments in the accounting and auditing profession make it important that the auditor follow a reading program. This should cover current professional journals, new books in the field, literature of public accounting firms, and tax and other government regulations.

3. *Master's Program.* Increasing numbers of internal auditors are taking graduate courses, some leading to the M.B.A. degree. These provide the auditor with a broad base of management and business theory, quantitative and computer techniques, and advanced accounting and auditing concepts.

4. *Passing Certified Public Accountant (CPA) Examination.* Passing this examination has long been a goal for many auditors, both in private work and in public accounting. Recently, there has been an increase in the number of books and coaching courses available to assist in passing the CPA examination. This CPA training should, however, be viewed as a supplement to CIA training, not as a substitute.

AUDIT PREPARATORY ACTIVITIES[2]

Each assignment should be planned carefully prior to its start. Sometimes there are pressures to begin auditing immediately because of the urgency of the assignment and availability of personnel. However, significant savings in time and effort can be obtained with adequate planning and preparatory work.

Although some of the preparatory activities described in the paragraphs below are often done during the audit process itself, it is important that they be done early. This helps the auditor to determine the scope and methods used in the audit, selecting from the alternatives available. It is especially worthwhile in larger companies with concurrent audits performed by different personnel. Defining the audit plan under these conditions serves not only to determine the best approach, but also provides for consistency in performance.

Determining Audit Objectives

The most important aspect of internal audit planning of an individual assignment is the establishment of the particular audit objectives. The scope of operational auditing may be as broad as the management process itself. Considering such factors as management's desires, the various audit approaches available, audit

---

[2]Reference should also be made to Chapter 7, where the conduct of certain personal relationships with management and auditees is discussed.

staff capabilities, the nature of prior audit work, and available resources and time, the specific objectives and limitations of the audit must be established at the beginning of each assignment.

These objectives should be clarified and staff auditors should understand them thoroughly. Once the purpose is determined, the scope of the audit can be defined. A strategy of audit should be developed and methods devised for carrying out the audit.

Scheduling and Time Estimates

A scheduling committee is frequently used to decide which audits should be done in the ensuing period and by whom. Key staff members, generally audit managers, attend these meetings and participate in the decision making. Preliminary time estimates are established and time frames set for performing each audit. In addition, changes are made in audits in progress in light of findings to date, personnel changes, and other priorities. Scheduling may cover a month, a quarter, or a longer period. Meetings are held at least monthly to reflect changes. An example of a scheduling sheet for personnel is given in Exhibit 10.10. This form is used to project assignments for each auditor for the next three-month period. It is also used to show scheduled annual leave, supervisory and administrative time, and formal training. As a control device, it serves as reconciliation of available worker-days with scheduled audit requirements.

Assignment of Personnel

The number and level of staff required depend on an evaluation of the nature and complexity of the job, as well as elapsed-time constraints. The job should be broken down into individual tasks in making the staff estimates. This not only makes the overall estimates more reliable, but serves as a benchmark for comparing actual with budgeted performance.

Employee skills and developmental needs should be considered in selecting specific auditors for the job. After deciding on individual segments of the audit, the talents needed to do the job are determined. In one segment of a job a computer-trained assistant may be needed to evaluate computer-generated data. During the preparatory stages this and other requirements are weighed carefully in justifying personnel requests. The training needs of staff are also considered, since each job serves as a basis for meeting developmental needs.

Preliminary Survey

Prior to starting actual field work, it is essential that a review be made of background and other pertinent material. This information is normally available in prior audit files and correspondence, and is analyzed and discussed for impact on the audit. Generally, the following items should be considered during this phase.

Requirements. The objectives of the audit and reporting requirements are reviewed. Specific and unusual audit requirements are pinpointed. Audit period covered, target dates, and tentative worker-day requirements are determined. The final report format is considered at this time, since proper planning at this stage will facilitate the writing process at a later date.

Review of Prior Working Papers. Permanent files should be studied in describing the background of the organization or function being reviewed, internal controls, and statistical data. The prior scope of audit and audit working papers and programs should be reviewed to gain familiarity with approaches used and results. In some companies an audit critique is prepared at the conclusion of the audit, evaluating the approaches used and making suggestions for future audits. If this was prepared, or staff are available who performed the prior work, ideas should be obtained for the current audit. Special attention should be paid to prior audit problems and methods of solving them.

Audit time taken in the prior audit is reviewed carefully to determine whether savings can be obtained. In this connection, it is useful to study the results of prior tests performed, deciding whether the tests should be reduced, eliminated, expanded, or performed on a rotating basis in future audits.

Review of Prior Reports. All prior audit reports issued for the entity being audited should be reviewed. Patterns in findings and their significance are analyzed, as well as the extent of corrective action taken. To obtain leads as to sensitive areas, reports on similar entities or functions in the company are studied. Related findings in other areas may also be useful. In some cases it may be beneficial to review articles in the professional literature which discuss successful approaches used by other internal auditors in developing findings in certain areas.

Organization of Entity. The auditor should obtain an organization chart of the entity being audited and review for structure and responsibilities. The mission or function of the entity is also obtained to determine its purpose. In addition, the number and names of employees by major department or section should be made available. This should include the name of the liaison person for contacts during the audit. Budget material and financial data are also reviewed as background material.

Other Reviews. Related reviews or audits completed, planned, or in progress should also be studied. This includes audits by the outside public accountant (including management letters), and reviews by federal, state, and local auditors. This also includes the results of reviews made by departmental or other company officials, trip reports, and reports of accomplishment. Any indication of known problem areas should be listed.

EXHIBIT 10.10. Personnel Scheduling Sheet

Division Office:

Worksheet for Audit and Personnel Schedule

Name of Auditor	Month:	Month:	Month:

Reconciliation of Available Auditor Worker-Days

Direct audit time (per attached monthly audit status reports)   ___

Leave and holidays   ___

Supervision and administrative   ___

Training   ___

Total worker-days   ___

Comments:

Contacts with Appropriate Personnel.   At this point, the auditor should have obtained sufficient knowledge about the audit to discuss the audit plan intelligently. He should be prepared to brief his supervisor and the audit manager as to the objectives of the audit, work to be done, and steps to be taken.

Officials of the entity under audit should be contacted as soon as practicable to set up an entrance conference date. At this time the auditor should request statistical and other reports available at all levels relating to the entity and program being audited. Reports are considered very helpful in identifying trends or patterns. Also, comparisons can readily be performed between entities or programs to determine significant variances.

CHAPTER ELEVEN

Directing and Controlling Internal Auditing Activities

STARTING THE AUDIT

At this stage of the audit there has been contact and the auditor has gathered sufficient general information about the organization and program to be reviewed. The auditor is now prepared to start the field work. Exhibit 11.1 is an example of a flowchart showing the audit process from planning to completion of audit.

Field Survey

This survey, like the preparatory survey, is critically important in determining the direction, scope, and extent of the audit effort. The auditor cannot rush in to begin examining documents and other test data. He must become familiar with the system prior to developing the audit program and starting the actual field auditing. He must determine the reliance that can be placed on the system and various subsystems of internal control before proceeding.

The survey also serves as a means for identifying new and innovative approaches to audit. Results of prior audits are studied carefully and related to audit procedures used. New techniques are considered in the light of changed operating conditions. Staff auditors are encouraged to make suggestions for improving the audit process to obtain better results.

The following are approaches used in the field survey, which emphasize the review of the effectiveness of internal control.

Organization. The auditor obtains organization charts of the entities being reviewed, including names of personnel assigned. Review of the organization enables the auditor to become familiar with functional responsibilities and key people involved in the operations.

Manuals and Directives. During this stage the auditor reviews applicable policy and procedure manuals, extracting data of interest in the audit. Federal and state laws and regulations and planned operating controls are studied.

EXHIBIT 11.1. Audit Flowchart

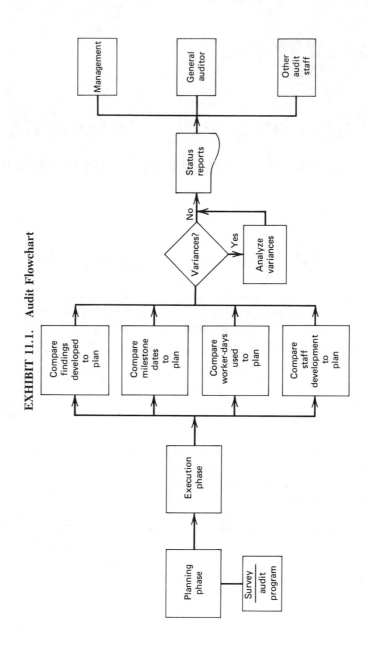

266

Correspondence files are screened for applicable material. This material is put into a framework for performing audits of compliance.

Reports. The auditor studies relevant management reports and minutes of meetings covering such areas as budgeting, operations, cost studies, and personnel. He also carefully analyzes the results of inspections or management reviews, and actions taken. These reports may provide leads for the audit, as well as a summary of problems faced and progress made in their solution.

Personal Observation. A tour of the activity should be made, with explanations obtained about the different operations. This familiarizes the auditor with the entity to be audited, basic operations, personnel, and space utilization. Compliance with company procedures can also be determined.

Discussions. The auditor should hold discussions with key personnel to determine known problem areas, results of operations, and planned changes or reorganizations. Questions should be raised based on preliminary data reviewed, and the viewpoints of management obtained. In all the discussions the auditor maintains a positive approach, eliciting the assistance of staff to contribute to achieving the audit objectives.

Flowchart Approach

The use of flowcharts is of major assistance to the auditor in the review of internal control. By providing a graphic summary of the documentation and flow of data, flowcharts enable the auditor to follow the complexities of a system more clearly. Also, weaknesses may be more easily detected by looking at a well-designed flowchart.

Flowcharts may not be needed in small or relatively simple operations of the company. In some cases abbreviated presentations can be made to depict the system. Flowcharting methods should be standardized wherever possible, and used consistently in the various audits. The use of flowcharts should be coordinated with the computer systems department and with the external auditor to prevent duplication and to facilitate the work.

Alternative Approaches. There are two theories used in developing flowcharts, one known as the method theory and the other as the end-result theory. The method theory looks at the means rather than the ends. Emphasis is placed on the system, with analysis of controls to prevent errors. Under this approach one goes through the system, and if it is acceptable, there is assurance that the end results are acceptable.

The end-result theory, on the other hand, starts with documenting an information system from the final information product, such as financial statements and budgets. The data that feed into this product are traced back to their sources. Only those data that affect the final product are identified. Not all information flows affect the final product, and under the method theory there is thus some tracing of systems that are irrelevant to final results. The proponents of the end-result theory state that there is thus some waste of time and money under the other approach. Any improvement in the cost effectiveness of internal control analysis would increase the efficiency of the audit as a whole.

Symbols. Exhibit 11.2 shows some typical symbols used in preparing flowcharts. Exhibit 11.3 is an example of a flowchart prepared for a relatively simple system for controlling mail receipts from customers. Major control points illustrated in the diagram are:

Mail clerk required to list cash received in the mail as a control for cash accountability.

Remittance advices are used as basis for recording receipts in cash book as well as subsidiary accounts receivable ledgers, thus providing a control for entries made.

Deposits are to be made intact on a daily basis. This serves as a check on proper handling of cash received and asures that cash is made available to the company as soon as possible.

Reports prepared monthly for management on aging and extent of accounts receivable balances provide a control over collection activities.

Receipted deposit slips and later bank statements provide control over final disposition of money received from collections.

Survey Conclusions

Based on the survey, the auditor prepares the audit program outlining the nature and extent of audit work to be performed. The results of the survey should be summarized in written form to the extent practicable and reviewed before proceeding in the audit. Exhibit 11.4 is an example of a report on survey conclusions.

AUDIT PROGRAM AND RELATED ACTIONS

The audit program is a tool for planning, directing, and controlling audit work. It is a blueprint for action, specifying the procedures to be followed and delineating steps to be performed to meet audit objectives. The audit program is the culmination of the planning and survey processes. It represents the selection by the auditor of the best methods of getting the job done. It also serves as a basis for a record of the work performed.

Examining Information[1]

The standards of The Institute of Internal Auditors state that the auditor should examine and evaluate information on all matters related to the audit objective.

[1]See also the discussion of the technical approaches of the internal auditor in Chapter 6.

EXHIBIT 11.2.   Flowchart Symbols

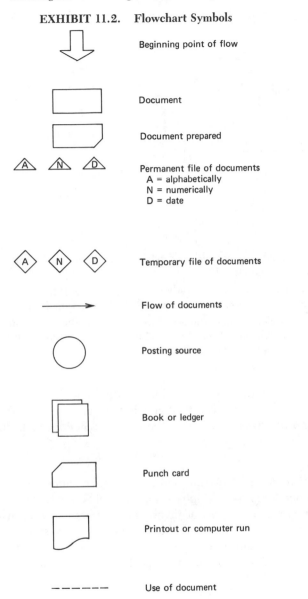

Beginning point of flow

Document

Document prepared

Permanent file of documents
  A = alphabetically
  N = numerically
  D = date

Temporary file of documents

Flow of documents

Posting source

Book or ledger

Punch card

Printout or computer run

Use of document

This information, or evidence, should be sufficient, competent, relevant, and useful.

The auditor must gather evidence to support both the positive and the negative conclusions resulting from the examination. He must be assured that all information in the working papers has been checked out for possible findings. He must also determine that there is sufficient evidence to support his conclusions. In carrying out the review, he must always evaluate the different

EXHIBIT 11.3.   Flowchart Cash Receipts by Mail

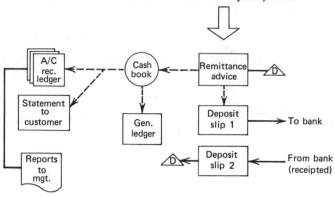

Weaknesses noted:

1. Remittance advices not recorded when received by mail clerk, thus no control over amounts deposited.
2. Deposits made twice a week rather than daily. Results in loss of interest because of delays in depositing large collections, and risks of theft of cash.
3. When mail clerk is sick, the accounting clerk handles incoming cash as well as recording collections. Lack of segregation of duties could result in misappropriation of cash and cover-up in the cash book.

types of evidence, discuss that evidence with the auditee, and obtain feedback to test his observations. The final conclusions are then based on a multitude of auditing procedures, selected by the auditor as needed to distinguish between fact and fiction.

Analytical Evidence.   The internal audit often includes extensive analysis of business operations, with emphasis on internal controls. This evidence is considered circumstantial, since it involves circumstances from which inferences can be drawn. By examining relationships in the system and determining whether internal controls are operative, the auditor arrives at conclusions with respect to the system and determines the extent of testing that needs to be done.

Supporting Evidence.   The auditor must decide on the specific type of corroborative evidence needed in the review. This may take the form of documentary evidence, testimonial evidence, or a combination of the two. For example, in determining why competitive bids were not obtained in acquiring equipment, the auditor reviews the purchase files for justification for sole-source procurement. In addition, he may discuss the problem with the purchasing agent and with the requisitioner to obtain additional information.

EXHIBIT 11.4. Survey Conclusions

Area: Inventory Shortages

Objectives: To determine whether inventory shortages are excessive and ascertain the causes

Survey Findings:

1. The inventory write-down based on a physical inventory at the end of the current year indicated a loss of $2,550,000, or 7% of the recorded inventory of $36,400,000. This was a 70% increase in the amount of the loss over that at the end of the prior year.

2. A new computer system was installed during the year, and there were problems in obtaining accurate stock records.

Suggested Approach: Test the accuracy of postings to the stock records, determine whether postings are current, and ascertain that cutoff procedures are acceptable.

Original Budget: 25 worker-days

Time to Date: 8 worker-days

Revised Budget: 50 worker-days

Approved:

Jim Carmody
Audit Manager

Structure of Best Evidence. In obtaining and evaluating information, the auditor must select the strongest evidence available. He realizes that if an employee tells him something, it is not as strong as obtaining a written statement. He also recognizes that oral or written statements have to be tested and verified. The following is a structure of best evidence which is useful to the auditor:[2]

Classifications	Strongest	Weakest
Relationship to agency	External	Internal
Techniques	Observation–confirmation	Inquiry
Origin	Corroborative	Underlying accounting data
Form	Written	Oral
Sophistication	Formal	Informal
Reality	Actual system	Designed system
Auditor	Self	Others

Auditing Procedures

While auditing standards are the same in any audit, auditing procedures will vary in each assignment based on the nature of what is being audited and the scope of the review. Auditing procedures are the specific acts performed or

[2]Alan Johnson "A Structured Theory of Management Auditing," *Footnote(5)*, Journal of the HEW Audit Agency, Winter 1971–1972, p. 17.

methods used to obtain the necessary data used for preparing the report. In internal auditing, procedures are related to various sources of information because of the emphasis placed on processes by the internal auditor. These procedures typically involve the following types of actions:

Comparing.   The internal auditor frequently compares related information and analyzes differences. For example, he compares actual costs with budgeted and standard costs, and reviews explanations for significant variations.

Vouching.   In addition to tracing items to subsidiary records, the internal auditor reviews support for entries and for amounts in reports. This involves the inspection of documents on a test basis. Judgment sampling or statistical sampling may be used as appropriate to arrive at conclusions as to the validity of information.

Confirming.   If documents prepared by third parties are sent to the auditor, they are considered especially reliable. In recent years auditors have extended their use of confirmations, especially in instances where internal control is weak or documents are missing from the file. An example is confirming payables to disclose unrecorded liabilities and the validity of account balances.

Scanning.   In some cases the auditor may wish to scan or examine the records and reports visually to determine if there are sensitive items requiring further attention. This procedure does not substitute for testing; it enables the auditor to become familiar with the system and pinpoint areas for inquiry.

Analyzing.   It is through analysis that the auditor breaks down a process or an item into its component parts. This breakdown facilitates the review through highlighting essential elements. It also serves to identify major causes for conditions.

   An example is the review of increases in maintenance costs. The auditor prepares a matrix of maintenance costs by departments and equipment and period, breaking costs down by labor, materials, and overhead. He then uses this analysis to determine trends, review differences, and determine causes for the increases.

Inquiring.   Information obtained orally is an important means of explaining the facts that are in the records or developed from other sources. It also enables the internal auditor to visualize the activities and processes that are in operation, and provides him leads for further review. The internal auditor can secure such explanations from individuals involved in the particular area being reviewed, as well as from individuals in other departments.

Observing.   There may be listed under this procedure all the impressions and observations that the auditor has experienced during the audit assignment. The internal auditor observes the physical layout of plant, storage of equipment and inventories, physical inventory procedures, coordination and utilization of personnel, and other operations of all kinds. These observations give additional meaning to reviews made of the underlying data. The importance of planned observations makes it desirable for the internal auditor to carry out his assignment in such a manner that he can move about and observe the various phases of the company's operating activities.

Recomputing.   The auditor is called on to check selected footings, extensions, and other calculations as part of his audit. His review of controls, including computer controls, will determine the nature and extent of testing to be performed. An example is in the use of dollar-unit sampling, in which it is necessary to check the footing of the total dollars in the universe prior to selecting the sample.

Program Criteria

Preparing an audit program requires planning, judgment, and experience. The internal auditor has obtained and evaluated preliminary information in his survey—now he has to use it.

The most important criterion is, of course, the system of internal controls. Based on the survey the auditor determines on a preliminary basis the reliance that can be placed on the system. He also selects the aspects to be further examined and the sensitive areas that require audit emphasis.

Materiality and relative risk are also criteria for developing the audit program. Materiality is based on the significance of an item compared to other items. In preparing the program the internal auditor may extend or limit his work in light of materiality. Although an area may not be material, it may be essential in light of relative risk. Under relative risk the auditor reviews those items that require increased attention because of adverse circumstances. For example, property leased from officers or employees of the company would be scheduled for review.

The reliability of evidence and types of information available should also be considered. The internal auditor will try to select audit steps that will produce the most reliable evidence.

Advanced audit techniques will also be used wherever practicable. Computer software packages are available for the auditor to carry out selected audit steps. Statistical sampling procedures, combined with computer techniques, enable him to obtain data quickly from large populations. These and other techniques should be considered in preparing the program.

Detail in the Program

An audit program usually includes a statement of objectives, audit steps, auditor assigned and provision for initials upon completion, working paper reference,

EXHIBIT 11.5.   Segment–Cash
Audit Objective–Determine Whether Excessive Cash Balances Are Maintained

Tasks/Subtasks	Person Assigned	Staff Days	Estimated Start/Comp.	W/P Reference
1. Schedule cash balances from bank statements for year.	AJ	3	3/1–3/4	A-1
2. Ascertain whether average cash balances appear excessive.	AJ	2	3/5–3/8	A-20
3. For accounts with excess balances, determine cycle for deposits and major expenditures during the month.	AJ	2	3/9–3/10	A-25
4. Determine whether deposits can be timed more closely with expenditures.	AJ	1	3/11	A-31
5. Ascertain whether company's policies for temporary investments of cash are being followed.	AJ	1	3/12	A-34

budget by audit steps, and estimated start and completion dates. Exhibit 11.5 is an excerpt from an audit program used by one company.

Audit guides or preliminary programs may be available in a given area. These should be used as guides only, with changes made as needed, based on the circumstances. Audit programs may be written in general form or may contain detailed steps, depending on the area and the level of auditor performing the work.

Program Modification

The audit program should be considered a model of the assignment in discussions with management and the audit staff. The auditors must, however, be responsive to new evidence, changes in staff assignments, and other changes in conditions. In the early stages of the audit it may be necessary to redirect the assignment as well as modify objectives.

PERFORMING THE AUDIT

When the survey and audit program are complete, the internal auditor is faced with directing and controlling the audit to obtain the desired results. The preparatory work will play an important role in the audit's success. However, the auditor is still faced with the day-to-day problems of performing field work.

Early Detection of Problems

It is especially important that problems be detected early in the assignment and solved as soon as possible. Difficulties in obtaining cooperation of one department's personnel, for example, may slow work in that area. Discussion of the problem with management as soon as it surfaces will facilitate the timely completion of the audit.

Technical Assistance

Complex problems requiring technical determinations may arise in the audit. These often necessitate extensive research, discussion with operating personnel, and coordination with higher-level supervisors, including the general auditor when necessary. Problems of this nature should be brought to the attention of the supervisor and assistance provided as needed.

Monitoring Visits

Supervisory visits should be made as frequently as is practicable to the audit site to review progress and provide technical direction to the work. These reviews supplement such reviews as are made by supervisory personnel who are part of the field staff. Review comments should be made in writing, covering such items as additional work or explanations required, questions raised, and changes to be made. The data and extent of the review are also indicated. The staff member then performs the additional audit work required and makes the necessary changes to the working papers, indicating action taken on the review sheet. Upon review of the auditor's comments, additional work done, and corrections, the supervisor indicates on the review sheet his clearance of each item or directs further action.

Audit Leads

Whenever the internal auditor discovers an audit lead, he should prepare a brief summary of possible deficiencies, sometimes called a point sheet. Whether or not this results in a finding depends on the results of additional review. A point sheet does not become a finding until the audit lead has been explored and an issue of substance established—a deficiency or an opportunity for improvement.

It is important that a point sheet be prepared as soon as the auditor has some indication that a substantive issue exists. This facilitates bringing such issues to the attention of all levels of supervision at an early point in the audit. It also serves as a control to assure that all leads are followed up. In addition, the point sheet file can bring out a number of minor issues that fall into a pattern, indicating a more serious overall condition. Lastly, the use of point sheets requires commencement of the writing process early in the audit, thus helping assure that the essential facts for developing a finding are obtained.

The supervisor should assure that the point sheet is documented to show

EXHIBIT 11.6. Audit Point Sheet

Name of Audit	Point Sheet Number	Date
Inventory	3	1/25/82

TITLE   W/P REFERENCE

Excessive Inventory Writeoffs   D5

Source
  Audit adjustments at end of year.

Statement of Condition
  Increased inventory writeoffs over those in previous years.

Cause
  Potential problems: Computer errors, physical security, location errors.

Effect
  Potential problems: Production shortages, excessive insurance, erroneous interim
  statements.

Recommendation
  Related to cause.

Comments and Final Disposition
  (Filled in prior to end of audit)

its eventual disposition prior to completion of the audit. If developed into a finding, the point sheet will be cross-referenced to the finding. If the lead is dropped, the reasons should be stated. Exhibit 11.6 is an example of a point sheet form.

Telephone Contacts

Telephone contacts are a useful method of monitoring jobs between supervisory visits. Often the press of supervisory work loads prevents visits to the site, and the review of job progress by telephone can be beneficial. In addition, the auditor in charge of the assignment is encouraged to discuss problems by telephone as they arise.

Specialized Audit Techniques

Staff members are encouraged to use such techniques as statistical sampling and computer auditing software packages where feasible. When these techniques can be applied to testing performed, sampling and other plans should be reviewed carefully to assure the most effective results with the least expenditure of resources. In some cases the assistance of other auditing departmental personnel with special expertise will also be necessary.

Periodic Reports

In larger audits, or those performed in various locations at the same time, it is useful to require progress reports on a weekly or biweekly basis. These reports provide useful information to the supervisor as well as a control for the auditor in charge. They include such information as budgeted and actual time to date, estimated time to complete, and number and description of leads and findings. Exhibit 11.7 is an example of a monthly audit status report. This is prepared monthly by each division office to provide the general auditor with information concerning the status of audits in process or scheduled during the next three-month period. A separate form is completed for each audit. This form is used to provide control over audits scheduled and in process and to assure that audits are started and completed on a timely basis. By requiring that each division office submit the form by the twentieth of each month, reviews can be made of the data and revisions can be made prior to the beginning of the next month.

Modifications

Changes are often needed in the audit plan as work progresses. Thus it is desirable to build some flexibility in plans to meet unforeseen requirements. During the assignment in the field the auditor may encounter such situations as an unexpected problem or event, the need to modify or drop an audit segment, the discovery of a new area for review, and changes in audit personnel. In some cases there may be slippage through taking additional worker-hours

EXHIBIT 11.7. Monthly Audit Status Report

Date:

Division Office	Audit

Section I: Scheduling Data

	Original	Revised	Actual
Entrance conference			
Exit conference			
Draft audit report			
Final audit report			
Elapsed Days			

Section II: Time Controls

	Current Fiscal Year	Other Fiscal Years	Total Worker-Days
Approved Worker-days			
Worker-days expended through end of this month			
Approved worker-days remaining			
Estimated worker-days required to complete			
Estimated worker-days required next 3 months			
Estimated worker-days required subsequent to next 3 months			
Current forecast of overrun (or underrun)			

Section III: Projected Worker-Day Requirements Next 3 Months

Part 1: Reporting Division Office

Level	Auditor	Month	Month	Month	Total Worker-Days

EXHIBIT 11.7. (Continued)

Subtotal: Reporting Division Office

Part 2: Auditors Assigned from Other Division Offices

Division Office	Names of Auditors

Part 3: Headquarters Office Direct Time

Part 4: Total Worker-Days Projected for Next 3 Months

Remarks

_____
Signature (Division Audit Manager)

_____
General Auditor Approval

Date

or elapsed time to finish a segment. In these circumstances, revised budgets are needed, and proper approvals should be obtained.

Increases in time requirements should be carefully monitored, with identification of those changes that are warranted because of new circumstances. This monitoring serves to indicate the techniques which were not scheduled or justified. In some cases the problem may have been inaccurate budgets, while in others there may have been problems in performance. Close control of the audit will prevent slippage caused by inadequacies in staff, delays in solving problems, insufficient supervision, and excessive attention to detail. Exhibit 11.8 is an example of a form used to approve changes in an organization when there is an extension of more than 15 days in elapsed time to do the audit, or when there is an expected overrun of 10% of the approved worker-days.

Meaningful Findings

The nature of findings should be reviewed during the audit to determine if they are useful. Are there many findings of a minor procedural nature? Are cost savings indicated and properly reported? Are findings related to operational effectiveness? Do operating officials believe that the findings are helpful? The answers to questions such as these will provide an indication as to whether findings developed are meaningful.

Post-Audit Critiques

Some companies have experimented successfully with the use of post-audit critiques. At the end of each job the auditor in charge evaluates the assignment in terms of such factors as approach, time spent, areas of emphasis, staffing, and suggestions for the next audit. The critiques serve as an excellent training device for staff, as well as a basis for planning the next audit. They serve to set out the techniques that proved successful, as well as the efforts that were unproductive. Also, post-audit critiques or other summary evaluations serve as useful information in the self-audit of performance. Exhibit 11.9 is an example of a post-audit critique prepared after the audit of purchasing.

WORKING PAPERS

Nature of Working Papers

The term "working papers" is used to describe the various schedules, analyses, and memoranda that are prepared by the internal auditor during the course of the particular audit assignment. In many cases also these working papers will include documents secured from company personnel or outside sources. The common characteristic in all of these situations is that the aforementioned documents are of such significance in describing the audit work and results that they are formally retained for subsequent reference and substantiation of re-

EXHIBIT 11.8   Revision of Audit Schedule and Approved Worker-Days

Change Request No.	Audit	Division Office	
	Requested Change	From	To
Entrance conference			
Exit conference			
Draft audit report			
Final audit report			
Elapsed days			
Approved Worker-days			
Justification			

_____
Division Audit Manager

_____
General Auditor

EXHIBIT 11.9.   Post-Audit Critique:
Audit of Purchases

Scope of Audit

Review of efficiency and economy of purchases in the Denver plant, including effectiveness of operations.

Audit Approach

A statistical sample was taken of all purchases in the plant for the past year. Review was made of support in the files for the purchases. In addition, the overall work load in the plant purchasing department was analyzed to determine reasons for the extensive backlog. For the next audit a stratified sampling approach should be used as more efficient, with separate strata for high-dollar items and items determined sensitive.

Sequence of Audit Segments

Additional survey should be performed prior to developing the statistical sampling plan. This should include study of results of supervisory reviews of purchasing activities, determination of items with acquisition problems, and analysis of items subcontracted on a cost or negotiated fixed-price basis. This would be useful in developing a better statistical sampling plan.

Time Budget

The original time budget was unrealistic, requiring a 25% adjustment for unplanned work. Some worker-days could be saved in the next audit by additional supervisory input at start of job to pinpoint problem areas, assist in developing the statistical sampling plan, and routinize work performed in reviewing purchasing files.

Staffing

The work was performed by one senior without the use of assistants. Because of the routine nature of some of the review, savings could be obtained by planning the audit to assign one assistant for at least half the audit.

Adequacy of Audit Program

The audit program appeared adequate, with the exception of the areas described above. For the next audit a more detailed program should be prepared and standardized for use throughout the company.

Areas to Be Emphasized or Deemphasized

Additional work should be performed in the area of sole-source procurement.

Contemplated Changes in Organization or Procedures

None are anticipated that will affect the audit.

Cooperation and Receptivity of Management

Good. However, it was observed that the Assistant Purchasing Agent was defensive about the findings, and it was necessary to obtain the agreement of the Purchasing Agent to obtain concurrence and remedial action.

Prepared by:	Approved by:
Robert White	Jack Jensen
Senior Auditor	Supervisor

ported conclusions and recommendations. The working papers thus constitute the bridge between the actual audit work and the reports issued. This bridge is such an important link in the entire internal auditing process that it needs to be carried out in accordance with appropriate professional standards. At the same time it is important to recognize that working papers are not an end in themselves, but a means to an end. They are created to fit particular audit tasks and are subject to a great deal of flexibility. The general test in all cases is whether they reasonably achieve the purposes of the internal auditor, regardless of their specific form. We will, therefore, in this treatment of the subject be more concerned with principles and concepts, rather than specific form.

Functions of Working Papers

We can perhaps better understand the problem of working papers if we look more closely at the major functions that these papers serve. These are as follows:

1. *Record of Work Done*. Irrespective of whether the audit work is being carried out in accordance with prescribed manuals, it is important that a record be established of the auditing work actually carried out. This record will include location of the particular activities reviewed, the extent of the audit coverage, and the results obtained. This record may be in some cases referenced to specific procedures set forth in the manual, or it may in other cases be independently developed.

2. *Use During the Audit*. In many instances the working papers prepared play a direct role in the carrying out of the specific audit effort. For example, the company trial balance of the accounts receivable ledger can be used as a basis of control over the mailing and receipt of customer confirmations. Similarly, a flowchart might be prepared and then used in connection with the further review of the actual activities carried on at the individual stages of the processing.

3. *Describe Situations of Special Interest*. As the review work is carried out, situations will be encountered that have special significance in terms of their bearing upon such things as compliance with established policies and procedures, accuracy, efficiency, people performance, cost-saving possibilities, income opportunities, and the like. These situations need to be described and evaluated.

4. *Support for Specific Conclusions*. The just-mentioned situations in some cases will evolve into the development of specific conclusions and recommendations that will be reported in some manner. It is an important function of the working papers to show how the final judgment was arrived at, and to provide the necessary support for the actual conclusion or recommendation.

5. *Reference*. The foregoing functions combine in various ways to provide the basis for needed later reference. The reference may be to answer additional questions that may be raised by higher-level internal auditing

management or by other company personnel. The questions may be in connection with the validity or scope of a particular conclusion or recommendation, or they may relate to new informational needs. There is also a need for basic background materials that will be applicable to all audits of the particular entity or activity.

6. *Staff Appraisal*. Working papers serve as a basis for evaluating the performance of staff members during an audit. The auditor's ability to gather and organize data, evaluate it, and arrive at conclusions is reflected in his working papers.

7. *Audit Coordination*. The internal auditor frequently exchanges working papers with the external auditor, each relying on the other's work. In addition, government auditors, in their review of internal controls, ask to examine the internal auditor's working papers. Frequently, the working papers serve as a basis for coordinating and selecting various areas for audit.

Types of Working Papers

With the wide range of operational activities reviewed and the equally wide range of audit procedures carried out it is inevitable that the form and content of individual working papers will vary greatly. These working papers do, however, fall into certain major categories, which we can identify as follows:

1. *Listings of Completed Audit Procedures*. Such listings usually follow audit manual sequencing and indicate dates the audit work was actually done, and by whom. Commentary-type notes may be included on the same listings or attached as supplementary notes. Frequently, standard forms are provided for this purpose.

2. *Completed Questionnaires*. Closely related are standard questionnaires covering particular types of internal control procedures. These questionnaires normally provide for yes and no answers and appropriate supplementary comments.

3. *Descriptions of Operational Procedures*. It is frequently desirable to describe briefly the nature and scope of a specific type of operational activity (or group of activities). This description then usually provides an essential basis for later probing and evaluation. It can be in flow chart or in narrative form, or in any kind of combination.

4. *Review Activities*. This type of working paper goes on to outline the scope of specific investigations that are made to appraise the effectiveness of one of the operational activities. Such investigations can include testing of data, observation of performance, inquiries to designated individuals, and the like.

5. *Specific Evaluations*. Supplementing the above-mentioned investigations are the specific interpretations and evaluations that need to be set forth as a basis for specific conclusions and recommendations to be in-

cluded in reports. These papers are of special importance because they directly support the representations made in final reports. These evaluations include human, operational, and financial factors.

6. *Analyses and Schedules Pertaining to Financial Statements*. In the review of financial statements, or particular portions thereof, there will be a special variety of working papers relating to the individual financial statement balances. These will include:

   a. Schedules relating general ledger accounts to financial statement balances.
   b. Analyses of individual accounts.
   c. Details of backup account data and supporting physical counts.
   d. Results of specific kinds of verification.
   e. Explanations of adjustments to the accounts.
   f. Notes as to pertinent supplementary information.
   g. Summaries of total financial statement balances and adjustments.

7. *Company Documents*. In many cases there will be basic company documents which pertain importantly to the audit work. Illustrative would be organization charts, minutes of meetings, particular policy statements or procedures, contracts, and the like.

8. *Drafts of Reports*. Within reasonable limits it is useful to retain and include in the working papers the several drafts of the written report. These drafts can be annotated to show major changes in these drafts, by the persons responsible for those changes, and in some cases the reasons for the changes.

9. *Supervisor's Notes*. During an audit the supervisor prepares review comments that require explanation by the auditor. In some cases, further auditing is needed. Action taken by the auditor is documented and referenced.

Working Paper Standards

Standards pertaining to working papers fall generally into two groups, those pertaining to substance and those pertaining to form.

Standards of Substance. From a substance standpoint the matters with which the internal auditor should be concerned include:

1. *Relevance to Audit Objectives*. A first requirement is that the content of the working papers be relevant to both the total audit assignment and the specific objectives of the particular part of the audit review. The inclusion of other materials, even though appearing to be impressive in a quantitative sense, detracts from the usability of the working papers.

2. *Condensation of Detail*. Again also, the condensation and careful summarization of detail can reduce the bulk of the working papers and make

their later use more efficient. To do this condensation effectively requires a special effort on the part of each staff person.

3. *Clarity of Presentation.* Closely related is the standard of presenting basic material in a manner that is clear and understandable. To do this effectively requires a reasonable amount of planning before the actual audit work is done.

4. *Accuracy.* An essential standard is the accuracy of all statements and quantitative data. Each staff person must recognize that the papers being prepared may be used at any time in the future to answer questions and to substantiate the later representations of the internal auditing department.

5. *Action on Open Items.* Questions are frequently raised in an audit or information disclosed that require follow-up. There should be no open items in the working papers on completion of the audit.

Standards of Form. The other kind of standards applicable to working papers concern matters of form. These include:

1. *Preparation of Headings.* The headings need to be prepared in a uniform manner. The center heading should include the title of the total audit assignment, the particular aspect of that total assignment, and the date applicable to the current materials. A smaller heading on one side should indicate the name of the person preparing the working paper and the date of preparation.

2. *Organization.* Materials covered need to be organized in a manner that will facilitate reading and understanding. This includes the use of appropriate headings, spacing, and adequacy of margins.

3. *Neatness and Legibility.* In addition, adequate standards of neatness and legibility make the use of the papers more efficient. They also confirm the qualities of care in the preparation.

4. *Cross-Indexing.* All working papers should be indexed and cross-indexed to provide a trail for the auditor and the reviewer. Cross-indexing assures the accuracy of information in the working papers, as well as in the audit report.

Illustrative Working Papers. Examples of working papers are included as Exhibits 11.10 to 11.13.

EXHIBIT 11.10.   Illustrative Working Paper 1

Review of Settlement of Subcontractor Costs:
Discussion with Senior Buyer-Subcontractor

A meeting was held on March 10, 1981 with Mr. Gerald Perkins, Senior Buyer-Subcontracts Purchasing Department, to discuss the subcontracts footnoted in Schedule D2. He made the following comments:

(1.) He agreed that additional follow-up was necessary with the government auditors, in the first case, and with the company subcontractor auditors, in the second case, to obtain more timely audits.

(2.) He stated that some subcontracts were negotiated without audit because of time pressures and reliance on the subcontractors' claims. He agreed that it would be beneficial to have audits done, based on past experience (D4)

(3.) Staff shortages (D3) and subcontractor delays prevented the timely negotiation of claims after the audit was completed.

Conclusion: Finding should be developed in the area of subcontractor administration. See report, W/P A5-A6.

L.D. 3/15/81   D1

287

EXHIBIT 11.11. Illustrative Working Paper 2

Review of Settlement of Subcontractor Costs
Subcontracts over $1 Million Completed
During 1979 and 1980
South Bay Company

			Dates			
Subcontractor	Amount	Work Completed	Audit Requested	Audit Completed	Final Price Negotiated	Comments
Pyramid Tooling	$2,401,000	8/10/79	9/15/79	—	—	(1)
Excalibur, Inc.	1,050,000	5/7/80	5/30/80	8/25/80	10/20/80	
Sentinel Mfg.	1,750,000	2/7/79	—	—	3/7/79	(2)
Haven, Inc.	4,250,000	11/14/80	12/5/80	—	—	
Stellar Engineers	3,650,000	1/7/79	2/15/79	5/10/79	—	(3)
ABC Construction	2,010,000	5/7/79	9/7/79	—	—	(1)
General Tooling	1,365,000	8/8/79	—	—	10/7/79	(2)

Notes
(1) Follow-up not made with subcontractor auditors.
(2) Final price negotiated without audit, although
    subcontract was cost-plus-fixed-fee.
(3) Audit report received but negotiation not
    held with subcontractor

Source: Subcontract files
J.T. 3/2/81   D2

EXHIBIT 11.12. Organization Chart

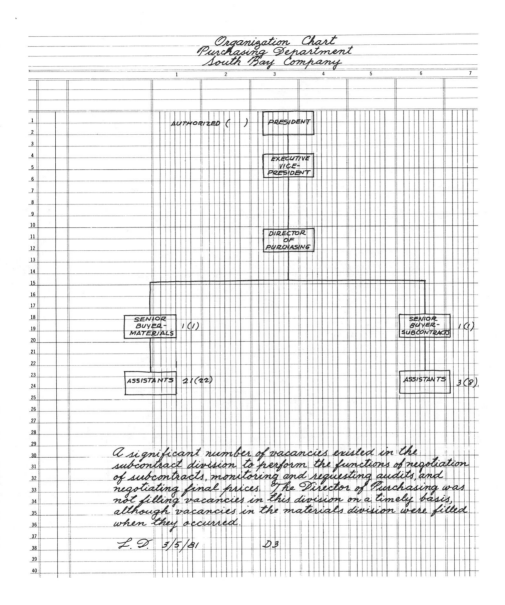

Organization Chart
Purchasing Department
South Bay Company

AUTHORIZED ( )

PRESIDENT

EXECUTIVE VICE-PRESIDENT

DIRECTOR OF PURCHASING

SENIOR BUYER-MATERIALS 1 (1)

SENIOR BUYER-SUBCONTRACT 1 (1)

ASSISTANTS 21 (22)

ASSISTANTS 3 (8)

A significant number of vacancies existed in the subcontract division to perform the functions of negotiation of subcontracts, monitoring and requesting audits, and negotiating final prices. The Director of Purchasing was not filling vacancies in this division on a timely basis, although vacancies in the materials division were filled when they occurred.

L. D. 3/5/81   D3

289

EXHIBIT 11.13.   Illustrative Working Paper 4

Prior Audit Adjustments for Selected Subcontractors
South Bay Company

Subcontractor	Date of Last Audit	Period Covered	Cost Claimed	Adjustments Per Audit	Negotiated
Sentinel Mfg.	8/15/80	1979	$3,850,000	$320,400	$280,000
General Tooling	6/4/79	4/1/78 to 1/31/79	1,650,000	121,000	92,000

Based on prior audit experience, significant audit adjustments were made and negotiated with the above two subcontractors — see w/p D2. Thus material savings may have been achieved if audits were performed.

Source: Subcontract Files

L.D. 3/6/81   D4

290

CHAPTER TWELVE

Internal Audit Reporting

PRINCIPLES AND ALTERNATIVES

Nature of Report Function

We come now to one of the most important phases of the total internal auditing process, the development and issuance of reports. Reports are the major means by which many different persons both inside and outside the company are apprised of the internal auditor's work and evaluate his contribution. The reports also constitute the most enduring type of evidence about the total professional character of his internal auditing activities. Effective reporting quite obviously depends on the quality of the work that has gone before. But it is also true that good auditing work can be nullified by poor reporting. Reporting is, therefore, one of the major concerns of internal auditors at all levels, especially to the general auditor, who is ultimately responsible for the effectiveness of the total internal auditing program.

We especially need to recognize that good reporting is more than just the preparation of the reports themselves. This is to say that the reports reflect the basic philosophy and related concepts of the total audit approach. This total approach includes the underlying objectives, the supporting strategies and major policies, the procedures covering audit work, and the caliber and performance of the audit personnel. The character of these basic components ultimately determines what there is to go into reports. In addition, the administration of these basic components is always carried out in a way that anticipates the later reporting, and to a major extent prepares for it. The reporting phase thus provides a natural opportunity to integrate the total internal auditing effort and to provide a basis for overall appraisal.

Purpose of Reports

The internal audit report has many important functions, both for the auditor and for management. These functions must be considered carefully in performing the audit work and in determining how to write the report.

1. *Conclusions Based on Audit.* The report serves to summarize the evidence obtained during the audit, with presentation of findings and conclusions. It thus represents the end result of the auditor's work.

2. *Disclosure of Conditions.* The report provides the organization with a summary of areas needing improvement. It can thus be viewed as an information device for management concerning the operations of the organization. It is also viewed by some as an evaluation of performance, disclosing those areas that are good and bad and the extent subject to possible improvement.

3. *Framework for Managerial Action.* The recommendations in the report represent the auditor's conclusions as to actions to be taken by management. Based on the conditions disclosed and causes identified, the recommendations serve as a framework for action in correcting deficiencies and improving operations. The report is also used for reference purposes, both in reviewing other areas of the company and in following up to determine the extent to which responsive action has been taken.

4. *Clarification of Auditee's Views.* The auditee may wish to state mitigating circumstances, or provide clarification of issues of disagreement. A clear statement of the auditee's viewpoint, with comments by the auditor, helps to pinpoint the issues for management and provides a basis for arriving at decisions as to actions needed.

For Whom Is the Report Prepared?

The consideration of the report phase brings to a head also the important problem of for whom the report is being prepared. At first glance the answer seems very simple—it is being prepared for management. But management exists at all levels, including the management of the organizational component being reviewed and the management at the higher levels to which the component management is responsible. Each management group has special needs and special interests, and the question becomes one of what relative recognition of these types of needs best serves the company interest. In more specific terms the question comes down to what the internal auditor's respective responsibilities are to the auditee versus the auditee's bosses. As we look more closely at this question it becomes more complicated; we must understand it as best we can and determine how to deal with it most effectively.

Problem from the Standpoint of the Auditee. The auditee—that is, the organizational staff or line component that is being reviewed, and its responsible management group—is motivated by a combination of company and local entity interests. The auditee management knows that its ultimate welfare is closely related to the total company welfare, but it knows also that its own rewards are largely determined by its own performance. This latter performance is again in turn a combination of the operational results achieved and how upper-level management thinks the locally responsible managers actually contributed. In everyday parlance local management strives to look good to upper-level management. What this all means in terms of the internal auditor is that the local managers want help, but want it on a basis that as little as possible discredits them with upper-level management. Hence, ideally, they would like to have the internal auditor work with them on a private professional basis. The internal auditor wishes to help local management do a more effective job. He knows also that if he is to do this he must have the full cooperation and partnership relationship. The internal auditor is, therefore, strongly motivated to deal with the organizational component in the way the local management wants it, and thus to achieve best what really counts—more effective local operations.

Problem from the Standpoint of Upper-Level Management. The upper-level management consists of both the managers to whom the local manager has line responsibility and the higher-level staff managers to whom the local staff managers have a functional responsibility. These upper-level managers have a very practical type of control need. They want to be apprised of significant deviations from established company policy and procedures. They also want to know of major operational problems and of important possibilities of carrying out the particular operational activities more effectively and more profitably. This is in part a need for protection and in part a desire to be helpful. As one of the means for achieving this control these higher-level managers look to the internal auditing department. From the standpoint of the internal auditor he wishes to provide these higher-level managers with the services they seek. Moreover, it is these higher-level managers who pass final judgment on the worth of the services of the internal auditor, and who influence and ultimately determine his compensation, organizational status, and overall progress in the company.

The starting point for a good solution to the conflicting demands is that both management groups must be provided with a more comprehensive understanding of the needs of each other, and also of the desire of the internal auditing group to serve both types of needs. That is, we need to increase the level of tolerance and flexibility on each side. A second way in which the problem can be minimized is through raising the level of what shall be considered sufficiently significant to warrant report coverage. In this way we can eliminate many of the more minor matters that should be, and can be, finalized at the local level, without the irritations that come from involving higher-level managers. A third attack on the problem can come through a more determined joint effort between the local managers and the internal auditor to work out needed follow up action *during* the course of the audit. The general effect of all these actions is to push the internal auditor more toward the "service to local management" concept. It stops short only of recognizing that there is still an important final reporting responsibility to higher-level managers.

Types of Reports

The reporting of results covers a wide spectrum of types. We can describe the more important ones as follows:

1. *Oral Reports.* In many situations the reporting of results will be on an oral basis. To some extent this is inevitable since a part of the actual audit

effort is carried on in conjunction with company personnel. In other cases it is a result of emergency action needs. It may also be a prelude to more formal written reports. To some extent there will always be oral reporting as a means of later supplementing written reports, especially when individuals being served have special needs. Oral reporting, therefore, serves a useful and legitimate purpose. It is recognized that it has the major limitation that there is no permanent record. As a result there are more likely to be later misunderstandings. What is important, therefore, is that this type of reporting be used carefully and not in lieu of later written reports.

2. *Interim Written Reports.* In situations where it is deemed advisable to inform management of significant developments during the course of the audit, or at least preceding the release of the regular report, there may be some kind of interim written report. These reports may pertain to especially significant problems where there is a need for earlier consideration. Or the reports may be of a progress nature. In either case they may be quite formal in nature, or of the more informal type of current memoranda. They can be reserved for very exceptional developments, or issued on a more extensive basis. Often, their distribution is limited to the auditee management, but this is not necessarily the case. Normally, interim reports are fully covered in the final regular reports, and are superseded by the latter. All in all, the interim reports represent a type of reporting which, when used with judgment, can be a good device to improve the total reporting process.

3. *Questionnaire-Type Reports.* The usual procedure is that some kind of a written report is prepared at the completion of an individual audit assignment. One type of final report utilizes a questionnaire, and is built around it. The type of report is normally used only for internal reporting within the internal auditing department. It works best where the scope of the audit review deals with fairly specific procedural matters, and usually at a fairly low operational level. This type of report can be useful under the right circumstances but it has a fairly limited range of overall usefulness.

4. *Regular Written Reports.* In the typical situation the particular audit assignment will include the preparation of a formal written report. The form and content of such written reports will vary widely, both as between individual audit assignments and individual companies. They may be short or long. They may be presented in many different ways, including the extent to which quantitative or financial data are included. We will in the later pages of this chapter discuss in more detail the problems and alternatives associated with this more common type of report.

5. *Summary Written Reports.* In a number of companies the practice has developed of issuing an annual (or sometimes more frequent) report summarizing the various individual reports issued, and describing the range

of their content. These summary reports in some cases are primarily for audit committees of boards of directors, but in other cases for higher-level management. These summary reports are especially useful to top-level managers who do not actively review the individual reports. They are also useful to the general auditor in seeing his total reporting effort with more perspective, and on an integrated basis.

Approaches to Written Reports

As stated above, the form and content of regular written reports will vary widely. We can, however, identify certain common approaches, and briefly appraise their merits.

1. *Encyclopedic Coverage.* Some internal audit reports strive to present a great deal of information about the activity that has been reviewed. The objective seems to be to provide an in-depth reference source to the audit report user. The information can be of a historical nature or pertain to the current situation. It may cover operational practices and results, or may deal with financial information. The latter is more commonly done in the case of audit assignments covering the review of financial statements. The major question here is whether providing such reference type information is really a proper function of the audit report. This is an especially valid question when one considers the time and cost required to provide such detailed information. On balance this type of approach is not recommended unless specifically requested by management.

2. *Description of Audit Work.* Another approach that is sometimes adopted is to provide a great deal of information about the audit work actually carried out. Audit steps may be described as well as the scope of actual verification and testing. To some extent this coverage overlaps with statements of procedures contained in audit manuals. The question here is primarily how interested a reader of the report is in this procedural detail, and what purpose it really serves. It is believed that most users of the reports are willing and eager to rely on the competence of the internal auditor for those technical dimensions. On balance, therefore, such detailed accounts of technical auditing coverage should be excluded, or at least minimized.

3. *Detailed Explanations of Audit Findings.* A closely related approach of some internal auditors is to go into fairly voluminous detail about the results of the various audit efforts. Although the coverage here may in some respects be impressive, it is again doubtful whether the lower level of items dealt with and the greater amount of detail serve a sufficiently useful purpose. There is, indeed, a very real possibility that the reader may be turned off by such an approach, and thus miss things that are really important. We, therefore, recommend the maximum summarization of audit findings that is possible.

4. *Focus on Significant Issues.* The more commonly used approach in written reports is to focus on the really significant issues. Significant as a term used here means types of issues that have an important bearing on policies, operational approaches, utilization of resources, worker-power performance, and results achieved (or achievable). Higher-level company managers are interested primarily in problems that are of such a nature and scope that they wish to be informed, and have the opportunity to contribute to solutions. Sometimes also, these significant issues relate to completed action, but in this case the issue would have to be still more significant to merit the actual reporting. The special advantage of this focus on significant issues is that higher-level managers can get the information they need without wading through excessive detail. It is the type of approach that leaders in internal auditing try to follow.

Elements of a Finding

The internal auditor must analyze the bits and pieces of information gathered during an audit to select those that should be included in the report. Is there sufficient information to develop a finding? How should the data be arranged? In answering these questions it is useful for the auditor to have a structure for a finding in mind. The elements of a finding, or common attributes, are discussed below.

Statement of Condition.   The first sentence of a finding summarizes the results of the auditor's review. It is developed from a comparison of "what is" with "what should be." The "what is" is the condition or appraisal made by the auditor based on the facts disclosed in the review.

Criteria.   The criteria, or "what should be," are used in judging the statement of condition. Without strong criteria there cannot be a finding.

Criteria vary according to the area being audited and audit objectives. The criteria may be the policies and procedures and standards of an organization. In a financial audit they may be generally accepted accounting principles. For audits of costs the requirements of laws, regulations, grants, and contracts may also pertain, such as Internal Revenue Service regulations.

For other findings, good management principles may apply, and there may not be as definitive criteria. In this case the auditor's professional knowledge and experience are important. In some instances the internal auditor must develop the criteria. For example, in an audit of effectiveness there may not be preestablished targets or measurements to be used as indicators. Standards may be couched in general or vague terms. Where there are criteria gaps, the following are suggested techniques for use by the auditor.[1]

---

[1]Allan L. Reynolds, "Examining Performance of Socio-economic Programs—The Criteria Gap," *Footnote (3)*, Journal of the HEW Audit Agency, Winter 1970–1971, pp. 23–25.

1. *Criteria of Extremes.* When performance is clearly inadequate or out-standing, it is relatively easy to appraise. When performance moves closer to the average, it becomes more difficult to judge. The auditor can some-times use extreme cases of inadequate performance as criteria for a find-ing.

2. *Criteria of Comparables.* Comparisons can be made between similar operations or activities, determining their success or lack of success and causes for the differences.

3. *Criteria of the Elements.* In some cases performance criteria can be stated in such broad terms that it is impossible to evaluate the progress. How-ever, breaking down the activity on a functional or organizational basis, or by elements of cost related to specific activities, may provide useful criteria.

4. *Criteria of Expertise.* In some cases the auditor can rely on experts to evaluate an activity. These experts may be outside the organization or may be part of the audited organization's staff.

Effect. The auditor must also answer the question "How important?" He must weigh materiality—if the finding is of no significance, it may not be a finding at all. Findings containing dollar savings, are, of course, of special interest to management. Similarly, findings that affect company operations and achieve-ment of goals are especially of interest.

Cause. The answer to the question "Why?" is especially important to man-agement. The reasons why there is a deviation from requirements should be explained. Once the cause of the condition is identified, there is the basis for taking needed management action.

Recommendation. The auditor must then arrive at a conclusion as to "What should be done?" The recommendation flows from the cause previously iden-tified in the finding. It represents the auditor's opinion as to what action or actions should be carried out to correct or improve the situation. Often, work-able solutions are arrived at in conjunction with personnel of the organization being audited.

Balanced Report Presentation

An important part of internal audit effort is devoted toward evaluating the efficiency, economy, and effectiveness by which management has accomplished its objectives. This involves the weighing of both satisfactory and unsatisfactory conditions disclosed during the audit. When conditions needing improvement are noted, methods should be developed to minimize the statement of findings in negative terms and yet produce results, that is, encourage management to take the needed action. The audit cannot be fully successful if the auditee is not receptive toward the auditor. Consequently, the auditor should adopt a positive reporting style that is balanced with favorable as well as unfavorable comments, present matters in perspective, and emphasize constructive rather than negative comments.

In providing balance in audit reports, the question is frequently asked: "How does one decide on the favorable comments to be included?" The answer to this question cannot be laid down in precise terms. However, the same criteria used in identifying significant findings can be used; that is, matters are reported which are considered significant based on standards of performance. For example, assume that the audit objective is to evaluate the timeliness of filling purchase requisitions. Comments presented in a finding should relate to the organization's ability or inability to fill purchase requisitions in a timely manner. Details on the use of special techniques to provide balance are presented in the following paragraphs.

Providing Perspective. Perspective is added by presenting the entire results of the audit in an accurate, complete, and professional manner. The auditor should avoid the temptation to cite only those factors which support the auditor's conclusions and to ignore those which distract from it. For example, perspective should be added when a dollar effect is noted. The report must disclose, as appropriate, the total dollars audited or recorded in relationship to the dollars of errors. The significance of the finding is made evident by this procedure. Also, when deficiencies are disclosed in only part of the area examined, balance is added by reporting those areas examined that did not contain deficiencies. This practice is in accordance with the policy of disclosing accomplishments as discussed below.

Examples of the above where perspective has been added are:

Original	With Perspective
Inadequate screening procedures resulted in the payment of duplicate claims totaling $50,000.	Improved screening procedures could have helped reduce duplicate payments of $50,000 in claims totaling $10 million processed.
The policies and procedures used for estimating materials and computer costs were not adequate.	We determined that the policies and procedures used for determining salary, travel, equipment, and overhead costs were adequate to assure accurate estimates. However, procedural improvements were needed in order to develop sufficiently accurate estimates for materials and computer costs.

Reporting Accomplishments. Reporting the auditee's accomplishments together with the noted deficiencies or aspects with improvement potential can add much to the usefulness of the audit report as a management tool. Since the evaluation process involves the weighing of both the satisfactory and un-satisfactory aspects of the auditee's operations in light of the audit objectives, such information should be made available in the audit report. The auditee's accomplishments should be disclosed in the summary of the report when the conclusions of the audit may be affected by the significance of the accomplish-ments, and in the summary or body of the finding when detailed disclosure of the accomplishments is desired or necessary.

Showing Needed Action. In situations where the auditee has taken, or made plans to take, timely action to correct or improve the situation prior to the completion of the audit, the audit report should disclose this fact. Needed action is that effort taken or planned which has a direct bearing on the reported activity subject to correction or improvement. However, other steps taken by the auditee in an attempt to correct or improve the situation may not be so obvious but nevertheless should be considered by the auditor as a positive reportable action. For example, the auditee may have contracted with its ex-ternal auditor for the purpose of establishing the internal controls needed in the computer system.

Reporting Mitigating Circumstances. Mitigating circumstances generally con-sist of factors relating to the problem or condition over which management has little or no control. Since these factors lessen management responsibility for the condition, they should be reported as part of cause. It is difficult to convince the grantee of the factuality of the audit report if it has a legitimate reason to argue that the blame should be shared. Situations that may be viewed as mitigating circumstances include the haste or urgency in which the program was required to be implemented, and lack of adequate funds for key personnel or material to accomplish objectives.

Including the Reply. The auditee's reply may contain information that pro-vides additional balance to the audit report. The auditee may indicate its ac-complishments under the program or cite additional facts and mitigating cir-cumstances. Also, the auditee may indicate the action it has or will take to correct the deficiency. In instances where agreement has not been reached on the finding or recommendation, the auditee should be given the opportunity to explain the basis for nonconcurrence.

Improving Tonal Quality. Good tonal quality is obtained by the use of positive and constructive words and ideas as compared to negative and condemning language. Findings that begin with phrases such as "failed to accomplish," "did not perform," and "was not adequate" emphasize the negative rather than the constructive aspects of the audit. In improving the tonal quality of reports, the auditor is encouraged to be innovative in expressing the ideas in a positive and constructive manner. The following are a few examples of how negative open-ing statements can be phrased in a positive and constructive manner.

Negative	Positive
The department failed in several of its training program operations.	Several opportunities exist for strengthening controls in training program operations.
The budgetary system was not adequate to assist management in the control of project funds.	The establishment of a proper budgetary system would assist management in the control of project funds.

In addition, negative titles and captions should be avoided since they do not add to the finding and may misrepresent the actual situation. Thus a negative title such as "Inadequate Cash Controls" should be replaced by "Cash Controls" or "Need to Improve Cash Controls" or "Cash Collection Procedures."

PREPARING AND FINALIZING THE AUDIT REPORT

Improving the Report Process

Skeleton Report. During the early stages of the audit it is desirable to develop a framework for the report, filling in as much of it as possible. Information and statistics on the background of the area being audited can be gathered during the survey stage. This will assure that the needed information is obtained early in the audit, and will prevent delays in the final writing process. In addition, the objectives and scope should be defined clearly at the start of the audit. These serve as useful guides for the audit staff in planning and carrying out the audit assignment.

As findings are developed and completed, they are inserted in the proper sections of the report, together with comments of the auditee.

Delegation of Writing. Staff auditors should be given every opportunity to write the findings in areas in which they are auditing. This gives them the opportunity to obtain writing experience, which is so important to their development. Also, by using a report-oriented audit approach, the auditor obtains needed information for the report while he is performing the audit.

Supervisory Assistance. The supervisor should become involved in the writing process early in the audit. He should review leads when developed to assure that there are sufficient criteria for a finding. He should check that the staff auditor prepares an outline of the finding in advance. He should discuss the possible causes and effect of the finding, and obtain agreement as to how it will be developed. In some cases an approach of hypothesizing as to possible causes and then verifying them in the audit is useful.

The supervisor should also review working papers to determine whether there are any leads that have not been followed up by the auditor. This will prevent the need for developing findings late in the audit. An example of a checklist for reviewing the quality of the report in various stages of its development is given in Exhibit 12.1.

Discussion with Auditee.[2]   As findings are developed the auditor reviews them with company employees, soliciting ideas as to their validity. He also discusses possible causes with them and data needed to prove or disprove the condition. In some instances company personnel will assist in obtaining information to develop the findings. They will also provide useful feedback as to whether the auditor's facts are correct and whether he is on the right track. Areas of disagreement can be pinpointed and resolved.

Discussing findings with company personnel has another benefit—it helps to get agreement and implementing action. When agreement is reached, the auditor may be able to limit the amount of detail included in his finding, thus shortening the writing process.

Organization of the Written Report

The choice of the significant issues approach now takes us to a consideration of how the written report should be organized. The organization will be based on a number of sections.

Date of Report.   The report should preferably be dated as of the time it is released. As a practical matter this is usually the date the final approval has been given to it by the general auditor, or his deputy, and the report put into typing. Under proper standards of efficiency for typing, reproduction, and binding, the date of actual transmittal should not then exceed about five days from the report date.

Addressee.   Under best practice the report will be addressed to the manager who has direct responsibility for the particular company activity that was reviewed. In some cases, however, the review is made in accordance with the specific authorization and instruction of a higher-level manager, and the internal auditor may have been directed to report to that manager. In other cases also the nature of the audit assignment may require some special procedure.

Opening Paragraph.   It is normally desirable to use the opening paragraph to state the nature and scope of the audit assignment, the period covered or other pertinent point of time, the length of time devoted to the field work, and the audit personnel who were assigned. In some cases it may be necessary to have one or two additional sentences describing the major parts of the audit work, but any substantial detail along that line should be avoided.

[2]See also the related material in Chapter 7.

EXHIBIT 12.1.   Quality Control of Report Development:
Checklist of Critical Phases

Development of Finding Outline

1. Determine if there is sufficient support to warrant the findings.
2. Review to determine additional evidence needed.
3. Ascertain that cause and effect are considered.
4. Determine whether there is a pattern of deficiencies requiring procedural change or an isolated case.
5. Review plans to assure that budgets are revised, as necessary, to assure adequate development of findings.

Preparation of First Draft

1. Review findings for adequate development.
2. Ascertain whether the findings are stated in specific rather than in general terms.
3. Assure that figures and other facts have been checked to the working papers.
4. Review working papers supporting finding for adequacy of support and disclosure of items of significance.
5. Check for adequacy of punctuation and spelling.
6. Ascertain whether there is sufficient support for the expression of opinion or whether a qualification or disclaimer is needed.
7. Determine whether cause, effect, and recommendations are adequately developed.
8. Discuss with subordinate methods of improving content and writing style.

Discussion with Management

1. Determine whether management was aware of the problem and taking corrective action.
2. Find out management's reasons for the conditions.
3. Ascertain whether there are facts or mitigating circumstances of which the auditor was unaware.
4. Determine management's ideas on how to correct the conditions.
5. Assure that management is aware of all significant items that will be present in the report.
6. Assure that efforts are made to obtain agreement on the facts and conditions.

Preparation of Final Draft

1. Ascertain that all prior recommendations for changes in report have been made.
2. Assure that management's viewpoints have been adequately considered.
3. Determine that the report is well written and easily understood.
4. Ascertain that summaries are consistent with the body of the report.
5. Assure that recommendations are based on conditions and causes stated in the findings.
6. See that management's viewpoints are fairly stated and adequately rebutted.
7. Review report for use of graphics, tables, and schedules to clarify conditions presented.
8. Assure that auditors who wrote the findings agree with any changes made.

Closing Conference

1. Assure that management has had an opportunity to study the final report.
2. Attempt to obtain agreement on any points of difference.

EXHIBIT 12.1.   (Continued)

3. Consider any suggestions for changing content of report, including specific wording.
4. Obtain from management current plans for follow-up action.

Issuance of Final Report

1. Assure that final changes are made in accordance with the closing conference.
2. Check report for typographical errors.
3. Review report for balanced presentation, with positive comments included on results of audit when applicable.
4. Make final reading of report for content, clarity, consistency, and compliance with professional standards.

Background Paragraph.   It is normally desirable to have a paragraph describing the general nature of the operational activity covered by the review. This is background orientation for the reader of the report, and is not intended to be complete in any reference sense.

Summarization of Key Issues.   When there are a substantial number of significant issues dealt with in the report it is normally desirable to include a listing of either all, or a portion of, the individual issues. This enables the reader to inform himself quickly as to the nature and scope of the issues dealt with in the report, without a detailed examination of the entire report.

Summary Evaluation.   It is also useful to provide a summary evaluation of the effectiveness of the operational performance of the particular company component or activity. This summary evaluation is usually expressed in very general terms. It usually also refers to the situation at the time of the last review—providing that there was a previous review—and comments on the extent to which progress has been made. In some companies this evaluation becomes very specific, and in one case known to the authors it takes the form of a specific rating—excellent, good, satisfactory. In this instance the audit reporting is being used primarily as an instrument of control by higher-level managers. Even in this company, however, there seem to be problems in applying this approach to all types of audit reviews, and in any event a considerable price is paid through the defensive posture that such an approach induces on the part of the auditees.

Presentation of Individual Issues.   The main body of the report is then made up of a series of subsections dealing with individual issues of special significance. The manner recommended for the presentation of each issue is as follows:

1. *A Heading that Reasonably Describes the Issue.* Illustrative would be a "Dispersion of Purchasing Activities" or "Quality Deviations in Production Process."

2. *Findings*. Under this heading the major findings of the internal auditor will be briefly described and interpreted. This will include the conditions found to exist, particular standards being violated, the significance of the resulting deficiencies, and judgments as to the causes of the unsatisfactory conditions. In other cases the findings may describe conditions that have significant improvement potential. This section may be relatively brief or be more extended depending on the significance of the particular issue. The objective should be to include only such information as will be directly pertinent to the later conclusion or recommendation, and to be as brief as possible.

3. *Conclusion or Recommendation*. The previous coverage of the findings will now provide the basis for a conclusion or recommendation. Conclusion is used here in the sense of a final statement that is important even though it does not involve a further recommendation. The most sought-after type of conclusion is that local management has already taken, or has agreed to take, certain corrective or improvement types of action. This type of conclusion is then only to keep higher-level managers informed of the problem and its solution. Or the conclusion may be limited to a statement that management recognizes the existence of the problem and is continuing its study of what should be done.

In other cases there should be, to the maximum extent practicable, a specific recommendation made by the internal auditor. One type of recommendation covers something the internal auditor believes that local management should do, but where local management is not in agreement. The other type involves recommended action that must be taken by a higher-level authority. In this latter case the local management's position on the question should also be stated. It is important to note that items involving local management action are often eliminated from the recommendation category if local management has agreed to take that action. However, in some of these cases it may be that higher-level needs to be informed that a particular condition did exist irrespective of the fact that the problem has been dealt with adequately.

4. *Comments of Auditee*. This section covers the reaction of the auditee to audit findings. Where there are differences of opinion or mitigating circumstances, the report includes the auditee's comments with rebuttal by the auditor as needed.

Closing Paragraph and Signature.   Finally, there should be a closing paragraph in which the internal auditor expresses his appreciation of the cooperation and assistance received during the course of the audit. There should then be a phrase like "Respectfully submitted" or "Very truly yours" and the signature. The latter signature should be manual—at least on the master copy—and by the general auditor, or his deputy. Frequently also, the name of the internal auditor actually preparing the report will be shown.

Distribution

The distribution listing provides information as to the specific executives who are to receive a copy of the report by formal transmittal. This is important because individual managers will be guided as to their responsibilities to answer questions involving their respective operational areas. The distribution list should be developed with great care. Over time this distribution list will tend to expand, and a continuous effort must be made to keep it within reasonable limits. It is, of course, assumed that direct subordinates of persons shown on the distribution list will have access to the report, but practical limitations here must be recognized.

Special Summary Digests

In addition to the complete report as just outlined there is the possibility that supplementary special digests be prepared for certain report users. The purpose of such digests is to provide summary information without requiring actual reference to the complete report. The approach is especially applicable when the complete reports are very complicated and voluminous. The General Accounting Office has adopted this procedure, and in this situation it appears to be very useful. The GAO reports cover many very extended investigations where the reports are necessarily very long. The reports in this case also are used by legislators, government officials, and other more general readers. The summary digest is also especially useful to these users in that it can be detached for separate use, without making the basic report incomplete. The procedure is an excellent illustration of developing effective reporting based on special user needs.

Validation of Findings and Conclusions

Among the important aspects of internal audit reports are the steps taken to validate the adequacy and accuracy of the reported findings, and the soundness of the related recommendations, prior to the finalization of the report. The major foundation for this validation is the audit work and review that is carried on at all levels by the internal auditing staff. But this major foundation needs to be supplemented by certain types of review and confirmation involving auditee personnel, including ultimately the auditee top management. The benefits of this supplementary validation are twofold. The first is that this provides a crosscheck on the accuracy, completeness, and quality of the audit work. Important facts may have been overlooked or erroneously interpreted. There may also be other factors affecting the particular matter that are known only to certain people. The exposure to the auditee thus provides an important check on whether the findings and recommendation will stand up under later scrutiny. The second benefit of the review is to induce a partnership relationship with local management. The opportunity for this kind of participation creates both a cooperative spirit and a more likely commitment to working out adequate solutions. Under the opposite approach there is the very real possibility that local management may be embarrassed and embittered by having its bosses informed of audit results at the same time it is, through the medium of the final report. Such developments will then cause the local management to have a defensive and hostile attitude toward working out needed solutions. The internal auditor is also likely to find a noncooperative auditee when he returns for another audit.

Closing Conference.   While the above-mentioned type of validation goes on to a major extent at all stages of the review, one of the most important ways in which this is effected is through the closing conference. This closing conference takes place at the close of the field work, and just preceding the planned departure of the field audit personnel. It includes the top members of the audit group and the top members of local management. At the conference major findings and proposed recommendations are reviewed. Frequently also, the next-higher-level audit manager will travel from headquarters to the field location to participate in this conference. To the extent that agreement has already been reached between audit personnel and local company personnel on particular matters, an opportunity is now provided to inform the top manager and to secure his further agreement. At the same time any question still open can be resolved. Sometimes the participants will have drafts of report coverage for review, but in most cases the discussion will be based on preliminary memoranda or point listings. It is possible that the discussions here may require additional audit work, but normally only in unusual circumstances.

The closing conference is a major opportunity for the internal auditor to confirm the soundness of the audit results and to make such modifications as seem to be justified. It is also a major opportunity to demonstrate the constructive and professional type of service the internal auditor is seeking to provide. It can be a major means for building sound partnership relations with the auditee. The objective should be to get as much agreement as possible so that more can be reported as completed action, and less as recommendations for necessary later follow-up. Other aspects relating primarily to the relations with people were discussed in Chapter 7 and should be reviewed to achieve the maximum benefits from this major auditee contact.

Reviewing of Draft Reports.   As previously noted, the closing conference may in some cases be based on drafts of text that will be included in the final reports. In some companies also there may be a further phase where draft reports are forwarded to the local management for their review and comment, prior to the finalization of the report. The use of draft reports in closing conferences has certain major disadvantages. These disadvantages are primarily the danger that the discussion will center unduly on words rather than on the substantive issues. In addition, the later independence to make modifications, including the usually necessary editing, is importantly restricted. On balance, therefore, it would seem best to avoid the use of draft material at the closing conference stage.

The submission of draft reports to the auditee management at a later stage has merit through the demonstration of genuine consideration for the auditee. However, there are again certain significant disadvantages. The first one is that the internal auditor tends too much to become the captive of the auditee as to the way thoughts are expressed and particular words used. The finalization of reports is then more likely to become a special kind of game. This leads to the second disadvantage, which is that there is excessive delay in finalizing the report. A major part of the effectiveness of the report is the extent to which it is issued promptly. Again on balance, therefore, it is believed that the closing conference provides an adequate basis for the finalization of the report at the headquarters office. This would not, of course, preclude telephone conversations during the finalization stage to confirm particular facts and interpretations.

Report Follow-Up

Reference has previously been made to the internal auditor's possible role in connection with the follow-up of reports. It sometimes happens that top management requests this follow-up role as the best means in its opinion to ensure that needed actions based on the audit are actually taken. In some cases also a particularly zealous general auditor will propose this procedure. The desirability of follow-up action in itself is very clear. The problem, however, is whether this is a proper responsibility of the internal auditor, and whether such action by the internal auditor will undermine the basic responsibilities of the managers who are in charge of the particular activities. It also puts the internal auditor more in the role of a policeman, and this tends to conflict with his ongoing partnership relationship with the auditee. In many companies, therefore, the internal auditor plays no specific role after his report is released, other than to respond to questions, and to review again the situation at the time of the next audit assignment. Many companies, however, have adopted some intermediate type of approach.

A typical intermediate approach is that the coordination of the total follow-up effort is placed in the hands of another office, usually the Finance Department or some more neutral administrative services group. The corrective action is then initiated by the responsible line or staff manager, but responses are made to the coordinating officer. If there are undue delays in dealing with the recommendation, the coordinating office issues follow-up inquiries. Under this approach, copies of responses can also be supplied to the internal auditor group for information, or the internal auditor can maintain other liaison with the coordinating group. There is no final answer as to how this total follow-up effort should be handled, but on balance it seems best to subordinate the internal auditor's formal role in it. The help of the internal auditor can always be asked for on a special basis, either by the coordinating office or by individual managers. In addition, the lack of action can be highlighted at the time of the next review.[3]

---

[3]See also the comments in Chapter 2 relative to Section 440 of The Institute's Standards.

Criteria for Effective Report Presentation

It is the internal auditor's responsibility to produce a report that is readable, understandable, and persuasive. The objective is to have a report that will command the attention of the managers who have the responsibilities for the various operational activities, and to induce them to press for appropriate action. The objective also is for a report that will build respect for the internal auditing effort. These professional criteria include the following:

1. *Professional Tone*. This professional tone avoids excessive casualness on the one hand and stilted formality on the other. It reflects dignity, perspective, and objectivity. It denotes the professional level and stature of the internal auditor.

2. *Accuracy*. Individual statements and related data must be accurate. Moreover, they must meet the standards of reasonableness, considering the complexity of what is being covered. There is probably nothing that can be so damaging to the internal auditor's image as the later discovery of an erroneous statement of fact, the inclusion of erroneous data, or unreliable estimates.

3. *Courtesy and Tact*. We need to remember that people involved in the findings and recommendations will be very sensitive as to any reflection on their capacity or performance. By being courteous and tactful one can do much to neutralize this sensitivity.

4. *Consideration*. Closely related is the ability to show proper consideration for the people involved. Where people have tried hard they appreciate having this recognized, even if they have failed.

5. *Persuasiveness*. Everything that is said should be handled in a way that will provide the proper setting and subsequent motivation to take the needed types of action. The key ingredients here are logic and fairness.

6. *Sentence Structure*. We need to avoid long and dangling sentences. Simple and shorter sentences are more easily understood, and hence are more effective.

7. *Paragraphing*. The thoughts expressed need to be arranged in paragraphs that deal with designated segments of that thought. Paragraphs that are too long are discouraging and hence resisted.

8. *Choice of Words*. Care in selection of the right words will be rewarding. We want words that reflect the particular shades of meaning desired, that do not have special emotional content, and that are not stereotyped.

9. *Good Grammar and Spelling*. Mistakes in grammar and spelling both distract and annoy the reader. There is then the risk that the force of the impact of the message on the reader will be undermined.

10. *Physical Processing and Binding*. The needed physical standards of a good report include accuracy of typing, attractive physical arrangement of text material, quality reproduction, and accuracy of report page as-

sembly. There is also a need for a quality cover of a uniform character, with an adequate label describing the audit assignment and the time period or date involved. A distinctive color for the binders also makes for their later easier identification when used in connection with other company reports.

In Exhibit 12.2 we illustrate the structure and substance of an internal auditor's final report.

EXHIBIT 12.2.   Illustrative Audit Report

April 20, 1982

Mr. Bruce R. Weston
General Manager
Bright Products Division
The Wonder Corporation
Central City, Penn.

Dear Mr. Weston:

In accordance with our agreed-upon arrangements we have completed an operational review of the supply activities of the Bright Products Division. This review covered operations during the period January 1 to December 31, 1981. The review was made by Roger G. Wilson and his assistant, Bruce A. White, during the period January 3 to March 31, 1982.

Scope

Our internal audit was performed in accordance with generally accepted internal auditing standards. Our review was limited to supply and related computer activities of the division.

Summary of Major Issues

1. The Supply Department had excess inventories on hand at December 31, 1981 of $875,000, resulting in unneeded cash investment and use of storage facilities.
2. Computer customers were being billed at rates that were excessive, resulting in a surplus in the computer center of $1,215,000 at December 31, 1981.

Supporting Findings and Recommendations

1. Excessive Supply Inventories
   Findings
   The Supply Department had excessive inventories on hand at December 31, 1981 of $875,000, resulting from the purchase of stock that was not needed. During 1981 the division averaged $650,000 of cash investment in excess stocks, representing $91,000 in unnecessary interest costs at the current market rate of 14%.

EXHIBIT 12.2. (*Continued*)

The excess stocks resulted in part from the fact that the division did not record unused stock returned from production. As a result, purchases were based on stock records that did not reflect the additional stock, and were therefore excessive. Although the records were adjusted at the end of the year to reflect physical counts, records used for purchasing during the year did not reflect actual on hand.

Recommendations

a. Procedures should be revised to provide for recording unused parts returned from production.
b. Purchases should be reduced until excess inventories are depleted.

2. High Computer Billing Rates

Findings

Computer rates billed the using departments were not adjusted at the end of the year to reflect actual costs. At the end of 1981 the computer center had a cumulative excess balance of $1,215,000, representing excessive amounts billed, which was being carried over as a reserve. As a result, departments were charged excessive rates for use of the computer, and the income for the period was understated. The computer department was not reducing rates billed in order to have a reserve to cover potential increases in costs or future reduced usage.

Recommendations

a. Procedures should be developed to adjust computer rates periodically to reflect actual costs.
b. The surplus should be credited to computer users and reflected in income.

Comments of Auditee

Division personnel agreed with both findings and recommendations and began to take corrective action. They stated, however, that with respect to the excessive computer billing rates some reserve had to be maintained, and would reduce the balance to $75,000 for carryover to the next period.

The internal auditing department wishes to express its appreciation for the very fine cooperation received during the review by the divisional management and personnel.

Respectfully submitted,

Charles W. Reiber
General Auditor

Distribution

R. C. Gulick	Group Vice President
J. R. Whelan	Vice President, Finance
G. E. Bender	Vice President, Purchasing
W. R. Timms	Vice President, Production
J. R. Miller	Vice President, Marketing
R. K. Nolan	Manager, Administrative Services

Reporting in Perspective

While the final payoff of the internal auditing process is the action taken by company personnel to increase the overall effectiveness and profitability of the company operations, a major means by which that action is achieved is the background, development, and execution of good reports. The reporting is a combination of technical skills and the ability to communicate these results to people in a way that will best assure their acceptance and active support. The importance of this part of the internal auditor's work in terms of service potentials underlines the desirability of the general auditor and his associates of giving it the most careful attention. It means especially that the general auditor should himself be actively involved. It means also that all levels of internal auditing staff should think in terms of ultimate report needs. In this connection the problems of report development should also be given proper attention in training programs.

The written report thus is a major tool of the internal auditor for greater management service. It is at the same time his credential when the report is subsequently circulated, referred to, and implemented. It is usually the major factor by which the reputation of the internal auditing department is established. It follows, therefore, that reports should be prepared with special care. It follows also that the department's influence will be better served by issuing better reports, even though this may mean that fewer reports will be released.

PART THREE

Operational Areas

CHAPTER THIRTEEN

Introduction and Basic Financial Control

AUDIT APPROACH FOR OPERATIONAL AREAS

Nature and Scope of Operational Areas

The modern internal auditor is primarily concerned with the operational areas in the organization of which he is a part. These operational areas will vary among individual organizations, depending on the kinds of products produced and services offered. These areas will also vary, depending on the way the particular organization chooses to conduct its operations. There are, however, a range of types of activities that are carried out in the typical business organization, and to a considerable extent in all kinds of organizations. The need, therefore, is to understand these various types of operational activities and then to utilize that understanding as a basis for developing a program for effective review. The chapters in Part Three deal with these commonly encountered types of activities and provide guidance for the related operational reviews.

General Approach to Be Followed

The development of any audit program and the carrying through of the related internal audit review must, if it is to be truly effective, be based on an adequate and effective thought process. We believe that we can contribute best to that thought process by raising the right kind of questions. This means that, while some descriptive and directive material is always necessary, the major emphasis will be on the nature of the more significant types of problems that are likely to be encountered. In that sense the material is intended to be provocative rather than prescriptive.

Manner of Treatment for Each Type of Operational Activity

Each type of operational activity that is reviewed by the internal auditor will have its own special character and unique aspects. And these differences will necessarily have to be recognized. However, as far as possible, we plan to deal with each operational activity in the same manner in terms of general approach.

We first describe the general nature of the particular activity, with emphasis on the function served and the objectives to be achieved. To the extent possible we also look at each activity in terms of the major stages of the operational cycle. Second, we look at the activity in terms of its major control points. As we will see, the identification of these major control points—linked as they necessarily are to the way we structure the various subobjectives—can usually be approached in alternative ways. There is also the further problem of controls within controls. As a third step we cover any special types of problems which exist in the case of that particular operational activity but which have not previously been discussed. Finally, as a fourth step we move to an examination of the internal auditor's specific role in connection with the activity. The purpose of the uniform approach is, on the one hand, to induce a consistent effort as respects each operational area, and on the other hand to provide greater ease of reference for the reader. In all cases there is the common objective to find all possible means of extending the range of management service on the part of internal auditors.

Audit Guides

While the detailed discussions of the various operational areas are intended to provide substantial assistance to the practitioner in developing audit programs for specific situations, there can be some additional benefit in restating some of this material in the form of specific audit guides. Such audit guides cannot provide the depth coverage of the detailed discussions, but they can serve as a convenient summary-type reference.

The audit guides will generally be of two types:

1. Specific kinds of audit actions to be taken.
2. Questions regarding individual aspects of the operational process being reviewed.

The first type will necessarily be quite general and will especially need to be adapted in the individual situation, both for the way the particular activity is actually being operated and to reflect the auditor's judgment as to the extent of the particular test or other audit action. The second type is a useful type of approach to open up a line of inquiry that is appropriate in the individual area or subarea involved. Needless to say, it is not intended that there just be a "yes" or "no" answer. The result desired is careful investigation and critical appraisal, with the subsequent determination of any significant deficiencies, and the opportunities for bettering the operation in some worthwhile manner.

It needs to be recognized also that audit guides can be expanded to almost any level of detail and that the extent of detail actually presented represents an unavoidable compromise between possibilities and practicabilities. Additionally, there is unavoidably some overlap between the various items.

Relation of Audit Guides to Scope of Review. As we have seen in Chapter 9, an operational activity can usually be reviewed as a single functional activity, or can be made a part of a broader review of an integrated operational location. For example, the purchasing activity is an activity that can be approached on a company basis or as part of a broader field operation, or in some combination of the two. If undertaken on a company or total functional basis, the emphasis will most likely be on the broader company-wide policies, and on the type of approach being made to the more important purchasing management problems. Another variation of this functional approach may also take place at a subsidiary or divisional level. In either case there may be some review of the actual purchasing activities at a number of individual field locations.

The other type of approach will be that of examining the purchasing activity at a particular field location as a part of the total operations carried on at that particular field location. This situation is good from the standpoint that all the various types of operational activities are seen in an actual working relationship.

An intermediate type of approach will be the examination of the purchasing activities only at a particular field location. The size of the overall operations at that field location may make this a practical necessity. The audit guides presented cut across all of the three approaches and will necessarily have to be drawn on in a manner appropriate to the scope of the particular review being made.

Types of Audit Guides Applicable to All Operational Areas. In developing audit guides for the various types of operational activity there are many specific guides that cover similar types of inquiry, even though the individuals and organizational units are different. To avoid significant duplication we are including certain standard audit guides at this point. This will make it possible to refer to these standard guides as we deal with the audit guides for individual operational areas, and then to supplement them as necessary.

AUDIT GUIDES

Common to All Operational Areas

I. Introductory
   A. The nature of audit guides as broad guide lines to the development of definitive audit programs should be recognized.
   B. The entire audit program needs to be adapted to the functional or organizational scope of the review.
      (*Note:* The audit guides will usually refer to the activity reviewed as a department regardless of whether the activity being reviewed is a functional activity or an integrated operational entity.)

II. Preparatory Activities
   A. At Headquarters
      1. Discuss timing and scope of planned review with the officer to whom the manager of the department reports. Determine if there are any questions or suggestions.

2. Review reports, working papers, and subsequent development aspects in audit files covering last review.
3. Determine what other individuals should be contacted before beginning the actual review, and arrange and complete such contacts. Determine if there are any questions or suggestions.
4. Make such advance arrangements with the department as are appropriate—living accommodations, work space, needed supporting actions, etc.—depending on the site location.

B. At the Office of the Manager of the Department
1. Explanation of scope of planned review.
2. Determination of manager's concept of his operations, its role, objectives, and special problems.
3. Determine if there are any questions or suggestions.

III. Organizational Factors
A. Organizational Relationships of the Department with Other Company Activities
1. To whom does the head of the department report?
   a. Is this reporting satisfactory in terms of that individual's other responsibilities?
   b. Is the organizational level sufficiently high?
2. Establish that the department is independent of the other company activities from which it receives input and to which it provides output.
3. Obtain and appraise for adequacy all statements of mission, organizational purpose, and major policy relating to the department.
4. To what extent is the responsibility for various types of activities by the department made clear?
5. To what extent do committees or other organizational components participate in the control over policy?
6. To what extent is the function decentralized to other operational components, with only a functional reporting responsibility to the central department? Are the responsibilities clearly stated? Is necessary coordination adequately specified?

B. Organizational Relationships within the Department
1. Obtain and review a copy of the organization chart for the department. Are the assignments of responsibility clear and reasonable for effective internal control?
2. If the department is decentralized on a line basis, review and appraise the manner in which responsibilities are assigned and coordinated.
3. Review and appraise the adequacy of supporting job descriptions.
4. Review and appraise the adequacy of manuals covering policy and procedures.

IV–IX. Operational Activities
To be developed, as required, for each operational activity.

X. Overall Appraisal of Departmental Effectiveness
  A. Examination of Reports Rendered
    1. To appraise adequacy of scope.
    2. To confirm accuracy of data being reported.
    3. Adequacy of backup for reported results.
  B. Program of Goal Achievement
    1. Adequacy of program for establishing and updating operational goals.
    2. Extent of achievement of projected goals.
    3. Extent of best utilization of available resources.
  C. Relations with Other Company Activities
    1. Adequacy of coordination with other company activities to achieve operational effectiveness and maximum company profitability.
    2. Evidence of close relationships with higher-level management for maximum contribution to overall planning and performance.
  D. Relations with Outside Parties
    1. Evidence of efforts to relate effectively to outside parties in current operations.
    2. Adequacy of effort to exploit longer-term dimensions of achieving greater mutual profitability.
  E. Appraisal of People Utilization
    1. Levels of turnover.
    2. State of morale.
    3. Order and efficiency.
    4. Cost performance.
    5. Proper use of qualifications of personnel.
    6. Effectiveness of key personnel.
  F. Appraisal of Fraud Control Efforts
    1. Are fraud potentials adequately considered by the company, both as respects fraud prevention and to minimize temptations to individuals?
    2. Have particular cases of fraud detection been properly handled in accordance with company policies and procedures and general sound business practice? Has proper consideration also been given to the need for modified procedures to avoid similar future developments?
    3. Did the internal auditing department provide all possible assistance to other individuals in the handling of fraud investigations currently in progress?
  G. Extent of Major Problem and Opportunities
    1. What, if any, are the major areas of difficulty? What are the causes and possible remedies?
    2. What are the major areas of improvement? What action is needed?

BASIC FINANCIAL CONTROL

Nature of the Financial Process

This chapter and Chapter 21 will deal with the financial operations that normally are the responsibility of the finance department in a modern business organization. In this chapter we are concerned with the basic operational processes that are in a very real sense part of the total concerns of operational auditing. In the later chapter we will be concerned with a higher-level type of financial policy that is linked more closely to major management decisions and related management policy. We see these financial operations at both levels as part of the continuing concern of the modern operationally oriented internal auditor.

Rule of Reason for Financial Controls

A general word needs to be said about the application of controls in the basic financially oriented operations of the company. We begin always with stating the kind of control we would ideally have in every individual situation. Whether that kind of control is actually practicable in terms of balancing costs and benefits is, however, a further question. In some situations geographical factors may make it necessary that a single individual carry out combined activities which under normal circumstances should be separated. In other situations the volume of a particular activity may be so small that it is simply not realistic in a practical business sense to hire additional personnel to achieve an otherwise desirable distribution of responsibilities. It is important not only that we understand the bases of the most effective control, and use them as guides, but also that we evaluate the degree of implementation in terms of the practical aspects of the individual situation. What we actually do is to get as close to proper principles as we can within the limitations of each situation. The philosophy needs to be kept in mind especially as one reads this chapter.

CASH PROCESSES

From a financial control standpoint cash is of special interest and concern because of the fact that in its most basic form it is the most transferable, and from a risk standpoint the most vulnerable type of item. Because of the greater risks involved there is the greater need for protection and control. There is also the ever-continuing objective to minimize the extent of the problem by eliminating the use of cash to the extent practicable. At the same time there are important managerial dimensions of using cash in the most effective manner. For all these reasons the various cash processes are of major concern to the management-minded internal auditor.

Sources of Cash

A discussion of the cash processes starts most logically with an identification of where and why cash is received in a particular company situation. In each case we can properly ask ourselves the question of whether this is necessarily so or whether it might be done differently. For example, is it really necessary that salesmen accept cash from customers? Or, if there must be collections, do they have to be in cash? Perhaps, however, cash is best in terms of accelerating and maximizing collections. On the other hand, we might either urge (but not require) a different procedure, and in certain cases actually require it. The important thing is that the reviewer critically appraise each situation and determine what degree of compromise from a control standpoint is justified because of other operational considerations.

In most situations the sources of cash also lend themselves to another type of control. This control is the extent to which estimates can be made of the amount of cash that should be received from the different sources. This does not take the place of regular records of claims which must be ultimately liquidated by cash received—as, for example, accounts receivable—but it supplements such records. Thus we might have initial expectations as to the amount of the cash collections to originate at a certain point at particular times. In cases where there are lesser degrees of control, the estimate of what ought to be becomes all the more important. An example of the latter would be miscellaneous cash sales, or perhaps service fees.

Receiving of Cash

The receiving of cash as a phase of the total cash process can be defined in various ways. As a minimum it covers the *first* receival of the cash from any party outside the company. Thereafter it blends with the handling of cash, as the cash received moves internally toward the centralized control which is normally exercised by a company. There is thus some unavoidable overlap, requiring a consideration of the total span of the cash process. It will be useful, however, to describe first the key principles of control which apply partially or completely to cash receipts. These controls focus both on the outside part, to be sure that we receive cash which should be received, and on the employee, to be sure that cash received is not improperly diverted.

1. *Accountability should be established at the earliest possible time.* The sooner we can bring cash received under control the better. This is accomplished by establishing the best possible kind of record of initial accountability. A common example would be the issuance of a serially numbered cash receipt, with one copy to the outside party. Another example would be the ringing up of the transaction on a cash register. Or a serially numbered ticket of some kind might be issued in exchange for the cash received.

2. *Relief of internal accountabilities should be tied to the cash receipts to the extent practicable.* Ideally, the receipt of the cash, which establishes a new accountability, will be linked to the relief of a previously existing accountability. Illustrative would be the collection of an account receivable. Another illustration would be the sale of merchandise controlled

on an item-by-item inventory basis, where the company employee must account for inventory or cash.

3. *Controls should be instituted to assure collection for services provided.* The first requirement here is that the customer pays for a service he is receiving. In some cases this might be a cash sale slip or a ticket, without which the customer could not receive a service. This might also need to be supplemented by physical protection over merchandise or restricted entry to areas where services are rendered, as in the case of a theatre. Internally, the control might require the segregation of responsibilities, as where one person sells the tickets, or issues the particular authorization, and another person collects the ticket or authorization.

4. *The outside party should be utilized where possible, as a further control.* In some situations the presence of the customer can serve to some extent to check on the action of the employee. For example, the customer presence will help provide assurance that the employee rings up a cash receipt on a cash register.

5. *Consolidation of cash receiving points.* From a control standpoint the fewer the number of cash receiving points, the more effective the control will be. Also the consolidation of the cash receiving, with the greater volume at the fewer points, makes it possible to separate responsibilties to a greater extent between different individuals. Obviously, these benefits must be weighed against the needs of properly servicing customers or other parties involved.

6. *Cash receipts should be separated from cash disbursements.* There is frequently the pressure to utilize portions of the cash received to cover current expenditures of one kind or another. Under normal circumstances this pressure should be resisted. More effective control and cleaner accountabilities are possible if the cash receipts process and the cash disbursements processes are completely separated, and where each is controlled by different means.

7. *Cash receipts to be channeled intact and promptly to the central cash depositories.* Closely related to the preceding principle is the desirability of depositing, or otherwise transferring, the cash received intact for the specified day or other period, and as promptly as is practicable. For example, a day's receipts should normally be deposited intact as soon as possible after the cutoff for the day. This is important for several reasons. First, a delay in deposit results in a greater risk of theft or diversion. Second, checks might be good now but not at a later point of time. Third, it is important to be able to identify a particular deposit with a given period of time. Finally, as we shall discuss later at greater length, undeposited cash is idle cash and is not contributing to the best possible utilization of corporate resources.

8. *Accountabilities should be properly established for all transfers.* Since the accountability for cash should be fixed at all times, it is important

when cash is transferred that the accountability of the transferor be properly relieved and that the new accountability of the transferee be clearly established. This is normally accomplished by some type of a cash receipt or transfer record.

9. *Records covering accountabilities should be independently operated.* The records by which the accountabilities for cash are established and controlled should be maintained by persons who are independent of the persons charged with the direct accountability. The latter persons should not have access to the records and hence not be able to improperly relieve their own accountabilities. Checks should be made periodically by an independent person to assure that cash has been properly handled and accounted for.

Cash Handling and Custody

The handling of cash, as has previously been noted, is interwoven to some extent with both the receiving and disbursement phases. There are, however, certain additional control aspects which can be best considered under the heading of cash handling and custody.

1. *Physical safeguards should be adequate.* The types of physical safeguards needed in individual situations will depend on the amounts of cash normally on hand and the extent of the risks that exist. In certain cases, locked cabinets may be adequate; in other cases small safes are needed; and in still other cases the most elaborate type of burglar proof vaults will be needed. These facilities then must be actually used. The access to these facilities must also be controlled through the care with which keys and combinations are made available. During operational periods the area used by the cashier needs to be adequately sealed off by cages or separately partitioned portions of office quarters. Finally, when cash is transferred there must be suitable protection, depending on the scope of the exposure.

2. *Adequacy of insurance coverage.* Cash on hand is subject to the risks of fire and burglary. Normal business prudence requires that these risks be covered by insurance at adequate levels.

3. *Cash on hand should be kept at minimum levels.* The greater the amount of cash on hand at any given location, the greater is the risk of loss in a physical sense. At the same time, having cash on hand which is in excess of actual needs means a loss of potential earnings through the lesser utilization of that cash. Keeping cash at minimum levels is therefore important for the company's interests. This holds true at any level in the organization, including the central depository itself.

4. *Earning potentials should be realized to the extent practicable.* Since "cash" is a broad term that goes beyond physical cash on hand to include all types of bank accounts, we need to recognize the earning potentials that can be realized, where practicable, through the placement of funds

in savings accounts or under other arrangements where some interest will be earned. In some cases, however, the maintenance of given bank balances may be the basis for credit lines or other services rendered by the banks involved. The objective is to exploit these potentials to the maximum extent possible. For other cases, it may be possible to maintain balances only sufficient to meet checks as they clear the account.

Cash Disbursements

Cash received and available in various forms is now ready for use by the company—for the purchase of operating facilities, payment of expenses, and for investments. The general objective is that these disbursements be for valid and proper purposes, that fair value has been received, and that they are in the correct amounts. The special control aspects can be summarized as follows:

1. *Separation of the Disbursement Function.* As previously noted, the cash receipts and cash disbursement phases of the total cash process need to be as separate as possible. Cash received has been channeled to the central cash depository, and now the disbursement phase can be separately handled and controlled.

2. *Adequacy of Documentation for Liquidation of Payables.* In the normal financial operations the major types of expenditures are processed through the creation of a payable, which is then subsequently liquidated by the cash disbursement. At the same time, however, the disbursement is normally reviewed in terms of the validity of the underlying payable, plus the propriety of the timing of the liquidation of that payable. The nature and scope of this documentation will be discussed further under accounts payable.

3. *Use of Petty Cash Funds.* A number of situations will arise when small cash expenditures must be made without delay. In other situations the amounts may be too small to justify the application of the formal disbursement procedures. In these circumstances cash must be advanced and be available to service those needs. Normally, this can be best accomplished when the funds are handled on an "imprest" basis. Under this procedure a designated amount is advanced, and then reimbursements are made to the fund from time to time covering exactly the total amount of expenditures, thus bringing the fund back to its original level. The receipts or other documentation supporting the individual expenditures provide the documentary backup for the reimbursement of the fund. The size of the fund should be large enough to sustain expenditures of the amounts reasonably expected, but with allowance for the time required to process the previously described reimbursements. On the other hand, as previously noted under cash handling, the size of the fund should be no larger than necessary. The level of the fund can be changed at any time, and from time to time the need for such change should be reappraised in the light of experience and new conditions.

Several other important matters relating to petty cash funds need to be mentioned. Since the individual expenditures involve cash it is extremely important that satisfactory evidence be obtained to support the expenditure. If such evidence is not directly available in the form of an invoice, cash register slip, or receipt, it will be necessary that a special receipt be prepared and signed, preferably by the recipient of the cash, but at least by the person making the expenditure. These supporting documents should be canceled at the time of reimbursement to prevent their reuse. There is the continuous temptation to relax on obtaining adequate documentation. There is also the temptation to use the cash for improper purposes, as, for example, personal employee needs. The matter of documentation can be monitored via the review at the time of reimbursement. The improper use, however, cannot be detected except by an actual examination and count of the fund. Both of these protective efforts need to be carried out on a continuing basis.

4. *Use of Branch Imprest Funds.* In other higher-level situations it becomes useful or necessary for a branch location to issue checks for local expenditures. Here again the imprest approach can be effectively utilized. Again, also the same principles apply as to the handling of the documentation, the usage of the fund, and as to the level of the fund itself.

5. *Control over Check Signatures.* In most situations it is useful to require two signatures on checks. This serves as a cross check of one person against another, both for the prevention of fraud and error and as to the care and judgment being exercised. In some situations, however, signature plates may be used, and here the important point of control becomes that of access to the plates and the condition of the usage of them.

6. *Designation of Payee of Checks.* It is important that all checks issued should be made payable to the specific individual or firm from which the products or services are obtained. The writing of checks to cash or to bearer would be strictly avoided, since cash can then more easily be used for unauthorized purposes.

7. *Maximum Separation of Duties and Responsibilities.* The cash disbursement process particularly highlights the desirability of breaking down the various aspects of the activities and assigning them to different individuals. Thus one person might review the documentation, another prepare the check, a third review the propriety of the combined set of documents, a fourth provide the primary signature, and a fifth the secondary signature. Each activity then serves as a cross check on the other.

Other General Aspects of Cash Process

A number of matters pertaining to effective control cut across the receival, handling, and disbursement aspects of the cash process. These are, as follows:

1. *Bonding of Employees.* Normal business prudence requires that all employees participating in any part of the cash processes be bonded. The

benefits to be derived are twofold. First, there is the actual protection to the company in the case of any defalcation or other improper diversion of company funds. Second, the fact of the bonding is more likely to motivate the individual employee to exercise a higher standard of care and integrity. To accomplish the latter there is the need that the bonding action be properly publicized.

2. *Maximum Exploitation of Mechanical Aids.* A considerable range of mechanical aids has been developed covering various phases of the cash processes. The types of assistance rendered include record keeping, physical protection, better control, and labor efficiency. The modern cash register is illustrative of a device that protects cash by restricting access, establishes a record of accountability and motivates good control through its visible record of a transaction. The special benefits of most mechanical aids is that they better assure a uniform handling of designated matters at the desired level of control. All of these opportunities need to be considered and adequately exploited.

3. *Keeping Records Up to Date and Prompt Reporting.* In all parts of the cash processes it is especially important that all records be kept up to date as a basis for both efficient current reference and prompt periodic reporting. There is at the same time the important psychological motivation to the people participating in the cash process as to the need for special care. Delays in carrying out various parts of the cash processes can generate greater physical risk and at the same time restrict the efficient utilization of cash resources.

4. *Control of Blank Checks and Other Supplies.* The proper control of papers and forms is always important in terms of physical protection and efficient usage. In the case of the cash processes this control becomes especially important since certain forms, as in the case of blank checks, might somehow be used for improper purposes.

5. *Independent Reconciliation of Bank Accounts.* The periodic reconciliation of bank accounts represents an important point of control over both the cash receipts and disbursement activities. It is important therefore that these reconciliations be made by persons who are independent of the regular receiving and disbursing operations. Bank statements and canceled checks should also be obtained or received directly from the depositories to assure that they have not been tampered with in any manner by any intermediary. Bank reconciliations also provide the opportunity to review various aspects of how receipts and disbursements are handled, and additionally to identify unusual actions.

RECEIVABLE PROCESSES

Nature of Receivable Processes

The receivable processes cover any type of company action that generates claims against individuals or companies. The claims are usually against parties outside the company, but at times can also involve employees and officers. The claims are brought into existence as an intermediary phase pending the ultimate collection of them in the form of cash or other types of consideration. Although these claims can originate in a variety of ways, the major category has to do with the sale of products produced, or services rendered by the company. We will therefore deal first with this category and then later touch on some of the other types.

The receivable processes that relate primarily to sales have a number of important relationships. There is the immediate necessity for policies covering the extent to which credit is first granted and then subsequently administered. Who should be extended credit? In what amounts? How aggressive should the company be in pressing for subsequent collection? A second type of consideration has to do with how these receivable activities bear on customer satisfaction and continuing customer goodwill. The company is unavoidably interested in how customers react to the modes of credit authorization, billing, and collection. The company is also interested in what it can learn through the receivable relationships about how the customers are reacting to company products and policies in a broader sense. Finally, there is the specific interest of the company in the efficiency of its various receivable activities and the effectiveness of the control.

The processes relating to receivables group themselves into three phases. The first phase has to do with the conditions under which the receivable comes into existence. The second phase covers the administration of the receivables thus created. The third phase consists of the means by which the receivable is finally liquidated. Our objective in each case will be to understand the general range of matters involved and to identify the major problems of control.

Generating Receivables

Since the account receivable normally arises out of the sale of company products or the rendering of some kind of service, the first interest has to do with establishing a direct linkage with that underlying basis. There is the objective of being certain that the receivable being created is backed up by the shipment of the product or the performing of the service. At the same time we want to be sure that all receivables are brought on to the record that should have been. Both objectives are more likely to be satisfied when the creation of the receivable can be directly linked with the relief of an inventory accountability or with the record of the performance of the service. We therefore strive to establish this linkage in a specific procedural sense.

As we have previously noted also, the generating of the receivable immediately involves the question of whether the company wishes to extend the required credit to the customer to cover the sale. Underlying this determination is the general credit policy of the company, but now the general policy must be applied to the particular customer in the light of that customer's credit standing and our own experience with him. When that credit acceptability has been determined, the regular sales and billing procedures are initiated. As a part of those procedures an invoice is prepared and the account of the customer charged.

The major control considerations that apply to the generating of the receivables are as follows:

1. *Independent Review and Approval of Credit.* When an order is received, the credit approval must be obtained. This approval should be provided by an independent department or person within the framework of established company policy and appropriate information about the particular customer. This latter information covers the financial standing of the customer and his general credit standing. It also includes up-to-date facts as to the company's own experience with the party, including his present receivable position. The approval itself is made by properly authorized individuals, depending on the amount involved.

2. *Determination of Product Availability.* All items ordered by the customer may not be available for shipment at this time, and hence cannot be included in current billings. The goods actually available must be identified on appropriate assembly and packing papers, which then establish the specific basis for shipment and billing. Other items not now available must be covered by backorder procedures for later shipments.

3. *Authorization of Prices and Terms.* Prices and terms may be completely standardized for all customers. In some cases, however, these will vary for different groups of customers and for different quantities being sold to those customers. For billing purposes the applicable prices and terms must be provided based on established company policy. Interpretations or special deviations must additionally be approved by properly authorized individuals.

4. *Multicopy Papers for Related Purposes.* Invoices need to be prepared in enough copies so that the same identical information can be used for a number of operational purposes. Thus one copy authorizes the shipment, another goes to the customer, another is used for the compilation of sales data, and still another goes to the accounts receivable department for posting. Controls can also be established covering the total of the individual invoices for a given period, usually one business day.

Administration of Receivables

The administration phase of the receivable process picks up where the generating phase ends and goes on to handle the receivable until it is paid or otherwise liquidated. The major control considerations during this new phase include:

1. *Independent and Controlled Accounts Receivable Records.* The actual accounts receivable records in some situations may be maintained manually and in others on various types of bookkeeping machines. In larger installations they will be handled on a computer. The principles, however,

in all cases are that the records be independently maintained and not subject to access by outside parties, especially by those who might have access to cash or to the customers themselves. In all cases also there must be control accounts, and possibly subcontrol accounts, which are supported by the individual detailed accounts.

2. *Current Posting and Control.* Ideally, newly generated charges, credits from cash collections, and all other miscellaneous charges and credits will be posted on a daily basis so that up-to-date information is currently available to serve the various operational needs in the company. At the same time accuracy is maintained through the current check on the agreement of detailed accounts with the control accounts.

3. *Prompt and Adequate Reporting.* In addition to information furnished currently, there should be periodic reports of current balances, together with aging analysis. The latter analysis shows the portions of the account balance which have been unpaid for different time periods—for example, current, one month overdue, two months overdue, three months overdue, and so on. This analysis is an important basis for the administration of the ongoing credit and collection efforts.

4. *Direct and Independent Mailing of Statements.* A basic feature from a control standpoint is that statements are mailed directly to the individual customers without any opportunity for diversion or modification by any other company personnel. This makes it possible for the statements to serve as a reliable cross check upon the accuracy of the individual accounts. It is also an important means of disclosing the delayed reporting of collections.

Disposition of Receivables

The receivables represent an asset claim against the particular parties involved. It is, therefore, important that this claim not be relieved except in a properly authorized manner. The four normal modes of relief can be listed, together with the major control considerations, as follows:

1. *Cash Collections.* The most usual development is that cash collections from customers will liquidate the previously generated receivables. Summary controls cover the relief of receivables and a corresponding charge to cash accountabilities. This is our previously discussed problem of achieving adequate control over cash receipts. At the same time assurance must be provided that discounts deducted are properly earned and accounted for.

2. *Merchandise Returns.* When products sold are returned for one reason or another, we have the reverse process of the original sale. First, there is the requirement that the actual return be authorized. Second, there is the requirement that the products actually be received and that they are in proper condition. Finally, there is the need to be certain that the

credit is in the proper amount. These three assurances when properly documented provide the basis for a sales return credit.

3. *Adjustments and Allowances.* Still harder to control are the many situations where a customer is granted some kind of a special allowance or credit. This may be for volume purchases, for the sale of particular types of products by the customer, or to adjust for product deficiencies. Where the allowance is pursuant to a specific arrangement the control is to confirm compliance with the arrangement. In many cases, however, the authenticity of the credit is based on judgmental factors as evaluated by an executive who then approves the credit within the limits of his own authority.

4. *Write-off to Bad Debts.* To some extent, there are normally some customers who simply fail to pay. Although every possible effort should be made to enforce payment, there may be bankruptcy situations, disappearance of the debtor, or other causes which leave no other alternative but for a write-off. Usually, provision has previously been made for such losses through the creation of reserves for doubtful accounts, and now the actual write-off is charged to that reserve. One specific interest at this point is that the write off has been properly authorized by a sufficiently high-level company officer. The other interest is that the accounts written off are covered by new controls and given adequate continuing attention in the way of such further collection effort as is practicable and reasonable.

Policy Aspects of Accounts Receivable

Having considered the operational framework of the receivable process, we need to look more carefully at several key policy areas relating to the handling of receivables.

Economics of Credit Levels. A continuing policy question is how liberal a company should be in its extension of credit. It is, of course, clear that the tighter the credit granting the lower will be the ultimate bad debt losses. But the judgment of what credit policy best serves the company's total interests cannot stop there. The sales made pursuant to the more liberal credit policy may be additional sales which otherwise would not have been made. But these sales will yield extra profits. Hence it may well be in the company's interests to generate these higher sales. Also, higher sales may generate additional production economies. It may be very difficult to measure the incremental benefits accurately but it is important to recognize the several dimensions of the problem. What it means is that a low record of bad-debt losses is not necessarily in the company's overall interests, and that hence we must examine the entire situation in greater depth.

Customer Relations Impact of the Receivables Process. A related important aspect of both the operation of the credit department and the total receivable process is the major impact that all activities have on good customer relations. We know on the one hand that it is in the company's interests to develop efficient internal procedures and operations. In this endeavor it is frequently desirable to streamline procedures and to reduce the degree of personal contacts and treatment in the handling of the various relationships. On the other hand, the receivable processes unavoidably involve customer relationships. We need therefore to handle these customer contacts in a way which minimizes customer irritation and builds positive customer good will. Examples of these contacts would include the handling of credit applications, clarity of billings, processing of credits and adjustments, and the various collection efforts. Real effectiveness here is to combine internal efficiency with courteous and reasonably cooperative customer relationships. Very often also customer dissatisfaction due to many different causes (and quite independent of the receivable process) may surface through the receivable contacts. Here the receivable personnel have a further opportunity to help channel these problems to company personnel who will solve them, and to thus build greater customer goodwill.

Other Accounts Receivable Processes

Although regular company sales activities provide the major source of accounts receivable, there are various other activities and developments that may lead to some special types of accounts receivable. Illustrative of this group would be:

1. *Advances to Employees.* Sales of regular company products or services would be normally included in the regular accounts receivable. However, there may also be advances of one kind or another—for travel, special business purposes, or possibly for personal reasons. While there is the special security of salaries and wages which are currently being earned, the extent of such advances is normally very closely controlled. Advances for personal purposes would especially require approval by properly authorized officers.

2. *Deposits with Outsiders.* In many situations deposits are required in connection with establishment of utility services or for other reasons. These deposits may be of a temporary nature or may be permanent as long as the service is being utilized. The record is important so that recovery of the deposit is made when the original need no longer exists.

3. *Claims.* Relations with vendors, carriers, or any outside service group can lead to claims asserted which need to be recorded pending actual reimbursement. Insurance claims will provide still another source of such receivables. Although an alternative approach is to forgo setting the claim up on the books, and recording the proceeds when received, more effective control is provided by the actual recording of the claim as a receivable.

4. *Accruals of Income.* A special type of receivable in a very loose sense exists when earned income is accrued prior to being due and collectible.

The objective here in an operational sense is to recognize income in the periods actually earned and to thus provide a better evaluation of current operational performance.

Special Aspects of Other Receivable Processes. While the nature and scope of the transactions and activities that generate these miscellaneous types of receivables can vary greatly, there are certain control aspects which are generally applicable to all. The first of these is that the conditions under which the particular type of receivable is created is clearly defined in both a policy and procedural sense. A special objective is to provide adequate safeguards that the receivable is actually brought on to the books at the earliest possible time, and in the proper amount, as far as it can be determined. The second control aspect is that procedures need to be established for the periodic review of the status of all of these miscellaneous receivables. What frequently happens is that these miscellaneous receivables get overlooked in a regular operational sense, and are not given adequate attention. It is necessary therefore to take specific precautions that will combat such tendencies.

Notes Receivable Processes

In some situations it may be that practice of a particular company to make sales for its products and services on a deferred payment basis. In such cases contracts may be executed which specify the timing of the payments. In other cases, notes receivable may be obtained. Notes receivable can, however, also originate as an outgrowth of the collection problems with regular accounts receivable. It may be that circumstances have developed where the regular account cannot be liquidated in accordance with the intended plan. It may be in such a situation that the company wishes to obtain what it regards as a more precise recognition of the receivable through the use of notes receivable. Also, it may be that interest can now be charged. In all these situations the circumstances need to be defined and properly authorized under which the notes receivable come into existence. Subsequently, there is the need for a regular monitoring of the collection of the notes on the dates specified, including the collection of such interest as has been agreed upon. Notes receivable also pose a further problem of custody, since the notes exist as separate documents. There is the possibility that since the use of notes receivable is a more unusual type of transaction, regular and systematic attention will not be given to them. Hence specific procedures may be needed to assure periodic review and possible action.

PAYABLE PROCESSES

Nature of Payable Processes

The operation of any company necessarily requires that there be expenditures. These expenditures are for materials, products, equipment, salaries and wages, and services of various kinds. All of these expenditures involve the creation of company obligations which are then either immediately liquidated, as in the case of a cash expenditure, or are liquidated at some future time. The payable processes have to do with the recognition of all of these obligations and the subsequent control and handling of them. When these obligations are liquidated the payable processes merge with the cash disbursement procedures discussed earlier in this chapter. The payable processes are thus generated by the underlying operating activities of the company but focus on the financial control of the total process. This financial control is concerned with the promptness and accuracy with which such obligations are formally recognized, the legitimacy and propriety of those obligations, and the procedures by which the stage is set for the final liquidation.

The payable processes involve activities that fit into fairly well defined groups. There is first, the activities which have to do with the creation of the payables. How do we control the amount of the payable and how do we determine the validity? Second, there are the various activities in administering the existing payables. What kinds of special problems are encountered in terms of current recording and control? Finally, there are the procedures by which the individual payables are prepared for actual payment, thus leading to the issuance of a check covering the actual liquidation. We will briefly discuss the payment processes under these headings.

Generating Payables

Payables can originate from a variety of sources. The normal and most voluminous source will be as a result of the purchase of products and services by the regularly established purchasing department, as discussed in Chapter 14. These products and services will relate largely to items purchased for resale, or for use in the production of products and services to be sold by the company. But as we have seen, they can also be for any operational need of the company. Additionally, many purchases of products and services are for various reasons procured directly by company personnel directly involved in other line and staff activities. In terms of value importance the item can range from the smallest type of purchase to the purchase of major capital items. In all cases the basic control issue is that obligations are incurred only within authorized limits. These authorized limits cover the kind of expenditure, the dollar amount of that expenditure, and the individual incurring the particular obligation. What we have here are delegations of authority from the basic source of authority—the board of directors—plus authorized redelegations. Needless to say, emergencies may develop when these authorized limits are violated, in which case the unauthorized action must be ratified to give it proper standing. However, such emergencies should be carefully evaluated to be sure that emergencies are real emergencies, not just a device to get around established limits of authority.

What Constitutes a Valid Payable?   Regardless of the source of the payable there are certain common objectives which exist from a financial control standpoint over all types of payables. These objectives can be described as follows:

1. *Is the type of expenditure reasonable?* The objective here is that the expenditure bears a reasonable relationship to the operations of the business. Normally, this relationship is self-evident, but in other cases it may be partially or completely obscure. In that case a question is raised that needs to be probed for a reasonable explanation. To the extent that such a reasonable explanation is not available, there is the greater dependence on the approvals recorded by individual company officers.

2. *Are quantities excessive?* A related question is whether the expenditure is of a reasonable magnitude in terms of the quantities or volume purchased. The pressures for higher levels may be to obtain lower prices or simply to provide higher reserves for operational needs. In either case there is a level of judgment involved, which is subject to reasonable evaluation. Again the more excessive the deviation from normal levels, the greater dependence that must be placed on the judgment and approval of the particular officers who authorize the particular expenditure.

3. *Are prices and terms correct?* The concern with prices and terms is twofold. One question has to do with their correctness in terms of previous agreements covering expenditures of which the present payable is one portion. The second concern is that the prices and terms are the best obtainable. In the latter case it may be that nothing can be done about the particular payable, but there may be the possibility of affecting future expenditures. Prices and terms as used here will include list prices, discounts, time of payment, freight basis, warranties, guarantees, and the like.

4. *Was proper value received?* There is always concern that the proper value has been received. One aspect of this concern is that the services invoiced have actually been rendered, or that the products invoiced have actually been received. The second aspect is that the goods or services were of the proper specifications, condition, and quality. There is the need for proper evidence to cover both of these aspects. If payables are to be validated prior to the receipt of value as described above, there will again be the need for adequate approval by authorized officers. There will also be the further need for supplementary controls to check on the later compliance with the temporarily waived requirements.

5. *Are approvals and supporting evidence adequate?* The validation of payables requires that there be proper documentary evidence to back up the concerns of the type previously described. This evidence will consist of basic papers such as purchase orders and receiving reports. It will also include the specific approvals of properly authorized and qualified officers. These specific approvals cover various aspects of the validity and in each case the question needs to be asked both as to whether the person approving has the authority to make that approval and whether the level of that authorization is adequate.

Intermediate Administration of Payables

In some cases the validation of the payable leads immediately to the cash disbursement phase. In other cases the validated payables are held for later liquidation. From a control standpoint it is desirable to recognize the payable formally at the earliest possible time. However, it may be more efficient to achieve this control through filing procedures and to defer the formal accounting recognition until either the time of payment or the end of an accounting period, whichever comes first. Under such an approach, however, there are certain matters that have to be handled, as follows:

1. *Coordination and Control of Incoming Papers.* Under a system of proper internal control the various papers relating to the individual payables will be flowing directly to the accounts payable department. These will include a copy of the purchase order from the purchasing department, the receiving report from the receiving department, claim forms from shortages or quality deficiencies, charges for transportation paid for our account, and original copies of invoices and statements received from vendors. All of these papers need to be filed in a manner that will facilitate later assembly to support final payments.

2. *Making Accounting Distributions.* All expenditures must ultimately be charged to the proper expense or asset accounts, as determined by the existing accounting policies and procedures. In some cases also, supplementary budgetary charges must be made. The analysis of the correct distributions requires an adequate knowledge of the total account structure. The actual distribution may also require special supplementary work sheets.

3. *Subsidiary Ledger Control.* Once the payables are formally recognized, the overall control of payables is achieved through one or more control accounts backed up by subsidiary ledgers. The latter must be periodically checked to determine that they are in agreement with the controls. Offsetting errors in individual accounts will be checked and reconciled when vendor statements are received. These detailed ledgers are commonly maintained on computers.

4. *Planning for Payment Dates.* Where the eligibility exists for the application of cash discounts through timely payments, the controls must be provided to exploit these benefits. Normally, the loss of discounts represents a severe financial penalty in terms of current interest costs. In other cases the terms of the payables will require payment by specific dates. Good relations with vendors depend in part on making payments at the proper times. Late payments and deduction of unearned discounts are especially irritating. All of this means that controls must be set up to assure completion of the final processing and payment in the manner and at the time intended.

Final Review and Payment

The final phase of the payable process is to prepare the payable for payment. The key control points at this stage are:

1. *Final Assembly and Matching of Supporting Documents.* Now the pertinent supporting papers—purchase order, receiving report, and invoice—must be brought together and checked for clerical accuracy and agreement. The total set is assembled in a physical sense and a request for a check then prepared.

2. *Deduction of Counter Claims.* Control procedures are now necessary to identify all outstanding claims against the particular creditor that should be deducted from the payment. In some cases amounts are to be withheld pending final inspection or usage. The request for a check is appropriately modified to reflect these deductions.

3. *Preparation of Check.* The request for check, supported by the previously described set of documents, is now subjected to independent review, and, when approved by a properly authorized individual, is routed to individuals who will prepare the actual disbursement check.

4. *Final Review and Release.* The check and supporting payable package is now ready for final review by independent reviewers. These independent reviewers will either provide one of the check signatures or will initial the authorization for an officer to sign. If a check has been mechanically signed the approval validates that action. At this stage the reviewers and signers are concerned both with the completeness of the supporting papers, and with the kinds of questions discussed earlier under general validation. When this phase has been completed, the check is referenced on the supporting documents, supporting papers are canceled in some way to prevent reuse, and the check is mailed directly to the vendors.

Separation of Processing Responsibilities

The payable process as just described is one that can vary in many respects in individual situations. Especially in the case of computerized systems there will be many different kinds of procedures. In any of these procedural arrangements the most critical aspect from a financial control standpoint is that the various processing activities are separately assigned to different individuals. The resulting separation and independence is important for purposes of clerical cross check, thus assuring greater accuracy. It also prevents manipulation by any one individual to create disbursements or relief of payable obligations where somehow he could personally profit. In such a separation the accountabilities of the individual persons can be more precisely fixed.

Other Payable Processes

While the greater part of the payable process will normally be concerned with the types of accounts payable just described, there are a number of other operating activities which generate various types of other payables. Although some of these focus more directly on the correctness of the periodic financial statements, there is a significant operational aspect. We will consider several of the more common supplementary payable processes.

Travel Expenses. A type of payable that has some very special characteristics is that of obligations incurred for travel expenses. Although the usual sequence is to advance funds to the individual travelers and to then credit those advances at the time properly approved expense reports are submitted, the basic nature is that of a company expenditure within the framework of the payables group. However, the fact of the cash advance does often create a supplemental operating problem in that such advances may be misused by the recipient. This misuse is commonly the use of the funds for personal purposes or the comingling of such advances with personal funds. In other cases the money may be legitimately used, but there is an undue procrastication in preparing the expense accounts which relieve the existing accountabilities. Systematic follow-up is, therefore, required on keeping the submission of expense reports up to date.

When the expense accounts are actually submitted, the need becomes one of validating the propriety of the expenditures claimed. A number of problems are involved of which the following are the most common.

1. The traveler may have incurred expenses beyond levels established by the company, or in the absence of such established levels, in excess of prudent levels.
2. Items may be claimed which are not allowable as expenses.
3. Amounts claimed may not be properly documented, leaving open the possibility that the items have been overstated.
4. Entertainment expenditures may be for persons not in the regular line of company business, and where the legitimacy of the expenditures may be very doubtful.
5. Approvals of responsible supervisors may not be obtained.

The handling of expense accounts is a very difficult one, especially where individual expenditures are a matter of judgment. Normally, it is desirable to have established policies covering the various types of expense. Also, the entire procedure should be continuously monitored. This means that questions must be raised when established policies are unduly violated or where the evidence is not sufficiently clear. Receipts and hotel bills should also be required to the extent practicable. These controls are necessary both to provide needed support for company expenditures, but also to minimize the always existing temptation of a traveler to use expense accounts for personal advantage.

Financing Activities. The financing activities will be discussed in greater detail in Chapter 21 as a part of the financial policy area. We take note here, however, that they do lead to the creation of some very important payables and related financial control processes. The financing activities pertain to two quite different, although obviously related, types of needs. One of these is for short-term purposes and includes principally loans obtained from banks and other short-term creditors. The other kind of financing activities has to do with long-term needs. The latter needs are satisfied either by equity financing or through bonds or long-term payable. In the case of the bonds payable the detailed procedures are normally carried out by banks which act as agents. Procedural controls maintained by the company would, therefore, not be elaborate in most of these situations. However, they will need to be sufficient to assure timely payments of both principal and interest.

Expense Accruals. The desire from an operational standpoint to determine financial performance again leads us to recognize expenses applicable to current periods which have not yet been processed as regular payables. These accruals are in effect a preliminary recognition of obligations which will later be fully recognized and then liquidated. Illustrative would be interest on notes and bonds payable, taxes, and salaries and wages. The control objective is to recognize all pertinent accruals and to measure them in as accurate manner as is practicable.

Notes Payable. In many situations the payable process may by agreement result directly in the creation of notes payable. This treatment is adopted usually when longer payment periods are envisioned and where interest may be involved. The vendor also may wish to be able to discount the notes with financial institutions or to use them as collateral for loans. In other situations the notes payable may come as a later development when accounts payable cannot be liquidated on a timely basis. From a control standpoint the interest would be in the conditions for the creation of the notes payable, and in the procedures which will adequately assure the meeting of future payment dates for both interest and principal. Adequate detailed supporting records will also be necessary for current reference and control.

PAYROLLS

Nature of the Payroll Process

The payable process includes expenditures for salaries and wages of company personnel. The expenditures of this latter type, however, require special consideration for a number of reasons. One of the reasons is the fact that salaries and wages usually represent the largest segment of the company's operating costs. A second reason is that these expenditures involve people and consequently the inevitable people problems. Payrolls are also of special interest because they relate so closely to the operational problems of all company activities and the efforts to achieve effective labor utilization. A final special aspect concerns the many interrelated legal considerations which come about through minimum wage legislation, unemployment insurance, and social security. Payroll costs are thus at the heart of the total company operations. Our interest at this point, however, is with the way payroll data are initially developed and subsequently processed. We are especially interested also in the way adequate control is achieved. The latter is of special importance because of the frequent cases of fraud which arise in connection with the payroll activities.

Tie to the Personnel Department.   As we saw previously, the personnel department is engaged in a wide range of activities that pertain to the administration of people relationships. At the same time the personnel records maintained constitute a major independent source of authority for the payroll operations. It is here in the first instance that the record of hires exists and the conditions of such hiring actions. Subsequently, changes in status and compensation are recorded. Administered here, partially or completely, are the various programs that generate special charges or credits. Finally, the record here covers termination from the company. From a control standpoint all of these records become a major source of reference and authority. Needless to say, it is extremely important to protect that independence in all the operations relating to the processing of payrolls. The actual processing itself is done by an operational group which is normally a part of the accounting group.

Tie to Computerization.   The preparation of payrolls in the typical situation involves a great deal of detail and clerical activity. It has, therefore, been an area where computers have had their earliest advantageous applications. Computers have the capacity to handle the many detailed calculations and summarizations required. These computer operations in their broader sense are dealt with more fully in Chapter 22. At this point we will be concerned with the basic problems and issues that relate to payrolls irrespective of the means by which the payrolls are actually processed.

Source of Payroll Data

Since payrolls have to do with employees and their compensation for work performed, the starting point is the requirement that the individual be a properly authorized employee. The individual must have been officially hired and not subsequently terminated prior to the starting date of the current payroll period. This fact is, of course, subject to independent verification through the personnel department. The second requirement is the evidence of work performed. In the case of salaried employees the documentary activities will vary depending on the policies of the particular company and the organizational level of the particular employee. At lower levels there will normally be time cards generated by the individuals under established time-clock procedures. In other cases there may be records maintained by supervisors at the various levels. But at higher levels the control is usually of a less formal type, depending more on general observation and the integrity of the individual. As to rates the records of the personnel department will again provide the most reliable independent authority for the presently existing salaries. Where overtime compensation is involved there is the further need for records maintained by supervisors and for adequate higher-level approval.

The situation in the case of hourly employees is normally handled in a more systematic manner. This will include at least time-clock cards covering time actually spent in the plant. In many situations also there is the need for information as to how much time is spent on individual projects, job orders, or other specific work assignments. Such records may be prepared by the employees themselves, and then subsequently reviewed and approved by supervisors, or be prepared directly by the supervisors themselves. When such supplementary records are maintained there is the opportunity for a cross check between the two sets of records for accuracy of the total time, including also the accuracy of the allocations of a cost accounting nature. The accuracy of rates used is again subject to independent confirmation with personnel department records. There is also the problem of individuals working on different jobs which carry different job classifications, and which therefore call for different bases of compensation. Here there is the special problem of possible manipulation, plus the managerial question of whether labor was effectively utilized. For payroll purposes, however, the authorization of the responsible supervisor is a key control.

Preparing the Payroll

Employees of the several categories are paid on different time period bases. Hourly labor will normally be paid on a weekly basis, certain salary personnel on a semi-monthly basis, and other salary personnel on a monthly basis. At the end of the designated payroll period the payroll department is now charged with the responsibility of preparing the payroll. This action has to do with the determination of what is owed and payable to each employee for work performed during the given payroll period. The key aspects of this preparation of the payroll can be briefly listed, as follows:

1. *Accumulation of Work Evidence.* Time cards and other basic records of work activity must be accumulated. This requires first that the source data are clerically accurate and properly approved by responsible supervisors. Where inaccuracies are found, the correction to be made must be determined and carried out. Required also is the summarization by individuals and organizational components. The clerical accuracy of this summarization must be assured by internal controls of various kinds, including segregation of clerical work and responsibility. The fact of whether individuals are bona fide employees is determined by cross reference to personnel department records and reports to the extent needed.

2. *Application of Rates.* Work performed must be compensated at proper rates. These rates are established by existing union contracts and by other company actions reflected in the records of the personnel department. When the authenticity of the rates has been adequately established tł

necessary calculations must then be made and the resulting amounts summarized.

3. *Accounting Distributions.* The amounts payable for services performed must be allocated to the proper operational activities in conformance with the established accounting requirements of the company, including those of a cost accounting nature. Although it is possible, and sometimes necessary, to defer the determinations of these distributions, the actions here should be accomplished as soon as is practicable because of their value as a cross check on the accuracy of the payroll itself.

4. *Application of Deductions.* Deductions will be required for a number of reasons. Illustrative will be those for social security, union dues, pension plans, and personal purchases. The charges for these different purposes must then under proper control be applied to the individuals affected.

5. *Determination of Net Pay.* Finally, the difference between the basic compensation earned and the deductions provides the net pay that is due to the individual employees. Again also there must be summarization and proof against the detailed data.

Payment of Salaries and Wages

The preparation of the payroll as just described leads directly into the question of how payment shall be made and the preparation of the various checks and other papers that will implement the payment mode. The preferable mode of payment to each individual is by check. This reduces the risk of handling cash and, of course, also provides an automatic record of receipt by the employee. In some situations, however, it may be necessary to pay in cash. In still other cases checks can be used but special check-cashing facilities must be provided. The payroll preparation procedures will normally tie into the policies and requirements that exist and provide for the preparation of the individual checks. Where cash must be made available a check will usually be prepared covering the aggregate amount. The summary journal entry will provide for the credits to the accounts for which deductions were made. These credits will then provide controls for the later preparation of governmental reports covering social security and unemployment insurance.

The checks or cash for the individuals covered by the particular payroll will now be distributed to them. It is important that this delivery be made directly to the various individuals so that there is no opportunity for any diversion or manipulation to take place on the part of any intermediary. Identification of the recipient is also important for the same reasons. Receipts should be obtained where payment is made in cash. Where cash is paid, or where check-cashing facilities are made available, there is the additional requirement of adequate physical protection. In the event that individuals are not available at the time of the regular distribution, the cash or checks should be taken back to a designated cashier location, and the individuals affected should then be required to present themselves in person to receive payment.

Basis of Internal Control for Payrolls

While extremely voluminous and extensively involved with the detailed complexities of varying rates, calculations, and deductions, the payroll process in principle is straightforward and subject to basic internal control considerations. First and foremost is the necessity that the handling of, or access, to cash be entirely separate from the creation of any part of the record that supports the cash payment. There is also the essential requirement that all parts of the process be broken down as between departments and individuals within individual departments so that the maximum cross check exists. The use of control totals at the various stages provides necessary control over voluminous detail. The latter is especially important in the payroll department itself where the payroll itself is prepared. A reviewer such as the internal auditor will in turn appraise both the adequacy of the existing cross checks as provided for in the basic design of the payroll procedures, and also the care with which the procedures are actually executed. Constant effort is required to enforce the proper level of care and also to reappraise the need for procedural modification to meet the needs of changing situations.

FINANCIAL CONTROL OVER SECURITIES

The handling of securities represents a special problem of financial control that has great importance, especially for a financial institution like a bank or investment company. In the case of a typical company the handling of securities may be delegated to a financial institution. Back of the handling problem are, of course, the broader questions of why securities are acquired, and if so of what type and of what amount. These broader questions pertain to the company financial policies and will be touched on in Chapter 21. In this chapter we are concerned with the problems of basic financial control. The problem that exists is how procedures can be established that will provide adequate accountability and protection for securities. The operational requirements here include the receipt of securities, the current access to them as required, and the release of them at the proper time for sale or other authorized purposes.

Receiving Securities

Securities purchased may be registered in the company name or be payable to bearer. While the latter have the advantage of greater convenience in the event of transfer, the risk of theft is much greater. However, in the case of securities left as collateral or for other special purposes by customers or other outside parties, the company may have had no election as to the form of the securities. In any event the receival of the securities by a company officer or employee marks the assumption of responsibility and accountability on the part of the company. What is then needed are records that properly establish accountability and physical facilities that will provide adequate protection. Where this custody is a significant activity of the company these facilities will be burglar proof vaults. In all cases the accountability of those individuals accepting custodial responsibility should be clearly established through the issuance of formal receipts. At the same time records of the accountability should be established both by the custodian and by an operational group independent of the custodian. These records should cover both the basic securities and the interest coupons that are attached to bearer bonds. The latter coverage is important both for the custodial responsibility and for the scheduling of clipping coupons as they become due.

Handling and Release of Securities

As time goes on there will be instances when parties other than the custodian will require access to the securities. Effective control in these circumstances first of all requires that the party to be granted excess is properly authorized. A second requirement is that the inspection of securities be carried out jointly by the custodian and the second party. In the case of interest coupons the procedure in a banking institution will normally be to clip and transfer coupons that are due to a collection department for collection and credit to the customer's account, with the relief of the custodian's responsibility being thereby formally established. When securities in a bond category become due the procedure would be similar. Securities may also be withdrawn for other reasons when properly authorized. In a company situation coupons and bonds that are due will necessarily be removed and transferred to a bank for collection. In summary, the important considerations from a control standpoint are adequate physical protection, plus clearly established accountabilities, with access to the securities being always on a dual basis. Adequate insurance and the bonding of all employees who participate in the handling of securities is also a basic requirement.

Review of Control Adequacy

As always the first requirement is that the procedures and facilities be adequate in terms of basic design. An outside reviewer like the internal auditor will wish to reappraise that aspect periodically because of changing conditions. Especially does the changing volume of security holdings and related transactions require changes both of facilities and operational procedures. Additionally, changing environmental factors may result in greater risk exposure. But good procedures and adequate facilities are not enough. The procedures themselves must be carried out with proper precision and care. The appraisal of these procedural operations is accomplished both by careful observation and by testing the record of previously executed transactions. In this connection the verification of securities and coupons on hand against the records of accountability as independently established provides basic assurance that securities have not been improperly diverted. An important aspect of the foregoing also is the appraisal of the trustworthiness and competence of the personnel carrying out the custodial activities. Also, one is interested in the efficiency of personnel utilization.

BASIC ACCOUNTING ACTIVITIES

Scope of the Accounting Process

The accounting function covers a wide range of levels. At its highest level it involves the development of major policies that are part of the broader financial and management policies. Illustrative would be the handling of the investment credit or the policies for taking up profits on installment sales. At its lowest level the accounting activity is a primary paper—as, for example, a cash receipt form—and the procedures for its use. In Chapter 21 we deal with the higher-level financial management policies which determine the directions of the supporting accounting activity. In the present chapter our concern is with the more operational aspects of the accounting system on a day-to-day basis. This system has both a design aspect and an implementation aspect. Although the two aspects are closely interrelated, there is the question of whether forms, records, and procedures are adequate as designed to deal with the various operational requirements. There is also the question of whether we have the right kind of people and whether they are applying themselves in the proper manner.

General Character of Accounting Activities

The basic accounting activities do not exist as an end in themselves but for the support of the total operating activities of the company. They are thus inter-woven with all of the operational activities discussed in other chapters. This interrelationship emphasizes the point that all company activities have a financial dimension that ties them in some manner to the overall accounting activities. Accountabilities must be established in various ways, information must be provided, and the basis provided for necessary control. Because these situations and the related requirements vary so greatly, as well as the views as to how the individual situations can be best administered, the accounting applications will also vary widely. This is especially true as more and more of the basic accounting activities are computerized and blended with broader operational needs. We will, therefore, be more concerned with principles and common characteristics, rather than with specific forms, records, or procedures.

General and Cost Accounting

The basic accounting activities include both those termed as "general" and those termed "cost." The former area has traditionally been concerned with the general aspects of assets and liabilities, and similarly with expense and and revenue, whereas the latter has focused more on the cost of individual products and services. Actually, the distinction becomes increasingly artificial since the latter is an extension of the other and to a considerable extent is motivated by common objectives. What we are really trying to do is to establish a total accounting framework that is sufficiently flexible to provide the types of data that can be useful for the total range of management needs. At the same time all of the special data need to stem from common sources, and in some manner be generally reconcilable. Some of the problems of a cost accounting nature that require special consideration are discussed under production in Chapter 16.

Internal Auditor's Interest in Basic Accounting Activities

The interest of the modern operational auditor in the basic accounting activities comes about in two rather different ways. The first of these lies in the recognition that the accounting activity is a part of the operations which must be reviewed just like any other operational area. There is an accounting job to be done to meet the needs of the total organization. At the same time the accounting activity costs money and we wish to achieve its proper service role in as economical and efficient manner as possible. Thus this operational aspect of the accounting activity confirms the need that the internal auditor continue to be concerned with it.

There is also, however, a second way in which the interest of the internal auditor in the basic accounting activities arises. In his review of the various operating areas one of the sources of input as to what is going on is the review of the basic accounting activities as they pertain to those operations. At the same time there is the question as to whether the accounting activity is servicing the particular operational area in the most effective manner. For these reasons the basic accounting activities become of great importance to the internal auditor in carrying out his new broader operational role.

Areas of Concern in Review of Accounting Activities

It will be useful in planning the review of the basic accounting activities to identify the major areas of concern. These concerns fall into two broad categories: (1) the component parts of the typical accounting system, and (2) the major operational dimensions. Admittedly, the lines between these component parts and the related operational dimensions comes to be blurred somewhat as various activities are integrated in modern computerized systems. However, it is still useful to know the subfunctions which are being integrated. Also, in smaller divisional and subsidiary operations the accounting system still tends to retain the more traditional approach.

Components of the Accounting System. The individual components that exist to some extent separately, or that represent the functions that are combined, are as follows:

1. *Primary Papers.* The accounting system begins in an operational sense through the creation, completion, and initial processing of primary papers. Illustrative is the preparation of a purchase requisition, or the execution of a cash receipt form. These primary papers need to be designed such that essential information and approvals will be picked up and recorded. They need also to be as simple as possible so that there

will be minimum misunderstanding and error. Finally, the procedures for their use, including their routing and ultimate disposition, must be properly designated.

2. *Journals.* The journal function is to provide a chronological record to the extent that such a record is needed. Illustrative would be a chronological register of purchases. The nature of this chronological record will vary widely and in many cases can be a file of primary papers under proper batch control. The test is whether later reference to the sequence of given transactions for a given time period is available to satisfy operational needs.

3. *Ledgers.* The data accumulated at the journal stage provide the source information for classification in the various accounts of the company—that is, for the various assets, liabilities, equities, and types of expense and income. General ledgers deal with the aggregate type accounts and where needed these aggregate accounts are supported by detailed accounts in subsidiary ledgers. The general ledger account "accounts receivable" thus would be supported directly, or through intermediate controls, by detailed accounts with customers. The key questions involve the adequacy of the tie-in with the source date and the controls to keep detailed subsidiary ledgers in agreement with the aggregate accounts.

4. *Auxiliary Records.* An accounting system will also include a number of auxiliary records, which are related to the basic ledger accounts but which perform auxiliary functions. Illustrative would be an insurance policy register describing the coverage of the various insurance policies and perhaps developing basic expense allocations. The key questions here will be whether the auxiliary records properly support the required operational needs, and whether they are efficiently maintained. In some cases the auxiliary records also include a subsidiary ledger function.

5. *Manuals.* The accounting manuals describe the total account structure and the policies and major procedures for the operation of these accounts. The issues involved have to do with the highest-level type of policy and ranging down to lower-level procedures. The key questions are the logic and practicality of the basic determination and then the clarity with which the required implementation is described.

6. *Reports.* Information developed by the accounting system is in part made available on an informal or individual request basis. In the main, however, it is through formal reports that information is provided to the various interested parties in the company. These reports cover a wide range of matters and levels of summarization. The problem is extremely complex but centers mostly around the adequacy of the information provided, the manner in which it is presented for effective use, the extent to which the information is provided on a timely basis, and finally whether it is being distributed to the right people.

Operational Dimensions of the Accounting System. Having looked at the accounting system in terms of its major components, we now come at the total system from the standpoint of its operational dimensions. These dimensions are not as well standardized as the components, but will typically include the following:

1. *Distribution of Work Assignments.* As in the case of every operational activity, the starting point is the manner in which work assignments are made to the individuals involved. Through these work assignments we can achieve the benefits of specialization, and at the same time the cross check between individuals that minimizes both error and fraud. In each operational situation and at various levels of organizational responsibility the challenge is to exploit these advantages fully.

2. *Competence of Personnel.* Different work assignments require different types and levels of technical competence. The extent to which individuals interface with other personnel calls for varying levels of professional qualifications. The objective is to obtain the kind of personnel in each instance that fits the need, avoiding a serious lack of competence, and at the same time a level of competence that is not significantly in excess of the particular requirements.

3. *Utilization of Personnel.* Closely related to the proper level of competence is the need to supervise and manage existing personnel in a manner that properly utilizes the existing productive potential. Included also is the need to avoid both significant under- and overstaffing. At the same time there is the need to avoid excessive overtime. All of these often conflicting factors need to be evaluated and combined with reasonable competence.

4. *Coordination and Support.* An effective accounting department operates as a partner and counselor to all other operational activities. The opposite extreme is to make the accounting product an end in itself and to function more restrictively than constructively. This means that the accounting group needs to reach out to the other operational activities to render help and support, and to join with them in the solution of problems.

5. *Extent of Decentralization.* A final important operational dimension is that of finding the right balance of decentralization. What this consists of is determining where and by whom the accounting work can be best accomplished. An illustration at a low level would be the extent to which a salesperson is charged with preparing forms and summaries that might better be done by the central accounting group. At a higher level there is the question of how much accounting work should be done at field locations versus centralization at the headquarters or other central location. Illustrative would be the handling of billing operations. The key factors for these decisions are the operating economies to be achieved versus the need to support local operations.

Operational Criteria for Appraising the Accounting System

To a considerable extent the review of the major areas of concern above have already provided essential criteria for the evaluation of the effectiveness of the accounting system. There are, however, some additional ways in which the accounting activity can be appraised. These are as follows:

1. *Cost of Operation.* One important criterion for evaluation is always the degree of economy achieved in carrying out the various parts of the accounting operation. One standard that can be used are comparisons with other companies, either through the direct exchange of data or through industry associations. However, such comparisons must be used with care because of different operational conditions. Another standard is the company's own past performance. Still another approach is the study of what costs would be under alternative types of approach, including various types of automation.

2. *Error Experience.* Some errors are unavoidable as a practical manner. In the last analysis we are dealing with human beings, and human beings are never perfect. Moreover, the greater the control structure the greater the cost. Nevertheless, excessive error experience indicates levels of weakness of some kind that need to be studied. The cause may be improper design or ineffective operation, or a combination of both. The objective is to strike the right balance between cost and the degree of error.

3. *Fraud.* Similarly, the extent to which fraud has developed will provide another rough measure of whether basic accounting controls, in combination with other operating controls, are adequate. We look more closely at the fraud question later in Chapter 26.

4. *Orderliness of Accounting Operations.* An important measure of the effectiveness of the accounting operations is the order and efficiency with which they are carried on. Order and efficiency is the result of having good people, properly trained, and properly supervised. It reflects also the soundness of the accounting procedures. Additionally, it normally reflects the existence of adequate facilities and modern mechanical equipment. A qualified observer can recognize the absence of confusion, the businesslike execution of the various tasks and the capacity for ready response to daily operational needs.

5. *Company Service.* The most basic test, however, of the effectiveness of the accounting group is whether the needs of the various operational activities are being adequately and properly serviced. The needs to be served cover a wide range. They include obtaining reference information being accumulated by the accounting system. They include also getting comprehensive and useful reports on a timely basis. Last but not least they include the receiving of help and counsel in dealing with the accounting dimension as it pertains to their own operational problems. The

measure of this service can best be evaluated from the user's standpoint. Is the needed assistance available and how easily can it be obtained? Frequently also, the development of supplementary records by a user group provides the clue to a less-than-satisfactory degree of cooperation. A reviewer approaches this problem by getting the user's viewpoint, and by critically appraising the existing needs for accounting information and controls.

AUDIT GUIDES

Basic Financial Control Activities

I. Introductory
   A. Reference should be made to the general discussion of audit guides, as discussed earlier in this chapter.

II. Preparatory Activities
   A. See standard Audit Guides.
   B. The organizational group involved will be the accounting department or that part of the finance group which has the responsibility for basic financial control activities.

III. Organizational Factors
   A. See standard Audit Guides.
   B. Matter of special interest in the review of manuals will include:
      1. Scope of chart of accounts and description of individual accounts.
      2. Policies and procedures relating to the areas dealt with in this chapter.
         a. Cash processes: receipts, disbursements, custody, petty cash funds, branch funds, and administration of bank accounts.
         b. Receivable processes: credit sales, maintenance of accounts, adjustments, bad debts, special receivables activities, and notes receivable.
         c. Payable processes: vouchering, internal review procedures, records, special payables, travel expenses, accruals, and notes payable.
         d. Payrolls: preparation, review, and payment.
         e. Handling of securities: receiving, custody, and release.
         f. General procedures: types of records, reports, and operational aspects (both general and cost accounting).
      3. Coordinative arrangements with other company activities.
      4. Handling of deviations.

IV. Internal Operations
   A. Cash Processes
      1. Cash receipts
         a. Review the sources of cash and appraise both the possibilities of

reducing or eliminating difficult-to-control conditions, and for better assuring effective establishment of accountabilities.

b. Determine that cash flows promptly and intact—without diversion for cash disbursements—directly to central depository control. Appraise the necessity of all deviations.

2. Cash handling
   a. Are physical safeguards adequate at all stages?
   b. Is insurance coverage adequate?
   c. Is cash on hand—in all forms, at all levels, and for all purposes—at lowest possible level?

3. Cash disbursements
   a. Are petty cash and branch funds utilized and operated on an imprest basis?
   b. Are standards adequate for documentary support? If not, why not? Appraise also the standards of review at the time of disbursement.
   c. Are credit cards adequately controlled and payments properly documented?

4. General
   a. Are all employees who handle or have any direct or indirect access to cash adequately bonded?
   b. Are independent work assignments in effect to the extent practicable, including the reconciliation of bank accounts?
   c. Are records of accountability separately maintained?
   d. Are cash funds periodically verified by independent parties?

B. Receivable Processes
   1. Regular accounts receivable
      a. Appraise the adequacy of procedures for credit authorization.
      b. Review sources and control of data used in billing.
      c. Are customer records independent and accurately maintained on an up-to-date basis?
      d. Are monthly statements mailed directly to customers?
      e. Are cash credits adequately linked to cash receipts processes?
      f. Are other types of charges and credits properly authorized and controlled—special charges and credits, merchandise returns, bad-debt write-offs, and the like?
      g. Are credit policies periodically reappraised for level of bad-debt losses versus sales revenues generated?
      h. Appraise in all possible ways the impact of receivable procedures on customer relations.
   2. Other receivable processes
      a. Review all special types of procedures—for example, advances to employees, deposits with outsiders, claims, and income accruals—to assure adequacy of conditions of their creation and the control thereafter exercised.

    b. Review and appraise the circumstances for accepting notes receivable, and the adequacy of subsequent control, including interest due.

C. Payable Processes
    1. General
        a. Review and appraise the adequacy of the controls over the creation of all types of company obligations. Is reasonable provision made for contingencies?
        b. What procedures exist for the subsequent administration and liquidation of these obligations? Are they adequate?
    2. Regular accounts payable
        a. Review and appraise the procedures for the receipt, coordination, and ultimate matching of supporting documentary papers.
        b. Are adequate control records maintained?
        c. Review and appraise the procedures by which the payables are ultimately approved and linked with the check payments. Is proper provision made for the deduction of all existing counterclaims?
    3. Other payables
        a. How are obligations covering financing authorized and subsequently controlled? Are supplementary controls adequate where interest is payable?
        b. How adequate are the policies and procedures for the handling of expense accounts? How carefully are these policies and procedures subsequently administered?
        c. Review the policies and procedures covering expense accruals.
        d. Review and appraise the conditions by which notes payable come into existence and the control exercised over them, including interest obligations.

D. Payrolls
    1. Are independently prepared personnel department records used properly as cross controls for the preparation of payrolls?
    2. Review and appraise the effectiveness of the primary procedures and records by which the record of work is accumulated and validated.
    3. Review and appraise the procedures by which payroll data are processed, authorized deductions made, payrolls finalized, and checks (or checks for cash) prepared.
    4. Are the procedures for payment adequate to assure the release of checks (or cash) to the proper individuals without the opportunity for diversion or modification?

E. Securities
    1. Are securities adequately safegarded from theft and burglarization?
    2. Review the adequacy of records established which are independent of those responsible for physical custody of the securities.

3. Is the receipt and release of securities properly documented?

4. Is access to securities restricted, and when necessary adequately controlled through witnesses?

F. Basic Accounting Activities

1. Are primary papers, journals, ledgers, auxiliary records, and reports adequately structured and administered in connection with the various accounting activities, and in a collective sense?

2. Review and appraise the operational effectiveness of the basic accounting activities—again in connection with particular financial processes and in total—as to:

a. Distribution of work assignments.

b. Competence of personnel.

c. Utilization of personnel.

d. Effectiveness of coordination and support of other company activities.

e. Reasonableness of decentralization.

3. Review and appraise extent of automation of accounting activities, especially with respect to use of computers.

4. Evaluate the basic accounting activities, as to:

a. Cost of operation.

b. Error experience.

c. Fraud experience.

d. Orderliness of operations.

e. Recipients' views as to service received.

V. Special Audit Tests

Audit tests of policies and procedures may also include a certain amount of test verification of cash funds, receivable balances, securities, payable balances, payroll authenticity, and the like. In addition, more extensive verification is frequently made of complete sectors of these assets and liabilities. As previously stated, these verification activities overlap to some extent with the financial auditing carried out for the purpose of the review of financial statements.

VI–IX. Not used.

X. Overall Appraisal of Basic Financial Control Activities

A. See standard Audit Guides.

ILLUSTRATIVE AUDIT FINDINGS: BASIC FINANCIAL CONTROL

Overly Large Cash Balances

A review of cash operations at the Dallas plant indicated that cash balances were in excess of needs. An analysis of receipts and disbursements showed that the plant controller was maintaining a cash balance large enough to meet all planned expenditures for the month. Since the major expenditures were made on the 15th and 31st of the month, cash was needed for only half a month's expenditures. By reducing cash on hand, interest savings of $25,000 a year could be earned on the excess.

Reducing Bank Balances Based on Float

A comparison of cash balances per books and per bank statements showed that excess cash was being kept in the bank. This resulted from float, or delays in cashing checks and presenting them to the bank for payment. It was recommended that the bank balances be restricted to need based on estimates of checks that will be presented for payment. This would result in net interest earnings of $150,000 a year, after deducting additional bank costs for services.

Excessive Bad Debts

Write-offs of bad debts in the Chicago division were 10% of divisional sales during the year, significantly in excess of other divisions. Divisional management had authorized the excessive write-offs without determining the causes and taking corrective action. It was found that the division granted credit to customers without sufficient study of their financial capability. Also, the division continued to extend credit to customers for long periods even though payments on account were not being made.

Unreasonable Payables

In performing an audit of material and equipment acquisitions it was noted that significant overruns in expenditures occurred from budget. An analysis of the payables function indicated that although purchases were properly authorized and approved, insufficient attention was being placed on the type of item acquired. Automobile fleet specifications were exceeded, both in size and cost of vehicles acquired. Unique types of equipment were purchased when standardized equipment was available. In addition, items with defects were accepted for payment without return to the manufacturer. Closer control was recommended over the generation and approval of payables.

Elimination of Manual Accounting Reports

Manual accounting reports continued to be prepared even though a new computerized system had the capability of producing the same reports. In some cases there was a duplication, primarily because personnel wanted information presented in a different form. By summarizing all accounting reports prepared, reviewing needs, and changing report formats, management was able to discontinue four reports prepared manually.

CHAPTER FOURTEEN

Purchasing and Transportation

PURCHASING

Purchasing as a Major Part of the Procurement Function

The starting point in the total operational cycle of a company is the procurement of the materials and services which are to be marketed either in their existing form, or used, processed, or combined in some other fashion to provide the products and services actually offered for sale. This procurement can involve raw material, processed materials, parts, subassemblies, services, supplies, facilities, people, and money itself. In many of these areas of procurement there are special problems which require special skills. Illustrative would be the recruitment of people—which would be handled by a personnel staff, or obtaining capital funds—which would be handled by a treasurer's office. A large portion of the procurement, however, is normally handled by a group specifically established for this purpose. Although, as we shall see, the scope of this group's procurement activities will vary, the items handled usually include most of the materials, parts, and supplies used by the company.

The importance of the purchasing activity is usually very great, with its purchases running typically a large part of the costs incurred by the company for the products and services marketed. It is, therefore, an activity that deserves a great deal of attention on the part of management. It is an important activity also because it interrelates in such a significant manner with other management activities. What is purchased is directly related to production efficiency. The volume of the purchases is also a determinant of inventory levels. The investment in inventories is a major factor in the achievement of a favorable return on capital employed. In addition, the purchasing function has direct operational relationships with such activities as receiving, warehouse operations, scrap sales, and accounts payable. For all of these reasons, the purchasing area is also an important area for review by the internal auditor.

Basic Purchasing Role

For those areas of procurement where the responsibility has been assigned to the purchasing department,[1] the basic role is, like any area of procurement, to provide the right products (or services) at the right price, at the right time, and at the right place. "Right" is used here to signify the "best possible," all things considered, as judged by the long-term interests of the company.[2] It is, of course, a determination that often cannot be precisely evaluated, and hence one that involves a great deal of judgment. This is especially true because of the major interrelationship with other operational activities, and the long time often required to appraise particular types of benefits or penalties. These key dimensions of the basic role are at the same time the objectives of the purchasing activity. It is these objectives in which we are interested in our discussion of the purchasing activity. Our interest in this basic purchasing role exists at several levels. At the lowest level is the clerical efficiency with which the procedural part of the operations is carried out. At the next higher level we are interested in the effectiveness with which individual activities cover more substantive matters such as the selection of vendors and the negotiation of prices. At the highest level our concern is with the extent to which opportunities are perceived for better relating the purchasing to the other major management functions.

Normal Cycle of the Purchasing Function

The purchasing function can be viewed as a cycle that includes a number of fairly well-defined steps. These are:

1. *Determination of Needs*. We must first determine what the specific need is that must be satisfied through the procurement action. This would include the identification of the product and its specifications, quantities, delivery requirements, and any other pertinent information.

2. *Authorization of the Purchase*. As a second step there must be an authorization to proceed with the purchase. Something is needed and now we decide we will actually get it.

3. *Making the Purchase*. The purchasing group then carries out its search for the vendor which it is believed will provide the goods sought, on the basis which is most advantageous to the company. The selection of the vendor then leads to the decision to enter into a definitive purchase agreement.

4. *Follow-up*. To the extent necessary there must now be such follow-up action on the part of the purchasing group as will best assure the delivery

---

[1]Department is used as a general term to describe the organizational component charged with purchasing responsibilities.
[2]Company is used to cover any type of business or nonbusiness organization involved in any kind of an operational activity.

of the needed goods in the manner that will satisfy management requirements.

5. *Completion of Delivery.* Actual deliveries are now made and a determination is made as to whether there has been proper compliance with
   the purchase agreement, or if not, what offsetting claims exist.

6. *Financial Settlement.* Finally, the settlement is made with the vendor
   on the proper basis, and the purchase transaction is complete—subject
   only to such continuing warranties by the vendor as may have been part
   of the basic agreement.

Major Control Structure

We discuss next the control problems around the previously listed operational
steps in the normal cycle of the purchasing function.

Determination of Needs

The basic control issue in the determination of needs is the extent to which
that determination is made on a sound basis and then accurately communicated
to the purchasing group. Typical sources of these determinations include:

1. A production schedule which, when exploded as a bill of materials, identifies the specific requirements in terms of individual product items,
   pertinent specifications, and conditions of delivery.

2. An inventory system with predetermined stocking levels for individual
   products, which then generates order requirements for individual items
   as the stock level reaches a given minimal point.

3. Special projects of either a capital or operational nature which carry with
   them particular kinds of requirements for goods and services.

4. Other operational needs which are evaluated in some way and translated
   into purchase requirements.

In any one of these situations a number of different types of questions arise,
which have to be considered in a manner dependent on the significance of the
particular item. There is, first, the question as to the general validity of the
underlying need. This would include both the purpose for which the particular
items are to be used and the soundness of the way in which the basic need is
translated into the definite requirements. Illustrative of this would be the need
for a particular item for warehouse stocks and the kind of decision formula
applied for the determination of the stocking requirement. Second, there is
the further question of whether the system as designed is actually being operated efficiently. Finally, there is the question of whether the determined
need is properly transmitted to the purchasing group in the form of an approved
requisition, or by other proper documentation.

Responsibility for Determination of Needs. How needs are determined is normally the responsibility of other company personnel. While these determinations initiate the purchasing process, the purchasing group does more than just process them. The purchasing department is very often in a good position to know what is sound in the way of an underlying method or policy for determining needs. It is also well qualified to serve as a kind of a check on unusual and abnormally high supply requirements. The role of the purchasing group also extends to the determination of needs in a different way. The purchasing group through its purchasing activities is in touch with market conditions and should be able to appraise new developments and trends in the way of shortages or oversupply. The individual buyer also knows more intimately the situations of the various vendors, especially the more important vendors. Thus purchasing personnel should be able to make an important contribution in advising other company personnel of the changing developments, and as to what bearing these developments might have on the current ordering actions. The purchasing group thus does in part share the responsibility for the proper determination of needs and should be as helpful as possible.

Procedural Aspects of Determination of Needs. The needs as determined must now be put into proper documentary form. Normally, there will be requisition forms or other types of advice which list the specific needs with the pertinent specifications, the required approvals, and any other information needed for other company purposes. Specifications should be used to develop standardized parts, wherever practicable. Although a substantial part of this procedure may be automated in individual situations, there is still the question of the propriety of the basic input to the automated process. In some cases standard and so-called "traveling requisitions" are used in repetitive situations to minimize excessive clerical effort and human error. The important aspects in all of the situations are:

1. Propriety of approvals.
2. Completeness of all information needed.
3. Accuracy of the clerical and processing effort.

Authorization of the Purchase

In some cases the determination of the need will at the same time become the authorization to purchase. But this is not necessarily so, because the authorization to purchase involves some further questions which are not normally the final responsibility of the people who determine the need. Typical of these questions would be:

1. *Is the item available within the company?* The purchasing group may have knowledge of the availability of the item elsewhere in the company. In other cases there may be enough question to justify making a specific search as to that possibility.

2. *Should the item be made rather than purchased?* This is a question that is normally under continuing scrutiny. Changing conditions such as increasing difficulties of procurement, increased volume, or increased cost will sharpen the interest in the make possibility and be the basis of initiating more depth studies. The impetus for the make-or-buy investigation can come from a number of sources, but possibilities here are part of the overall concern of an effective purchasing group.

3. *Can the purchase be made?* Conditions may have arisen where the items specified cannot be purchased, or perhaps only in a modified form. In such a situation there must be further discussions with the using organizational component.

4. *Are budgetary requirements complied with?* If not previously covered at the requisition stage, there will normally be the necessity for budgetary approval. This would be true especially if the purchase would result in an overbudget condition for the requisitioning activity.

5. *Are there financing problems?* Since the purchase will establish a definitive financial obligation, the question may arise as to whether the purchase at this time is within the company's financial capabilities. In some cases it might be necessary either to defer the purchase or to reduce the quantities.

Procedural Aspects of Authorization of Purchase. The actual authorization of the purchase can be handled either as a part of the requisition form or as a supplemental or separate form. The important thing is that the designated approvals have been secured and that the purchasing group has raised any questions that would be in the company interest before proceeding with the operational execution of the actual purchase. In most cases this would be handled as a supplementary set of approvals to the basic requisition.

Making the Purchase

We come now to the heart of the purchasing activity—the search for the vendor and the making of the definitive arrangement for providing the items needed. In selecting the vendor the important considerations include at least the following:

1. The diligence of the search which has been made for all vendors who would reasonably seem to be a possible qualified source. This will include both new vendors and vendors who have supplied other items.

2. The extent of field contact which has been made to look over facilities and to discuss operational capabilities and related problems with existing and potential vendors.

3. The individual vendor's reliability in terms of past procurements, general reputation, and financial standing.

4. The weighing of the various factors that comprise the determination of

the value to be received. This will include price, terms, absorption of delivery costs, treatment of tooling charges, maintenance of reserve inventories, capacity to satisfy delivery requirements, quality, service backup, product development activities, and the like.

5. The extent to which there are supplementary considerations such as community relations, support of small business, competitor disclosure risks, sales reciprocity, or government direction.

6. The extent to which the company desires protection for supply through dual or multiple sourcing.

Exploiting Competition. Except in the case where the price with a single vendor is to be determined later, the selection of the vendor is at the same time the fixing of the terms of the purchase arrangement with that vendor. The basic control factor is, therefore, the extent to which the purchasing group has fully exploited market opportunities through competitive bidding. Has every legitimate competitive pressure been used to get the maximum value for the company? Here it must be recognized that this normally desirable objective could conceivably be carried too far. This could be where the vendor so much needs the business that the purchaser is in a position to exploit that power by forcing the price down to an unfair level. The more enlightened company, however, recognizes that it is in the company's long-run interest to have a solvent and reasonably prosperous vendor. These conditions are in fact the basis for securing quality products and in being able to rely on the vendor. But the company must at the same time recognize its own problem of competitive survival and find that proper balance of toughness and fairness. To achieve these ends it must seek continuously to have a strong and healthy competition among its vendors.

What this means is that the solicitation of competitive bids must be standard procedure to the maximum extent practicable. The only exception is for the special situation where there is no satisfactory second source, or where emergency pressures do not allow adequate time to get the competitive bids. But such situations should be minimized in every way possible by better planning and by a deliberate effort to develop alternative sources. It is also important that the solicitation of competitive bids be done often enough for the same item to take advantage of new developments in the field. In addition, the bid solicitation must be in good faith and the basis for the actual award, as opposed to the possible situation when it might be a cover-up, or be manipulated to support an already determined selection. A good purchasing group will, therefore, continually strive to expand and to make more effective its effort to seek competitive bids, and it should be prepared to justify the extent to which that approach is not in fact followed.

Negotiated Fixed-Price Contracts. Despite the objective to seek competitive bidding to the maximum extent possible, the fact must be faced that in some situations the vendor choice will be dictated by other factors. It may be, for example, that a particular vendor alone has the know-how, experience, or patent position. Or the choice may be dictated by our customer, as is often true in the case of government work. Under such circumstances the vendor may have an established price and that will be the price if we want the product. In other situations there will be a negotiation of the pricing arrangements. The approach here is normally a more detailed showing of costs which it is estimated will be incurred, plus a factor for profit. In some cases these costs estimates are subject to field review, especially if there is to be any later incentive-type price redetermination based upon actual cost experience. Cost estimates prepared by company personnel should also be used to the extent possible. It is also frequently possible for finance personnel to assist purchasing personnel in the various stages of the price negotiations.

Cost-Reimbursement Types of Procurement. In certain situations the experience with a product may be so limited that it is not even possible to negotiate intelligently any kind of a fixed-price type of contract. In that case resort must be made to an arrangement where the payment is determined by actual costs plus an agreed-upon profit factor. Several important cost control problems exist with this type of procurement. First, there is the difficulty of defining which types of cost are to be reimbursed. This includes the problem of defining what costs are to be considered as direct charges and what kinds of overhead items will be proper. In the case of overhead there is the further problem of how they will be allocated to the particular products. A second major type of difficulty lies in the lack of sufficient motivation to reduce costs as compared to the fixed-price type of contract. In fact, there can often be a reverse type of motivation. The third major difficulty is with the determination of the profit factor. Especially to be avoided are percentage approaches that result in higher profit when costs increase, again providing the wrong kind of motivation. All of this means that cost-type contracts are to be avoided to the maximum extent possible, and that, if we have no other alternative, they be handled with extreme care. Again, finance people are normally brought in to help define cost relationships and to review the propriety of claimed costs. The monitoring of work and costs in progress is especially important in cost-type contracts.

Procedures for Making the Purchase. The procedure for the handling of this phase of the purchase transaction can vary, but in a typical situation include:

1. "Logging in" the authorization to purchase and assigning it to a member of the purchasing group, usually called the buyer, depending on the size of the proposed purchase and the type of item. Specialization of buyers is normally the practice but the extent of it will, of course, depend on the size of the purchasing operation.
2. Vendor records are normally cross-referenced for the various types of items and these will be consulted for possible sources.
3. The responsible buyer consults with his superior and with the company user to clarify any questions he might have about the procurement.

4. Bids are solicited by means of standard forms, but these may be supplemented by telephone contacts.

5. Bids are received and summarized on standard forms and the lowest bid, all things considered, will be determined. Factors in the selection of the bid are noted. If the recommendation is made without competitive bidding, the supporting reasons are attached.

6. The recommendation of the buyer is reviewed by the superior to the extent required.

7. The "authorization to purchase" record is completed and cross-referenced to the purchase order number as listed in the register of purchase orders issued.

8. The purchase order is mailed to the vendor with a copy provided on which he is to acknowledge acceptance and to return to the purchasing department.

The purchase order is normally a serially controlled document. It is prepared in multicopy form so that information copies can be forwarded to other interested company activities, such as the user, receiving department, and accounts payable. It contains the standard contractual terms, plus any approved modifications. The purchase order normally states all warranties and may provide the alternative right of rejection or repair in case the goods do not meet the specifications. It also may provide a measure of damages in the event the goods are defective.

Whereas the transportation costs may be the responsibility of either the vendor or purchaser, the mode of transportation and, where applicable, the routing via a selected carrier are normally the prerogative of the purchaser. These directions will also be included as a part of the purchase order. We deal in greater length with the transportation problem later in this chapter.

Follow-Up

The continuing concern of the purchasing group is now that the products purchased are actually delivered in accordance with the purchase order agreement. In many situations the dependence of other company activities on agreed deliveries is so great that all possible steps must be taken to ensure the wanted result. Frequently, it is desirable for the buyer or his representative to visit the vendor facilities to check on progress. Other company personnel may also be brought into the picture to act in an advisory capacity or to verify quality performance. The emphasis here is on taking all preventive measures in any way which will best assure the wanted final result. In other cases the buyer will be in touch with regular company activities to review interim progress with repect to deliveries. If and when problems develop of delays or below-standard specifications, the buyer can act as a liaison with the vendor. Another term sometimes used for the follow-up activity is "expediting."

Procedural Aspects. The extent of the procedures will necessarily vary with the complexity of the delivery schedules and the length of the delivery period. Normally, some type of visible follow-up record will be utilized to keep the purchasing group apprised of key performance dates. Each buyer will be responsible for monitoring the progress of those purchase orders which he handled. Regular written reports are also useful in some situations.

Completion of Delivery

Under best practice there will be a separate receiving activity which will establish the facts as to what has been received and in what condition. In the case of certain products there will also be necessary inspections for conformance to agreed-upon specifications and level of quality. In some cases more elaborate tests will be necessary, with approvals by responsible operating executives. In some cases also it may be necessary to hold the questioned items for later vendor inspection. Thus the determination is made for acceptance or rejection, or for various types of claims. There may also be claims against the transportation agencies that have acted as carriers. Now, subject to any continuing warranties, the basis is established for the expected financial settlement.

Procedural Aspects. The key procedural requirements are that the receiving and inspection activities are organizationally independent of the purchasing group and that the records of these activities are transmitted directly to the accounts payable activity. At the same time all records of claims of any kind should be clearly stated and also transmitted to the accounts payable group. To the extent that there are other types of proof of receipt—as, for example, the continuing operation of a particular manufacturing operation—it mst be adequately demontrated that the goods were received and in proper condition.

Financial Settlement

The financial settlement will actually be carried out by the separate accounts payable group. Here there will be the final matching of the original purchase order with the receiving data, and subject to the consideration of deductions or adjustments, the final approval for payment and subsequent disbursement. The negotiation of the adjustments is normally made by the affected buyer, but in certain cases it may be desirable to bring finance people into these negotiations. We covered the settlement procedures when we discussed the basis financial controls in Chapter 13. Our interest at this point is to recognize the financial settlement as the final step in the purchase transaction. Although the purchasing group is kept informed, as necessary, the important control aspect as it relates to purchasing is that it not be under purchasing control.

Other Matters of Special Interest

Our review of the major control points now needs to be supplemented by a consideration of some related matters that bear importantly on the effective control of the purchasing activity.

Organizational Status. One of these broader issues is the question of the organizational status of the purchasing function. Although it must be recognized that the volume and importance of the items purchased determine in the first place the importance of the purchasing function—and to that extent its organizational status—there is still the question of whether the purchasing group has been accorded the level of organizational status it really deserves. In the typical situation a vice president ranking is warranted at the corporate headquarters level with counterpart organizational status in component operational units. What is needed is an organizational status that will best assure the ability to attract a person who will have sufficient stature, and which will provide the proper degree of independence and position for effectively relating with other staff and line members of the top management group. At the same time the responsibilities should not include collateral activities such as receiving, warehousing, and payment, which are needed as legitimate and constructive counter-controls.

Centralization versus Decentralization. A related organizational problem is the extent to which the purchasing function should be centralized at the corporate headquarters level versus the extent to which lower-level operating subsidiaries, divisions, and other profit centers should have their own purchasing activities. Another possibility is that purchasing personnel may be physically located at the lower levels but organizationally be directly responsible to the central purchasing group. To a considerable extent the answer here depends on the overall picture of the company with respect to decentralization. If this is a centralized company, it will be logical that purchasing will also be centralized; and if the company is strongly profit-center oriented, we would expect to find separate purchasing groups in the individual profit centers. Even in the latter situations there will normally be the need for some kind of a central purchasing group. In the first place, there will always be the need for some central group to develop and administer certain types of company-wide purchasing policy. Also, such a central group can provide needed central research and special expertise in a staff capacity. Second, in many situations there is a need for the central coordination or central control of certain procurements on a company-wide basis. To the extent that there are local purchasing groups it would seem to be preferable to have them report to the local management group in a line sense and to the central purchasing group on a so-called dotted-line functional basis. The important thing is that the respective jurisdiction and related responsibilities of the central purchasing group versus the field purchasing groups be clearly stated. If this is done properly it is usually possible for the total company purchasing operations to operate effectively, and to serve adequately the needs of both the operational component and the central headquarters. All of this assumes that the central purchasing group will exercise adequate control over the field units. Part of this control will be built in as a part of the day-to-day operational relationships, but will normally be supplemented by the review of reports and periodic field visits.

Purchasing Jurisdiction. Another type of organizational problem concerns defining and administering the jurisdiction of the purchasing group. This problem appears in a variety of forms but perhaps the most common one is determining what types of purchases will go through the purchasing department. In some cases the conclusion may be reached that it is more efficient for a particular operational group to satisfy certain types of procurement needs through its own direct efforts. The personnel department has already been referred to as such a case. Another illustration would be that of an advertising department obtaining media space directly, or through an advertising agency. In making the official determination of jurisdiction the basic issue is whether the purchasing group can make a contribution, either as a result of its actual experience in a given area of procurement, or because a professional purchasing approach can be expected to yield special benefits.

Another type of problem exists when the official determination is clear enough but there is an evasion of some kind. One frequent type of evasion is when the user jumps the gun, so to speak, and in effect carries out his own investigation of the particular type of availability and then comes to the purchasing department only to legitimatize the effort through a perfunctory handling of the actual purchase through the purchasing department. Here the possibility of the contribution of the regular purchasing group is precluded. The best remedy in this kind of a situation is that the purchasing department turn back the request. The need to get the expenditure authorized properly to fit into regular accounts payable routines will then serve as a discipline to let the purchasing department do its proper job in the future.

A more commonplace type of problem is the avoidance of regular purchasing controls by effecting the procurement through petty cash, credit cards, or other types of operating funds. Such funds have presumably been set up for relatively limited purposes, usually for small expenditures and those of a special nature. The problem arises when those purposes are abused through a more extended use of them, and in this instance for the procurement of items which should go through regular purchasing channels. The result is a loss of control over these procurements and the loss of advantage that can come through the more consolidated procurement. The basic control here is that the ground rules be clearly stated, and that these rules are enforced through the procedures under which these established operating funds are reimbursed.

Emergency Purchases. Another variation of the evasion problem is that of emergency purchases. This particular problem exists when the operational activity simply does not act on a timely basis. Because of the delay the purchasing group is then placed in the situation where it does not have enough time to do its job efficiently. The problem is usually confused by the fact that emergency needs are to some extent unavoidable, and that in those situations there is no choice but to compromise through completing the purchase on the best possible basis within the time constraints. As a result, prices will usually have to be accepted which might have been reduced through competitive bidding. It can lead also to the undesirable situation where purchase commitments are made without price agreement; that is, the vendor is asked to proceed with the production or shipment of the item and then to advise the company what the price will be. As we have seen, emergency needs are often unavoidable. There may be a breakdown of equipment, or perhaps an unexpected rush order from one of the company's customers. The issue here is for the need to make a fair determination of what volume of emergency needs is in fact reasonable, and in taking steps to eliminate the portion that is due only to various kinds of inefficiency.

Purchasing for Employees. It is inevitable that company personnel will seek help in one way or another from purchasing personnel in making their own personal purchases. This is especially likely to be true if the items involved are the same as are being purchased for company use. It is a practice that is especially common in the case of company officers. Normally, this is not too serious a problem, but it can get out of hand. The main concern is that such service be extended on an equitable basis—that is, to individuals at specified organizational levels—and that it not be permitted to affect the ability of the purchasing group to discharge their regular responsibilities in an effective manner. Consideration must be given not only to the dilution of buyers' efforts, but also to the nuisance to vendors, including the administrative difficulties of effecting delivery and payment. Normally, the more this practice can be restricted the better it will be.

Analytical Role in Purchasing. Although the effectiveness of the purchasing representative is determined to some extent by his so-called trader skills, there is perhaps no type of activity that depends so much on basic analytical ability. This analytical ability is a combination of a vigorous and imaginative search for facts, and the related capacity to relate those facts to specific procurement situations. In his special product area the buyer needs to know what goes into the making of the product, the nature of the manufacturing processes, and the major operational problems that affect the completion and delivery of the product. He also needs to know what things should cost and what are good levels of cost performance. Related also is a knowledge of how the product will be used and what types of problems can arise in that utilization. His job is to put all of this knowledge together in the most advantageous manner possible in terms of ultimate company interest. Perhaps the most important aspect of this entire process is that he can be instrumental in finding better ways to accomplish the objectives as opposed to simply trying to squeeze profit out of a vendor. A good illustration of his work along these lines is the so-called "value analysis" of products where consideration is given to how different material and/or different processes might be used to take cost out of a product without impairing its usefulness. Under this kind of approach the buyer is also more likely to win the cooperation of vendors, and it should similarly provide attractive possibilities to other company personel. Fortunately also, this particular capacity on the part of the buyer tends to increase over time as his knowledge is augmented by further experience and breadth of contacts.

Controlling Undue Influence.   A particularly troublesome operational problem in the purchasing area exists in the temptation for purchasing personnel deliberately to favor particular vendors. Since the purchasing department's decision as to which vendor shall receive the order is one that has such a major impact on the financial interests of that vendor, it is to be expected that the vendor will exert a great deal of pressure on the person in the purchasing group who can control that decision to any significant extent. The types of pressure run from legitimate sales presentations and persistent follow-up to friendship factors, to entertainment, to gifts, and on to various types of actual bribery. Frequently, the line between the proper and improper is a hard one to draw—as, for example, in the case of a Christmas gift—and the standards of what is right and wrong often tend to deteriorate over time. Most well-managed companies recognize the danger that exists and endeavor to control it by strong policies prohibiting the acceptance of all favors, including the publicizing of those policies both to the purchasing personnel and vendors. The dangers here in any event increase the importance of good purchasing supervision and review, and continuous alertness to anything that appears to be an unwarranted favoritism to particular vendors.

Measuring the Effectiveness of the Purchasing Activity

A central problem that concerns both the management of the purchasing department and other company management is how to measure the effectiveness of the purchasing function. At the level of internal administration there can be the usual measures of the volume of purchasing handled, the number of purchase transactions effected, the length of time to handle the various types of operations, and the costs of these activities. These measures are, of course, most meaningful when they are compared with the performance at other purchasing operations where similar types of purchases are made. Useful comparisons can also be made with the performance of previous periods. It is important, therefore, that these measures be applied through a series of monthly and quarterly reports.

But the real problem in measuring the effectiveness of the purchasing activity is that each purchase transaction involves judgment, and that it is difficult to measure the quality of that judgment. Savings here are also passed on to the user groups in the way of lower procurement costs and are reflected in the operational results of those other groups. Still another difficulty is that the contribution of the purchasing department in many cases is a joint effort with other company personnel. Yet, despite the difficulties involved, there is the clear necessity to do something reasonably precise in measuring this larger and more important contribution of the purchasing group. The question is how to do it in a meaningful way.

The starting point of the measurement effort is, as we would expect, to establish meaningful objectives. The dollar volume of purchasing expected to be routed through the purchasing department is the gross base from which we must determine possibilities for savings through purchase price reductions. As we have seen previously, one type of possibility exists through the expansion of the competitive process, which in turn depends to a major extent on the development of additional vendor sources. Another possibility exists through working with individual vendors to develop new approaches that can provide the basis for lower costs. As we have seen also, the latter effort involves working with company personnel, and determining how their needs can be served in different ways. Throughout this entire effort the emphasis is on lower-cost approaches which will not reduce the value to the user. In all cases we are seeking to increase the number of options available. Finally, there is the possibility of interpreting market conditions so that buying can be done at the most advantageous time possible.

Once having analyzed the foregoing types of possibilities, to the extent possible, the basis is provided for establishing meaningful objectives. Needless to say, all of the purchasing group needs to participate in this effort because it will largely be individual buyers who can speak to the real possibilities in particular product areas. It will also be these same individual buyers who will actually effect the savings. The objectives thus established now become the basis for a periodic reporting of results actually achieved against these objectives. The savings reported to be achieved then have to be supported as well as possible with credit to other parties as is appropriate. Although the entire sequence is to some extent unavoidably inexact, experience has demonstrated that more will be accomplished by the program of savings objectives than simply to proceed in the usual manner. Certainly, other company personnel have better visibility of the nature of the purchasing effort and, therefore, have a better opportunity to support it.

Internal Auditor's Role

The role of the internal auditor in relation to the purchasing function will follow generally the pattern that would exist for any operational activity, but we restate it with particular application to the purchasing activity.

1. To understand the nature and scope of the purchasing function.
2. To check on the administrative efficiency of the purchasing activity in terms of presently designated policies and procedures—at the same time determining the extent of actual compliance with those policies and procedures.
3. To appraise those policies and procedures in terms of possible improvement.
4. To seek to identify the management service potential as purchasing works in a collaborative partnership fashion with both vendors and operational managers of the company.

5. To seek to contribute to increased company welfare through identifying any other means by which the purchasing effort can be made more effective.

Put in summary terms, it is the role of the internal auditor to see the purchasing department through the eyes of top management, but with an understanding of the problems of the purchasing department, the company users, and the vendors. He seeks to appraise efficiency and control in a basic operational sense, but at the same time to determine whether its full potential for contribution to company interests is being adequately exploited.

AUDIT GUIDES

REVIEW OF PURCHASING

I. Introductory

    A. Reference should be made to the general discussion of audit guides, Chapter 13.

II. Preparatory Activities

    A. See standard Audit Guides, Chapter 13.

III. Organizational Factors

    A. See standard Audit Guides, Chapter 13.

    B. Establish that the purchasing department is independent of receiving, inspection, stores, and accounts payable activities.

    C. Matters of special interest in the review of purchasing manuals will include:

        1. Standards of vendor relationships.

        2. Competitive bidding requirements.

        3. Extent of multiple sourcing.

        4. Reciprocity.

        5. Extent of local purchases.

        6. Coordination with user organizational components.

        7. Authorized levels of approval.

        8. Conflict of interest and acceptance of gifts.

        9. Follow-up responsibilities.

      10. Special types of purchase orders for applications that are more extended—over long time periods, or covering usage at a number of locations.

      11. Handling of employee purchases.

      12. Handling of deviations from established procedures.

IV. Authorization for Purchase

    A. Review the procedures for authorizing purchases. Points of special interest include:

1. Who initiates?
2. What approvals are necessary for particular types of items and amounts in terms of either quantities or dollar value?
3. What forms are to be used?
4. How are supplementary approvals handled when actual purchase cost exceeds original estimates?
5. What provision for changes in specifications or quantities?

B. On the basis of actual tests, verify and appraise:
1. The extent to which the procedures are complied with. (Where they were not complied with to any significant degree, what were the causes?)
2. Do the procedures appear to be adequate?
3. Where there are unusual authorizations in terms of types of products, quantities, source restrictions, and the like, does it appear that these are questioned and discussed?

V. Internal Operations

A. General
1. Are the facilities adequate:
    a. For reception and interviews with vendor representatives?
    b. For internal operations?
2. Are the internal operations being carried out in a manner consistent with established organizational responsibilities, policies, and procedures? If not, what are the causes, and what kind of corrective action seems to be warranted? This part of the review would include such questions as:
    a. Should the organizational responsibilities be modified?
    b. Should operational policies be reappraised?
    c. Should operational procedures be revised?
    d. Do we need different people?
3. To what extent do the operations reflect a high degree of efficiency and morale? Factors of special interest are similar to question 2 above.
4. Are internal records and files of various types adequate in terms of special purpose and relation to other records and procedures? Are they being maintained efficiently?
5. Is the total purchase cycle adequately controlled as to receipt of authorization, assignment to buyer, making of purchase, follow-up, and completion—so that the status of individual procurements can be easily determined?
6. Are purchasing forms properly safeguarded and controlled?
7. Are purchasing actions being processed on a timely basis?
8. Is the computer used for controlling orders, expediting, and reporting?

B. Relating to Vendors

1. Are adequate vendor records maintained showing supply capabilities and continuing purchasing relationships?
2. How adequate is the effort to develop new vendor sources?
3. How adequate are the field contacts with vendors to keep abreast of these vendor situations and to maintain cordial, high-level relationships?
4. Are vendor financial capabilities adequally investigated through banks and credit agencies?
5. What efforts are being made to evaluate vendor performance for price, delivery, and quality? And are adequate files pertaining to these factors maintained?
6. How adequate are the efforts to work with vendors to study cost reduction possibilities?
7. With respect to competitive bidding:
   a. Are competitive bids solicited in all cases possible?
   b. Are bids invited from at least three qualified vendors?
   c. In the case of recurring purchases are competitive bids solicited with needed frequency?
   d. Are all factors directly or indirectly related to price properly considered?
8. If price lists of vendors are used, are they updated with reasonable frequency?
9. With respect to negotiated purchase prices:
   a. Is the need to purchase on this basis adequately justified?
   b. Are adequate cost breakdowns made available as a basis for negotiation?
   c. Are all possible cross checks utilized in the way of comparison with products involving similar materials and processing, or via "in-house" estimates?
10. With respect to cost-type procurement:
    a. Is the need to purchase on this basis adequately justified?
    b. Are clearly defined and reasonable agreements reached as to recoverable costs prior to award of the purchase?
    c. Is profit reasonable and established in such a manner as to best motivate the lowest possible level of cost?
    d. Is cost performance adequately audited for compliance with established agreements?
11. Is the selection of the vendor and the basis of the proposed procurement reviewed and approved by a higher-ranking member of the purchasing group?

VI. Special Audit Tests

A. In addition to such observations and queries as have been made relative to specific aspects, it is desirable to test a representative number of purchase transactions by following them through all steps in the purchasing cycle. The sample should be picked at random from the original input of authorizations to purchase. Points of special interest at all stages would include:

1. Compliance with all policies and procedures.
2. Reasonableness of timing at the various stages.
3. Evidence of care and maximum protection of company interest.
4. Evidence of good team work in the total purchasing group.
5. All possible evidence of good value received.
6. Excessive rush or emergency orders.
7. Possibilities for combining separate purchases.
8. Orders for unauthorized items—as, for example, capital equipment.
9. Necessity of commitments in advance of price agreements.
10. Effectiveness of internal records and related procedures.
11. Leads for matters to be investigated in the review of other operational activities.
12. Any evidence of vendor favoritism.
13. Overall evaluation of the competence of the management of the purchasing activity.

VII–IX. Not used.

X. Overall Appraisal of Purchasing Effectiveness
  A. See standard Audit Guides, Chapter 13.
  B. Appraisal of relations with both vendors and company personnel should focus especially upon reduction of costs through substitution of materials, modifications of production processes, different delivery arrangements, and the like.

TRANSPORTATION

Transportation as a Part of the Procurement Activity

Transportation services are an important group of services which must be procured by the company. Although to some extent the company may elect to provide these services with its own facilities—as, for example, through the use of company-owned trucks—there is still normally a large volume of transportation services to be obtained from outside parties. Outside parties include principally railroads, ships, barges, truckers, express agencies, airlines, and the U.S. Postal Service. The procurement here may be associated with the procurement of purchased goods, with company shipments to customers, or with any type of internal transfer of materials. Its overall importance will depend on the range of operations of the particular company, but it will normally represent a very substantial type of operating cost. It is a type of procurement that has many special complexities, but which like any other operational activity presents opportunities for effective control.

Nature of the Transportation Process

Transportation in its most basic sense has to do with moving the various materials from the place of origin to a newly desired location in the most efficient manner. Materials include raw materials, processed materials, parts, facilities, products, or any other tangible item. Efficiency means the combination of price, other terms, timing, and physical conditions, which best serve the company's interests. We are concerned at this point only with the transportation services obtained from outside parties, although any company-provided transportation activity should always continually be reviewed as to the alternative of securing that service from an outside group. As managers, and in turn as internal auditors, we are interested that transportation activities are carried on in a manner that best serves the total company interest.

The functions of the transportation group, commonly designated in the company organization as the traffic department, fall into two general groups. The first of these groups has more to do with the development of transportation policy and in carrying out the various studies and investigations that pertain to major decisions. What mode of transportation should be used in the various situations? What routings are best? What can be done in the way of new approaches to reduce transportation costs? The second group of activities on the other hand concerns the day-to-day operations which are carried on pursuant to the aforementioned policies and key decisions. These are the operational activities that have to do with daily carrier relations, shipments, follow-up, and the like—including the maintenance of current files and records. The latter activities also lend themselves to decentralization to field offices or to other lower-level operational organizational components.

The basic operational cycle is generally similar to that which we found in the case of purchasing:

1. The determination of the need.
2. The determination of the specific arrangement for obtaining the transportation service.
3. The notification of the transportation arrangement to be used.
4. Any necessary follow-up.
5. The financial settlement.
6. The handling of claims.

These operational stages, and the particular objectives associated with them can also again become the basis for looking at the structure of control and the related control problems of major significance.

Determining the Need for Transportation Services

Like purchasing, the starting point of the transportation problem is the identification of the need. There is first the validity of the need itself. Here the main question is whether there are other operational approaches that would eliminate or modify the asserted transportation need. For example, could delivery be made at a closer location? Or could we establish a storage point to eliminate a larger number of small shipments? There is also the question of whether the need has been accurately defined. Is the asserted urgency realistic? In many of these situations the transportation representative can provide good advisory counsel. It is always necessary that he know the exact nature of the need if he is to satisfy that need in the most economical manner. From a control standpoint we are interested in everything that will best induce this careful determination. Although this determination of need may be the basic responsibility of other operating personnel, the transportation personnel have a professional interest in it and to some extent a share of the responsibility.

Determining the Specific Transportation Arrangement

The heart of the transportation function is the study and search that goes into the determination of the specific transportation arrangement that will best satisfy the properly defined need. Here the special expertise of the transportation professional is fully utilized. Typical features that might be applicable will include:

1. The savings to be achieved by using the proper commodity rate.
2. The decreasing costs of shipping in carload or truckload quantities.
3. Possibilities of pooling shipments with other shippers.
4. In transit stopovers or in transit privileges that can be obtained at a small extra cost.
5. Delivery schedules.
6. Risk of damage or theft.
7. Extra services for premium rates.
8. Customer preferences in connection with outbound shipments.
9. Reciprocity pressures.
10. Availability of special equipment.
11. The relative costs of different modes of transportation in relation to the existing operational need.

In some cases costs can be saved by hauling for compensation for wholly-owned subsidiaries or for others, as allowed under the Motor Carrier Act of 1980. Before this Act, private fleets of trucks were restricted to hauling their own goods. Also, although it was permissible for a subsidiary to haul for another subsidiary, it had to be gratuitous. Under the new Act, a company may become involved in for-hire transport for unrelated companies, or obtain contract carrier authority to haul for its subsidiaries. In the past, subsidiaries often approached freight movement methods independently, and the new regulatory changes have created opportunities for joint freight operations.

The transportation department weighs these various considerations to arrive at the final conclusion that seems on balance to be the best. There will also, where necessary, be continuing discussions with customers, vendors, and company personnel. For repetitive shipments the same decisions will apply until there is some indication that some significant dimension of the evaluation has changed. In all situations the importance of this step from a control standpoint is that this is where the decision is actually made and that, therefore, this decision should reflect the greatest possible degree of efficiency and good judgment. The focus is on all evidence which indicates that the various factors pertaining to the decision have been recognized and properly evaluated.

Making the Transportation Arrangement

The determination of the transportation arrangement may at the same time become the actual notification to all interested parties, or in other cases this notification may be handled separately. The parties to be notified in different situations may be vendors, customers, or our own company personnel. In the case of a purchase the selected routing will normally be included on the purchase order. In the case of outgoing shipments, the proper bills of ladings will be prepared, or other company personnel instructed to do so. The control objective is a clear and timely notification of the underlying decision. In the case of repetitive shipments this becomes the operational implementation of standard routing instructions.

Follow-Up of Specific Execution of Transportation Arrangements

The extent of follow-up efforts depends on the urgency of the need for the materials being transported. In some cases this requires the monitoring of actual loading operations and interim reports on the progress of the shipment up to the point of actual delivery at the final destination. In other cases the failure of the materials to arrive at destination at given points of time would initiate the follow-up effort. The control objective is that the follow-up effort is adequate in the circumstances.

Settlement of Completed Transportation

In certain situations the transportation cost may be paid by the vendor or the customer. If, according to the applicable agreements, this cost is to be absorbed by them, the problem of the validity of the settlement is theirs—subject only to claims that we may have against the carrier involved. In other situations the basis of purchase or sale may be that the cost of transportation is to be borne by us, and we will ultimately be billed that cost either by the carrier or by the vendor or customer who has paid it on our behalf. Although these costs will ultimately be paid through an accounts payable department—or in some cases through credits to customers who have paid them for us—the review and approval of these charges are normally made by the traffic department. One reason for this practice is that the accounts payable department does not have rate information on the purchase order. But the more important reason is that the review and approval of the freight costs require special expertise. In addition, a great deal of money is involved and special effort is warranted to be sure the company is not overcharged. The normal practice is, therefore, for the transportation department to make a general review of the billings prior to payment, covering the clerical and more obvious basis of the billing, and then to conduct an audit of the rates on a more thorough basis at a later time. This second review in many cases is subcontracted to an even more specialized outside service group.

Handling Claims

Claims against carriers are of two broad types, those arising out of incorrect billings, and those for damage to goods while being transported. In both cases it is the usual practice for these claims to be handled by the transportation department. The control aspects here are that the operating group which originally identifies the claim promptly records it and transmits it to the department. Such operating groups would include receiving departments, inspection departments, and accounts receivable activities. The transportation department must then establish adequate controls over the filing of these claims and the subsequent follow-up of them. The key concerns are that we maintain our record of the claims and that we give them adequate follow-up attention. From an internal control standpoint it is preferable that claims be controlled through the regular financial accounts.

Organizational Aspects of the Transportation Activity

Like an operational activity, the effectiveness of the transportation activity is closely related to its organizational status. Certainly, the importance of the transportation function would argue for a high-level status. In a great many cases the close relationship of the transportation activity to purchasing is recognized by making transportation a part of the purchasing department. There is no harm in this arrangement as long as the role of the transportation group is not restricted to serving the normal purchasing operations. The transportation activity as we have seen involves outbound shipments and intracompany shipments as well.

Quite commonly also, the transportation function is decentralized to a considerable extent. Normally, the central group will cover the staff functions and such operational activities as involve the entire company. The operational activities pertaining to the operational components—subsidiaries, divisions, and other operational groups—will then be decentralized. Although these decentralized groups may report on a line basis to the local management, there is necessarily a strong functional tie to the control group. The objective is to centralize those aspects that need a total company approach and at the same time to give local operating management the direct support it needs.

Company Welfare Potentials

At many points we have seen the possibilities of significant contributions by the transportation group to the overall company welfare. Very often, these potentials are lost sight of in the actual company situation in the volume of day-to-day work that is carried out by the usual traffic department. It is important, however, that all parties recognize the wide range of potentials. Especially do these potentials come out of a close collaborative relationship between the transportation group and the other operating activities. We list some of these areas of company service as illustrative:

1. The decision regarding the building of a new plant, or the relocation of an existing plant, is significantly affected by available transportation alternatives and their related costs. Pertinent is the impact on vendor supply, transfers of partially processed materials from one plant to another, and customer service.

2. The utilization of plant capacity and the location of particular types of production processes will involve the same types of considerations.

3. Similarly, the location of warehouses depends on proximity to plants, vendors, and customers.

4. New approaches to the use of existing transportation services might have important marketing implications—as, for example, the use of air freight. Also, the increased volume may be a basis for pressing for further rate reductions.

5. New types of shipment may materially reduce handling costs—as, for example, the use of containers for small parts.

6. It may be possible that costs can be reduced through the company acquiring its own facilities.

7. The more careful study of rate structures may indicate different ways in which the company can qualify for lower rates—as, for example, different-size shipments, the use of different commodity classifications, and the like.

There are of course the efficiencies of a well-administered operational activity, which are significant and should be fully exploited. Our purpose here is to demonstrate that there are additional potentials which also need to be studied and adequately explored.

Measuring the Effectiveness of the Transportation Activity

It may again seem that the nature of the transportation services is so interrelated with other company activities that it is not practicable to set up meaningful goals and objectives, and thus that it is not really practicable to measure the effectiveness of the transportation group. Again it needs to be emphasized that there is much to be done along these lines. At the lower operational level there are standards that can be established as to what can be done in the way of individual performance. These are the considerations covered by the usual personnel and expense budgets. But at the higher level also it is desirable to project plans for providing more value for transportation expenditures. These can be reductions of cost or other types of added value provided to company operating activities. Normally, these plans are expressed in terms of specific projects to be studied and are then grouped in the best possible fashion. These plans then provide the basis for a periodic reporting of accomplishments with adequate backup to support the claimed savings.

Internal Auditor's Role

The role of the internal auditor should follow an approach similar to the one outlined at the close of the discussion of purchasing. In summary, this should include:

1. Understanding the transportation process.
2. Reviewing the efficiency of the administrative operations and related compliance with current policies and procedures.
3. Appraising the effectiveness of existing policies and procedures.
4. Endeavoring in all ways possible to determine how the transportation group can increase its contribution to the total company welfare.

AUDIT GUIDES

REVIEW OF TRANSPORTATION ACTIVITIES

I. Introductory
   A. Reference should be made to the general discussion of Audit Guides, Chapter 13.

II. Preparatory Activities
   A. See standard Audit Guides, Chapter 13.

III. Organizational Factors
   A. See standard Audit Guides, Chapter 13.
   B. Establish that the transportation department is independent of the accounts payable department.
   C. Matters of special interest in the review of manuals will include:
      1. Standards of relationships with carriers.
      2. Extent of authority for local transportation arrangements.
      3. Coordination with user organizational groups.
      4. Authorized levels of approval.
      5. Restrictions on receiving of gifts.
      6. Follow-up responsibilities.
      7. Handling of deviations from established procedures.
      8. Jurisdiction over all arrangements with outside truckers.

IV. Authorization for Making Transportation Arrangements
   A. Review the procedures for making transportation arrangements. Points of special interest include:
      1. Who initiates?
      2. What approvals are necessary for particular types of arrangements and in what amounts?
      3. In what way is the making of the arrangement finalized?

B. On the basis of actual tests, verify and appraise:

1. The extent to which procedures are complied with. (Where they are not complied with to any significant degree, what are the causes?)
2. Do the procedures appear to be adequate?
3. When there are unusual types of arrangements, does it appear that these are questioned and discussed?

V. Internal Operations

A. General

1. Are the facilities adequate?
2. Are the internal operations being carried on in a manner consistent with established organizational responsibilities, policies, and procedures? If not, what are the causes? What kind of corrective actions seems to be warranted? This part of the review would include such questions as:
   a. Should the organizational responsibilities be modified?
   b. Should operational policies be reappraised?
   c. Should operational procedures be revised?
   d. Do we need different people?
   e. Do we need better training and supervision of the existing people?
3. To what extent do the operations reflect a high degree of efficiency and morale? Factors of special interest are similar to those of question 2.
4. Are internal records and files of various types adequate in terms of special purpose and relation to other records and procedures? Are they being maintained efficiently?
5. Is the operational cycle adequately controlled as to authorization, assignment to personnel, making of transportation arrangement, follow-up, and completion—so that the status of individual transportation assignments can be easily determined?
6. Are official documents properly safeguarded and controlled?

B. Relating to Carriers

1. Are adequate records maintained of business given to individual carriers?
2. What efforts are made to evaluate carrier performance?
3. How adequate are the efforts to work with individual carriers for cost-reduction possibilities?
4. How thorough is the effort to evaluate the value aspects of alternative routings and other transportation arrangements?
5. Is the selection of carriers reviewed and approved by a higher-ranking member of the traffic department with reasonable frequency?
6. Are records and controls adequate to minimize demurrage?

C. Relating to Approvals for Payment of Carrier Billings

1. Are procedures adequate to determine whether charges are for company account? Are portions chargeable to vendors or customers properly controlled?
2. Are billings in accordance with originally authorized transportation arrangements? If not, are proper deductions made?
3. Are weights properly confirmed?
4. If claims are to be made, are they adequately recorded for subsequent handling and control?
5. Is the follow-up of claims adequate?
6. Is adequate provision made for the more thorough post-audit of all freight bills?

VI. Special Audit Tests

A. In addition to such observations and queries as have been made relative to specific aspects, it is desirable to test a representative number of transportation decision actions, by following through all steps in the operational cycle. The sample should be picked at random from the original input of authorizations to make transportation arrangements. Points of special interest at all stages would include:
1. Compliance with all policies and procedures.
2. Reasonableness of timing at the various stages.
3. Evidence of care and maximum protection of company interest.
4. Evidence of good teamwork in the total traffic group.
5. All possible evidence of good value received in the decisions.
6. Effectiveness of internal records and related procedures.
7. Leads for matters to be investigated in the review of other operational activities.
8. Any evidence of favoritism to individual carriers.
9. Overall evaluation of the competence of the management of the department.

VII–IX. Not used.

X. Overall Approval of Transportation Effectiveness

A. See standard Audit Guides, Chapter 13.

B. Appraisal of relations with both carriers and company personnel should focus especially on reduction of transportation costs through development of new types of equipment, new conditions of shipment, use of company equipment to haul for others, and the like.

ILLUSTRATIVE AUDIT FINDINGS: PURCHASING AND TRANSPORTATION

Standardization of Parts Needed

The company could increase efforts to standardize electronic parts needed for production. This would reduce purchase costs, eliminate duplication in parts control efforts, and improve quality. The company had standardized parts in the heavy-equipment divisions, but had not attempted to standardize parts in the computers division.

Backlogs in Filling Orders

The purchasing department had significant backlogs in filling requisitions, resulting in delays in meeting production requirements and making deliveries to customers. A statistical sample of one month's requisitions indicated that the delays were caused by excessive time taken to process the requests and place orders with available suppliers.

Sole-Source Procurement

Purchases were being made from sole-source suppliers without adequate justification. In addition, insufficient competitive bids were being obtained. As a result, excessive prices were being paid for certain items.

Buying Items of Too High Quality

Controls over specifications needed strengthening to assure that the company was not acquiring a higher quality of items than needed. In a test of machine parts purchased it was found that parts with a useful life of 20 years were being acquired when the life of the equipment was only 5 years. By substituting machine parts with a lesser life, significant savings could be achieved.

Pinpointing Responsibility for Change Orders

Payments were being made for change orders that were caused by errors of suppliers rather than company design. Additional analysis and review of change orders as to cause were needed to prevent the unwarranted payment of additional costs that were the responsibility of the supplier.

Need to Monitor Subcontract Costs

Excessive prices were paid to subcontractors under cost-type contracts because there was insufficient monitoring of performance and costs claimed. Procurement personnel were not monitoring cost-type subcontracts any differently than they were monitoring fixed-price subcontracts.

Need for Private Fleet of Trucks

Savings in freight costs could be obtained by maintaining a private fleet of trucks to ship finished goods. This equipment could be used to haul goods for subsidiaries of the company and others under the new ICC regulation granting contract carrier authority.

CHAPTER FIFTEEN

Receiving, Inventories, and Scrap

RECEIVING

Nature and Importance of Receiving

The receiving process is a continuation of the operational cycle that was begun through the procurement of needed materials and services. It starts at the point the carrier makes delivery to the company premises or at some other designated point. It is here that the determination is made that goods are received in the quantities, specifications, and conditions covered by the underlying purchase order agreement. In addition, the receiving process includes the physical care of the goods received and the forwarding of them to the user or to company stores. The importance of the function is in providing an essential link between the basic procurement and the ultimate placement of the particular products where they will be available to satisfy the operational need. Delay or error in providing this link can often result in serious delays and operational problems in the other affected company activities. The proper receival also is a basic prerequisite in establishing the validity of payments to vendors as a part of the accounts payable process. From an operational standpoint it is apparent that the receiving activity should be carried out with maximum efficiency.

One of the challenging aspects of the receiving process is the fact that it must deal with so many different types of incoming materials. The material itself may be a liquid or a solid, packaged or in bulk, small or bulky, of low or very high value, and there may be special requirements in the way of protection. The materials may also arrive in a variety of forms, as by freight car, air, trucking, or messenger. We mention these well-known variations to emphasize the broad range of operational problems that a receiving organization faces in carrying out its operations.

Organizational Setting of the Receiving Activity

Because of the role of the receiving activity in the final financial settlement with vendors, it becomes extremely important that this particular phase of the operations be carried out with proper organizational independence. This organizational separateness is desirable, first, to assure a separate and professional concentration on this important activity. But from an internal control standpoint the independence from the purchasing activity especially minimizes the risk of someone in the purchasing department controlling both the order and the evidence of satisfying the requirements of that order. The organizational independence is also an important check on vendor performance as a basis for the final determination for payment by the accounts payable department. Needless to say, the organizational independence should in no way lessen a cooperative relationship with all other interested groups—the purchasing department, the company user, the transportation department, the stores department, and the accounts payable department.

The organizational placement of the receiving department should be sufficiently high to give it reasonable status with other operating activities. Normally, the receiving department would be a part of the production staff, or perhaps the production control department. Although there is a need for company policies and procedures to apply to all receiving operations, there will be a high degree of decentralization to the different field locations. However, at any individual geographical location there should be only one receiving group, and as far as is practicable, a single receiving area.

Control Cycle for Receiving

We are now ready to look at the operational cycle of the receiving activity as a basis for understanding the key control points. Normally, this operational cycle would be:

1. Notification to the receiving department by the purchasing department of the placing of an order.
2. Delivery of the materials by the carrier.
3. A count of quantities received.
4. Inspection of materials to the extent required.
5. Delivery to the user or to the stores department.
6. Reporting of receiving results to accounts payable and other interested company groups.

We will look at these individual steps to determine the nature of the control problems involved.

Notification to Receiving Department.   This is accomplished by the transmittal of a designated copy of the purchase order issued by the purchasing department. As discussed later, this copy may or may not show quantities. The copies received are filed in some kind of an open order file pending receipt of the materials. The essential control feature is that this receiving copy be forwarded promptly and that it be utilized as a continuing alert for the expected receival.

Delivery by Carrier. In some cases the goods may arrive at a local transportation terminal and be picked up by the company or by its trucker intermediary. More frequently, however, the carrier will make delivery to the company premises. The first control point here is how the carrier obtains access to the company premises. This aspect is part of the domain of plant security, which controls all movement of materials in and out of the company property area. Now railroad cars will be switched onto the proper sidings, and trucks will be directed to the established receiving docks. Assuming that there is no delay, the railroad car or truck is unloaded and the materials are transferred to the custody and responsibility of the company. At this point there is an appropriate check of what is being delivered—weight, number of packages, and the like. Empty cars and trucks (except as they may contain material for other parties) are cleared and then leave the company premises. The controls here are again those of plant security plus the importance of unloading in a manner that will best facilitate any subsequent more detailed count and inspection.

Counts Covering Materials Received. The receiving department is now ready to make such further detailed counts of the material received as appear to be reasonable and appropriate. The influencing factors here will be the degree of confidence in the particular vendor, the extent to which there are sealed containers with stated quantities, the practicability of counts, and the values involved. Obviously, a considerable degree of judgment is involved in making the determination of what kind of a count verification is needed. It should also be noted that there are secondary checks on quantities as materials are put into stores or by user operational activities when the materials are put directly into production. In the case of bulk materials the reliance is on weights, and the question becomes one of the independent confirmation of the weights asserted by the shipper or carrier. From a control standpoint our interest in all cases is that a reasonable standard of verification is applied and that the verification is carried out with reasonable promptness.

A special question exists at this point as to whether the purchase order copy sent to the receiving department should show the quantities ordered. The rationale that supports omission of these quantity data is that the receiving personnel will then be forced to make a more independent and more accurate count of quantities received. However, this course of action often causes delay and sometimes confusion, especially to the accounts payable department.

Inspection of Materials Received. In the case of many materials the inspection is carried out as a part of the counts and other verification of quantities received. In other cases, however, more elaborate and substantive types of inspection are required. In these latter situations the inspection action is carried out by representatives of the separate inspection department, frequently called the quality control department, which is normally responsible for inspection activities at all stages of the production process. When this further inspection is necessary, the goods received are usually moved from the first receiving area to a new area that is under the exclusive jurisdiction of the quality control department. The concerns from a control standpoint are that the materials are moved to the inspection area with reasonable promptness and that they are then inspected with the same reasonable despatch. Because of the extra movement of the materials it sometimes becomes a more difficult control problem to keep the individual vendor shipments separate and intact, but it is most necessary that this be done.

Intracompany Delivery of Materials Received.   The materials as received, and as subsequently inspected, are now ready for transfer to either the stores department or directly to the using operational department, subject only to the identification of deficiencies in the way of quantities, specifications, or damage. At this point the basis for all claims thus identified is established and recorded. If the inspection of the carrier or vendor is necessary, the items to be examined will have to be segregated and held for that later review. Also, there may be certain delegations from the vendor, including certain types of rework to bring the parts up to the required standard. The important control considerations are that claims are generated on the basis of competent authority, that appropriate record controls are established, that additional costs which may be incurred will be kept track of for later recovery, that defective materials are adequately tagged and segregated, and that good items then move promptly to the proper destination. With respect to the latter action, there also needs to be the acceptance of the quantities by the transferee for continuing accountability.

Reporting.   The operational cycle of the receiving department is now complete except for the very important reporting to all interested parties of the results accomplished. This reporting is best accomplished through the use of standard type multicopy receiving reports covering each incoming shipment and properly referenced to the applicable purchase order. Some of these copies are for liaison information purposes, but as previously noted the copy to the accounts payable department is especially important because it will be used as a basis of determining proper payments to vendors. For the purchasing department it will also set the stage for the negotiation of claims against vendors, and for the traffic department the basis both for passing upon billings from carriers and the processing of related claims. From a control standpoint it is, therefore, critical that all of these papers are accurate and that they are promptly transmitted to the parties who will make use of them.

Administrative Aspects of Receiving

The work of the receiving department has two important but somewhat different dimensions. One is the prompt and accurate preparation and transmittal of the forms by which interested parties are informed, accountabilities established, and financial actions supported. The other is the orderly handling and control of the actual materials received. The latter dimension is especially difficult because it involves both a wide range of physical characteristics of individual items received and the pressures of fluctuating volumes which are sometimes beyond day-to-day capacities. The two dimensions are, however, closely interrelated in that problems which develop in the case of the second dimension can undermine the capabilities to care efficiently for the first requirement. The necessity of proper standards of orderliness and control in a physical sense in turn brings us to an interest and concern in two underlying causal factors. One of these causal factors is the adequacy of the facilities provided for the receiving activity. Included here will be the amount of space provided, the extent to which unauthorized access to it can be prevented, the adequacy of unloading docks, and the adequacy of the various types of auxiliary equipment. The second causal factor is that of people. Are there enough people, are they adequately trained, is there proper supervision, and is the overall management direction of a sufficiently high standard?

Fraud and Dishonesty. The causal factors and the related administrative dimensions are also especially important because of their bearing on their relationship to the minimization of fraud and dishonesty. Defects in the procedural system can open up the possibilities for fraudulent payments to vendors and carriers. These defects can be in the basic design of the procedures or in the laxity with which properly designed procedures are actually applied. Similarly, a breakdown in the orderly handling and control of materials in a physical sense can induce the fraudulent diversion of various types of materials. In the latter case there is still the problem of getting the materials out of the plant, but to some extent that also may be possible. We have here simply another reason for pressing for effective receiving operations.

Management Service Potentials of Receiving Activity

We are interested always for any operational activity to identify and exploit whatever potentials that may exist for management service. In the case of the receiving department, we do not have the level of lofty potentials we found in the purchasing department or in the transportation department. Still we find an important range of management service in a more day-to-day operational sense. Here the emphasis is on the efficiency with which the current services are provided, as the receiving link fits into the total company operational cycle, and as the receiving department works in a cooperative fashion with other operational activities. The appraisal of services should include the timeliness of processing goods and the reliability of quality and quantity checks. If statistical sampling is used in the checks, the internal auditor should review the appropriateness of the sampling plan. There are, in addition, the normal management possibilities of the department properly identifying its current and evolving needs for facilities and people.

When then we come to the problem, as we always must, of the best possible manner of measuring the effectiveness of the receiving activity, we are led to conclude that objectives as to improving the level of operational efficiency are the most meaningful. These would be expressed for the most part in expense and manpower budgets. This approach would still not preclude the development of special projects of a more innovative nature, but they will exist to a lesser extent than was the case with many other operational activities.

Internal Auditor's Role

The role of the internal auditor in relation to the activities of the receiving department will necessarily be determined by the level of management service potentials just described. As usual, the internal auditor will first want to familiarize himself with the nature and scope of the receiving process, including the existing policies and procedures that have been developed for the conduct of this activity. He will then be especially concerned with the level of efficiency with which the activities are being carried out within the framework of the established policies and procedures. This does not mean that there will not be opportunities for finding areas of improvement in the existing policies and procedures, but the opportunities may be more limited in that respect. As always, however, he will be interested in people utilization. Also, he will want to appraise the overall competence with which the total activity is being administered. Thus in all respects the internal auditor will be seeking to determine how the receiving activity can further contribute to management needs and total company welfare.

AUDIT GUIDES

REVIEW OF RECEIVING ACTIVITIES

I. Introductory
   A. Reference should be made to the general discussion of audit guides, Chapter 13.

II. Preparatory Activities
   A. See standard Audit Guides, Chapter 13.

III. Organizational Factors
   A. See standard Audit Guides, Chapter 13.
   B. Establish that the receiving department is independent of the purchasing department, the stores department, and the accounts payable department.
   C. Matters of special interest in the review of manuals will include:
      1. Preparation and distribution of receiving reports.
      2. Delegation of authority to sign and approve receiving reports.
      3. Criteria for determination of verification of quantities.
      4. Handling of partial deliveries by vendors.
      5. Action in case of shortages.
      6. Action in case of damaged materials.

7. Coordination with inspection department.
8. Handling of unidentified receipts.
9. Safeguarding of materials received.
10. Procedure for transfer of materials after count.
11. Are the policies and procedures adequate? If not, in what respects should they be improved?

IV. Internal Operations
   A. General
      1. Are facilities adequate? If not, what are the deficiencies?
      2. Is auxiliary equipment adequate? If not, in what respects?
      3. Are the internal operations being carried out in a manner consistent with established organizational responsibilities, policies, and procedures? If not, what are the causes, and what kind of corrective action seems to be warranted? This part of the review would include such questions as:
         a. Should the organizational responsibilities be modified?
         b. Should organizational policies be reappraised?
         c. Should operational procedures be revised?
         d. Do we need different people?
         e. Do we need better training and supervision of the existing people?
      4. To what extent do the operations reflect a high degree of orderliness and control in the physical handling and storage of the materials? If not, what are the causes for the deficiencies?
      5. Are internal records and files adequate in terms of special purpose and relation to other records and procedures? Are they being maintained efficiently?
      6. Are receiving report forms properly safeguarded and controlled?
      7. Do relations with other company operational activities reflect a proper degree of cooperation?
      8. If there is a significant amount of overtime, appraise the causes and relate to needs for regular personnel.
      9. Is there an excessive backlog of work?

V. Special Audit Tests
   A. Irrespective of such observations and queries as have been made relative to specific aspects, it is desirable to test a representative number of completed receiving reports where the material is still on hand, to check the accuracy of counts and procedural handling. Points of special interest would include:
      1. Adequacy of count.
      2. Reasonableness of timing.
      3. Handling of special situations.
   B. Also test a representative number of completed receiving reports. Points of interest would include:

1. Reasonableness of timing.
2. Handling of special problems—shortages, damaged material, and other differences between goods ordered and received.
3. Leads for matters to be investigated in the review of other operational activities.
4. Overall evaluation of the competence of the management of the receiving department.

C. Review of effectiveness of checks of quality and quantity of goods received. Points of special interest would include:
   1. Appropriateness of the sampling plan if statistical sampling is used.
   2. Checks of functional accuracy of instrumentation used in testing.
   3. Follow-up on exception reports for shortages, damages, and defective material to see that claims are filed.

VI–IX. Not used.

  X. Overall Appraisal of Receiving Effectiveness
     A. See standard Audit Guides, Chapter 13.
     B. The level of appraisal focuses predominantly on operational efficiency and quality of coordination with other company activities.

INVENTORIES

Nature of Inventory Control Process

Materials received may go directly into the production process, a phase of the operations discussed in Chapter 16. In other cases the materials received will go into inventories and be held there until wanted for further use. These inventories are commonly known as stores. The materials can be of any type—raw materials, supplies, parts, subassemblies, and the like. They may be for later use in some phase of the manufacturing process, for maintenance or other operational purposes, or they may be for sale to customers. At the same time they may have come from outside vendors, and hence through the receiving department, or they may have come from one of the company's own manufacturing processes. The common characteristic is that there is an interim period before they will be wanted for further use and, therefore, they are to be held in stores during that interim period. The stores activity is related to a number of other operating activities, including receiving, inspection, production, maintenance, and sales. The function of the activity is to hold the materials involved with proper physical care and to make them available at the time needed.

Relation to Maximizing Return on Investment

To a major extent our interest in all operational activities is to reduce the costs of operation for the particular activity or to provide a range of service that makes possible the reduction of the costs of operations in other company operating activities. This is again true in the case of the stores activities. There is, however, a special dimension in this case which comes about because of the investment of company funds in inventories. The supplementary interest is to control inventory stocks so that the minimum investment is required, at the same time giving appropriate consideration as to how well the total company needs are being served by the particular level of inventories for individual items. The accomplishment of this supplementary objective involves many significant trade-offs and a host of detailed factors. It is an area where the use of modern computers in combination with the tools of the new management sciences have made important contributions.

Control Cycle of the Stores Process

Despite the fact that the actual role of the stores inventories is to become involved in the broader operational activities at many different times, it will again be useful to break down the process into the specific steps that comprise its typical role. These steps can be summarized as:

1. The determination of the types of materials, and the quantities of them, which are to move into stores.
2. The acceptance of the materials by stores.
3. The storage of these materials in such a manner that they will be properly safeguarded and available at the time they are later needed.
4. The collection and release of specific materials on request by properly authorized parties.

We discuss next the problems of control under these headings.

Determination of Need. It is possible that the occasion for the storage of materials may have come about in an unintended manner. To illustrate, goods might be returned by a customer or by an internal user. Also, particular production runs may have been excessive. Normally, however, the determination of what will become input to stores will be determined in a deliberate manner. Illustrative of this would be any managerial judgment, whether by a user or by the stores department itself, that a given quantity of a specific type of item will be needed to such an extent in the future that there ought to be a certain quantity held in stores to supply that later need. The real question here is, first, how soundly the operational need has been determined, and second, how soundly the basis for supplying that need has been developed. We use the term "soundly" because in each case the determination normally involves a number of conflicting factors, and also because the two parts of the question are to some extent unavoidably interrelated. As an example, there may be a certain need for a repair part. But it may be quite uncertain as to how many breakdowns there will be and at what time. There is also the question of how serious it would be if the repair part is not available when needed, or if subjected to various periods of delay. There may also be influencing factors such as the level of supervision of workers on the machine or the standards of inspection and maintenance. Although experience is a considerable guide, and there are various good statistical approaches to the determination of the future need, there is still a great deal of judgment involved.

The stores department now looks at the estimated demand and endeavors to determine how it can most economically maintain an inventory to service that need. First, consideration must be given to the required lead times for the individual items, that is, how long it will take from the time an item is ordered to the time it will be received and available for issue. Second, consideration must be given to various types of costs. One group of these costs is the cost of processing individual orders. Another group has to do with the cost of carrying inventories, that is, occupancy costs, interest on investment, insurance, obsolescence, and the like. Here also the estimated costs of being out of stock must be considered. Finally, the lower purchase costs for larger quantities, together with related transportation costs, must be considered. These factors combine to provide judgments as to the necessary minimum level of inventories and the order point and quantities to be ordered which will be most economical. These determinations can to some extent be made through optimizing the results via different types of mathematical formulas, but the explanation of this practice is beyond the scope of this discussion.[1] It should be said, however, that the use of mathematical models requires a great deal of care, with respect to both the coverage of the models and the satisfactory determination of the various input factors. Even then there is no substitute for judgment in their application.

Importance of Determination of Need.   Despite the difficulties involved the fact remains that the way needs are determined, and then evaluated, is the basis for the placement of actual orders from which results the physical input to the stores department. The key point of control, therefore, is to take every possible step to assure the soundness of the determination of what is really needed. Because of the repetitive nature of the problem there is a practical necessity of following some kind of a standard decision-rule approach. But it is particularly important that this decision-rule judgment be competently devised and also that it be periodically reappraised in the light of continuing experience. It must also normally be applied on an individual item basis, with the greatest effort being directed to the high-value types of items. The responsibility for this important phase is one that is jointly shared by the user and the stores department, and more often the latter because there may be multiple users of the same item. Normally, the help of specialized staff is also utilized, as, for example, from an operations research staff or the finance department.

[1]For a more detailed discussion of a management sciences approach to inventory management, see *Research Bulletin 16*, "Internal Audit of Inventory Control and Management" published by The Institute of Internal Auditors.

Acceptance of Materials by Stores Department. The material as ordered, or produced within the company, now comes to the stores department. The depletion of stocks will have already provided alerts, especially as to delays that have developed in the filling of replenishment orders. Liaison with the receiving department, purchasing department, and other sources will then be in order. The actual receival is essentially the count of the items for which it accepts accountability and a reasonable inspection of the materials to see that they are in proper condition. Acceptance would normally be indicated by signature on either the purchase order or receiving report copy. Still another type of receival will come from materials previously released from stores, but for various reasons not used, and now returned to storage. The acceptance of accountability will in this case provide a credit against the previous charge.

The receipt of the physical items with the supporting paper is now normally the occasion for entering the receivals of the various material items in some kind of a book inventory record. This inventory record may be kept only in terms of quantities, but in its most complete form it will also carry money values. These latter values will be determined by purchase order costs or in the case of the company's own production at established internal transfer prices. The purposes of these values are to be able to price later releases and to establish later total inventory values. Current balances will normally be maintained for quantities so that availability information can be provided promptly, and also for money values to the extent required for the pricing of releases. Any or all parts of this inventory record are very often computerized. The total control interest is to make sure that the physical acceptance of the materials has been prompt, orderly, and accurate, and that the related procedural aspects have been promptly and accurately carried out.

Storage of Materials. The storage of individual materials in a stores department is part of a total design determination of where various items can be physically accommodated for interim storage and still be found promptly and made available for transfer out as needed by other operational activities. The space actually available at the storage area is, of course, the first constraint. But there are different ways to utilize space to achieve maximum efficiency. Pertinent considerations here include:

1. Placement of bulky items in more remote areas.
2. Proper stacking.
3. Effective use of shelving, racks, and bins.
4. Adequate provision for aisles.
5. Protection of flexibility for varying inventory levels for particular items.
6. Use of conveyors or open cars on tracks.
7. Clear location identification.

Assuming that items are placed to best suit their physical and frequency of movement characteristics, the collateral need is for a location identification that will make it easy to find items as needed for later release. All of this needs to be worked out in an orderly and systematic manner. The locations assigned are then noted on the individual book inventory records.

Collection and Release of Materials.   The release is initiated by some type of authorizing paper. This can be a requisition form for internal use or a shipping order in the case of a customer sale. In all cases the particular authorizing paper needs to be completed properly and carry the approvals of the persons duly authorized. These papers are then used as a basis for collecting (sometimes called picking) the items specified. In some cases where the collecting is widely dispersed it may be necessary to use intermediate forms for the various parts of the collection. Although this may seem like a fairly simple and straightforward operation, there is a great deal of possibility of error and hence it must be done very carefully. The items collected are usually placed on conveyors or movable vehicles and then brought to the area where they will be released. If they are to be shipped, the shipping activity is usually conveniently adjacent.

The handling of the inventory records may vary in some respects. At the time that the authorizing papers are received it may be the practice to check the availability before the instructions for the physical collection are actually transmitted. When this is done, it also provides an alert for items in short supply and a determination as to whether enough new supplies are on order. In any event, the items actually collected for release must be entered into the inventory book records as credits. At this time there is to some extent another cross check on the accuracy of the book records, as where items shown by the records to be on hand are not actually there, or where more items were collected than are shown by the book record. This is also another alert to short-supply conditions, as a basis for investigatory action.

The major control interests again center about the efficiency with which the physical aspects of the collection and release are handled, and then the efficiency of the supporting procedures, including both the preparation of the various forms and the maintenance of the book inventory records.

Organizational Considerations

The nature of the responsibility of the stores department for the materials in its custody makes it imperative from an organizational standpoint that it be independent of the activities from which it either receives or to which it issues materials. If also it is to be charged with part or all of the larger responsibility for inventory levels and inventory obsolescence, it must clearly have a high-enough organizational status to participate as a sufficiently influential partner in these determinations. From a high-level internal control standpoint this is most desirable. Within the stores department operations itself there is also an excellent opportunity to assign responsibilities in such a way that there is effective internal control. For example, the persons who physically handle stock should not maintain the actual records by which the accountability for physical quantities is established.

Obsolete Materials

It is inevitable in any stores activity that there will be cases of damaged or obsolete materials. In these cases the first requirement is that the lack of regular usability be approved by the proper authority, and then that the materials be removed from the regular stores area. At the same time the stores department is relieved of accountability for these items. The ultimate disposition of these items is part of the larger problem of the scrap and surplus materials activity which will be discussed later in this chapter. The second and the more important requirement is that the causes of the damage or obsolescence are studied to determine what can be done in the future to minimize this kind of problem. In some cases the problem may be due solely to the current operating activities of the stores department, whereas in others the causes may run to other operational groups that have misjudged their material needs.

Facilities Considerations

Some reference has previously been made to facilities considerations as they relate to the various stages in the stores operational cycle. We need, however, to further emphasize the importance of adequate facilities. With respect to the total storage area, the importance is first in terms of providing enough room, so that there can be orderly arrangement of materials and proper access to them. The second aspect of importance is to provide the needed security. Here there must be floor-to-ceiling partitions and the ability to control entrance to the area. At the same time there must be adequate provision for the controlled input and release of materials to prevent pilferage. However, the use of storeroom clerks and locked facilities must be weighed in terms of costs versus benefits and the importance of ready access to materials when needed. Adequate shelter must be provided to protect the stores from the weather. The facilities needs extend to the types of internal shelving, bins, and special restricted areas. They include also the equipment used to move materials in and out of the assigned storage locations, and for lifting and stacking. Finally, there must be adequate fire protection facilities, usually in the form of a sprinkler system. All this means that the carrying out of an effective stores activity begins with adequate facilities.

Use of Public Warehouses

In some situations the lack of availability of sufficient storage space may make it necessary for the company to make use of public warehouses. Most often this will be high-cost space and the first question that arises is how soon ways can be found to provide the needed storage space in our own facilities. The second question concerns the adequacy of the control measures that are likely to be sacrificed through this outside storage operation. Especially is this likely to be true in being able to get particular items at the times they are needed. The more difficult coordination and operational handling will thus normally combine to argue for the elimination of the continued use of public warehouses.

When actually used, however, their use should if possible be restricted to homogeneous types of items to which current access will be most limited.

Inventory on Hand

Reliable information as to inventory on hand is necessary for overall inventory control and management. In addition to use in preparing financial statements, physical inventories are taken to correct perpetual inventory records, to check on bin levels as a basis for buying decisions, and in some cases, as with crude-oil producers, to measure production. The adequacy of the location system can be determined during the taking of inventories, including whether duplicate materials are stored under different descriptions. The existence of obsolete, defective, and slow-moving stock may be apparent when the inventory count is made. In addition, observation of the reliability of counts is important, including the use of valid statistical sampling plans if items are counted on a test basis.

In addition, differences between physical and book records of inventories are important indicators of the operational efficiency of the inventory control system. Analysis of significant adjustments may indicate weaknesses in computer processing, ineffective security measures and pilferage, posting errors, and inadequate physical count procedures. Management is interested in explanations of the differences as a basis for taking corrective action in controlling inventories.

Internal Auditor's Role in Relation to Inventory Activities

The internal auditor's interests in the inventory activity exist at two levels. At the day-to-day operational level his broad concern is that an existing system is being administered efficiently in both a physical and procedural sense. Included here are the individual concerns as to establishing accountabilities for materials, having adequate information about them, providing adequate physical care, promptness of the various operational actions, effective utilization of people, and economy of operational costs. At the higher level his broad concern is that we are bringing the needed level of expertise to the devising of the best possible approach to the inventory problem. This best approach will include the application of applicable management science techniques and the computer-based systems which not only permit the actual implementation of the new approach, but also cover many of the operations previously carried out manually. We have here a particularly challenging type of dual responsibility for the internal auditor.

AUDIT GUIDES

REVIEW OF INVENTORY ACTIVITIES

I. Introductory

    A. Reference should be made to the general discussion of audit guides, Chapter 13.

II. Preparatory Activities

    A. See standard Audit Guides, Chapter 13.

III. Organizational Factors

    A. See standard Audit Guides, Chapter 13.

    B. Establish that the stores department is independent of purchasing, receiving, inspection, and accounts payable departments.

    C. Matters of special interest in the review of manuals will include:
        1. Determination of ordering criteria.
        2. Receiving of materials into stores.
        3. Storage of materials.
        4. Release of materials from stores.
        5. Coordination with other organizational components.
        6. Authorized levels of approval.
        7. Handling of deviations from established procedures.
        8. Handling of obsolete and damaged material.
        9. Inventory records.
      10. Physical verification of inventories and book records.

IV. Determination of Needs

    A. Currently Existing Design
        1. Who is responsible?
        2. What is the basis of the determination?
           a. Is the coverage of pertinent factors adequate?
           b. Has the mathematical basis of existing models been backed up by adequate expertise?
           c. Has it been approved by an adequate level of authority?
        3. Are the various types of materials adequately covered?
        4. What supplementary day-to-day approvals are specified as the results of the designed approach are translated into actual procurement orders?

    B. Current Operation of the Design for Determination of Needs
        1. How often is the basic design reviewed, and is this reasonable?
        2. Review the adequacy of input data used in the basic design.
        3. Review a representative number of individual inventory balances to determine the extent to which the basic design appears to be producing reasonable results. Have write-offs for obsolete materials been reasonable?
        4. Are stipulated approvals being actually required?

V. Internal Operations

    A. Incoming Materials
        1. Are the items being handled adequately from a physical standpoint?
        2. Is security adequate?
        3. Are accountabilities being properly transferred through counts and sign-off of transfer papers?

    4. Are book records promptly and accurately posted?

B. Storage of Materials
    1. Are facilities and equipment adequate?
    2. Is the overall approach sound for the location of specific materials?
    3. Are materials being promptly moved to assigned locations?
    4. Is storage area orderly, and is there adequate access?
    5. Is security adequate?
    6. Is fire protection adequate?
    7. Do book records show assigned locations?

C. Release of Materials
    1. Is collection of materials for release phase adequately handled:
       a. As to authorizing paper to collectors?
       b. As to care in collecting individual materials, both as to accuracy of count, and physical handling?
    2. Is release procedure adequately handled:
       a. As to reasonable recheck of accuracy of collection?
       b. As to procedural transfer of accountability?
       c. As to posting of inventory records?
       d. As to adequacy of security?

D. Maintenance of Book Inventory Records
    1. Are records properly maintained?
    2. Are abnormal book record developments adequately investigated?
    3. Are low-stock developments used as alerts for checking on new supplies?

E. Miscellaneous
    1. Are authorizing forms numbered?
    2. Are supplies of authorizing forms properly safeguarded?

VI. Special Audit Tests
A. Tests of Book Inventory Records Based on a Representative Number of Individual Items
    1. Establish validity of receival entries to source papers. Evaluate implications of any differences.
    2. Establish validity of release entries to authorizing paper—requisitions, shipping orders, and subsequent evidence of accepted accountability by transferee. Evaluate implications of any differences.
    3. Review development of current balances.
    4. Investigate any correction or special entries for authority and causes.

B. Tests of Specific Physical Stock Based on a Representative Number of Individual Items
    1. Verify count and condition of the physical stock.
    2. Check physical count to related book record. Evaluate implications of any differences.

C. Analysis of Significant Differences between Book and Physical Inventories
   1. Identify and appraise existing causes.
   2. Determine extent of corrective measures taken.
D. Tests of Valuation Bases of Inventory Items
   1. Determine impact of inventory valuation on income and ad valorem taxes.
   2. Review obsolete, damaged, defective, and scrap materials for appropriate writedown in order to minimize taxes.
   3. Determine adequacy of insurance coverage based on reliable valuation.

VII–IX. Not used.

X. Overall Appraisal of Stores Effectiveness
   A. See standard Audit Guides, Chapter 13.

SCRAP

Nature of the Scrap and Other Excess Materials Processes

The processes pertaining to scrap and other excess materials cover a wide range of situations. The more common of these situations will include:

1. Materials that exist as a result of the regular production or construction processes, but which have no further use in the normal operations of the company.
2. Spoilage of material in the production processes or other operating activities.
3. Worn-out equipment.
4. Materials no longer needed for the purposes acquired.
5. Materials that have become obsolete.

The excess materials function includes all of those activities covered by such terms as scrap, salvage, and obsolete materials. The activities may come about through underlying production processes, construction operations, or any other part of the company's operations. There is quite clearly a wide diversity among the individual situations. At the same time, however, the common character of these situations is that there are materials of some kind which are no longer needed in the regular operations of the company, and that these materials should, therefore, be disposed of in as advantageous a manner as possible.

Importance of the Total Process. In many cases the materials that need disposition are of very significant value and, therefore, the handling of the related activities will have an important bearing on the company's overall profitability. The importance of this relationship is also all the greater because it covers two

different dimensions. One of these dimensions is the more day-to-day operational side and the efficiency with which the operational features are carried
out. Included are the activities of careful handling, maintaining of accountabilities, and maximum realization through sale. The other dimension is the
management analysis of the causes of why the particular materials came into
existence and the evaluation of alternative approaches that might lead to the
minimization of excess materials. Both dimensions are important, and we note
that they are unavoidably related. It is, however, the evaluative second dimension that has especially important possibilities for managers and internal
auditors.

Cycle of the Excess Materials Process

Despite the fact that there is such a wide range of diversity as respects the
individual situations, it is still useful to identify the broad stages in the overall
cycle of operations. This can provide a framework for the examination of any
situation involving excess materials. This approach can again enable us to focus
on the special control problems that are associated with each stage. Such a
general framework can be said to be:

1. An understanding of the particular operational activities or conditions
   which are the causal factors for the generation of the particular excess
   materials.
2. Bringing the generated excess material under appropriate control.
3. The interim care and control of the excess materials prior to actual disposition.
4. Effecting disposition with maximum realization of revenue.

We look next at the major control problems under these four major headings.

Generation of Excess Materials

All excess materials come about as a result of something. What we need to do,
therefore, is to first understand this something as completely as is practicable.
If it is a manufacturing process, we will want to understand the nature of that
manufacturing process and why the excess material is generated. If it is an
inventory situation, we will want to know how the determinations are made
that provided the input to these inventories which then led to the resulting
excess materials. A similar need for understanding would be true in the case
of a construction situation. The questions here lay the groundwork for evaluations of how effectively the causal operating activities are being carried out.
All of these operating activities cannot always be studied in the depth needed.
Indeed, many of the evaluations are more properly a part of reviews focusing
directly on other activities. Nevertheless, it is important to utilize all approaches
to identify potential problems in any of the related operational areas. Our
extension here from the excess material vantage point can be most useful, even
if it does no more than alert those who should be looking at the problem. For

the internal auditor this can be an important means of developing questions for further examination when later reviews are made of the other affected operational activities.

Related also to an understanding of the operating activities responsible for the generation of excess materials is that a more accurate determination can now be made as to the exact types and quantities of materials that can be expected to be available. In a manufacturing process, for example, there will often be a fairly direct relationship between production volume and the amount of particular types of scrap generated. In some cases, the activities of a quality control group can directly provide the basis for our expectations as to scrap material.

Bringing Excess Materials under Control

At this second stage we now want to establish such supplementary control over the excess materials as is practicable. At this point we move more definitely into the operational aspects of the control effort. There is first the need, to the extent practicable in the individual situation, to remove physically the particular excess materials from the area of the causal operating activity, and to put them in a new location under the custody of those parties handling the excess materials activity. This is highly desirable for a number of reasons. One is that prompt and efficient disposition of them requires that they be put in the hands of someone who is directly responsible for that disposition. Also, in many situations it is important to remove them from the regular production areas so that they will not erroneously be used as good material. In some cases, however, the excess material may be too bulky and removal may not be practicable or even necessary. In any event, however, the accountability for the excess materials should pass from the regular operational activity to the new parties through appropriate and properly approved transfer procedures. Thus, in the case of a stores activity, the items would be released by that activity and accepted by the new and separate disposing group. The transfer papers, when properly approved, and signed by both parties, would establish the credit to the stores activity and the charge to the disposing group. The adequacy of the control at this stage is that all of these physical and procedural measures are complied with as promptly and efficiently as is practicable in the individual circumstances.

Interim Care and Control

The interim physical care and control of the excess materials in operational terms are essentially that there is adequate protection of the excess material from weather, deterioration, or theft. The parties charged with the responsibility for excess materials will both need to protect their basic accountability for those materials and to take such other actions as will best protect the company's interests in the ultimate disposition. The latter interest will in some cases comprehend activities such as sorting, treatment, packaging, and other preparation which will be in anticipation of particular types of disposition. From a control standpoint we are interested in whether the various types of interim action are in fact taken and the general efficiency with which they are actually executed.

Control over Disposition

The central objective is now to carry out the disposition of the excess material in a manner that will be most advantageous to the company. This generally means maximum realization in terms of value received, subject only to exceptions where there might be offsetting community or social types of problems. Here also is the two-dimensional level of the problem. The first of these involves the evaluation of the manner of disposition and the other is relatively operational. The former dimension especially provides some challenging opportunities as to how the company's interests can be served more effectively.

Manner of Disposition.   The determination of the manner in which we should dispose of excess materials comes down to an evaluation of the revenue possibilities that exist, under alternative ways of selling the material, after giving consideration to the extra costs that will have to be incurred to put the materials into the necessary form for the particular type of sale. Thus, for example, we can sell scrap material in the form received from the underlying operational activity or we can sort it into specific types of materials or grades of material, and sell the sorted materials separately. Or it may be a condition of a particular type of sale that materials be treated, baled, or put in some other particular form to be acceptable to buyers. Very often this determination at the same time identifies the particular kind of a buyer that we will seek for our disposal effort. Also, it may be that, if the material is prepared in a certain manner, we might be able to use it in some way in our own company operations. All of this involves the making of proper studies that can establish the profitability of the various approaches and enable the company to do it the best way. This would include also the updating of these studies as necessary to reflect changing market conditions and changing internal costs. In the latter case changing volumes of generation, the development of new equipment for handling excess materials, and other internal practices can directly affect the cost levels. The control focus on all these aspects of disposing of materials is to find the right combination at the point in time that will provide the company with the maximum net revenue.

Price Maximization.   Once the particular manner of disposing of the excess materials is determined, there is still the need to be certain that we have received the best available price. To the extent that there are competing buyers, we are able to utilize the approach of seeking competitive bids. In other cases there may be established markets where reliable price quotations are available. In still other cases the disposition may involve negotiations with individual buyers based on an evaluation of the services provided and the ultimate recoveries. In many situations the determination of these pricing arrangements is not done with enough care, and especially is not reappraised in the light of changing conditions.

Operational Considerations. Even after the manner of disposition has been determined, and also the applicable pricing arrangements, there is still an important area of control in making the actual disposition. There is first the necessity of being certain that quantities released from company control are accurately determined and agreed to by the buyer. In some cases this will be on the basis of count, and in other cases on the basis of weight. In some cases there also will be questions of establishing the right grade or other specifications. In all these cases it is important that this be based on a company determination, or if not by the company, by an independent agency. It is obviously unsatisfactory to rely on later determinations by the buyer alone. We will also wish to be certain that the transfer of accountabilities be supported by properly prepared papers and signed by authorized persons. In addition, there is the clerical control that quantities of the various items and grades are extended accurately at the agreed-upon prices. The control at this operational level is both one of adequate physical custody and proper procedural backup.

Organizational Factors

The organizational status of the group charged with the disposition of excess materials will depend directly on the scope and volume of the total disposal activities. In some cases these activities may be so important that we in effect have another full-fledged business operation. In other cases, however, it may be a subordinate part of the total company operations. What we need, then, is a sufficiently high organizational status that will attract people who can provide the necessary level of management. We also need to assure adequate independence from the operational activities that provide the input of the various excess materials. We want the excess-materials group to provide a needed organizational check on these related operational activities by giving visibility to the quantities and value of these excess materials.

Internally, in the excess-materials group, we also have important needs for good internal control. Accountabilities must be carefully established as between those who receive, store, and dispose of the excess materials. The responsibilities of those individuals who dispose of the materials must be carefully administered to minimize both collusion with purchasers or honest error. The fact that the parties who buy excess materials tend to have a lesser degree of integrity and character makes this control effort all the more important.

Role of the Internal Auditor

The excess-materials function is by its nature one that offers a wide range of opportunities for service to management. At the level of day-to-day operations we have the type of situation where the internal auditor is especially qualified to pass on the adequacy of the controls. There is a basic physical character to these operations which needs proper standards of care and protection. There are also the clearly needed procedural controls to fix accountabilities and to assure efficient and honest final disposition. But there are, at the same time, even greater possibilities for management service in identifying and evaluating the various ways in which approaches might be changed. Here are the possibilities of improvements in the various operational activities to reduce the amounts of excess materials actually generated. Here also are the possibilities of doing something to those materials that will increase the final net realization for them. The excess-materials area is indeed a challenging area for the internal auditor. While there are important and necessary protective services to be provided, these protective services become an excellent base for the more extended analytical and management-oriented types of service.

AUDIT GUIDES

SCRAP AND OTHER EXCESS MATERIALS

I. Introductory

    A. Reference is made to the general discussion of audit guides, Chapter 13.

II. Preparatory Activities

    A. See standard Audit Guides, Chapter 13.

III. Organizational Factors

    A. See standard Audit Guides, Chapter 13.

    B. Matters of special interest in the review of purchasing manuals will include:
        1. Relations with operational activities providing input.
        2. Receiving of materials.
        3. Storage of materials.
        4. Release of materials.
        5. Authorized levels of approvals.
        6. Efforts to increase revenue realization.
        7. Making of sales arrangements.

IV. Review of Input Factors

    A. Review of Conditions of Input from Each Significant Source Activity
        1. Does the nature of the source appear to be reasonable? Is the type of generation being given adequate management attention for possible alternative approaches?
        2. Is the generation of the excess material adequately controlled for transfer of proper quantities?
        3. Is physical care and handling adequate?

B. Company-wide Aspects
1. What assignment of responsibility exists for the company-wide review of inputs for consideration of all operational interrelationships that might be advantageous?
2. How effectively is this approach being implemented in actual practice?

V. Review of Conditions of Disposal
A. As to Individual Materials
1. Is the particular material being disposed of in a form or manner that is most advantageous?
2. Are there additional things that might be done by the source activity to make possible a more advantageous disposal?
B. Company-wide Aspects
1. Is there adequate coordination with the purchasing department for possible use of excess materials in lieu of current purchases?
2. Is adequate technical expertise being utilized as to ways in which excess materials might be treated or repaired for more advantageous disposal?
3. Are adequate cost studies being made as to the possible benefits from different approaches to the disposal problem?

VI. Internal Operations
A. Receipt of Materials
1. Are the materials properly handled in a physical sense?
2. Is security adequate?
3. Is accountability properly transferred through appropriate verification of quantities and approved transfer papers?
B. Storage of Materials
1. Are materials properly cared for prior to disposal:
a. For protection from damage or deterioration?
b. For security?
2. Are facilities adequate?
3. Is there adequate information control as to materials available for disposition?
C. Making of Sale Arrangements
1. Are bids solicited to the extent practicable?
2. Are alternative ways of disposal adequately investigated and evaluated?
3. Are customary arrangements for disposal reviewed with reasonable frequency and with adequate standards of care?
4. Is financial capacity of vendees properly established?
D. Disposal of Materials
1. Are counts, grades, and condition factors properly established by company representatives or by independent parties?

2. Are materials handled with adequate care?
3. Is transfer of accountability properly covered by approved papers?

VII. Audit Tests

    A. Tests of Materials on Hand

    From the book records and/or by direct observation select representative lots of materials.

      1. Determine time received and appraise reasonableness of delay in disposal.
      2. Appraise physical care and security.

    B. Test of Disposition

    Select a representative number of completed disposal actions.

      1. How was the vendee selected? Does he appear to be a responsible party?
      2. How were the sales arrangements determined? Do they appear to be reasonable?
      3. Were transfer papers properly completed and approved?
      4. Were applicable monies properly received?
      5. When was the applicable material actually received for disposition? Has action timing been reasonable?

VIII–IX. Not used.

  X. Overall Appraisal of Excess Materials Function

    A. See standard Audit Guides, Chapter 13.

ILLUSTRATIVE AUDIT FINDINGS: RECEIVING, INVENTORIES, AND SCRAP

Ineffective Sampling Approach

In making quality control inspections of incoming material the receiving department judgmentally sampled about 30% of items received. The auditor recommended the use of statistical sampling, which would reduce the costs of the receiving function because of the lesser number of sample items required. In addition, the inspectors were able to arrive at more reliable conclusions because a representative selection was made of items to be inspected.

Delays in Handling Defective Parts

Significant delays were being experienced in processing goods through the receiving department, resulting in instances of slowdowns in production. The auditor found that items reported questionable during inspections were set aside for long periods without taking needed action. In addition, priorities were not being set for processing items that were needed immediately in production. As a result, production schedules were being disrupted and user needs seriously affected.

More Effective Warehouse Operations

The company maintained three storerooms for materials, of which two had storekeepers and one was self-service. Losses from pilferage and unrecorded withdrawals in the self-service store were approximately $12,000 a year. Since the stock in all three storerooms was comparable, it was recommended that all stores be on a self-service basis, with estimated net savings of $20,000 a year.

Delays in Responses to Bill of Materials Changes

Significant amounts of inventory on hand were obsolete because of changes in bill of materials requirements, which were not coordinated on a timely basis with the stores department and with purchasing. In addition, other items were not acquired on a timely basis, resulting in delays in starting production.

Needed Extension of Order Point Controls

A review of procedures used for determining inventory levels indicated that the company was adequately calculating and using order point and quantity needs in determining inventory levels of 70% of the inventory on hand. For the remainder, the auditor found that significant savings could be achieved in an additional 20% of the inventory by extending the use of the calculations of need.

Excessive Physical Inventory Adjustments

Recorded adjustments to stock records in the current year were $7,500,000 out of total inventory of $80,000,000, a 20% increase in adjustments over those in the previous year. A review of the increases indicated that posting errors had risen with the use of a new computer system, cutoff procedures used in the physical inventory were not adequate, and storage procedures were ineffective for sensitive items of material. Adjustments were being made in the records without sufficient analysis by management as to causes.

Fraudulent Diversion of Scrap

Analysis of revenue from scrap, waste, and damaged goods indicated that the Toledo plant experienced a $50,000 decrease in revenues from the preceding year. Although the amount of scrap and waste generated was the same, there was lack of control over the disposition of the assets. By obtaining the assistance of guards to examine outgoing vehicles on a test basis, the auditor found that some scrap was being hidden in garbage trucks leaving the plant and was being sold for personal benefit.

CHAPTER SIXTEEN

Production and Maintenance

PRODUCTION

Nature of the Production Process

Production, as a term, applies to all situations where materials are combined or modified in some significant manner by the people of a company through the use of appropriate facilities and equipment. This scope of the production process is also often referred to as the manufacturing process. The production process covers a wide range of situations. A moment's reflection as to the various kinds of manufacturing companies and the great number of different kinds of products and services produced by them makes us realize the magnitude of the range and the difficulty of generalizing our thinking about them. However, there is the common characteristic of taking inputs of material and labor and, with the use of facilities and equipment, combining all of these elements in such a fashion that the resulting products are ready for internal use or for sale to the outside world. The administration of this sector of the total management operations is identified as the area of production management.

Importance of the Production Process

The importance of the production process will vary with the individual company. In some cases, as in the case of retail store chains, it may be quite insignificant. In other cases, as, for example, an automobile manufacturer, or a producer of metals, it is the major segment of the operations in terms of costs incurred and number of people involved. It is at the same time in most situations a very complicated area because of the range of types of activity that are carried out. There are, for example, the various developmental activities that pertain to the way materials are to be obtained and processed, the facilities and equipment to be used, and the required training of people. On the operational side there are the necessary movements of materials, the use of machines, the supervision of people, the coordination of various subactivities, the needed inspections, and the final packaging and transfer of completed units. Related are the problems of coordination with other important company activities such as purchasing, finance, personnel, and marketing, as the total company operations are integrated for total company profitability. It is to be expected, then, that the production process is of vital concern to management as a part of the total managerial problem of the company. The challenge to the internal auditor is particularly interesting because of the great need for effective control over the production operations.

Cycle of the Production Process

Despite the wide range of different types of production situations, which exist not only between companies but also within an individual company, we can identify a cyclical pattern with definite stages in the cycle. These stages are:

1. The determination of the demand for the needed products sought from the production process. That is, what is to be produced, and when?
2. The planning of what should be done to produce the products so specified.
3. The procurement of the needed inputs to carry out the planned production activities.
4. Receipt, installation, and testing of equipment and production processes.
5. The actual processing of the planned products.
6. The final transfer of the completed products for other company use or for sale to customers. Included here also is the release of scrap and excess materials, discussed in Chapter 15.

We propose to discuss the nature of these individual stages in more detail with particular emphasis on the problems of control. We then go on to discuss additional aspects of the production process that cut across the entire cycle, and require more extended consideration.

Determination of Needs for Products. The starting point for the production activity is the determination of the items that need to be produced and when they will be wanted. This determination includes the specifications of those products and their quantities. It is a determination that is the responsibility of the company management, and it involves an appropriate simultaneous evaluation of a great many factors. The latter would include all of the pertinent cost and revenue considerations as determined by the interested staff and operational groups. What is the size of the market? How will the product be sold? What prices can be charged? What will be the cost of producing the product? What are the related procurement problems? What other supporting activities will be required?

Viewed narrowly and perhaps traditionally, the production activity begins only after this determination of needs has been completed. This is essentially a responding type of role for production. However, it is not the approach that is followed by modern management. Instead, the production group is now viewed as a partner in the determination of needs. Under this approach its role would include at least the following:

1. Counseling with the management decision group as to the ability to produce the desired products in terms of timing and costs, and the evaluation of possible alternatives.
2. Initiating information as to new technical developments that might increase capacity and/or reduce costs, thus providing new options to the company.
3. Conducting research and engineering studies in the area of facilities, processing, and product design which may increase production capabilities or reduce costs.

The substance of this partnership relationship is that the production group is itself an influence in the determination of the needs for the products it will then actually produce. The first important control aspect is, therefore, that the production group is making its best possible contribution to the determination of needs, so that those determined needs will be in the company's best overall interests.

Planning for Actual Production. Although the previously described participation in the determination of needs has already initiated the planning process to a considerable extent, the actual determination of those needs is now the basis for the more definitive planning effort. Typical considerations here would include:

1. Evaluation of existing capacity to produce the products wanted in the necessary volume within specified time periods.
2. Determining how existing capacity might be expanded through more intensive use of equipment, additional equipment, extra people, overtime, extra shifts, and the like—with appropriate consideration of costs, timing, and quality of product.
3. Construction or purchase of new facilities, with the related factors of timing and costs of bringing the new capacity on stream.
4. Determination of particular types of manufacturing processes to be used, in relation to product specification alternatives.
5. Determination of needs for machine tools, tooling, and other equipment, and scheduling of programs to supply those needs.
6. Developing appropriate placement of equipment and supporting services to assure the efficient flow of production with the planned processes, facilities, and equipment.
7. Determination of personnel needs and planning for hiring and training.
8. Determination of material needs based on bills of material and coordination with the purchasing department as to procurement availability and timing.

9. Arrangement of necessary supporting services, as, for example, heat, refrigeration, water, and electricity.

The essential control considerations at this stage are that plans are adequately developed to cover the pertinent aspects for the particular product or products needed, that supporting actions are initiated, and that procedures are established whereby the progress of those plans can be satisfactorily monitored. The latter action is especially important when there are engineering, development, or procurement requirements for individual parts or phases that are prerequisites for other parts and phases, and that must, therefore, be completed on a timely basis.

Procurement of Needed Inputs. With the input needs having been adequately identified, the next stage is the procurement action itself. Although the production group is normally not charged with direct responsibility for procurement, what is important is that other groups which actually make the procurement are adequately coordinated. The groups affected would include the purchasing department for the procurement of materials and equipment, the construction department for any new facilities, the engineering staff for necessary engineering services, the stores department for materials already on hand, and the personnel department for the recruitment and training or transfer of needed personnel. The coordination would include the preliminary contacts during the planning stage, the transmittal of definitive requirements, and continuing liaison to deal with possible problems that might arise during the actual procurement. The interest from a control standpoint is that these activities are carried on in an orderly and efficient manner.

Receiving, Installation, and Testing. The inputs as procured now flow to the production group. The receiving of tangible items may be direct from vendors, from stores, or from other internal sources. Then they must be properly inspected to determine the conformance to previously designated quantities and specifications. Where installation of some type is required—as in the case of tooling and equipment—this is now carried out. Also, such equipment must be tested to determine whether performance meets designated specifications and standards. The problems here will vary greatly depending on the complexity of the particular production process or subprocess. Very often, however, it is the important and even critical phase when errors are detected or unexpected operational problems are identified and adequately handled. In other cases there is the problem of developing needed skills and overall ability to turn out high-quality products. The control focus at this stage is to carry out these important preparatory activities in a thorough and efficient manner. Failure to do so can result in later excessive costs and serious delays.

Actual Production. Assuming that all of the different needed inputs, facilities, equipment, materials, people, and supporting services have been procured, made available, installed, and adequately tested, the stage is set for the actual production activities. These activities are the ultimate realization of the earlier planning activities, and in fact in many cases are necessarily interwoven as we progress through a lengthy total production program. These activities involve a number of specialized subactivities and functions, which include:

1. The handling and effective utilization of materials.
2. The administration and effective utilization of labor.
3. The utilization and control of a range of supporting services.
4. Scheduling and control of the individual production activities.
5. Appropriate inspection and quality control activities at the various stages.
6. The maintenance of plant and equipment.
7. The control of the production activities in terms of levels of physical performance.
8. Achieving adequate cost control.
9. Continuing liaison with company activities that supply the various inputs.
10. Coordination with ultimate users of the product for progress and special developments.

The various activities are overlapping and interrelated in many respects. But together they combine in the processing of the applicable inputs for the ultimate completion of the particular products in the form and at the times desired by the users.

Final Output.   With the actual processing complete, the product is now ready for transfer directly to vendors, to the stores department, or to some company operational area outside of the regular production group. This completed product may be something that is now ready for sale to a consumer, it may be a component to be used in the completion of a larger product, or it may be some type of material that is used in the subsequent processing operation outside the company. The product may also be one that is used by the company itself, as, for example, the use of electric power by an electric power company for its own office building purposes. The technical dividing line of where the production process actually stops is not always entirely clear, but for our purposes is what has been organizationally designated as the production department.

Completed production, as described, is now ready for final inspection and transfer to the parties who are now to take custody. There are here again the usual problems of adequate physical care and handling; the carrying out of these physical movements with reasonable promptness; the accuracy of the physical counts, weights, and other pertinent measures, for the transfer of accountability; and the proper completion of papers confirming the changed accountabilities, including the appropriate approvals. From a control stand-point, the concern is that all of these activities are carried out in accordance with standards that are appropriate to the individual situation.

MAJOR PROBLEM AREAS OF PRODUCTION

The viewing of the production process in terms of the overall operational cycle is useful to understand the flow of the production factors in a sequential sense. Even here, however, it is necessary to recognize that within the production process individual operations go back and forth within the overall cycle. There are, in addition, many problem areas that cut across all stages of the operational cycle to some extent and that need to be examined and understood in greater depth. These problem areas in turn overlap and are interrelated. They are also areas that involve a high degree of technical expertise. We need to look briefly at the more important of these problem areas as a basis for better understanding the production process and the related problems of control. In this connection we need to understand the relationships of the various production activities to other company activities outside the production group.

Product Development and Design

As we saw previously, the production cycle begins with the determination of the particular demand for the products and services to be produced. The role of the production group is both to respond cooperatively as other company personnel need information or assistance and to do a number of things of its own initiative. What the production group is endeavoring to do is to employ its technical expertise in product development and design in any way that will enhance the company interests. At the one end of the spectrum is the study of the properties of various types of materials—both old and new—and how they might be utilized more effectively. At a higher level are the possibilities of new approaches to the processing of these materials and new types of fab-rication. All of this may apply to final end products, to components of products, or to some aspect of how components are combined or assembled. The benefits achieved may be to serve new uses or to serve existing uses in a less costly or more efficient manner. A large portion of this type of work is done by the special engineering and research activities, which may or may not be a part of the official production group, and which we discuss in more detail in Chapter 17. In other cases there may be extensive testing activities, including the development of prototypes. But the regular production group should also be continuously seeking for new ways to improve the various production processes and to get more value for costs expended. The heart of the problem is how best to induce this kind of creative and aggressive approach at all levels of the production group. We need here both the proper motivation of individual persons and the intercommunication that makes possible the larger efforts of the total group.

Determination of Processing

While the research and development effort continues for new approaches to the processing activities, there is the practical problem today of choosing between available alternatives. The determination here at the same time is often linked to the determination of what materials to be used and the choice of specific equipment. In some cases the processing decision may lead into the question of facilities, as, for example, the determination that the product will be made from a forging or a casting. Involved also are the factors of the volume of product to be processed, the amount of time available, and the related costs. The cross-evaluation of all these factors involves a great deal of technical expertise, which in turn is derived to a considerable extent from previous production experience. There is, however, also a very practical side to the determination, which comes down to the question of what it costs under the alternative approaches. What new facilities will be required, or what modification of existing facilities? What is required in the way of additional equipment and related tooling? What materials will be required? What will be the labor costs, considering the types and numbers involved and the production time? All of these determinations for the various alternative processing approaches must be estimated as accurately as possible, taking into consideration the impact on the quality and ultimate usability of the item actually produced. The first problem is to develop the various analyses in a comprehensive and accurate manner with maximum objectivity. The second problem is to do all of this in accordance with time schedules that will support the time requirements of the other parts of the larger production schedule.

Facilities

The determination of facilities needs, as we have seen, has been a part of the decision in finalizing the product design and the subsequent processing. There are, however, a number of more specific problems that arise in connection with the actual implementation. These additional problems include:

1. How much space is required, and of what type? What will be the penalties of compromises in these preferences?
2. If there is existing company space, what is the priority of other company uses? What will it cost to adapt this space to the given production need?
3. If space is to be acquired, what is available and what will be the costs of adapting it to our needs?
4. How important is the geographical location of the facilities in terms of such factors as labor supply, community living conditions, distance from suppliers, closeness to point of delivery for later use of the product, related availability of transportation services, cost of land, and taxes?
5. If new facilities are to be constructed, what is the timing and cost? Is the company able to provide the necessary capital? Should it, in terms of other competing capital needs?

6. To what extent should newly constructed facilities be for the current special purpose versus protection for later types of usage?

7. What services will be required for the facilities, as, for example, power, water, and sewage disposal, and to what extent will they be available?

8. What provision needs to be made for special lighting, humidity control, heating, ventilation, and the like?

9. What social or community issues need to be considered?

Many of these issues will be of such significance that they must be resolved as a part of the total product and process decisions. In other cases they can be determined more independently, based on careful analysis of the pertinent factors. Always, however, there will be the interrelationship with the activities and needs of other company activities. The problem in summary is to recognize all of the pertinent factors and to evaluate them accurately and objectively in terms of the best long-term interests of the company. Again there is also the necessity of doing all of this in accordance with acceptable time schedules.

Equipment and Tooling

As in the case of facilities, the determination of the need for equipment and tooling has been a part of the earlier planning of the product design and the related processing. But now more detailed decisions have to be made as to the types to be utilized, the specific operational characteristics and features, and the number of them. In many situations this will in effect become the determination of the vendor source, since many features may be unique to equipment produced by particular makers. Here again the determination will be heavily determined by technical expertise, but there are special problems that require other types of consideration and analysis. Typical special problems include:

1. What is the economic payoff of alternative types of equipment and tooling in terms of speed of processing and reduction of labor and overhead costs?

2. For the same type of machines and tooling, what is the economic payoff for different size machines and individual optional features?

3. What is the right balance between special-purpose and general-purpose equipment and tooling? What factors affect this determination?

4. To what extent should equipment and tooling be purchased, leased (where leasing is possible), or made by the company itself?

5. How far should the company carry the automation approach, with consideration of risks when products demand changes?

6. To what extent should existing equipment and tooling be reworked?

Again it is clear that these are a wide range of factors that must be considered which go beyond the technical expertise and involve marketing, personnel, and financial aspects. But in any event these determinations must be made on the basis of as complete and accurate data as are available, and on a timely basis.

Plant Layout

The determination of the problem of equipment and tooling has necessarily taken into consideration the manner of utilization in terms of plant layout. But the plant layout problem not only includes the locational placement of machine tools, but also covers storage areas, tool cribs, aisles, conveyors, and other supporting services. The central objective is to facilitate the inflow of materials, the accomplishment of the various processing operations, the transfer of partially processed products between processing centers, necessary inspections, and the release of completed items. The achievement of this objective is measured by the efficiency and cost with which the total production process is carried out. It involves some very important decisions because once the plant layout is conceived and implemented, it is a very costly and time-consuming task to make changes. Changes in plant layout are also very disruptive to current production activities.

Basically, the plant layout tends to be either of two types:

1. The integrated sequential processing approach, with the placement of equipment and services supporting that approach, of which the automobile assembly line is a good example.
2. The grouping of equipment around particular types of processing, as, for example, a departmental grouping of grinding machines.

However, there may be various types of combinations of the two approaches at various stages of the production process. From a management standpoint the first concern is that the design of the plant layout is comprehensive, that is, that it takes into consideration the various dimensions of the actual production process, so that it has the capacity to function efficiently on a day-to-day basis. The second concern is that every reasonable effort is then made to make the selected plant layout work out efficiently. A good test of the first requirement is how well the proposed plant layout has been documented to cover the various factors. A good test of the latter is how much delay or confusion seems to exist in the actual operation. A further clue to the efficiency of the plant layout determination is how often the plant layout has to be changed, and whether the causes for the new change could have been reasonably foreseen.

Material Handling

To a major extent the needs for material handling are linked to the earlier decisions involving product, facilities, processing, equipment, and plant layout. But again, there are additional specific problems that must be handled. The central objective is to minimize the cost of handling materials, while efficiently supporting the particular sequence of production processing.

The problems of material handling can first be viewed in terms of the different kinds of material that are normally handled. Materials must be moved from the stores department or the receiving department to the production area. In other cases the material may be directly unloaded from ships or railroad cars. In some situations the material must be stacked in a specified manner, or placed in tanks or containers that feed the actual production processes. In some situations partially processed material must be transferred to other machines or to other production areas, which can be for both short or long distances. Finally, there is the final movement of the completed items back to the stores department, or for shipment. The problems of material handling can also be viewed in terms of their relationship to the individual worker who is operating the machine or working on the assembly line. This latter relationship then extends to the efficiency of the total production operations and the related scheduling activity. The latter efficiency in turn depends on the type of materials handling equipment which has been acquired and the performance of the materials handling personnel. This personnel performance reflects the adequacy of the training received and the degree of application of the individual workers. As we can see, the materials handling function involves a substantial degree of special expertise but offers splendid opportunities for operational review and constructive service.

Production Planning and Control

The stage is now set for the actual production operations. The production planning and control picks up from the types of basic planning previously discussed and goes on to cover first such further planning of the actual production, as is necessary; second, the transmittal of appropriate instructions to the production personnel; and third, the monitoring of the ongoing production activities. In total it is a facilitating activity which has as its objectives an efficient and timely flow of the work through the production operations to make possible the scheduled delivery of completed products. The manner in which this function is carried out will necessarily depend directly on the kinds of products being produced and the way the production activities are organized. In one situation we may have some kind of a job-lot type of production, with all production operations geared to the individual job lot, whereas in another situation we may have some kind of continuous processing or assembly. In either case the cycle of the operations may be very short or very long.

Production Planning. The production planning can be said to begin with the determination of forward schedules—for the day, week, month, or quarter, depending again on the type of product. The determination of these schedules will normally involve the participation of many company activities, as, for example, marketing, purchasing, stores, personnel, and finance. Production personnel will, of course, themselves be heavily involved, and in most cases top management will participate, especially to resolve the cross pressures of the various interested groups. On the basis of this determination, to which the production planning and control group has agreed, the quantities and timing of the various needed inputs will be calculated. This will cover usage of materials on hand, what items are to be procured, what hours or production shifts will be needed, how much overtime, what new hires, and what supporting services. In some cases also a determination will have to be made as to which particular machines and other equipment will be needed. Here, consideration must be given to the economies of larger runs to minimize the cost of setting up machines for the running of particular products. In total, the production planning job is to identify all of the needed inputs and to deal with them in whatever way will result in the greatest efficiency in terms of costs and timing.

Production Control.   Specific instructions can now be issued to all affected parties as to what is to be done. This will be accomplished by various types of transmittal papers and communication devices, and in many cases can be done to a major extent through computerized systems. The degree of detail will depend on the complexity of the particular kind of production and on the degree of decentralization. But whatever is done now provides the basis for the subsequent control of the actual operations. How this control is achieved will again vary widely, but the objective is to provide needed information as to the progress and current status of the production activities so that customers can be advised, as necessary, and that operational developments that might delay production schedules can be promptly identified and dealt with, In some cases the major control will be exercised through a work order sheet or packet that accompanies the individual job, and on which are recorded the various operations completed. In other cases the control will be maintained through records maintained at the work area supervisory office. In still other cases there will be more elaborate types of centralized control. The overall results achieved reflect the adequacy of the basic design of the system and the promptness and accuracy with which the system is maintained. The results achieved now also blend with the broader aspects of the general operational control maintained over the production activities. The interests from a control standpoint are that the design of the production control system is reasonably suited to the existing production situation and that it is efficiently operated. There is often a tendency to make these systems too elaborate, thus resulting in an excessive operational effort. The problems of maintaining the existing system and errors made are usually good clues to systems deficiencies.

Operational Control

With the underlying planning and control functions now established we are ready to consider the broader problems of the actual production operations. Our interest here is to examine the major aspects of these actual operations, and to understand how they can best be controlled to achieve the most effective production results. These individual operational aspects are the utilization of material, the utilization of labor, effective use of supporting services, and adequate cost control. These elements are brought together through good administrative management.

Material Utilization.   In most production situations there is some important utilization of materials, although this will obviously vary greatly. To the extent, however, that materials—raw, processed materials, or components of any type—play an important role, the key objective is the maximize the utilization at the lowest possible cost. Typical ways in which this can be achieved are, as follows:

1. Insistence on receiving materials which are of the right specifications and quality, subject only to deviations that are approved at higher management levels in consideration of other company needs and benefits.
2. Requisitioning of materials in the proper quantities to permit the most efficient utilization.
3. Adequate care of materials after delivery to the production areas, whether in original form or during various stages of processing.
4. Care in the processing of materials to minimize waste and spoilage.
5. Where mix of material ingredients is flexible, varying that mix to exploit to the greatest extent current market prices for the individual ingredients.
6. Adequate reporting of material utilization, based, where possible, on established standards.
7. Adequate reporting of scrap and spoilage, based on available standards.

The focus from a control standpoint is on the manner in which material needs are determined, how material is cared for after receipt, and on the extent of losses sustained through deterioration, spoilage, or other operational developments.

Labor Utilization. Although the proportion of the production cost that is labor will again vary greatly, it is normally a factor of great importance. The objective is also again to achieve maximum value at the lowest possible cost in a legitimate and long-term sense. The effective utilization of labor is particularly complex because of the fact that we are dealing with the human factor. Further complexities exist because of the fact that all actions relating to labor have important long-term dimensions, and it is frequently very hard to estimate accurately the actual impact of many of those long-term dimensions. The effective utilization of labor would typically include:

1. The care with which labor needs are planned to support agreed-upon schedules.
2. Timely recruitment and adequacy of training for the requirements of the specific assignments.
3. Adequacy of working conditions and employee facilities.
4. Assignments to meaningful work to the maximum extent practicable.
5. Utilization of group effort to extent practicable.
6. Fairness of compensation, and linkage to performance results in every way possible.
7. Supervision that combines competence with effective personal relations.
8. Fairly determined standards of performance, and prompt reporting against those standards.
9. Transfers between production jobs in an orderly and controlled manner.

The control aspects of labor utilization center about the way labor requirements are defined and then how the application of the labor effort is administered. In most cases the technical aspect has been determined previously through appropriate engineering analysis, and the utilization can be evaluated by someone like the internal auditor in a reasonably satisfactory manner. In most cases there is a major procedural aspect and always there is the question of how effectively the human relationships are being achieved. All of these latter aspects are of the type where the internal auditor can make important contributions.

Supporting Services. In the normal production situation there will be an important group of supporting services which are important both in terms of cost and their contribution to the final production results. The objective here also is to achieve the needed results in the most effective manner at the lowest possible cost. Typical areas of interest would include:

1. For important types of manufacturing supplies the same kind of approaches as have been described for materials.
2. Prudent use of power.
3. Adequacy of light for proper execution of individual production operations.
4. Quality of support by material handling personnel.
5. Quality of food facilities.
6. Adequacy of rest facilities.
7. Quality of plant maintenance.

Costs and Cost Control. Whereas control in the first instance should be exercised, to the extent practicable, on a quantitative or physical basis, at some stage the basis of control will be through costs. Ultimately also, the total production activity will be evaluated on the basis of what it has cost to produce products of the wanted specifications and quality. Costs serve a number of different purposes and they are developed accordingly in different ways for those varying purposes. For our present purposes, however, we are interested in costs as a basis of operational control. For this purpose we will be concerned with observing certain criteria to the maximum extent practicable. These criteria would include:

1. Clear identification of the cost with the basis of how it is incurred. For example, the cost of power as purchased and to the extent used by a particular activity.
2. Fixing of cost responsibility on the basis of the control exercised. As in the example above, the usage of the power determines the costs for which there is responsibility.
3. The grouping of costs so that cost performance is realistically related to operational performance, as in the case of cost centers.

4. The establishment of fair standards and/or other cost performance objectives.
5. Prompt and accurate reporting of actual results against those standards.
6. Analysis of variances as a basis for prompt corrective action.
7. The careful examination of individual costs to determine their degree of variability under different operational conditions.
8. Equitable bases for the allocation of common costs.

Almost always, some compromises have to be made with respect to the above-stated criteria. In such situations an effort should be made first, to keep the compromises at a level where they do not significantly undermine the total control effort. Second, every possible endeavor should be made that allocations of common costs are made on a reasonable basis. In some cases, also, it is possible to use established market price for internal transfers and thus better measure the performance of both the supplying and receiving activity. Thus regular market rates could be used for power used instead of costs actually incurred by a company power facility. The problem that often exists is to extend the development of costs to include complicated allocations that may be attractive to the cost accountant but that have little or no value for the meaningful control of individual production activities. The challenge to any reviewer is, therefore, to assess the reasonableness of the approach.

Reporting and Analysis of Cost Performance. Once the plan for the identification and measurement of costs is established, the effectiveness of the cost control is determined largely by the subsequent reporting and review of cost performance. The important features here will include:

1. Prompt and accurate preparation of reports.
2. The frequency of reports and the detailed coverage are related to the level of management that has direct control and responsibility.
3. Later and more consolidated reports covering longer time periods to flow to the higher levels of responsible management.
4. Prompt review of significant deviations and investigation of causes for deviations by direct discussion with responsible subordinates.
5. Vigorous appraisal of causes for poor cost performance and the development of effective action programs to deal with those causes.

The primary interest of an outside reviewer such as the internal auditor is to determine first, whether an adequate basis for cost control exists, and second, whether that basis is being administered effectively. This is an area where the competence of the internal auditor is especially well established.

Engineering, Research, and Quality Control

The various types of engineering, the technical research activites, and the maintenance of the inspection and quality control function are closely related to the production operations, and in many situations may be a part of the production group. In other situations, however, they may exist as separate organizational groups and serve as a more direct control over the production activities. We recognize them here as an important adjunct to the regular production activities, but because of their special nature, we deal with them in Chapter 17.

Waste Control

Waste control is a term that can be used in a very broad or in a more restricted sense. We use it here to refer to smoke or residual waste created as a result of the regular production operations. It is a problem that has always been of some significance, and in the case of certain kinds of companies of very serious dimensions. These have always been the direct relationship to the total production operations and always the problem of how the disposition of the waste can be achieved at minimum cost. In our own day these previously existing problems have been expanded to include the impact upon the social environment. Society has now become acutely aware of the problem of pollution of air and waterways, and is now exerting major pressures on industry to find ways to reduce that pollution. To what extent these pressures may be unreasonable is not the question for us to decide. The pressure is there, and the ways available to industry to deal with the problem involve major operational changes and substantial costs. How best to deal with this problem is now a major challenge to many companies.

To a major extent the problem of dealing with production waste is a technical problem requiring changes in the production processes. It is a problem of feasibility combined with the costs that will be involved. The attack on the problem will usually be along the following lines:

1. Changing the material content of products, processing materials, or the manner of processing the material, to reduce the amount of waste, or to reduce its objectionable features. Using oil instead of soft coal in the production of electricity is an example.

2. Developing new ways to reuse the offending materials, such as the recycling of paper products.

3. Developing better ways to dispose of the waste materials or to reduce their objectionable features. Illustrative of the latter would be the treatment of waste; of the former, the building of special underground receptacles.

The operational concern with this problem will be to make certain that adequate steps are being taken to deal with the problem. There are in the first place the economic potentials of finding better ways to make use of the waste. In the second place there is the need to avoid punitive governmental measures or public ill will, which can be even more costly than some kind of current action.

Plant Safety

Most production operations pose some problem of physical safety or health; and in certain situations the problems can be of the utmost importance. The mining industry is a very good example of the latter type of situation. The significance of the problem is clear enough in terms of its cost impact upon the company through damage to property and disruption of operations. But that significance is still greater when one considers the impact on human welfare. It is, therefore, imperative that we understand the problem and deal with it effectively as a part of a well-managed production operation.

Basic to an understanding of an adequate plant safety problem is a recognition of the various types of operating conditions that can be the cause of accidents or disease. Factors relating to the facilities will include the failure to use fire-proof or fire-resistant materials, the lack of provision for ventilation, lack of fire exits, and the like. In the equipment area the causes will include the lack of adequate inspection programs, the failure to cover or shield moving parts, faulty design and layout, and the like. Or the problem may stem from the way production processes are designed and the types of materials used. Equally important are the factors that relate to the individual workers. For example, adequate allowance may not be made for fatigue. The problem may also be one of inadequate training as to the need for safety and inadequate reminders as to safety requirements.

The attack on the problem is through the development of an adequate safety program. Here the aspects to be considered will typically include the following:

1. The review of all facilities and equipment for safety hazards, and the determination of needed protective measures.
2. The review of all operational processes and activities to identify and evaluate problems of safety or health. Alternative approaches should be considered that might reduce these hazards, and determinations should be made of what is needed in the way of protective devices.
3. Systematic programs for the education of all personnel as to the needed conduct and precautions for their particular jobs and for general application within the production area.
4. Continuing surveillance for compliance with established requirements.
5. Careful investigation of all accidents.

The development of an adequate safety program in part involves certain technical expertise. To a major extent, however, its elements are reasonably understandable by the thoughtful observer. Its success is a combination of careful design and persistent follow-up. Unfortunately, it is the type of activity that can easily be neglected, especially when there have been no current accidents. It is, therefore, the type of program that must be carefully reviewed on a regular basis.

Unionization

The subject of unionization is dealt with in more detail in Chapter 20. We include it here only to confirm its importance as a problem of management as we seek to achieve effective production operations. The problem is important first, through its impact on production costs. Union contracts stipulate the general levels of compensation and go on to cover the rates for the various types of production services. There is, in addition, the cost of union stewards, whose services are primarily in the interest of the union. The problem is equally important in that the control over the individual workers and groups of workers is subjected to important constraints. Jurisdictional limits of particular types of activity are clearly defined and enforced. Administrative and supervisory actions must be carried out in a manner that will not lead to asserted grievances. When grievances are asserted by individual workers, it is part of the responsibility of production management to hear these grievances and to resolve them within the framework of the union agreement. In all these matters there will necessarily be dealings with the appropriate union officials. The relationship with the union is also complicated by the fact that it views both the current contract and the potential developments with an eye to the next contract negotiations, which make this aspect such an important dimension of achieving effective production operations. For all these reasons, any outside reviewer must take unionization very much into consideration as he appraises current conditions and develops recommendations.

Modern Approaches to the Production Process

Although the total field of management operations has been changing significantly in recent years, the intensity of that change in the production area has been particularly impressive. We single out several of these developments that are of special importance:

1. *Increasing Use of Automation*. The rising cost of labor has created special pressures for the development of facilities and equipment that will minimize the requirements for human intervention. At the same time, the increasing progress in the world of technology has provided new capabilities for the development of the more automated type of equipment. We see, therefore, an increasing investment in highly specialized automated equipment. This development has major implications with respect to operational control and capital investment decisions, and in worker relationships.

2. *Computer Developments*. The development of modern electronics has provided new capabilities for controlling the new more automated equipment. In addition, the new electronic developments have made possible the design of systems that not only control manufacturing processes themselves but also link them to other related company activities. This has also resulted in the elimination of many previously existing forms and paper procedures. We look at this area as a part of Chapter 22.

3. *Greater Use of Operations Research*. The new computer developments with their new capabilities to handle voluminous data at high speeds have made it possible to apply new management techniques that were not practicable heretofore. The use of linear programming to schedule machines for the best utilization, or to determine the most economical mix of alternative material ingredients, is illustrative.

All of these developments combine to make the production processes more efficient and to reduce costs. They all have an important bearing on the nature and scope of the control exercised.

Role of the Internal Auditor in the Production Process

The production operations have come to be one of the most important areas of potential service on the part of the modern internal auditor. The scope of the opportunities can perhaps be best described by identifying the key levels of managerial activity, as follows:

1. The highest-level type of managerial planning, where the production role is determined in relation to the needs and activities of other management functions, especially with respect to purchasing, marketing, and finance.
2. The managerial problems of production performance as they involve day-to-day coordination with other operational activities, and of the various components of the production group itself.
3. The operational problems of the individual production units in terms of effective utilization of materials, labor, and supporting services.

The role of the internal auditor at all three of these levels is first, to appraise the efficiency with which existing policies, procedures, and established plans are being carried out. His second role is to look for new approaches that hold varying degrees of promise for ensuring more efficient and more profitable production operations. The wide range of activities involved and the large proportion of dollars expended make this an especially attractive area of management service. Although there is a major technical dimension to most of these production activities, there are still excellent opportunities for constructive service in supplemental ways. By working in cooperation with those who have technical expertise this further contribution can be made.

AUDIT GUIDES

PRODUCTION ACTIVITIES

I. Introductory
   A. Reference should be made to the general discussion of audit guides, Chapter 13.
   B. Because of the magnitude of the production activities in most com-

panies, the review will often deal with a particular type of production activity, or with the total production activities at a single field location.

II. Preparatory Activities
   A. See standard Audit Guides, Chapter 13.
   B. The production process should be physically observed and studied to the extent practicable.

III. Organizational Factors
   A. See standard Audit Guides, Chapter 13.
   B. Matters of special interest in the review of manuals will include:
      1. Manner of receiving production requirements.
      2. How input needs are transmitted to other company groups who will procure such inputs.
      3. Internal planning criteria.
      4. Receival of inputs.
      5. Control of processing operations.
      6. Relations with support activities.
      7. Relations with quality control, especially as to jurisdictional control.
      8. Internal production records.
      9. Inventory taking requirements.
      10. Reporting requirements.
      11. Union relations.

IV. Determination of Needs for Products to be Produced
   A. Type of Initiative Taken
      1. To what extent does the production department carry out its own activities to study new manufacturing approaches for current products?
      2. To what extent does the production department counsel with other management components as to new developments relating to production capabilities?
   B. As a Partner in Long-Term Planning
      1. To what extent does the production department participate in the long-term planning effort?
      2. Is the opportunity adequately provided to the production department to make its contribution in such areas as needs for facilities, equipment, personnel, and costs?
      3. Is the production department adequately consulted as to the feasibility and cost of products newly proposed or being modified?
   C. In the Development of Current Production Plans
      1. Do these determinations include the active participation of all interested parties? Is this participation adequate?
      2. Does the production department have final authority as to the

feasibility of production plans? If not, how are the limitations given adequate visibility?

V. Internal Planning for Approved Production Requirements
   A. Basic Processing
      1. Appraise the organizational status of the group and its internal organizational arrangements.
      2. Is the processing group provided adequate opportunity to evaluate alternative approaches before facilities and equipment are committed?
      3. Does this group appear to be adequately staffed and operating in an orderly and efficient manner?
      4. Is documentation adequate to support processing decisions?

   B. Facilities (see also Audit Guides, Chapter 18)
      1. Appraise the organizational status of the group and its internal organizational arrangements.
      2. To what extent are alternative ways of satisfying facility needs adequately explored?
      3. How adequate is the coverage of all pertinent factors in documenting a particular selection?
      4. Is collaboration with other company activities adequate?
      5. Is the scheduling and subsequent control of the facilities project adequate?

   C. Equipment and Tooling (see also Audit Guides, Chapter 18)
      1. Appraise the organizational status of the group and its internal organizational arrangements.
      2. How adequate is the evaluation of alternative types of equipment in terms of capacity, maintenance, and operations performed?
      3. Are levels of authority for acquisition of equipment and tooling reasonable?
      4. Is collaboration with other company activities adequate?
      5. Are the scheduling and subsequent control of the acquisition projects adequate?

   D. Plant Layout
      1. Appraise the organizational status of the group and its internal organizational arrangements.
      2. Appraise the adequacy of analysis and supporting documentation for major plant layout determinations.
      3. How adequate is the coordination with other interested company activities in arriving at plant layout determinations?
      4. Are the planning and control of the actual work adequate?
      5. Are approvals adequately established for projects of the varying magnitudes?

E. Material Handling
   1. Appraise the organizational status of the group and its internal organizational arrangements.
   2. How adequate is the collaboration with all company activities served?
   3. Appraise the adequacy of the analysis and documentation for major decisions as to how material handling needs will be satisfied, including the choice of equipment.

F. Production Planning and Control
   1. Appraise the organizational status of the group and its internal organizational arrangements.
   2. How adequate is the participation of the group in the determination of production schedules?
   3. Appraise the procedural system whereby detailed input requirements are determined and transmitted.
   4. Appraise the policies and procedures by which work assignments are determined, and then actually transmitted within the production department.
   5. Appraise the adequacy of the system by which the production control group will maintain control of the status of production activities.

VI. Current Production Operations
   A. Material Utilization
      1. Are materials properly received and cared for pending actual processing?
      2. Is there excessive waste or spoilage in the processing of materials? If so, why?
      3. Are spoiled materials used or salvaged in the most effective manner possible?
      4. Is material usage in accordance with approved bills of material?
      5. Is reporting of material utilization adequate?

   B. Labor Utilization
      1. How adequate is the selection and training for the particular kinds of jobs?
      2. Is there excessive idle time? If so, what are the causes?
      3. Is there excessive overtime? If so, what are the causes?
      4. Does supervision appear to be adequate?
      5. Are standards established wherever possible? Are they fair?
      6. Does morale appear to be good? If not, why not?
      7. Are relations with the union satisfactory? If not, what are the problems, and how should they be dealt with?

   C. Supporting Services
      1. Are supporting services adequate? (For example, material handling, light, temperature, work area facilities, food facilities, rest facilities, and the like.)

2. Are there excessive delays? If so, why?

D. Production Control

    1. Is the established production control system working effectively? If not, why not?

    2. Are various production and support groups working with each other in a cooperative fashion? If not, why not?

    3. Are schedules being met? If not, why not?

E. Inspection (see also Audit Guides, Chapter 17)

    1. Are inspection procedures adequate?

    2. Are inspection activities carried out in a careful manner?

    3. Is spoiled or defective material adequately tagged and segregated?

F. Reporting and Cost Control

    1. Appraise the reporting system as it applies to the various parts of the production operations at the various levels of supervision, with particular reference to:

        a. Scope.

        b. Adequacy of variance analysis.

        c. Timing of release.

        d. Focus on controllable costs.

        e. Persons to whom directed.

        f. Degree of summarization.

    2. How effectively are the reports being used as a basis for needed managerial action—with particular reference to:

        a. Promptness of review.

        b. Probing of causes for deviation.

        c. Corrective action.

VII. Other Manufacturing Activities

A. Waste Control

    1. Is the organizational status of the group charged with this responsibility adequate?

    2. Has the problem of waste control been adequately recognized by the company?

    3. How adequately is the study of the waste control problem being pursued?

    4. What opportunities appear to be available in dealing with the waste control problem, and what, if anything, is being done with them?

    5. What evidence do you see of any injurious impact of present waste disposal practices?

B. Plant Safety

    1. Appraise the adequacy of the organizational status of this group and its internal organizational arrangements.

    2. How adequate does the safety program appear to be as judged by:

      a. Existing hazards?

      b. Past experience as to problems?

    3. Is the program being coordinated adequately with operational groups?

    4. Is the program being adequately integrated with training and supervisory programs?

    5. Is there adequate top management support?

VIII. Direct Audit Tests

    A. Handling of Production Orders

       Select a representative number of actual requests for production, and check to the extent practicable the quality and timing of the execution at its various stages:

      1. Basis of origin of the production request.

      2. Manner of acceptance by the production department.

      3. Determination of needed inputs and use of bills of material.

      4. Transmittal of requests for needed inputs.

      5. Receipt and testing (where required) of inputs.

      6. Determination of machines to be used and related internal actions.

      7. Dissemination of internal production instructions.

      8. Production of specified products.

      9. Inspection.

    10. Release of products produced.

    B. Cost Reporting

       Select a representative number of internal cost reports, and determine to the extent practicable:

      1. Accuracy of data reported.

      2. Timing of release of reports.

      3. Actions taken on the basis of the reports.

IX. Not used.

  X. Overall Appraisal of Production Effectiveness

    A. See standard Audit Guides, Chapter 13.

    B. As previously indicated, the review will normally be dealing with only a portion of the production activities, and the overall appraisal will therefore focus on that portion.

MAINTENANCE

Nature of Maintenance

Maintenance consists of activities relating to the inspection, servicing, and repair of facilities in the organization, including buildings, equipment, and tooling used for processing, and service equipment. It may be a repetitive-type operation, or a highly sophisticated system used by management in coordination with production and facilities activities. It also includes the responsibility for making the necessary supporting arrangements with suppliers of equipment and subcontractors.

Maintenance activities can be divided into four types: emergency repairs, preventive maintenance, corrective maintenance, and maintenance elimination. Emergency repairs are usually required when there is a breakdown of equipment needed currently in operations. A system of preventive maintenance, or scheduled repairs, serves to keep equipment in good running order and to reduce the idle time resulting from breakdowns and the time required for emergency repairs. Some companies go beyond preventive maintenance and employ corrective maintenance. This program involves the analysis of maintenance activities and costs to identify unfavorable aspects in the use of some assets. Based on this analysis, recommendations are made for changes in use or content and design to improve productivity and decrease maintenance. The last type of maintenance is often called maintainability or maintenance elimination. It involves monitoring maintainability needs during design, production of the asset, installation, and final use. Through this approach, the nature and extent of upkeep and repair are determined in the planning phase, with specifications incorporated in the design to conform with maintenance objectives.

Importance of Maintenance

Recently, maintenance has received additional attention as an operating and cost objective in business. Managers are increasingly recognizing the need for developing plans and programs for attaining maintenance effectiveness. Maintenance costs may exceed the initial acquisition costs of assets. On the equipment side, there has been a significant increase in the costs of the assets themselves because of inflation and other factors. It is thus important that these assets be used as long as possible through added attention to maintenance. Together with this there have been increases in costs of maintenance labor and parts. These changes have made it increasingly necessary to plan and control maintenance expenditures to maximize benefits.

Control Cycle

The maintenance function can also be viewed in terms of the individual stages in its total cycle. This framework is useful in evaluating the processes by which maintenance is carried out. The individual stages are as follows:

1. Planning maintenance strategy.
2. Determining needs and scheduling.
3. Providing personnel and materials.
4. Budgeting and controlling performance.

Planning Maintenance Strategy

Many companies are now developing broad policies and strategies for maintenance, rather than treating it as an ad hoc operation. This involves an appraisal of current maintenance practices, need for changes in light of company objectives, and development of a maintenance strategy based on production and other operating needs. The level of maintenance required is important in planning. The level should be selected to obtain longer life of equipment without spending excessive amounts. In addition, the company's policies should be flexible to allow for periods when maintenance may have to be deferred because of shortages of funds or other conditions.

In addition to overall considerations, the company needs to consider operational requirements of specific assets prior to deciding on maintenance. This includes determining basic performance parameters, the operating cycle, and needs as to availability. Maintenance requirements have to be set for the asset, including personnel requirements, spare parts needs, and frequency of work. In some situations the best policy for a unit may be to use the throwaway approach when there is a breakdown rather than preventive maintenance. In planning for maintenance of specific assets it is also desirable to be involved in the design stage. This enables the user to specify criteria for design in accordance with maintenance objectives.

Determining Needs and Scheduling

It is important the management have procedures for determining needs for maintenance and setting priorities. Often, there are limited resources available and conflicting requests for service. Under these circumstances it is important to keep all items of equipment maintained at the optimum level. On the one hand, management wishes to maximize the useful life of an asset by an effective maintenance program. It recognizes that to optimize return on investment excessive maintenance has to be avoided as well as insufficient maintenance. It also wishes to avoid downtime, which can be costly to the company in terms of delays in production and lost sales. It is also faced with the necessity to make unexpected emergency repairs, which can disrupt the planned maintenance schedule. Because of these considerations it is necessary to determine the right time to schedule maintenance work.

By considering factors of safety and economics, some unnecessary tasks can be eliminated. Study of lubrication needs and results of alternative schedules for lubricating can often result in savings. The company may well determine the feasibility of deferred maintenance in some cases. However, the savings on maintenance charges may not offset the costs of lost production, spoilage, idle time of production workers, excessive wear, and overtime.

Management must, of course, have valid records and reports of maintenance needs in order to have an effective system. A significant number of items of equipment may be nonoperational although not so classified. Under these circumstances tests may be required of equipment to determine if it runs. In some cases equipment will be in running order but have defects that could cause deterioration and breakdowns at a later time. If the defects are not reported, they represent a hidden, or unnoticed, backlog of maintenance needs that are not being given attention.

An effective work order system is important in achieving the orderly scheduling of work based on need. When there are backlogs of maintenance work, priorities are set based on work orders properly authorized. There are two types of work orders: (1) blanket or open work orders used to cover routine maintenance, and (2) job orders which cover individual maintenance projects. Priorities should be indicated in the work orders, such as immediate, when convenient, or deferred. In some companies the work order system is computerized and machine records kept for scheduling each item to be maintained.

Providing Personnel and Materials

The maintenance department is a service activity that benefits other departments of the company. As such, the department should be independent, and adequate personnel and materials should be provided to perform the function effectively. In some cases it may be more economical to contract outside the organization to get the work done, especially if the service is needed for limited periods only. In other cases the equipment may be highly specialized, requiring qualified technicians. It may be preferable in these circumstances to use the vendors' service personnel, even after the initial warranty period, to obtain their expertise. When contracts are entered into, the work should be adequately controlled and service charges verified.

For work performed in-house, the primary element of an effective maintenance program is a well-organized and trained work force. This should include an adequate number of craftsmen with the required skills to carry on the technical work. It should also include adequate salaries and incentive plans to retain and motivate the maintenance workers needed. The incentive plans should take into consideration the measurement of the results of the maintenance activities. As a basis for achieving effective results management must also see that spare parts and materials are available when needed. In planning and controlling maintenance inventories the same principles are involved as in other types of inventories. There is thus the need to assume that sufficient materials are available to prevent unnecessary costs and losses due to interruptions of activity. Inventory levels, however, should not be excessive because of the risk of obsolescence and unnecessary carrying costs. There are certain unique problems in maintenance inventories because the demand for some items is not repetitive. However, for preventive maintenance the use of standard items is predictable. The use of computers in materials planning and control is especially beneficial in achieving effective management of maintenance materials.

There should be adequate physical inventories and storage of maintenance items. Materials and spare parts should be kept whenever possible in storerooms, and should be readily accessible to maintenance workers. The usage experience of the items should be continually monitored to assist in determining stockage levels. In addition, when there are changes in equipment the related spare parts and materials should be disposed of if no longer needed. At the same time, there should be a coordinated approach to acquiring needed maintenance materials if a different type of equipment is acquired. For newly acquired equipment, the company should have a system for correction of defects in parts when covered by warranties.

Budgeting and Controlling Performance

The many changes in fixed assets and the unknowns in technical requirements make it difficult to budget realistically for maintenance. Changes in production methods or misuse may shorten an asset's useful life. The sheer number of different types of equipment and changes in plans to replace them present problems in preparing meaningful budgets.

It is important that accountability be set for preparing the budget and performing within prescribed limits. This is especially desirable in controlling the number and extent of overruns. Because of the nature of the maintenance function, overruns can frequently occur, and managers must be responsible for obtaining analyses of the causes of them. These analyses serve to identify areas needing additional monitoring in the maintenance process, as well as improvements needed in budgeting. They also serve to justify the costs incurred, such as when extensive overtime is used to meet production deadlines. In some instances savings can be achieved by contracting out instead of performing the work in-house, or vice versa. For example, with a large fleet of vehicles it may be more economical to hire full-time mechanics than to have the vehicles serviced by outsiders.

It is important that a company have an accurate costing system to assure that materials and labor are charged to the right work order. Controls over transfers of costs between work orders should be instituted to prevent concealment of overruns. Also, there should be adequate control over unused materials to discourage stockpiles of material and charges to the wrong jobs.

It should be recognized that costs are only a factor in evaluating performance. Management is interested in keeping equipment running, in having an effective maintenance force to handle problems, and in preventing unnecessary repairs. The operating efficiency of the maintenance department, however, is of paramount importance because of the unique nature of the maintenance role and the problems in utulizing available funds to obtain the best results.

Role of the Internal Auditor in Maintenance

The internal auditor can make a significant contribution to management in his review of maintenance activities. On the one hand, the operational approaches used in reviewing production, inventories, and personnel are applicable. On the other hand, the internal auditor can review the overall effectiveness and efficiency of maintenance efforts. Since maintenance is basically a service function, its contribution to facilities management and production can be reviewed and evaluated. In addition, the internal auditor can determine the operability of equipment, through study of reports and tests made. In addition, by looking at accounting information, he can analyze personnel and material costs as a basis for obtaining savings. In addition, he can review preventive maintenance schedules and determine adherence to maintenance policies in effect for various types of equipment. In total the internal auditor seeks to determine how well existing policies, procedures, and operational activities serve the various interests of the company. This includes, as far as practicable, an evaluation of available alternatives that might provide still greater benefits.

AUDIT GUIDES

MAINTENANCE ACTIVITIES

I. Introductory
   A. Reference should be made to the general discussion of audit guides, Chapter 13.
   B. Because of the interrelationships with facilities and production activities, reference should also be made to the audit guides for those sections.

II. Preparatory
   A. See standard Audit Guides, Chapter 13.

III. Organizational Factors
   A. See standard Audit Guides, Chapter 13.
   B. Matters of special interest in the review of manuals include:
       1. Methods of setting maintenance levels.
       2. Coordination with facilities policies.
       3. Determining needs.
       4. Setting priorities.
       5. Managing backlogs.
       6. Receival of inputs.
       7. Control of work.
       8. Relations with production and quality control.
       9. Internal maintenance records.
       10. Setting materials and spare-parts levels.
       11. Inventory taking requirements.
       12. Reporting requirements.

IV. Operations
   A. Planning
       1. Are maintenance strategies supported by studies and valid data?

    2. Are maintenance policies revised with changing conditions?

    3. Are activities coordinated with those of other departments?

B. Determining Need

    1. Are needs for recurring maintenance specified and supported?

    2. Is there adequate support for types of maintenance: for example, choice of lubricants and tests to determine how often to lubricate?

    3. Do breakdowns and other symptoms indicate insufficient maintenance?

    4. Determine whether controls assure that facilities are not over-maintained.

C. Preventive Maintenance

    1. Does the company have an effective preventive maintenance program?

    2. Are standards set, and are they realistic?

    3. Is the preventive maintenance program followed? Are deviations adequately explained?

D. Contracting Out

    1. Are decisions as to performing maintenance in-house or contracting out documented as to justification?

    2. Are maintenance contracts periodically evaluated for costs and benefits?

    3. Is the expertise of manufacturers used to solve maintenance problems?

E. Scheduling Work

    1. Are schedules based on periodic studies of maintenance needs?

    2. Are schedules used as a basis for ordering materials and determining personnel requirements?

    3. Are schedules revised currently to reflect changed priorities due to breakdowns, shortages of spare parts, and other factors?

F. Materials and Spare Parts

    1. Are materials and spare-parts inventories set at economic levels?

    2. Are acquisitions and disposals of assets reflected in changed materials requirements?

    3. Are excess materials used on jobs returned to the central storeroom?

G. Cost Control

    1. Are cost overruns controlled and analyzed as to causes?

    2. Are budget revisions adequately supported and justified?

    3. Does the job costing system equitably reflect direct and indirect costs applicable to maintenance?

V. Audit Tests

A. Test a representative number of maintenance orders for the actions taken at various stages:

1. Basis for the maintenance request, including check of manufacturer's responsibilities.
2. Coordination with the production department.
3. Time required to schedule and perform the work.
4. Determination of needed inputs.
5. Receipt and testing of inputs.
6. Costs incurred based on budgets.
7. Inspection.
8. Return of asset to production.
9. Workability of asset, including auditor inspections.

B. For backlogs of equipment awaiting repair, determine whether schedules are being met and follow-up is made.

C. Determine whether service provided by contracted maintenance is effective and timely.

VI–IX. Not used.

X. Overall Appraisal of Maintenance Effectiveness

A. See standard Audit Guides, Chapter 13.

B. Review comparative studies made by management of results of preventive maintenance activities.

C. Discuss maintenance policies and activities with representatives of the production department.

D. Examine records of machine breakdowns by department and by type of asset.

ILLUSTRATIVE AUDIT FINDINGS: PRODUCTION AND MAINTENANCE

Unjustified Variation in Tolerances

The internal auditor found differences in tolerances used in the manufacture of a component of agriculture machinery. The Atlanta plant was using a ⅜-inch tolerance, whereas the Charleston plant was using a 5/16-inch tolerance. The auditor recommended the use of consistent tolerances, and since the ⅜-inch tolerance was acceptable under company standards, savings of $25,000 a year were obtained.

Concealment of Overruns

A review of charges for production labor indicated that unsupported transfers were being made between jobs to avoid overruns. Transfers out were made after the completion of the job, and usually had the explanation "to correct prior errors." However, there was no evidence of prior errors in record keeping.

Instead, the transfers were being used by production supervisors to conceal ineffective use of personnel on some jobs.

Delays in Servicing Customer Parts Needs

The internal auditor found that additional coordination among the sales department, the production department, and the maintenance department would help to increase sales. Some cancellations in customer orders during the year were caused by delays in deliveries of essential parts. Delivery dates promised by salespeople were not being met because of lack of communication of priority needs, unrealistic production expectations, and maintenance delays.

Faulty Standards for Maintaining Production Equipment

The company was scheduling maintenance of production equipment based on hours of usage. Parts were often replaced on a time basis regardless of condition in order to assure that there would be no breakdowns. The internal auditor recommended that a study be made to determine maintenance needs by parts. Based on reliability studies 25% of the components were receiving unnecessary maintenance.

Idling of Fleet Units through Unreported Defects

The internal auditor physically tested a selected number of fleet automobiles to see if they were in working condition. He found that some automobiles were inoperable because of defects that had not been reported. As a result, vehicles were unused for long periods of time without being scheduled for repair.

Excessive Delays in Completing Repairs

A test of a representative number of maintenance orders indicated that time schedules were not met for 34% of the orders. This resulted in a slowdown in production and delays in deliveries to customers. Analysis of the late orders showed a need for improvement in scheduling jobs and ordering spare parts and materials on a timely basis.

Insufficient Analysis of Cost Overruns

A review of selected cost overruns indicated that additional analysis was needed by maintenance management to determine the causes of the overruns and take corrective action. In some cases significant overruns were incurred because of emergency scheduling of jobs, use of higher-paid maintenance workers than budgeted, and the requisition of excess materials that were not returned for credit upon completion of jobs.

CHAPTER SEVENTEEN

Quality Control, Engineering, and Research

QUALITY CONTROL

Nature and Importance of the Process

The quality control activities are to a considerable extent a part of the production process, but they extend into the engineering function, and reach also to the point of final sale and delivery. In its simplest terms, the quality control function has as its mission the achievement by the company of specified quality levels for all of its products. It is a concept that can be applied to any operational activity, or even to the total aggregate of the company's operations, but it is used most commonly to refer to the production activity. The need for quality control arises from the fact that there is variability in all parts of the production process, starting with the materials themselves, extending to all aspects of the processing, and finally to the completed product. These different types of variability must be kept within certain ranges at the different stages so that the final product will be able to function in a manner that is desired by its users. This means that the final product must conform to a given range of specifications. The achievement of specified quality levels is in effect maintaining the individual and collective kinds of variability between acceptable ranges. Individual components must comply with such acceptable ranges in the way of particular attributes such as length, thickness, width, weight, finish, texture, durability, and the like. Also, the finished product must represent a combination of these individual components in such a way that a new set of composite requirements is met. Determining what these specifications and related ranges of variability should be leads us into some of the most basic of management decisions. Here the factors of marketing needs, production feasibility, and cost must be balanced in a manner that ultimately makes possible a sound and profitable company operation.

Scope of the Quality Control Process. When we think of the quality control process we are perhaps prone to think only of the activities where completed products are inspected for final acceptability. Although this final inspection is an important operational activity on its own own merits, it is only a minimal part of a comprehensive quality control function. The broader spectrum of levels that are involved can be viewed as follows:

1. Actions that are taken in various areas which will ultimately have a bearing upon the quality of the later actual production. Such actions might pertain, for example, to training programs, product design, processing, or equipment used. They might also involve the examination of vendor facilities and the related production operations.

2. The inspection of the different materials and components as first received by the company. The inspection here is both concerned with protecting the quality level of the final products, but is also a basis for vendor payment.

3. The intermediate types of inspection as materials are transferred from one operational group to another. The inspection here is also to protect quality levels, and additionally to assure a proper transfer of accountability.

4. The inspections that take place at various stages in the production process. This is at the same time a check on how well the applicable processing operations have been carried out. It may also in some cases be a basis for piecework compensation.

5. Final inspections as finished products are released by the production department for shipment to customers or transfer to stores. At this point the total effort of the production department is validated in the form of good final product.

The broad conceptual distinction that emerges from this spectrum is that quality control at its lowest level is catching defects or substandard conditions after the fact, and then getting the products out of the flow of good products. At a second and higher level, quality control is working in every way possible to prevent substandard production by determining and eliminating causes. Here the focus is on building quality into the product as opposed to policing the flow of finished products.

Importance of Quality Control. The fact that a large amount of money is expended in maintaining a quality control group makes the quality control activity very important in an expense control sense. But the importance is many times greater when quality performance deteriorates. The production of nonacceptable products immediately involves the loss of material, labor, and support services which have now been wasted, subject only to scrap recoveries. Second, if the defective product moves along further in the production process it usually causes the wastage of the further processing. Thirdly, and more often the most important cost of all, is that incurred in delivering an unsatisfactory product to a customer. Here the cost may range from loss of customer satisfaction to positive ill will, and even to damages for losses sustained because of the defects. In many cases human life may be at stake. What all of this means is that the quality of product has a major impact on the welfare of the company. As a consequence it is a function that needs the most careful attention by managers, and again in turn by the internal auditor.

Quality Control Is Everybody's Business.   The aforementioned relationship of the quality control activities to the total welfare of the company emphasizes the important point that maintaining proper quality control is everybody's business. Although the execution of the quality control function must be carried out in an efficient manner, it is clear that the preventive type of activity on the part of the quality control department involves every activity of the total pro- duction department, and in many cases the activities outside the production department. This is to say that everything that is done has a bearing directly or indirectly on the quality result of the final product. We thus have a broadly based operational problem which becomes a general management responsi- bility. Put another way, the quality control department is a special arm of management to coordinate all of the lower-level managerial responsibilities in the total company interest.

Cycle of Quality Control Operations

Again it will be useful to look at the total activity in terms of a control cycle. Such a control cycle can be viewed as follows:

1. The determination by the company of the specific level of acceptability of the individual component or finished product.
2. The determination by the quality control department of how the particular problem of quality assurance will be achieved.
3. The execution of the quality control action with appropriate clearance.
4. The monitoring and evaluation of results.

Determination of the Specific Level of Acceptability.   We have already noted the fact that determination of the specific level of acceptability is a management decision that requires the cross evaluation of a great many factors—engineering, marketing, production, and finance. There are always conflicting pressures as to what the specific level of quality should be, but somehow this question must be resolved in the manner that best serves the company interest. An engineer may wish to overdesign a product so that it will be the more sturdy and durable. The marketing people may be overly concerned with appearance factors. Pro- duction people may lean toward more manageable types of processing. But the finance department will be viewing the matter more from the standpoint of costs and the related recoverability of those costs at a profit. The resulting determination is necessarily a compromise type of integration. These deter- minations made at the final product level will then largely determine the ranges of the determination at the lower component and operational levels.

Several points also need to be emphasized. One is that quality is a relative term and that although different people might have different concepts of what is good or bad, good quality for the company is the level judged by the company management to support its established strategy best. Whether that management judgment is the best is an issue which is, of course, subject to continuing reappraisal and always on the basis of appropriate consideration of all pertinent factors. Meanwhile, the particular determinations are what we use in carrying out the quality control effort. The second point that needs to be emphasized is that the quality control department has an important contribution to make as the decisions are reached as to what the particular levels of quality should be. The key quality control personnel are normally engineering trained, and, in addition, have a wide range of experience as to what are realistic levels of feasibility for achieving specific quality levels. Thus they are often in a position where they can temper the expectations of other company personnel in a realistic manner.

In terms of special control interests the important points are to make certain that specified ranges of quality levels have in fact been established, that they have been determined on the basis of a reasonable consideration of all pertinent factors, and that the quality control department is participating in the actual determinations.

Determining How Quality Levels Will Be Achieved.   With the particular quality levels specified, the quality control department now faces the problem of how it will actually develop a program to achieve those specified levels. This program will be a blend of the different types of activities outlined in our previous discussion of the scope of the quality control function. In an operational sense these different types of activities fall into two general groups.

The first group of activities center about the actual inspection of specific components or products at specific stages of their processing. Here the matters to be determined will include:

1. Where will the inspection activities be carried out?
2. What facilities will be required?
3. What is the scope of the inspection activities?
4. What equipment is to be used?
5. What are the personnel and organizational needs?
6. How will the results of the inspection activities be utilized as a means of controlling the underlying production operations?

The second group of activities are concerned with the various types of preventive actions which can be taken to provide better assurance that the actual production operations will be more effective. The matters involved here would include:

1. To what extent should vendors be visited and worked with to assure that materials and components received from them are fully acceptable?

2. What opportunities exist in the way of providing more efficient facilities and equipment?

3. What training programs would be useful?

4. To what extent is better management support needed?

5. What other conditions might be changed to contribute to the effectiveness of the various processing operations?

From a control standpoint the interest is that the quality control department is developing programs to cover both the regular inspection and the preventive types of effort, and that in each case these programs are definitive and comprehensive.

Quality Clearance. At this next stage the quality control group actually implements the previously described determinations and carries out the related actions. This is the operative stage when work responsibilities must be assigned, personnel supervised, and actual work productivity achieved. Moreover, operations must be carried out on a timely basis so as not to delay the ongoing production operations. Timing is also very important with respect to identifying operational problems that develop, and that may affect the quality level of the resulting product at any given stage. The objectives are thus both to provide a reliable basis for the clearance of the particular products and to determine the existence of operating conditions from which defective products are emerging.

The actions in the preventive area obviously must precede the regular clearance-type inspections, but in a continuing production program there will come a time when they will be operating simultaneously. They can also at this point provide a useful kind of cross interaction. During this operational phase the key considerations are that the two types of effort are administered in an efficient manner and that they are sufficiently flexible to respond to new developments. Day-to-day developments can include changed sources, product modifications, new standards of quality acceptability, delayed production by vendors or company components, pressures for release of cleared materials, pressures for relaxation of inspection standards, and the like. Part of the administrative efficiency is to take all of these developments in stride through good administrative direction. At the same time there is the necessity of doing the job properly and at the lowest possible cost.

Monitoring and Evaluation of Results. The final stage of the control cycle has to do with carefully observing the extent of deviations from acceptable quality levels, studying their implications, and taking whatever action is needed. In the current inspections any deterioration in the level of product quality must be an immediate basis for probing as to causes. Perhaps a new worker is not doing his inspection job properly. Perhaps the testing equipment has become inaccurate. Perhaps the cause may be some adverse development in the production of the particular items. But whatever the cause there is the need to identify it so that all possible corrective action can be taken. In certain situations it may be necessary to stop production until the problem is resolved. Similarly, in the preventive area there is the continuous question as to whether the planned preventive measures are proving to be adequate to deal with the problems. If not, they must be expanded or modified. If these changes require operational coordination or the participation of higher-level management, this too must be handled. The evaluation function is therefore, the major control means of detecting threats to the quality control objectives.

Organizational Status of the Quality Control Department

The effectiveness of the quality control activity, as one could expect, is closely linked to the organizational status of the quality control department. In many companies the quality control group is part of the production department, and this arrangement can work satisfactorily if the reporting responsibility is to the head of that production department, and if that executive is in the top management group. In other companies the quality control department is separated from the production department entirely and made responsible to a higher-level corporate office. The important factors are that the quality control department can command the proper respect in the total organization, and that it can when necessary serve as a positive counter-control in relation to the production operations. It can often happen that a production group will become unduly obsessed with making production schedules. In such situations there may be too much of a temptation to disregard proper quality levels. At this point the protection of company interests may well be that the quality control department has the organization power to turn back units produced and, if necessary, to shut down parts of the production operations. The actual needs here depend on how serious a situation may be caused by the release of the below-standard product. Releasing a pair of shoes as either a first or a second quality may not be very critical, but if the product is an aircraft engine, there is quite a different set of concerns. What all of this means is that the organizational status of the quality control department must be adequate in the particular situation to protect the company's interests properly.

Statistical Methods for Quality Control

The achievement of the quality control objectives is made possible in the most efficient manner by the use of statistical methods. The first requirement is that a particular manufacturing process or set of related processes is brought under adequate direct control through the specification of levels of performance and continuing measurements of performance against those specifications. Under such circumstances it is practicable to inspect the product results on a statistical sampling basis. The essence of statistical sampling is that the results obtained from a sample can be interpreted to apply to the larger group from which the sample was drawn. With the help of those trained in statistics we identify the limits of the larger group (referred to as the particular universe) and then select a representative sample. From this sample, and depending on its size, we are able to conclude that within given ranges of probabilities the overall results will be of the desired specification. This provides a basis for clearance of inspected items at any level of probabilities that we wish to establish. On the basis of the more limited inspection effort the company can exercise needed control over the underlying production operations. By charting the results of an ongoing sampling program the deterioration of some phase of the production process can be detected and then corrected with minimum loss.

What Is an Adequate Quality Control Effort?

One of the most difficult question faced by anyone appraising the adequacy of a quality control program is to know exactly how far one should go in terms of depth and overall coverage. It is relatively easy to generalize but hard to know exactly where the line should be drawn. In the preventive area this difficulty is especially great because many of the actions taken cannot be precisely evaluated in terms of the final results. In the inspection area, although it is much easier to relate results to actions taken, there is still the difficult determination of the level of confidence that is needed as to the quality of the final products. All of the quality control aspects cost money and it is necessary that we be able to justify the level of expenditures in terms of benefits received. The key considerations include the following:

1. A clear indication from top management as to the extent that stressing quality is a major part of the company's marketing strategy.
2. The proper support of a company-wide effort to provide conditions that support the production of final products at the desired quality levels.
3. The design and implementation by the quality control department of an efficient quality control program, including the use of up-to-date equipment, control charts, statistical sampling, and good administration.
4. The continuing appraisal by the quality control department of the scope of its program in relation to total company needs.

On the basis of such an effort, which is carried out by the quality control department, with the support of top management and the collaboration of other company personnel, there can be a reasonable expectation that the right balance will be achieved in a cost/benefit sense.

Internal Auditor's Role in Quality Control

The internal auditor's role is subject to the initial handicap that there is a significant technical base to much of the quality control effort. There are, however, at the same time usually good potentials for company service. One dimension of this company service is that various operational developments provide continuous readings on the adequacy of the total quality control effort. Illustrative are levels of scrap generation, stoppages of current processing, backlogs of products to be inspected, customer complaints, and the like. These provide a good clue to problems that relate directly or indirectly to the adequacy of the quality control problem. The causes may be faulty design of the program or inadequate implementation. The evaluation of the design of the quality control program is in part technical, but at some point depends on practical management considerations, an area in which the internal auditor has greater capabilities. The evaluation of the adequacy of the implementation is still more within the internal auditor's capabilities. The focus here is on the administrative handling of the day-to-day elements of the quality control program. In this area the internal auditor is well fitted to appraise the manner in which the quality control department is organized, the clearness with which job responsibilities are defined, and the manner in which the personnel are supervised. These opportunities are covered in more detail in the audit guides that follow.

AUDIT GUIDES

QUALITY CONTROL ACTIVITIES

I. Introductory
   A. Reference should be made to the general discussion of audit guides, Chapter 13.
   B. Because of the interrelationships with production and engineering activities, reference should also be made to the audit guides for those sections.

II. Preparatory
   A. See standard Audit Guides, Chapter 13.

III. Organizational Factors
   A. See standard Audit Guides, Chapter 13.
   B. Matters of special interest in the review of manuals will include:
      1. Organization and objectives.
      2. Means of obtaining specification ranges.
      3. Relations with company activities, vendors, and othe parties outside the production department.
      4. Relations with activity components within the production department.
      5. Approach to statistical sampling.
      6. Handling of rejects.
      7. Reporting of results.
      8. Levels of approvals.
      9. Handling of disputes.
      10. Collaborative management activities.
      11. Records to be maintained.

IV. Operations of the Quality Control Department
   A. General
      1. Is the quality control department adequately advised of all quality specifications?
         a. Are they approved by a proper level of authority in the engineering department?
         b. Are changes received promptly?
         c. What provision, if any, is made for deviations?
         d. Does the quality control department collaborate in the determination of the quality control specifications? If not, why not?
      2. Is there evidence of a reasonable planning effort:
         a. As respects the overall approach?
         b. As to current day-to-day operations?
   B. In the Preventive Area
      1. Does an adequate program exist as to how a preventive program will be set up to minimize the underlying causes of below standard quality, including appropriate collaboration in the related company areas:
         a. Product design?
         b. Facilities planning?
         c. Processing?
         d. Plant layout?
         e. Equipment and tooling?
         f. Material handling?
         g. Purchasing department?
         h. Production operations?
         i. Marketing group?
         j. Personnel department?
      2. To what extent is there a direct relationship with vendors to determine acceptability of source and for later review and counsel? Is this effort adequate?
      3. Relations with company activities, vendors, and other parties outside the production department.
   C. In the Area of Current Product Inspections:
      1. Are facilities areas adequate?
      2. Is adequate equipment used?
      3. Are materials received properly from producing or delivering activities—both physically and procedurally as to accountability?
      4. Are inspection areas neat and orderly, and is material adequately protected?
      5. Are materials and products properly identified as to stage of inspection?
      6. Are charts showing quality performance kept up to date and accurate?

7. Are adequate records maintained of work handled?
8. Is statistical sampling based on adequate coordination with qualified statisticians?
9. Have levels of statistical sampling been approved by persons of sufficiently high authority?
10. How adequately are substandard results followed up?
11. Are rejected materials properly segregated, tagged, and reported for vendor chargebacks?
12. Is staffing and work supervision adequate?
13. Are findings adequately coordinated with the preventive program?
14. Are working relationships with production personnel and other involved company personnel on an efficient and cooperative basis?

V. Special Audit Tests
   A. Tests of Purchase Orders Based on a Representative Sample to Determine:
      1. Adequacy of evidence that there was a proper check of compliance with stated specifications.
      2. Adequacy of evidence of proper charge back of deficiencies.
   B. Tests of Rejected Lots on a Random Basis to Determine:
      1. Whether proper chargebacks were made to vendors
      2. Extent of ultimate receipt and handling by the scrap disposal group
   C. Tests as to Relations with Recipients of Inspection Activity to Determine:
      1. Extent of their agreement as to scope of coverage.
      2. Extent of problems encountered with quality control department and manner of resolution.

VI–IX. Not used.

X. Overall Appraisal of Quality Control Effectiveness
   A. See standard Audit Guides, Chapter 13.
   B. To what extent has an adequate plant-wide support program for quality been developed?
   C. Are quality specifications being met?

ENGINEERING

The direct tie of the quality control program to the underlying engineering determinations leads naturally to a consideration of the engineering function. This area is one that has a major technical core and some question might be raised as to what the nonengineer can make in terms of a worthwhile contribution. Even here, however, there are important areas of an administrative control nature which lend themselves to review and analysis by the general practitioner. At this particular point in the chapter our concern will be with the engineering role as it responds to current *operational* needs. Although there is also clearly a *research* dimension of the engineering role, the treatment of that phase will be postponed until the final section of this chapter.

Nature and Scope of the Engineering Process

The engineering process has to do with the design, construction, and operation of structures, machines, engines, and other devices used in industry and in everyday life. Its specific nature will vary greatly depending on the area of concentration and the industry in which it is applied. The vast field would include aeronautical, agricultural, chemical, mining, industrial, and still other types of engineering. In a particular company, engineering may cover a wide spectrum of activities. One way in which this spectrum is broken down is in terms of the specific subareas in the manufacturing process. Thus we would have engineers concentrating on the design and operation of products, facilities, processing approaches, plant layout, equipment, tooling, work methods, and the like. In each of these areas there will be different degrees of specialization. A second way in which the spectrum can be viewed is in terms of how close or how remote the engineering activity may be from the actual operational application. For example, in the area of the product itself we can at the more remote end of the spectrum be studying the development of new materials or new types of forces that might eventually contribute to the further development of existing products. This kind of focus is generally referred to as basic research. At the other end of the spectrum we are working with the specifications of a new model of our existing products, which involves little if any substantive change in those products. In between are all kinds of intermediate types of applications. The latter type of spectrum applies in a similar manner to other subareas, such as facilities, equipment, and the like.

Importance of Engineering

In most companies the engineering function is very important and in some companies—as, for example, in an aerospace manufacturing company—it is by far the most important factor for operational success. In these situations it is important in terms of the large expenditures actually made, but more important, for the specific contribution that it makes. It is the engineering activity that provides the necessary knowledge in a design sense, and the translation of the design concepts into workable production operations to make possible a product that actually provides the services customers want. Although products must be made by a production department, financed, and marketed, the engineering function provides the necessary technical base without which nothing else could exist. It is for all of these reasons that the engineering activity has such high prestige in most company situations, and that any contribution to its further effectiveness is so much sought after by the company management. This further effectiveness is obtained in two major ways. One is through the more efficient internal administration of the engineering activities. The other is through close cooperative interaction between the engineering activities and the other company activities which directly or indirectly use or are affected by the engineering services.

Control Framework of the Engineering Process

The engineering operational cycle covers:

1. The definition of mission.
2. The implementation of that mission.
3. The follow-up support.

Our control effort, therefore, is concerned with these three areas.

Definition of Mission. Although the particular type of engineering service needed can vary widely, from the specifications for a single simple component part to the design of a spacecraft, the particular purpose needs to be defined. This defined need then becomes the mission for the particular engineering activity. The starting point, therefore, from a control standpoint is to see to it that the mission is defined as precisely as is practicable under the existing conditions. At the same time a range of projected cost should be established, with as much accuracy as can be achieved at this stage. In exploratory types of situations it may not always be possible to know what we are seeking, but we can know the problem we are attempting to solve, and we can define the areas of contribution to the solution of that problem. As work progresses it may be necessary to redefine the mission in the light of new developments. At any point in time, however, the truth remains that we seek maximum mission definition as a basis for the supporting engineering effort. Past estimates will be at the same time appropriately revised.

Role of the Engineer in Mission Definition. We should at this point also ask the question of who has the responsibility for defining the mission. The answer here must basically be that it is the responsibility of management at the appropriate level to do this. Meaningful missions can exist only when they reflect the evaluation and final judgment of the weight of all management considerations. Also, no single functional activity is in a position to do this as effectively as the responsible management group. But this does not mean either that the engineer should have only the responsibility to execute missions defined for him by others. On the contrary, it is highly desirable that he provide all possible input to the management decision, both in the way of contributing creative ideas, and in counseling as various alternative approaches are discussed. His special expertise is thus properly exploited in helping to reach decisions which on balance appear to best coincide with the overall company interests. It should be said also that the participation of the engineer in the definition of mission

ensures a needed preliminary standard of the actual feasibility of carrying out
the mission.

Preliminary Exploration of Mission. In many cases the mission is of a type
where the process by which the mission has been defined is sufficient to establish proper feasibility. In many other cases, however, this will not be true.
In the latter situations the mission may seem potentially sound in terms of
feasibility and cost, but it may require further study before one can be sufficiently certain. The second phase, then, is to make that further study on a
limited expenditure basis as a means of confirming the soundness of the total
mission before pouring into it the full-scale effort. In most situations this will
be a prudent approach and can avoid large expenditures which may later prove
to be wasted. Exactly when this preliminary exploration is advisable and what
the scope of it should be are difficult judgments. There will always be risk to
some extent, and the question comes down to the scope of the risks to be taken
in the light of the potential benefits and the related urgency of the company's
need. The control dimension here is that this evaluation is made in an orderly
manner on the basis of reasonable evidence. Although precise lines cannot be
drawn in making such judgments, the fact of extremes in either direction can
more easily be identified.

Implementation of Mission. Assuming that there is now reasonably satisfactory
assurance of the feasibility of the mission, the next stage involves carrying out
the defined mission in a full-scale operational sense. Depending on the overall
complexity of the mission, and the period of time that will be required, the
operational steps needed include:

1. Breaking up the mission into individual tasks and work assignments.
2. Determining what inputs will be needed and when in the way of facilities,
   equipment, personnel supplies, and other support factors.
3. Laying out a schedule of completion for each of the tasks, and for the
   combination of all tasks in the total mission.
4. The actual assignment of work responsibilities with appropriate guidance
   instruction.
5. Current administration and control of progress in terms of both physical
   accomplishment and costs incurred.
6. Reporting of progress both as to physical and cost performance.
7. Evaluation of problems and new developments and appropriate collaboration with other interested company activities, including possible modification of mission definition and/or budgetary adjustments.
8. Completion of mission, including the preparation of the necessary blueprints, charts, instructions, manuals, and so on, which provide the basis
   for the utilization of the engineering work in the ongoing company activities affected.
9. Final reporting of financial performance.

The implementation has been outlined in terms of a single mission or project. But where, as in many cases, this project approach is not possible, the total operations of the engineering group for a given period of time—a year, a quarter, or a month—can be viewed as a total project. In this kind of a situation all stages of the cycle may be operating simultaneously to some extent, but the performance of the total group still needs to be controlled as a composite of many projects. The control aspects of this entire implementation can be viewed as the efficiency with which each of the dimensions of that implementation are carried out and how they combine to produce the final results in a satisfactory manner at an economical level of cost.

Follow-Up Support.   In a narrow sense the engineering mission has been completed, but in a more realistic sense it is not complete until the engineering services have been adequately utilized by the user group. Normally, this involves interpreting the engineering blueprints and instructions and helping to deal with new problems that may develop. A particular part may be thought to be designed adequately for a particular purpose, but in later assembly a problem may develop. Or, perhaps, something has changed in the conditions of that use. At this stage there may be the need for deviations or for engineering changes. At worst the situation may require doing the engineering work over again. In all of these situations the engineer will, of course, be deeply involved, and be participating in the new decisions.

As we know, in many situations the role of the engineering group will extend beyond the production activity to providing backup service to the marketing group, and even directly to the customer. The scope of this service can include diagnosis of customer needs in connection with the sales effort, counseling with marketing personnel, working with dealers making installations of technical equipment, and servicing products in the hands of customers. In some situations the personnel performing these services may be organizationally under the control of the marketing group, but in any event there would be a necessary collaboration and interaction with the engineering group that originally handled the underlying engineering design. In a sense the engineering job is never finished because of the fact that continuing experience with company products is always providing additional evaluation of the worth of the underlying engineering effort. The control dimension of this total follow-up effort is first, to determine the adequacy of its scope, and second, to appraise the efficiency with which it is being carried out.

Organizational Status of the Engineering Department.   Because of the importance of the role of the engineering group the organizational status of the engineering department becomes all the more significant. Our first concern, therefore, is that the engineering department have the organizational status that will make possible the full scope of its important contribution. Normally, this requires independence from all other company activities, including the production department, and a direct reporting to the chief executive officer.

Having said this, we must go on to say, however, that this need is usually well recognized, and that the practical problem can sometimes be that the engineering department comes to wield too much power in the company operations. The relatively greater precision with which the engineer can speak and the natural desire on the part of most people for reliable and efficient performance contribute to this possibility. The result can then be that engineering considerations unduly dominate the related marketing and financial considerations. What is actually needed is engineering excellence, but excellence that is combined properly with marketing needs and financial soundness. What this means is that engineering must be a competent force but at the same time a partner in the achievement of the company's best overall interests.

A particularly interesting dimension of the organizational problem for the engineering function is the extent to which it should be decentralized. Supporting the centralization approach are the usual arguments of economy of operation with the larger group, the ability to better attract the various types of needed expertise, and the necessity in many situations of control over particular product dimensions. On the other hand, operational components with their profit center responsibilities and pressing operational needs can argue with merit the desirability of having the engineering function directly under their own control. The right answer in any individual situation will depend on the particular circumstances. Normally, however, there are some engineering activities that can be carried out more effectively at the lower organizational levels, and which to some extent should be under local control. The practical judgmental question is to determine how far to go in this respect, and then to work out the appropriate coordinative and policy relationships that will make the composite effort function efficiently.

Other Management Problems Relating to Engineering

As we have already seen, the engineering function combines basic importance and uniqueness of operations in an especially challenging manner. Certain of these unique aspects require some further elaboration if we are to be able to contribute to making this a more useful company activity.

Nature of the Work Force. The activities in the engineering function have special characteristics. Engineers are involved with relatively precise elements—the material content, physical characteristics, forces that act on these materials, and other operational relationships. They deal with these elements in a very defined, factual, and often scientific manner. It is a type of activity that is often both very specialized and detached in the sense of relating to other people. It also involves a great deal of technical knowledge. All of these forces combine to give engineering a certain professional character. It is this professional character that poses special problems from an overall company management standpoint. Professionals tend to require special types of rewards and overall treatment. Recognition by their professional associates and the pursuit of professional goals displace to some extent the normal motivation and loyalties that exist for other company personnel. As a result the administration of engineering personnel is subject to special problems. In essence we must deal with engineering personnel in a more sensitive manner and with adequate recognition of the pulls and pressures in the professional direction.

Developing Cost Consciousness.   Stemming from the emphasis on professional standards and excellence comes a common tendency to unduly subordinate cost considerations. The concern for engineering excellence in a technical sense can overshadow the importance of costs incurred both to carry out the engineering work and as respects the later production and operation of the product involved. As a result there is the very real possibility of overdesign, that is, building in design characteristics that go beyond the determined need. There can also be a tendency toward uniqueness of development, as opposed to the ever-important maximum standardization. All of this combines to make the engineering function less amenable to financial implications and makes it more difficult to work within the normal cost and cost-efficiency sense. This means, therefore, that the reviewer must recognize the problem and strive to deal with it all the more intelligently.

Collaboration Emphasis.   The engineering input to most operational problems has very great potentialities. It is necessary, however, that the input be properly utilized through good collaboration with other company activities. In the production area it can provide the basis for better processing of materials. In the purchasing area it can provide analytical assistance for more effective purchasing. In the marketing area it can strengthen market development and good customer relations. The key, then, is the development of an effective program of collaboration with these other company activities. The objective at all times needs to be how engineering can be used as a means of best supporting other company activities, as opposed to establishing a position to which all others must conform. Again a recognition of the potentials from this approach can perhaps better set the stage for finding ways to achieve it.

Engineering Changes.   In the discussion of the follow-up activities there was reference to problems or other new developments that could necessitate changes in the engineering specifications. When such changes actually become necessary, the changes must be handled procedurally in a way that will clearly define the scope of the various changes to the affected parts, provide for the appropriate approvals, and be numbered so that all interested parties can accurately determine the point of applicability. Other interested parties would include the various production activities, purchasing, stores, and customer service. This is especially important when the change being made is significant in the operability of the company product, as, for example, in the case of an aircraft engine. When these changes are voluminous, there is a still greater problem in developing a procedural system that is both accurate and up to date for use by other company activities, and in some cases also by customers.

Methods Engineering and Time Study

Our discussion of the engineering function requires some special consideration of one of its important activities, that of methods engineering and time study. This activity, sometimes referred to as industrial engineering, can extend to any type of operational activity in the company, but is especially concentrated in the production area. Its role stems from the fact that in any significant repetitive operation there is a best way to carry out that particular operation. Through careful analysis of the elements of the particular operation, and with the assistance in many cases of time and motion study, that best way is determined. The result can be both less fatigue for the worker involved and increased productivity for lower cost, higher quality, and more efficient operations. The potentials along these lines demonstrate the importance of developing a comprehensive methods engineering and time study program and then administering that program in an effective manner.

Framework of the Total Effort. The starting point for the methods engineering program is to study the particular job, as, for example, operating a particular machine, or carrying out a particular part of a more extended assembly operation. We need to know both the purpose of the job and how it is being accomplished. Typical elements to be examined and evaluated will include:

1. The individual labor operations and their sequence.
2. The possibility of combining the operations with a different process.
3. Adequacy of equipment.
4. The work layout.
5. Materials used.
6. Supporting services.
7. Inspections and other interruptions.

Tools utilized in the foregoing would include time analysis and possible use of motion pictures. The objective in each instance would be to determine the extent to which there is wasted effort and what could be done differently to improve the total result.

The job analysis and related time study also become foundations for determining what proper standards should be for particular types of operations. In some cases this effort can be extended further to involve the manner of compensation—both as piecework and for group incentive compensation.

Problem of Employee Acceptance. A special problem that exists in the development of any kind of a methods engineering project is the resistance that may be encountered from employees. The problem here stems from the fear on the part of the employee that somehow the findings are going to be used in a way that will be adverse to his interests. Although he is not sure whether this adverse interest might be lesser pay for the same work, harder work, more automated work, or the like, he may feel that his control over his own working

conditions is being undermined. Quite clearly, the first requirement is, therefore, to achieve the worker's confidence and genuine cooperation by convincing
him of the legitimate objectives of greater productivity, which can then be
shared by both company and employee. The second requirement is to demonstrate over time that the benefits are actually being shared in a reasonably
equitable manner. In dealing with these two requirements it is necessary that
management participate actively in the launching and overall administration
of the program. This management effort can then be effectively supported by
the right kind of a methods engineer. But both ingredients are necessary.

Role of the Internal Auditor in Engineering

Previous comments have set the stage for a conclusion that the internal auditor
can make an important contribution in the field of the engineering activities.
As indicated, there is admittedly a major technical base to all types of engineering activities, but whereas a familiarity with those technical aspects can
be useful, that familiarity is not a controlling prerequisite. In many company
situations some members of the internal auditing staff may have had engineering
training. In other cases members of the staff may have had some actual production experience, with a good exposure to the engineering function. In any
event it is believed that careful observation of engineering activities can provide
an adequate basis for important areas of management service. This is especially
true if the internal auditor works in a cooperative fashion with engineering
management.

The more specific areas of management service relate to the manner in which
the engineering department interprets its mission, makes its plans, organizes
its resources, and administers its operations in an orderly and businesslike way.
These various types of operational activity require the use of standards and
systems of measurement and control that are ultimately judged in terms of
providing quality services at a reasonable cost. The internal auditor is interested
in how adequately programs are developed for carrying out this function, and
then as to how efficiently those programs are being implemented.

AUDIT GUIDES

ENGINEERING ACTIVITIES

  I. Introductory
    A. Reference is made to the general discussion of audit guides, Chapter
       13.
    B. Because of the interrelationships with production and research activ-
       ities, reference should also be made to the audit guides for those
       sections.

 II. Preparatory
    A. See standard Audit Guides, Chapter 13.

III. Organizational Factors

    A. See standard Audit Guides, Chapter 13.

    B. Matters of special interest in the review of manuals will include:

        1. Organization and objectives.

        2. Acceptance of work projects.

        3. Preparation of budgets and budgetary control.

        4. Assignment and scheduling of work.

        5. Operational reports.

        6. Approvals for release of blueprints, specifications, manuals, and other instructions.

        7. Security.

        8. Relations with other company activities.

        9. Personnel control.

      10. Engineering changes.

      11. Records to be maintained.

IV. Operations

    A. Planning

        1. Review and appraise the basis of the planning effort:

          a. As to adequacy of collaboration with other company activities.

          b. As to internally generated study projects.

        2. How adequately is the planning basis translated into operational projections:

          a. As to personnel?

          b. As to other costs?

        3. How adequate is the program for reviewing performance against plans:

          a. As to costs incurred?

          b. As to results accomplished?

    B. Input of Work Assignments

        1. From other company activities

          a. Are authorizations at a sufficiently high level?

          b. Are work assignments adequately defined?

          c. Does the engineering department collaborate adequately in the finalization of work requests?

          d. Are projects reasonably documented?

          e. Are expenditure limits adequately fixed?

        2. Internally generated work projects

          a. Who approves? Are approval levels adequate?

          b. Are internal proposals adequately coordinated with other interested company activities, and when of appropriate significance, with top management?

          c. Are projects reasonably documented as to purpose, expenditure justification, and as to basis of control?

    C. Assignment of Work

1. Is the procedure for breaking down the work assignment adequate?
2. Are instructions properly transmitted to component organizational units?
3. Is adequate provision made for coordination of the individual work assignments?
4. Are cost and time estimates established to the extent practicable?

D. Interim Administration of Work Assignments
1. Does day-to-day supervision appear to be adequate?
2. Are there adequate periodic progress reports covering work assignments—including time charged to individual projects, costs incurred to date, and estimated time and cost to complete versus original estimates?
3. Is internal coordination adequate?
4. Is there adequate liaison with the ultimate company users?
5. Are work conditions reasonably adequate as to facilities, filing of materials, control of confusion, and the like?
6. Are project records adequate, and are they being adequately maintained?
7. Are supporting reproduction services adequate?
8. How adequate are the controls over personnel scheduling and utilization?

E. Completion and Release of Engineering Results
1. Are results transmitted in the form that is most suitable for their utilization?
2. Is the completion of the work adequately conforming to planned time schedules and costs?
3. Are cost and performance records properly compiled and evaluated?
4. Are continuing personnel requirements reevaluated?

F. Follow-up Activities
1. Is liaison with the using activity maintained to ascertain that the engineering provided is adequate?
2. Are the engineering data being provided considered satisfactory by the users? If not, why not?

G. General
1. Are engineering changes authenticated promptly to cover new developments and needs?
2. Is the engineering change program being administered in an orderly and efficient manner? Is information adequately disseminated to all interested parties?

V. Audit Tests

A. Test a representative number of requests for engineering service to appraise performance to date of completion.

B. Verify the accuracy of time and costs changed to a representative number of projects over the period under review.

C. Make inquiries of a representative number of company users to ascertain extent of problems encountered in dealing with the engineering department.

D. Examine representative change orders to ascertain the extent to which changes were caused by faulty design.

E. Review methods engineering studies made for validity and implementation of results.

VI–IX. Not used.

X. Overall Appraisal of Engineering Effectiveness

A. See standard Audit Guides, Chapter 13.

RESEARCH

The research activities are closely related to the engineering activities. Research exists basically for the purpose of generating new knowledge, which then at the proper stage of development will provide input to the engineering group for operational application. The internal auditor's potential contribution again lies in the area of developing more efficient administration and control. Even though the area may be even more technically oriented than the engineering activity, the general recognition that the research group especially needs the administrative and control type of assistance provides, perhaps, for a better receptivity than will exist in the engineering area.

Nature of the Research Process

New knowledge can actually be of any kind and pertain to any kind of human activity. As viewed by management the research activity will pertain to some aspect of the overall company operations and should have as its central purpose the development of new knowledge that will increase the profitability of some aspect of the company operations. Although the broader spectrum can include production, marketing, personnel, and the like, at this point we are concerned only with the technical type of research which applies to the production operations. However, even in this one area there is still a wide spectrum of applications, including such subareas as product design, processing, equipment, material handling, and all other types of production activity. These individual production activities will again break down into smaller areas—as, for example, different kinds of existing products, new products, and new product features. The objective in all cases is to develop new knowledge that will be useful in some way. This may be by reducing manufacturing costs, adding or strengthening the operational characteristics of the product, or perhaps making it more attractive in appearance.

Another way in which we need to view the research role is in terms of its degree of proximity, in a time and developmental sense, to its actual production utilization. The degree of remoteness from the actual production application is important because the greater the degree of that remoteness, usually the greater difficulty in assessing the extent and worth of the ultimate usability. But whatever the specific focus of the particular research, the evaluation is based on the probabilities that a given type of application will be forthcoming and on an estimate of what the payoff will be at that time. To what extent will the new application enable us to reduce costs or to increase revenues as a basis for improved profitability? This evaluation is a difficult one because of the long time period that is frequently involved, the uncertainty as to how the application will actually work out, and the lack of knowledge about the market demand for the company's product. In some cases also the problem is the uncertainty as to whether the new knowledge will be such that it can be implemented at a reasonable level of production costs.

Still another characteristic of the research process is that even when we think we know the application that is being sought and have a pretty good idea of its potential value, we are often unable to know how far we have progressed toward the achievement of our research objective. In a particular situation we may find our solution to the problem in a month, or it might take several years, or it may prove to be an unsolvable problem, at least in terms of acceptable cost. Thus we may not be able to say at a particular stage of the research how far we are toward completion. This evaluation is made still more difficult by the fact that people frequently have individual attachments to particular research projects, and consciously and unconsciously have biased or erroneous views. In addition, there is the fact that solving the problem is not the total question. Equally pertinent is whether and to what extent there is prudent justification for the further costs to be expended.

All of these factors combine to make the management and control of the research activity one of the most difficult of operational areas to handle. But it is precisely because of these difficulties that it represents the challenging problem that it is. It is in turn one of the areas where top management especially needs help. This then provides the basis for the special interest of the internal auditor.

Importance of the Research Activity

Despite the difficulties involved in the management and control of the research activity, the need for the research contribution is so great that ways must be found to deal with the problem. The basis for that need in its simplest terms is competitive survival. The world is moving forward at an accelerating pace with the development of a new and improved technology from which emerge new products, new product features, more efficient types of equipment, better processes, and other operational developments. If, therefore, a company is to be competitive in an overall sense it must be competitive in terms of its research effort. Assuming that the direction of the research effort has been established, the problem then takes on a new importance. This latter problem is to manage and control the research effort to which the company has committed itself. It involves a determination of what types of research shall be undertaken, the amounts of money that will be expended, and finally the controls exercised to assure that maximum value is being received from the given expenditures. In total the company must achieve the research results that it needs to support its competitive objectives, while accomplishing those objectives at a price that it can afford.

Control Cycle of the Research Process

The control cycle is similar to the one discussed for the engineering process, but can better be described as:

1. Definition of mission.
2. Initial implementation.
3. Current administration.
4. Periodic reevaluation.

Definition of Mission.   Perhaps in no other area of operational activity is there such a need for a clear definition of mission. Lacking this definition the research effort can go off in nonproductive directions based on the more restricted judgment and personal interests of the individual researchers. At the same time it must be recognized that the definition phase can be carried too far. Here the focus of the research may be so narrowly directed that it overlooks the more general areas which may offer the greatest rewards. In addition, there is the very real risk that we may unduly restrict the creativity of the researcher, which is often the priceless ingredient. The solution of the dilemma is that the determination of the particular mission must come about through an effective interaction between other company personnel and the research group. In this interaction joint consideration should be given to all of the pertinent factors. These would include:

1. The scope of the needs for new knowledge and the specific ways the new knowledge will benefit the company.
2. The technical possibilities and probabilities of satisfying those needs through the research effort, together with realistic estimates of the time dimensions and cost expenditures that will be required.
3. The total research capabilities of the company in terms of personnel and budgetary allocations, and the alternative merits of competing research projects within those total capabilities.

These factors will normally be discussed on a preliminary and informal basis, and then, depending on the scope of the operational application and the dollar value, will be further documented and reviewed by higher-level personnel of both the research group and other company activities. The interactions may focus on a single project or a combination of them. From a control standpoint the objectives are that there is this orderly and comprehensive interaction, and that from it emerges a reasonably adequate definition of the composition and magnitude of the research mission. This definition should clarify the extent of involvement in basic research as well as applied research.

Initial Implementation.   With the mission defined in the best possible fashion the research department is ready to receive the properly approved authorization and to initiate actual work on the project. At this point the project needs to be broken down into its various component elements and a determination made as to the requirements for facilities, personnel, equipment, materials, and supporting service, with cost estimates for each element. This will be followed by direct operational assignments to the component organizational units and personnel of the research department. At the same time records will be established to cover the operational activities which are now to be carried out. In each case there will be appropriate consultation with the personnel to whom the assignments are made so that responsibilities and operational objectives are well understood.

Current Administration.   The actual research effort now goes forward in the form of the various activities, such as testing, analysis, compilations of data, and studied interpretations. Meanwhile, time spent on the various projects is recorded and accumulated, other costs incurred are also recorded, and periodic reports are issued covering total costs incurred to date in relation to work accomplished. During this time also there is such interaction as is needed with other personnel both within the research group itself and in other company activities. This collaboration serves the purpose of providing such additional information as may be needed. At the same time it serves to inform other interested parties of problems encountered and progress made so that there can be a useful interaction for a more meaningful ongoing pursuit of the research objectives.

Periodic Reevaluation.   The complicated nature of the research process makes it essential that individual research projects be reevaluated at appropriate intervals. How often that will be depends on the nature of the particular research and when points of reevaluation can be meaningful. Normally, these points have been previously determined at the time the mission was defined and the project authorized. At these designated reevaluation points consideration must be given to costs expended, results achieved, the estimated cost to complete, and the current expectations as to final benefits. Participating in the reevaluation should be both the representatives of the research group and the persons who took part in the original project decisions. The conclusions may be to cut back the project, to continue it as it is, to make modifications, or to expand the project. If in the latter case new funds are required, these needs will again have to be subject to the same considerations as were discussed in connection with the earlier definition of mission. New authorizations will have to be subject to the same kind of original approval requirements.

The foregoing periodic reevaluation is basic to the effective control of a research activity. It is important first, that a reasonable plan of such periodic reevaluations be set up, and second, that they be carried out in accordance with the plan and on a comprehensive basis. It is also desirable that *all* projects be reviewed at a given point in time—monthly, quarterly, or at least annually—to be sure that no projects are overlooked. It is recognized that the precise scope of individual projects sometimes overlaps, and also to have a continuing type of evolution, all of which complicates the administration of a project control effort. Nevertheless, the periodic reevaluation approach, coupled with the redefinition and amendment of projects, provides the most effective way possible to keep the research effort under reasonable and proper control.

Organizational Status of the Research Department

The size of the research department and the organizational status that is given to it in the total organization will depend directly on the kind of business in which the company is engaging, and how important the research function is to the success of the company. In a company whose products have a significant technological basis, the research activity will need to be given the same high-ranking organizational status as exists for the engineering department. Again this is necessary to be able to attract the right kind of research management and to enable it to interact with the other major operational and staff functions in an effective manner. Although the activities of the research department are closely related to the engineering department and to the production department, it is important that the research department be independent of both of them. The danger otherwise is that the research effort will be unduly diverted to deal with urgent operational problems. Although the separation of the research activities can be carried so far that it unduly insulates the research group, it is essential that it be able to operate in a detached manner, and be free from the pressures of the day-to-day regular operations.

The issue again arises as to the extent to which the research effort should be decentralized. Normally, the case is stronger for the centralized approach because as one moves backward from the operational level to more basic problems there is a more likely greater commonality in the research focus. It is then logical to exploit the economies of scale and to have a centralized research group serving all operational groups. The exception is where the company has operational components which are in a really different kind of business, and where those operational components are being operated on a decentralized basis in other major respects. This is the kind of situation that exists in the modern conglomerate. Here a centralized research group will be quite inappropriate. In intermediate types of situations there may also be some decentralization of the research activity, but in these situations there should at least be a protective functional type of control to avoid wasteful duplication of research efforts.

Special Management Problems

To a considerable extent the special managerial problems discussed in connection with the engineering activity are again applicable, but with variations in intensity. As to the degree of professionalism that exists on the part of research personnel, this problem will normally be of even greater magnitude. The more remote tie to actual operations also further weakens the company-loyalty dimension and pushes the individual into the more separate world of his profession. Similarly, the researcher will tend to become even more interested in the results of the research as an achievement of professional excellence and be less concerned with either the cost of that achievement or its ultimate potentials in a profit and loss sense. These tendencies further complicate the management problem. From a control standpoint the best solution appears to be a good underlying project authorization procedure with supporting cost reports, combined with continuous interaction with responsible managers of the other company activities. This interaction can normally have the benefit first, of better assuring right directions for the research effort, and second in securing a better kind of commitment from the research personnel. It is also most important that the support of this collaborative effort come from the top executive himself.

Organizational Approach.   The nature of the research operations has an interesting and important impact on the internal organizational structure of the research department. The special problem here is to exploit the benefits of normal-type organizational structure in the way of assigning work responsibilities, but at the same time to protect as much as possible the basic creativity and productivity of the individual researcher. On the creativity side there is the special need to have more than the usual degree of independence for the researcher, and to free him from as much administrative work as possible. As to productivity, there is the need to recognize that work assignments may revolve to a greater extent around the work focus of the individual project. The result is that the research activities frequently do not fit nicely into traditional organizational structure. The important thing here is to be aware of the special needs and to find the right balance between the completely structured and completely unstructured types of organizational approach.

Role of the Internal Auditor in Research

In many respects the review of the research activity offers some of the greatest potential rewards in a very real operational auditing sense. At the lowest level the internal auditor can ascertain compliance with stated operational procedures. These will normally include the authorization of research projects and the accuracy of the cost records and reports that cover the work implementation. At the next level it is also possible to appraise the level of administrative efficiency in terms of the way people are going about their jobs. At a still higher level it is possible to determine the extent of collaboration with responsible people outside the research department, and to appraise the tangible results of that collaboration in the form of curtailment, modification, or expansion of specific projects. At the highest level it is possible to evaluate to a reasonable extent the total research effort on the basis of what it has cost and what it has produced. The latter would include new products, improvement in existing products, and improvement in various aspects of the projection process. The achievement of these contribution efforts is obviously not easy, but they can be accomplished to a major extent by the internal auditor without his being a technically trained engineer or scientist.

AUDIT GUIDES

RESEARCH ACTIVITIES

I. Introductory
   A. Reference should be made to the general discussion of audit guides, Chapter 13.
   B. Because of the interrelationships with production and engineering activities, reference should also be made to the audit guides for those sections.

II. Preparatory
   A. See standard Audit Guides, Chapter 13.

III. Organizational Factors
   A. See standard Audit Guides, Chapter 13.
   B. Matters of special interest in the review of manuals will include:
      1. Organization and objectives.
      2. Manner of receiving authorized work projects.
      3. Preparation of budgets and budgetary control.
      4. Assignment and scheduling of work.
      5. Operational reports.
      6. Manner of releasing research results.
      7. Security.
      8. Relations with other company activities.
      9. Personnel control.
      10. Records to be maintained.

IV. Operations
   A. Planning
      1. Review and appraise the basis of the planning effort:
         a. As to adequacy of collaboration with other concerned company activities.
         b. As to initiation of projects within the department.

    2. How adequately are plans translated into operations:
       a. As to personnel?
       b. As to other requirements?
       c. As to costs?
    3. How adequate is the departmental program for reviewing overall performance against plans:
       a. As to costs incurred?
       b. As to results accomplished?

B. Input of Work Assignments
    1. What approvals are required:
       a. From personnel of research department?
       b. From persons outside the department?
    2. Is the supporting documentation adequate:
       a. As to feasibility?
       b. As to cost estimates?
       c. As to value of ultimate benefits?
    3. Is there adequate collaboration between departmental personnel and concerned persons outside the research department?
    4. Are cost estimates made?
    5. Are points set for periodic reappraisal by the approving group?

C. Assignment of Work
    1. Are projects broken down adequately as to feasible work assignments?
    2. Is the internal organizational structure sufficiently well adapted to project requirements?
    3. Are instructions adequately transmitted to personnel receiving assignments?
    4. Are time and cost estimates assigned to these personnel?
    5. Is adequate provision made for needed coordination both within the department and with other company activities?

D. Interim Administration of Work Assignments
    1. How adequate is day-to-day supervision?
    2. Are work habits reasonable?
    3. Are there adequate periodic progress reports covering work assignments, including time charged to individual projects, costs incurred to date, extent of results achieved, and evaluation of costs and probabilities of completion?
    4. Is coordination adequate:
       a. Within the department?
       b. With other concerned activities?
    5. Are work conditions adequate as to space, special facilities, needed equipment, and freedom from confusion?
    6. Are project records adequate, and are they adequately maintained?
    7. Are supporting services adequate?

8. Are designated periodic reevaluations carried out as scheduled, and on a comprehensive basis?
9. How adequate are the controls over personnel scheduling and utilization?

E. Completion and Release of Research Results
1. How are research findings communicated to concerned company groups, and is the procedure adequate?
2. In the case of partial findings, how are original projects handled as to redefinition, modification, or replacement by new projects? Is this procedure adequate?
3. Are completed projects closed, including records, handling in regular reports, and evaluation of results?
4. To what extent are there research projects which are to continue indefinitely? How is control achieved for these projects, and how adequately?
5. Is desirability of patent coverage adequately explored and implemented?

F. General
1. What is the scope of the security program? Is it adequate?
2. Are agreements in force for establishing company rights to all research results?

V. Audit Tests
A. Test a representative number of individual research projects:
1. For compliance with established procedures and policies.
2. As a basis for evaluating the adequacy of the applicable policies and procedures.

B. Examine departmental budgets and related reporting for adequacy of:
1. Bases of development of budget.
2. Current performance levels.
3. Analysis of deviations.
4. Evidence of corrective action.

C. Determine via discussions with representative company users what problems are thought to exist in getting more help from the research department, and what the best means of dealing with those problems might be.

VI–IX. Not used.

X. Overall Appraisal of Effectiveness of Research Activities
A. See standard Audit Guides, Chapter 13.
B. How do total research costs compare with other competitive companies on the basis of results achieved?
C. Are results of applied research compared periodically with objectives, and plans revised as needed?

ILLUSTRATIVE AUDIT FINDINGS: QUALITY CONTROL, ENGINEERING, AND RESEARCH

Excessive Sampling

A review of the statistical sampling plan used for testing the quality of instruments made in a plant indicated that the sample sizes were excessive. Sampling plans were not updated to reflect improvements in production techniques. Also, sample sizes were increased for larger universes without justification. As a result, in one quality control test a sample of 2000 was being used when 500 would have been sufficient. In addition, plants were inconsistent as to methods of determining sample sizes, resulting in oversampling for three production items and undersampling for one.

Correction of Defects

Insufficient analysis was being made of the causes of defects found during quality testing. As a result, the number of defects in five of the items tested continued at high levels without correction. As a result of the auditor's recommendations, a study was made of the causes of the defects. It was found that additional coordination was needed between the quality control department and production. Improvements were also needed in engineering design.

Deficiencies in Engineering Design

A review of change orders on the manufacture and installation of new production equipment indicated that the contractor was being awarded additional amounts for overruns that were caused by design deficiencies. One change order for $175,000 had the explanation "unforeseen requirements." A review of the correspondence file showed that the overrum had been caused by faulty engineering design that had not been corrected.

Utilization of Research Personnel

Improvement was needed in planning the utilization of research personnel under conditions of fluctuating work loads. During February there was a loss of a large government research contract, resulting in an excess of personnel until additional research contracts were awarded. Additional planning and coordination would have prevented idle item through use of personnel on company-sponsored research of a current or long-range nature.

Erroneous Charges to Research Projects

Salary costs of research personnel were being charged to projects on a funds available basis rather than on a work-load assignments basis. Project directors justified the practice in view of the similarity of research objectives of some projects. A test of salaries charged to selected research projects indicated that $135,000 was charged to projects that were dissimilar in nature. Further analysis showed that the inappropriate charges were made because of overruns on other projects. As a result, unauthorized research effort was expanded on some projects, whereas insufficient research was expended on other projects because of the nonavailability of funds.

CHAPTER EIGHTEEN

Facilities

NATURE OF THE FACILITIES PROCESS

An important group of operational activities is concerned with facilities. At the highest level these operational activities have to do with the managerial decisions covering the commitment of company capital for facility purposes. At the lower level they involve the day-to-day care and utilization of individual pieces of equipment. The relationship of these operational activities is in some respects closer than usual to the later financial audit problem. At this point, however, our focus is on how the operational activities pertaining to facilities can be handled to serve best the total interests of management.

The processes relating to facilities combine physical and financial considerations in a closely interrelated fashion. In a physical sense the facility process involves the use of tangible assets for the support of the daily operations of the company. These tangible assets include land, buildings, machines, equipment, tools, and furniture. These facilities provide a range of services that deal with the housing of operations, the direct production of goods and services, and supporting the operations in a great variety of ways. A key interest here is to make sure that the facilities actually provide these services effectively in a physical manner. The other dimension of the facilities problem has to do with the financial aspects. Typical concerns are whether the facilities represent the best possible use of company capital, whether the facilities are provided at the lowest possible cost, and whether they are utilized in a manner that results in maximum profitability for the company. Supplementary financial problems involve the accounting for the facility-type assets and the allocation of facility costs to operational periods as depreciation expense. The physical and financial objectives obviously overlap but are nevertheless recognizable dual aspects of the problem of effectively controlling the facilities processes.

Importance of the Facilities Process

The special importance of the facilities process is the result of the special character of facility expenditures. In most company situations a major portion of the expenditures is made for facility purposes. Consequently, it is very important that these large expenditures are made wisely. This is especially important also because expenditures currently made will very often not be recovered for a long period of time. The assets acquired will be with the company for many years, and during that time there will be relatively little one can do about making major changes. Because the physical facilities also represent so much investment, there is the further importance of providing adequate physical care and control. There is the very practical need that the company obtain all of the services from the facilities that were intended. Finally, the large investments, which have to be spread over the time periods and then to the various types of operational activities, mean that they have an important impact on operational profitability, and in turn on all related operational decisions.

Control Cycle for Facility Activities

It is again useful to view the facilities process in terms of the individual steps in its total cycle. The individual steps can then again be the basis for our examination of the problem of achieving effective control over the related operational activities. They are as follows:

1. The determination and initial justification of the need for facilities, as made by the operational groups with primary responsibility.
2. The analysis and appraisal by higher management of the merits of the facilities proposal, with the resulting approval or rejection.
3. The actual acquisition of the approved facilities, including the final acceptance of them.
4. Administering the facilities during their productive life.
5. Effecting the final retirement or other disposition of the facilities.
6. The post-review at some point in time of the facilities utilization to appraise the adequacy of the results achieved.

We will discuss this control cycle in terms of a major capital project.

Determination of Needs. The first step in the process is that a particular operational or larger management group comes to the conclusion that their operational needs will be better served through the acquisition of certain facilities. The purpose may be to make possible the manufacture of new products or to improve the manufacture of current products. The purpose may be to increase capacity, improve the quality of production, or facilitate other aspects of the operational activities. At this point the case must be established for the acquisition action through a careful study of all of the related factors, with the documented support emerging in the form of a facilities proposal, often referred to as a facilities or capital project. The points covered in such a proposal normally include:

1. Description of the proposed facilities and the purpose for which they are to be acquired.

2. The estimated cost of the proposed facilities in reasonable detail.

3. The timing of the acquisition and the estimates of costs to be incurred over the months and years involved.

4. The extent to which the proposed capital expenditures are within an already approved capital budget.

5. The extent to which presently existing facilities are affected in terms of both physical factors and undepreciated account balances.

6. The economic justification for the proposed capital expenditures in terms of costs, anticipated revenue, and ultimate profitability. Included here also would be comparisons with continuing present facilities, if any, and alternative types of facilities that were considered.

7. The cash flow estimates during the total period of acquisition and service.

8. If a supplement to a previous project, the reasons for the need for the supplement, and the effect on previous projections of profitability.

9. Approvals of local management personnel.

Projects will of course be prepared in the form specifically designated by the particular company and will include supporting analysis in accordance with applicable company procedures and policies. Normally, the company central group having either direct or functional responsibility for facilities matters will have worked with the local group in preparing the project proposal. In addition, there may have been some preliminary coordination with higher-level management personnel.

The control considerations at this stage are first, that the stated company requirements have been complied with properly, in terms of both technical compliance and quality of actual implementation. A second interest goes beyond this phase and includes the appraisal of the overall adequacy of the existing policies and procedures. Possible improvements may be perceived in the way of providing additional information that will be needed in the later review stages; or there may be better ways of handling individual aspects of the project proposal.

Higher-Level Review and Approval. The project proposal now moves to higher management levels. The levels involved will depend on the size of the particular company and the size of the project, but ultimately there will be the review by a senior management committee, the approval by an authorized company executive, and possibly the review and approval by the board of directors. The review and approval process covers the detailed examination and evaluation of the proposed capital expenditure. The primary basis for this review will be the documentation submitted, but other available knowledge will be utilized, including especially the experience and judgment of higher-level operational and staff executives. The impact on other company activities and objectives will also need to be taken into consideration. The total review normally includes:

1. *Total Resources Potentially Available for Capital Expansion.* This is not an exact figure but covers a general range of dollars. It reflects the consideration of two factors: (a) the amount of debt or equity capital which the company can reasonably be expected to be able to raise under current conditions, and (b) the attitude of the company as to how much risk it wishes to assume in the way of capital investment. The risk aspect also includes the scope of the commitment for debt service, if the resources are to be provided through debt.

2. *Company Strategy.* The degree of support for capital expansion depends on the extent to which the proposed investment supports the strategic plans of the company. Although these strategic plans may change over time, they exist in some form at a particular point in time, and facility proposals are either consistent or not consistent with those strategic plans.

3. *Projected Profitability of the Particular Project.* The project documentation, as we saw previously, already includes the projected costs and revenues that have been developed to establish the estimated profitability of the proposed capital expenditure. Now these cost and revenue data are subjected to review and analysis to further appraise their validity. At the same time consideration must be given to discounting the various cost and revenue factors so that their timing can be properly taken into consideration. This is necessary because we cannot offset a dollar expended now with a dollar of revenue in the future without adjusting those dollars to the same period of time through discounting the future revenue dollars at a proper interest rate.

4. *Acceptability of the Rate of Return.* Each company has a cost of capital that is based on the cost of debt plus the cost of equity capital, as determined by the market evaluation of the company's capital stock. The rate of return should at least match the "cost of capital" rate if the new investment is to be a wise use of capital.

5. *Judgment Factors.* In addition to the foregoing financial analysis there is always properly the independent judgment by management as to the desirability of the proposed capital expenditure. This independent judgment reflects the experience and other perceptions of the management, and it supplements and goes beyond the basic supporting analysis.

6. *Assessment of Priorities.* Every capital project necessarily competes with other capital projects for final approval. Although a particular company may appear to have plenty of funds available for investment, there are always alternative ways to utilize the company's resources. The objective is to find the investments that best serve the company's interests. The evaluation of the merits of each facilities proposal, therefore, reflects that final assessment of priorities.

From a control standpoint the key considerations are first, that an adequate set of policies and procedures exist for the higher level review and approval of capital projects, along the lines just outlined. Second, it is necessary that the company make these policies and procesures effective in actual practice through a careful and rigorous review effort.

Acquisition of Facilities.   Assuming that the project has been approved by the proper levels of authority, the next stage is to acquire the facilities covered by the project. Acquisition can be accomplished in various ways—by purchase, lease, company construction, or by any combination of these three approaches. If purchased, the purchasing department may handle the entire acquisition —although with appropriate coordination with other company personnel—or it may only handle specific portions. When facilities such as buildings are to be acquired, the acquisition will normally be handled by specially created facility construction groups. The price paid for the acquisition may be a standard figure, be the result of direct negotiation, or be based on actual cost. These alternative approaches were discussed briefly in connection with purchasing. Since the facility acquisitions can involve so much money, the particular approach adopted is all the more important. We come back to this problem later in the chapter and deal with it in greater depth.

Facilities can also be leased. The advantages achieved through this particular approach include the lower capital requirements and the greater possibilities of accelerating and maximizing the tax deductibility of the current expenditures. The determination to utilize this approach requires very careful analysis and consideration of all related factors. It requires also that competent legal assistance be available to cover properly the different conditions that have to be dealt with in protecting the company's interest.

Finally, there is the possibility that the company may deem it best to construct the particular facilities with its own personnel. In such situations, the complexity of the particular acquisitions will determine whether the work is done by a regularly established operational activity, or whether a special group is created for this single purpose. Where buildings are constructed by a special in-house group, the administration of the activity will involve many of the same types of problems as exist in the regular purchasing department. Normally, when a company does its own construction it will still purchase many items, use a number of subcontractors, and lease various types of supporting equipment. The construction decision is, therefore, not the normal all-or-nothing type of determination, but rather a composite of different combinations of internal and external operations. The key decision is more one of which party shall have the responsibility for the supervision and resulting cost of particular areas of the total construction project. Certain portions of the construction may be subcontracted—as, for example plumbing, electrical work, cement work, and the like—or a general contractor will be sought who may do portions himself and subcontract others.

Control Aspects of Acquisition.   From a control standpoint the first interest is that the mode of acquisition has been determined on the basis of adequate consideration of the various available alternatives. the factors to be taken into account include:

1. Skills available in the company.
2. Ability to secure such supporting personnel as may be needed.
3. Timing requirements.
4. Level of estimated cost efficiency.
5. Impact on other company operations.
6. Extent of competition between outside contractors.

The second interest is that the particular outside source selected is both capable and reliable, and that the basis of compensation is reasonable. These considerations are particularly important because the recourse of sending back an unacceptable product is not enough protection in the case of many facility acquisitions. In such situations company operational schedules and commitments to its own customers may depend directly on the performance of the supplying contractor.

A third interest centers about the control over the progress of the project, both from timing and cost standpoints. Specific control machinery is needed to monitor all projects so that delays in scheduled completion and cost overruns can be detected promptly, thus providing a better opportunity for needed corrective action. Where costs are exceeding estimates by more than acceptable limits (usually fixed at from 5 to 10% of original estimates) there will be the need for a supplementary project. This provides an important control in that the reasons for the cost overrun will have to be documented, and an opportunity is thus provided to appraise the extent to which the extra cost was due to faulty performance.

Testing and Acceptance. The facility acquired may be of such a nature that the acceptance of it is no more complicated than for any regularly purchased item. In other cases, however, the facility may require extensive examination and testing to determine its acceptability. These activities may also be required at interim stages, as well as for the final completed project. They represent important steps in the determination of where the supplying contractor's responsibilities end and as to when compensation for work done will be forthcoming. These steps will, therefore, normally be defined with great precision. From a control standpoint there is first, the need that the terms of acceptance be clearly defined in advance. The second requirement is that the designated steps be carried out properly. The testing must be done in the manner specified, with appropriate care, and be evidenced by appropriate approvals or other documentaton. If there are any qualifications these also can be extremely important in the event of any subsequent malperformance and the related collection of damages.

Administering the Facilities. Once the facility has been accepted, the company has the ongoing responsibility for the care of the asset. There is at the same time the broader managerial responsibility to get the maximum value from the facility. As we noted earlier, this requires coverage of both physical and accounting matters. The administration problems normally include:

1. Providing adequate housing facilities for the types of assets that need to be kept indoors.
2. Protection from physical forces—weather, water, humidity, excessive heat or cold, dust, and the like.
3. Adequate security from theft.
4. Maintenance of appropriate insurance coverage.
5. Safety protection for employees.
6. Fire protection.
7. Adequate maintenance and repair.
8. Unit records for control purposes—location, availability, maintenance requirements, and the like.
9. Established accountability to persons or organizational components.
10. Supporting accounting records for depreciation and related cost accounting systems.

These administrative matters extend into the broader problems of operational care and control discussed in greater detail later in this chapter.

Retirement of Facilities. Although some types of facilities go on indefinitely—as, for example, land—in most cases there comes a time when the particular facility is worn out, needs to be replaced, or to be modified substantially for some other reason. At this stage there is some kind of managerial determination that the company interests will be better served if the existing facility is partially or completely retired. This can be a very simple and clean-cut type of action or a very complicated one. An individual small machine may be removed and then junked or sold. At the other extreme, a building may be remodeled. In general, however, certain types of activity are involved, with varying degrees of complexity, depending on the particular facility item. These are:

1. *Managerial Determination That the Particular Item Should Be Retired.* At this point a judgment is reached that the costs are no longer justified by the benefits being received. This determination is often made as a part of the decision to acquire a new facility.
2. *Related Determination of What Is to Be Done with the Old Facility.* This is the necessary decision as to whether the facility will be transferred to another company location, put in stores, be junked, be sold as a used item, or be somehow incorporated in the construction of the new asset. Again this decision may also often be made as a part of the new facility proposal.

3. *Physical Implementation of the Retirement.* The particular facility is now actually taken out of service, and transferred to the predetermined location for other use or disposition. If within the jurisdiction of the scrap department it will be put in the hands of that department. Or the disposition may be so important or so unique that it is handled in a special manner.

4. *Accounting Implementation of the Retirement.* At this stage also all current records must reflect the fact of the retirement. Unit records need to be adjusted so that accountabilities are properly relieved. Similarly, the more formal accounting records must be adjusted to reflect the retirement.

From a control standpoint the first interest is that retirements are made in accordance with adequate authority, as evidenced by an established policy or based on a proper management decision. We do not want physical retirements without the proper authority; nor do we want the authorized physical retirement to be overlooked. The second interest that then follows is that the retirement is made properly in both a physical and accounting sense, based on adequate procedures and careful adherence to those procedures. There is always the concern that the company interests are maximized in every possible way.

Post-Review of Project Results. There is one final phase of the control cycle which has special importance in terms of management review and appraisal of previous experience. This consists of a reexamination of the individual facility acquisition to determine how the particular item did actually work out over its life span. At the time the facility was proposed with its supporting analysis there were expectations established for certain kinds of results. The question is now whether those expected results were actually realized, and to what extent. In making this determination two subsidiary questions are involved: (1) as to the point of time at which such a determination should be made, and (2) as to whether it is feasible to make such a determination at all. As to the former question, it must be recognized that partial results may be inconclusive. However, it will not be sufficient to wait many years until the asset is worn out. It can very well be that the general results can be reasonably appraised one or two years after the acquisition of the asset, depending on the particular asset and the original estimated timing of the expectations. A judgment must therefore be made as to what is a reasonable time for demonstrating that the new facility is going to produce results along the lines originally indicated.

As to the second question, there is always the problem of whether new developments since the date of the acquisition have significantly affected the outcome of the original plan. In many cases these subsequent developments substantially reduce the value of a post-review. But having recognized the limitations, there is still much that can be said in support of such a review. The major benefit is that everyone can learn from past experience whether any aspect of the total procedure can be improved. This is true especially with respect to the kind of analysis and supporting documentation that was developed. It can apply also to the manner in which projects are initiated, reviewed, and finally approved. The results of this feedback can then lead to modifications in the policies and procedures that will apply to future proposals. But there is a second benefit that is also very important in terms of more effective control. The benefit here is that the persons or organizational components which develop the proposal know that they will be subjected later to the post-review. This knowledge serves as a disciplinary motivation to be more thorough and objective in their initial support of the project. This is a most useful check on what is sometimes overenthusiasm for a desired facility, which can lead to proposers being too optimistic in the estimation of future expectations.

Facility Areas of Special Concern

Although the internal auditor has an important contribution to make at each stage of the facilities control process, the relative importance of his role will vary as between the individual stages. This is necessarily so because some of the activities described involve the most important management functions and responsibilities. In the case of major facility investment decisions the judgements and related actions are the highest-level kinds of top management responsibilities. There will also be major supporting staff roles in the areas of finance, marketing, and management sciences. In these situations the assistance of the internal auditor can be useful, but there are unavoidable practical limitations. However, major opportunities to assist management do exist in the administration and procedural support of these major magagement decisions. In subsequent portions of this chapter we deal with three of the supporting areas where the internal auditor can make an especially significant contribution. These are:

1. The control of cost-type construction activities.
2. The physical care and accountabilities for individual facility items.
3. The impact of facilities costs on operational responsibilities.

CONTROL OF COST-TYPE CONSTRUCTION ACTIVITIES

All facility acquisitions involve cost to the acquiring company. The question is how that cost is to be determined, and how that determination will best coincide with the company's interests. The range runs from the standard established price for a particular small tool to the construction of a building, where the company's cost is determined by the costs incurred by the contractor builder.

Two different types of questions are involved. The first of these is whether the particular set of arrangements was the best possible solution for the acquiring company in its effort to secure the facility it desires, and at a given time, a given place, and the lowest possible fair price. The second question is whether the costs have actually been incurred in accordance with the established arrangements and whether costs incurred are being used properly to suport the final determination of price. The latter question is one of typical audit verification of fact, but it includes whether reasonable value was obtained for the cost expenditure. In total the choice of the particular acquisition arrangements and the implementation of that choice is the management problem to be resolved. It is the type of problem where the internal auditor can be particularly helpful.

Types of Acquisition Arrangements

The varying extent to which supplier costs play a part in the determination of the acquiring company's costs can be illustrated by listing some of the typical types of acquisition arrangements.

1. *Standard Price.* Here the suppliers costs are not disclosed. The acquiring company makes its acquisition decision solely on the basis of whether the purchase at the standard price is in the best interests of the company. If there are alternative sources or substitute products available, the company may make its own analysis of value content, and this analysis to some extent involves estimates of what the supplier costs actually are.

2. *Negotiated Price.* When the acquiring company has sufficient bargaining strength, essentially because of other available alternatives, the price may be negotiated. In such a situation the costs of the supplier can play an important role. In some cases cost data may be supplied by the vendor. In other cases it will be estimated by the acquiring company.

3. *Lump Sum with Redetermination.* In certain situations it may be practicable to negotiate a tentative price for the facility item but to make this tentative price subject to redetermination at some later point of time. In such situations the acquiring company would normally have the right to review internal records of the supplier to verify or appraise the propriety of the cost data used for the redetermination, but the scope of this review will vary. The objective of this type of pricing arrangement is to preserve the incentive and overall benefit of a fixed-price arrangement, but to give consideration to the inadequacy of present knowledge as to what costs should be.

4. *Cost-type Contracts with a Percentage Fee.* The most extreme of the cost-type acquisition arrangements is that price will be determined on the basis of costs actually incurred by the supplier plus a profit that will be determined as a gives percentage of the total costs incurred. The supporting rationale is that costs cannot be determined in advance but must ultimately be fully recovered, and that the contractor needs to recover a profit that is related proportionately to the costs incurred. It is an arrangement that protects the supplier, but to the acquiring company it has the defect that it does not sufficiently assure effective motivation to control or reduce costs. In fact, the result may be just the opposite. Therefore, usually, it is employed only as a last resort.

5. *Cost-Type Contracts with Limitations.* A more highly regarded cost-type arrangement is where limitations are placed either on the costs incurred or the profit. One approach is to fix a maximum price that would be applicable if and when costs and agreed-upon profit exceed that maximum point. Another approach is to cover all costs but to provide for a fixed profit fee. These approaches provide better protection to the acquiring company but do not fully solve the problem of cost performance.

6. *Cost-Type Contracts with Incentives.* Still another approach in the effort to deal with the problem of motivating better cost performance is to set up incentives for either costs or profit, or in some combination. The arrangement may be for cost performance to be compared with previously established cost estimates, and then that either or both savings and cost overruns will be shared in a designated manner. Or the arrangement might cover the size of the fee depending on cost performance. The incentives may also be related to the extent to which the contractor completes his work in accordance with agreed-upon time schedules.

7. *Time and Material Contracts.* Other types of cost contracts may take the form of fixed rates for particular kinds of services, with final compensation depending on hours expended, plus supplementary material costs. The rates used may or may not include profit and overhead. These contracts are frequently used in connection with certain kinds of installation work, excavation, and grading.

Validation of Contractor Costs

As we have seen, the role of costs incurred by contractor suppliers varies greatly. It is clear, however, that increasing uncertainty as to what the final price should be leads to a greater dependence on contractor cost data. It follows also that as we depend more on contractor costs, the need increases for an assurance of the validity of those costs. The construction cost for a building facility is a common illustration of that kind of a situation. If, then, costs are to be the basis for compensation to the contractor, we need to look carefully at the various factors which determine that needed validity. These factors include the following:

1. *For What are the Costs Being Incurred?* The starting point is the identification of the specific facility items to be completed for the company. All costs incurred must ultimately be judged in terms of their relationship to that end product.

2. *What Services Are to Be Provided by the Company?* Individual items may be provided by either the contractor or the company, and therefore, what is to be done by each party needs to be clear. Examples would be testing of ground, building permits, licenses, and providing equipment. It may be that the company can supply certain kinds of equipment, material, or supporting services on a more economical basis than can the contractor.

3. *What Costs Are to Be Charged Directly to the Project?* Of central importance is the necessity of a clear understanding of what costs are to be charged directly to the contract. These would include labor, equipment, materials, and services that are acquired by the contractor directly for the project. These items should be at the actual net cost to the contractor, or in the case of contractor's own equipment, at prevailing market rates.

4. *What Costs Are to Be Reimbursed through Overhead?* There will be many kinds of cost for services performed by groups which are at the same time serving other contractor business. Also, certain kinds of costs incurred by the contractor—as, for example, corporate taxes—are normally considered to be recovered through the profit fee. Quite clearly an agreement is needed as to just where the line is to be drawn, and what types of costs are not to be recoverable in any part through the cost reimbursement channel.

5. *How Shall Overhead Costs Be Allocated?* When the project needs are being served by a person or organizational component which is at the same time serving other company business, there is the difficult problem of determining a basis of allocation that is fair and equitable. Possibilities exist that the contractor may select bases that charge the contract unduly. There may also be a tendency for the contractor to shift the approach when conditions change so that recoveries will be maximized. Efforts may also be made to use improperly direct charge and overhead allocation approaches simultaneously for the same cost center.

6. *What Premium Costs Are Authorized?* In many situations there may be the question as to whether premium costs are justified. One common example of such costs would be higher cost types of transportation to accelerate delivery. Still another would be the use of overtime labor. The problem can arise because of noncontrollable developments and the resulting need to spend extra amounts to prevent possible future delays. On the other hand, the premium costs may be necessitated by contractor inefficiency and be made to avoid penalties for the delay of promised completion. The propriety of such payments must, therefore, be carefully established.

7. *Do Costs Reflect Adequate Levels of Prudence?* Implicit in all of the previously listed types of inquiry is the requirement that not only is the cost claimed an authorized type of recovery, but also that it is both an actual cost and has been incurred in accordance with a reasonable level of prudence. It is not intended that the contractor be reimbursed for his inefficiency or for his negligence. It is expected also that all aspects of the cost recovery effort will be in good-faith and with integrity.

Operational Problems of Controlling Costs

We turn now to the manner in which the review effort covering a construction program can best serve management interests. In a narrow sense the review effort will validate the cost that will become the basis for the determination of compensation in accordance with the terms of the contract. In a broader sense the review effort is concerned with making the construction program more efficient and taking the kinds of steps that will be reflected sooner or later in lower company costs. This review might be carried out in part by accounting personnel or entirely by the internal auditor. In any event the internal auditor will be interested directly or indirectly in all aspects of the review.

Precontract Participation.   In many situations a contract is finalized and work actually begun before the reviewer comes into the picture. By that time the opportunity has been lost to inject into that contract the conditions that would better define the relationships with the contractor. By that time, also, the most favorable opportunity has been lost to establish foundation understandings with the various interested parts of the contractor organization. In a more efficient situation the internal auditor participates in the development of the contract with its various stipulations as to the validity of costs. This is done in part before bids are solicited, so that the various bids will be on a comparable basis. The general bases of cost reimbursements are thus known to the contractor at a time when questions, if any, can be raised and clarified. In the case of a major project it will be desirable for a survey team (which should also include the internal auditor) to visit the favored contractor prior to the time an actual contract is finalized. This makes it possible to clarify any areas of misunderstanding and to develop more intelligently the contractual coverage. It also provides a good foundation understanding of the contractor's organization and mode of operation, which will then become useful in the later review of actual costs claimed. The importance of all of this precontract activity in assuring a more effective later review cannot be overemphasized.

Establishing Initial Relationships with Contractor.   The scope of the contractor's organizational setup will depend on the size of the contractor. Although there will necessarily be some kind of an office at the job site, the higher-level organization will vary. In some cases there may be just a contractor central office and in other cases an intermediate field office. In any event the internal auditor will need to establish his relationship with the several offices very promptly after the signing of the contract. Building on the knowledge obtained from the earlier precontract survey, the objective now is to understand in still more depth the manner of operation, and to take any steps possible to achieve both a clear identification of applicable costs, and the highest possible level of administrative prudence. The early presence of the reviewer exercises a positive psychological motivation to contractor personnel. These initial relationships may serve also to identify areas where the company services could be utilized, and thus reduce the requirements on the contractor. Finally, all necessary arrangements can be made for the actual review of the various types of costs that are now about to be generated.

Labor Costs. Since a major portion of the costs incurred will relate to labor, a number of matters require careful attention. At the job site these include:

1. Reasonableness of manning levels.
2. Recruitment of right levels of skill.
3. Adequacy of work records.
4. Adequacy of supervision.
5. Control over absenteeism.
6. Accuracy of field payrolls.
7. Quality of work practices.
8. General order and efficiency.

At higher-level offices there will be similar problems of effective labor utilization, but more in the category of administrative supervision and control. At this higher level, control over what are proper direct charges and what are overhead allocations becomes especially important.

Material Costs. In most construction programs the efficient use of materials will be of great importance. The matters of special interest include:

1. Supporting documentation in the way of contractor's purchase orders, supplier's invoices, and receiving reports.
2. Reasonable evidence of propriety of quantities ordered.
3. Fairness of prices—including charges for materials transferred.
4. Reasonableness of standards of materials.
5. Prudent use of materials.
6. Adequacy of care of materials awaiting use for protection from weather and theft.
7. Purchase of materials that can be supplied at lower cost by the company.
8. Proper follow-up of claims against vendors.

Equipment Rentals. Necessary equipment—over and above that which is supplied by the company—is either rented by the contractor for use on the contract or provided directly by the contractor at agreed-upon rates. Items of special interest in this area include:

1. Supporting documentation in the form of rental agreements.
2. Determination that items included in the rental rate are not being charged as additional costs, as, for example, fuel and maintenance.
3. Whether there is excessive equipment, as judged by the amount of idle time.
4. Possibilities that company costs can be reduced through ownership of equipment.
5. Adequacy of protection of equipment from weather and theft.

Subcontractors.   In most cases the contractor will subcontract portions of the work, as, for example, electrical work, plumbing work, and the like. The expenditures in this form can be of major significance and therefore, require adequate standards of control on the part of the subcontractor. Here the same kinds of problems exist as were faced by the company when it made its arrangements with the contractor. What the company internal auditor is concerned with is that there is an adequate procedure for the solicitation of bids, the continuing appraisal in each case of the most appropriate type of acquisition arrangements, and then the review and appraisal of the actual operational implementation. In some cases the arrangements made will be subject to specific approval by the contractor and in those cases the reviewer will wish to determine whether these requirements are being complied with.

Other Costs.   To the extent that there are other costs charged at the job site, these costs will be reviewed for their propriety both as to type of cost and whether the levels of expenditure reflect adequate prudence. Costs generated at intermediate field offices or at the contractor's home office will also be reviewed most carefully. The items charged here involve the often difficult determinations of whether the charges are proper on a direct charge basis or as an allocation of overhead. In all cases also there is the concern as to whether the levels of expenditure are reasonable. More intensive reviews in this area are desirable to identify any controversial issues so that they can be resolved as quickly as possible.

Project Administration.   Although the examination of the foregoing types of cost will already have indicated to a great extent the overall level of efficiency with which the construction contract is being administered, the internal auditor will also be looking at the contract administration in a total sense. His interest here is to determine what additional steps might be taken to benefit the company. The benefits here include the possible reduction of current costs charged to the contract. But they include also the quality of the construction effort, how the quality level might be improved at reasonable cost levels, and greater service capabilities at the time of completion. Normally, other company representatives will be charged with the primary responsibility for these operational activities, but the internal auditor can frequently provide additional assistance as a result of his more specifically assigned responsibilities. In this effort he should, of course, work closely with the responsible company representatives.

Control of Change Orders.   The desire to improve the facility will in many cases lead to the authorization of change orders covering some aspect of the existing construction specifications. These changes may or may not involve significant costs. In any event, the decisions to make the changes are new contractual commitments that modify the existing contract. They, therefore, need to be handled with care and supported by the properly authorized level of approval. Where changes involve the loss of value of previous work, the decision to make the change requires special consideration of those facts. The reduction or expansion of the scope of the work can at the same time affect maximum contract limits and orginally agreed upon incentive rights. These aspects also must be carefully considered. Finally, an adequate procedure is needed to communicate and implement the changes so that the proper adjustments can be made to scheduled procurements of labor, materials, and equipment.

Winding Up the Contract. The completion of the contract at the earliest possible date will usually be desired by the company. The contractor may or may not be similarly motivated, depending on whether incentive provisions are applicable, or whether personnel are needed elsewhere. In some cases, however, there can be delays in the final windup that require special pressures on the contractor by the company. When the construction is actually brought to completion and the company has determined that it can accept the facility, the major operational problem is to be certain that all items which can be returned are so handled, and that proper credits have been made to the contract. At the same time, contractor-owned equipment needs to be removed and the premises cleaned up in an adequate manner. Finally, there is the necessity of a careful determination that the facility is complete in terms of the agreed-ıpon specifications.

OPERATIONAL CARE AND CONTROL OF FACILITIES

Because facilities in the aggregate represent such a concentration of investment, it is important that they be cared for in accordance with proper standards, and that they be adequately controlled in an operational sense. The purpose of this section is to deal with these aspects in greater detail. The problems of both care and control will obviously vary greatly as we consider the spectrum of types of facilities, ranging from a simple small tool to a major building facility, and considering their different kinds of characteristics and various dollar values. But there are some common features that serve as convenient references points. There is first, the need that individual groups of facilities have the proper type of physical care. Secondly there is the need for adequate control as to accountability. Third, there is the ever-present need that facilities are being utilized in a reasonable manner. We will look briefly at these key concerns that apply to some extent to all types of facility items.

Physical Care of Facilities

The problems of physical care tend to group themselves as those involving security and those of protecting physical usability. In the first category we have the situations where individual facility items can be stolen, used in an unauthorized manner, or physically damaged. The problems will vary and the appropriate safeguards must be tailored to the individual situation. Thus small tools will usually need to be kept in locked areas so that they will not be stolen or taken for use in an unauthorized manner. In other cases the equipment may be so valuable that protection is needed against a person who may damage it by not being sufficiently trained. In still another situation the problem may be one of sabotage, as might be true in the case of computer facilities or highly automated processing equipment. The attack on these problems will normally involve locked internal areas, rules for removal and/or use of the individual items, and the use of specially designated security personnel. Measures taken in individual internal situations tend to merge into larger situations and eventually into the total plant security programs. Problems of protection will always exist as long as there are human beings, with their weaknesses for misappropriation and urge to do what seems at the particular moment to be expedient. And now, in a more restless world, there is the increasing risk of deliberate sabotage. The practical question that comes through in all of these situations is to take such protective actions as are reasonable in terms of the costs of those protective actions in relation to the risks involved and their probabilities. The second concern is that the measures provided are carried out in the intended manner. It is an important part of the internal auditor's role to appraise both of these dimensions of the security problem.

Problems of Usability. The second group of physical care problems center more around assuring the proper usability of the particular facilities. The problems in this group also tend to break down further into (1) the protection from deterioration through improper exposure, and (2) the protection of operational efficiency through repair and maintenance—although these two types of problems often overlap. The first type of problem is quite often the one that is fairly obvious. The problem may be as simple as providing protection to equipment from rain or snow. Or it may be a type of deterioration that is not so outwardly visible, as, for example, the storage of machine tools without proper protective greasing. But even though the problem is usually more visible and better understood, there are still many situations where the proper measures are not taken.

The problem of repair and maintenance was touched on earlier in connection with the discussion of production activities. What was said there is also generally applicable to all company facilities. It has been repeatedly demonstrated that expenditures made to keep all types of facilities in proper condition, if done on a prudent basis, can avoid heavier repair expenditures at later points of time. The regular painting of buildings is illustrative. Similarly, the proper maintenance of operating equipment can prevent more serious breakdowns. The key here is to recognize the problem as it exists for individual types of facilities, and to develop systematic plans and procedures for carrying out the protective programs. Again the internal auditor can make an important contribution by identifying such situations where this is not being done.

Accountabilities for Facilities

The value of the various facilities items and the fact that there is in many cases a great deal of mobility makes it important that the responsibility be adequately fixed for the custody of individual items. This assignment of responsibility may be to a particular person: for example, an automobile to a salesperson or to an organizational unit. To a major extent this establishes the accountability of the individual or organizational group for the particular facility item, with the related responsibility of caring for and protecting that asset. At the same time the central accounting group has certain needs related to its administration of company financial statements. For the latter purposes the investments in fixed assets must be initially recorded and subsequently adjusted. Depreciation must also be calculated for determining reserves for depreciation. In both cases also the internal financial reports must reflect the responsibilities of organizational components for asset productivity and related depreciation expense. These higher-level financial needs, together with the needs for operational account-ability, combine to require the development of basic procedures for the iden-tification and control of individual facility items.

Property Records. At the time facilities are acquired, individual items should be identified by affixing some kind of a brass tag or decal which will carry the company's name and an assigned number. What an individual "item" should be is normally determined by the expectation of transferring or retiring that particular item. Thus a machine tool would have an assigned number, but major attachments might have separate numbers. At the same time a record card or sheet is established describing the particular item, the date acquired, its source, its cost, and its organizational location. In many cases computers can be ad-vantageously utilized for this purpose. The unit record is actually a subsidiary ledger of the controlling accounts of the general accounting system. At the same time, however, it will provide the initial basis for fixing day-to-day ac-countability. The term "initial" is used because this record may be supple-mented by additional records at the field location to control changing account-abilities within the jurisdiction of the responsible organizational unit. It should be noted also that the basic property records described will apply only to items capitalized, that is, charged to fixed asset accounts. All companies necessarily establish a minimum limit for items to be capitalized to avoid cluttering up the property records with items of very small value. Items not so capitalized are charged directly to expense. However, again supplementary records at the field level may be utilized to establish day-to-day accountability for these expensed items, depending on the need.

The basic property records established through acquisitions must subse-quently be adjusted as changes take place. These changes take the form of either a transfer to a different assigned organizational location, a further increase in the capitalization through an expansion or improvement of the original item, or through a retirement. A special problem here is that changes in location and retirement must be reported promptly and accurately if the records are to be reliable and up to date. To a major extent these changes are reported as part of new capital expenditures, since such other changes are often directly related to the new acquisition, but in all cases a properly designed and properly enforced set of policies and procedures is required to achieve complete coverage. Similarly, location-type supplementary records need also to be kept up to date if they are to achieve adequately their intended purpose.

Verification and Appraisal of Property Records. An important means of determining how well the system of basic property records is actually working is to carry out an independent verification of them through a physical inventory. This is an activity that can be carried out by any independent group, but usually is also done by the internal auditor. Through such an inventory the accuracy of the individual unit records will be established, and differences found can be used as a basis for making appropriate corrections. The differences will be either of the type where the record has not been adjusted properly for an actual transaction, or of the type where the facility item is actually missing. The former situation would exist where a particular facility item has been transferred to another location, or retired, without appropriate notification to the central records group. New acquisitions can also be in error, but this type of development is more unlikely since there was a direct expenditure used as a basis of creating the supporting property record. Or the item may be missing and no trace can be found of its whereabouts, in which case the item must be written off as a loss, subject to accumulated depreciation. But the differences developed have an importance that goes beyond the correction of the records. These differences provide the basis for probing for the underlying causes of the shortage. Does the reporting procedure in a design sense need strengthening at some point? Or is the cause a lack of proper supervision of personnel who failed to report the physical transaction?

Another important benefit derived from the physical inventory is that the internal auditor has an excellent opportunity to learn a great many useful things about the efficiency with which various facilities are being handled. He can observe, for example, how effectively individual items are being cared for and actually utilized. He will also be led to items which are idle and possibly stored away from normal operational activities. This will set the stage for determining whether the facilities are surplus or possibly obsolete. Thus the physical verification automatically provides the basis of a good appraisal of both the property records system and other broader operational practices.

Loaned Property

We have in the previous discussion assumed that all company property for which the operational component is responsible was physically at the particular location. This may not be true, as in the case where property is loaned to customers or to suppliers. In such situations there is the added complexity of controlling the property at the distant location. What needs to be clear is that the customer or supplier accepts full responsibility for the care and custody of the loaned item. Added procedural controls are also necessary to ensure that the item is returned when the purpose of the usage has been completed. At that time also a determination needs to be made as to whether any special claims are warranted. In some cases there may be rental rates established, or the benefits to the company may accrue in other specified manners. During the interim there may be some type of verification by the company organizational component involved, and the internal auditor will determine the necessity and practicability of making his own verification. It should also be added that facility items may be at company locations but owned by other parties. Here the conditions are exactly reversed. The internal auditor should review the particular arrangements and determine whether they were reasonable and whether the company is properly discharging its commitments.

IMPACT OF FACILITY ACTIVITIES ON MANAGEMENT

The management aspects of the activities pertaining to facilities have been identified to a considerable extent at various points in the previous discussion. Some further discussion is warranted, however, and it will be the purpose of this section to explore these management aspects in more detail. Facility activities, as we have seen, are particularly challenging because they involve such a wide range of management interests, extending into some of the most critical decision areas pertaining to asset utilization and forward investment.

Facilities as a Source of Operational Costs

The most immediate aspect of the facility activities is that they are an important basis of generating operating expense. This operational expense is a responsibility of the individual manager and of direct interest to him, both where his operating performance is being judged through expense budgets in relation to results produced and where he is being appraised on the basis of net profit achieved. The manager is, therefore, directly concerned with the operational costs pertaining to the facilities—as, for example, service costs, maintenance, and repairs. In many cases here he may have to balance short-run considerations against longer-run benefits, as in the case of preventive maintenance expenditures, but on an overall basis he is interested in keeping these costs at minimum levels consistent with results actually achieved in the way of services performed by the facilities. In this connection the manager is interested in depreciation approaches and methods of allocation, since depreciation expense is also a factor in the determination of the operational results. This situation prevails whenever a manager is evaluated on the basis of profit performance.

Facilities as an Investment Cost

When a manager is charged with profit and loss responsibilities he is also responsible for maintaining a satisfactory return on assets employed. In such a situation the facilities investment is in effect charged to him and that investment directly affects the level of his managerial performance. For this additional reason the manager has a direct interest in the facilities assigned to him and whether they best fit his needs in terms of ability to use the facilities productively. He is also very much interested in the basis on which those responsibilities are assigned to him, that is, on a cost basis, depreciated cost basis, or on some other basis. Thus from both an operational and investment standpoint the manager evaluates the suitability of existing facilities and studies the possibilities of getting operational results with fewer, more, or different types of facilities. Because of this managerial interest it follows that the internal auditor will seek to assist him in whatever way he can by thinking in the same terms.

Related Managerial Considerations

In the last analysis everything related to facilities comes down to costs and the related profitability in terms of results produced. There are some kinds of things, however, where the evaluation is more long term and sometimes more obscure than described above. To some extent also the facilities items takes us into the noneconomic areas of social responsibility. Illustrative would be the incorporation in facility specifications of protective features, even though at a higher cost. Another example would be a modern foundry with extra cost features solely to provide more pleasant working conditions. Still another example would be the construction of an especially fine office building to serve as a useful public relations image. These cases are mentioned to demonstrate the far-reaching managerial implications of facility decisions and activities. Again, because they are part of the managerial impact, the internal auditor is also interested in them.

Decisions in the Case of a New Facility

All of the managerial considerations ultimately come to focus on the question of whether the management interests would be better served if existing facilities of various types are either modified or replaced. The starting point for such determinations is first, the degree of assurance that existing facilities are being used in the most productive manner possible. This is a question that can never be answered precisely but one that can be answered within reasonable limits. The more difficult question has to do with what can be accomplished by modifying or replacing the facilities. The answer to this question involves a range of factors that are controllable in different degrees. Thus we can perhaps reasonably project the operational economies of a certain type of new facility. But the volume to achieve those economies may depend on market potentials that are much more difficult to predict. Involved also are the possibilities of new technological developments that may significantly affect the kind of facilities now best suited to the company's needs. There may be new materials or new processes. All this means that facility investment decisions become most critical as they bear on the future welfare of the company.

Role of the Internal Auditor in the Facilities Process

The various types of opportunities for the internal auditor have been noted at various points. These opportunities, as we have seen, range from the lowest-level type of operational activity to the most critical new facility determinations. As usual also, the opportunities include the determination of compliance with existing policies and procedures, the appraisal of the efficiency with which the policies and procedures are being implemented, and finally the questions of whether the policies and procedures might themselves be improved. There exists also in the case of facilities the special opportunity to contribute to the making of higher-level types of management determinations, that is, the determination of the directions of new facility investment. The internal auditor will be able to make his most immediate contribution in some of the more procedural and day-to-day operational areas. At the same time the internal auditor needs to be alert as to where he can contribute in the more significant policy and decision areas.

AUDIT GUIDES

REVIEW OF FACILITY ACTIVITIES

I. Introductory

    A. Reference should be made to the general discussion of audit guides, Chapter 13.

II. Preparatory

    A. See standard Audit Guides, Chapter 13.

    B. The role of central headquarters will normally have to do with the development of policies and procedures, plus the control of major decisions relating to the acquisition and disposal of facilities. Operational responsibilities will then normally be assigned to specific field locations.

III. Organizational Factors

    A. Organizational Relationships at the Central Headquarters

        1. How is the responsibility assigned organizationally for studying company facility needs?

            a. Is the responsibility of each manager sufficiently emphasized?

            b. Is adequate staff support provided?

        2. What organizational components are involved in the review and approval of facility projects?

            a. Are levels of approval responsibility reasonable?

            b. Is adequate coordination of all interested staff and line groups provided for?

        3. Where is the organizational responsibility assigned for the development of policies and procedures relating to facilities activities?

a. Is this at a sufficiently high level?

b. Is there adequate coordination with the assigned responsibility for facilities acquisition?

4. Is there a specially designated construction group?

a. Is it placed sufficiently high in the organizational structure?

b. Is its jurisdiction sufficiently clear?

5. Obtain and appraise all statements of mission, organizational purpose, and major policy relating to organizational assignments in the facilities activities area.

6. Who maintains basic unit property records?

a. Is the level in the organization sufficiently high?

b. Is there adequate coordination with:

1. General accounting group?

2. Persons where the property is located?

7. Review and appraise the adequacy of job descriptions relating to personnel charged with facility-type responsibilities.

8. Review and appraise the adequacy of manuals covering facility policies and procedures. Matters of special interest in addition to those already mentioned above would include:

a. Control of construction activities.

b. Receival and acceptance of facilities.

c. Authorizations and supporting procedures for transfer of facilities.

d. Authorizations and supporting procedures for retirement of facilities.

e. Protection and care of facilities.

f. Adjustments for missing items.

g. Depreciation policies and procedures.

9. Who is responsible for initiating and monitoring later evaluations of project results?

B. Organizational Relationships at the Field Location

1. Who is charged with assessment of facility needs?

a. Is the organizational level sufficiently high?

b. Is management at the location sufficiently involved?

2. Who is charged with the responsibility of administering facilities activities?

a. Is this organizational level sufficiently high?

b. If decentralized to other individuals, is that decentralization reasonable, and is the total effort adequately coordinated?

IV. Review and Approval of Capital Projects

A. Documentation of Projects

1. Review and appraise the manner in which capital projects originate and the care exercised in their preparation.

2. Is coordination with other company activities adequate during the preparation stage?

3. Review and appraise the completeness and adequacy of the supporting documentation.

B. Processing of Project for Final Approval

1. Is the scope of required supporting approvals adequate to assure adequate participation by company activities which have either a potential contribution to make or whose activity interests are affected?
2. Are higher-level reviews and approvals adequate in giving consideration to overall company interests?
3. Is there reasonable evidence that parties approving project are reviewing all aspects with care?
4. Is processing handled with reasonable dispatch?

C. Control of Project Implementation

1. Review and appraise procedures for reporting status of projects, with special focus on:
   a. Adherence to time schedules previously stipulated.
   b. Costs incurred in relation to stage of completion.
   c. Estimated costs to complete in relation to project authorizations.
2. Are reasonable requirements in force as to limits of overruns, and for submission of supplementary projects?
3. Are supplementary projects adequately documented, especially as to reasons for needed supplement?
4. Are supplementary projects subject to same review and approval procedures? If not, why not?

D. Post-Evaluation of Completed Projects

1. Are reviews being initiated as a regular procedure at a reasonably appropriate point of time?
2. Review and appraise the adequacy of the post-evaluation procedure.
3. Are the findings reasonably utilized:
   a. As a basis for manager evaluation, both for those who sponsored the project and those who were involved with it at later stages?
   b. To determine possible modifications in the policies and procedures for the development, review, and approval of projects?

V. Construction Activities

A. Precontract Coordination

1. How adequate is the determination of what portion of construction activities shall be done by outside contractors?
2. Are alternative contractor sources reasonably evaluated?
3. Is adequate consideration given to the alternative types of contracts that may be negotiated?
4. How adequate is the participation in the foregoing determinations by other company activities, including the internal auditor?

5. Review and appraise the adequacy of field visits and discussion with contractor as to scope of costing arrangements.

B. Contract Administration

1. Is adequate opportunity provided to finalize costing arrangements prior to the commencement of actual contractor activities?

2. Do current contract activities include:

   a. Conformance to previous agreements as to types of cost to be claimed and manner of actual determination?

   b. Relationship of costs to facilities to be provided as covered in the contract?

   c. Adequacy of procedures for selecting persons or subcontractors who provide service?

   d. Control of receipt of good and services for use on the contract?

   e. Adequacy of source documentation?

   f. Extent to which costs incurred indicate reasonable level of care exercised by source, and adequacy of value received?

   g. Extent to which claims or penalties need to be assessed against the contractor?

   h. Protection and physical care of materials, supplies, and partly completed work?

   i. That full credit has been received for materials, supplies, and equipment returned to contractor suppliers not actually needed for use on the project?

   j. Adequacy of control over change orders and conformance of contractor activities and costs claimed to contractual requirements?

VI. Care and Control of Facilities

A. Physical Protection and Care

1. Are the various types of facilities reasonably protected from deterioration to which they are subject, considering costs of providing such protection?

2. Is security adequate, with appropriate consideration to the risks involved for different kinds of facilities and costs involved?

B. Usability of Facilities

1. Are programs adequate to assure best possible operational use of various types of facilities:

   a. As to design of programs?

   b. As to extent programs are implemented with care, proper timing, and efficiency?

2. To what extent is there evidence of inadequate utilization of particular facility items:

   a. Buildings?

   b. Processing setups?

   c. Machine tools?

   d. Supporting equipment?

C. Accountabilities
    1. Are the various facility items tagged in an appropriate manner with brass plates or other number identification?
    2. Review and appraise the adequacy of the property records maintained for the various types of facility items.
    3. Are procedures adequate for the reporting of transfers and retirements?
    4. What procedures are in effect for the control of property loaned to outside parties? Are they adequate?
    5. Are property records verified at reasonable points of time through physical checks, carried out by independent parties?
    6. Are differences disclosed by physical inventories used:
        a. To properly adjust property records?
        b. To appraise weaknesses in the design and/or implementation of the policies and procedures appliable to facilities?

VII. Special Audit Tests
  A. Directly Assigned Audit Activities
    1. Cost-type acquisition contracts In this situation the internal auditor has very often been directly assigned the responsibility of verifying contractor costs as a basis for reimbursing the contractor. In this situation the internal auditing department has the supplementary responsibility of appraising the adequacy of its own basic auditing activities. This supplementary review should be by a separate internal component of the internal auditing department. If the prepayment audit activities are carried out by another company group, the internal auditor would make actual audit tests of these activities.
    2. Verification of property records through physical inventories. The same kind of situation applies here as discussed above.
  B. Other Audit Tests
    1. Select representative approved projects at various stages of implementation and check the individual actions taken at the various points as to compliance with established requirements, timing, and general level of quality.
    2. Select representative post-evaluation reports and verify bases for conclusions reached.

VIII. Appraisal of Effectiveness of Facilities Activities
  A. Scope and Quality Level of Policies and Procedures Relating to the Acquisition and Utilization of Facilities
    1. How adequately do policies emphasize the need for careful determination of needs?
    How adequately does the acquisition of facilities require coordination and approval in keeping with significance of the individual acquisition?

    3. Do the policies and procedures for care and control of assets have adequate scope?

B. Quality of Implementation
    1. To what extent do existing assets reflect effective implementation, as judged by productivity of facility items and their conditions?
    2. Are the number and magnitude of supplementary facility projects justified in terms of noncontrollable developments?
    3. What do the overall results of post-evaluation reports tell us?
    4. To what extent do inventory differences demonstrate inadequate attention to facility accountabilities?
    5. Are managerial responsibilities adequately related to facility matters?
    6. Are the various managerial implications of facility costs adequately understood and considered?

C. Effectiveness of Personnel
    1. Are the personnel assigned to various types of activities relating to facilities adequately qualified to discharge the assigned responsibilities?
    2. Is the supervision of personnel assigned to facility activities adequate?
    3. Are the various personnel discharging their responsibilities in an effective manner?

D General
    1. What major problems, if any, appear to exist for the company as respects the proper utilization of facilities? What should be the attack on these problems?
    2. What specific types of improvement seem to be indicated? What are the alternative ways in which this improvement might be achieved?

ILLUSTRATIVE AUDIT FINDINGS: FACILITIES

Purchasing Equipment Already Available

The internal auditor while reviewing the fixed asset accounts noticed purchases of large boilers previously physically observed as unused at one of the field locations. Inquiry disclosed the need for regular physical inventories of equipment and maintaining of unit records for review at time of new purchases.

Buying Equipment instead of Leasing

The company continued to lease items of equipment even though it was more economical to buy the equipment under options available in the lease agreements. It was found that four items of photocopying equipment and three word processors could be purchased at an annual net savings of $18,000.

Excess Number of Automobiles

It was noted that automobiles at the south plant were being underutilized for extended periods. Based on a study of mileage records and staff needs, it was recommended that three automobiles be transferred to the north plant and that one automobile be sold as excess.

Obsolete Facilities

The company had not taken action on facilities that were obsolete to production needs. Company files indicated that savings of $150,000 a year in production costs, as well as personnel and space costs, could be achieved over the next 20 years if facilities were modernized. Based on a study it was recommended that the facilities be traded in on new equipment, and procedures were strengthened for reviewing facilities to determine whether they were obsolete.

Pilferage of Sensitive Equipment

Significant inventory shortages in audiovisual equipment indicated the need for increased security to prevent pilferage. The auditors recommended that the sensitive items of equipment be stored in a secure place and controlled by sign-out procedures.

Repairing Defects Covered by Warranty

The internal auditor noted that six items of electronic equipment had been repaired by the maintenance department, although the items were still under warranty. Repair orders were not being checked against warranty agreements prior to approval, resulting in unnecessary costs for repair of the equipment.

CHAPTER NINETEEN

Marketing

THE NATURE AND SCOPE OF THE MARKETING FUNCTION

The marketing function of the company has emerged in recent years with a new breadth of coverage and increasing importance. Once viewed more narrowly as including only the sales activity, it now comprehends the broader developmental and related activities that support and go beyond the basic sales effort. In recognition of this greater scope the interest and concern of management with this function has been simultaneously extended. In turn, the internal auditor has broadened his interest beyond the earlier financial control orientation and is doing more to serve management in this area. Since the marketing function involves to a much greater extent the characteristics of creativity, personal skills, and other intangible qualities, the role of the internal auditor might seem at first glance to be less fitting than has been the case in some of the more traditional areas. The answer here is that wherever management's greatest concerns are, there is the corresponding need for the independent review and appraisal of the internal auditor. More specifically, the answer is that while the central character of the marketing function embodies much that is intangible, there is at the same time the need for a systematic approach to dealing with these more intangible activities. In this latter area the internal auditor is in an excellent position to make an important contribution. He must, however, move more cautiously since the creative core must be properly recognized and adequately preserved.

The range of the marketing activities in a particular company can be appreciated only through an understanding of the nature and scope of the marketing function. This takes us back to the basic purposes of the company itself. Here we start with the truth that the existence and ongoing success of any company is justified only to the extent that it makes possible the satisfaction of the needs of people in an effective manner. The need may be satisfied through a product that is tangible or that exists in the form of some kind of service. The product may be used by particular individuals, companies, governments, or any users—referred to as the customer. What the marketing function is all about is to accomplish this need satisfaction in the most effective and economical manner possible. In more specific terms it means attracting and satisfying customers and at the same time doing it on a profitable basis.

In an individual company the marketing function begins by identifying particular types of customer needs where the company has some reasonable capability to satisfy those needs and where there is a reasonable expectancy that this can be done profitably. Policies, programs, and procedures must then be developed that will provide the means for actually achieving the identified purpose. Finally, all of the foregoing plans must be implemented in an efficient manner. All of this encompasses what one might well call the total management function. In our own terminology, however, we do not go that far. The marketing function centers on the issues just indicated but merges as a partner with the production, engineering, personnel, and financial functions to support the higher-ranking general management role.

Importance of the Marketing Function

The importance of the marketing function comes about because it emphasizes a particular point of view in the collaborative process just mentioned. Products must be properly engineered, they must be produced efficiently, people of proper skills and numbers must be recruited and administered in an effective manner, and in all cases the costs generated must be controlled in a prudent manner in relation to revenues obtained so that adequate profits are earned. At the same time the products must be sufficiently useful and attractive to the consumers, that they will be purchased at competitive prices and in adequate quantities. Also, the products must be presented to consumers in a sufficiently effective fashion to exploit the product potentials. Each function plays its important part and no one of them can fail without dragging down the total management effort. But in many respects the marketing function has many claims to special importance. Perhaps this comes about partly because the marketing job cannot be standardized to quite the same extent as its sister functions. Hence the marketing job in many respects seems to be more difficult and to require a special type of expertise.

In the case of the individual company this importance of the marketing function can perhaps be seen most clearly. In a conceptual sense the determination of the marketing strategy becomes the central core of the overall company strategy with its related goals and objectives. Thus it becomes one of the most important, if not the most important type of company decision. At the same time the decisions in this area become the more difficult because they must combine the more intangible creative factors with objective depth analysis. This latter analysis involves both the testing of market potentials, as through modern scientific market research, and the related support in the enginering, production, personnel, and financial control areas. These interrelationships must be worked out both in the planning/decision stage and in the subsequent implementation. The special importance of the problem lies in the necessity to give proper weight to the marketing point of view but still not to allow it to dominate unduly the role of the other related functions. Maintaining this proper balance is the difficult job of top management. The fact of both the difficulty and importance sets the stage for a new and expanding role for the internal auditor as he continues to seek to enlarge his own area of management service.

Control Cycle

The marketing function can, like the other activities we have discussed, be viewed as a total cycle with individual operational stages. This framework is applicable to the company as a whole, or it can apply to the review of the marketing activity of a division, subsidiary, or any other organizational unit that has a product type responsibility. The individual operational stages of the total cycle are as follows:

1. *Determination of Product/Market Strategy.* At this stage the concern is with how market needs are evaluated, how a determination is made as to which particular needs will be satisfied, and in what manner all of this will be accomplished.

2. *Product Planning and Development.* Now the broad product/market strategy must be translated into the planning and development of specific products, for ultimate production by the company.

3. *Sales Promotion and Advertising.* The potential purchasers must be informed about the products and be appropriately conditioned for a definitive sales effort. This sale promotion effort includes the use of advertising media.

4. *Sales and Distribution.* Now the definitive sales effort must be made as to the type of distribution channels to be utilized. This question also involves the related problem of where, and to what extent, inventory stocks will be maintained.

5. *Customer Support.* The sale then involves a range of customer support activities starting with order handling and billing, going on to include customer familiarization and service, and the handling of possible claims and adjustments.

DETERMINATION OF PRODUCT/MARKET STRATEGY

The starting point in the total marketing cycle is to determine what products will be supplied and to what markets. This involves an evaluation of company resources and capabilities versus the requirements that exist for obtaining needed and desired sales volume. At the highest level it is the question: "What business am I in?" Thus IBM Corporation can ask itself whether it is in the computer business or in the communications business. At a lower level the question may be whether it should build an economy model of an existing higher priced product. In principle the question is: What range of products will be marketed and to what types of customers? One seeks to determine how the existing company resources can be used to exploit best the potential market opportunities.

Scope of Marketing Capabilities

On the one hand, the company needs to examine carefully its various marketing capabilities. High on the list here would be the extent of the experience gained and results already achieved in marketing particular types of products. The success in establishing an important market position with a cosmetic product should normally be a sound base for the introduction of another cosmetic product. Similarly, contacts established with a particular group of marketers —as, for example, supermarkets—can be a good base for expanding the product line to include other items sold by those same stores. Or the capability may exist in selling products in the industrial market, especially to a particular industry. This capability has a number of important dimensions. The first is the familiarity gained with the kinds of problems that are involved in the particular type of market. The second dimension is the contacts that have been made with the individuals or organizational entities that are customers for other products. The third is the reputation established with customers who, it is expected, can be transferred in part to new products.

Back of marketing experience and results achieved are the broader types of resources that will be needed to sustain a given product effort. This includes first, the financial resources that, it is expected, will be required to develop new products that can successfully penetrate a given market already in the hands of entrenched competitors. Included also will be the depth and general capabilities of the management team. These can be general strengths or more specific capabilities in a given technological area. All of these specific capabilities combine to provide the base from which one can determine the total capability to exploit effectively a new market opportunity.

Market Requirements

The second set of factors to be evaluated concerns the market requirements that exist for the products under consideration. Typical considerations in this area include:

1. *Total Demand Believed to Exist for the Proposed Products*. Where information is available on an industry basis or through the financial reports of publicly owned competitor companies, these sources can be utilized. Otherwise, the estimates must be based on other factors. At the same time the currently existing demand must be projected in the best possible fashion to estimate future demand. It is the potential growth of the particular market that is most critical. This part of the estimate is, of course, the most difficult since it involves a judgment of both what customers will want and what they can afford. This includes also the extent to which the market demand is for stable necessities, or products that can be dispensed with or deferred.

2. *State of Competition.* The projected market demand establishes market potential, but there is still the question of what portion of that potential one can obtain for a particular company. The answer here requires an appraisal of the competitive situation. This appraisal involves first of all the existing competitors. How many are there? What is their relative size? What is their relative strength? Is the competitive climate conservative or aggressive? Pertinent also is the question of how easily new firms can enter the market as additional competitors. Requirements for capital, money, know-how, and sales outlets are the factors that operate here to determine the ongoing ease of entry. Finally, there is the extent to which particular consumer demand can be satisfied by other types of products. Paper may take the place of glass for packaging purposes. Or home entertainment may displace traditional theaters.

3. *Timing Requirements.* An important question centers around the time required to penetrate a market with enough volume to be profitable. In most cases customer acceptance must be earned in the face of already established customer loyalties. In other cases it will be necessary to recruit and develop a dealer organization. Many of these operations require a considerable period of time.

4. *Transportation Feasibility.* In many cases the geographical dimensions of the market may be directly determined by the transportation costs that will be involved in supplying customers. In the case of books, the problem is relatively simple, but for the cement industry the transportation costs are a major factor.

5. *Money Requirements.* The time and effort required to penetrate new markets must finally be translated into the financial cost of securing the needed market volume. Money is required to finance the various promotional and developmental activities that frequently extend over long periods of time. Operating losses must, therefore, be expected before profitable operations can be achieved, all of which can require major financial support.

Finalizing the Evaluation

The determination of the specific product/market strategy now is made based on the comparision of the existing capabilities and the assessment of the scope of the market opportunities. In financial terms it is the weighing of projected costs and revenues at a level of risk that is acceptable to the particular company. Out of this evaluation will come the decision as to whether the company will seek to establish itself in a broadly based market or whether it will try to carve out a particular kind of a niche. The latter strategy is to find a particular sector of a market and to establish a strong position in that particular sector. At the same time the product developed will be one that is especially designed to fit that smaller market sector. The product may be of a special size or with special operational characteristics, or there may be distinctive types of service provided. Or the niche may be to serve a particular type of customer. Illustrative of these possibilities are the following:

1. A special line of products for a particular type of purpose.
2. An economy model of a product.
3. Simplified design for ease of maintenance.
4. Serving a special geographical area.
5. Faster deliveries.
6. A special operational characteristic.
7. Distinctive appearance.
8. Catering to a particular buyer group.
9. Special innovations.
10. Brand claims established through advertising and sales promotion.

To the maximum extent possible the objective will be to create a situation where the competitor does not think it sufficiently worthwhile to compete in the particular sector. To the extent that this is not possible, the objective will be to capitalize on the situation while the competitor is catching up. In the latter situations the company must be preparing at the same time to expand its product market strategy in new directions, as needed. Obviously, the situation must be subject to continuous reappraisal as market conditions change. At the same time also a company's capabilities will be changing as experience is gained and the company grows in size. Supplementary evaluative efforts will include general forecasting as to the general state of the economy, more specific forecasting of the trends in particular types of markets, market research as to changing customer preferences and needs, and always the studies of current and projected profitability of alternative product/market approaches.

Control Considerations

From a control standpoint the first requirement is that the basic importance of the product/market strategy be adequately recognized. History provides many examples of companies that have drifted downhill by taking for granted the continuing merits of a previously existing strategy. The best evidence of the recognition of the importance of a product/market strategy is that it has been reduced to writing and has been made known to the proper parties within the company. The second requirement is that definitive steps are taken to reappraise periodically the need for modifying existing product/market strategies. These definitive steps include the kinds of special study efforts previously described and the vigorous examination of the results developed. The real vitality of this latter type of examination is evidenced by changes actually made over time in the product/market approach. In this current dynamic world, a lack of change is likely to be proof of inadequate study.

PRODUCT PLANNING AND DEVELOPMENT

The operational stage of product planning and development follows the determination of the product/market strategy and is closely interrelated. There is, however, a real difference between the two efforts. Whereas the product/market strategy is the broad conceptual plan of the company's approach to the market, the product planning and development phase is the actual implementation of the underlying plan. This implementation effort is now concerned with planning and developing the actual products that are consistent with the strategic plan. It also goes on to extend the studies, which were the basis of the determination of the strategy, to support the more specific individual products. But both the conceptual plan and the implementation effort are necessary if the company's resources are to be used in a really effective manner. In General Foods the product/market strategy is the development of convenience-type foods for the sophisticated modern housewife, and the implementation is the development of an increasingly broad line of individual items that can be prepared and served with minimal effort.

Nature and Scope of Product Planning and Development Efforts

The total product planning and development effort extends from the most basic type of research to the ultimate management of the individual products, and at all stages includes the coordination of other related company activities. We will look briefly at the major phases.

Basic Research.   Within a presently existing product/market strategy there is normally, and quite properly, a continuing interest in basic research. This includes developing better materials used in the products, better functional characteristics, and new ways to produce the products at lower cost and/or of better quality. Such research work will normally be carried on by such a research activity as was discussed in Chapter 17. We refer to it here again, however, as the initial stage in the product planning and development process. In General Foods the research might center on how new processes can be developed to preserve the quality of the food better in the face of exposure to various types of physical conditions. In an automobile business the research might center on how to make exterior enamels more lustrous and durable through using new materials or through better painting processes. But in all cases the product planning and development group should be a major generation of pressure on the research group to obtain new and improved products.

Application of New Technology to Existing Products.   As new technological knowledge is developed, another important type of research effort has to do with applying that new knowledge to existing products. Thus the development of new types of plastics immediately opened up the possibility that a range of items previously made of more expensive materials (like steel) or less durable materials (like fabrics) might now be made of the new plastics. Similarly, the development of the dry-freeze process for food, with its new advantages of better preservation of flavor and greater shelf life without refrigeration, opened up the immediate possibility of utilizing this new technological development for a wider variety of food items. Another good example is the development of improved paper cartons for packaging foods. In all these situations the product planning and development group can provide a basic force for the exploitation of these possibilities.

Expanding Customer Convenience. Many types of product development have to do with expanding the range of service for consumer needs. Some of these developments may again reach back to the supporting research effort, but in many cases they may result primarily from the imaginative thinking of the product planner. Again using the automotive industry as an example, the addition of certain extras involved more extensive technical efforts, as, for example, air conditioning, power steering, and exhaust purifiers. Other extras may involve very limited technological expertise and may be designed primarily to provide an imaginative appeal to the customer, as, for example, the more generous providing of arm rests.

Appearance Changes. A closely related type of product application has to do with changes in the appearance of the product, new colors, new finishes, or perhaps more attractive packaging. Here the effort is to make the product more appealing in an aesthetic sense, and in many cases to induce new purchases even when the product already owned is functionally still very efficient. This takes one into the world of style, where new designs are valued in terms of a variety of ego, status, and other personal values. In many industries, for example in the clothing industry, this becomes a major part of the product planning and development thrust.

More Extended Market Research. The product planning and development stage is a time also when earlier market research efforts are expanded in major depth. Now the market research is directed to learning more about individual consumer preferences, and to evaluating how consumers are responding to both new types of products and new types of product developments. Such market research can precede the development of new product applications, and it can be used at various stages to check on the advisability of extending new product developments to wider geographical markets. New developments in modern statistical techniques combined with the use of high-speed computers have increased the value of these marketing research efforts. While the results obtained still are imperfect in many respects, the usefulness of the approach is no longer seriously challenged.

Timing Considerations

An important aspect of the product planning and development effort has to do with the timing of the individual phases of the total activity. The source of the problem lies in the fact that many products have a limited life cycle. Whereas a product such as Listerine seems to go on forever, there is normally a cycle of market acceptance that begins at the time of the product introduction, rises slowly during the early promotional stages, rises more sharply as an expanding group of customers accelerates consumer acceptance, rises more slowly as market saturation is approached, levels off for a period of time, and finally trends downward as newer products begin to overshadow the original product. The exact shape of the cycles for individual products will, of course, vary, as well as the periods of time involved, but the pattern is similiar. What this means in that an effective product planning and development effort will be charting and projecting the life of the various products, and at the same time developing a group of upcoming products that will reasonably fill the gaps produced by aging products. This is especially important since the normal company wishes to maintain a sustained growth rate, in terms of sales and profitability. To provide a program that serves the purpose, the supporting effort must take into consideration the timing requirements for the development and testing of individual product candidates, and what number of new products must be in process at the various stages.

Organizational Considerations

The product planning and development activity, like any other important activity, needs to have an adequate organizational assignment in the company. It is especially important, however, in this case because of the greater needed assurance that the product development function is given its power attention. It is also important because of the greater than normal need for a collaborative participation by other important company activities in the product development effort. This is normally accomplished by placing the product planning and development group at a relatively high organizational level. Usually, the group will report to a senior vice president for either administration or marketing. In addition, it is desirable that the necessary coordination with other concerned company activities be further assured through the creation of a product planning committee consisting of responsible representation from the other interested company staff and line groups. The product planning and development group will then have the primary responsibility of providing leadership for this important activity in which all company activities have such a substantial stake. It will initiate and study proposals and programs while responding to the proposals of other company groups. On a day-to-day basis it will work in a cooperative manner with the research, engineering, production, sales, and finance groups, testing the feasibility of its own proposals and seeking their counsel. Through the aforementioned committee structure a further opportunity is then provided to present definite proposals and programs to the management of these same functions and to the top company management. Although this entire effort focuses primarily on the effective implementation of the existing product/ market strategy, it also provides a continuing opportunity to reappraise the need for major changes in the basic strategy.

Product Management Responsibility. The situation that emerges after new products have been approved is that the production, promotional, sales, and financial profitability evaluation activities pertaining to individual products are fragmented and diffused to the responsible functional groups. At the same time it has been recognized that something is needed as a basis for looking at the combined activities on an individual product basis. The solution to this problem has been to create product managers who are assigned one or more of these individual products and are charged with the responsibility of coordinating the functional pieces in terms of total effective management of the individual products. These product managers can be placed in any high-level staff group, but very often are positioned just below the senior marketing executive. Their unique character from an organizational standpoint is that they have no line responsibility over the production, promotional, sales, or financial organizational components but are still charged with a kind of management responsibility in terms of profit and loss. They must, therefore, accomplish their objectives by nondirective means. Despite the limitations of authority, the approach has been very successful. There is, however, a great dependence on the skill with which the product manager handles his assignment, especially in a human relations sense.

Control Aspects of Product Planning and Development

The achievement of effective control over the product planning and development activity begins with a recognition of the importance of this activity. Here the foundation action is the establishment of the activity in the way of adequate organizational status and mission. The second important control consideration is the development by that organizational group of programs for assuring the needed flow of new products to replace aging products, and to provide such an increase in good products as will assure the wanted company growth. Finally, there is the test of how vigorously these programs are being carried out. The ultimate proof of the total development effort is, of course, company profits, but frequently the accurate assessment of causal factors is not that simple. However, comparisons with competitor products provide a useful guide as to whether a product planning and development effort has been well conceived and executed.

SALES PROMOTION AND ADVERTISING

The product as planned, developed, and now produced by the manufacturing group should now be available for sale. At this stage a substantial effort is necessary in the way of familiarizing the potential customer with the product, and in creating a receptivity on his part that will support the more definitive sales effort. This conditioning effort is the sales promotion function. It is a broad function that includes the advertising activity. In recognition of the common character of all sales promotion activities, we first discuss certain general features that are applicable to the total range of the sales promotion function. We then go on to supplement the more general discussion with more detailed consideration of problems relating directly to advertising and to other specific types of sales promotion.

Nature of the Sales Promotion Process

The common objective of all sales promotion activities is to induce a sale. The objective may be for an immediate sale or it may be only to plant an idea that will later be further implemented to be contributory to the making of a later sale. Advertising tomorrow's special sales offerings at a department store is at one end of the spectrum, and institutional advertising of a public relations nature is at the other. In some cases the results achieved can be immediately measured with some reasonable degree of accuracy, but more often there is an intangible character to the effort that defies accurate measurement and evaluation. Usually, there are a number of other factors operating—other causes, new situational developments, and the like—that make it impossible to say exactly how much the particular sales promotional action contributed to the sales actually achieved. The lack of precision here makes it possible for many types of claims to be made as to what the actual contribution was, some of which are often overenthusiastic and unrealistic by more conservative standards. Sales promotional activities are directed to human beings, who, as we know, are to a considerable extent unpredictable, and this is a further source of the difficulty. The link to human beings does, however, emphasize the necessity of being imaginative and creative in developing the various sales promotional approaches.

Importance of the Sales Promotion Activities

Despite all the problems of measuring the effectiveness of sales promotional activities, a company is for all practical purposes forced to continue them. Not only does our managerial instinct support the wisdom of much of the sales promotional effort, but actions along these lines by competitors require an individual company to do likewise. As a result, large sums of money are expended for advertising and other types of sales promotion. The problem of management is then how much actually to spend, on what particular types of sales promotion the moneys should be expended, and how one can best obtain assurance that the company has received maximum value for these expenditures. Somehow, claims of the suppliers of the services must be evaluated; somehow, proper directions of effort must be specified; and, somehow, there must be controls to assure prudent cost levels. It is part of the mission of the internal auditor, in whatever way is practicable, to help management answer these difficult questions.

Organizational Considerations

The need for adequate organizational status for the sales promotion activity is dictated by the level of expenditures and the type of sales promotion. The advertising component particularly needs the kind of organizational placement that will enable it to interpret directly the company's highest-level product/market strategy. This is especially true also because the advertising activity frequently takes on a larger public relations role. By nature the advertising results have great visibility and are apt to come under fire from executives who have different tastes or different points of view. The higher-level organizational status here enables the responsible sales promotion executive to deal on a basis of greater equality in justifying the approaches taken. Although the need for this higher-level organizational status may not be so important to many of the more routine types of sales promotion, the interrelationship between all sales promotional activities, and the frequent trade-off between them and other company interests argues also for the merits of the higher organizational position. In the typical situation the sales promotion activity will report to the senior marketing executive.

Control Cycle of Sales Promotion

Although there is a wide range of types of sales promotional activities, they do individually and collectively reflect an operational cycle with common points for needed control. These are, as follows:

1. *Determination of Objectives.* The starting point for any sales promotion effort is a determination of what one expects to accomplish. This determination involves first the answering of such questions as: Whom are we endeavoring to influence? Where are these individuals? How can we reach them most effectively? At the same time the different ways to accomplish the sales promotion are evaluated as between available alternatives on the bases of cost and expected results. Where there has been previous experience with particular approaches, that evidence is utilized. Out of this evaluation comes the selection of the specific approaches and a determination of what we should achieve at a given level of cost.

2. *Approval of Budgets.* Budgets always play a key role in assuring better planning and control, but they are especially important for sales promotional activities. The reason is that personnel in this function typically are less concerned with costs and more motivated by the built in enthusiasm they have for the effectiveness of particular sales promotion approaches. Thus it is most important that the proposed program be carefully documented as to just what will be done and at what cost. This proposed program is then subjected to further review and after any modification is approved. This approved budget and program now set the limits of expenditure for the actual implementation of the program.

3. *Determination of Suppliers*. To a varying extent the approved programs will require the procurement of goods and services from outside parties such as advertising agencies, media, designers, and vendors. In some cases portions of this procurement can be handled through the regular purchasing department, but in many cases the procurement is so specialized that it can best be handled by the sales promotion group itself. In any event the usual principles of sound procurement are applicable. We seek to deal with financially sound suppliers, to utilize competitive bidding to the extent practicable, and to be assured of reliable specifications, quality, and delivery. In cases where there is an extended and complicated relationship it will be desirable to reduce the mutual understandings to writing in proper contractual form.

4. *Receiving Product or Services*. The product or service may be a one-time proposition and subject to the usual standards of good receiving. In other cases the product or service may be rendered over a considerable period of time. The company has two types of concern. The first is that maximum value has been provided through quality performance at prudent cost levels. The second is that what was supposed to be provided is actually received. In certain cases the receiving is clean-cut, but in other cases supplementary evidence may be needed. Where there are deficiencies of any kind there is the need that claims are asserted to protect the company.

5. *Settlement*. The settlement stage then follows from the receival and involves a determination that billings are in accordance with previously agreed upon arrangements. These arrangements include prices, specifications, and timing of delivery. In many cases there may be extra charges, and the question of their propriety must be carefully examined.

6. *Evaluation of Results*. The final stage is the review and evaluation of what was accomplished—at least to the extent that such an evaluation is practicable. The results accomplished can provide an important guide to continuing sales promotion activities, with respect to both the adoption of the same approach and the use of the same supplier. This is especially important because there is such a qualitative aspect to all sales promotion activities.

The controls at these individual operational stages will be individually appraised for each sales promotion effort. This appraisal focuses first, on the adequacy of the existing procedures and controls in a design sense, and second, on the care and vigor with which they are implemented. In the sales promotion business there are always bound to be crises and special emergencies, and in such situations deviations may be necessary in the company interest. It is important, however, that every reasonable effort be made to enforce the controls, and that when deviations are necessary they be carefully documented and approved by as high a level of authority as is practicable at the time.

Advertising and the Agency Relationship

Because the advertising part of the sales promotion activity is so important, and because it has some very special types of problems, it will be desirable to supplement the previous discussion. A special characteristic of the advertising function is the fact that it is normally accomplished through advertising agencies. These agencies exist as separate business entities which stand between the company and the various media used—the magazines, newspapers, radio broadcasting stations, and television stations. It is these firms that have the relations with the media and that are normally responsible for payments to them for space or time used. Their other functions are to study company advertising needs, to determine how advertising outlays can be best utilized to satisfy those needs, to propose specific advertising programs, and to implement approved programs through creating effective copy and supporting production work so that the actual execution can be accomplished by the individual media. The agencies thus function both as an advisor and a subcontractor for the company, working primarily with the head of the sales promotion group, or the advertising component thereof. The agencies will also normally have such other company contacts as are needed, including top management itself.

Basis of Compensation. In compensating the advertising agency for these services one starts out with the proper objective that the agency ought to be fairly reimbursed for its efforts. The agency should be able to pay its suppliers and its own operating expenses, and in addition earn a fair profit commensurate with the level of its professional contribution and the efficiency of its own internal management. The problem is how this fair compensation will be determined. Traditionally, the major basis of compensation has been a 15% discount given by media to the agencies—a discount not directly available to the company itself. In some cases this percentage allowance has been supplemented by certain types of special costs, as for artwork, mats, plates, and so on. Also, extra compensation will be charged for specially defined extra services.

The basic media allowance type of arrangement has been good in the sense that the agency has been protected by this assured revenue. It has been bad, however, in that there is a kind of built-in incentive to increase the use of advertising media. Even when advertising budgets really need to be expanded there is apt to be the lurking suspicion that the recommended increase is motivated to a substantial extent by the direct relationship to the increased discount allowances. There is the weakness also that there is not necessarily a good correlation between the amount of revenue obtained through the media allowances and the scope of the work performed by the agency. It can cost just as much to produce the copy for an advertisement that will run only once as for one that will run a dozen times. Also industrial advertising does not involve the extensive use of media as is the case with consumer advertising. As a result of these problems there has been a greater trend in recent years to develop a more tailored type of compensation that is mutually negotiated to compensate fairly for the scope of the services actually performed. But the entire matter is still in a state of transition, and great care must be exercised, both in the determination of the actual compensation arrangements and in being certain that these arrangements are properly carried out.

Agency Selection and Advertising Plan. The advertising agency used by the company is usually selected on the basis of competitive presentations of the nature and scope of the program to be provided. Frequently also, different agencies are used for different divisions or for different product lines even within the same division. Although the actual choice of the particular agency is usually a very high-level management decision, the internal auditor can be very helpful in working out the various compensation arrangements. This is especially important because the internal auditor will normally later be auditing the agency billings, and at that time there will have to be a final determination of exactly what the billings should cover. The fact that an agency is being selected at all is usually because of dissatisfaction that has developed with the previous agency. Here too, the experience of the internal auditor with that previous agency may have been a contributing factor to the decision to make the change.

After the agency has been selected and the contract finalized, the usual procedure is that budgetary ranges are discussed, and then that the agency prepares and presents a proposed program for the year ahead This program includes the basic creative approaches, alternative types of copy, media to be used, timing of usage, and estimated costs. After the necessary discussions, the agreements reached constitute the action plan, subject to change over the year in the light of new developments. The action plan is very important from a control standpoint because it both details what is to be done and the extent of lead times and commitments that have to be respected in making any later changes in the scope of the program.

Agency Operations. The agency now proceeds to implement the agreed-upon advertising program. The internal operations include the creative work (essentially the development of ideas and supporting copy), art work, preparation of mats and plates, final selection of media, relations with media, accounting, billing and collection, and general administration. From the standpoint of the company, the major concerns are that:

1. The work done is carried out in a capable professional manner, properly coordinated with the company.
2. Billings made for media services cover advertising properly authorized by the company, at the best available rates, and for services properly authorized under the contractual agreement, and that costs reflect good value.
3. The internal operations of the agency are carried out efficiently and in a businesslike manner, including their own procurement of materials and services.

4. Relations of the agency with dealers and customers covering cooperative advertising are carried out in an efficient and cooperative manner.

5. The entire advertising relationship is well coordinated and administered.

Company Financial Control   The financial control of advertising expenditures by the company becomes very important when large sums of money are being expended. This financial control begins with the budgets allocated to individual agencies for particular product, institutional, or other special-purpose programs. Subsequent financial control then includes:

1. Continuing updating of the state of program progress as to the extent that programs can be curtailed in the light of new conditions, and at what cost. The factors here include agency preparatory work, and commitments to outside suppliers and to media.

2. Extent to which advertising compensation is earned through actual usage—insertions in periodicals, radio and TV time, and so on.

3. Amounts of actual billings payable, and the adequacy of the supporting documentation.

4. Continuing assurance that agency operations and billings are consistent with previously established agreements.

5. Current and projected conformity to established budgets.

These financial control concerns are satisfied in two ways. The first of these is through the adequacy of the records and related procedural controls maintained in the company by the advertising and accounting departments. Practice will vary as to just what portion of the record controls will be maintained by the advertising group or by the accounting department. In any case, however, the two efforts must mesh together in an accurate and systematic manner. The second type of financial control is accomplished through the field review of the operations of the agency itself. This review may be accomplished in part by company advertising personnel, but is usually handled to a major extent by other more specialized personnel, such as the internal auditor.

Internal Auditor's Role in Advertising.   It is the normal role of the internal auditor to cover all of the above-mentioned areas of activity. In his review of the company activities he will appraise the adequacy of the records and procedures by which the above-mentioned financial control is achieved. At the same time he will also appraise the effectiveness with which those records are being maintained and how well procedures are actually being carried out. In his audit of the agency operations he will carry out a similar type of appraisal plus the further determination of how the agency records and procedures mesh with the company records. The examination of the financial controls also provides a good basis for other management service. One of these further opportunities is to appraise the effectiveness of the coordination of the agency with the company activities, and to detect possible overlap and duplication. An excellent opportunity is also provided to develop input for management in its continuous appraisal of how satisfactory the particular agency relationship is proving to be.

Other Sales Promotion Activities

Although the general nature of all sales promotional activities has previously been outlined, there are many unique problems that exist in the case of particular types of sales promotion. In actual practice the number and kinds of individual types of sales promotion are limited only by the imagination and ingenuity of the sales promotion personnel. As a result, there is a wide range of special problems that exist. These problems are often more complicated because they operate through more than one level of product distribution; that is, a particular promotion may involve ultimate consumers but may necessarily be administered through jobbers, dealers, or agents. We will consider a few of the more common types of promotion and some of the related special problems.

1. *Sales Promotion Services Purchased.* These would include such diverse purchases as the services of a sales demonstrator in a retail store, the display of company signs, or the skywriting by an air pilot. The common problems are the fairness of the initial arrangements, the quality of the services performed, and the evidence that the services were actually rendered. This is much like any procurement except that more may be required in the way of coordination in arranging the purchase and in obtaining the particular products and services.

2. *Display Materials Furnished.* The problems here center about the prudent procurement of the particular materials, the proper receipt of them, the care with which they are handled and protected while awaiting use, the manner in which they are distributed, and the effectiveness of the subsequent care and use by later recipients. Many times the controls over the purchase and custody of these materials are very weak. When distributed to outside parties, there are apt to be various types of waste, especially when the materials come at no cost to the recipients. In some cases the display materials may be sold to the recipients, and in that case further controls are necessary to assure proper billing and collection. However, such billing prices are usually deliberately set at nominal levels and often do not induce adequate responsibility. Depending on the cost of the particular types of materials and the volume involved, the possibilities for waste are of major significance. It is important, therefore, that there are appropriate policies, records, and procedures for handling such materials. It is similarly important that the later implementation be carried out in a careful manner.

3. *Free Samples.* The problems here are similar to that of display materials. The added problem, however, is that the free samples are normally desirable items for a greater number of persons, and hence are more easily diverted from their intended purpose.

4. *Premiums*. There are many types of promotion through the use of premiums. One with which we are all familiar is Green Stamps. Here the
   control problem is to treat Green Stamps like money and to control their
   issue through careful procedures. In other cases the customer will submit
   something as proof of purchase and be entitled to the premium. Frequently, a small payment is required from the customer which either
   partially or fully pays the cost of the premium. Here the control problem
   is to enforce the conditions specified and to administer the entire operation in an efficient manner as a separate activity.

5. *Coupons*. In certain businesses a popular type of sales promotion is to
   give coupons which then entitle the customer to a reduced price for the
   particular product. The dealer or agent who has accepted the coupon then
   claims reimbursement from the sponsoring company. The control problem here is to control the creation of the coupons, to see that they are
   distributed properly to the persons who, it is hoped, will use them, to
   prevent the coupons from being used improperly—as, for example, for
   the purchase of a competitor's product—to handle properly the final
   reimbursement claims, and finally to cancel the coupons to prevent their
   reuse. There are many difficult problems here to avoid improper usage
   both because of the large number of people often involved, and the
   impossibility of pressing too hard with the kind of controls that are really
   required.

6. *Combination Sales*. Frequently, combinations of several company products will be offered at a specially reduced price. The final seller may,
   however, abuse the arrangement by breaking up the combination and
   selling the individual components at the full price. The attack on this
   problem is to provide enough visibility of the intended arrangement that
   the final purchaser acts as a control on the seller. This visibility can be
   accomplished through advertising or marking of the individual products.

7. *Special Discounts and Allowances*. A very commonly used type of sales
   promotion is to establish a temporary special price by announcment in
   some manner to the ultimate consumer. The intermediary retailer and/
   or distributor is then protected through an allowance payable upon proper
   evidence of the sale under the conditions stated. In other cases the
   allowance may be only to the distributor or retailer to stimulate a special
   sales effort on his part. The key control problem is again the adequacy
   of the evidence that the specified conditions have in fact been carried
   out. A special complication is also involved when allowances apply to
   inventories on hand, and where, therefore, there must be an adequate
   check on the accuracy of the affected inventory.

8. *Contests*. Another popular type of sales promotion is the awarding of
   prizes to salespeople, dealers, distributors, and other intermediary groups
   on the basis of designated types of action. The action desired here is
   increased sales through the stimulation of special sales efforts. In other

cases the contest may involve ultimate consumers and seek additional sales through the purchase requirement for eligibility in the contest. The control problem with contests centers about the necessary assurances that the specified conditions have been complied with. Often also, the administration of the contest is placed in completely independent hands to assure complete integrity in the entire effort.

9. *Shows and Presentations.* In many types of business the introduction of new models and lines is supported by various types of shows and promotional meetings. The first requirement is that there is something important enough to present to justify the presentation. In the automobile business, for example, the introduction of new annual models, or the introduction of an entirely new type of car is such an occasion. The second requirement is that the presentation be well planned and executed.

Common Problems of Sales Promotion Projects

Although the individual sales promotion projects can take many forms, there are always certain common problems. The first of these is that the particular project provides reasonable promise that it is sound in that it will achieve results that justify the expenditures to be incurred. As previously noted, sales promotional people tend to be overly optimistic and enthusiastic about results expected to be achieved. What is needed as a counterbalance is usually a more detached and objective type of evaluation before definitive action is agreed upon. Second, there is the problem of whether the proposed approach can be implemented in an administrative sense without excessive abuse and waste. Nothing is gained when special payments and allowances are diverted or otherwise appropriated without achieving the originally intended conditions. Finally, there is the problem of actually carrying out the particular project in an efficient manner. Many a sales promotion program has been sound in concept, and designed in a way that it could be administered properly, and yet failed because of the lack of care and discipline with which it has been administered. All sales promotion projects require a continuing critical cross check along the lines of these problems. Granted that all things can never be perfect, and that the outside reviewer cannot be in the position of preventing worthwhile creative efforts, there is still a tremendous range of service that can be provided by a person such as the internal auditor.

SALES AND DISTRIBUTION

The sales promotion effort has now set the stage for the necessary ultimate sale. Unless this latter action is achieved in adequate volume and at proper prices the company cannot earn the profits needed for its ongoing survival and progress. It is, therefore, most important that the sales effort be wisely planned and efficiently carried out. This involves, first, the determination of how the products are to be sold, and through what channels of distribution. It is only then that the supporting sales effort can be developed and executed. Linked also to the sales effort is the question of the later program of customer support, into which the sales effort actually merges. The sales effort thus stands as a vital key phase of the marketing process, but with increasing recognition that its character and effectiveness are determined to a major extent by other marketing considerations. We look first at some of those other marketing dimensions and then come back to a more specific focus on the basic sales effort itself.

Underlying Distribution Determination

An individual company normally has a number of alternatives available as to how it should market its products. In some cases the means selected have been to deal directly with the consumer. In such a situation the contact may be through the company's own representatives on a direct basis. In other cases the contact may be via the mails, radio, television, and the like. In still other cases it has been decided to use the services of intermediate parties—brokers, agents, dealers, stores, wholesalers, distributors, and so on. In determining which types of distribution should be selected, in what numbers, and in what combinations, the company weighs the relative advantages and costs, subject to what it can afford in terms of time and money. Moreover, these determinations are always being subjected to continuing reevaluation as further experience is gained, and as conditions change. A small company, or small-product division of a company, may at one point of time have no alternative but to depend on a particular type of intermediary. Later, however, it may be able to justify a more direct kind of marketing effort. Subject to reevaluation, also, is the selection of particular intermediaries in terms of the quality of services rendered.

Question of Stock Availability.   The choice of distribution channels at the same time has some other far-reaching implications. One of these questions is that of stock availability for customers. This is a question that covers where stocks will be maintained, what they will include in the way of product-line components, in what quantities, under whose surveillance, and at whose financial cost and risk. In evaluating these questions there is a dual type of concern. The first is with the functional efficiency with which customer needs are adequately taken care of. The second is with the level of the costs incurred. Under which of the alternative approaches can costs be minimized, assuming full consideration of the quality of the services, and the present and long-run benefits expected? The problem here is complicated by the fact that intermediaries, to the extent used, are by definition independent businesspersons and not subject to direction in the same manner as company employees. Although there is always the expectation that common interests will lead to mutually agreeable actions, there may be differences of judgment, and sometimes also limited financial capabilities.

Pricing.   Directly related also to the channel of distribution question is the problem of pricing. In broad dimensions the pricing function is one in which both marketing and finance have a joint responsibility, although for convenience we will discuss this problem in more depth in Chapter 21 when we deal with the various financial policy matters. We mention pricing here also, however, because it plays such an important role in the relations with the intermediaries selected for the distribution of company products. These intermediaries are, first, very interested in the ultimate consumer prices, for the reason that they directly affect the volume of sales that can be generated—and thus in turn their own profits. The intermediaries are also interested in what margins they will be granted out of which they must earn their own profits. In principle, the prices to the intermediaries are set at a point where the intermediary will be motivated to provide properly the services needed and to apply a vigorous and sustained sales effort. Therefore, the company must carefully weigh the various considerations and endeavor to fix fair standard pricing levels for the various types of intermediaries. Individual pressures, however, may prevent the achievement of either the desired stability or uniformity.

In setting pricing the legal aspects are extremely complex and require the assistance of an attorney when problems arise. The legal restrictions as to price discrimination are especially important to the marketing function. The Sherman Act of 1890 outlaws monopolies and contracts in restraint of trade. The Clayton Act of 1814 outlaws price discrimination, where it tends to lessen competition or create a monopoly. The Robinson-Patman Act of 1936 makes specific the types of price discrimination which are violations, such as forbidding quantity discounts or other price differentials unless they reflect costs of manufacturing and selling goods. A seller may discriminate in price, however, to meet a legitimately lower price of a competitor. There is other legislation, such as the Federal Trade Commission Act of 1914, which also regulates unfair competition. It is important that management be familiar with these, and the corporate attorney review the marketing policies for adherence to the law.

Making the Sales Effort Effective

In the typical company situation the sales effort will involve the use of sales personnel, even though the role of those personnel may vary widely. In some situations it will be necessary to generate sales on a day-to-day and month-to-month basis. In other situations the sales may take the form of longer-run contractual relationships. In still other cases the sales effort may be directed more to helping intermediaries to generate sales to their customers. In all cases, however, there is the problem of achieving the existing sales objective and doing this at the lowest possible cost over the long run. We will look briefly at several of the most important types of effort that need to receive attention.

Organization of the Sales Effort.   One of the basic decisions that must be made in the administration of any sales effort is the way in which it should be organized. One aspect of this organizational problem is how the levels of authority will be structured. The alternatives involved at this stage include:

1. *How Many Levels of Authority Should There Be?* This is essentially the question of how many individuals can be effectively supervised, and hence how many supervisory levels will be necessary.

2. *How Broad Should Be the Product-Line Sales Responsibility of the Individual Salesperson?* On the one hand, the cost of salespeople and their travel pushes one toward utilizing the individual salesperson for a greater range of products while he is there with a customer. On the other hand, the fact must be faced that the broader the line, the less effective the job that can be done by the salesperson for particular products. Related here also is the question of how those charged with ultimate responsibility for individual product profits can be assured that they get needed sales effort in relation to other company products.

3. *Where Should Salespeople Be Physically Located?* The need for supervision of sales personnel will push the company in the direction of more centrally located groups. On the other hand, factors such as better contact with customers, reduction of travel costs, and resistance to too much time away from families, will push the company in the direction of regional and even smaller district offices.

The second aspect of the organizational problem is the broader problem of the extent to which the sales effort should be decentralized. Under the centralized approach all sales personnel, irrespective of the physical location of the individuals involved, and irrespective of the number of intervening levels of supervision, will report on a direct-line basis to the central sales executive. Under a decentralized approach individual subsidiaries, divisions, or departments may have a broader type of profit responsibility that will include the direct-line control over their own sales personnel. In this case the central sales group may have some kind of dotted-line functional responsibility, primarily in the way of policy. The particular arrangement selected by an individual company will depend to a considerable extent on the total company approach to decentralization, and the extent to which there are special considerations that push the company toward greater or lesser centralized control of this particular activity.

Managing Sales Personnel. Regardless of how the sales effort is organized, there is still the problem of how to maximize the performance of the sales staff with minimum cost. The kinds of matters that are typically of special interest include:

1. *What Should Be the Qualifications of the Personnel?* The questions here include experience, special skills, educational levels, and presentability. The answers depend on the complexity of the products sold, the dollar value of individual items, the customers to be dealt with, and the opportunities for career development.

2. *What Kinds of Training Are Needed?* The problem here is related to the preceding question and applies especially to new recruits. However, in many situations there is the need for continuing training to cope with new developments.

3. *How Shall Salespeople Be Compensated?* At the one extreme is the fixed salary, and at the other the straight commission approach. Other questions involve the level of the compensation, the potentials of assigned territories, the protection of territorial jurisdiction, and the extent to which travel costs are covered. Usually, the actual arrangements reflect a blending of the various factors. In all cases, however, the problem is a difficult one, both in terms of adequacy of design and as to actual implementation.

4. *How Shall Sales Personnel Be Coordinated and Controlled?* The questions here include the extent to which higher organizational levels should supervise the personnel for which they are responsible, how accessible they are to these lower-level personnel, and what reporting is required. In the latter instance, information is needed both for control purposes and to utilize properly the very important field intelligence.

5. *How Best Motivate Sales Personnel?* All the foregoing questions have a particular administrative type of purpose. In addition, however, the manner in which they are carried out has a great deal to do with how effectively salespeople are actually motivated. The extent to which this motivation can be accomplished is very much at the heart of a successful sales effort, and hence needs to be considered most carefully.

6. *How Best Can Customer Goodwill Be Assured?* Important also is the recognition that although we want to make sales, we must in the long-run interest of the company, make those sales in a way that will best assure continuing customer goodwill. For example, the pressure of increasing commissions, or meeting established budgetary objectives, can lead to overselling. Although the company currently has the benefit of the sale, the aftereffects may prevent continuing sales.

Credit Policy Management

The management of credit policy to a major extent is a problem of financial management. Here the emphasis is on minimizing bad-debt losses and achieving the proper balance between such losses and profit generated by the related sales. Increasingly, however, credit policy management is viewed as a marketing tool. In these situations the extension of credit is tailored to generating new customers and expanding sales from existing sources. In some cases this generation is linked to the limited financial resources of potential customers, in other cases to customer cash-liquidity problems, and in still other cases to the greater convenience provided for customers.

Related marketing considerations are the sensitivity with which credit extension is made responsive to all the changing needs of different types of groups of customers. In this connection, goodwill and product loyalty are typically generated by a continuing appraisal of customer credit needs, stable and dependable availability to customers of credit actually needed, fairness of administration of credit policies and procedures, and demonstrated interest in customer welfare. Quite clearly, all of these marketing-oriented actions need to be closely coordinated with the policies and procedures of the finance department. But it is highly essential that the marketing opportunities be properly identified and presented to blend with more conventional financial objectives to serve best the overall management interests of the organization.

Dealer Support Efforts

In many situations the company will decide not to carry out the sales effort to the ultimate consumer with its own personnel. The advantages gained include the better community representation, and the greater motivation that is achieved through a person running his own business. In other cases the volume of sales is not sufficient to support the use by a company of its own salespeople. In this type of situation the sales effort will take the form of assisting intermediaries in dealing with the ultimate customers. Although there usually is the fact of the sale by the company to the intermediary (unless the products are provided on a consignment basis), there is the broader recognition that the company's interests are not well served until the intermediary actually makes sales to the real consumer. The emphasis here, then, is on helping the intermediary to run his business in a manner that will best assure these later sales. At times also the company sales representative may assist the intermediary in making individual sales, especially where a particular sale is very important. The management counsel provided will typically cover ordering the right products, and in the right quantities, how to store products, how to display them effectively, training and management of personnel, business operations, facilities maintenance, and the like. The scope of this counsel provided emphasizes the need for a company representative who has both the special technical skills and is well qualified in a general business sense. In addition, the company representative must be one who is sufficiently personable and persuasive to overcome the various types of resistance that may be encountered. The challenge is to help the dealer to do what is in his own ultimate self-interest, but to do it in a way that preserves the motivation and goodwill of that dealer. Unless this can be done with reasonable success the alternative may finally have to be to sacrifice the potential advantages of this type of marketing arrangement, and to revert to direct company-controlled distribution.

Operation of Regional Sales Office

As previously noted, the company may find it advantageous to establish field sales offices of one kind or another away from the central headquarters. In a large sales operation the field sales office organization may involve several organizational levels, that is, with certain field offices reporting to higher-ranking field offices. These field sales offices are operational entities that can be very important in an overall company sense. Two kinds of problems are usually involved. The first group of problems centers about the extent to which the operations conform to policies, procedures, budgets, and other types of designated controls established by the central sales office. Involved also may be similar controls established by other company groups, as, for example, personnel, accounting, and the like. The second group of problems goes beyond these prescribed controls and has to do with the general level of operational efficiency. This will include general housekeeping, quality of supervision, office hours observed, contacts with visitors, and the total management climate. The field sales office is a geographically detached operation where there cannot be the day-to-day contacts and observation possible by higher-level management as will exist at a central headquarters location. Therefore, an outside reviewer, such as the internal auditor, plays an especially important role in appraising the adequacy of the operation and its potentials for improvement.

CUSTOMER SUPPORT

The final stage in the total marketing cycle brings us to the final user of the company product. This may be the consumer who uses the company's toothpaste product, the individual who buys a company's automotive product, or another company that buys the product of the producing company for its own operational use. We are concerned at this final stage of how the various contacts are carried out with this user. The objective is that the sale is supported with such further information and service as will fully meet the needs of the user. The objective recognizes that the continuing good will of the customer/user is necessary to the long-run growth and success of the supplying company. Also, there is at all times the recognition that the sale is really not complete in terms of company welfare until the needs of the user are adequately satisfied over the life of the product. The problem is a difficult one because certain standards of care are necessary on the part of the user if the product is to function properly. But more and more there is greater recognition of the company's responsibilities and interests in this area.

Components of Customer Support

The total range of the customer support effort covers a variety of actions actually beginning before the sale is consummated, here blending with the sales promotion effort, and extending after the sale to the final utilization of the particular product. Clearly also, the range of the customer support effort will vary greatly, depending on the complexity and value of the individual product. The toothpaste example stands at one end of the spectrum and computer hardware at the other end. However, the following listing can serve as a useful framework for considering the scope of the problem in any individual situation.

1. *Preliminary Information about Products for Evaluation by Prospective*

Customers. One starts with the fact that the customer has a specific kind of need. At this point he needs information about the company's product as it pertains to satisfying that need. In some cases also, the company may, at its own suggestion or by invitation, study the user's problem in some depth as a basis for developing recommendations as to how company products would relate to the satisfaction of those user needs. Sometimes also, the user will be given the opportunity actually to try out the particular product on a trial basis.

2. *Stock Availability.* Both as it pertains to the actual decision to make the purchase, and to the later use of the purchased product, the question of the adequacy of the stock availability becomes important. How long will it take to get delivery of additional or replacement units, including parts and components that become part of the later-mentioned service support? Assuming a regular type of stock availability, what can be done on a special basis when emergency situations arise?

3. *Product Familiarization.* Once a product is purchased, an important aspect of the customer support effort includes the extent to which the operation and maintenance of the product are adequately explained to the user. Is the supporting instructional material adequate? Has the operation of the product been properly demonstrated? Are customer personnel being given needed training? In some cases this may mean that company personnel need to be on the ground making the initial installation, testing, and actually operating the product, and counseling customer personnel.

4. *Backup Service and Support.* At the later stages of use by the purchaser the adequacy of the backup service may be a critical question. The breakdown of a particular machine may shut down an entire production line. Similarly, the breakdown of a farm tractor may endanger the harvesting of a valuable crop. Here the backup service may be getting delivery of a needed replacement part, or it may be the need for a company technician to diagnose and correct the problem. In many situations the adequacy of this service backup can be the most important part of the total customer support.

5. *Warranty and Handling of Claims.* An important cost consideration to the user can in many situations be the extent to which the producer company reimburses the user for the failure of the product or its components. This type of customer support recognizes that customer satisfaction includes both good functional operation of the product and low cost. Related also is the way in which the warranty policy is administered. Are there resistance and argument as to the validity of claims? Is there undue delay in making the claims good? Fair and prompt service here become important aspects of good customer support.

6. *General Liaison.* The final aspect of customer support has to do with maintaining good relations with customers without waiting for actual problems to arise. What is involved is a realistic demonstration of interest, by determining from time to time how the customer is faring with the

product. This is important as a means of developing the desired customer goodwill. It is also important as an input for continuing product development.

Role of the Internal Auditor in the Marketing Function

In recent years the marketing function of the typical business corporation has come of age in terms of management sophistication and overall management depth. Its broader dimensions and major interrelationships with all other company activities have been recognized. No longer is the marketing function thought of only as the sales activity, but instead as embodying the central mission of the company. It has now become the focal point of the total management effort. As such, the internal auditor has necessarily reappraised his own role in relation to the broader marketing function.

The actual role of the internal auditor in the marketing area can perhaps be said to involve three different levels. At the most elementary level there is the concern for the more financially oriented protective role. This is the concern with accountabilities for products sold and the cash and receivables received in payment, as dealt with in Chapter 13. At the second level the internal auditor is concerned with the extent of compliance with marketing policies and procedures as they affect the efficiency of the various administrative operations and controls. Examples of this would be the administration of an established plan of compensating sales personnel or the adequacy of the development and use of sales data. In these areas the role of the internal auditor has developed more recently, but is now coming to be more generally accepted.

The third and highest level involves the more important policy determinations of the type that have been described in this chapter. In these latter areas the role of the internal auditor is increasing, with major progress being made in individual company situations. It is an area where there is great potential for internal auditing service. Certainly, the capability exists in the way of rational analysis, and there is the special strength of the detached vantage point, combined with an opportunity to see the marketing operations close up. The special skill that needs to be developed is the appreciation of the creative and dynamic dimensions of the marketing role. This will require some special care on the part of the internal auditor, but if properly handled the stage can be set for a new level of potential management service. One of the subareas in the total marketing area is the possibility of reviewing and appraising more objectively the scope of the customer support program. All of these potentials are dealt with in further detail in the audit guides that follow.

AUDIT GUIDES

MARKETING ACTIVITIES

I. Introductory

    A. Reference should be made to the general discussion of audit guides, Chapter 13.

B. In the review of marketing activities it needs to be recognized that many of them are mixed in some way with other company activities.

C. Special care needs to be exercised because of the creative and personal skill aspects of most marketing activities. The internal auditor seeks to find a proper balance between these aspects and traditionally more conservative procedures.

II. Preparatory

A. See standard Audit Guides, Chapter 13.

B. Because of the greater diffusion of marketing activities there will be special difficulties in identifying all parties of interest. The sensitivity of many of the issues involved will also call for added care on the part of the internal auditor.

III. Organizational Factors

A. See standard Audit Guides, Chapter 13.

B. There is a special need to identify and coordinate the key marketing functions previously discussed.

C. Matters of special interest in the review of manuals include:
1. Marketing objectives.
2. Product development criteria.
3. Procedures for product development.
4. Product management responsibilities.
5. Promotional policies.
6. Sales policies.
7. Coordination of marketing activities.
8. Budgetary development and administration.
9. Customer support policies.
10. Market research policies.

IV. Operational

A. Product/Market Strategy Development
1. Is the company (or divisional) product/market strategy in writing? If not, why not?
2. Has either general management or marketing management focused adequately on the product/market strategy determination? If not, why not?
3. Does the existing product/market strategy—to the extent it has been identified—appear to be sound and reasonable? If not, in what respects?
4. How adequate is the provision for periodic reappraisal of the major product/market strategy? What could be done to improve this process?
5. How adequate is the provision for obtaining market intelligence—changing customer needs, changing product technology,

competitor actions, industry trends, and so on? What can be done to make these efforts more effective?

B. Product Planning and Development
1. How adequate is the organizational set up for product planning and development?
2. To what extent is the responsibility recognized by other company activities to provide input for the product planning and development effort?
3. How effective is the coordination between the product planning and development group and other company activities in the initiation, screening, and actual development of new products and product improvements?
    a. Research department?
    b. Sales group?
    c. Finance?
    d. Production?
    e. Market research group?
4. Is there an adequate procedure for the formal presentation of new product proposals and the overall product planning and development program?
5. How efficient is the internal operation of the product planning and development program?
    a. Are organizational assignments clear and adequate?
    b. Are work activities scheduled and controlled?
    c. Is supervision adequate?
    d. Is there a suitable reporting system?
    e. Are personnel properly qualified?

C. Product Management
1. How does the company assure coordination and maximum profitability of individual products being marketed?
2. How adequately does the product management effort assure desired results without conflicting unduly with assigned responsibilities of other organizational components? In what ways could there be improvement?
3. Is the product management effort efficient in an internal operational sense?
    a. Are organizational assignments clear and adequate?
    b. Are personnel properly qualified?
    c. Is there a suitable reporting system?
    d. Is supervision adequate?

D. Sales Promotion and Advertising
1. Does the organizational setup provide adequately for the coordination of all sales promotion activities—including advertising?
2. Are the coordination relations with other company activities adequate?

3. How adequately are sales promotion objectives analyzed and related to specific types of sales promotion?
4. Are budgets carefully developed, and when approved used as a basis of project control?
5. Are outside procurements carried out effectively?
    a. Is proper use made of the regular purchasing group?
    b. If handled directly, are suppliers properly screened and evaluated?
    c. Is competitive bidding used to the maximum extent practicable?
    d. Are receipts of products and services adequately monitored to assure compliance with agreements?
    e. Are prices charged reviewed for accuracy?
6. Is there adequate provision for final evaluation of individual sales promotion projects and programs?
7. Are the internal operations of the sales promotion department carried out efficiently?
    a. Are organizational assignments clear and adequate?
    b. Are personnel properly qualified?
    c. Is supervision adequate?
    d. Is there a suitable reporting system?
8. With special reference to advertising agency relationships:
    a. Are arrangements properly covered by written agreements?
    b. Are billings adequately supported as to company authorization, actual rendering of services, and at best available rates?
    c. Are controls adequate as to expenditures authorized, services actually rendered, and extent to which programs can be curtailed?
    d. Is company liaison with agency adequate?
    e. Are adequate field reviews being made of agency operations?
9. In the case of other sales promotion programs, consider whether the scope and volume of activity require special procedural handling, including the use of outside parties.

E. Distribution Activities.
    1. Review the scope of the distribution plan.
    2. In the case of company operated distribution centers see the coverage under Section VI of these Audit Guides.
    3. In the case of distributors, dealers, and other intermediaries:
        a. Review the adequacy of contractual arrangements which cover the rights and obligations of the two parties.
        b. Review the adequacy of the arrangements in terms of customer support.
        c. Appraise the adequacy of the programs for backup assistance to these intermediaries.
    4. Appraise the total approach to the alternative use of company-operated distribution centers versus the use of intermediaries.

F. Sales Activities
   1. Review and appraise the relative merits of the organization of the sales effort:
      a. As respects physical location of sales personnel
      b. As to levels of authority
      c. As to extent of product specialization
      d. Extent of decentralization to other organizational components of the company
   2. Is a comprehensive sales development program in effect for:
      a. Adequacy of qualifications for recruits?
      b. Subsequent training?
      c. Manner of compensation?
      d. Coordination and control of sales operations?
      e. Motivation of sales personnel?
      f. To assure adequate customer goodwill?
   3. Review and appraise the operation of any program of dealer support. Is it coping adequately with the special problems of independent businessmen?
   4. Review and appraise the operations of major regional sales offices.
      a. As to conformity with company policies and procedures and legal requirements.
      b. As to general efficiency of operation and use of personnel.

G. Customer Support
   1. Is preliminary information issued covering company products adequate?
   2. Are customers being adequately serviced in terms of available stock?
   3. Are programs adequate for familiarization of customers with products purchased?
   4. How adequate is the program of backup service?
   5. Review and appraise the handling of warranty claims—especially as to attitudes, accuracy, and timing.
   6. Is there an adequate program of general liaision with customers?

H. Coordination with Credit Department
   1. Is the credit policy adjusted based on profit and market considerations?
   2. Are credit limits set to maximize net returns?

V. Field Audits of Advertising Agencies

   A. Preparatory Activities
      1. Examine all available contractual arrangements and note pertinent provisions covering scope of services to be furnished and bases of payment.
      2. Discuss agency relationships with responsible company executives and liaison personnel.

3. Review reports being received from agency and utilization by company for control.

4. Review budgetary plans and other company authorizations for advertising services.

B. Examination of Billings Rendered

1. Review scope of billings to determine compliance with contractual arrangements, budgets, and other company authorizations.

2. Trace billings for media services to underlying billings from the individual media.

a. Is the rendering of the service by the media adequately evidenced?

b. Are rates the best available for the services rendered with due consideration to times rendered and volume?

c. Are commissions accurately computed?

3. Determine that all other costs billed are properly recoverable and reflect full value.

C. Internal Operations

1. Do the day-to-day operations appear to be well supervised and administered?

2. Are records and procedures adequate for the control of work carried out and expenditures incurred?

3. Is outside procurement handled in accordance with recognized procurement standards?

4. Are media relationships covered by adequate procedures to assure propriety of rates charged, authorized services, and evidence of rendering of service?

5. Are coordinative relationships between the various activities of the agency adequate?

D. General Relations with the Company

1. Are relations with the company adequate both in terms of day-to-day timing, and in degree of integrated coordination?

2. Are relations with dealers and customers carried out adequately, both in terms of basic professional service, and cooperative approaches?

3. In what other ways do you feel that the services of the agency could be improved to serve the company's interests better?

VI. Other Special Audit Tests

A. Special Promotional Programs

In situations where there is a special promotional program of significant magnitude, audit it in major detail:

1. As to scope of underlying objectives and arrangements.

2. As to actual operation of the program.

3. As to results achieved.

B. Representative Product Planning Developments
    Select a representative number of product planning and development
    cases, and review them from their first inception through the various
    subsequent operational stages.
    1. Who did what at each stage?
    2. How effectively were the individual cases handled?
C. Regional Sales Offices
    Select a representative number of regional sales offices and audit their
    total operations for a given period of time:
    1. As to compliance with all applicable policies and procedures.
    2. As to general efficiency of operation.
D. Distribution Centers
    Where there are distribution centers, operated either by the company
    or a distributor, examine their operation:
    1. For compliance with all applicable policies and procedures.
    2. For efficiency of operation.
    3. For adequacy of service provided.
E. Customer Support
    Select a representative number of customers and review with them
    directly the adequacy of the various factors outlined in the chapter
    text.

VII–IX. Not used.

   X. Overall Appraisal of Marketing Effectiveness
       A. See standard Audit Guides, Chapter 13.

ILLUSTRATIVE AUDIT FINDINGS: MARKETING

Unprofitable Sales Offices

An audit of company sales offices disclosed that three of them were incurring
significant operating losses. In all three cases major customers had relocated
their operations or changed their lines of business, and future business prospects in the areas served were limited. It was recommended that the central
sales office monitor overall company sales office needs more currently and
determine whether the three sales offices should be closed.

Delays in Filling Orders

A statistical sample of sales orders for the last three months indicated that
substantial delays were experienced in filling customer orders. This resulted
in canceled orders and in some cases the permanent loss of customers. The
delays were caused by excessive time required for administrative processing
of the orders, as well as overly optimistic delivery dates promised the customers.

Product Defects

The company was not correcting defects in the manufacture of a product, resulting in excessive returns and repair costs under warranties. It was found that the sales department delayed in providing information to the production department concerning the nature and extent of the defects. In addition, the production and engineering departments did not analyze the defects on a timely basis to determine the causes and take corrective action.

Invalid Survey of Product Demand

Analysis of a field survey performed in market research indicated that a statistical sample taken was not representative of prospective purchasers of the product. As a result, information obtained as to demand for the product was invalid for use in the company's product decisions.

Prices Set Too Low

Salespeople were being given authority to set customer prices without limitation from the central sales office, resulting in too-low markups for some customers. In addition, practices followed by some salespeople resulted in price discrimination. It was recommended that the central sales office either control the setting of prices or provide salespeople with additional guidance as a basis for arriving at acceptable prices.

Ineffective Credit Controls

Excessive sales were being made to customers who were bad credit risks, resulting in a high ratio of bad debts to sales. On the other hand, sales were unduly restricted to other customers with a prior record of payments on time. Additional credit statistics were needed as a basis for setting credit limits to maximize profits.

CHAPTER TWENTY

Personnel Activities

NATURE OF THE PERSONNEL FUNCTION

This chapter is intended to deal primarily with the review of the activities of the personnel department. The name of this department may vary in individual situations, but it will be the department that is charged with the responsibility of assisting management in carrying out the personnel or people function. It is primarily a staff group since it is the basic responsibility of all managers to deal with people, although in certain situations the personnel department may administer service activities on a line basis. What is distinctive about this chapter, however, is that in discussing the areas where the personnel department is assisting management, we unavoidably are discussing matters of direct managerial responsibility. We will, therefore, be talking about a function that is carried out jointly and in a special collaborative manner.

The chapter builds on the basic material relating to human needs, as discussed in Chapter 7, but goes on to involve the actual company operations more directly. On the other hand, we do not cover the basic financial aspects of payroll procedures which were included in Chapter 13. We are concerned with all the relationships with people in the company at all organizational levels, as the personnel department seeks to provide assistance and services to all other staff and line components.

Scope of the Personnel Department Role

A proper understanding of the role of the personnel department must again start with the recognition that people problems are a major part of the basic responsibility of each manager. Managers accomplish things through people. Under normal circumstances, therefore, it is the responsibility of each manager to select, administer, develop, and reward people. But we know also as a practical matter that managers of the various line and staff activities in the company need assistance if they are to do their job effectively. In many areas there are opportunities for the utilization of professional counsel in the personnel area. It is also necessary that policies and procedures be developed on a company-wide basis so that there will be a proper standard of quality, an equitable application to all organizational components, and the protection of legal and broader social responsibilities. Certain personnel data also need to be developed on a company-wide basis. Finally also, there are frequently particular company service activities that can be best handled on a centralized basis. For all these reasons there is a proper and substantive need for staff assistance. It is the role of the personnel department to provide that staff assistance in the most effective manner possible.

What Is the Personnel Function?   The nature and scope of the staff assistance role can be viewed also in terms of the nature of the personnel function itself. One way of describing the personnel function is to say that it has to do with the relationships with all employees of the company from the time the employee relationship is first established until it is terminated in one way or another. This is, of course, a broad and far-reaching description, but it properly emphasizes the fact that the personnel function is all inclusive and that it is interwoven with the total management process. Still another way to describe the personnel function is that it has to do with the most effective matching of people with job needs. There is work to be done and people must be identified who can do that work. What "effective" means in this instance is a matching that strikes the balance that is most satisfactory from two points of view: (1) the needs of the company to achieve its established objectives, and (2) the personal needs of the people involved. Again it is clear that we have a broadly based function that goes directly to the heart of the total management function.

Special Problems of the Personnel Department.   What this all means is that the personnel department has a unique opportunity to assist management. Everything it does in one way or another affects managerial performance and success. But this close interrelationship brings with it a special problem. This special problem is that the department can very easily cross over the line of where its staff role should end and go on to assume a role that infringes on the basic responsibilities of individual managers at any level. A related special problem is that the personnel function can come to be an operation of policies and procedures that is unduly detached from the real operational conditions and needs. Too often the personnel department is accused of developing overly elaborate procedures that destroy an image of real workability in a partnership sense. At its worst the personnel department can develop gimmicks or shallow approaches that do more harm than good, and tend to operate in a kind of vacuum. The solutions here call for staffing the personnel department itself with people of adequate ability, judgment, and stature, and then to have these people work with other company personnel in a close and collaborative manner. There is, indeed, an important job to be done and the challenge is to find a way to do that job properly.

Major Areas of Application

In a general sense the area of application for the personnel function is people, whoever they are and whatever they do in the company. In its most important respect there is a common focus on people problems. At the same time the conditions of employment, the nature of the job performed, and the economic level of compensation result in significantly different problems. It is not possible to recognize all of these varying situations in any general discussion, but there are three major categories that need to be recognized. These are as follows:

1. *Hourly Paid Labor.* This group of people is distinguished principally by the fact that the workers are paid on an hourly basis, and that in most cases they are unionized. The work done by this group is located mainly in the production area, but extends to other allied service and operational activities.

2. *Salaried Clerical.* This group is paid on a salary basis and is less likely to be unionized. The clerical work done can be scattered practically anywhere through the company.

3. *Management Personnel.* At some level in each company the salaried personnel are classed as management personnel. The distinguishing characteristics of this group are the scope of assigned responsibilities and the more complicated patterns of administration. The group covers gradations that run from lower levels up to the top management executives.

Because of the commonality of many of the principles of personnel administration among the three groups, the plan is to discuss the more basic considerations first as a whole, with only limited reference to the three separate groups. We then return to a further elaboration of some of the special problems. as they pertain to the individual groups.

OVERALL OPERATIONAL PATTERN OF PERSONNEL ACTIVITIES

Common Elements

Although the various needs of the company will cover a wide spectrum, there is a common operational framework for all types of personnel. This is:

1. The identification of personnel needs, both in terms of the current situation and the future at various points of time.
2. The inventory, analysis, and appraisal of current personnel resources, for purposes of comparison with needs and determination of the existing gap.
3. The various activities that pertain to the means by which the gap, as previously determined, is to be bridged.
4. The many activities that have to do with the administration of the current work force.

We propose to discuss the personnel activities in this sequence, and then to deal separately with certain special problems.

Identification of Personnel Needs

The company has presumably established an organizational structure that is applicable at the present point of time. This organizational structure reflects the managerial judgments as to how the work is to be broken up and assigned to particular individuals at all levels. From this basic organizational analysis the next step is the development of more detailed job descriptions. As we have seen previously, job descriptions become a key building block in the administration of any company activity. These job descriptions then become the basis for the development of specifications for the particular kinds of individuals that are needed. Each job has its specific requirements in terms of knowledge, skills, personality, and experience. When all of this is done on a company-wide basis we are able to determine what the total company requirements are for numbers of the various types of people.

The type of analysis described above, as applied to the current situation, is at the same time extended into the future. Sometimes this future projection is very limited in scope and relatively informal, but in a well-managed company it is done in a systematic manner and will extend at least through the planning period that is appropriate to the particular type of business. For this planning period the growth and changing nature of the business will be projected, the related organizational requirements will be determined as best possible, and personnel needs estimated. This is a process that will normally be carried on at all levels and by all managers on the basis of common company assumptions—growth, scope of business activities, and the like.

From a control standpoint the determination of personnel needs is basic. It is important that it be done on a careful and systematic basis, and that it be updated periodically to reflect changes in future plans. Unless this estimate is carefully made, all subsequent supporting implementation will lack direction. It is also important to note the close tie-in of the forward personnel determinations with the organizational planning and development discussed in Chapter 5.

Available Resources for Satisfying Personnel Needs

The next step is to take inventory of the available resources so that the company can determine the extent to which it is presently able to satisfy its personnel needs. This inventory again has both its current dimension and its projection through the same planning period as was used in identifying the future needs. Individuals are viewed first in terms of their capacity to fill designated jobs at this particular point in time, and then in terms of what the company thinks they would reasonably be capable of doing with further development in successive years through the planning periods. Thus needs and resources are compared through a time spectrum that encompasses the entire planning period and that discloses at each key point in that time spectrum the excess or shortage of resources. Normally, a company will have a shortage gap that can exist at the present time and that will grow larger as needs grow at a faster pace than the resources. The identification of the gap during the successive years of the planning period provides the important information of what the company will face in the way of a people problem. It sets the stage for determining the nature and scope of the program which must be carried out to close that gap. As might be expected the importance of determining the gap and developing the needed action programs is greatest in the management personnel area, but it is important in the other two areas also. Illustrative would be shortages of particular types of technical personnel or special labor skills.

From a control standpoint the assessment of available resources becomes the key backup to the earlier determined needs. Again, it is most important that the procedures for making this assessment and comparing it with previously determined needs be both well designed and carefully executed. Again also, it is the responsibility of every manager to contribute his best possible input to this process.

Activities to Provide Needed Personnel Resources

The activities to bridge the current and projected gaps between personnel needs and personnel resources fall into two major categories. One means is through the recruitment of new personnel to the company. The other approach is to accelerate the development of the company's own personnel. The personnel department can provide assistance for both approaches.

Recruitment and Selection of New Personnel. The recruitment process begins with a judgment of where the prospective candidates are likely to be. Particular trade skills may tend to concentrate in particular geographical areas, managerial resources will generally be greatest in urban centers, and persons with modern business school training can best be found at the leading business schools. Closely related is the judgment as to how the potential employees can best be contacted. Typical methods are newspaper advertising, employee referrals, trade journals, employment agencies, and direct visitations to the colleges. Usually, a reasonable amount of care and thought will determine the most appropriate approach for the particular kind of recruits being sought.

Once potential candidates have been identified, and recognizing that employment is always a two-way decision between the company and the candidate, one comes to the problem of how the actual selection shall be made. At this point there is no single approach and we have a combination of techniques and practices, subject always to the very important judgment factor. Typical approaches used include:

1. *Completion of Application Forms.* The usefulness of the application form is that needed information can be conveniently obtained along such lines as age, education, professional achievements, and work experience. There is something learned also by how an application form is completed. In the management category the applicant is more likely to submit his own résumé, and here especially is a basis of appraising the person by the way that résumé is prepared.

2. *References*. A second important method used in the selection process is the written or direct contact (usually by telephone) with references furnished by the applicant. The direct contacts provide an especially good basis for asking more probing questions about the candidate's qualifications. From a control standpoint, however, it must be remembered that the reference has usually been selected by the applicant, thus ensuring to a significant extent that the reference will be well disposed toward the applicant. The company official, knowing this, must be all the more frank and persuasive to be sure that he is getting a truly objective report. Also where possible, the employer will seek to find independent references on whom he can more fully rely.

3. *Special Tests*. A variety of special tests have been developed to evaluate personality and particular types of aptitudes for different types of work. Clinical tests by psychologists are also sometimes used. These provide a useful supplementary bit of input but need to be used with caution, particularly in the psychological areas where the validity of the testing techniques is not as great as could be desired. However, progress is continually being made in the development of more effective testing.

4. *Personal Interviews*. Probably in most cases the major reliance is on the personal interview between the applicant and the company official or officials. Most managers have developed a reasonably competence in sizing up an applicant on a face-to-face basis and determining whether he is likely to fit well into the particular job situation. It also works out best when the interviewer is able to induce the applicant to speak freely, thus involving the art on the part of the interviewer to be a good listener. Needless to say, however, it is easy to make mistakes and to be misled by favorable first impressions. Nevertheless, the personal interview is a major means of supplementing the careful use of the other methods.

From a control standpoint the concern is that policies and procedures are in effect that will reasonably assure matching of the job opportunities with the best qualified candidates. This means that each major type of job need must be separately evaluated and handled. It means also that all available means of evaluation be utilized, but at the same time handled with great care. Interviews especially need to be made by a number of qualified persons to provide an adequate cross check.

Training and Development.   In the normal company situation the employees recruited must be provided with additional training and development throughout the greater part of their career span. The general need for such training and development is recognized by all, the real problem being how much of it there should be and how it can be done most effectively. This training is initiated at the time of recruitment, and the extent to which it is needed is directly related to the qualifications of the new employee. As a minimum there will be the training that provides necessary instruction to carry out a particular job assignment. Thereafter the training may be of a remedial or supplemental nature to assist the employee in taking on a more advanced assignment. In other cases the training may be of a broader nature and pertain to the development of better human relations, providing administrative skills, or for other managerial purposes. The objective in all cases is to achieve a greater usefulness and capability on the part of the individuals to whom the training is made available. All of this training is over and above the development that comes about through normal job experience and as a result of the regular supervisory efforts of the various bosses.

Fundamentals of Training. The achievement of effective training depends directly on the extent to which we can develop competence in the learning process. This is a professional area that cannot be reduced to precise formulas, but there are important principles that need to be understood and properly handled. These include:

1. *Receptivity on the Part of the Trainee.* A necessary first requirement is that the trainee recognize his need for training, and want to receive the particular assistance that is being offered. The trainee must see the training as relevant and worthwhile in terms of his goals and objectives, thus giving him the motivation to take advantage of it.

2. *Quality of the Training Materials.* The training materials themselves must be sound in a professional sense. Ideally, they have in fact been tested in that respect. At the same time they must be presented in a manner that is consistent with their quality. Especially must the materials have credibility to the trainee.

3. *Time Requirements.* The time requirements depend on the degree of difficulty of the training to be imparted and the capacity of the trainees themselves. But within reasonable ranges the training must recognize these time requirements and respect them. Otherwise, the training effort will be largely wasted.

4. *Participation and Involvement.* It is well known that effective training depends on a proper degree of participation on the part of the trainee. As learners we need to be involved and to have some kind of two-way interchange. In some situations it is possible to provide some type of feedback whereby the trainee can check on his progress. In the case method approach the trainee is able to participate directly in the discussion. These participative processes have been proven to be more effective than the conventional lecture approach.

5. *Reinforcement.* Closely related is the necessity for the trainee to perceive his definitive progress, and in some way to feel that he is being rewarded for that progress. This reinforcement can take place during the actual training session—as where a teaching machine program confirms the mastery of a particular increment of training—or it can be where the employer specifically recognizes the trainee's increased knowledge and competence which has come about through the training program.

Problems of Training.   For the most part, the problems of training are where the previously outlined principles are not adequately handled. What is likely to happen is that training is carried out because of a higher-management-level edict, but without the development of well-planned and well-executed programs. Under these circumstances training programs become sterile, busywork-type programs that are not meaningful to trainees, but instead become a source of irritation and ridicule. The blame for such failures involves two major groups. The first group is the personnel department that is charged with the responsibility for planning and carrying out such programs. The second group is management itself in delegating too completely the training function. Here again it must be recognized that training is part of the direct responsibility of management at all levels, and that management must involve itself sufficiently in the training process to be certain that it is being carried out effectively.

Control Problems of Training.   The key control aspects of effective training can be summarized, as follows:

1. The need for continuous management involvement and support.
2. The design of training programs that are both properly coordinated with operational needs and based on adequate professional standards.
3. The careful and sensitive administration of the actual training programs to assure good motivation and interest.

Although effective training does depend on professional know-how to a considerable extent, the fact remains that much of it is good sense and conscientious administration. The review of training by the outside reviewer can, therefore, be most rewarding. The benefits achieved are especially important when one recognizes the amount of time and money that is expended in these programs and the impact on human productivity that is involved.

Utilization of Personnel

Managers attempt to achieve effective utilization of personnel in various parts of the company. This includes the proper assignment of personnel to jobs in accordance with abilities. Also, sufficient subordinates and clerical staff should be assigned to assure that employees are working in accordance with job sheets and standards. Managers want the personnel function to be cost effective and are thus interested in personnel assignments.

In recent years management has placed increasing emphasis on work measurement as a basis for improving the productivity of hourly employees. Work measurement programs are designed to disclose such factors as outmoded work routines, poorly organized systems, excess staffing, and duplication. Through time and motion study, work systems are reviewed to develop preferred methods, standardize systems, and determine the time required by the average worker to do the task. Various other systems are used, such as work sampling and methods time measurement. The latter analyzes operations into basic motions required to perform it, and assigns to each motion a predetermined standard. Work measurement is also being used in clerical office routine. The purpose is to reduce paperwork costs through improved work flow, methods, and layout. In addition, an effort is made to improve operating controls through establishing schedules, relating tasks, and measuring employee and supervisory effectiveness. Paper simplification and office mechanization are some of the methods recommended to increase productivity and reduce costs.

Management is also interested in controls to assure that there is not an excess of personnel in certain classifications and shortages in others. The timing and duration of excesses need to be reviewed, as well as whether hiring and transfers are based on actual need. Records of idle time need to be maintained and studied for trends and analysis of the causes. The use of overtime in the company should be well controlled, with proper authorization in advance. Excessive overtime may be a symptom of improper scheduling of work, shortage of certain classifications of personnel, deficiencies in technical performance, and inordinate demands of customers, supervisors, and using departments.

PROBLEMS OF CURRENT PERSONNEL ADMINISTRATION

We come now to a wide range of current administrative activities that are carried out by a typical personnel department, supplementing the activities previously discussed. We will deal with these current administrative activities under the following headings:

1. Job analysis and evaluation.
2. Compensation administration.
3. Performance evaluation.
4. Transfers, promotion, and termination.
5. Employee records and reports.
6. Personal guidance activities.
7. Employee benefit programs.
8. Employee services.
9. Workmen's compensation and safety.
10. Labor relations.

Job Analysis and Evaluation

Reference has previously been made to the development of job descriptions and specifications as a basis for determining a company's personnel needs. From an administrative standpoint it also becomes necessary to rate the individual jobs in terms of relative difficulty and importance. This requires some kind of a yardstick that usually takes the form of a manual. In this manual various factors or dimensions are identified—as, for example, type of skill required, extent of responsibility, scope of effort, and nature of working conditions. These factors must then be measured in degrees of difference and some kind of weights assigned. These general measures are then available to be applied to specific jobs. At this point we require a detailed set of specifications to cover the individual job. At the same time appropriate job titles need to be developed.

The most difficult part of the job analysis and evaluation procedure is now the application of the general criteria to the individual job on the basis of the particular specifications. This is generally accomplished by the assignment of points in recognition of the degree of application of the various criteria. The concern here is with relative rankings of individual jobs. It is a determination that is bound to involve a great deal of judgment and hence one that must be made with extreme care and objectivity. The individual jobs are normally grouped in a number of grades or other broad classifications. The number of such grades can be relatively large or small but it seems usually to work best when about 15 to 25 are used.

Compensation Administration

While the job analysis and evaluation process is technically something that stands apart from the matter of compensation, in practice the two processes are closely interwoven. The compensation phase actually begins with a determination of the general level of pay in the community and industry of which the company is a part. Here the company faces the first question of its general approach to the meeting of that general pay level. On the one hand, its own level of compensation must be sufficiently high to attract personnel of the quality desired and in the proper numbers. On the other hand, an unduly high level of compensation will ultimately be reflected in excessive costs and noncompetitive product prices. Once the general level of compensation has been determined, the compensation levels must be fixed for the various job classifications and grades previously established during the job analysis phase. In the case of each grade it is customary to fix a minimum and a maximum with the expectation that this will provide needed flexibility in the application to particular individuals. At the same time, flexibility is provided for the giving of merit increases during the time span that an individual job falls in a particular grade.

The combined job classification and compensation grades together thus provide a necessary orderly framework by which a company can reasonably evaluate and control employee relationships. At the same time, there are many troublesome problems that arise in actual practice. Specific individuals will, for example, feel strongly that the nature of their work calls for a higher job classification than has been assigned. In some cases changing conditions may provide legitimate support for that position. In other cases the problem may be that of a restless employee who is qualified to do more responsible work but where there is presently no opening for his higher-level skill. A more general problem arises when employees come to believe that merit increases periodically granted are due to them. Here management flexibility can be unduly restricted. In situations where unions are involved, the determination of the job classifications and the related compensation become a contested part of the contractual negotiations and the subsequent administration of the contract. Thus on many fronts the job classifications and compensation become the sensitive point in the resolution of conflicting individual and company needs.

Control Aspects of Job Analysis and Compensation. From a control standpoint it may be useful to summarize briefly the essential control requirements as they pertain to the combined processes of job evaluation and compensation administration. These include at least the following:

1. A plan of job classifications that is based on a well-thought-out set of evaluation criteria.
2. A level of general compensation, as applied to the various job classifications, that is reasonably competitive.
3. Individual jobs carefully evaluated in terms of the existing criteria.
4. Regular reviews periodically made as to the scope of compensation for individual employees.
5. The overall plan of grades and related compenstion as appraised at appropriate intervals for changes in existing conditions.

Performance Evaluation

The administration of employees necessarily requires in one way or another some kind of evaluation of performance. This evaluation is in part a continuing process and in part a periodic undertaking. In its most basic sense it can be said to serve two key purposes. One of these purposes is to provide a partial basis for determining the best possible future utilization of the individual. This will include possible transfer, promotion, and increased compensation. The second objective also has to do with achieving the most effective future utilization of the employee, but concentrates more on what can be done to help the individual overcome any existing limitations and to increase his overall competence. It will again be seen that in both cases we are dealing with important direct management responsibilities. The personnel department role comes about in the way of helping to provide supporting procedures and policies.

Supporting Procedures. The personnel department has typically provided assistance by establishing a policy whereby all managers and supervisors will be responsible for at least an annual performance review. Typically also, forms will be provided for use at the several major supervisory levels that will detail the various factors to be considered and measures of performance to be evaluated. The factors will normally include job competence, personal qualifications, and the ability to work with people. Each of these factors will normally be evaluated on the basis of a scale or captions which run from unsatisfactory through acceptable, fair, good, very good, and outstanding. Provision will also be made for problems being encountered and consideration of what can be done to deal with such problems. The performance review is prepared by the immediate superior and is then reviewed and approved by the next-higher level of management. Under some procedures the completed review is shown to the person being reviewed, and his confirming signature may also be required. The completed forms are then placed in personnel files maintained by the personnel department, and are available to management personnel when wanted.

Problems of Performance Reviews. The achievement of an effective performance review program begins with a comprehensive and well-designed review form. The problems, however, are much more deep seated. Typically, the individual supervisor or manager dislikes the role of playing judge over the evaluation of his subordinate. When it comes to reducing something like this to writing and sharing it with the subordinate it becomes all the more unlikely that there will be the needed degree of objectivity and candor. Most individuals also experience real difficulty in adequately perceiving their own shortcomings, and to cut through this natural resistance becomes both difficult and unappealing for a reviewer. As a result, reviews tend to fall far short of what they might to be in terms of overall usefulness. Especially is this true as one moves up the managerial hierarchy, as it seems that the higher one goes, the less inclined managers are to complicate sensitive personal relationships by discussing performance evaluations. The answer is not to abandon the process. Rather, the best solution is to recognize the problem and to do the best possible to make an improvement. Generally, this has come to mean that the coaching approach is most likely to be acceptable to all parties involved, and at the same time has the greatest potential.

Transfers, Promotions, and Terminations

In any ongoing company situation there is a changing pattern of personnel needs. Some of the problems relate primarily to individual situations, whereas others arise out of more broadly based changes in personnel requirements. In all of these situations the personnel department serves as a central source of information as to available personnel resources, and as a planner and counselor in helping managers and supervisors solve their various problems. A particular individual is not working out well in his current assignment. What can be done to improve the situation or to find another situation where his contribution can be more effectively utilized? Or someone leaves the company, or a new job is created, thus opening up a new job assignment that needs to be filled. Who then are the individuals in the company who have the kind of experience and other qualifications that would make them eligible for consideration? The personnel department is uniquely equipped to provide a list of such candidates and to be able to help in making a final selection.

On a larger scale a new expansion of activity in a particular sector of the operations may bring with it the need for a substantially greater work force. Where are these people to come from, and how can we best go about it to provide the people as they are needed? Or conversely, there may be a major cutback of operations that will necessitate a substantial reduction of personnel in a particular department or division. Perhaps also, a new computerized system may lead to a major cutback in certain clerical areas, but at the same time may mean expanded needs in certain other areas such as programming and system input. In all of these situations the personnel department can render major assistance in developing plans whereby the disruptive process can be minimized and whereby the company's ultimate needs can be best satisfied. Especially where terminations may be involved, there is the need to anticipate this aspect, and to develop types of separation arrangements that will be both as equitable as possible and consistent with ongoing community responsibilities.

Employee Records and Reports

As we have seen, at various times the personnel department serves as a major central source of information regarding employees. When an individual joins the company, his original application and supplementary investigation becomes part of the basic company records. Subsequently, as individual job actions take place—transfers, new assignments, compensation changes, promotions, and so on—the papers pertaining to these job actions are processed by the personnel department and become part of the basic personnel records. As we have seen, performance reviews and evaluations become a part of these central employee records. Finally, when the employee leaves the company, or is retired or terminated, the circumstances of this final development are made a part of the records. The maintenance of these records thus becomes a primary responsibility of the personnel department. This enables the department to function as a major reference source to the entire company, and to be able to assist most effectively as a planning and counseling group.

The responsibility for all employee records and the processing of all changes in the employment status of the individual employees now sets the stage for a reporting responsibility along any lines desired by management. Information needed may relate to the composition of the work force and its changes over time—age, sex, religion, race, and the like—or it may relate to significant operational considerations. The particular interest may be for information as a basis for the control of overtime, absenteeism, or turnover. Or the information sought may pertain to levels of compensation and the trends in this area. How many merit increases are being granted and how often? What percentages of the individuals in the respective grades are at or near the upper and lower limits? How many people are being promoted from within as opposed to outside recruitment? What is the scope of the formal training activity in each sector of the operations? It is apparent that any of these needs can be served through the record resources of the personnel department.

Personal Guidance Activities

The responsibilities of the individual manager in developing his subordinates have been stressed repeatedly. There are occasions, however, when the subordinate needs to have a place where he can go that is independent of his primary boss–employee relationship. The question may relate to the clarification of a particular personnel policy, and perhaps in its direct application to a specific aspect of the relationship with his boss. Or the need may be for counsel in working out some aspect of that boss relationship. In still other cases the employee may be interested in exploring alternative types of job opportunities in other operational areas of the company, or in appraising various types of career patterns. The personnel department can in these kinds of circumstances provide useful assistance to individual employees, both in the way of providing needed information and in acting as an independent friend and counselor. Needless to say, this requires a particular kind of professional competence and skill on the part of the individual representative of the personnel group. It requires also a high sense of confidentiality and integrity with respect to the kinds of matters disclosed by individual employees. Important also is the necessity to retain a friendly but neutral attitude and to avoid becoming a partisan advocate in opposition to the individual manager or higher-level management.

Employee Benefit Programs

In recent years there has been a widespread development of many types of programs which in one way or another supplement the basic wage and salary compensation paid to the employee. In some cases these programs have come out of union negotiations. In other cases they have been devised as means to provide better for the needs of the employees, thus enabling the individual employees to be relieved of problems that might otherwise threaten their efforts to serve the company effectively. In still other cases the objective seems to be to motivate the employee in some way to provide higher levels of service. In many cases the establishment of particular programs by other companies has brought with it the competitive necessity that one's own company do likewise. All of these supplementary programs are referred to loosely as fringe benefits. Needless to say, they all cost money and the cost of each must be appraised individually as to its worth in ultimately serving the company's interests.

The nature and scope of these supplementary fringe benefit programs cover a wide range. Some of them are very closely related to the basic compensation. Illustrative of this type would be bonuses paid out of profits, stock option programs, savings, and stock purchase plans where employee contributions are matched by the company in some manner, insurance coverage at no cost or at below-market rates, hospital and medical protection, vacations, paid holidays, and the like. Other programs, while still being of the same general character, are less significant and are not so closely identified with the basic compensation. Illustrative of these would be credit services, food services that are partially subsidized, recreational services, and special types of home management and counseling services. Some programs, while technically part of the employee benefits, are hardly thought of as compensation at all. Illustrative of these would be company newspapers, purchasing associations, and social centers. All of these programs, however, need to be developed in accordance with sound standards of design and then properly administered. It is the personnel department that typically assumes these responsibilities.

Control Criteria of Employee Benefit Programs. The various employee benefit programs not only cost a great deal of money but also are all the more important because they involve so directly the relationships with employees. The important control considerations that need to be carefully administered include:

1. The careful design of the program in terms of costs and expected benefits.
2. The adequate communication of the way the program is to operate, including especially the basis on which available alternatives should be evaluated by each individual.
3. The careful administration of all aspects of the program.
4. Periodic reappraisal of whether the program is achieving its proper objectives, and what possible modifications should be made in it.

Service Activities

In the typical company situation there are a number of activities of a service nature that can be carried out most efficiently and economically on a centralized basis. Illustrative of such activities are plant protection and security, maintenance of reception areas, local transportation, first aid services, safety, printing, photography, and communication services. The distinction between these activities and employee benefits is that they represent services that are necessary to the ongoing operations of the company, and when carried out on a centralized basis must be made the responsibility of some staff group. In some situations such responsibility is assigned to a separate administrative services group. In other cases the personnel department is selected to provide this role.

What happens in either case is that the particular activity needs to be handled as a kind of a special business. The objective on the one hand is to provide the particular types of service to all company users in the way that will best suit their various operational needs. At the same time the theory of the consolidated operation is that this will be done at the lowest possible cost to the company. The possibility that always exists, however, is that the service group becomes too secure in its kind of monopoly position and is not adequately motivated in the normal sense to do as energetic a job as it should in meeting the various user needs. In this connection the role of an independent outside reviewer like the internal auditor can be especially useful. Moreover, the existence of the regular outside review is in itself a useful kind of motivation to the service group to check more critically on its own operation on a day-to-day basis.

Workmen's Compensation Activities and Safety

The general problem of safety was previously discussed in some detail in Chapter 16. We return to it here because of the usual relationship of the personnel department to this important activity. In addition, the administration of the workmen's compensation program deserves special recognition as an important aspect of the total personnel department activity. The underlying safety problem as we have previously seen is a combination of effective engineering—that is, the design of good protective devices of a physical nature—and working with people for greater safety consciousness. It is the latter area where the skills of the personnel department can be especially effective. The people approach begins with the careful selection of people to avoid the type that tends to be unduly prone to accidents. It goes on to develop a staff type of service that educates and alerts all employees to the desirability of safety and the means of best achieving safety conditions. Finally, there is the need to reinforce the fact of each manager's responsibility for promoting safety in his own particular area of operations. Since the personnel department also administers the handling of all workman's compensation claims arising out of actual accidents, the personnel department is in an excellent position to utilize these facts in the further efforts to develop an effective safety program. At the same time the facts in this area can be communicated to all interested parties in meaningful reports. The final test, of course, is the extent to which accidents are actually eliminated.

Labor Relations

Any discussion of personnel department activities would be incomplete without some recognition of the role in the handling of labor relations and the day-to-day problems as they relate to the existing unions. It is, of course, natural that this close interrelationship with unions should exist since the personnel department is dealing with such a wide range of matters affecting every employee. At the outset these personnel relationships involve the conditions out of which union relationships emerge. Prior to the unionization of either hourly or salary workers it is the conditions of compensation and the conditions of other kinds of treatment which provide the foundation from which the proposals for unionization emerge. Here the personnel group serves both as the sensor to the developing problems and the counselor as to how the force of particular problems can be neutralized. Similarly, after a union is established, the process is repeated as the pressure for new types of contractual arrangements are generated. Here current actions continuously set the stage for the renegotiation and modification of union contracts. But irrespective of these future implications, the personnel department is also actively engaged in the current administration of the union relationships. Interpretation of and compliance with individual contractual provisions must be continuous. Rules must be enforced and actions pursuant to these rules properly documented. When grievances are asserted at any level in the work force, these must be dealt with in a manner that is fair and equitable. In all of these relationships with the union the personnel group has a major opportunity to blend the ever-basic managerial roles of other company personnel with the needed uniformity of company-wide policies and procedures.

SPECIAL PERSONNEL PROBLEMS FOR MANAGEMENT

The discussion of the functions of the personnel department provides an appropriate opportunity to touch on certain broader types of personnel problems with which management is currently being challenged. These further problems go beyond the previously discussed current operations of the personnel department, but do involve areas where there are major assistance potentials for the personnel group. At the same time the internal auditor can, through better understanding of these problems, be alert to the impact on operational problems that he is reviewing. We will deal very briefly with seven of these major types of management problems that involve the continuing effective utilization of people.

1. Increasing unionization.
2. Minority-group development.
3. Women in industry.
4. Adapting to higher human expectations.
5. Utilization of computers.
6. Continuing management development.
7. Achieving good morale.

Increasing Unionization

The major development of unionization has, as we know, been in the so-called blue-collar or day-labor area. The basis for this development has been the belief on the part of labor that it was not receiving a fair share of the productive results made possible by its operational collaboration with management. Other contributing causes have probably also been the greater desire of laborers for self-expression and greater control over their own activity. At the same time enterprising labor leaders have recognized their opportunities to build up their own strength and power. The impact of all of this development on management has been primarily the constraints of union demands and the lesser degree of management flexibility. On the other hand, there have been some benefits in the way of a more orderly process of dealing with labor needs. In most large companies the unionization of direct labor has become a fact and the management problem is how to deal with unions in an effective manner. Although there are still some situations where day labor is not unionized, there is continuing pressure on the part of unions for the further control.

The same forces that have generated the unionization of day labor now also appear to be operating to try to bring various types of salaried employees into the unions. Clerical-type salary workers have become increasingly a target for union organizers and some limited success has been achieved. More recently there has been some unionization of professional groups such as engineers. These developments again have effects similar to the earlier direct labor unionization in the way of widening the gap between the partners of the total company effort, and in placing further constraints on management flexibility. Our own purpose is not to pass judgment on the very complex issues that are involved, but to recognize the problem as one where management needs all possible assistance. This assistance comes first in providing information and counsel about conditions where unionization may be developing as an issue, and then subsequently in dealing with existing unions. Because of the internal auditors' continuous exposure to operations a special opportunity exists to render such assistance.

Minority-Group Development

A major development of recent years has been the view that minority groups have not shared equitably in the economic and social progress of our society. To the greater extent this focus has been on the black portion of our population, but it has also extended to the status and progress of other racial and ethnic groups. The black dimension of this problem has, however, been the most volatile and has received greater attention because of the more violent type of protest which has often been associated with the problem. The basic complaint is that the blacks in our population have in total been substantially exploited, and that major corrective action is needed in providing better living conditions, better education, and better economic opportunities. This is a view shared not only by the blacks themselves but by a great number of whites. The development has had a significant impact on the modern business company and its operations. It is a problem that every well-managed company is seeking to understand and to cope with more effectively. Suddenly, the extent to which black persons are being utilized within the company is being carefully examined and new efforts are being made to accelerate the degree of utilization.

Again it is not our purpose to pass judgment on the causes and responsibilities of this very complicated problem. We are concerned primarily with the fact of the existing pressure for greater utilization of black personnel in higher-level jobs, and the kinds of operational problems that are involved. These problems include the usually existing needs for more training, the often sensitive personal relations involved with the minority workers, the reactions of other company personnel, and the overall impact on the levels of product quality and customer service. Here the conflicts that normally exist between various internal management objectives pose major problems of evaluation and ultimate reconciliation.

Women in Industry

Another more recent problem has to do with the extent to which women are utilized as compared with male personnel. The concern here has two dimensions. The first of these is that women be given equal opportunity to have particular types of jobs, that is, that they are not discriminated against when they are equally qualified to do those jobs. The second dimension is that, when women are given particular jobs, they be fairly compensated. The standard here is especially the compensation given to a male when he does a similar type of work. The pressures to combat both types of discrimination have come primarily from associations of women. These associations have exerted their pressures directly on the management of various organizations, and have additionally made a strong appeal for general public support. The problem of management has been how to respond to these new pressures in an orderly and effective manner. One of the difficulties is the very frequently controversial judgmental question as to the extent to which the performance of the female employee really conforms to the ends of the job. There is also in many cases the counterpressures of male employees who feel that their earning needs have a higher priority. In all phases of the problem, management quite clearly needs the kind of assistance that can be rendered by the independent reviewer.

Adapting to Changing Human Expectations

The previously discussed problems of a more effective treatment of minorities and women extend also into the broader dimensions of changing human expectations, and how management can best adapt to those changes. What has been the most basic development in this area has been the change in attitude of youth, and the strong protest against certain conditions of our times. The general view of youth seems to be that in achieving economic and material goals, there has been an undue disregard for environmental factors and more basic human needs. The impact on business has been twofold. One result has been the new pressures to raise the standards of environmental protection to an extent that is both frequently very difficult in terms of feasibility, and at very high cost. The other impact has been to divert many young people from an interest in business careers. Instead, many of the brightest of the younger minds have been attracted to social causes and governmental activities. Business, while initially disregarding this change of attitude, or at least believing that it was a temporary phenomenon, has now begun more vigorously to find solutions to bridge the gap. For example, it is now much more common for business organizations to give the new younger employees the opportunity to participate more directly in the new causes. This trend has been helped also by the further recognition by companies of a higher degree of responsibility in these areas of greater social responsibility. At the same time the younger employees have been given more opportunities for personal self-expression and flexibility. In all of these ways modern business has sought to adopt itself more realistically to the greater expectations of modern youth. But the entire problem is very complicated, and management needs every possible assistance in working out the proper solutions.

Utilization of Computers

On various occasions reference has been made to the development of modern computers and the impact on particular types of operational activities. In Chapter 22 we deal more directly with the review of computers and the related processing and systems activities. Our interest at this point relates to one especially important type of application to the personnel activities and then more broadly to the total human problems of computers. As we saw in our discussion of planning and placement activities relating to personnel, the identification of the existing human resources becomes of extremely great importance. Both in terms of effective personnel utilization and in providing maximum growth opportunities to the individual employees, it becomes most important to be able to determine accurately and promptly the kinds of talents and skills that are available in the company. This problem has always been dealt with in some fashion but often in a very inefficient manner. Now, however, the ability to develop computerized data banks, with immediate access and retrieval of pertinent personnel data, has made possible a new level of efficiency. What happens is that each indivdual's record is incorporated in the data bank with coverage of such factors as age, marital status, education, type of skills, kinds of experience, language capabilities, work preferences, and important personality traits. When a particular type of job needs to be filled, the data bank can then be tapped for an immediate listing of all individuals who meet designated requirements. A powerful type of tool is thus made available for better personnel utilization.

The broader impact of computers has been to automate many types of operational activity that were formerly carried out by specific individuals. In some cases the effect has been to restrict the number of personnel needed, and in other cases the nature of the job requirements has been significantly modified. Frequently, new types of skill are also required. At the same time the success of the particular computer application depends directly on the adaptation of the various individuals to the new requirements. What all of this means is that developing new computer systems, and putting them into operation, requires a collateral type of personnel planning and development that will anticipate the problems of adjustment, and deal with them effectively over an adequate time period. Individual companies have demonstrated that this can be done but there is still much room for improvement. The challenge to the personnel function is to assist operational management to exploit the benefits of the new computer technology, but to do it in a way that protects the necessary collaboration and cooperation of the various types of people involved.

Management Development and Motivation

While the activities relating to basic training and development have been dealt with earlier in the chapter, we continue this discussion of the personnel function with supplementary coverage of management development at the level of middle and higher management. Although people are important at all organizational levels, the maintenance of proper managerial standards becomes especially critical at the higher management levels. A number of important dimensions of this problem need to be recognized:

1. *There Is the Special Need to Provide Proper Motivation to Higher-Level Managers.* In part this can be done through imaginative programs of executive compensation which provide rewards that are related to their efforts to increase company profits. These programs can be made still more meaningful when they can be linked to organizational control of the operational factors determining profits, as in the case of profit decentralization. Still other kinds of motivation can be provided through effective leadership by superiors, and the creation of the kind of climate that induces full utilization of talents.

2. *Changing Management Conditions Require New Types of Knowledge.* The greater use of computers and the new management sciences (which is made possible through computers) is illustrative of a kind of situation where new knowledge is needed. Similarly, the new kinds of environmental and social problems that are emerging also bring with them the need for new knowledge and philosophies.

3. *A Greater Need Exists for Skills in Relating to Other Company Personnel.* Because of changing human expectations there is an increasing need for self-analysis and for the greater understanding of the complexity of human relationships. Higher-level managers especially need to be able to relate effectively to their colleagues at all levels.

These problems are illustrative of the changing needs and the increasing importance of providing continuing executive training and development. In some cases this is accomplished through in-house programs, whereas in other situations use is made of outside programs established to serve this kind of need. What is important is that the problem be recognized and dealt with in a comprehensive manner.

Achieving Good Morale

The effectiveness of any organization is directly related to the level of morale. Morale as here used refers to the extent to which employees are satisfied with the way they are treated, and the enthusiasm they have for achieving established organizational goals. High morale thus not only makes for greater operational productivity, but also makes the efforts of individuals more rewarding to themselves. Hence it is something that is eagerly sought after by all managers at all organizational levels. The basis for good morale is a combination of many factors. Included here are soundness of organizational goals, good supporting policies, competent managers, evidence of fairness and integrity, functional facilities. well-designed operational procedures, a climate for self-expression, and a reasonable consideration for individuals and their problems. The managerial problem involved is to appraise continuously the success being achieved in doing things in a manner that promotes the highest level of morale practicable in the particular circumstances. There is also the related need to detect low morale and to determine its causes. The tie to people sets the stage for potential assistance on the part of the personnel department. The tie to operational conditions also makes it possible for the internal auditor to make useful observations and to develop constructive conclusions and recommendations. Quite clearly, this type of contribution requires both special sensitivity, and much good judgment on the part qf the individual internal auditor.

Role of the Internal Auditor in the Personnel Function

We have gone to some length to describe the nature and scope of the personnel function and its unique blending of basic managerial responsibilities with needed staff assistance. We have done this because we believe that the review of the personnel department and its related activities provides a unique opportunity to serve management. In addition, every type of operational review carried out by the internal auditor relates in a number of ways to the activities of the personnel department. The combined insights gained by the internal auditor provide a useful basis for a number of specific types of contribution. These contribution potentials include at least the following:

1. The appraisal of the operational efficiency of the various types of programs, operational procedures, and records carried out by the personnel group.
2. The extent to which the personnel group works in a collaborative fashion with the staff and line managers who have the primary people responsibilities.
3. The appraisal of the soundness and operational effectiveness of the personnel policies adopted by the company.
4. The extent to which otherwise sound personnel policies and procedures are being applied effectively in a managerial sense in individual operational areas of the company.

Admittedly, the total area is a sensitive one, and the internal auditor must proceed with extreme care. Clearly, however, the opportunities are there for important managerial service. Personnel activities, indeed, can be viewed as one of the new frontiers of internal auditors for management service.

AUDIT GUIDES

PERSONNEL ACTIVITIES

I. Introductory
  A. Reference should be made to the general discussion of audit guides, Chapter 13.

II. Preparatory Activities
  A. See standard Audit Guides, Chapter 13.
  B. Because of the sensitivity of personnel activities, special care is needed on the part of the internal auditor.

III. Organizational Factors
  A. See standard Audit Guides, Chapter 13.
  B. Matters of special interest in the review of manuals will include:
    1. Personnel planning.
    2. Recruitment policies and procedures.
    3. Training policies.
    4. Job analysis and evaluation.
    5. Compensation policy.

IV. Personnel Planning and Development
  A. Personnel Planning
    1. Review and appraise the adequacy of the policies and procedures for the current determination and projection of personnel needs.
      a. Does each manager adequately participate?
      b. Is there proper coordination with all interested staff and line components?
    2. Review and appraise the adequacy of the assessment of currently existing employee resources and the developing expectations over the planning period.
      a. Does each manager evaluate the personnel for which he is directly responsible?
      b. Are results systematically matched with needs to show existing and projected gaps?
  B. Recruitment and Selection
    1. Is recruitment centralized and/or coordinated properly to avoid duplication of effort?
    2. Review and appraise the procedures followed for the various types of recruitment.
      a. Do organizational components being served participate adequately in the final selection?
      b. Are customer groups satisfied with the service being provided? If not, why not?
      c. Are records and files to recruitment being efficiently maintained?

C. Training and Development
1. What is the nature and scope of the training program?
   a. How adequate are the materials being used?
   b. Appraise the professional qualifications of the people administering the training program.
2. To what extent do other company line and staff managers participate:
   a. By demonstrating support for the program?
   b. By actually participating in the instruction and training?
3. Are company organizational components satisfied with the training being provided? If not, why not?
4. Are personnel being trained satisfied with the training experience? If not, why not?

V. Current Administration of Personnel Activities

A. Job Analysis and Evaluation
1. Review and appraise the design of the currently existing approach to job analysis and evaluation.
   a. How adequate are the criteria used?
   b. Are weighting factors reasonable?
   c. Is the number of classifications adequate?
2. Are adequate specifications developed for individual jobs?
3. Are the evaluations of individual jobs adequately made on the basis of the existing criteria and weights?
4. Are job evaluations periodically reexamined for changing conditions?

B. Compensation Administration
1. Is the general level of compensation reasonably sound, and is it based on adequate surveys?
2. Are individual job compensation levels adequately tested on a continuing basis?
3. Are the individual cases of actual compensation reasonably distributed within the various job classifications?
4. Are employees reasonably satisfied with the current job analysis and compensation administration? If not, in what respects is there dissatisfaction?

C. Performance Evaluation
1. Do adequate review forms exist for use at the several levels of organizational responsibility?
2. Are policies and procedures reasonably adequate?
   a. Are reviews required periodically?
   b. Are reviews discussed with and approved by the next level of supervisory responsibility?
   c. Is there adequate evidence of the communication of review results to the affected subordinates?

      d. Are subordinates satisfied with the adequacy of the reviews being made by their superiors?

      e. Is there reasonable evidence that the reviews lead to specific developmental action on the part of the subordinate?

    3. Are reviews available for later reference, and are they being used adequately for personnel planning?

D. Transfers, Promotions, and Terminations

    1. How effective is the coordination of individual organizational components with the personnel department when personnel changes come about?

      a. Are candidates identified for consideration before personnel actions are finalized?

      b. Is other assistance adequately rendered?

    2. Is the personnel group adequately advised when there are to be major expansions or contractions of volume in individual operational sectors?

    3. Does the personnel group take adequate measures to minimize the disruptive impact of personnel expansion and contraction?

E. Employee Records and Reports

    1. Are employee records adequate in terms of design, and are they efficiently maintained?

    2. Are individual personnel files kept up to date and available for current reference?

    3. Are job action changes—transfers, promotions, merit increases, new hires, terminations, and the like—promptly processed?

    4. Do reports rendered adequately cover needed information for the control of the various aspects of the personnel function?

      a. Are these reports satisfactory to company users?

      b. Are the reports reappraised periodically for scope of coverage, timing of release, and parties to whom distributed?

F. Personal Guidance Activities

    1. Are employees made aware of the availability of counseling services?

    2. Is there reasonable evidence that such personal counseling is being carried out in a professional manner?

    3. Are employees satisfied with the counseling services being made available?

    4. Is management being made adequately aware of the types of problems which are developing (over and above any violations of personal confidence)?

G. Employee Benefit Programs

    1. Appraise the adequacy of the total program of employee benefits, including consideration of programs carried on by competitor companies.

2. Is the design and operation of each individual program sound and effective? If not, what are the areas of needed improvement?
3. Are employees satisfied with the programs, both individually and collectively? If not, in what respects is there criticism or complaint?
4. Are individual programs reappraised periodically?

H. Employee Services
   1. Is the personnel department the most appropriate choice for the assignment of each particular type of employee service presently being handled?
      a. Are there other organizational components that might provide this service more effectively?
      b. Is the personnel department reasonably equipped to provide the particular type of service?
   2. Is the individual type of service being provided in an efficient and effective manner:
      a. As to quality and availability of the service?
      b. As to economy of cost?
   3. Are company users satisfied with the services being received in each case? If not, why not?

I. Workmen's Compensation and Safety
   1. Is the scope of protective devices adequate? If not, in what respects is improvement needed?
   2. Is a reasonable effort made to select personnel in such a manner as to avoid individuals who appear to be subject to greater than normal accident exposure?
   3. Review and appraise the adequacy of the program to alert personnel to accident problems and to induce a positive approach to safety.
   4. How adequately is the safety program related to individual managerial responsibilities?
   5. Are workmen's compensation activities efficiently and promptly administered, including comprehensive reporting and utilization in the development of the broader safety program?

J. Labor Relations
   1. Are personnel procedures closely attuned to labor relations requirements and implications:
      a. For conformance to existing contractual requirements?
      b. As a basis for possible changes in those contractual requirements?
   2. Are grievance procedures adequate, and are they carried out effectively?
   3. Do personnel department representatives participate adequately in the development of all aspects of the union relationships?

VI. Special Audit Tests
   A. Detailed Reviews of Individual Employee Benefit Programs

Over a period of time individual employee benefit programs should be subjected to detailed examination and review.

B. Detailed Reviews of Individual Service Programs

Similarly, the operations of individual service activities should be subjected to detailed examination and review.

C. Testing of Particular kinds of Processing

A particular type of job action—as, for example, getting a new hire into the records, or perhaps a change of job status—should be examined from the time of its inception to final completion. The focus here will be on types of problems encountered and time required for execution.

D. Direct Employee Tests

A useful type of special test is to review directly with representative groups of employees their satisfaction with selected types of personnel activities.

VII. Special Personnel Problems for Management

A. Special problem areas include:

1. Increasing unionization.
2. Minority-group development.
3. Women in industry.
4. Adapting to higher human expectations.
5. Utilization of computers.
6. Continuing management development.
7. Achieving good morale.

These problem areas were described briefly on pages 546–551.

B. Although no detailed audit guides are practicable to cover these broad areas, the internal auditor should be alert to the implications involved, and report significant observations and conclusions.

VIII–IX. Not used.

X. Overall Appraisal of Personnel Activities

A. See the standard Audit Guides, Chapter 13.

B. The people aspect of personnel activities broadens the scope of this overall appraisal.

ILLUSTRATIVE AUDIT FINDINGS: PERSONNEL ACTIVITIES

Reductions in Administrative Personnel

Reductions in the number of administrative personnel were not made subsequent to a cutback in operations. As a result, unnecessary expenditures were made for administrative services no longer needed. The plant manager was aware of the excess personnel but had not made reductions on the basis that additional contracts might be obtained. At the time of our review the plant manager stated that the plant had been unable to obtain the contracts, and he agreed that cutbacks of personnel with annual salary costs of $125,000 could be made.

Better Assignment to Training Classes

The company did not have effective procedures for assigning staff to training classes, often selecting personnel based on availability rather than need. Some employees thus received extensive training, whereas others were not being given training courses needed for their work and for advancement.

Savings through In-House Courses

The company was incurring high tuition fees for enrollment of individual employees in courses sponsored by various organizations. Based on the number of enrollees, it was found that similar training could be provided on a group basis through company-sponsored courses, thus saving a significant amount in training costs. In addition, in some cases the individual taking a course outside the company could provide training to other members of the staff.

Using Idle Time

Based on time and observation studies of personnel in data processing the auditor found that many employees had idle time throughout the month. The auditor recommended that these personnel rotate their functions to provide resources to run a new terminal being acquired. By better use of existing personnel there was no longer the need to hire an additional person to work on the new terminal.

Decreasing Overtime

Three departments of the company were incurring excessive amounts of overtime compared to other departments. Although some of the overtime was warranted because of backlogs, savings could be obtained if additional emphasis was placed on work-load planning, scheduling, and monitoring. Also, in one department there was the need to hire two additional employees rather than granting overtime for extended periods.

CHAPTER TWENTY-ONE

Financial Management

NATURE OF THE FINANCIAL MANAGEMENT FUNCTION

In Chapter 13 we dealt with the basic accounting activities of a day-to-day operational character. In this chapter we are concerned with the higher-level activities that are carried out by a finance group in a modern company. Over the last several decades the finance function has emerged as one of the foremost types of support to top management. The function stemming historically from the accounting role has now gone on beyond the earlier base to encompass the responsibility for financial liquidity, the management of capital resources, and the coordination and integration of the total company effort for maximum profitability. This expanded role has been a natural result of the fact that all of the company operations have a major financial dimension. The development of new techniques combined with modern computer capabilities has also helped to make this new role possible. But perhaps the most dramatic development has come through the broader and more management oriented approach which has been adopted by finance managers themselves. Under these circumstances the internal auditor must similarly expand the scope of his own review so that he can effectively serve management. He must be able to review the finance group operations in the same way that he reviews any other company activity. At the same time also he must be able to identify and deal with the higher-level financial policy dimensions of the other company activities that he reviews. For all these reasons the modern internal auditor is vitally concerned with the area of financial management.

Organizational Setting for Financial Management

If the finance group is to effectively serve top management in the various financial areas, there must first be an adequate organizational setting. This organizational setting includes the level at which the finance group is placed in the organization, and the related channels of relationship with the senior management group. It also includes the extent to which the finance group is integrated. In the normal situation the senior finance officer reports directly to the chief executive officer of the company. The senior finance officer will in these circumstances be a vice president, a senior vice president, or an executive vice president, depending on the number of levels existing in the particular company. Under these conditions the senior finance executive will properly have direct access to the chief executive and be on an equal level with the other executives who report directly to that officer.

In some companies the finance group is split between the treasurer role and the controller role, with the responsible heads of these two groups reporting directly to the chief executive officer. When this is done the chief executive officer himself has the additional responsibility of integrating the two important financial roles. However, this is likely to be a burden on the chief executive officer as he carries out his total management role. It is therefore believed to be more satisfactory to have one executive who coordinates and integrates the total finance role.

Internal Organization of the Finance Group. Assuming that there is a vice president–finance who is responsible for the entire finance activity, the next question is how the finance group itself should be organized. Although practice will vary, it is normally desirable to separate the roles of the treasurer and controller. The treasurer's role will cover the responsibility for the cash received as soon as it can be brought under central control, and the subsequent disbursement or other utilization of that cash for company purposes. It will also usually include responsibilities for bank relationships and investments. It may also include responsibilities for tax services, insurance, real estate, pension funds, stock purchase plans, and other financially based services. The controller's role, on the other hand, will normally be concerned with the accounting activities—including the preparation of reports, the analysis and interpretation of financial data, and the development and administration of budgets and profit plans. Also, there may be other activities assigned—insurance, taxes, liaison with outside auditors, and so on. In some cases also, the data processing activities may be assigned here, although more will be said about this particular matter in Chapter 22. It may also be that some of the responsibilities mentioned above may be assigned to managers reporting directly to the vice president–finance.

Plan of Treatment of Financial Management

The total financial management activities can be classified and discussed in various ways. Our own approach will be to deal first with the activities that pertain most directly to current operations. This will include major accounting policies, report interpretation, profit analysis, and cash management. The second major section will focus on the planning role. This will involve a consideration of the organizational relationships, budgets, and profit plans. In a third section we concentrate on problems of determining and administering the capital expenditures program. In the fourth section we turn to the problems of determining and satisfying the company's capital needs. Finally, we deal with some other matters not previously covered—taxes, insurance, and pricing.

ACTIVITIES PERTAINING TO CURRENT OPERATIONS

Accounting Policy

When the basic accounting activities were discussed in Chapter 13, our interest centered primarily on the procedural and basic operational aspects. At this higher financial management level, however, we need to consider in more depth the accounting policies that underlie the basic accounting activities. Here accounting policy merges into financial policy and then into management policy itself. It is impossible to identify all such policy matters, but the important ones will at least include the following:

1. *Credit Policies.* There is first the determination as to whether credit will be made available to customers. For example, the motor companies have traditionally required cash on delivery of cars, but parts are payable on a monthly basis. Where credit is extended, the conditions must then be established for when and to whom such credit is to be offered, and at what levels.

2. *Operational and Product Costing.* The policies as to cost allocation determine how costs flow to individual operations and then to products, affecting the values of inventories and what becomes cost of sales for the current accounting period. The problem of allocating the cost of the central company headquarters is illustrative. The use of direct costing is another example.

3. *Capital versus Revenue Expenditures.* Where and how the line is drawn between charges to expense and property accounts in the case of small items purchased or for various types of repair will substantially affect the expense and profits for the accounting period. There is a trade-off here between theory and practical considerations.

4. *Depreciation Rates.* Once depreciable assets are acquired, these assets must be written off through allocations to current operations. But the manner in which this is done and the level of conservatism applied can vary greatly. The rates used may or may not be the same as those used for income tax purposes.

5. *Deferment and Accrual of Various Expenses.* The determination of what portions of cash expenditures are fairly applicable to future periods, and the accrual of expenses where cash has not been expended, involve many different types of questions and levels of conservatism.

6. *Treatment of Tax Credits.* The investment credit allowed by the federal government illustrates a kind of situation where policies will vary as to the accounting treatment to be followed. Under one policy approach the credits may be used in full as a reduction of the current year's taxes; whereas under a second policy approach they may be used to reduce the asset cost, and thus be brought into the income account over the life of the asset via lower depreciation charges.

7. *Accrual and Deferment of Income.* In many cases income has not yet been received but is fairly accruable. On the other hand, there may be book income which is properly applicable to future periods. In both cases the selection of methods and the level of conservatism creates important policy problems.

8. *Providing Reserves.* The possibilities of later liabilities or losses in existing assets may be so great that prudent accounting will require the creation of reserves. How these reserves should be set up and in what amounts can involve major policy determinations.

9. *Consolidation of Subsidiaries.* Although consolidation of subsidiaries is normally desirable when practicable, the determination of that practicability can reflect various degrees of judgment and conservatism.

In all these kinds of situations the internal auditor will be concerned with the reasonableness of the particular policy both in terms of generally accepted accounting principles and level of reasonable business conservatism. Although some of the issues involve decisions made at a very high level, the standing of the internal auditor in the accounting and financial field provides a special competence for making recommendations.

Report Analysis

Reports have been identified in Chapter 13 as a major dimension of the total accounting system. In our present discussion of financial management it can also be said that reports, together with their supporting analyses, can be a major means by which the management is given the information for effectively controlling and guiding the company. These reports take a great many forms to serve many different types of purpose. This comes about because of the varying needs of company managers and their particular levels of responsibility. Some reports will deal with specific operational aspects such as cost performance, product margins, changes in individual assets, and profit analysis. Other reports will be concerned with overall results of the individual profit center or of the company as a whole. The scope of the individual reports will range from a basic standard format, to the inclusion of various kinds of standardized and special analysis. In some cases the data they contain will be predominantly financial, whereas in other cases the coverage will be a blend of operational and financial information. Although it is not practicable to cover all these variations in the present discussion, it will be useful to emphasize certain aspects of reports and their analyses which should be generally useful.

1. *Focus on User Needs.* The basic purpose of all financial reports is to serve the managerial needs of the particular users of those reports. Hence the starting point is an understanding of what those needs are. These needs arise out of the specific operational responsibilities of the users. The needs also are directly related to the level of responsibility and the amount of detail that is needed. Related also to this level of responsibility is the

time element. The more detailed the scope of the information, the more quickly the report should be available. Admittedly, some reports serve a number of different uses. However, there should be the constant effort to think of the scope of the report in terms of the person who is going to use that report.

2. *Ease of Interpretation and Use*. Although perhaps implied by the foregoing point, the objective of ease of interpretation and use needs special emphasis. There is a natural tendency for those who prepare reports unconsciously to develop them in terms of their own professional standards and capabilities. To some extent those reports may become satisfying to the makers, but not useful to the recipient. The key elements here that need attention are clearness and maximum simplicity of headings, arrangement, and supplementary analytical content.

3. *Respect for the Responsibility of the Individual Manager*. Each manager who has a given sphere of responsibility normally has a desire to have a reasonable opportunity to do his job before his superiors inject themselves into the problems involved. When reports covering these problems are exposed simultaneously to his superiors, he lacks the opportunity to assess the causes, and to develop immediate or planned solutions. The proper approach is that there be some difference in timing of the release of reports.

4. *Quality Analysis*. Reports quite commonly include analytical comments either as a part of the basic report, as a separate attachment, or as a later document. The objective here must be that such supplementary analysis is really meaningful to the user. There is a tendency for such analysis to become stereotyped on a recurring basis. Again, the needed approach is to seek to provide the user with additional information that will help him to understand his problems, and to be able to take the best possible action.

5. *Emphasis on the Future*. One purpose of financial reports is to provide historical information for the record and for later reference. But the more important purpose is to be a constructive force for current action which will make possible a better future. In part, the latter is accomplished by looking at the past and interpreting the implications of the past. In part also, this is accomplished by developing forward estimates and projections. These forward estimates can also be combined with historical data. For example, the actual operational results for the months thus far elapsed can be used at each month end to provide a more enlightened basis for a new estimate of the year as a whole. The benefit here is that by recognizing the indicated future directions managers can know better what actions should be taken now to improve the future results.

Scope of Analysis. The general objective of analysis to provide additional information which can be meaningful to managers has a number of important supporting dimensions.

1. *More Information as to What Actually Happened.* This is provided through additional details and through identification of relationships not otherwise apparent to the user of the reports.

2. *Identification of Causes.* The more specific objective here is to identify the different factors which were the causes of the larger results, and to measure their relative significance.

3. *Comparison with a Standard.* Here the focus is on the evaluation of how good or bad the performance was in relation to some kind of an implicit or explicit standard.

4. *Guide to Action.* Finally, to the extent practicable, the purpose of good analysis is to provide guidance to the user as to what he might do to serve the large organizational interest. The success at this stage depends directly on how well the preceding purposes have been achieved.

Profit Analysis

The preceding general discussion of reports and report analysis leads directly into a brief examination of the basic concepts of profit analysis. Because profits and profitability become the central issue in so many operational and policy decisions, the financial manager is very concerned with all the means by which he can better measure this aspect. At the outset, however, it needs to be recognized that profit analysis has certain limitations which need to be understood. One of these limitations is that profits frequently do not provide adequate recognition of other forces and developments that are of vital concern to the future welfare of the company. A given profit center may for example, be showing adequate profits but may at the same time be losing sales position, be failing to provide adequate service support for products sold, be high-pressuring customers, and be producing products of marginal quality. Although eventually these other factors will be reflected in declining profits, the current profit results may not be affected. Hence profit standards need to be supplemented by other types of operational standards. A second limitation of the profits concept is that it comes out of an accounting process which itself has certain basic deficiencies. Illustrative of these deficiencies is that costs of depreciable assets are on a historical basis rather than on a current value basis, that allocations of costs may be unavoidably arbitrary, and that average costs cloud the impact of fixed and variable costs and of incremental costs. What this all means is that normal accounting data are frequently not directly useful as a basis for decision making, and must be adjusted and restructured in various ways. All of this does not mean that accounting data are no longer important. It simply means that we must use them with special care and adapt them in a way that will eliminate the limitations as much as possible.

Volume–Cost–Profit Analysis. A very commonly used technique of profit analysis is the separation of fixed and variable costs and the projection of these costs at different levels of sales volume to show the resultant profits, including the point at which there is a break-even of profit and loss. In diagram form this appears as shown in Exhibit 21.1. Conceptually, this chart illustrates that fixed costs and variable costs result in a varying total cost pattern under different sales volume conditions, and that profits are a function of the extent to which sales cover those total costs. In practice it is very difficult to measure fixed and variable costs accurately. This is because costs are variable to different degrees, and also because this degree of variability will vary over different periods of time. Also, sale estimates represent a changing mix of products and prices over different levels of volume. However, the application can be useful to some extent.

Flexible Budgets.   The entire subject of budgets is dealt with later in the chapter as a part of the planning activity. Flexible budgets, however, represent a special type of approach that pertains importantly to report analysis and control. Since costs have different degrees of variability under changing conditions, we need to study individual costs, and to determine what they should be at different volume levels. To the extent that this can be done, we have a better basis for profit analysis and control. Also, we have a means for measuring the extent to which actual cost variances are due to changing volume, thus making possible a more effective search for causes that are under the control of the particular activity. Again there are limitations as to how far one can go in this direction. There is an unavoidable judgment factor in estimating what costs should be at different volumes. Also, there is a practical limit to the number of volume levels that can be covered. However, it is a useful approach when applied with reason.

Incremental Profit Analysis.   When analyses are made of the profitability of alternative decisions, the limitations of the usual types of cost data have been noted. What is pertinent to a particular decision is what *additional* revenues will be generated under the proposed course of action, and what *additional* costs will be incurred. The extent to which these incremental revenues exceed

EXHIBIT 21.1.   Break-Even Profit Analysis

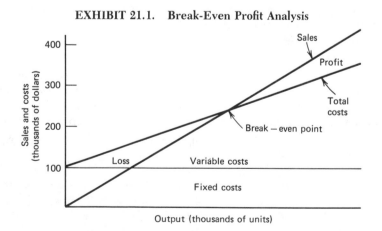

the incremental costs is the measure of the worth of that particular course of action. Quite clearly, the estimating of these incremental revenues and costs is very difficult, especially when the estimate must be projected over longer future periods. Nevertheless, it is an approach that is very useful in carrying out adequate analysis as a basis for decisions. Decision makers too often are unduly influenced by irrelevant past costs, and thus fail to think in the necessary incremental terms. A good illustration of such a situation is when a determination is being made as to whether a particular machine or manufacturing process should be replaced.

Cash Management

The management of cash is another one of the important activities of the financial manager of a current operations nature. It is the focal point of the broader problem of working capital management, which includes the management of receivables, inventory, and payables, thus involving the total problem of financial liquidity. It also relates to the problem of capital needs and how the desired funds will be obtained. In the simplest terms cash management has to do with the most efficient utilization of cash, after consideration of all of the other related needs of the enterprise. It covers all the means by which one can increase cash availability, how the cash flows can be regularized to minimize the need for outside borrowings, and finally the investment of surplus cash to maximize supplementary earnings.

Increasing the Availability of Cash. In the discussion of the cash and receivable financial processes, we discussed the types of actions that provided the most effective control. These same actions are closely related to the objectives of increasing the availability of cash. These and other types of action can be summarized as follows:

1. Billings to customers should be made as quickly as possible after a determination is made as to what is actually being shipped to the customer.
2. Every possible legitimate means should be used to accelerate payment by the customer.
3. Control over collections should be achieved at the earliest possible time, as, for example, routing collections to a regional center, or using a lock box address to which the local bank has access for deposit purposes.
4. Transfers of cash balances need to be made promptly so that funds in excess of needed minimum balances are accumulated at key points for investment purposes.
5. Disbursements should be controlled so that the company meets but does not accelerate stipulated terms of payment.

To the extent that these types of action involve procedures under the company's control, the needed type of policies and procedures should be established and then effectively monitored. Where bank actions are involved, the counsel of the company's banks should be solicited. Assistance in achieving maximum availability of cash is a proper expectation as a part of good banking service.

Regularizing Cash Flows.   The operational requirements of each individual business will determine the relative cash inflows and outflows over the year. It is essential that the financial manager understand the nature of these various types of flow, and to be in a position both to appraise their relationships and the possibilities of modifying them. The starting point for this type of financial management is to develop a cash budget that identifies and summarizes the aggregate results. From such an overview it then becomes clear whether shortages exist at various points of time. With these special needs identified, consideration can then be given to what other courses of action might possibly be taken to eliminate the problems. It may be that there are securities which can be converted into cash. On the operational side it may be possible to cut back temporarily on normal policies for the levels of inventories. Or a pending capital project might be temporarily deferred. Whether these are the courses of action that should be taken, when consideration is given to the penalties involved, is something that will have to be determined on the merits. The important thing, however, is that the various possibilities are explored so that the company can decide on what is best. If then there are still shortages in the availability of cash, that need is known so that plans can be made most advantageously to obtain funds from banks or other lending agencies. Needless to say, such plans will be implemented only at the time the funds are actually needed. But the financial manager is aware of the potential needs and is prepared to deal with them.

Investment of Surplus Cash.   Under the procedures previously outlined, all cash not needed to maintain minimum balances and established branch imprest funds will show up at the central cash depository, or in a small group of banks that constitute the central cash depository. Determinations will now have to be made as to how large such balances should be to provide adequate support for the total company operations. Advantageous buying developments might lead to greater cash requirements. Or a pending strike might cause a major reduction in sales. Available cash beyond reasonable reserves, however, should now be used in a productive manner by investment in interest-bearing securities. The choice of the particular securities is determined to a major extent by the time it is expected that the money will be invested and the general state of the money market. Normally, the objective will be to maximize the return within the constraints of an acceptable level of risk and an assured liquidity of the securities or money-market funds. In many cases this liquidity can be achieved with securities such as Treasury bills that have maturities corresponding to the expected time needs of the company. Here also, the counsel of banks and other financial institutions is available to the company, and should be utilized.

THE PLANNING ROLE IN OPERATIONS

Nature of the Planning Role

The activities pertaining to current operations merge into and overlap with the planning role now to be discussed. This planning phase is best exemplified in the development of the profit plan. Although the annual budget is a part of current operations, we wish to emphasize the planning aspect of that combined planning and control process. The capital budget covering forward capital expenditures is also clearly directly related to the financial manager's planning role. However, the planning of capital expenditures involves special problems and we will therefore defer this particular matter to the next section of the chapter. At this point, however, a preliminary word needs to be said about the financial manager's role in supporting management's policy of decentralization through the creation of profit centers.

Financial Control of Profit Centers

In Chapter 5 we discussed the possibilities of management decentralizing its responsibilities through the utilization of profit centers. When this is done, the control exercised by the central management is effected to a major extent through budgets and profit plans. This in itself brings the finance group actively into the total managerial control carried out by that central management. In fact, the very decision to create profit centers on a meaningful basis requires close collaboration with the finance group to determine the feasibility and practicability of profit measurement. The problem that frequently exists is that the profit centers share common facilities or services, and that, therefore, the accuracy with which profit center costs and profits can be determined becomes difficult or even impracticable. In other situations also, the profit centers sell products or furnish services to each other, and here there is the difficult problem of determining meaningful transfer prices. What this all means is that the finance group must play an active role, both in determining what profit centers should be set up and in developing the policies and procedures by which the profitability of their operations are measured and evaluated. The latter aspects become an integral part of the administration of both budgets and profit plans.

Annual Company Budget

If we go back in years, many companies made little use of the budgetary process, disregarding such usage altogether, or perhaps having the chief financial officer develop a projected profit and loss statement. Today it is unusual to find any large organization that does not make substantial use of annual operational budgets. A complete budget covers all the company activities, and comes together as an integrated final result in which all the individual pieces are linked. That is to say that the expense budgets of individual cost centers, and the revenue budgets of the revenue producing components, come together in profit center budgets—to the extent that such intermediate profit centers exist—and in turn come together in the total budget of the company. These detailed and aggregate budgets necessarily combine the operational and financial dimensions of the various activities, just as will the later reports covering actual performance. The responsibility for the total budgetary process in some cases is delegated to a special organizational component reporting directly to the chief executive officer, or to an intermediary such as a vice president–planning or a vice president–administration. More commonly, however, the responsibility for coordinating and administering the budget rests with the chief financial officer. This latter situation is a natural development when one considers the major role played by the finance group.

Role of the Budget Process.   The budgetary process serves a number of important purposes, but one of the most important purposes is to assist the company to achieve better planning of its current operations. If the budget is properly developed, it provides an opportunity for individual managers to think thoughtfully and analytically about the effectiveness of the operations for which they are responsible, and to then develop plans for improving the operational results. This is a type of action which, if properly achieved, can well justify the entire budget process. Once this planning has been accomplished, the budget becomes a major basis of control both for the manager who developed it, and for the higher-level managers. Even then, however, as we shall see, the control must be carried out in a proper manner. Where the budget is viewed primarily as for control, or is improperly used as a control device, the planning role is likely to be significantly undermined.

Relationship to the Accounting System.   It is a basic requirement that the budget structure be the same as that of the accounting system. One aspect of this is that a well-designed accounting system and the supporting reports have recognized the scope of organizational responsibilities established, and the related accountabilities. These same organizational responsibilities are then used in connection with the establishment of budgetary responsibilities and objectives. Although the line is always not as clear as we would like to have it between controllable and noncontrollable factors relating to those responsibilities, and although it is sometimes not practicable to eliminate all noncontrollable items, nevertheless we should seek in both the budgetary and accounting structure to focus on controllable responsibilities. The second aspect of the tie immediately follows, which is that actual performance as developed by the accounting system must be comparable with the budgetary data. If this were otherwise, there would be no practical possibility of using the budgetary process either as a useful planning or control purpose. When there is a high degree of decentralization of the company operations to individual profit centers, the accounting and budgetary structures combine especially to provide the basis for effective financial and general management control.

Developing the Budget

The question is frequently raised as to whether budgets should be developed from the top down or from the bottom up. The answer is that we need to do both. We know that eventually a budget should represent the mutual agreement of all levels of company management in a total integrated budget, insofar as the budget pertains to their respective mutual responsibilities. But in achieving this final result some things must come down from the top, and some come up from the bottom. Where there are gaps, they must be negotiated on a mutually acceptable basis. The part that comes down from the top should in the first instance be the overall company objectives as to the level of *desired* improvement—sales objectives, cost productivity levels, and profit goals. Subsequently, also, certain assumptions must be developed and approved on a company-wide basis. Illustrative would be such conditions as the level of expected general business activity, estimated industry sales, the expected level of inflation, assumptions as to labor cost levels, and the like. The individual company activities will then develop their own budgets within the framework of those assumptions. However, the latter development must proceed in a predetermined sequence. Thus sales budgets must be developed and agreed on before production and expense budgets can be developed.

Role of the Finance Group.   The development of budgets is clearly the primary responsibility of the line and staff organizational components which are responsible for the particular activities involved. This primary responsibility cannot be shifted to the finance group. On the other hand, the finance group has a responsibility to provide assistance, to the extent possible. This assistance usually takes the form of providing needed historical data, and in laying out forms and procedures for the development of the budgetary data. Personnel from the finance group should also be available to assist the operational managers in the analysis of pertinent data of all types as a basis for the development of meaningful operational objectives. It is absolutely necessary, however, that the finance personnel do not dominate the budget determinations, and in effect themselves set the objectives. Otherwise, the commitment on the part of the responsible managers is not a genuine one, and we end up with form rather than substance. There is always the very real danger that the special skills of the finance personnel, and their eagerness to put together a budget that will be attractive to top management, will lead them to exert undue influence on the responsible managers.

Level of Budgetary Objectives.   In developing their respective portions of the budget, individual managers are always faced with the problem as to how much task and challenge they should take on. They can on the one hand opt for levels that will be relatively easy to achieve. On the other hand, they can be too optimistic and set objectives that are unrealistically high. Or the objectives can be set somewhere in between. The question is what level best serves the total company interest. On balance, the right answer here is that objectives should be at levels that are difficult to achieve, but still attainable. A necessary condition here is that the objectives are backed up by sound plans to achieve those objectives. A second necessary condition is that the risks are adequately understood both by the individual managers and their superiors. The latter condition additionally involves the question of how the budget will be used later as a control device. If experience has demonstrated that the budget will be used in a rigid manner, and that blame will be assessed in a punitive way when there are budgetary shortfalls, individual managers will tend to build protection into their budgets. If, instead, higher-level management uses the budget in a control sense with understanding of changing conditions, the individual manager will have the confidence to go on the line at budget development time with full disclosure and high-level objectives.

Reconciliation of Gaps. In developing the budget for a major operational activity, the detailed budgets prepared within the framework of certain company-wide assumptions will, as we have seen, move upward through the several organizational levels and eventually come together in the total company budget. But at any stage there may be gaps between the objectives proposed by the individual managers and those sought by the next higher-level managers. At this point the problem of the gap must be resolved in some manner. How this is accomplished is critical to the success of the budgetary process. Very often the wrong thing is done. This wrong thing is where higher-level managers either change the lower-manager budgets to match their own ideas, or where they put undue pressure on these lower-level managers to do it. Under proper procedure there is a meaningful joint probing of the issues, supplemented normally by a reexamination of the underlying buildup of the budget with the responsible manager's subordinates. What is essential is that if the budgetary levels are raised, there is a sound basis for the upward revision, as agreed to by the lower-level managers, who are going to be faced with the responsibility of performing in accordance with those higher objectives.

Administration of the Budget

If the budget has been properly developed along the lines just described, it now becomes a useful means of controlling operations at all levels. When managers are committed to the budgetary objectives they will themselves seek every proper means to achieve those objectives. It must be recognized, however, that conditions do change, and that the efforts toward compliance with the budget can become so intensive as to lead to actions that are not in the company interest. Thus if sales revenues decline because of changed economic conditions, such a shortfall should not necessarily be offset by cutting out an important training program. The budget must be viewed as having a reasonable amount of flexibility. It is guide, but not a straitjacket. In dealing with such situations there is special need for close relationships between the responsible manager and his superiors, coupled with a mutual concern for what can, and what should not be done, to reverse a current and projected budgetary deficiency.

Formalization of Budgetary Adjustments. When conditions develop that are different from those existing at the time the budget was agreed on, there are various ways in which this kind of a situation can be handled in a procedural sense. One way is to adjust the budget to reflect the new conditions. The revised budget objectives are then directly comparable with current and projected performance. The second approach is to leave the original budget objectives as they were, but to explain the effect of the changed conditions as a part of the supplementary variance analysis. In the case of deficiencies that are of a reasonably controllable nature—that is, essentially a measure of bad performance—the adjustment of the budget is normally considered to be undesirable. To do so would in effect relieve the responsible manager of his poor performance, and eliminate the pressure to recover this deficiency in the ongoing months. In the case of causes that are clearly noncontrollable, and where they are at the same time of a really significant nature, the case for budget adjustment has considerable merit. The use of the flexible budget to adjust for volume changes in a manufacturing operation is illustrative. At a higher level, the company might adjust the sales budget to reflect changes in industry volume, thus focusing on the level of penetration versus competition in an available market.

Internal Auditor's Relation to the Budgets

The interest of the internal auditor in the total budgetary process has a number of important dimensions. The first of these exists when he reviews the total budget procedure. This is done in depth when the internal auditor reviews the activities of the budget department. This will include the design of the basic policies and procedures, the scope of instructions issued, the timing of the development of the various parts of the budget, the manner in which the budget department coordinates the development of the budget, the way in which the budget is finalized, the types of reports used to evaluate budgetary performance, the more formal reviews that are made, the manner of adjusting budgets, and the general overall efficiency of the budget department itself. Since the budgetary process is such an important means of developing good management at all levels in the company, the internal auditor seeks in every way possible to identify specific ways in which that total process can be more effective.

The second kind of interest of the internal auditor in the budgetary process arises in connection with his review of any line or staff operational activity. At this point he is interested in the budget and the backup materials as a source of information about the plans and objectives of the particular operational activity. He is also interested in the later performance reports to find out about new problems and conditions that have been encountered. Finally, he is interested in the manner in which the budget is being used as a basis for effective managerial control. What kinds of exposure is made down through the particular activity as to budgetary deviations? What kinds of review meetings are held and what is accomplished at them? What evidence exists that a maximum effort is made to counter budgetary deficiencies at all levels?

Third, there is the direct interest that the internal auditor has in the budgetary process as he develops and administers his own budget covering the internal auditing department. This firsthand involvement has an additional benefit in that he has an opportunity to observe directly the way the total company procedure is designed and administered.

Profit Plan

In some companies the annual budget may be called *a* profit plan, and in those situations where there is no formal planning system beyond the one year it may be called *the* profit plan. Normally, however, the profit plan covers a longer period of time than the budget. The profit plan is like a budget in many respects, but is different in that it concentrates on long-term planning, and is not as detailed or precise as a budget. Moreover, it does not involve lower-level managers to the same extent as does the annual budget. As to its timing, there are various alternatives. It can be developed just prior to the development of the annual budget, in which case the annual budget then becomes the detailed implementation of the first year of the previously finalized profit plan. Or it can be developed simultaneously with the annual budget, in which case the profit plan can be viewed as a plan for the years after the budget year. Or the profit plan can be developed immediately after the finalization of the budget, and cover the desired number of years beyond. The first approach appears to be preferable, as it can then be dealt with before people become so deeply involved in the more detailed budgetary process. A basis is also thus provided for a more meaningful budget.

Importance of the Profit Plan

The time horizon of modern business is being continually extended. One of the reasons for this is that we are able through the use of modern quantitative tools to probe the future more effectively. A second reason is that the development of our more advanced technology requires longer periods for design, construction, and to prove out from an operational standpoint. With this longer planning horizon, it becomes increasingly necessary that management think more carefully about its future directions. What new types of demand are developing? What new kinds of technology will be available? What new markets will exist? What new approaches in an operational sense will be possible? In short, where are the revenue opportunities, the possibilities for increased productivity, and the basis for continuing growth and increased profitability? Although these determinations are basically general management responsibilities, the considerations involve financial dimensions at every turn. What will the alternative types of action cost? What are the revenue potentials? What kind of funds will be required to support these endeavors? Thus the finance group must be actively involved in the total profit planning process.

Development and Administration of the Profit Plan

The profit plan development begins at the highest management level. It normally consists of a statement by the chief executive officer of the scope of the total plan and how it is to be formulated. The supporting policies and procedures, and the subsequent coordination of the total development process, may in some cases be assigned to a vice president–planning. In other cases this responsibility will be assigned to the chief financial officer. In any event the finance group must be closely involved, both in working with other company activities and in developing the portion of the profit plan covering its own activities. Plans submitted by the individual line and staff operational activities will then be reviewed and discussed, and will finally come together as a total profit plan for the company.

The subsequent administration of the approved profit plan will vary. In some situations quarterly or semiannual reports of progress may be required. In other situations the interim reviews focus on the performance as covered by the annual budget. In either case the major formal review comes at the time the next profit plan is developed. At that time the new plan should be adequately reconciled with the plan presented the previous year and satisfactory explanations provided for changes and new directions. Again the well-developed planning materials become an important basis for high-level management control.

Internal Auditor's Interest in the Profit Plan

In most respects the internal auditor's interest in the profit plan process parallels the approach discussed in connection with the annual budget. He is interested in the basic central administration of the profit plan, he is interested in the profit plan as it pertains to the particular company activity which he is reviewing, and he himself should be participating directly in the process as he prepares a profit plan covering his own internal auditing department. It must be recognized, however, that the annual budget will have a greater impact on his current operational auditing. But at the same time we need also to recognize that the degree of involvement in, and concern with, the profit plan in its various phases is an important measure of how adequately the internal auditor will be able to understand management needs, and to service those needs effectively. For that reason he should make a special effort to be more concerned with profit planning.

PLANNING AND CONTROL OF CAPITAL EXPENDITURES

In the development of the profit plans just discussed, the managers will necessarily be considering the kinds of facilities that they will be using in achieving the planned operational results. These facilities may be a major prerequisite for expanded operations, new product directions, or cost savings. Closely related also will be the cash budgets being developed and the resulting planning of needs for capital expenditures. This planning will reflect the greater cash needs at the time of constructing or purchasing facilities, followed by new cash availabilities when the investment in these facilities is being recovered in later years. It is, therefore, clearly very important that capital expenditures be planned carefully and with full consideration of all the various aspects of the total management effort. This planning process then merges into the controls that are necessary to assure that the definitive capital expenditure decisions are properly made and executed.

In Chapter 18 we discussed some of the basic operational problems relating to the determination of facility needs, and the procedures by which projects were prepared and reviewed. At this time we focus more on the financial policy aspects of the total capital expenditures process. The finance group is very concerned with capital expenditures because of their major tie to the ongoing profitability of the company. A further type of concern arises through the impact of these capital expenditures on capital needs, both in terms of maintaining adequate short-term liquidity, and of the soundness of the longer-term capital structure. These concerns are all the greater because of the fact that decisions made covering capital expenditures have such a long-term impact.

Stages in the Development of Capital Expenditure Decisions

The decisions relating to capital expenditures normally come about through a series of stages, which are, as follows:

1. *As Reflected in the Determination of Company Strategy.* The choice of company strategy, as discussed in more detail in Chapter 3, if done on a sound basis, necessarily took into consideration the kinds of facilities, and their value, which would be required to support the particular strategy in a satisfactory manner. There was also presumably a consideration of whether providing the needed facilities was within the financial capabilities of the company. There exists at that point, therefore, a kind of general approval of a fairly definitive facilities program. This general approval then remains valid until there are developments that require a revision of the strategies to be pursued.

2. *Developing the Capital Expenditures Budgetary Plan.* During the period when the profit plans are being developed, the various types of forward action proposed will normally involve the replacement of or addition to facilities. It is then necessary for management to consider all of these needs for facilities as a total problem. This must be done to be sure that aggregate capital expenditures do not exceed the financial capabilities of the company. It must be done also so that the proper priorities can be evaluated as between the competing needs of individual operational components. Thus the development and finalization of the profit plans involve at the same time the development of the capital budget. This capital budget, as it is normally termed, consists of the total planned capital asset programs. These programs cover estimates of the total cost

of the capital projects together with the funds required for the individual years during which the individual programs are being completed. The applicable portions of this plan will then also be reflected in the annual budgets. However, none of these preceding actions constitutes authorization for actual capital expenditures.

3. *Delegation of Project Approval Authority*. Normally, actual capital expenditures will be approved in the form of facilities or capital expenditure projects. In that connection determinations must first be made as to what approvals and concurrences will be required for projects at various dollar levels. The higher the level of responsibility of the individual manager the greater his authority. A particular divisional profit center might, for example, have an authority up to $50,000, and he might delegate an authority of $10,000 to a lower-level profit center department. It is then necessary in the subsequent control over these delegations to be sure that projects are not deliberately broken up to keep them within the authorized limits. There is also the possibility that expenditures of a capital nature will be charged to expense to avoid the restrictions of the delegated authorities. However, the counter control to this practice is the resulting unfavorable impact on the profit performance of the particular organizational component.

4. *Development and Submission of Specific Projects*. Specific projects for capital expenditures are now developed and processed in accordance with established procedures. These projects are reviewed by the responsible line and staff personnel and unless rejected, and after possible modification, are approved by those individuals previously authorized. These projects will normally pertain to types of capital expenditures covered in the capital budget, and if not, should be supported by appropriate explanations of the special circumstances.

5. *Later Control and Evaluation*. The approved projects are now subjected to continuing control for progress and conformity with authorized cost levels. If and when it becomes evident that there will be overruns beyond a designated percentage, supplemental projects will be required. Post-audits should also be made after the completion of the projects. These matters were discussed in more detail in Chapter 18.

Financial Evaluation of Capital Projects

Financial evaluation of individual capital projects centers around analysis of the level of expected profitability of the related capital assets. The first requirement will normally be that the expected profitability is consistent with established company objectives as to the level of return on investment (ROI). This established ROI objective constitutes a benchmark that is commonly used as a cutoff point for minimum acceptability of every proposed project. The second key aspect of the financial evaluation is the comparison of the expected profitability of competing projects so that they can be ranked as to their respective levels of attractiveness. The objective is to allocate the company's capital resources in a manner that will be most profitable. There will always be certain cases when a project will be approved for special reasons. Illustrative would be compliance with governmental regulations, safety requirements, or powerful competitive threats. All choices, however, are on the basis of maximizing long-run profitability.

Evaluation of Profitability.   In the usual evaluation of profitability of individual projects there are two types of considerations involved. The first of these has to do with the accuracy of the estimates that go into the project. These estimates include the cost of the facilites and the time that will be required to make the facilities operational. The estimates include also the benefits that will be derived from the use of the facilities in terms of cost savings and/or revenues generated. The accuracy of these estimates is dependent both on the degree of difficulty inherent in the particular estimate and the competence of the people doing the estimating. Where new processes are involved, the estimates will necessarily be more difficult. Also, when revenue projections extend a number of years in the future, the estimates unavoidably are subject to much risk and uncertainty. In addition, there is the very common problem of the objectivity of the estimates. When the management of a particular organizational component has concluded that a given facility is what is needed, it is very easy to yield to the desire to present that proposed capital expenditure in the most possible favorable terms. For all these reasons the supporting estimates and related analysis must be subject to especially careful review and appraisal.

Types of Evaluation.   The second key aspect of the evaluation of profitability is the type of test applied. These tests vary as to their degree of complexity, and as to their relative merits. The most commonly used types are as follows:

1. *Payback.* This type of evaluation centers on the number of years required to recoup the investment covered by the project. It is not really a measure of profitability, but rather a measure of liquidity and risk exposure. Nevertheless, it is frequently used to measure the relative desirability of competing capital investment proposals. It is calculated by determining the number of years required for the cost savings or revenue benefits, on an "after-tax" basis, to equal the amount of the proposal capital investment. Assuming that the estimates are sound, it is a very simple and well-understood measure. Its limitations, however, are that it includes no consideration of how long or in what amount the ongoing benefits will be to the company after the payback point. This means also that there is no measure of overall profitability or return on investment. It is useful only as a crude measure.

2. *Accounting Method.* This type of evaluation attempts to project the profitability of the proposed investment through the existing accounting process. Here the estimate of the income to be generated is related in

percentage terms to the investment being made. In some cases the income estimate is before depreciation and taxes, in other cases after depreciation but before taxes, and in still other cases after both depreciation and taxes. On the investment side the amount used may in some cases be the original investment, and in other cases the average investment over the life of the asset. These alternative approaches lead to some confusion, and this is one of the disadvantages of using this measure. Moreover, the averaging of the investment may not fairly measure the use of the asset. The most important limitation, however, is that the method gives no consideration to the time element for the return of the funds.

3. *Time-Adjusted Methods*. The time-adjusted methods meet a major deficiency of the previously discussed accounting method by taking into consideration the value of money. These methods recognize the fact that dollars represent interest earning potential, and that the longer we hold on to dollars the longer they can have earning power. Similarly, the sooner dollars are returned to us the sooner we will have an earning capability. This means that all dollars involved in the outflows and inflows processes pertaining to the project are adjusted in terms of current dollars. Once this is done, all projects can be put on a comparable basis.

The two commonly used time-adjusted methods are the discounted cash-flow method and the present-value method. The discounted cash-flow (CDF) method provides for the determination of the rate which when applied to the expected later inflows of cash (from the utilization of the asset) will make those inflows equal the original investment. This determined rate can then be compared with the rates calculated for other projects and with the required ROI rate. This rate should normally be higher than the company's cost of capital. The cost of capital is the combined cost of outside financing from debt and equity, where the cost of equity is induced through the relationship of the market price of the stock to current earnings per share.

In the present-value (PV) method the expected future cash flows are discounted at a predetermined rate, and the resulting present value is obtained and compared with the original investment. Since any difference will be in terms of dollars, those dollars must be related to the original investment to develop an index of profitability. The latter index can then be compared with the index for other projects. On balance the DCF approach is simpler and is more commonly used.

Role of the Internal Auditor Relative to Capital Expenditures

The increasing concern of management that the decisions relating to capital expenditures be made on a sound basis has motivated the finance group to develop the policies and tools which will enable them to provide management with the guidance that is needed. Similarly, the internal auditor must now understand both the problems involved and the nature and scope of the newly developed techniques and procedures by which the financial implications of capital expenditure decisions are identified and evaluated. He is interested first that the new approaches are being used. It is no longer enough to rely on the older techniques and managerial intuition alone. The internal auditor is also interested that the new approaches are being used intelligently. We do not want to swing from one extreme to the other. What is needed is the competent use of the new approaches, but combined with the proper use of managerial experience and judgment. The internal auditor has a unique opportunity in his review of the financial management activity to make such a balanced judgment.

DETERMINING AND SATISFYING CAPITAL NEEDS

Responsibilities Relating to Capital Needs

A major responsibility of the financial manager is to evaluate the company's needs for capital. He does this at the beginning by participating in the determination of company goals, and in the choice of the supporting strategies. At that time he helps provide information as to what the capital needs will be under various alternatives. That role is continued as capital budgets are formulated. It is continued also through his counsel and analysis as major policy and operational decisions are considered. Out of this background the financial manager is thus in a good position to estimate the company's total capital needs over the years of the planning period. These capital needs include the short-term needs—for current liquidity—and the longer-term capital needs, which, while involving different problems, are very closely related. Then with the knowledge of the existing and future capital needs it is the further responsibility of the financial manager to determine how those needs will be satisfied. The objective is to satisfy the existing needs at the lowest possible cost. However, all the different company interests must be considered, and the means finally utilized must be consistent with the total company welfare.

The foregoing role of determining and satisfying capital needs requires a great deal of special expertise on the part of the responsible officers of the finance group. It also requires the additional assistance of outside bankers and other financial institutions. Although it might seem that all of this would not greatly involve the internal auditor, we believe it is essential that a general understanding exist on his part of the major types of issues involved. Such a general understanding will especially enable him to review individual operational activities which in various ways relate to these higher-level responsibilities.

Short-Term Capital Problems

The short-term capital needs of the company stem to a considerable extent from the nature and scope of the particular business. A public utility has certain kinds of operations, while a retail merchandising chain has others. But even in the case of businesses in the same industry there can be substantial differences in the strategies followed. One company may have decided to provide its customers with special types of credit, whereas another may emphasize the savings that result from a no-credit policy. One company may emphasize supply availability and then establish more warehouse locations and more extensive inventories. Beyond these individual strategies there are then the many operational decisions that generate the need for various amounts of cash funds. Should a particular promotional program be undertaken? Should sales be generated through a sale? Or should a particular staff activity be expanded?

Finally, there is the level of efficiency that is achieved in the management of each type of asset. This efficiency can be reflected, for example, in the cash management previously discussed, in a well-managed credit department, or in the more scientific determinations of inventory levels to be maintained. It can come also through the tight control of expenses. The objectives are to seek assurance that operational strategies are based on adequate study and that the levels of efficiency are the best possible under the circumstances. A sound basis is then provided through the cash budgeting process for the determination of the specific short-term capital needs.

Satisfying the Company's Needs for Short-Term Capital. At the same time that the company's needs for short-term capital are being determined, there must be consideration of the feasibility and cost of obtaining the funds needed to support the various policy and operational decisions. There is, therefore, a continuous interaction and trade-off. Needs in one area are also considered in relation to the possibility of generating funds somewhere else in the business to satisfy the first mentioned needs. At some point, however, a company determines that it does or does not need outside funds, and the periods of time during which those outside funds will be required. At that point the company is ready to explore the manner of obtaining the needed funds. Typical sources will include:

1. *Coverage via Long-Term Financing.* Quite often the company's needs for working capital will be included as a part of the long-term financing carried out for more basic capital needs. This approach has the advantage of avoiding a relatively short-term maturity.

2. *Use of Commercial Banks.* In the usual situation arrangements will be worked out with a commercial bank. The specific arrangements will include the scope of the total credit line, stipulations as to balances to be maintained, the interest rate charged, the maturity of the loans, the larger credit line if involved, and the type of security provided. How liberal or stringent these specific arrangements will be depends on the availability of loanable funds and the credit standing of the particular company. Typical types of security will include marketable securities, accounts receivable, and inventory.

3. *Business Finance Companies.* In addition to the commercial banks there is another group of lending institutions which have tended to develop specialized financing techniques suited to the varying needs of the individual company. The approaches used include the purchasing of accounts receivable, advances on accounts receivable (with or without notification of the borrowing to the customer), and direct financing assistance to the company's customers.

4. *Other Financing Institutions.* This group includes a number of other types of financing institutions. These can be life insurance companies, leasing companies, or governmental or semigovernmental agencies of various types.

Long-Term Capital Needs

Initially at the time a company is created, and later as it grows and expands, the longer-run needs of the company must be determined and somehow provided. The basic needs again depend on the type of business that is involved, the basic strategies adopted, the operational decisions supporting those strategies, and the general efficiency of all of the total operational activities. The specific needs usually relate both to the capital expenditures planned and the increased permanent working capital needs resulting from new levels of operational growth. A major source of these capital needs will be the company's own internal operations. More specifically, there will be funds generated by profits, plus depreciation which is charged as an expense but not actually disbursed. Closely related also is the company's policy as to the level of dividends paid out. A profitable company that is growing has the basic justification of retaining earnings by being able to demonstrate that the reinvestment of those profits is in the interest of the corporation and its stockholders. Mention should also be made of the possibilities of a company divesting itself of capital assets, where particular operations are deemed not to be sufficiently profitable. There is the possibility also of selling certain assets under lease-back arrangements.

Satisfying Long-Term Capital Needs. When, however, all of the above-mentioned types of sources have been exhausted, and there is an indicated need on a sound basis for additional capital funds, the company must go outside to investors for such needed capital. The alternatives available relate to the type of security to be offered to investors and the manner in which the offering shall be made. The type of security depends in part on the state of the investment market, that is, the type of security wanted by investors. It depends in part also on the financial structure of the company and the feasibility of increasing debt as compared to equity. The manner of offering includes the question of whether the stock should be privately sold to a large investor or offered publicly to all investors. Included also is the possibility of offering rights to its own stockholders to acquire stock at a given price. The private placement has the advantage of avoiding registration with the Securities and Exchange Commission, and in freeing the company from the risk that a public offering will not be completely sold. The financial manager will take into consideration all of the pertinent factors and choose the route that seems, on balance, to be in the best interests of the company.

Considerations of Financial Structure. In satisfying long-term capital needs the question of what is good for the company in terms of ongoing financial health, and the question of what the market will accept, come together in the capital structure of the company as it exists before and after the proposed financing. This involves the amount of debt versus equity with appropriate consideration to the types of debt and the types of equity. This requires some review of the nature of these different types of securities and their relative advantages and disadvantages.

Traditionally, debt has been preferred as a source of capital. The reasons for this preference include the deductibility for tax purposes of interest paid, greater market acceptability, preservation of ownership control, and the greater leverage.[1] The disadvantages and limitations are that a fixed obligation exists for both principal and interest. Where sales and earnings are subject to fluctuation the coverage of established interest requirements can involve considerable risk. The common stock type of equity in general carries advantages and disadvantages which are the counterpart of those for debt. Preferred stock is another kind of equity that ranks ahead of the common stock as a claim on assets and carries a designated rate of dividend, but not payable unless covered by earnings. There are additionally various types of bonds and stocks that embody different types of features. One of the most popular types of an intermediate security is the convertible bond. This is a bond in the sense of being a fixed obligation, but it is one that can be converted into common stock at a given price. Although the latter price is set above the prevailing market price of the common stock, it has the potential of extra profit if and when the stock price rises to and exceeds the conversion price. Because of this latter feature convertible bonds can be sold at a lower interest rate. Their disadvantage to the company is the potential dilution of the common stock equity.

The decisions as to what the financial structure will be represent some of the most fascinating activities of the finance group. They do, however, represent an area where there are major opportunities for serving the company's total interests. The interests here involve particularly the cost of the capital obtained, the risks to which the company is subjected, and the impact on stockholder profits. A basic requisite to achieving these benefits is the special expertise of the financial manager, but augmented through the outside counsel that is normally available. The total benefit is achieved only, however, when this

---

[1]Leverage will exist where profit rates exceed the interest rates paid and the difference accrues to the benefit of the stockholders. The common stock in these circumstances is said to have leverage.

expertise is coordinated closely with the other operational activities of the company. Here too, it is the team effort that yields the greatest returns.

TAX ACTIVITIES

In different company situations there will be a wide variation in the range of activities carried out by the finance group. It will, therefore, clearly not be practicable to cover them all. We have, however, selected three areas that are of special significance from a financial management standpoint—taxes, insurance, and pricing. These are also areas where the internal auditor will be making both direct reviews and relating to them as a part of other audit reviews.

Scope of Tax Activities

The tax activities of a company cover a wide range of different types of taxes, all of which are payable to many different governmental bodies. As to type they include property taxes, use taxes, sales taxes, franchise taxes, and income taxes. The taxes may be payable to local municipalities, counties, states, or the federal government. Here again much specialized expertise is involved. But here again an important aspect is the way the effort is organized and administered. Important also is the dependence on good operational procedures, and especially a close linkage to the total accounting activity. All of this administrative and operational effort is of the type that calls for effective control. In addition, there is the major tie of tax activities to the development of operational policies and the making of various operational decisions. There are also great potentials of company benefit through a well-coordinated effort. We will look briefly at the more typical types of tax activities.

Property Taxes. In most local jurisdictions the property tax is a major source of governmental revenue. Because it represents such a major operational cost it is essential that the company take every legitimate means to protect the fair assessment and administration of property taxes. The level of property taxes is normally one of the factors initially considered by the company when it buys or develops property in specific geographical locations. At that time the governmental unit with taxing power will often provide special tax-relief benefits as an inducement to the company. Subsequently, it is important to maintain good liaison with the taxing body so that changes in any initial arrangements are fairly considered. Similarly, the revision of assessed values needs to be monitored carefully to reflect changes due to capital additions and retirements, or for any other reasons. In most cases a kind of continuing negotiation takes place through which the company makes sure that its position is properly presented and fair treatment obtained.

Definitive tax bills subsequently give effect to the foregoing arrangements. These tax bills need to be examined for their correctness in all respects. Where accruals have already been made to reflect the correct operational costs for the accounting periods affected, these will be adjusted to the extent necessary, and the obligation properly recognized in the accounts. Where there are questions of any kind, they will be referred to the proper parties for investigation. Major increases in the level of the tax billings would, for example, raise questions as to what were the causes and the degree of propriety. Effective controls are necessary to assure the identification of all developments where company action could be beneficial.

Sales Taxes. The pressure for additional revenues is leading more and more to the levying of sales taxes by cities and states. The first important issue here is the correct interpretation of the law to determine the types of items to which it is applicable. This applicability, in turn, determines the company's obligations as an agent of the government. The remainder of the problem has to do with the actual collection, the establishment of adequate records and accountabilities, the safeguarding of funds collected, the correctness of the later reporting, and the payment of the taxes owed. The reviewer of these operations must be sure that policies are clear, procedures adequate, and operational aspects well controlled.

Social Security and Unemployment Taxes. The social security taxes call for both deductions from the wage and salary payments made to employees and the payment of amounts which are the direct obligation of the employer. The unemployment taxes payable to the states in which the company has operations are also of the latter type. The deductions must be made in accordance with the provisions of the Social Security laws, and as a part of the payroll procedures discussed in Chapter 13. The tax liability that is directly the responsibility of the company must also be accurately calculated in accordance with the legal requirements. Reports must then be prepared and filed on the dates due, together with the actual payments. The review by the internal auditor should cover all aspects of the policies and procedures to assure both a correct compliance with the applicable legislation and that everything is done with maximum efficiency.

Franchise Taxes. There are a variety of taxes levied of a franchise nature. These taxes are levied principally for the right to do business in a particular area—city, county, or state. The basis of assessment will vary greatly, and in some cases may become a special type of income tax. The first requirement is that the various reports to be prepared are properly identified and scheduled, thus minimizing the possibility that filing dates will be overlooked and lead to penalties. The second requirement is that the provisions of the report requirements are properly understood and carried out in preparing the reports. In preparing those reports a combination of legal and financial expertise is essential. In many cases there are options, or relationships with other company policies and decisions, that need to be identified and evaluated.

Income Taxes. In overall importance the federal tax, plus income taxes levied by other governmental jurisdictions, is clearly the dominant part of the total tax activities. This importance is the result of the heavy tax rate involved, and the related need to minimize this impact in every way possible through properly considered managerial decisions. The income tax activity is closely interrelated with the total accounting activity. This is true because all of the data used in the computation of income taxes payable flow directly or indirectly from the accounting system. Normally, there is also an effort to design the accounting treatment of given types of transactions in a manner that coincides with the treatment for tax purposes. Where certain matters are treated differently than in the regular accounting system, the basic accounting data must be used as a starting point, and there must be a careful reconciliation with the figures used for tax purposes.

The tax department or other organizational group charged with the income tax responsibility is frequently headed by an individual who is both a qualified accountant and a lawyer. This is important because tax work is a blend of accounting and legal work. The tax group organizes the supporting data for the computation of income tax obligations, and then actually prepares the returns. Subsequently, as the governmental representatives make audits, the tax group deals with these representatives. If and when the need for adjustments is asserted the tax group handles these matters to a conclusion, including such tax litigation as may be necessary. Inasmuch as large amounts of money can be involved in the final resolution of the company's tax liability, there is a great need for the highest level of professional competence.

Impact of Income Taxes on Operations. In making any operational or policy decision of any significance, an important consideration in weighing the alternative approaches is what the income tax consequences may be, especially where the tax law may not be entirely clear. These questions have their first beginning when a company determines its corporate form of organization and continues on to include such matters as the manner in which inventory is valued, the types of sales arrangements, manner of purchase, depreciation of capital assets, retirement of plant, supplying capital needs, corporate distributions, and executive compensation plans. In dealing with those various matters there are usually various opportunities for effecting tax savings, provided that the possibility is recognized on a timely basis and properly implemented. The tax group must, therefore, be aware of all of these operational developments and have the opportunity to provide information relating to the tax impact. This includes also the role of helping management to do what needs to be done in an operational way, but in a way that minimizes the income taxes payable.

Role of the Internal Auditor in Tax Activities

The internal auditor is first, interested in the extent to which the tax group is administering its basic operational activities in an orderly and efficient manner. The second interest is in how effectively the tax group is working with other operational activities to assure proper consideration of tax issues in their respective policies and current decisions. Through the internal auditor's wide contacts in the company there is a continuing opportunity to contribute to the achievement of effective company coordination in all tax matters.

INSURANCE ACTIVITIES

Nature and Scope of Insurance Activities

Another important type of activity frequently carried on by the finance group has to do with insurance. The insurance function in its most basic sense is a major part of the total company effort to manage risk. The total business operations unavoidably involve risk. Profits are, indeed, the reward for the assumptions of risk in committing capital to the selected operational areas. But where risks can be eliminated or minimized through various types of action the prudent business manager weighs the cost, and determines what course of action appears to best serve the company interest. One of the ways to do this is by purchasing insurance for protection of various kinds. The most common form is the coverage of possible losses of assets like cash, inventory, and facilities. One can go further, however, to cover such items as the collectibility of accounts receivable, loss of profits from interrupted business operations, or life insurance on key officers. The responsibility of the insurance group is to develop policies for management approval covering the extent to which such insurance protection should be purchased. Subsequently then, the insurance group has the responsibility for administering the approved policies. Again a great deal of special expertise is required on the part of the people who administer this activity.

Developing Insurance Policy

The development of insurance policy starts with an inventory of the types of risks to which the company is subject. Although to some extent risks may seem to be unavoidable, there is usually a way that they can be eliminated or substantially reduced if we are willing to pay the cost. In some cases we will pay that cost and in other cases the cost may be too high. For example, in the case of capital assets, the property may be so widely dispersed in a geographical sense that the company may conclude that it will assume directly the risk of fire and other similar hazards. In that case the company will either absorb losses directly into operations or it will accrue reserves at customary insurance rates and then charge actual losses to those reserves. Thus the insurance group appraises the types of existing risks and determines whether it shall seek outside insurance. This then leads into the more detailed determination of the particular features that are desired in the way of insurance coverage—what inclusions and exclusions, and what ranges of dollar limits. For example, do we want full coverage for auto damage or are we willing to accept a deductible provision? Do we want liability coverage at the $100,000 level, $300,000 level, or $500,000 level? In all these determinations a major level of professional competence is required and care in the identification and evaluation of the various issues and alternatives. To some extent also, additional counsel can be obtained from insurance agents and brokers.

Administering the Insurance Activity

The policies as now determined provide the basis for the actual procurement of the wanted insurance coverage. This first involves selecting the carriers to be used. In making that selection a number of factors are necessarily considered. This will include the range of the coverage that a particular carrier can offer, the financial resources of the carrier, the reputation as to the efficiency and fairness with which claims are settled, and the rates charged. Again, insurance brokers, who usually represent a number of carriers, can be helpful in appraising the various alternatives. As a basis for the final negotiation for the purchase of insurance coverage, the insurance group will wish to have complete data as to the value and location of the assets, and other pertinent operational data. The objective will be to seek maximum leverage in achieving the most advantageous rates practicable. Out of these negotiations will then come definitive contracts for the agreed-upon coverage at mutually acceptable rates.

Ongoing Administrative Activities. During the life of the policy there will now be a varied range of ongoing administrative responsibilities. In some cases coverage should be adjusted periodically on the basis of regular reports as to the status of the insured assets. In other cases the changes in coverage are linked to other operational developments—as, for example, new facilities may be purchased and old ones retired. Usually, coverage is automatically adjusted in such situations but there must be notification within a given period for the purpose of adjusting future billings. All these requirements must be complied with, and adequate procedures must be designed so that the various operational developments are identified and properly reported to the carriers. As billings are received for insurance coverage, they must be carefully reviewed both as to the accuracy of rates charged and the correctness of the coverage provided. All these review activities must also be closely tied into the regular processing of the invoices for actual payment, and the proper distribution of costs to the various operational activities affected.

Handling Claims. The insurance group will also normally play an active role in the reporting of all developments that provide a basis for a claim by the company under the existing coverage. This prompt reporting requires the proper cooperation of the operational activities directly affected. It is especially important because the carrier must usually be given the opportunity to take any steps that may assist it in reducing the final loss claim. The insurance group then works with the operational people in developing the actual claim, and after its submission to the carrier coordinates any later audit and negotiation that precede the ultimate settlement. At this stage the supporting data and related information must be provided as needed. However, it may also be necessary for the insurance group to provide additional pressure to assure a final settlement that is fair to the company. Again these settlement activities must also be closely coordinated with the accounting operations.

Educational Role of the Insurance Group

The cost of insurance is very closely related to the loss experience of a particular company. If losses run at a very high level, higher rates must be charged by the carrier if it is to maintain its own profitable operations. In an extreme case of high losses the carrier may even elect to cancel the coverage completely. These possibilities make it very important that the company operations be carried out in a way that will minimize losses, thus reducing the amount of claims which will be filed. A well-managed insurance department recognizes this problem and endeavors to bring about the right kind of conditions. It does so by developing educational material that can describe the things that should be done. Departmental personnel can also make periodic field visits to ascertain firsthand what problems may exist. At the same time the insurance representatives can provide direct counsel to the operational managers. The liaison also makes possible a more up-to-date understanding of insurance needs and possible solutions.

Overall Appraisal of the Effectiveness of the Insurance Activity

An impressive thing about the insurance activity is that it relates in some way to almost every phase of the company operations, and that it has to do with each level of those operations. This makes it a necessity that the insurance group maintain effective coordination with the highest level of management. It includes also the need to tie in closely with the basic accounting activities. The effectiveness of the insurance department is, therefore, dependent on combining professional expertise with good coordination with all company activities. The department must be prepared to respond to the needs of the various operational activities and at the same time to take the initiative in suggesting new possibilities and approaches. The appraisal of the insurance activity centers on the extent to which the insurance group is carrying on this total coordination. As it happens also the internal auditor comes across the insurance problem as he reviews the various operational activities, and this provides further input for the specific review of the activities of the insurance group. The internal auditor's interest is that the insurance department has developed sound policies and procedures and that they are being carried out in an effective manner.

PRICING ACTIVITY

Basis of Interest

The profits of a company, as we know, are determined by the excess of revenue over cost. In various chapters we have been concerned with the managerial efforts to control costs, so that they will be at levels that make the greatest

possible contribution to the success of the company. We have also considered
at a number of points the need to maximize revenue. It is as a part of that
latter concern that we look briefly at the problem of pricing. To a major extent
this problem of pricing is part of the broader area of marketing management,
an activity dealt with in Chapter 19. However, pricing also has a major financial
dimension and in most companies the recommendations to management for
pricing action are finally determined by the finance group. We view pricing
as a joint responsibility of the marketing and finance activities, but we have
found it more convenient to defer consideration of it to this point.

Factors Bearing on Price

Prices are the dollar figures set by the company for its products and services
when offered to customers for purchase. How wisely these determinations are
made quite obviously has a major impact on the company's profitability from
both a short- and long-term standpoint. It is, therefore, most important that
we understand the factors that need to be considered in establishing prices.
It is also important that we understand how better information about those
factors can be provided, as a basis for more advantageous pricing. In this
connection there are three areas that need to be examined. One of these is the
state of customer demand. A second is the competitive situation. The third is
the particular company situation. Although all three areas are interacting, each
has its specific type of influence, and we will look briefly at them.

Customer Demand.   We know that customers have various kinds of needs and
desires. They also have different levels of economic capacity to make purchases
that will directly or indirectly satisfy those needs. As products and services are
then offered to them they will make some kind of evaluations and elect to make
particular purchases. The extent to which they purchase the offerings of a
particular company will depend on a variety of factors, of which one important
factor is the price that company has established for the given item. From the
company's standpoint an important consideration in price determination is the
volume that will be purchased at different prices. If we can answer that question,
we can project the revenue impact at particular levels of price, and give proper
consideration to that dimension in our effort to achieve the highest possible
level of profitability.

The answer to the question of what customers will purchase at various prices
involves a number of matters we have previously discussed—the design of the
product, the quality achieved in production, the goodwill of the customer, the
effectiveness of our salespeople, the advertising and promotional appeal, and
the like. We also may have a great deal of experience as to how customers have
reacted in the past to specific types of pricing action. Additionally, we need
information of the kind normally now obtainable to a significant degree from
modern marketing research. This research can take a number of forms. To
some extent it will include the analysis of economic capability, including the
levels of purchasing power and expected trends in the economy. To some extent

also it will include surveys of customers' needs and preferences. In other cases it will include actual market tests in representative local markets. The objective in all cases is to contribute to the accuracy of the estimates that are made of the volume that will be purchased over time at various levels of price.

Competitive Situation. The second area that needs to be examined is that of the competitive situation. The interest here is twofold. In the first place the extent to which customers are going to purchase the products and services of our own company at given prices will depend importantly on what competitors are doing in the way of offerings in terms of attractiveness of products, availability, and price. Our estimates of volumes at various prices must, therefore, take into consideration the number and types of options open to the customer. Involved also is our relative strength as respects basic product merit and effectiveness of various aspects of the marketing program.

The competitive situation also touches us in another very important respect. When a particular company sets prices it must take into consideration how competitors will respond to that price action in terms of their own prices. If our company is the leader in the industry, we may have less difficulty making this prediction. On the other hand, in a more equal competitive relationship we may through our own pricing action induce various types of retaliatory response. This retaliatory response will then change the scope of the options to customers previously discussed. Still another possibility is that a high-level profit margin may be so attractive that it will attract new competitors. In the short run this may not be a problem but in the long run it could be very serious.

Company Situation. The third area that needs to be examined is the particular company's own situation. At the highest level are the company's goals and objectives, and the supporting strategies—as, for example, an objective for more rapid growth through lower pricing. At the operational level are the conditions of existing stocks, production facilities, and the effectiveness of the production and marketing activities. The latter factors are reflected in current and projected costs. These projected costs will reflect the impact of new operational programs. Additionally, they will reflect the impact of different volumes that result from the various alternative price levels. This latter impact is due to the fact that all individual types of cost have different degrees of variability for different volumes. Thus to the extent that some costs are fixed (or not completely variable) unit product costs will be lower for higher volumes. Therefore, the evaluation of various pricing alternatives must take into consideration the effect on profit of both the factors of cost and revenue levels.

It is thus clear that cost plays an important role in the determination of prices. In specific situations it may even be the controlling guide. For example, some items are made to order on the basis of actual costs plus a given margin of profit. Cost is also a powerful psychological force in the short run when price reductions are being considered. Also, we know that unless costs are covered on a long-run basis, we eventually want to abandon the type of business involved. But having said all of this as to the role of cost, it should be clear that sound pricing policy and action is based on an evaluation of all of the three areas discussed above—consumer demand, the competitive situation, and the company situation—and that these three areas have major interlocking relationships. It is because of these three factors that the determination of prices which best serve the total company interest is so difficult.

Typical Pricing Problems

The broad scope of the pricing policy decision can perhaps be best appreciated by an identification of a number of typical pricing problems.

1. *Product Differentiation.* If products can be differentiated from competitor products by some unique aspect that consumers value highly, prices can be higher than competitors as long as that differentiation can be maintained. Examples include unique styling, a special operational characteristic, or by being in the market first with a new product. Sound marketing policy, therefore, seeks to offer such product differentiation.

2. *Product-Line Relationships.* When there are a number of related products in a given product line, there is the question of whether profit margins should be uniform or to what extent they should be different. Illustrative would be a luxury model in an automobile line versus the standard model. Wider margins are usually sought for the more deluxe models, but there are practical limitations.

3. *Price Differentials.* A number of different types of price differentials normally exist. That is, different prices will be available to different kinds of buyers (like wholesalers versus retailers), for different quantities (quantity discounts), for promptness of payment (cash discounts), for purchases at different times (early orders before the season of normal demand), and the like. The question is the basis for such differentials and how they should be determined.

4. *Legal Constraints.* In all pricing action there is the ever-present potential threat that prices may in some way discriminate against particular buyers or groups of buyers. There is also the risk that the prices set may appear to reflect some agreement with competitors that can be interpreted as being of an antitrust nature. It is here that the assistance of competent legal authority must be utilized.

5. *Selling on the Basis of Price.* There can be many types of market strategy. One strategy, however, is to use pricing policy as a specific strategy. At one extreme prices may be set low to create special buyer appeal, subject always to the risk that competitors will meet those prices. At the other extreme high prices may be used to create the impression of special quality. There is the question, therefore, of the choice of strategy and then what specific prices support the selected strategy.

6. *Incremental Profit Pricing*. In many situations it may be possible to take on new business at lower-than-usual prices when the new business will still yield extra profit, without endangering the regular business. An example would be covering new markets overseas. Still another example would be a second brand to appear to a lower-price market. A major question here is whether the additional sales, at the lower prices, will in some way undermine the market for the regular products.

7. *Sequential Pricing*. When a product with unique appeal is introduced, there is the possibility of initially exploiting this appeal through higher prices. This is especially applicable when production capabilities are still at relatively low levels. Subsequently, when production capabilities are expanded, the price will then be reduced to attract larger demand. Consideration must be given, however, to how the original buyers will react to the later reduced price. What seems to be in the short-run interest may not be the best policy in the long run.

8. *Standard Volume Pricing*. A company may decide to fix prices at a level which over a number of years at a reasonably expected volume will yield the desired level of profits. Although volumes over the different years will yield different profit margins, the advantage is the stability of pricing policy that is thereby achieved. For the company that is the industry leader, this is an especially attractive policy. For other companies, however, this option is less available because of the fact that prices must be set at levels that are competitive with the industry leader.

Role of the Internal Auditor in Pricing Policy

The previous brief discussion of pricing clearly indicates that the problems in this area involve the highest levels of management, and are linked to basic strategy policy decisions. It might, therefore, seem that the internal auditor has very little concern about what goes on in the pricing area. We believe, however, that the very fact that pricing is such an important management responsibility is why the internal auditor should seek to be of assistance. But if he is to be of assistance, the first step must be a general understanding of the issues that are involved.

When we turn more directly to the specific manner in which the internal auditor can be of assistance, we see two major ways in which this can be done. The first type of assistance can center about the kinds of factual input that are provided to management as a basis for policy development and actual pricing decisions. On the cost side the needed input is not only good historical cost data—a traditional concern of the internal auditor—but also estimates of future cost levels, developed for the different levels of volume that must be projected by management at various pricing levels. On the revenue side there is the needed input relating to the analysis and testing of market demand. There is also the necessary study of economic trends for the total economy and for the specific industry. There is also the study and projection of possible action by important competitors. With respect to all these input factors, the internal auditor can be useful in appraising the scope and quality of the actual data developed. The objective here is to provide management with the best possible basis for pricing decisions.

The second major way in which the internal auditor can be of assistance is in the area of policy implementation. After the pricing policy has been determined, there should be adequate procedures for its extension throughout the company. Where the policies must be translated into specific prices, the procedures must cover that phase also. In some cases there may be in addition the need for particular types of deviations to meet specific types of situations. The internal auditor is concerned that the procedures and related controls are properly stated, and that they are adequate. Finally, there is the efficiency and care with which the pricing policies are implemented in terms of lower-level organizational performance. At the same time the problems of specific implementation may provide important information as to both the feasibility and desirability of specific pricing policies. The internal auditor can make significant contributions in all these areas.

AUDIT GUIDES

FINANCIAL MANAGEMENT ACTIVITIES

I. Introductory

   A. Reference should be made to the general discussion of audit guides, Chapter 13.

II. Preparatory Activities

   A. See standard Audit Guides, Chapter 13.

   B. To a considerable extent the individual financial management areas will be handled as separate reviews.

III. Organizational Factors

   A. See standard Audit Guides, Chapter 13.

   B. These organizational factors need to be adjusted to the particular subarea being reviewed.

   C. Matters of special interest in the review of finance manuals will include:

      1. Accounting policy.

      2. Financial reports.

      3. Profit analysis.

      4. Cash management.

      5. Budgets.

      6. Profit plans.

      7. Capital expenditures.

8. Supplying capital needs.
9. Taxes.
10. Insurance.
11. Pricing.
12. Coordinative arrangements with other company activities.
13. Handling of policy deviations.

IV. Activities Pertaining to Current Operations
   A. Accounting Policy
      1. Review and appraise the manner in which major accounting pol-
         icies are developed, including depth of study and adequacy of
         coordination.
      2. Appraise the adequacy of the scope of existing policies, including
         those applicable to:
         a. Credit.
         b. Product costing.
         c. Capital and revenue expenditures.
         d. Depreciation.
         e. Deferments of expense.
         f. Treatment of tax credits.
         g. Accruals of expense.
         h. Creation of reserves.
         i. Treatment of subsidiaries.
   B. Report Analysis
      1. Review and appraise the total group of financial reports regularly
         issued, with particular reference to:
         a. Focus on user needs.
         b. Ease of interpretation and use.
         c. Respect for individual manager responsibilities.
         d. Quality of analysis.
         e. Adequacy of attention to the future.
      2. Review the adequacy of analysis in the interpretation of financial
         reports.
   C. Profit Analysis
      1. Review and appraise the existing program of profit analysis.
      2. Are adequate efforts made to recognize the limitations of profit
         analysis and to provide supplementary data?
      3. Are flexible budgets used to the extent practicable?
      4. Are incremental types of analysis utilized for guidance to man-
         agement?
      5. Is the total effort adequate, in the way of developing various
         types of profit analysis?
   D. Cash Management
      1. Is the importance of the cash management activity adequately

recognized in terms of assigned responsibilities and quality of personnel?

2. What steps have been taken to increase the availability of cash? Are they adequate?

3. Have cash flows been studied for maximum possibilities of regularization?

4. Is a cash budget regularly prepared and released to all interested parties?

5. How effective is the program for the investment of surplus cash?

V. Planning Role in Operations

A. Annual Budget

1. Has top management established and provided adequate backing for a budgetary program? Appraise whatever is being done of an annual planning nature.

2. Is the responsibility for coordinating the development and later administering the budget placed at an adequate organizational level?

3. Is the organizational structure reasonably supportive of an effective budget program?

4. Is the planning aspect of the budget adequately emphasized?

5. Are there adequate procedures covering the manner in which budgets should be developed by the individual organizational components?

6. Does the finance group provide adequate assistance through providing historical performance data, explaining procedures, and providing any other needed experience?

7. Are the budget data developed along the lines of accounting reports, so that budgetary performance can be periodically measured and evaluated?

8. Are individual budgets as developed accepted by the respective managers as their own commitments and plans?

a. Are existing gaps reconciled on a mutually satisfactory basis?

9. Review and appraise the extent to which interim performance reports are used for management analysis. What evidence is there of resulting corrective action?

B. Profit Plan

1. Apply the same guides as listed under the annual budget to the review of the profit plan activity.

2. Is the profit plan properly tied into the annual budget?

3. Review and appraise the adequacy with which new profit plans are reconciled with previous profit plans.

VI. Planning and Control of Capital Expenditures

A. Capital Expenditure Budget

1. Is a capital expenditures budget prepared? If not, appraise the extent of the existing need.

2. Review and appraise the adequacy of the manner in which the capital expenditures budget is prepared and administered.

B. Control of Individual Capital Projects
   1. Is there an adequate and reasonable plan of delegations of authority?
   2. Are projects processed, reviewed, and controlled as previously outlined in Chapter 18?

C. Financial Evaluation of Capital Projects
   1. To what extent are methods used which adjust for the different time value of money?
   2. Are the results of these newer scientific methods adequately communicated to management?

VII. Determining and Satisfying Capital Needs

A. Short-Term Capital Needs
   1. Does the determination of short-term capital needs reflect adequate coordination with all company activities and exploration of merits of other actions that could minimize these needs?
   2. Do qualified personnel effectively explore the various ways in which the determined short-term capital needs can be satisfied?
   3. Are short-term needs properly coordinated with long-term capital needs?

B. Long-Term Capital Needs
   1. Is the determination of long-term capital needs properly coordinated with the capital expenditures budget?
   2. Do qualified personnel effectively explore the various ways in which the determined long-term capital needs can be satisfied?

VIII. Tax Activities

A. Policy
   1. Are the tax implications of policy and major operational decisions given adequate visibility through effective coordination with all company activities?
   2. What evidence exists as to the sufficiency of forward tax planning?

B. Operational Efficiency
   1. Are the organizational responsibilities for the various types of taxes specifically assigned at a sufficiently high level? Is there adequate qualified staff?
   2. Review and appraise the procedures for the development of required tax reports.
   3. Are tax due dates adequately identified and scheduled?
   4. Are relations with tax authorities effectively handled?
   5. Are tax actions adequately coordinated with the accounting group?

IX. Insurance
    A. Policy
        1. Are the risk-reduction possibilities through insurance given adequate visibility to management by the insurance department?
        2. What evidence exists as to the adequacy of the consideration of insurance factors?
    B. Operational Efficiency
        1. Review and appraise the effectiveness of the selection of carriers and the negotiation of specific insurance coverage.
        2. Review and appraise the linkage and coordination of insurance matters with the affected operational activities, and with the accounting group.
        3. Are claims efficiently handled?
        4. Are adequate efforts made to carry out programs to reduce losses, to ultimately reduce insurance costs?

X. Pricing
    A. Development of Pricing Policy
        1. What is the procedure for developing pricing policy? Does the finance department participate in a reasonable manner?
        2. Review and appraise the manner in which cost and revenue estimates supporting pricing action are determined.
        3. Is the coordination between the marketing and finance groups adequate?
    B. Operational Control
        1. Review and appraise the procedures by which price lists are developed and distributed.
        2. How adequate are the efforts to determine the propriety of prices actually used?
        3. Are procedures for the control of deviations adequate?

XI. Specific Audit Tests
    Supplementary specific audit tests will be applicable in connection with the various operational phases of the areas discussed.

XII. Overall Appraisal of Financial Management Activities
    A. See standard Audit Guides, Chapter 13.
    B. The overall appraisal can be made separately for each financial management subarea, and also for the area as a whole.

ILLUSTRATIVE AUDIT FINDINGS: FINANCIAL MANAGEMENT

Needed Revision of Depreciation Methods

Modifications of depreciation methods were needed to obtain better valuations of capital equipment and to achieve savings on income tax. Depreciation policies established by the treasurer's office had not been modified under changed conditions. It was found that eight items of equipment were being depreciated over 10 years when the company's current plans for usage of the equipment were only 6 years. Improved coordination was needed between production, the accounting office, and the treasurer's office to assure that depreciation methods are periodically reviewed and changed as needed.

Delayed Deposit of Cash Receipts

A survey of two weeks average daily bankings of the five branches of the company indicated that delays were encountered in making deposits. Deposits by two branches were accumulated and made the next morning, even though total daily receipts from customers were as high as $200,000. Under the extended hours recently adopted by the bank, deposits made by 4 P.M. would be credited that day. It was recommended deposits be made the same day as receipts, resulting in interest savings of $20,000 a year.

Inconsistent Methods for Developing Personnel Requirements

Procedures for developing budget requirements needed strengthening to provide management with more effective control of operations. There was no formal procedure which established the budget cycle from preparation through execution and evaluation of performance. Because of limited budget guidance, differences in forecasting methods existed. In forecasting personnel requirements the engineering research group relied on past historical performance only, whereas the economics research group developed more realistic requirements by using a combination of historical experience and an evaluation of each employee's anticipated performance.

Budgeting on an After-the-Fact Basis

In developing budgets there was no recognition of organizational changes during the year, resulting in budgeting partially on an after-the-fact basis. At the end of the first quarter a decision was made to consolidate two divisions. Experienced costs of the two divisions for the quarter were added together and used as a basis for the budget for the new organization, without change to reflect proposed economies.

Need to Identify Certain Overhead Costs

It was found that there was insufficient segregation of functional costs in overhead to serve as a basis for controlling costs. Costs of bidding, public relations, and downtime were not segregated in the accounting records; and operating groups did not separately budget for these functions. These costs should be identified in the records, and comparisons made with budgets that are sufficiently detailed to serve as cost control.

Coordinating Needs for Low-Dollar-Value Equipment

The company's policy required operating groups to submit budgets for the purchase of fixed assets with a unit cost of $500 or more. However, it did not provide for the separate budgeting of quantity acquisitions of capital-type items with unit values under $500, nor did it provide for coordinating the acquisition of annual capital item requirements of these items with the purchasing department. During the last year the company issued 341 purchase orders to acquire 754 items of desks, tables, chairs, and cabinets at a cost of $225,000. In addition to the inordinate number of purchase orders used, tests showed that over two-thirds of these purchase orders were issued to only three vendors. Better prices might have been obtained and substantially less costs incurred through separately budgeting for quantity acquisitions and coordinating the requirements with the purchasing department.

Invalid Data Used in Pricing

An analysis of losses and decreased profits for four product lines indicated that invalid data were used in pricing. For two of the products short-run factors were used for inflation, although prices were in effect for two years. For the other two products, overhead rates had not been projected to reflect increases resulting from higher costs and decreased activity.

CHAPTER TWENTY-TWO

Computer Operations

NATURE OF COMPUTER OPERATIONS

Computer operations, or electronic data processing (EDP) as it is commonly called, represents one of the most important areas of operational activity that supports the total management effort. Although it is a development of the last quarter century, it has assumed a central role in the total spectrum of managerial and internal auditing practice. Computer operations is an operational activity that includes two major groups of subactivities. The first of these comprises the planning and development activities that deal with determining the kinds of uses to which computer capabilities will be put. The computer applications must be determined and developed, and the right kind of equipment procured. The second type of activity has to do with the actual processing of the data in accordance with previously developed programs. The latter activity is thus directly operational in a more conventional sense.

In addition to these activities, our interest in this chapter is with the newer forms of distributed data processing and various management information systems. In addition, we discuss the problems of computer crime and the approaches used by the internal auditor to prevent and detect its occurrence.

Because of the complex nature of data processing activities, it is often difficult for the internal auditor to cover all phases of the function. He is interested in such diverse areas as justification for type of equipment and application, lease versus buy considerations, design and planning, security, utilization and billing rates, controls over input, processing and output, logistics and housekeeping, reports generated, and effectiveness of system in meeting needs. Often, the audit resources available may not be sufficient to cover all the various phases. Under these circumstances the internal auditor selects manageable segments of the function, performing reviews of various phases on a rotating basis in light of need and importance.

Importance of Computer Operations

The computer operations are of special importance for at least three reasons. The first reason is that the typical company has a total operational group that is becoming increasingly large. Annual budgetary expenditures in many companies run into millions of dollars, and a large investment of capital is involved. With such a commitment of people and money it is to be expected that there is an increasing concern as to the operational effectiveness of this effort. The second reason for the importance of computer operations is the direct relationship that exists between them and every other type of operating activity that is reviewed by the internal auditor. Many of these other operating activities may depend upon or relate to the computer operations in some way. Third, our review of computer operations is important in that it further sets the stage for the internal auditor himself to use the computer as a tool in carrying out various types of auditing tests and inquiries—as discussed in Chapter 8.

Management Orientation of Chapter

The design of computer systems and the subsequent processing of data are very technical and specialized. It is obviously impracticable in a single chapter to provide this kind of information. Instead, the chapter is concerned primarily with the general nature of the major types of computer activities and their significance from an operational control standpoint. We are concerned also with the managerial implications, especially with how computers can be useful to management. We believe that this approach will be most useful to the generalist, such as the internal auditor, who must look at computer operations as he would any other company operational activity. Although all internal auditors are necessarily learning more about the technical aspects of computer operations, it is also assumed that there will be one or more persons on the internal audit staff who will provide more specialized assistance.[1]

Changing Character of Computer Utilization

Modern computers, as we have noted previously, represent a relatively recent development. Their real birth came during World War II when the needs of our military establishment led to an acceleration of the underlying technical research and development. In the postwar period the new capabilities were then introduced into the commercial field. At this stage most commercial processing of data had been limited to the electromechanical types of equipment, and built around the use of punched cards. The immediate payoff was then to replace this older type of equipment with computers, retaining punched cards only as one of the means for preparing data for actual computer processing. In all of these installations the emphasis was on using the new capabilities of speed and accuracy to make clerical types of activities more efficient. At the same

---

[1]For a more detailed coverage of the technical aspects of computers and computer processing, the reader is referred to the manuals on Systems Auditability and Control, published by The Institute of Internal Auditors.

time computers made it possible to handle the ever-increasing volume of such activities, and thus to avoid an almost impossible bottleneck that would otherwise have come to exist. Typical applications included the preparation of payrolls, the billing of customers, the handling of accounts receivable, and inventory records. These applications provided immediate and definitive benefits.

Subsequently, however, there has been an increasing movement toward the utilization of computers for a broader range of applications. In part this has been due to the fact that the more clerical types of applications have been fairly well covered. But it has also become increasingly recognized that there can be a major range of benefits from the utilization of computers for other managerial purposes. These broader applications have to a considerable extent been linked to the use of the more complicated mathematical and scientific concepts (generally referred to as management science), which, with the new computer capabilities, have made it feasible for the first time to make the necessary voluminous calculations and combinations on a timely and accurate basis. There has also been a new capability to link together a number of separate operational activities in an integrated type of system relationship. Thus computer operations as a field of operational activity now comes to have a much broader scope in terms of ongoing management interest.

Management's Concern as to Computer Utilization

Under these new conditions the concern of management relative to computer operations can be more clearly defined. This concern has at least two major aspects. The first of these is whether the range of opportunities for computer utilization is being adequately exploited. Since business is competitive, no individual company can afford to lag behind in the achievement of the benefits that modern computers can make possible. At the same time there have been problems of overly ambitious types of computer utilization, with resulting excessive costs and operational disasters, all of which naturally make management very cautious. The objective, therefore, is to find the level and range of computer utilization that is sound and profitable. There is also the related need to determine exactly what has to be done to achieve that objective. The second type of concern is more operationally oriented. Here the focus is on the day-to-day efficiency of the actual computer processing. Are existing computerized systems functioning in the proper manner? Is the processing of data being done in a manner that provides the needed services on a timely and economical basis? Are we relating to outside parties on an accurate and timely basis? All of these important types of management concerns in turn define the areas in which the internal auditor can make his contribution through his operational auditing effort. In essence we seek to determine whether management needs are being adequately served by the existing computer operations and whether this is being done at a fair and reasonable cost.

PLANNING AND DEVELOPMENT ACTIVITIES

Nature of Planning and Development

From a chronological standpoint the planning and development activities pertaining to computer operations must precede the actual processing of data. That is, there must be operational instructions covering the processing to be done before the actual processing can take place. It is, therefore, logical that we first examine this aspect of computer operations. The range of these planning and development activities is, of course, very great. In its simplest form they can consist of the writing of a simple computer program for data processing; at the other extreme they can focus on long-range research. In total, however, they represent the foundation for the total computer effort. It has been said that the computer itself is a kind of robot, providing only the basic electronic impulse, and responding only to the instructions it receives. It is, therefore, through the planning and development that the process becomes meaningful. The planning and development effort here includes both the design of the mechanical means by which the data can be processed—that is, the operational features of the basic computer and the various types of peripheral equipment—and the programs that direct the computer hardware to process data in a manner that will achieve the information objectives. In combination, and as properly integrated, these planning and development efforts provide the basis for the more specific operational activities.

Systems Types of Computer Applications

Some further consideration of the various types of computer applications will be useful as a basis for better understanding the total planning and development effort. In general, there are two broad categories of applications. One of these categories has to do with operational systems of varying scope, and the other focuses more on providing specific information for individual decisions of various kinds. Although the two categories are closely interrelated, and sometimes combined, the operational type is concerned with the handling of data as a definitive part of the operational activity of the company. It also commonly takes the form of a systems application. The term "systems" is used here to cover the type of situation where different operational activities, or individual parts of a single operational activity, are linked together in some manner. The complexity of the particular systems application depends on the complexity of the particular activity, and the extent to which it relates to and involves other operational activities. The system can also be of a clerical processing nature or involve any type of production or other operational activity.

Clerical-Type Processing Activities. As previously stated, the earliest types of applications involved the types of activities that were of a clerical nature. The characteristics present were the existence of a large volume of paperwork which was of a standard and repetitive nature. As a result it was possible to develop precise methods and procedures for the handling of the particular operations. The preparation of a payroll is a good illustration. Here the various types of input data—hours, rates of pay, and various types of deductions—can be defined and subjected to prescribed types of combinations, calculations, and summarization. A similar situation exists in the maintenance of an inventory record, where individual inputs can be defined and combined on an ongoing basis with subsequent output withdrawals. In all cases provision can be made for the flagging of transactions that go beyond the established decision rules and that must receive special supervisory attention. As time goes on these clerical-type applications are further refined and modified to meet changing operational requirements. There is also the opportunity to modify such applications to make use of the various types of new equipment and processing techniques that are continuously being developed.

Production Processing Applications. Another type of computer application that has major value is in connection with the carrying out of particular production operations. Here the operational situation normally involves a substantial volume of processing which again is subject to precise rules and specifications. These specifications may relate to the quantities and proportions of the various types of materials, temperature, humidity, time, and the like. The programs developed give effect to these prescribed rules, and control the ongoing production processing until the desired production is completed, or until there is an interruption because of some planned or unplanned development. Processing applications can range from the operation of a single phase of the production to the linkage of a number of phases. The judgmental question here is the determination of the feasibility and practicability of extending the scope of the individual system, considering always the related costs and benefits.

Broader Types of Operational Systems. At a more sophisticated level the computer application is extended to cover a wider area, and to link together additional operating activities. Now previously individual applications—commonly referred to as subsystems—are combined in larger systems. The individual subsystems at the same time may cover new types of operational activities. An example of the latter development is a computerized system for purchasing. In some situations the normal needs of customer departments for goods and services can be defined in standard terms. Sources for these goods and services can then be sought out and purchasing terms established. This can then lead to the development of prescribed decision rules and procedures which can be incorporated in a computer program for handling specified types of procurement. Other subsystems in certain situations can be developed for the entry of customer orders, stock availability, billing, accounts receivable, and production scheduling. At some later point some of these subsystems can be linked together in still larger systems. Ultimately, it is conceivable that the receiving of customer orders can lead automatically into the determination of stock availability, to generate the billing, and to spark the resulting necessary production and purchasing support action. It is the extension of operational systems that represents new major frontiers in computer utilization.

Computer Applications to Support Management Decisions

The second broad category of computer applications has to do with the support for various types of management decisions. The support here can take the form of making a specified calculation, answering a question, or providing some kind of analysis. It can involve processing that will be completed by the computer at a later point of time, or it may involve direct communication with the computer. In certain types of applications there may be data banks established where given types of information are stored and made available as requested. Illustrative would be the data bank covering the specified qualifications of designated groups of company personnel.[2] When a person is needed for a given position, the necessary qualifications are identified and the computer queried as to which company personnel possess the needed qualifications. Another important type of support for managerial decision is where the results can be determined based on varying management assumptions. Thus the merits of a given capital project can be tested in relation to varying assumptions about the revenue that will be produced by the new investment. Similarly, the effect of alternative pricing decisions can be tested on the basis of varying sales estimates. It is recognized here, of course, that the computer results are dependent on the merits of the assumption used. The value, however, lies in the way the computer capabilities can be used to provide a rapid cross check of the impact of the various assumptions, and thus help narrow the boundaries of the problems to which the manager must ultimately apply his judgment.

Organizational Setting of the Planning and Development Effort

The effectiveness of the planning and development effort for computer operations, as is true for every operating activity, depends to a major extent on where the responsibility is placed in the organizational structure. We know, in principle, that this planning and development effort has as its central mission the service of management needs. This means that it must have an organizational status that enables it to do that job at a level corresponding to its capabilities. This will include the ability to attract a person to head this activity who has the proper qualifications, plus a supporting staff of adequate numbers and qualifications. It means also that the personnel of that staff must have adequate access to the managers whose needs are being served. One question here is whether the planning and development of computer operations should be a part of one of the other staff groups, or whether it should be entirely separate. In the past the practice has been to place this responsibility with the finance staff. However, there has been some question as to whether this resulted

---

[2]See Chapter 20.

in a developmental effort that was too much oriented to the finance point of view, and also as to whether the service was as available as it should be to other company activities. For this reason some companies have created new independent organizational units, frequently called management information systems (MIS), and have placed the developmental activity there.

Centralization versus Decentralization. A second organizational problem that is of great importance is whether the planning and development effort in a company should be centralized at the company headquarters, or whether it should be decentralized to the operating divisions and departments. The argument for centralization stresses the company-wide character of the computer developments, and the possibility of exploiting the advantages of a more specialized and more professional computer development group. The argument for decentralization is that the divisional operations may be relatively unique and often large enough to justify their own efficient coverage of computer needs. The argument here also is that managers at this level will not be adequately served by a more distant and less directly involved central staff.

The best solution is usually some kind of compromise. It is clear that some computer applications will have a company-wide character. Certainly, the trend would appear to be more and more in this direction. Hence there must be a capable central group to identify and develop the solutions to these needs. On the other hand, some computer applications need to be worked out at a level that is closer to the field operations. It is also highly desirable to support the lower-level operational manager so that computer potentials can be more directly exploited. Hence there should be some personnel attached to the division - or departmental staffs. To whom these individuals should report is still another question. There are both advantages and disadvantages for a reporting responsibility to the divisional manager versus a reporting to the central computer group. But in any event, as a minimum, there should be a functional relationship of the local computer personel to the central computer group. The local computer personnel should also in any event seek to serve the local management needs, and at the same time retain coordinative relationships with the central developments.

It should be noted that what has been said about the partial decentralization of the planning and development activity to lower-level operational groups applies equally to other corporate staff groups. Here too, a good case can be made for having a smaller development staff that concentrates on the specific problems of that particular group. But again also, that subgroup would work in a coordinative relationship with the central computer group.

Committee-Type Coordination. An approach sometimes used to coordinate the planning and development efforts in a company is through the use of some kind of a central committee. This particular approach has commonly been used in the transitional stages when the need for central coordination is first recognized but the company is not ready to establish a strong central computer group. Such committees are usually made up of representatives from the key central staffs and the major operations groups. They may deal with either or both the development of company-wide program applications and the acquisition of computer hardware by any individual organizational component. The committee may be advisory or have final approval authority in the designated areas. When used in a strictly advisory capacity they frequently lack sufficient authority to cope with the normal tendency of individual organizational components to go their own way. On the other hand, when they do have enough authority it is usually then better to set up more formal organizational arrangements. But these committees have served a useful purpose to condition the various internal groups to the need to look at computer activities on a company basis rather than just in terms of the needs of individual units. The mounting cost of computer hardware and systems development has accelerated this trend.

Operational Phases of the Planning and Development Effort

A review and appraisal of the planning and development activities pertaining to computer utilization requires some understanding of the operational phases that are involved. We deal here with the situation as it is likely to exist in a relatively large company and with the problems arising in connection with the more complicated types of systems applications. It is indeed these more extended systems situations that present the major difficulties and risks. But it is this type of application that is becoming increasingly typical as the computer development effort seeks for the more rewarding opportunities.

General Research and Study. The first beginnings of the planning and development effort actually take place as a company studies the future types of computer utilization. This includes the forecasting of technological developments and the types of computer equipment that may be expected over the future. It is a type of activity that is carried on to a major extent by the computer manufacturers themselves, and it is also the focus of interest in professional associations. But it is also carried on by an individual company as it projects its own utilization of computer equipment. This more general type of research then in the individual company leads into the more directed research as to the kinds of systems that might be potentially feasible and effective in the specific company situation. Normally, broad company needs have been identified in the way of operational control and customer service, and a planning group is continually searching for the specific directions for the approach to the better coverage of these needs. In recent years there has been increasing emphasis on the development of a coordinated management information system and the problem is how to proceed to develop such a system in the particular company situation.

Determining the Feasibility of Individual Systems Applications. Although there are some proponents for the view that a management information system should be approached as a total one-time problem, the more prevalent view is that priorities are established, and that one then moves to the coverage of those priorities, with an evolving plan as to how various developments will eventually form a larger system. Assuming that such priorities have been established by management, the computer development group then moves to a conceptual plan for the specific systems application, and to the more serious study of the feasibility of the proposed system. At this point there needs to be an in-depth examination of the affected operations as they now exist and the manner in which the proposed system will function. Normally, there will be the requirement of covering the services presently provided, but also there will be the possibility of extending the role of the system to provide new types of services. The study at this point will take into consideration the transactions that take place, the information requirements, the operational needs of all interested parties, the impact on personnel needs, the types of equipment required, and the costs to be incurred.

The judgment of whether an investment should be made in a given systems application is in principle the same as any capital investment. The essence of that judgment is an evaluation of the operational benefits to be achieved versus the costs to be incurred, including an evaluation of the related risks. The time required for such an evaluation will depend on the complexity of the application, but it must be adequate to allow enough time for proper consideration of all the related factors. Of equal importance, it must involve the participation of all the key people who will be affected by the application. This participation is necessary both to get the proper input for a sound evaluation and to obtain their support for the new system. If the feasibility is properly established, the proposed application is ready for final management approval.

System Design and Specification. The materials developed in the feasibility study will now be used as a basis for a more in-depth determination all of the operational aspects of the systems application. Now the system must be developed in great detail, starting with the basic information inputs. What information will be collected, where, when, and in what form? How will this information input be received into the computerized portion of the system and with what equipment? What people will be affected and what will they do, and when? All of these details must be reflected in flowcharts supported by adequate notation as to the manner in which the operation will function. Similarly, the stages of the later transfer and processing of the data must be covered, including finally the manner in which the results are to be made available as needed at all stages. Consideration must also be given to interim and final formal reporting, and to ongoing data retention needs. In this design and specification there is the need for close collaboration with all parties who will either be participating in the later operation of the system, or who will be using it for direct or indirect operational purposes. The great danger is that decisions will be made in isolation, without recognition of the practical operational problems. Also, there is no substitute for taking enough time to do the job right, despite the pressures that often exist for accelerating the completion of the application.

Programming. The system design and specification now become the basis for the actual programming. The first decision here is as to the programming language that will be used. Normally, it is desirable that this determination be made on a company-wide basis to assure maximum compatibility with existing and planned equipment, and with current programs. The next important requirement is that there be a close collaborative effort between the programmers and the systems analysts to ensure a proper understanding of the system, as designed, and to provide a further check on the soundness of that design. The programmer will be concerned with how the capabilities of the computer equipment can be best utilized, and as to how the programming instructions will best assure an efficient processing of the data. To the extent that already exising subprograms can be used—as previously developed, or available from manufacturers or other outside sources—they should be used to the extent practicable. The combined results will then be tested at the various stages, and there must be the ever-necessary debugging of any errors. Although much progress has been made in simplifying the programming effort, this part of the development activity still remains one of the most time-consuming aspects.

In a well-managed programming activity there will be a major dependence on proper documentation in accordance with well-defined standards. These standards need to be set forth clearly in some kind of manual. Such standards become the basis for training purposes, and for the development of adequate documentation on a consistent and high level as actual programming is carried out. The documentation itself should normally move from the summary stage to the more detailed backup, with the total tie-in being clearly indicated. It would typically include program summaries, flowcharts, pertinent narrative explanations, diagrams of computer logic, identification of records developed at the various operational stages, codings and program decks, and supporting detailed instructions.

Installation and Testing. The system as designed and programmed is now ready for installation. This is a most critical phase because there is no absolute assurance that the total system will work satisfactorily, and, therefore, a transition from the old system must be effected in a manner that will not endanger the ongoing operational activities of the company. There is, in addition, the problem of getting operating people to adjust to the new system. In some cases the system can be phased in on a piecemeal basis, but in other situations this is not possible. In all other cases the problem is critical enough to work the two systems simultaneously for an appropriate overlap period. Also, every possible type of preparation should be made in the way of advance instruction and training. Despite the best of efforts, however, some difficulties and delays will normally be encountered. Accordingly, every possible provision should be made for backup support to protect the orderly continuation of the essential company operational activities.

Ongoing Operation of the System. At the time the system is actually installed, and before the key computer personnel move on to other assignments, it is important that all documentauon be reviewed and put into order for later possible use. In the normal situation the operational conditions will change and further modifications in the application will be required. In other cases further experience will demonstrate the need for some kind of improvement in the system. When this happens it is important to have the basic documentation in the proper form for reference. It is also important that the modifications in the existing system be made with the same care as was exercised in the original design, and then properly incorporated in the basic documentation.

Organization of the Development Activity

The internal organization of the planning and development effort can vary greatly. It is also less likely to be structured and rigid. This is true because the personnel in the development group are higher-level professional types who tend to operate in a more fluid and collaborative fashion. Nevertheless, as the group expands there is the need for a certain amount of organizational structure. In developing this structure there are two different dimensions of the activity. One of these is looking into the future—as, for example, the distinction between long-range research versus more immediate system development, and versus actual programming. The other dimension has to do with the type of systems application, and the extent to which the applications have to do with either particular functional areas or particular operating divisions. A typical organizational structure would be as shown in Exhibit 22.1.

Utilization of Project Teams for Systems Development

Emphasis has previously been given to the need for close collaboration in systems development with the people who are going to be affected by the particular systems application. The people involved include the working per-

EXHIBIT 22.1.   Organization of Planning and Development
of Computer Operations

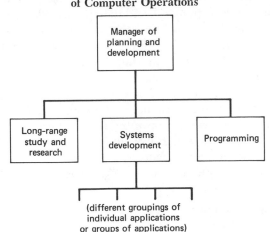

sonnel who will be relating directly to the system, and also the managers responsible for the various affected organizational groups. One of the ways in which this collaboration and coordination can be best assured is through the use of project teams. Such project teams can be effectively utilized both at the stage of determining feasibility and at the later stages of design and installations. The project teams themselves include key representatives from the various operational areas affected. In a given systems application, for example, the system might involve such operational areas as production, stores, marketing, engineering, and accounting. In such a situation each of these groups would designate a qualified person to work with the project head, normally a member of the computer development staff. These individuals can then provide needed operational expertise as to the problems and requirements of their respective operational groups. They can also provide needed liaison with the operational groups so that conclusions reached will be acceptable to those activities. The use of such project groups for the development of individual systems projects is becoming increasingly common, and is proving to be most effective. It also represents an important type of organizational development.

Relating System Development to Personnel Needs

In earlier chapters[3] we have stressed the need for understanding the human dimension of all operational relationships. In the development of computerized systems this is especially true. The problem here has two aspects that are closely interrelated. The first aspect has to do with the problem of assuring a needed level of cooperation to make an individual systems application effective in an operational sense. People tend to be apprehensive of the impact of a new system, and this can lead to both a lack of cooperation, and even a degree of actual hostility. In many cases a major contributing factor to the failure of a particular systems application has been that type of resistance. The need, therefore, is to recognize this type of apprehension and to deal with it properly. One of the ways that this is done is by adequate communication whereby people do understand what is going to happen, and when, and why. In that way distorted rumors can be liquidated, and there is also adequate time for mental adjustment. A second way to achieve the needed cooperation is by a clearly demonstrated intention to deal fairly with each affected employee. This leads into the second major aspect of the human problem, which is the effective utilization of people.

Effective utilization of people in new computer developments means basically the proper planning of personnel requirements under the changing conditions that come about as a result of the new system, and then taking such actions as will minimize the severity of any major impact on existing personnel levels. Actually, the problem is not usually as serious as one might initially expect. Although one of the reasons for approving a new systems application

[3]See especially Chapters 7 and 20.

may be to reduce personnel, two factors tend to counter such a reduction. One of these is that the new system normally contemplates an expanded range of services—which in itself can require more personnel—and the other is that volume is also usually growing. It is, of course, true that different types of people may be required for the new system, but again it may be possible to train many of the existing personnel for the new types of positions. Also, possibilities may exist for the transfer of existing personnel to other company activities. If, however, in the most extreme case these efforts—plus normal attrition—are not enough, the final resort must be to a fair kind of termination arrangement for the few individuals thus affected.

Closing the Gap between Computer Personnel and Management

The importance of close collaboration between computer personnel and operational personnel in the planning and development of computer applications has been emphasized. This collaboration becomes especially important in the case of the company managers. What frequently happens is that managers may not reach out sufficiently to work with computer personnel. This may be because these managers think they are too busy, or because they lack enough knowledge about computers to feel comfortable in the liaison relationships. At the same time, computer personnel frequently come to live too much in their own private world, with their own special technical knowledge and jargon, and tend to be too concerned with the technical achievements of the system. They may even at times come to believe that they themselves know best what the management problems are, and how they should be handled. Unfortunately, this understanding of management needs is often not that good. In any event it is the managers who have to do the actual managing. As a result of the existing gap, the computer effort is often misdirected and not properly utilized. One of the greatest needs, therefore, is to bridge this gap and to establish a close working relationship between the responsible managers and the computer personnel. To accomplish this there must be a better understanding of each other's needs, and a more positive effort on both sides to find a way to work together.

Role of the Internal Auditor in Planning and Development

The foregoing review of the nature of the planning and development activities sets the stage for an important role on the part of the internal auditor. We see at least two major types of contribution.

As a Participant in the Development of Individual Systems. Traditionally, the internal auditor has taken the position that he should not participate in the development of systems and procedures, lest he lose his objectivity in subsequently appraising the operation of the particular system. As we have previously seen, however, Section 120.03 of the "Standards for the Professional Practice of Internal Auditing" provides that "the internal auditor's objectivity is not adversely affected when the auditor recommends standards of control for systems or reviews procedures before they are implemented." Despite this conciliatory statement, the Standards go on to say that "designing, installing, and operating systems are not audit functions" and that "the drafting of procedures for systems is not an audit function." In the case of computer applications, however, it seems to be increasingly clear that it is most desirable for the internal auditor to maintain participatory liaison with major systems developments. The practical reasons are that systems are too costly and too complicated to be modified on a post-operational basis. Therefore, if the internal auditor's contribution is not made during the developmental stage, it is likely to be too late. It is also a very real fact that, through the internal auditor's familiarity with the total range of company operational activities, he is in an especially advantageous position to make an important contribution.

If one accepts the soundness of utilizing the internal auditor's input during the development of EDP systems, the problem still exists of how that contribution can best be made. The practical problem is that the assignment of full-time liaison personnel by the internal auditing group may be too much of a drain on the internal audit resources. On the other hand, the EDP group may otherwise be so occupied with their developmental work that they may fail to keep the internal audit group properly advised on a timely basis of the stage of the various types of important decisions. A practical compromise, used successfully by many organizations, is to establish in advance for each major development project appropriate milestone points, at which time the progress of the development of the system will be reviewed and evaluated together in joint meetings. The internal audit group in this way is periodically alerted to the manner in which control aspects are being recognized and dealt with. Meanwhile the internal audit group can be concerned with its regular internal auditing program. The planning and follow-through of such milestone meetings is therefore strongly recommended.

General Appraisal of Planning and Development Activities.   The second major type of contribution of the internal auditor can come in the way of an overall appraisal of the computer development activities. Since the ultimate test of those activities is the accomplishments in the way of actual computer utilization the internal auditor should review the extent of the completed applications and compare the level of accomplishment, as far as is possible, with what has been done in similar business situations. At the same time consideration should be given to the nature and scope of applications currently in progress and under study. This phase of the appraisal leads naturally into a further appraisal of the professional competence and operational effectiveness. The basis of this further appraisal is the success of the development group in dealing with the various types of subactivities discussed earlier in this chapter, and in its handling of the related problems. Here a useful type of evaluation can come through the reported relationships with other company personnel. A really effective development group will have established a reasonable degree of both cooperation and professional standing with the key personnel of the various line and staff activities involved in previous studies and installations. In all these appraisal efforts the internal auditor seeks to be constructive since he knows that an effective planning and development effort in the area of computer operations is a basic essential for the ongoing welfare of the company.

COMPUTER PROCESSING OPERATIONS

The development of the specific programs as a part of the planning and development activity has now provided the basic instructions. These instructions will now be applied to the actual transaction data for the carrying out of the computer processing operations. Here is the final step in the total computer operations to provide managers and other operational personnel with the information needed for their operational purposes. Although this final step does not involve the same degree of intellectual input as did the preceding developmental activity, it is still clearly an essential step, and therefore, one that needs to be carried out in an efficient manner. The operations at this point are relatively more technical than most operational activities, but they are subject to a major extent to normal administrative methods and criteria. There is also quite clearly a close relationship to the developmental activities since the efficient processing of data depends directly on properly developed programs.

Nature and Scope of Computer Processing Operations

The computer operations break down chronologically into three major phases—the input of the data to be processed, the actual processing operations, and the output of the processed data in some form. At the input stage the focus is on putting the particular transaction data in a form that will be acceptable to the computer hardware. In some cases this input can be accomplished directly through either consoles at the operations center, or through field terminals that are connected with the operations center. In other cases the data will be recorded on punched cards, which will then provide the means of feeding data directly, or indirectly into the computer via magnetic tape. What is actually done will depend on the volume of data involved and the degree of urgency that exists. At the processing stage the data fed into the computer are analyzed, combined, and manipulated in the manner prescribed by the applicable program. During this process additional data may be drawn from various data storage areas, and other data may be returned to those storage areas. Finally, the processed data are released by the computer directly in the form of printed reports, or as magnetic tapes that will then be used to prepare reports. In some cases output will also be used as further input for subsequent processing. In some cases also, the output will take the form of visual displays or short written messages.

Batch and Real-Time Processing. The nature and scope of the processing operations will vary greatly depending on whether we are dealing with a batch or real-time type of processing. In the former case a package or batch of data is received for processing, and this batch can be processed later at a time when machine time is available. This availability takes into consideration the various types of priorities in the particular company. In the case of the real-time processing the user has direct access to the computer (or at least what seems to him to be direct access) and he will be able to receive an immediate response to his inquiry. Another type of real-time processing exists in the case of production processing where the production process is being immediately controlled on the basis of current data developments. The common characteristic here is that information is obtained from the computer on such an immediate basis that current operational activities can be continuously controlled and modified as needed. From a computer processing standpoint an important distinction is that computer capacity must be specifically provided so that it can be available to support the real-time demands that are made on the computer.

Organizational Setting of the Computer Processing Operations

We are again most interested in where the organizational responsibility for the computer processing operations is placed in the total company organization structure. Although it might be thought that the problem here is the same as exists in the case of the planning and development activity, this is not necessarily so. It is quite possible to regard the computer processing operations as an entirely separate service activity, which can be available to users anywhere, like heat and electrical services, irrespective of where the planning and development effort is assigned. Nevertheless, there has traditionally been some tendency for the computer processing operations to combine the developmental effort as an adjunct activity. This has been true especially when the developmental effort was relatively limited and confined to particular operational areas. Thus at a time when the emphasis of the computer operations was upon clerical-type activities—and when also those clerical-type activities were predominantly in the accounting area—the responsibility for computer processing operations, plus the planning and development activities, was most often placed with the accounting and financial group.

Because of the relationship of broader computer utilization to the location of the hardware, the assignment of the responsibility for the computer processing operations takes on special importance. In any event the responsibility issue is important because that responsibility carries with it to some extent the greater power to control priorities as to the way the processing time is allocated. Even when that power is administered on a statesmanlike basis there is always the possibility that some other operational activities will be skeptical. As a result it has become more common to remove the responsibility for computer processing operations from the finance group, and to place it with an organizational component like a management information group where the neutrality of its use is more officially assured. In such a situation the central headquarters planning and development group and the computer processing operations group normally report to the same company officer.

Extent of Decentralization. Quite another issue is involved when one considers whether the computer processing operations should be centralized, or, if decentralized, to what extent. The argument for centralization is that this makes possible the maximum economies of scale. These economies come as a result of being able to use the types of computers which are the largest and most efficient, and which have the most sophisticated features. The centralization also makes possible the best possible utilization of existing computer capacity, as opposed to the often existing ups and downs of individual scattered installations. Another argument is that this centralization of the processing will more surely result in uniform standards of systems development and program compatibility. The rationale for decentralization is that there is excessive risk in depending on one central processing unit, and that also there may be major offsetting costs of getting the data transmitted to the central location. Still another argument is that the various operational divisions and departments need to have the computer hardware where they can get from it the processing service when they need it. To a considerable extent operational managers fear that a central processing group will become a bottleneck, and that they will be a victim of a priority allocation system which does not fully meet their own operational needs.

The handling of the dilemma described above has led in many cases to an intermediate compromise. This compromise has been to set up a limited number of regional processing centers, which then serve all operational components of the company in the given regions. Most of the economy of scale advantages are thus achieved without the major risks of a single central bottleneck. There has been a major effort to provide good service to all users and to convince the various operational managers that the computer hardware does not really have to be where they can see and touch it, or to control it directly. In fact, all computer processing installations are increasingly being located in low-cost locations some distance from central or regional administrative headquarters. One of the ways in which this separation of the managers from the actual hardware can be justified is through the previously mentioned partial decentralization of the planning and development activities.

Control Aspects of Computer Programs

The programming activity was discussed previously as a part of the total planning and development effort. We return at this point to a further discussion of programs to focus on their control aspects. What is important here is that the programs themselves can, when properly developed, provide important controls as to the quality and accuracy of the data processing. Fortunately also, the objectives of the systems development personnel and the programmers are the same as for the internal auditor—that is, efficient total computer operations.

These control considerations apply first in the basic design of the system with the determinations of where input data are to take place, under what conditions, and under whose responsibilities. The problems here are the same as will exist in any operational situation, but focus more sharply on the requirements of developing accurate and complete input data for the computer processing.

An important aspect of this effort to develop good input data concerns the editing controls that are built into the actual programs. The purpose of these controls is to identify invalid data and to prevent the actual input of those data into the computer processing. Such editing controls are of two major types. The first type has to do with the completeness and form of the data as, for example, that proper codes are used. The second type, in turn, is concerned with various qualitative factors. Illustrative of the latter would be conformance to reasonable dollar limits of particular data, and conformance to specific company operational relationships. The scope of these editing checks will vary greatly, but they have the common purpose of avoding the most common types of error in the specific operation situation. Quite clearly, these editing controls have a great payoff since they prevent the actual processing from being cluttered up with the otherwise existing errors. The objective, therefore, is to determine that proper editing controls have been developed to the maximum extent practicable.

Testing of Computer Programs.   Even with the best of program development there will be the need to test the actual workability of specific programs. This again is an important part of the control which is supplied by the programming group, but which at the same time also serves the control interests of the processing center. The program testing may take the form of processing data which are at the same time being processed by another method and then comparing the results. Or the testing may be on the basis of sample batches of live data. Other testing involves the injection of erroneous data to determine the accuracy with which the editing controls or other design features deal with the actual situation. In other cases a controlled answer, independently determined, can be used to check the performance of the program. In general the objective is to determine whether the system actually works in the intended manner; and if not, to find the problems and to solve them before reliance is placed on the program for use in the later actual computer processing.

Key Control Areas for Computer Processing

With programs in hand and ready to be applied to transactional data, we come now to the actual computer processing. We will discuss this actual computer processing in terms of the key stages and operational aspects that are critical from a control standpoint.

Facilities.   The interest in facilities centers about their adequacy and their cost. The key factors here are the amount of space, floor support for the weight of the machines, raised floors for placement of cables, air conditioning to control humidity, light, and ventilation. There must also be adequate protection for control of unauthorized access, including the provision for the security of tape files, programs, and records. From a cost standpoint the benefits of detachment from regular company operational activities, plus the special physical requirements, normally argue for locating the facilities in a relatively outlying area. This then at the same time results in a lower cost. It is also important that the planning of current facilities give consideration to future growth needs.

Internal Organization. Computer processing, like any other operational activity, depends on good internal organization. The first essential requirement is that there be a clear separation of the actual machine operations from the control function. Supporting activities for preparing the data, like key punching operations to prepare cards or tapes, should also be separately grouped. The tape libraries should also normally be a separate responsibility. These operational activities in total may report to the same manager, as does the systems development activities, but they should in any event be completely separated. A typical operational activity is shown as Exhibit 22.2

From an organizational standpoint it is thus important that the responsibilities of these subgroups be carefully defined, that they be staffed with competent personnel, and that they are effectively supervised.

Input Controls. In each major type of computer application there are specific controls instituted to cover exactly what data are received for processing, that they are properly prepared, and that they are entered into the computer accurately. At the point the data are created there must be prescribed clerical procedures and well-designed forms. The person creating the data thus receives maximum direction, and possible errors are then more easily detected and minimized. In some cases it may be desirable also to provide for a specific review of these data before they are converted into machine-readable form.

EXHIBIT 22.2. Organization of Computer Processing

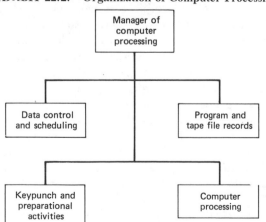

Clear instructions are also important where entry is made directly into the computer, as in the case of a real-time application. In the many situations where data are punched into cards or onto magnetic tape the problem then centers on the accuracy of that key punch operation. This accuracy can be tested on a visual basis, a statistical basis, or to the extent deemed necessary established by a complete rerun verification. In other situations specific types of calculations have been devised to check the accuracy of specific critical portions of the data. In all these approaches the cost of the verification must be balanced against the seriousness of the potential errors.

At the point where the data are entered into the computer the accuracy of that input in a real-time system will automatically be tested by the computer as it proceeds to develop the answer to the inquiry. In the case of batch operations, a test of the accuracy and completeness of the input can be tested through various kinds of control totals—as, for example, of total dollars, total numeric figures, number of individual documents, and the like. Programmed tests can also be used covering the valid use of coding, missing data, the proper combinations of specific data, and reasonableness of the aggregate totals. Various internal tests can also be devised to help ensure that the right tape files, and the portions thereof, have been used in connection with the data being received. Many of these same types of control are also applicable when data are later moved during the processing to provide input at a later stage.

Machine Controls. As the computer technology progresses more and more control capability is actually built into the computers themselves, thus reducing the necessary scope of programmed controls. A somewhat different kind of problem arises, however, in the possibility of the malfunctioning of equipment. The first attack on this latter problem is, of course, the proper level of quality in the design and manufacture of the equipment itself, and including the subsequent installation. The second line of attack is through proper care and maintenance of the equipment. Beyond all this, however, is the fact that there are both electronic components and some parts which move mechanically, and which, therefore, are unavoidably subject to malfunction. Also, there may be outside causes such as power failures, defective cards or tapes, and improper usage. The approach to equipment checks can be through the duplicate processing of particular lots of data and then comparing results. A common type of built-in control is through the use of "parity checking." Under this approach an extra parity bit is added to an identifiable group of data, and then at various stages of the processing a determination can be made as to whether a bit may have been erroneously lost or added. Other built-in controls, as developed by equipment manufacturers for their particular equipment, include such techniques as "read after writing," "echo readings," "duplicate circuitry," and the like. The internal auditor's interest here is primarily to know that such controls do in fact exist, and the type of cross check that is accomplished.

Receiving Data and Scheduling. In the batch-processing type of operation the first step is the receiving of the job from the customer-user. At this point the essential control is the determination that the data received are in the proper form for processing. At the same time it must be established that the job is covered by programs already on hand or that if a new program is to be used, that it too is in proper form. The next step is to fit the job into an established operational schedule. On the one hand, the scheduler is seeking to utilize equipment in the most efficient manner possible. On the other hand, there is the need to establish and administer priorities as they apply to the customers being served. In the latter case the customers must be satisfied that all of this is being done in a fair and equitable fashion. It also becomes important to be able to know the status of a particular job at any given point of time. The approach used here is usually through control logs and records of machine runs. In a real-time type of operation provision must also be made for the recognition of access priorities for those using the system. This type of priority can be programmed so that the priorities will be administered in accordance with the determined policies on an automatic basis, without operational intervention.

Running the Job.   The actual processing of the individual jobs will now consist of loading the individual machines, transferring data between individual sub-processes, moving tape reels, assuring that supplies are available as needed, and the like. The processing by an individual piece of equipment is for the most part automatic. However, when there are stoppages of any kind, there must be backup personnel to do whatever is necessary to determine the nature of the difficulty and to correct it. Some limited control activities may also be carried out by the console operator. To some extent also there is the need for current machine maintenance services.

Output Control.   Once the processing has been completed the results need to be released. In a real-time system this process is going on continuously but there may be periodic reports summarizing the activity or providing the current status of stored data. In a batch-type operation the results will be in the form of updated computer tapes and related reports. Normally, however, machine-generated materials will be arranged in a form that will better fit the user's needs. The control considerations are first, that the results developed are made available to the right people—the operational managers affected or their properly authorized representatives. The second and equally important thing is that the completed results are in satisfactory form. The final test of this is obviously the degree of satisfaction on the part of the user. It is, therefore, desirable that problems encountered be subject to a systematic review of the causes.

Tape Library Services.   In normal operation there will be certain records of the company users that will be kept on hand by the computer center for continuing use. These records will consist in the main of programs and tapes of company data used in connection with those programs. In a well-ordered operation these tapes and related records will be under the exclusive control of a tape librarian, and will be released for operational use as needed. From a control standpoint the important considerations are that they be properly labeled and stored in a fashion where they can be easily found when needed. It is important also that these tapes not be released except for properly authorized purposes. The computer center has a direct responsibility to the users for the careful custody of what can be very important and valuable records.

Risks

Our discussion of the key control areas for computer operations may also be conveniently reviewed in terms of risk exposure. These computer risks may involve the computer operations, computer programming, systems development, and all other aspects of data processing. Because of the extended impact of the risk problem, increasing attention has been given to risks in the data processing function.

1. *Access Control.* To prevent unwarranted access, permission to enter the facility should be limited to those who need access. Data processing facilities should be inspected and physical safeguards identified in use, such as guard service, locks, and a badge system. Programmers and systems analysts should not be allowed in the computer room. The location of the central computer facility should not be included in directory listings or maps. There should be a computer security administrator, and personnel should be given an educational program on security matters. Sensitive activity should be independently authorized. Duties should be assigned and records kept so that employees can be held accountable for their actions.

2. *Fire and Water Damage.* This involves the major interruption of use of the facility because of intentional or unintentional destruction by fire or water. The disaster plan should be reviewed to determine if it is current and sufficiently detailed. Fire protection should be in accordance with generally accepted standards. Appraisals made by fire marshals and insurance companies of the adequacy of fire devices should be reviewed. There should be an adequate insurance program covering the risks of natural disasters and sabotage. A secure off-site facility should be available for storing duplicate copies of software and other records. The construction of buildings should be examined to determine whether they are of noncombustible materials. The site should be located in a place to minimize the risk of flood damage or leaks. Fire and smoke detectors should be installed.

3. *Interrupted Processing.* This represents a temporary interruption of the facility, such as through a power failure. If possible, an uninterrupted power system and backup generator should be installed. Electric power serving the central processing unit should be separate and protected, and fluctuating electric loads should be prevented by using a special transformer. Insurance should include business interruption and extra expense.

4. *Theft*. This pertains to the theft of hardware or software, or the use of the computer to commit embezzlement or defalcation. Company procedures should prevent the sale or use of programs by employees for their monetary gain. In some instances the use of a paper shredder may be necessary to destroy sensitive computer listings and other items. Controls over computer terminals should be reviewed to prevent unauthorized use of the equipment.

5. *Accidental Loss*. A common danger is that data will be lost or accidentally destroyed as a result of confusion and error. The protection against these risks lies chiefly in the proper assignment of responsibilities, the existence of adequate procedures, and effective supervision. Additional safeguards include good labeling of all tapes and records and adequate custodial control. Further security for this kind of risk is a program for retaining basic tape files for specific overlap periods while updated files are currently being developed. These planned relationships for retaining files are frequently referred to as grandfather, father, and son relationships.

Distributed Data Processing

One trend in the development of EDP technology and processing has been in the direction of dispersing tasks among a group of geographically separated computers. This has been facilitated by the new smaller-size computers available at low cost. Basically, distributed data processing means putting computing units where the operational work originates, and then establishing communications links among all units. It is thus a form of decentralized computer operations, as discussed earlier in the chapter, with emphasis on increasing productivity through division of responsibility.

Advantages.   There are various functional advantages to using distributed data processing. Systems can be more easily designed and developed, with less complex software. Growth can occur in smaller increments with less disruption. Modules can be individually less complex under a decentralized system and have fewer failures.

In addition, there are various economic advantages. Personnel costs may be reduced because of improved system response and more efficient correction of errors. Resources can be shared to prevent duplication of services. Less investment may be required to start a system. Cost performance ratios can be improved by economics of specialization to address the needs of specific user groups.

There are also certain psychological advantages to the decentralized system. It can be tailored to meet the needs of specific users. The user has control over the computer, and can get preference when needed. In addition, the system can be developed along organizational lines to facilitate meeting goals.

Disadvantages.   The distributed system may require more planning and controlling than the centralized system. Decisions have to be made as to allocating data among dispersed processors. A study has to be made of hardware and operating systems and how to connect them. There are often many design problems involved with multiprocessor systems. In addition, some jobs may be too large and complex for local systems. Also, there may be problems in restricting growth in the absence of strong centralized control.

Analysis of System. Although the analysis and evaluation of a distributed basic processing system are complex, there are various approaches that are useful to the auditor. He reviews the design method to determine whether it is comprehensive and relates to organizational objectives as well as technology. An adequate system of documentation should extend from the design process. There should be program testing standards for reviewing test results based on specific criteria.

Key factors in evaluating effectiveness should be determined, such as major activities and their measurement; key resources and how to measure their consumption; and critical time budgets and standards for accomplishment of objectives. The needs of users for information flow should be met throughout the organization. Statistics from the operational system should be obtained and related to performance predictions to determine effectiveness of results. These techniques will be helpful, although it must be recognized that in large complex systems conventional methods of monitoring progress may not be practicable.

Word Processing Systems

Another type of development in EDP technology involves the increased capability to correct errors and make other types of modification in words and related data with greater ease and at earlier stages in the regular processing. As a result in keeping with developing technology, the modern automated office is often equipped with a word processing system. Typewriters can then make corrections in response to the press of a few keys. The internal auditor is interested in these systems because of their cost and potential for increased clerical productivity.

Word Processing Hardware. One type of hardware in widespread use is the electronic typewriter, which has limited editing capability and memory. Some versions have removable memory, communication capabilities with other machines, separate printers, and removable magnetic memory media.

A more advanced system has display capability, equipped with video display or cathode ray tube (CRT). These systems may have additional features, such as extended logic, software programming, and mathematics capabilities. A further developed system, called the shared logic system, has multiterminals which are attached to a central processing unit. The terminals share discs, tape storage, communications, and in come cases optical character readers with the central processing unit. Usually high-speed, computer-type printers are available for printouts. These shared systems are especially feasible for high-volume requirements.

Acquisition and Use. Appropriate representatives from administration, data processing, and telecommunications usually participate during this phase to obtain the views of all affected. Action plans are developed with suitable milestones.

1. *Conducting Feasibility Studies.* These studies should consider the type of documents typed and volume, organizational structure, number of copies made, and time devoted to typing by secretaries, stenographers, and typists. In addition, turnaround time is important for providing service to executives. Attitudes of personnel toward the automated equipment should be ascertained.

2. *Selecting Equipment.* The equipment selected will be based on the needs disclosed by the feasibility study and the capabilities of the equipment. In some cases the equipment must be compatible with existing typewriters as to print. Vendor support and training are important, as well as ability to adjust to changes in needs and equipment in the future. Relative cost has to be considered, and options available to buy the equipment.

3. *Preparing for Installation.* Because of the noise generated it is important that there be a separate room for the facility, including suitable insulation. Special power lines and air conditioning may be needed. In addition, personnel should be prepared for the new work arrangements and supervision required. New job descriptions and salaries are usually needed.

4. *Running the System.* Problems may be encountered in starting the new system. A review should be made to determine whether objectives have been met—user needs satisfied, cost effectiveness of system, and attitudes of employees. Policies and procedures should be reevaluated for the ongoing system. Excess capactiy and utilization of the machine should be determined.

Lease or Purchase of Computer Equipment

In carrying out the computer processing operations a company has the alternative of either purchasing or leasing its major computer hardware. If it purchases the equipment the company must, of course, commit the necessary capital and then depreciate its purchased asset over the useful life. If leased, a rental is paid to the manufacturer or an intermediary leasing group. The determining factors have generally been first, whether the company had other higher priorities for the use of its available capital, and second, the extent of the risk in making the purchase. This risk is essentially that the development of more advanced computer equipment may prematurely make obsolete the equipment purchased. Although companies have evaluated this problem in different ways, the greater tendency in the past has been to go the rental route. It appears, however, in more recent years that the purchase alternative is being looked on more favorably than previously. A possible explanation for this is the belief that the computer technology has stabilized itself to a greater extent. In strict theory the risk of obsolescense must be covered by someone, whether by the purchaser or through a rental that will reimburse the lessor for assuming the risk. The more basic answer would seem to lie in the company's own evaluation of its future computer needs, and in what alternative uses it has for its capital funds. There is no single answer; what is important is that each company periodically analyze its own situation in a careful and objective manner.

User Relations

The providing of satisfactory service by the computer processing group is similar to the problem faced by any service group. This is to provide the particular service on an effective basis and at reasonable cost. "Effectiveness" as used here includes both the quality of the actual processing, and doing it at a time that meets the existing operational needs. The problem is especially important, however, in that the relationships of managers to computer activities are never satisfactorily understood. As a result, there is more than the usual sensitivity on the part of managers about the computer services they need. All of this means that the computer processing group must go out of its way to try to satisfy the various user requirements. One additional way in which the computer group can do this is by working with the users in an advisory manner as to how to prepare their data in a way that will facilitate the later processing. It is also desirable in all respects to maintain a close liaison with the users. When problems develop at the computer center, as is bound to be the case over time, the liaison can be utilized to keep the users informed, and to demonstrate that a genuine effort is being made to provide the proper kind of service. Involved also is the question of cost, a problem that is discussed later in this chapter.

OTHER COMPUTER OPERATIONS

Up to this point we have dealt separately with the two major parts of the computer operations, the planning and development activities and the computer processing activities. Although these two types of activity can be placed at different places in the total organizational structure, it is quite common for them to report to the same officer. Our interest in this final section of the chapter is to examine some of the problems that are encountered when this is done. It also provides an opportunity to cover certain operational aspects that are common to both types of activity.

Organizational Aspects of Integrated Computer Operations

One advantage of bringing together the developmental and processing activities in the same organizational group is to better assure an efficient liaison between them. The larger advantage, however, is that computer utilization is best dealt with on a totally integrated basis. Although they *are* different types of activity—requiring separation in an organizational way—there is some risk that they can become too isolated from each other. Under such conditions there can also be some costly overlap because of the natural inclination for each group to develop some special staff expertise in the area of the other group. An organizational integration also provides a better opportunity to associate with the computer operations effort any separate related organizational groups in such areas as operations research, or any of the so-called management sciences. Here again, there are often problems of overlap that may otherwise exist.

In many companies the developmental and operational activities are themselves fragmented and dispersed in various organizational components of the company. This is often the case in a company where individual divisions have at earlier points been predecessor companies, and which still enjoy a high degree of autonomy. The creation of a totally integrated computer operations can in such a situation be a means of bringing all the computer-related activities together in one organizational group. This then permits the development of a more company-oriented approach, and in most cases has proved to be very beneficial. The integration at the same time demonstrates the company's total concern with computer utilization. Last, but not least, it justifies high-level placement in the total organizationl structure, a situation that in turns calls for a top manager of the higher managerial qualifications. It is at this point that most companies make the move to set up a vice-president-level officer in charge of a management information services group that is independent of any other functional staff—for example, finance—and that reports directly to the chief executive officer.

Planning and Budgeting for Integrated Computer Operations

The kind of organizational integration and placement just described now sets the stage for more definitive planning of longer-range objectives for computer utilization. Objectives can be developed and, after appropriate review by top management, can lead to the establishment of priorities and more detailed operational plans. This longer-range planning then leads into the development of profit plans that become an integral part of the total profit planning procedure of the company. These profit plans, in turn, tie into the annual budget. This is a most desirable development because it provides better assurance that the computer group will do the planning that it should. It also better assures the needed participation of management in the development of those plans.

Evaluating Computer Performance. The discussion of profit plans and budgets brings us face to face with the problem of evaluating computer performance. We start out with the very proper assumption that the computer group should make its proposals and then be held accountable for results in the same way as any other operational activity of the company. This is a discipline that forces both more careful thinking when proposals are made, and increased effort to achieve those objectives. But it also must be recognized that greater problems do exist in projecting costs than normally exist for other company proposals. It is also much harder to project the benefits with any real degree of accuracy. The evaluation job is, therefore, a difficult one. It serves to emphasize the degree of involvement that must take place on the part of management, at all levels. It also emphasizes the importance of bridging the gap between management and computer personnel mentioned earlier. An effective partnership between the two groups must exist, and out of this there can come a better basis for management to evaluate effective computer performance.

Billing Computer Costs

The incurring of substantial costs in carrying on the computer operations quite naturally raises the question of whether those costs should be billed to the various organizational components of the company, and if so, on what basis. The question becomes especially pertinent when the organizational components receiving computer services are profit centers. The first part of the answer to this question focuses on how one can measure the extent of the service actually received. In the case of actual computer processing, this problem appears to be reasonably manageable. Here specific services in the way of data processing are rendered, and there is a generally available commercial standard as to what those services are worth. In this connection the computer processing center can operate as a cost center or it can operate as a profit center. When, however, we deal with the planning and development activities we have a very different type of problem. First, it is often difficult to draw the line accurately between those benefits received by the particular organizational component, versus the benefits that accrue to other organizational components, or to the company as a whole. Development staff directly attached to the organizational unit—and thus presumably serving the direct interests of that organizational unit—would present no problems. But the problem does exist with the cost incurred by the central headquarters group. In the latter case billings, if made, will necessarily have to take the form for the most part of overhead allocations.

The second part of the answer to the original question has to do with the effect on the utilization of computer services. In the case of processing operations no serious problem appears to exist, but in the area of planning developments there are additional complications. Although we do not want to have computer development services wasted, we do want managers to exploit properly the available benefits from computer utilization. Hence an approach to the billing of charges that might discourage the use of the development services will be unfortunate. This is particularly important when managers may already be uncomfortable in working with computer personnel. The presence of this motivation factor thus provides another reason for shying away from specific charges for development service provided by the central group. Overhead allocations, on the other hand, might actually induce better utilization, since there would be the feeling that the service was being paid for and that, therefore, the managers might just as well be using it.

Use of Outside Computer Services

A special kind of problem frequently encountered is the extent to which organizational components should be permitted to purchase computer services outside the company. The basis for such a desire on the part of a particular operational component might be cost, quality of service, or the lack of service availability from the company operation. This can apply either to development work or to computer processing, although it more often arises in connection with the latter. Although there might be special circumstances justifying such an outside procurement—for example, a strike, a breakdown, or a special emergency overloading—in general, it would seem to be desirable to keep the work inside the company. In the case of computer processing, the company can then best exploit the economies of scale. In the case of development work, we thus best protect the growth of the competence of our own personnel, as well as assure the quality of the later support service for the particular systems application. What is really important, however, is that the company probes properly the causes for company people wanting to go outside. Such probing may provide important information as to ineffective operational practices that should be corrected.

Role of the Internal Auditor in Company Services Integration

The internal auditor's role relates to both development and processing activities. On the broader front the special role would then seem to be to help the company achieve a properly integrated setup. The problem is quite often a difficult one because the very integration process itself runs counter to the very human desire of an individual operational manager to hang on to something he has, as opposed to giving it to a new separate organizational group. Top management in such a situation is often restricted in how far it can go toward integration, and how fast. A key reason here is that top management is reluctant to take the risk of pushing the operational manager into a situation where his operations may suffer, or even where there could be an alibi for not achieving established objectives. The internal auditor's independent organizational status and familiarity with all operations puts him in a very advantageous position to present evidence that will support the integration effort. A possible problem here may exist in that the internal auditor may be reporting to the chief financial officer, but even integration under the banner of the chief finance officer can often be a first step. Again, it should be emphasized that proper computer utilization is a key management need and it is therefore a high-ranking part of the internal auditor's total effort to serve management effectively.

MANAGEMENT INFORMATION SYSTEMS

The close relationship between computers and effective management information systems discussed previously makes it appropriate to consider in more detail the factors that contribute to such systems. At the same time the role of the internal auditor, over and above assigned primary organizational responsibilities, will be further developed. All of this begins with the recognition that improved techniques of data processing have made it possible to obtain large quantities of information at high speed in the form desired. With the increase in storage and processing capacity of computers, there is additional impetus toward developing a total information system for all activities of a company. Also, as the use of real-time systems expands, information becomes available as events occur. Financial statements, for example, can be available soon after the end of the month. Daily operating reports can be available at the start of the next day. The increased information and the speed with which it becomes available enable management to operate more effectively.

Recent professional writings have emphasized the importance of providing managers with sufficient information at the right time to enable them to perform their job. A new information technology has developed, on the basis that an effective way to influence executive action is to direct the flow of information. The internal auditor reviews the management information system in light of its objectives, evaluating its usefulness to management in conducting the affairs of the company. This review is performed of the system whether it is a simple manual type or a complex computer system.

Developing the Management Information System

Review of Past Information.   Any study to develop an information system should begin with past information generated in the company. This study should identify information flows associated with decision-making activities throughout a business organization, and evaluate these flows as a basis for designing changes. The internal auditor obtains a listing of major reports and other information and determines how long it has been since a study has been made of the system and its usefulness. He reviews the study and follow-up action to determine whether there are indications that managers are performing with a lack of relevant information.

Determining Requirements.   As a basis for evaluating a MIS, basic objectives of the system should be determined. The need for data in a segment of a company's operations is identified and related to the decision-making process. From this, an attempt is made to develop the model MIS to meet the specific needs of the organization. Such factors as the characteristics of the system, degree of sophistication, and cost have to be considered. In some cases special research has to be performed to arrive at the best system. Discussion with managers is often required to ascertain needs. Comments are obtained as to the nature of the decision-making process and the problems to be solved. The internal auditor reviews that analysis and flow charting of the types of decisions made. He reviews conclusions to determine that they are responsive to management desires and also reflect objective requirements for information.

Responsibility for Developing. In some companies the information systems work is primarily under the responsibility of staff specialists. Because of the complexity of large computers, the role of specialists is emphasized in developing the systems. The work of the specialists is coordinated closely with operating management in determining requirements. In other companies the control of MIS is in the hands of operating personel, with reliance on specialists for their assistance. Under this approach, it is believed that leadership responsibility should be in the hands of operating managers, who will have control of the systems that span their areas of profit responsibility. Regardless of control over the development of MIS, there should be close contact with managers, determination of relative priorities, and coordination of requirements where systems cut across departmental lines.

Collecting Data. The final step involves matching requirements with the sources of data. Data are classified and coded in a manner to allow storage for subsequent retrieval. The data are then transformed or transposed into specific information for planning or operating purposes. The internal auditor tests the procedures for originating, storing, retrieving, and transforming data which are part of the information system. He reviews the manner in which available sources of data are utilized to facilitate the preparation of needed information. He also tests the storage and retrieval system to assure that data are readily available.

Reports

The subject of reports as an element of internal control was treated in a separate chapter. "Reports . . . are a major means of control by management. Inadequate reporting can lead to unwise decisions or ill-considered action. As with records, reports must be prompt, accurate, concise and complete."[4]

The internal auditor's review of controls extends to the total information system within the company. He is interested in the various types of information available to executives in setting goals and evaluating performance. Without effective reports, management's ability to control operations is significantly impaired.

Proper Analysis. Statistical and other data generated should be appropriately analyzed as part of the information system. In addition, conclusions should be drawn where practicable based on the analysis. In some instances sufficient data for analysis purposes may be available as part of the reports prepared. In other cases, special studies may be required by management to determine the causes of problems as a basis for recommending corrective action. The internal auditor examines reports and subsequent studies and evaluates the extent that data are sufficiently analyzed for management use.

[4]Bradford Cadmus, *Operational Auditing Handbook*, (New York: The Institute of Internal Auditors, 1964), pp. 11–12.

Control over Number of Reports. The internal auditor evaluates the extent that approvals are required for new reports. He should also determine that periodic review is made of the various types of reports and number of users. This review should involve circularizing users to determine continuing need. An effective method sometimes employed is to ask the users to return a card if the report is still required. Of course, for some activities there may be a requirement for additional reports. As discussed elsewhere in this chapter, it is important that sufficient information be provided management in the decision-making process; the review of the number of reports should take this into consideration.

Decisions to Combine Reports. In some cases reports may be effectively combined to provide required information, thus enabling savings in preparation. Also, areas covered may be shrunk, or reports may be made less complex. The important point is that periodic studies should be made to assure that information is tailored to meet specific requirements and only those requirements. Although cost savings may be obtained in some cases, it should be kept in mind that managers are entitled to information in the right form.

Special Reports. The need for many reports can be planned in advance, but there are often occasions when management wishes to have special reports. These reports are needed for various reasons, such as to solve problems, obtain information as a basis for new products or expansion, and to accomplish various short-term goals. Data may be readily available for preparing the reports, requiring only sorting and processing. In other cases detailed studies have to be made and sources of data determined. The internal auditor reviews the extent of special reports and the types of information requested. Comparison should be made with information in recurring reports to ascertain whether the data are already available in different form. Also, it may be found that some types of special reports may be useful to management on a continuing basis.

Timeliness. It is especially important that information be provided management on a timely basis. Historical reports that indicate past deficiencies are important, but of more use are reports that indicate current trends and problems. These enable executives to make current studies and take corrective action on a timely basis. The internal auditor assures that reports are prepared in accordance with schedules and that the timing is responsive to management needs.

Accuracy. The internal auditor reviews the accuracy of various reports and other information as part of his scope of audit. Frequently, he is called on to verify special reports because of his training and experience, for example, a bid proposal report for a new contract. The use of computers may simplify the auditor's traditional auditing procedures followed in reviewing reports. For example, data already stored in the computer may be processed and arranged in a special format. Under these circumstances, the auditor's general tests of the electronic data processing system may suffice with a minimum of additional work.

Special audit work may be required on various interim financial reports to test their accuracy. Year-end financial statements are normally audited by the external auditor and the internal auditor often assists in this review. However, management may require assurance that interim financial reports used as a basis for various operating decisions are accurate, and may call on the internal auditor for partial assurance.

Use of Reports.   Management must use the information made available in order that the objectives of the MIS are achieved. The decision maker requires information as a basis for selecting among alternatives; it serves no useful purpose to generate the information unless it is used. There are various specific actions that can be taken by management to improve a situation once all the information is in. Management can provide more guidance or training, supply better incentives, and make more personnel, facilities, and funds available. In some cases personnel are replaced, the goals are changed, and a new program is devised. Regardless of the course of action, the internal auditor reviews on a selective basis the use made of the information by management. He notes instances where the information does not appear useful or is disregarded. He reviews the effectiveness of controls over the use and evaluates the extent to which proper analysis is made of continuing need for the information. He also evaluates whether proper justification is included in the files when decisions are made that are not supported by information available.

Cost of Information.   The benefits of reports have to be weighed against the costs involved and resources available. Some information can be obtained by simply reclassifying data and reporting it in a different form. Other information may require extensive data gathering and computer programming, making it more expensive. This may be especially the case if the information is requested after a system has already been installed. The type of report format also affects the costs. Economies can be obtained by using simple computer listings rather than ornate reports. On the other hand, more sophisticated reports may be required for special purposes. The internal auditor evaluates the extent to which sufficient consideration is given to the cost of the reports in view of significance and operating objectives.

Application to Specific Areas

Total Information Systems.   One approach in developing information systems is to determine requirements of all company functions on an integrated basis. Under this approach, a company-wide review is performed of information and data requirements, rather than isolated studies. This approach is often used with adoption of a new computer involving radical changes in existing systems.

Because of the difficulties in evolving a fully integrated system, managers attempt to develop information for major segments of the company's operations, as described below.

Major Information Systems. Three major information systems in a company are financial, personnel, and logistical systems. Financial information is based on the flow of dollars through an organization. Personnel information concerns the people working in the organization. Logistics information concerns the flow of materials through an organization, covering procurement, production, and distribution. These systems may be divided into subsystems with their separate information network. There may be other less important information systems, such as research and development. The internal auditor reviews the scope of management information systems to ascertain the extent that important areas are covered. He looks for overlap in the information generated, and ascertains whether studies are made to integrate the information. In some instances this integration can be obtained in the data collection and processing stages as well as in the data presentation.

Example: Personnel Information System

A study was initiated of personnel operations in a medium-size company to improve the personnel information available to management. Since the company had already acquired facilities to expand in the next five years, there was a need for additional information on personnel requirements and capabilities. The study illustrates the methods of determining needs for specific reports; it also provides the internal auditor with a basis for evaluating the current information available in specific areas.

There were two reports prepared for management under the fairly stable operations of the company—number of employees on hand in each department and turnover by department. It was determined that additional reports were needed to assist the executives in personnel decisions. The following are the reports recommended in the study classified by specific personnel functions.

Determining Personnel Needs. A report was required for one-year and five-year projections of personnel requirements by department; a supplementary report by department showing levels of employees required; and a report showing flexible requirements for personnel under different levels of production. This information would enable management to determine needs for additional personnel in the expansion period.

Recruiting. A summary report was required of the background and capabilities of staff in specialized skills; a report of experienced recruiting costs per hire, locally and nationwide, compared with industry statistics; and a report of the number of hires per interview at colleges and as a result of advertising campaigns. The purpose of these reports was to determine primarily which skills were available in the company and the level of workers to be hired. Comparative costs of recruiting were needed to enable management to decide on the level of effort to be placed in recruiting and where and how to recruit.

Training. A report was needed on training needs; a report on training accomplished during the quarter; a report on company-sponsored training, historical and scheduled; and an inventory of employees with specialized training. These reports would provide management with information useful in developing the abilities of staff and in planning training programs.

Promotions or Demotions. A summary of performance appraisals was required; a report of unsatisfactory performance or actions; and recommendations for personnel actions from department heads. This information would be used in making decisions as to promotions and demotions, or removing employees from the payroll.

Compensation. A report of industry-wide salaries and wages was needed; a report on costs of fringe benefits; projected costs of alternative fringe benefits; and ratios of salaries and wages to total costs and sales. This information would enable management to determine salary and wage levels and make decisions concerning alternative fringe benefit plans relating to retirement and health.

COMPUTER CRIME

We discuss fraud and investigations in more detail in Chapter 26. However, it will be useful to discuss computer crime in this chapter on computer operations because of the impact of such crime on computer security.

Nature of Problem

Management is becoming increasingly aware of the potentials for computer crime with the growth of computer technology. Some recent crimes (Exhibit 22.3) have dramatized the current dangers of computer fraud. The risks for business are especially increasing with the expanded number of employees who can access computers through remote terminals. Also, more students are learning how to use computers and are finding weaknesses in systems that enable them to break computer security. The greater use of personal computers has also made easier tapping into data transmission lines, with the possibility of transfers of money from one bank account to another.

The incentive for computer crime is also increased because of the potential for large take per crime—in some cases millions of dollars. In addition, computer crimes are often difficult to detect, and the punishment may not be great even if management decides to prosecute. As a result, computer crime has become tempting as computer usage expands.

EXHIBIT 22.3   Examples of Computer Crimes

Case	Methods Used	Amount Taken
Wells Fargo	Funds were deposited in an account at one branch by using the bank's interbranch account settlement process to withdraw funds from a different branch; the account imbalance was hidden by making other fraudulent transfers later on, and the process continued	$21.3 million
Dalton School	Teenage students at Manhattan's Dalton School allegedly used their classroom computer terminals to dial into a Canadian data communications network and destroyed the files of two of the network's corporate customers	Zero
Union Dime	A teller at a New York savings bank used correction entries to embezzle money from accounts, transferring funds from other accounts to cover the shortages	$1.2 million
Equity Funding	Computers were used by management to report phony insurance policies that were sold to reinsurers	$27.3 million

Achieving Computer Security

The increased evidence of computer fraud has encouraged companies to develop good security practices. Although these practices do not guarantee the prevention or detection of computer fraud, together they help to achieve increased computer security.

Design Emphasis.   It is during the basic design of the computer system that data security should be emphasized. Often, systems developed by computer manufacturers are extremely flexible and are thus difficult to control. To satisfy the concerns of management, security measures must be introduced during the program design phase, at the expense of flexibility and availability.

Separation of Duties.   In accordance with good systems of internal control, sensitive computer duties should be separated wherever possible. Individuals should be accountable for their own actions, and checks should be made on others. Access to other employees' areas of responsibility should be restricted. Some examples are as follows:

Changes to a program library should be made by only one person.

Programmers should not both specify and write a procedure, write and test a procedure, and write and execute a procedure.

Employees should not have access to an asset and the records for control of the asset.

Approval authority should be separate from initiating authority.

Physical Security. Secret passwords are stored within the computer's memory system to prevent unauthorized use of the computer. In addition, entrance to the computer building and to individual computer rooms is restricted to those needing physical access. Some companies use TV cameras to record personnel entering, with guards at a central location reviewing TV monitors. Also, records may be kept within the computer's audit trail of all significant actions of users to access the computers. This serves as a means to detect unauthorized attempts to gain entry.

Scrambling Devices. By encrypting or scrambling data during transmission from one computer to another, only a computer with a special device can unscramble the message. The need for encryption software and hardware has increased with the growth of personal computers, which make it easier to tap electronic funds transfer systems fraudulently.

Risk Analysis. Studies can be made of a computer system to assess the risk of computer fraud. Estimates can then be made of the cost of measures to prevent fraud. These studies can be made either by personnel within the company or by outside consulting groups.

Audit Checks. Special audit software packages, as described in Chapter 8, are now available to review computer data. These packages enable management as well as internal auditors to make computer inquiries that would be likely to uncover fraud. In addition, special cross checks can be added to determine the reasonableness and consistency of transactions. For example, the computer can be programmed to disclose if individual salaries of workers are above a certain amount, or if the computer is being used in off hours.

Management Emphasis. There has been increased involvement of top management in setting up sophisticated antifraud measures. The Foreign Corrupt Practices Act has added incentive to management efforts because of the penalties involved. In most companies management has relied on computer professionals to provide adequate control over EDP. They, in turn, were involved more in day-to-day operations than in developing preventive measures. Currently, however, management and professionals have worked together more closely to develop strong antifraud programs in the computer area, such as those described in the preceding paragraphs.

AUDIT GUIDES

REVIEW OF COMPUTER OPERATIONS

I. Introductory
   A. Reference should be made to the general discussion of audit guides, Chapter 13.

B. The review endeavors to cover both the extent to which the company is fully utilizing computer application potentials and the operational effectiveness with which the various computer activities are being carried out.

II. Preparatory Activities

A. See standard Audit Guides, Chapter 13.

B. The familiarization with existing procedures and processes will be especially important.

III. Organizational Factors

A. See standard Audit Guides, Chapter 13.

B. Planning and development activities and processing activities need to be considered, both separately and as a total activity.

C. Matters of special interest in the review of manuals include:
1. For planning and development activities:
   a. Authorization of feasibility studies.
   b. Approval of actual program developments.
   c. Interim and final reporting.
   d. Standards of documentation.
   e. Planning of personnel impact.
   f. Planning of equipment requirements.
2. For computer processing activities:
   a. Relations with other company activities.
   b. Priority policies.
   c. Operational standards.
   d. Security.
   e. Billing.
   f. Use of outside services.
   g. Records and reports.

IV. Planning and Development Activities

A. Research and Long-Range Planning
1. To what extent is a systematic effort being made to keep in touch with new developments in the field of:
   a. Basic computers?
   b. Peripheral equipment?
   c. New types of applications?
2. What internal effort is being made to appraise computer utilization potentials for the company?
3. Has a long-range plan for company computer utilization been prepared? And is it adequate?
4. Is this long-range plan being reviewed periodically with top management?

B. Scope of Accomplishments
1. Review and appraise the presently existing range of program applications.

2. What are the specific accomplishments of completed programs in each of the past five years? What is the trend?
3. What applications are currently under study?

C. Operational Integration (Company-wide)
1. Appraise the adequacy of the central coordination of planning and development efforts.
   a. Is there excessive overlap and duplication between various development staff units?
   b. Are company-wide systems developments being dealt with?
   c. Are computer personnel being properly utilized?
   d. Are staff efforts sufficiently consolidated to be able to attract needed personnel with special expertise?
2. Appraise the adequacy of decentralization.
   a. To service management needs of individual staff and operational groups.
   b. To provide adequate input from local groups to the central group for broader company systems.
   c. To provide backup help from the central group to local groups.

D. Appraisal of Operational Efficiency
1. How adequate is the staff in terms of numbers, types of expertise, and personal qualifications?
2. Is adequate support being received from top management for investigative study activities involving various company operational activities?
3. Are managerial coordination activities being effectively exploited?
4. Is developmental work adequately documented?
5. Are equipment needs adequately validated, and necessary procurement achieved most advantageously?
6. Are installation plans properly developed?
7. Are personnel implications fully discussed with management and the personnel group? Are adequate plans made?
8. Are programming requirements being properly coordinated?
9. How adequately are completed and installed applications monitored for later design improvement? Is documentation properly updated?
10. How well is the internal administration of staff being administered?

E. Miscellaneous
1. What kind of training programs have been developed for management education?
2. What kinds of internal training programs are being carried out?
3. How adequate is the continuing liaison with the internal auditing group to permit its contribution on a timely basis? Are milestone review points established for individual programs to enable the internal auditors to use their time most effectively?

V. Computer Processing Activities at Individual Processing Centers

   A. Operational Integration (Company-wide)

      1. Are computer processing activities consolidated adequately as a basis for reasonable achievement of potential operational economies, such as:

         a. Purchase of equipment of more efficient size and with most advanced operational features?

         b. Best possible machine utilization?

         c. Uniform programming and operational practices?

      2. Are users being properly serviced under the existing arrangements of operational consolidation?

   B. Facilities

      1. Are quarters adequate in terms of physical operating requirements for current and anticipated volume?

      2. Are space costs reasonable (as compared with alternative possible locations)?

      3. Is proper provision made for controlling access to operational areas?

      4. Is there adequate protection from fire and other possible physical damage?

   C. Procedures and Controls

      1. Are there adequate procedures covering the preparation of data for processing?

      2. Are procedures adequate for the review and approval of incoming jobs and related programs?

      3. Are priority policies clearly stated, and periodically reviewed?

      4. Do organizational arrangements adequately separate data input, processing, control, tape libraries, and data release?

      5. Are procedures and control adequate in such key operational areas as:

         a. Completeness and accuracy of data input?

         b. Scope of program controls?

         c. Utilization of machines?

         d. Status of individual jobs?

         e. Transfer of data as a part of the total processing?

         g. Protection of tapes during processing?

         h. Procedures for machine stoppages and interruptions?

         i. Custody of programs and tapes left on premises?

         j. Completeness and accuracy of output data?

         k. Authorized release of output data?

      6. Is there adequate security over:

         a. Access to computer room?

         b. Data transmission?

         c. Access to remote terminals?

D. Operational Efficiency
  1. How adequately are procedures and controls monitored and enforced?
  2. How adequate is the overall supervision?
  3. Are housekeeping standards well maintained?
  4. Are people being fully utilized?
  5. Are machines being adequately utilized?
  6. Is overtime excessive?
  7. Is the current work load being handled effectively? If not, what are the causes?
  8. Are costs reasonable in relation to available standards? What is the trend?
  9. Are operational manuals complete and up to date?
  10. Are operations consistent with the organization chart? If not, are organizational changes needed?

E. Customer Relations
  1. Is work being processed in accordance with customer-agreed schedules?
  2. Are input and output customer relations satisfactory?
  3. Are customers satisfied in terms of:
    a. Processing time?
    b. Quality of processing?
    c. Cost?

F. Leasing Arrangements
  1. Do current leasing arrangements appear to be reasonable?
  2. Is there adequate evidence that purchase/lease alternatives are being periodically reevaluated?

VI. Integrated Computer Operations
  A. Is the degree of integration adequate in terms of potential operating effectiveness? What are the specific problem areas?
  B. What specific road blocks exist for more effective integration?

VII. Specific Audit Tests
  In addition to such audit tests as have been made in accordance with the preceding review of computer operations, it will be desirable in certain situations to carry out more elaborate tests. These tests can include:
  A. The detailed examination of one or more selected program applications from the first development to the operational stage.
  B. The development of special test decks to verify the accuracy of the processing of data with given programs.
  C. A more extensive survey of internal customer relationships in the areas of both development and computer processing. This will involve direct contact with these customer–users.

VIII. Continuing Involvement of Internal Auditor

    A. In Planning and Development Activities

        1. Is adequate liaison being maintained with planning and development group?

        2. Are all possible contributions being made in building in effective control?

        3. Is counsel being provided as to areas of development that have maximum company potential?

    B. In Processing Operations

        1. Does the internal auditor receive copies of all current production and performance reports of the computer processing activities?

        2. Is adequate liaison being maintained?

    C. For Total Computer Operations

        1. Is the internal auditor adequately supporting the organizational integration of all computer operations?

        2. Is the internal auditor aware of policy changes, and does he adequately participate in their determination?

IX. Not used.

  X. Overall Appraisal of Computer Activities

    A. See standard Audit Guides, Chapter 13.

    B. The special importance of computer potentials calls for increasing attention to this overall appraisal.

ILLUSTRATIVE AUDIT EXAMPLES: COMPUTER OPERATIONS

Information Requirements Not Properly Defined

During the systems implementation phase of a new computer system, the internal auditor found that some departments were not making significant requests for new information. Review indicated that these departments had not analyzed their requirements in light of additional capabilities of the new computer. As a result, the planning did not assure that the potential of the computer for providing information could be realized for all activities of the company. In addition, the early determination and coordination of requirements would prevent untimely requests for changes in programs. It was recommended that controls be strengthened over the timely determination of information requirements in all departments.

Magnetic Tape Management Required Attention

A review of tape libraries indicated that magnetic tapes were not being kept clean, resulting in stops in computer runs. In addition, many tapes were stored with only a few feet of writing, resulting in uneconomical usage. It was recommended that improvements be made in the management of magnetic tapes to assure effective and economical operations.

Unused Reports

Reports were being generated that were no longer needed by company activities. In addition, excess quantities of reports were being distributed. A study of the condition indicated that activities were not notifying data processing of changes in requirements. Although the company had procedures for periodic circularization of report users, operating heads were not notifying data processing on an interim basis. In the case of one division, reports continued to be generated although a reorganization of activities eliminated the need for some of the reports. It was recommeneded that controls be strengthened to assure the timely elimination of reports no longer required.

Delays Caused by Inadequate Scheduling

Computer jobs were not being scheduled and prioritized effectively, resulting in delays in obtaining requested computer runs. It was found in some instances that an excessive number of jobs were being loaded with tape drives, exceeding the capacity of the computer. Additional emphasis was needed on scheduling job runs sufficiently in advance and assigning priorities based on importance.

Duplication of Information

Reviews of reports prepared in a department indicated that a manual report duplicated data available in a computer report. Analysis indicated that management required information in a different format, with more summary and trend data. These requirements had been superimposed after the request for the computer report. The internal auditor found similar manual reports and analyses prepared in other departments which could have been generated by the computer. It was recommended that consideration be given to additional or revised computer applications to meet the report requirements of management.

Computer Not Fully Utilized

Significant savings could be achieved by running the computer in two shifts instead of three. The internal auditor noted that the computer was not being fully utilized during the evening and night shifts. Discussion with computer personnel indicated that planned usage of the computer had not materialized because of the sale of a division of the company. As a result of a study recommended by the internal auditor, management decided to shut down the night shift, with an annual savings of $125,000.

CHAPTER TWENTY-THREE

International Operations

INCREASING INTERNATIONAL INVOLVEMENT

Our modern life has become increasingly international in character. We know more about people and their life in all countries and areas of the world. We have more interchange with them in the way of travel and other contacts. There has been a greater and greater recognition of the responsibilities of the more developed countries for those other countries where there are pressing needs of various kinds. On the business side the magnitude of the international relationships are reflected in increasing levels of investments outside the home country, and in the increasing volume of sales between the various countries of the world. This increase in the level of international business has been due in the main to the pressures to seek new markets as a means of achieving continuing profitability and growth. Also, with the increasing advances in communication and transportation it has become possible to look at the entire world as a major potential area of business activity.

Impact on Management

The new international scope of business operations has at the same time increased the nature and scope of management responsibilities. The basis of these increased responsibilities lies in the greater volume of activities, the more extended geographical scope, and the special complexities of the new markets. Although it can be argued that management has always faced the problems of adjusting to new conditions, the scope of these problems in the domestic markets has not been of the same magnitude. Now there are new critical problems of planning, organizing, staffing, directing, and controlling. The success of management, as it deals with the expanded international operations, is how well it understands the new problems and how well it deals with them.

The complexity of international operations is increased by the fact that each country is different in various ways, and that usually these differences are very substantial. Generalizations, therefore, are bound to have limited value. At the same time, however, there are some common types of problems that can be identified and examined. It is these types of common problems that are considered in the present discussion. This should provide at least a starting point for going on to the consideration of the actual problems of a particular country. In should also confirm the necessity of caution in the individual situation, and the need for maximum flexibility.

Internal Auditor's Interest

The interest of the internal auditor in international operations stems directly from the fact of the increased management needs, and the consequent necessity of understanding the new types of operational problems so that the proper type of management service can be provided. The internal auditor again, as always, will be concerned with how effective control can be best provided under the new operational conditions. Our approach to providing some understanding of these special problems is to consider first the special characteristics of international operations, then to move to the question of the alternative ways to carry on international operations, and finally to examine the specific operational areas—marketing, production, personnel, finance, and organization and administration. We then consider the more specific impact of the special operational problems on making effective audit reviews. In Chapter 9 we considered the problem of how the internal auditor should structure his own organizational activities to serve best the international operations of the company.

Special Characteristics of Overseas Operations

The effectiveness of a company's international operations is closely related to the recognition of the special characteristics of the particular overseas situation. These special characteristics need to be recognized when a company first considers the extension of its operating activities to a particular country. Subsequently also, these characteristics need to be given consideration as the operations continue, and as further developments take place. The following types of problems are typical:

1. *Cultural Differences.* The first problem usually encountered is that of a different language. As a result, the participants in the business process must either know both languages (or in many countries a still greater number of languages) or they must depend upon the ability and integrity of intermediaries. Frequently also, it is difficult to find words in one language with meanings that have exact counterparts in the second language. Back of language are the still more important factors of customs and values. People do things differently and attach different degrees of importance to various attitudes, responses, and actions. An innocent violation of a native custom can have damaging consequences. Similarly, the manner in which real agreement is reached can vary. A "yes" may be only a courtesy, or perhaps a desire to avoid a negative response, instead of being a real commitment. Thus it becomes more difficult to carry on business relationships in an efficient manner. At a still deeper level are the social traditions and religious ties, which include various

types of restrictions and deep-seated value standards. It may, for example, be considered quite proper to take advantage of another party in a business relationship if that other party has not taken a specific type of protective action. These cultural differences especially affect the nature and scope of the business relationships.

2. *Economic Level.* The viability of any desired business operations must clearly take into consideration the economic level of the particular country. The economic level determines both the kinds of products and services that are needed by the society and its ability to make the related purchases. Important also is the structure of the particular society in an economic sense. In some situations there is a relatively small group at the top with substantial wealth, but backed up by a disproportionately large group at the level of poverty, or near poverty, levels. In some situations also, all of this is coupled with a paucity of natural resources. Or the problem may be a failure to utilize good natural resources. This lack of utilization is frequently related to other constraints of a social, religious, or political nature.

3. *Geographical Situation.* Also important to the viability of the desired business relations is the geographical situation. This will include the ease of accessibility in terms of distance and the surrounding terrain. It would also include such factors as climatic conditions over the year and their effect on local economic activity and related business operations. Involved also will be the adequacy of communication both between the country and other countries, and within the particular company itself. In many situations these geographical factors become the major problem.

4. *Political Factors.* Closely related to the preceding types of problems is a wide range of political factors. The type of government in a particular country can range from a highly centralized and autocratic rule to one that is reasonably democratic. The country may have a good record of political stability or it may be subject to frequent change. There may or may not be the continuing threat of revolution, expropriation, or even violence. Important also are the policies of nationalism and protection. There may be major efforts to foster local industry through restrictions on imports by means of high tariffs or exchange controls. A company operating in the country may be subject to increasingly burdensome restrictions as to the percentage of content not locally produced. Other restrictions may pertain to the percentage of foreigners who can be employed and upon what terms that employment must be based. Related also is the extent to which governmental officials apply policies with equity or on the contrary sell their favors to the highest bidder. All of these political factors can combine to have disastrous effects on international operations. The problem is especially troublesome because the shifts on the political scene are often not subject to reasonable prediction.

5. *Investment Values and Profits.* All of the foregoing matters discussed relate to the degree of attractiveness from an investment standpoint. Can

investment in the particular country have adequate profit potentials? Will the assets held in that country be secure? Can profits earned be recovered by the parent company? Present also are the problems of inflation, with the risks that claims stated in local currencies will not be adequately recovered. There may also exist the possibility of punitive taxation. In other situations the nationalization of industry may involve inadequate compensation for the properties taken over. In international operations these investment risks become increasingly great as more and more capital is committed to the expanded operations.

6. *Management Limitations.* The difficulties already discussed are also augmented by still another type of problem. This problem stems from the built-in difficulty which the foreign company normally has in adjusting to the new situation. In the case of the United States this problem frequently takes the form of an undue belief that methods and practices proven to be successful here can be similarly applied in a different country. To a major extent, Americans have had the view that they know best how things should be done overseas. Actually, however, Americans have been somewhat provincial in their learning of foreign languages, in their study of the histories of other countries, and in their overall interest in the cultures of the rest of the world. Americans going abroad often also lack an adequate sensibility to the thinking and feelings of the people in the host country. Lacking the experience and sensitivity of many other internationally oriented countries, it is not surprising that a great many mistakes have been made. Overcoming this lack of experience is, therefore, one of the special problems of expanding into the international area.

Potentials of International Operations

The preceding discussion of the special characteristics of overseas operations may appear to be so negative as to suggest the avoidance of this kind of broader company operation. On the contrary, however, it seems clear that the business potentials of most large companies is closely tied to expanded international operations. It is in the lesser developed areas of the world that rising economic levels provide the new markets for continued growth and profitability. Similarly, there are increasing trade potentials among the so-called "developed" countries. Our examination of the special characteristics is therefore not intended to be negative, but rather to induce a more perceptive and efficient handling of the various types of problems. Admittedly, international operations cannot always be successful. Also, there will still be the cases of expropriation and inadequate compensation. On balance, however, the international operations provide the best promise of future success for most growth companies.

Alternative Ways to Do Business Overseas

Assuming that there has been some kind of a judgment that a company should expand into the international field, there are a number of different ways in which this can be done. These different ways cover a wide spectrum both as to the extent of actual investment and managerial involvement. In the simplest type of situation the company may do nothing but honor orders that originate from unsolicited overseas buyers. However, even in this situation the company will find itself collecting foreign drafts and to some extent arranging needed transportation services. Such developments then set the stage for a more deliberate participation in international activities. Typical stages of company efforts and the major types of options can be described as follows:

1. *Creation of an Export Department*. The increasing volume of orders from overseas will at some point usually lead to the creation of a special export organizational responsibility, frequently termed an export department. Such a department will concentrate on operational problems related to making sales overseas, and will in most cases move on to a consideration of what should be done to promote such sales effectively. These promotional efforts typically include advertising of various kinds, and perhaps salespeople who will carry on promotional work in various countries. In some cases this type of operation will include the special modification and packaging of the products for better adjustment to overseas needs.

2. *Appointment of Overseas Agents*. As a company's products become better known, the company will receive inquiries as to the possibility of foreign individuals or firms acting as overseas agents. In such situations the particular overseas agent may maintain inventories, extend credit, or provide service to the final purchasers of the product. Frequently also, the export department will itself actively look for qualified overseas agents. Subsequently, the export department may develop a group of representatives who will work with the overseas agents to help them market and service the company's products more effectively. In some cases these representatives may be stationed overseas. But usually this type of operation will involve very little investment overseas on the part of the home company.

3. *Establishment of Overseas Sales Companies*. In some situations the company may feel that it is not getting adequate distribution in a particular country through its overseas agents. An alternative is to establish its own sales company or branch operation in that country. Frequently, this kind of a move includes the maintaining of inventories of the company's product, and in some cases the extension of credit. Such a company might still make use of local dealers or agents, or it might sell directly to the user, depending to a considerable extent on the type of product. Usually, there will be no substantial investment in permanent facilities at this stage.

4. *Local Manufacturing by the Overseas Sales Company*. At a still more advanced stage the home company may decide that it will either partially

or completely manufacture the product in the overseas country. In some cases this may come about as a result of governmental pressure, with the alternative often being to withdraw completely from that market. In an industry such as the automobile industry the first step will normally be the assembly of vehicles, and later the manufacture of individual component parts. Now the overseas company comes to function as a real member of the industrial community, with substantial facilities and with substantial employment of local nationals. The extent of the actual investment can, of course, vary widely. It can also take the form either of building new production facilities or the acquisition of already existing facilities, including the acquisition of a local company which owns facilities.

5. *Licensing of Other Overseas Companies*. If a company does not wish to make the investment in facilities itself, one alternative frequently utilized is to license another company in the particular country to produce, partially or completely, the product of the home country. When this is done the licensee is provided with the necessary technical know-how and backup assistance to do the job properly. At the same time controls are established in a manner appropriate to the type of product. These controls are principally to ensure proper specifications, and to protect the worldwide reputation of the licensor. The home company then receives a payment of some kind to compensate it for costs incurred, and to provide an acceptable profit. Relationships of this type have the major disadvantage of weaker control—versus direct ownership—but do have the offsetting advantage of less capital investment.

6. *Joint Ownership of Manufacturing Companies*. Still another available alternative is to share the ownership of the overseas manufacturing company with local nationals. In such a situation the degree of ownership of the home country can vary from a minority to a majority position. Usually, a company will be reluctant to make a substantial investment without keeping a majority ownership position, thus better protecting the financial interests of the company, but in some countries the governments will not permit such arrangements. The benefits of the partial local ownership lie in the greater acceptance of the situation by the country, and possibly more lenient regulatory control by the government of that country. The disadvantages are the necessity of keeping the local group satisfied. The needs and desires of the home company may also not always coincide with the local ownership group—as, for example, with the level of dividends paid. Also, if the company wishes to sell products or product components from one overseas company to another there can be controversial questions as to what should be the proper level of transfer prices. Because of these problems, many companies resist the joint ownership approach. In some cases, however, it may be the only alternative available.

Impact of International Operations on Managerial Activities

The managerial activities of an individual company in the overseas areas will vary greatly, depending on the type of operation just discussed. These activities will also be affected to a major extent by the magnitude of the overseas investment and the volume of sales operations. For our present purposes, however, we will assume that we are dealing with a large corporation which has extensive international operations, with either, or perhaps both, total and partially controlled ownership. As previously stated, we will focus on the special problems of the international operations in the various major functional areas—marketing, production, personnel, finance, and organization and administration. The functional problems are obviously closely interrelated, and the special actions taken in one functional area are directly influenced by the actions taken in another functional area. However, it will still be useful to look at the special impact in each area.

Impact on Marketing Activities

Marketing activities in international areas cover generally the same spectrum as discussed in Chapter 19. However, the special characteristics of the international operations create certain significant additional difficulties. Typically, these difficulties include:

1. *Appraisal of Market Potentials.* We know that the starting point of an effective marketing function is to determine the existing and potential needs of a given prospective market. In most international areas this kind of market appraisal is extremely difficult. Reliable factual information as to existing purchases and consumption is harder to obtain, and in many cases is not available at all. Often also, the company's products are of a different type than those being currently consumed, and hence the information obtainable is relatively speculative. In addition market trends are subject to abrupt change in the light of political determinations—as, for example, imposition of restrictive import duties, nonavailability of exchange, and changing policies for local manufacture. All of this means that market appraisals are significantly more unreliable.

2. *What Products to Sell?* The initial assumption may be that the product or products marketed domestically will also be salable in the new international market. But this is not necessarily true. The currently existing product may require major modification to suit the needs of the new market—as, for example, for ease of maintenance service, level of cost, or special durability. In other cases products must be adapted to the tastes and customs of the local society. There is also sometimes the very real possibility that it is more strategic to sell managerial or technical know-how rather than export the physical product itself. Included here will be licensing agreements or management service contracts. The company needs to study these various alternatives as a basis for making the

choice that has the greatest net promise of company benefit over an appropriate time span.

3. *What Channels of Distribution to Be Used?* When making the product decision the company must also be determining where and how the product is to be supplied. The question of where the goods will be produced is discussed below. But there still is the question of where and the extent to which inventories should be maintained, and then the channels of distribution to be used in marketing the selected products. Essentially this is the question of whether the company should work through a primary wholesaler, a secondary jobber, a retailer, or go directly to the consumer. In general, the further the company reaches toward the consumer, the greater the extent to which the company will have to perform the supporting backup functions itself. The factors that weigh heavily in these determinations are: (a) the skill and experience which are already available in the company, (b) the relative cost of the several alternatives, and (c) the degree of urgency to accomplish the desired levels of volume. These are difficult determinations because tbe basis for the decisions is usually not adequate, and hence there is a major reliance on judgment and intuition.

4. *What Kind of Sales Promotion?* Related closely to the decision as to the channels of distribution to be used is the question of what kinds of sales promotion there should be. The important thing here is that the sales promotion be geared to the particular market, as opposed to the approach being used in the domestic market. The basis of effective customer appeal is again linked to customs and value standards. Because of the risks involved, the use of local professionals is normally desirable. There are also frequently significant language problems. In many cases also it is desirable to share sales promotion efforts with intermediary jobbers and retailers, both as a cost-reduction device and to ensure effective implementation.

5. *Customer Service.* We know also that adequate customer service is essential to continuing market acceptance, especially in the case of technically oriented products. One special problem here is that local intermediaries may lack the needed technical skill to do this job adequately. A second problem is that users may not properly use or maintain the products. When all of this is coupled with usage conditions which are relatively noncontrollable—as, for example, climate and terrain—the problem of customer service becomes extremely serious. This means that the company must take the necessary steps to deal with the special difficulties. One major approach is through various types of special training programs. A second approach is through more simplified and self-explanatory service instructions, perhaps using pictures or diagrams to a greater extent. In all cases there will normally have to be a closer liaison with the various parties involved.

Impact on Production and Supply Activities

The marketing activities of the company are directly dependent on having the products supplied in accordance with the proper specifications and quality levels. This supply function involves a number of decisions as to how and where the items will be produced, together with appropriate operational implementation In the case of international operations the special impact on the production and supply activities will include the following:

1. *Feasibility of Overseas Production*. To a major extent the question of establishing overseas production facilities is an integral part of the total determination of the extent of overseas operations. However, in some cases it can also be treated as a separate option. The factors bearing on this determination are the availability of the necessary capital, the cost of the product in the ultimate market (taking into consideration also the transportation costs involved), the profitability of the capital investment, and the risks of security pertaining to that investment. When governmental pressures are involved the determination must also especially reflect the long-run impact of establishing the production facilities versus being precluded from the particular market. To an increasing extent, however, the typical company moves toward a greater investment in overseas production facilities.

2. *Location of Overseas Production*. In some cases the company may have the option of establishing production facilities in selected overseas areas, and then servicing the various countries in the broader regional area. The benefits achieved are frequently favorable operational conditions in the selected country, the saving of transportation costs, and the achievement of greater economy of larger-volume production. The deterrents are the greater risk exposure in the selected country, and the resistance of those countries where there will be no production facilities. The alternative is, of course, smaller plants in a greater number of individual countries, but with the resulting higher costs.

3. *Specialization of Individual Overseas Plants*. When there are production facilities established in a number of overseas countries, the company has yet another option. This option is to make the individual plants either a total integrated or specialized plant. In the first case the plant will produce the entire product or group of products, and thus be relatively self-sufficient. In the second case the plant will specialize on one or more products of a larger unified product group, or on one or more components of a total product. In this latter case one country is dependent on other countries for either components or other products of a larger unified product group. The advantage is that production economies can be achieved through the greater specialization. But the disadvantage of the dependence on the other countries may be critical. Thus the unavailability of supply of a needed component—due perhaps to a political takeover

or a strike—can conceivably paralyze production capabilities in all other countries.

4. *Type of Production Facilities.* A related question regards the kind of production facilities to be provided, in terms of the types and quantities of labor personnel. In a particular country the limited availability of skilled labor may dictate the need to use simple types of production equipment. At the same time an abundance of unskilled labor at low cost will mitigate against the use of highly automated (and more costly) types of capital equipment. These offsetting factors must, therefore, be carefully weighed. Consideration must also be given as to how the existing conditions may change over the years ahead.

5. *Purchasing Activities.* Local production operations will in turn generate a range of purchasing activities. The special difficulties are that these procurements are carried out normally among a relatively limited and less qualified group of suppliers. In addition, there are the problems of language and customs to contend with. Different standards may also exist as to the reliability of deliveries. These problems are compounded as a production operation moves, often under specific governmental pressure, to increase the percentage of local content. In these circumstances there must usually be an extended effort to work with local suppliers to help them develop the necessary production capabilities. In total there is a more uncertain and more tenuous procurement capability.

6. *Local Research and Product Development Effort.* A previously identified question relates to the extent that products are best suited for the individual country and regional markets. There is then the further question as to where the underlying research and product development effort should be carried out. It is asserted on the one hand that a centralized domestic effort cannot be sufficiently responsive to the various overseas needs. On the other hand, a too decentralized effort can result in a significant duplication of effort and excessive cost. There is also the loss of the greater economy of scale made possible by a larger development effort. The best solution seems to be to find the right middle approach, and then to effectively coordinate the local efforts with the centralized home-country effort.

7. *Special Operational Problems.* Carrying on production operations in the typical overseas location will involve a range of special operational problems. One of these special operational problems is that of labor relations. Locally available personnel not only may currently lack the needed skills, but also and more important, may lack the basic capabilities for acquiring these skills. In addition, there are the problems of customs and attitudes. Also, in many countries there are major union problems and burdensome governmental regulation. Similar operational problems arise in connection with available water, utility services, sanitation facilities, and the like.

Impact on Personnel Activities

The labor problems relating to the production operations lead into the broader personnel problems of the total international activities. These problems are directly determined on the one hand by the kind of society existing in the particular country with its social, religious and political concepts, its culture, and its stage of economic development. On the other hand, the problems are determined by the company's needs for given types of working personnel. Typical problems include:

1. *Social Stratification.* In most underdeveloped countries there is some form of major social stratification. In some cases this stratification is between the elite groups (those possessing wealth, education, and social position) and the nonelite group (those people substantially at the subsistence level, without education, and without social position). In other cases the stratification is on a racial or religious basis, with one group being in a dominant position versus another group. Illustrative is the plight of the blacks in South Africa, or the Jews in Russia. The problem here is then that an operational manager is restricted in his use of personnel apart from what he would do on the basis of straight productive ability.

2. *Paternalistic Dependency.* In a society with major social stratification, there is likely to be a strong feeling of dependency of the lower-ranking group on the higher-ranking group which provides the employment and protection. Therefore, when the international component of the company becomes the employer, it is called upon to provide a wide range of social services—living quarters, health services, credit, help with personal problems, and the like. The employment of personnel at all organizational levels, therefore, involves a very broad range of obligations and programs for implementing services.

3. *Governmental Control.* At the same time legal rights may be established for the local personnel. These legal rights commonly include guaranteed tenure, subject only to termination with substantial indemnities. Working hours, pay levels, and holidays may also be covered. Again, the acquisition of personnel carries with it substantial obligations and commitments.

4. Union Power. The paternalistic dependency mentioned earlier, coupled with the politics of the existing government, may combine to generate increasingly powerful unions. This development constitutes an additional major restriction on managerial flexibility.

5. *Basic Attitudes and Capabilities.* Supplementing the forces of legal rights and union power are the frequently existing basic limitations of the personnel in terms of native capabilities and attitudes. A manager of an international operation wishing to achieve a desired level of efficiency and productivity will commonly find himself thwarted in this endeavor.

6. *Developing Local Managers.* All of the problems just covered apply to

all local personnel, but become especially significant in the endeavor to develop local managers. On the one hand, the company is desirous of eliminating the higher costs of maintaining home country personnel for the various overseas assignments. Additionally, the company may be under great pressure from the government to increase the proportion of local nationals as managers. On the other hand, however, the company is reluctant to settle for managers who have inadequate competence and motivation. They are especially reluctant to entrust corporate resources to individuals who lack both the home-office company experience and the home-country standards of values. The problem is to do all possible to bridge this gap.

7. *Problems of the U.S. Manager.* This is not to say that the U.S. manager himself presents no special problems. We have already noted the high cost—this being due to the higher U.S. pay levels plus the extra allowances for living quarters, the education of children, and periodic home leaves. We have noted also the frequently existing problem of insensitivity to local country needs. A further problem is that the U.S. manager may enjoy his special status in the country so much that he is not adequately motivated to develop a replacement. If and when the U.S. manager is brought back to the home country, there is the final difficulty of bringing him back into the total company operation on a mutually advantageous basis.

Impact on Finance Activities

The financial activities of any company have always been the means of integrating the various operational activities in that company. Again in the case of the international activities this same role is continued, and becomes even more important. Again, the financial activities represent an area where the internal auditor has special competence. And again, the financial activities represent a means by which the internal auditor can have access to the broader operational problems of an international character. The special problems pertaining to these international financial activities normally include:

1. *Soundness of Investment Decisions.* All of the marketing, production, and personnel dimensions must somehow come together in the decision to invest funds in a given overseas location. This may be an initial investment—as, for example, the establishment of either an overseas sales company or the more extensive acquisition of production facilities. As we have previously seen, each of the functional dimensions presents special difficulties. It follows then that the investment decision itself is much more difficult, and involves much more risk than the similar type of domestic decision. As a result the profit potentials must be proportionately greater. Then losses in one venture can be offset by higher than normal gains in another. This same investment decision problem is then

continued as further investments are made in given overseas areas to support expanded operational activities.

2. *Financing Problem*. As previously in the domestic situation, capital must be provided to support both short-term and longer-term operational needs. The special problem, however, in this case is to evaluate the possibilities of local financing in local currencies, thus providing a hedge against depreciation in the home currency. In some cases funds can be moved between overseas countries in a way that will reduce taxation. Use can also be made of available governmental financing agencies.

3. *Local Financial and Accounting Activities*. The financial results of the overseas operation must ultimately be prepared in such a manner that they can be consolidated—whenever that consolidation option is exercised by the home headquarters—into the total company financial statements. This means that the basic accounts must be maintained in a prescribed manner. In addition, it is expected that financial and accounting operational policies and procedures will be consistent with the standard company approach. An objective here also is to assure to the greatest extent practicable the prudent and honest use of company resources. There is also the important requirement that accounting and financial procedures meet the legal requirements in the particular country. A special complication arises here when the country requirements include either excessive detail or different data than those developed by the company approach. There is also the special problem when prevailing commercial practice in the particular country includes types of actions not condoned by home-country policy. An example here would be special payments or gifts to governmental representatives for needed permits, licenses, allocations, and the like. Another example would be the failure to report data so that tax payments are reduced. Finally, there are the usual requirements of order and efficiency of the internal accounting and related clerical operations at the overseas location, all of which must be done for the most part by available local personnel. Thus the total local financial and accounting activities combine to have many special problems and complications.

4. *Budgets and Profit Plans*. At a higher level of financial control the various overseas locations are normally subject to the same type of budgetary and profit plan control as is applied to the domestic operations of the company. Since individual countries are separate political entities, they are normally at the same time profit centers. The special complications arise when products and components are purchased and sold, and the determination of transfer prices directly affect the amount of profit earned in the individual country. Another special complication here is the necessity of working first in terms of the local currencies and then converting these reports into the home-country currency. This requirement similarly applies to the actual accounting reports. In all cases there are the problems of selecting the rates for conversion, including the coverage of profits or

losses due to changing currency rates. A further special difficulty exists in the case of budgets and profit plans in that the future is so much more vulnerable to change than is usually the case in the domestic situation. Here the financial manager must be especially alert to current political and economic trends.

5. *Profit Routing and Recovery*. In strict theory an individual profit center will seek to maximize its own earned profit. In practice, however, there may be other types of influence which are operative. One type of influence is that, to the extent that there is an option, a company will normally seek to have profits earned in countries with the lowest tax rates. These options exist within reasonable limits in the way transfer prices and other inter-profit center charges are fixed. In other cases the company may find that it can maximize company profits by directing the flow of materials in a certain manner, even though this arrangement may penalize a particular profit center. An illustration of this is the allocation by a petroleum company of both crude oil stocks and refined gasoline to selected areas and countries. Later then, when profits are earned, there may be possibilities that taxation may be reduced through the routing of profits to tax haven companies which can be created in certain countries. Also, there is always the question of when profits should be transferred to the home country. The factors to be considered here include local country restrictions, taxation costs, existing overseas needs, and the pressures for profit recovery in the home country.

6. *Protection of Asset Values*. As we have previously seen, all overseas investments are subject to a range of risks, especially with respect to political security and loss of monetary value. The financial manager is therefore concerned with all possible steps to minimize these risks. With respect to political security, a company will normally take advantage of all available investment guarantees from the home-country government. Some protection is also provided by the courts of the local company, although the independence of such courts may be quite uncertain. Generally, the greater security will come from the usefulness of the company to the individual country, and the resulting leverage which is thereby provided against unfair treatment. This usefulness will include the providing of jobs, the training and development of local nationals, and the assistance in creating an industrial base. With respect to maintenance of value in the face of inflation of prices and currency devaluation, the approaches will typically include incurring local debt, currency swap transactions, reducing import requirements, raising local prices (to the extent possible), and reevaluation of assets. Problems of this kind are increasingly common in many overseas countries.

Impact on Organization and Administration

All of the foregoing aspects of international operations finally come together in terms of the question of how a company should organize to deal with its international operations, and how it should administer the various activities. The central objective is to find the combination that best serves the overall company interests. Supporting this central objective is the subobjective of achieving adequate control, at the same time giving the individual overseas country and broader regional area the opportunity to exploit the potentials of their markets in the most effective manner. Included also is the desire to utilize fully the types of contribution that can be made by the various domestic line and staff activities. The problem is a difficult one for several reasons. One of these reasons is that the nature and scope of the overseas involvement change over time, thus requiring different kinds of supporting efforts. The second reason is the ever-judgmental character of what kind of organizational arrangements and administrative approaches do in fact best serve the company interests.

Organizational Structure.   In terms of organizational structure, it appears that companies generally move through certain fairly well defined stages. These are, as follows:

1. *Reliance on an Export Department.* During the phase when overseas operations involve only the taking of orders for domestic product, or in other cases the more active promotion of the sale of domestic products overseas, the organizational structure of the company will normally include a separate export department. This export department will normally be small and will typically be positioned somewhere in either the marketing or finance group. The overseas market is here viewed only as a supplementary outlet for existing domestic products.

2. *Direct Domestic Division Involvement.* During the next phase individual domestic divisions become interested in overseas operations and they proceed, each on its own, to extend their activities into the various overseas areas. These activities will typically include the development of production facilities—with varying types of local ownership participation. In these circumstances the export department will usually still continue to exist but will give way to the jurisdiction of the operating divisions. That is, they will not normally compete in the same country market with the same products being produced locally under the aegis of the domestic division. Thus the expansion of the domestic divisions causes a gradual shrinkage in the scope of the operations of the export department. The benefits achieved are that there is a more aggressive exploitation of the overseas markets. The disadvantages are the greater cost of the parallel overseas operations of the several divisions. There is also some possible confusion as to who really speaks for the company in a particular country.

3. *An International Division.* The aforementioned overlapping and the lack of a coordinated company effort becomes increasingly serious as the volume of overseas operations grows larger. The solution then usually developed is to create an international division that will have operational

jurisdiction over all overseas operations, including the activities of the export department. Now the international division also either directly services the needs of the company operational units in the individual countries, or functions as an intermediary for obtaining help from the various domestic divisions. The advantages are a more deliberate and coordinated focus on international operations. The disadvantages are the cost of the new international division staff and the greater isolation of the domestic divisions. To a major extent also the international operations are viewed too much as only a supplement to the more seriously regarded domestic operations.

4. *Multinational Organizational Approach.* At this later stage the single international division gives way to an organizational arrangement whereby the world is looked at as a whole and broken up into major regional areas. Thus there might be a North American region, a South American region, a European region, an African region, and a Far East region—each with its own operating divisions. The corporate headquarters will then serve all regions in the same manner. Under this approach the corporate headquarters will view its locational setup more and more as a matter of geographical convenience than as linkage with a particular country. The company would view itself essentially as a worldwide global corporation. This appears to be the ultimate stage of organizational development.

Administrative Approach

The administration of international activities involves all of the usual problems that exist in the domestic area. In addition, there are again special problems. The following are typical:

1. *Stronger Case for Decentralization of Authority.* It might perhaps be argued that the special difficulties involved in international operations would push a company in the direction of a tighter and more centralized control of its decision-making process. Actually, however, other factors exist that have a more powerful influence in the opposite direction. In the first place, the distances involved, and the more difficult communication that exists, despite the new modern technological capabilities, make it imperative that local managers have greater authority to make many more important decisions on the ground. Telephone communication, for example, in many situations is most erratic. In the second place, international problems to a greater extent are unique problems that have to be resolved on the basis of local conditions, locally available information, and local experience.

2. *Attitudes of Local Nationals.* To a major extent the local administration of international operations must be carried out by local nationals. The special problem here is that these local nationals cannot be dealt with in the same way that one would deal with home-country nationals. The local personnel will quite naturally think and act to a significant extent in terms

of their own culture and environment. In the typical situation they will not be changed rapidly. There are also the special legal restrictions of the particular country. Hence there is the necessity for the higher-ranking home-office managers to move cautiously and more slowly. This problem can exist at any level, including the situation where local national partners have come into the picture through joint ventures, or through the acquisition of local firms.

3. *General Attitude of the Local Society*. To a certain extent the company from the outside may be welcomed by the particular country as bringing new benefits to it. At the same time there is often a kind of hostility to a newcomer, especially when there is a feeling that the local resources are somehow being exploited for the profit of the outsider. There is in this connection a continuing trend toward increased nationalism in most countries. The problem for the foreign company—foreign, that is, to that particular country—is, therefore, that it must demonstrate over time its genuine interest in helping that country, while making a fair profit. In some cases individual companies have not done this. Even when a particular company is sincere in wanting to play a constructive partner role, it may have some difficulty in convincing the local public that this is so. It seems clear that host countries will expect more of a true partner role of guest companies in the future.

SPECIAL PROBLEMS OF THE INTERNAL AUDITOR

In most respects the work of the internal auditor in the international situations will be similar to what is done in the domestic area. However, the more difficult management problems add further dimensions of complexity to the work of the internal auditor. Additionally, he too must adjust to the problems of greater distance, different languages, special cultures, and the like. If local nationals are utilized as staff, there are the greater problems of coordination and control. The special problems include at least the following.

1. *Special Need to Interpret Company Accounting and Other Operational Procedures*. Since the local accounting and other operational activities are being carried out for the most part by local nationals, the role of interpreting company policies and procedures becomes all the more important. Internal auditors need to be well acquainted with the official policies and procedures and to be prepared to carry out the needed educational and training role. The accounting and financial records will also necessarily have to be prepared in the local currency, and the resulting reports will then have to be converted into U.S. dollars. When this conversion is made locally—as is normally the case—procedures covering such conversion also have to be covered by proper instructions, and then carried out satisfactorily. In all of these local activities there are

usually also special problems of achieving adequate standards of quality and efficiency.

2. *Compliance with Legal Requirements*. Although compliance with legal requirements is always important, this aspect takes on special importance for an outside company, which is very often under greater than usual scrutiny. Also, penalties for noncompliance are frequently more burdensome than would be the case in the home country. This type of problem is also complicated by the fact that locally domiciled companies may not fully observe the existing legal requirements. In these situations local managers may sincerely oppose full compliance. On the other hand, the total company reputation is at stake and there can be no satisfactory policy other than uniform worldwide compliance. In this instance there is the special reliance on the internal auditor to help assure such a result.

3. *Achieving Adequate Standards in Administration of Resources*. A number of different pressures and risks may exist which call for a special effort to ensure that adequate standards are maintained in the administration of resources. The pressures may range from a type of laxity in the case of assets to the deliberate exploitation of company resources for private advantage. In some cases local attitudes and value standards may contribute to such pressures. Greater protection may also be needed against outside thievery of various kinds. All of these pressures and risks must therefore be understood and adequately handled.

4. *Appraisal of People*. Since distances are relatively great between the home country and the individual overseas locations, and since also there is the special problem of local nationals, it is to be expected that the internal auditor will play a greater than usual role in the appraisal of operational personnel. Also, as we have seen, locally based home-office personnel have their special problems, ranging from being too insensitive to local needs to the other extreme of becoming too native in their manner of operation. The internal auditor can thus serve as an important outside objective evaluator for all personnel.

5. *General Perception of Problems and Opportunities*. An even greater opportunity is presented to the internal auditor in appraising all types of operational activities and in perceiving various types of possible improvements and new opportunities. The discussion of the special problems of management in the various functional areas was in fact designed to provide additional capability in that direction. As in the domestic situation there is the challenge to serve management in this larger way. The relative lack of exposure to the international operations by home-country management makes this effort all the more important.

Carrying Out the Internal Auditing Role

As we have seen from the foregoing discussion, there are unusually great potentials for the internal auditor in the international area in the way of providing management service. As a practical matter, however, two kinds of difficulties have frequently been encountered in achieving these potentials. One of these difficulties is that there has often been a greater degree of resistance on the part of those managers responsible for international operations to open this area to the internal auditor. In part this resistance seems to have been the relatively high cost of sending internal auditors overseas. Frequently also, the resistance seems to come from viewing the internal auditor as a threat to the operational independence of the overseas locations, especially when those operations have necessarily been less orderly and subject to more deviations from official company practice. The solution here is somehow to convince these managers, including the company top management that ultimately makes the final decision, that the internal auditing effort really serves their own best interests.

The second difficulty has in some cases been the internal auditor himself. What has sometimes happened is that the internal auditor has lacked the specially needed sensitivity and diplomacy capability to do the job effectively. This deficiency has also often been linked with the lack of understanding of both the special problems of international operations and the related need of the overseas locations for a greater degree of operational flexibility. The solution here is a greater effort to familiarize himself with the existing environmental factors at the particular overseas location, and then to couple the new knowledge with a greater degree of judgment as to how those environmental factors can be dealt with best. All of this means that when the opportunity develops for extending the internal auditing effort into the international area, special care is needed in carrying out those assignments. Since the special opportunities do exist in the international area, the challenge is to exploit fully these new opportunities for greater management service.

AUDIT GUIDES

INTERNATIONAL OPERATIONS

I. Introductory

   A. Reference should be made to the general discussion of audit guides, Chapter 13.

   B. Since international operations involve the same functional activities as domestic operations, the audit guides for the previously discussed operational areas need to be used as a starting point. The audit guides here deal only with the unique aspect of the review of international operations.

II. Preparatory Activities

   A. See standard Audit Guides, Chapter 13.

   B. Because of the higher than usual travel costs, and the lesser later opportunities for communication with domestic personnel, special care is required in carrying out the preparatory activities. This special care covers both more complete coverage of particular background aspects, and more extended contacts with all parties of possible interest.

C. The greater detachment and autonomy of the usual overseas location call for special care on the part of the internal auditor as he makes his initial contacts.

III. Organizational Factors

A. See standard Audit Guides, Chapter 13.

B. All organizational factors need to be evaluated in terms of their adequacy to cope with the special problems outlined in the preceding discussion.

IV. Operational Activities Reviewed

A. See previously proposed audit guides for the particular operational activities being reviewed.

B. Special audit problems include:

1. Marketing
   a. Are all available sources of information as to nature and scope of existing market potentials being utilized?
   b. Are current and planned product offerings suitable for the markets being served?
   c. Have the distribution channels been selected on the basis of all relevant factors?
   d. Is sales promotion appropriate in terms of special market characteristics?
   e. Evaluate the adequacy of customer service and related customer relationships.
   f. Evaluate existing marketing problems and relate to available marketing opportunities.

2. Production and Supply
   a. Evaluate the alternatives of local production versus procurement from other sources, including the headquarters.
   b. Is local production being carried out in a manner best adjusted to local conditions?
   c. Evaluate the effectiveness of local purchasing in the light of the existing availabilities and conditions.
   d. Is the local engineering and research activity adequate? Is it properly coordinated with the home-office effort?

3. Personnel
   a. Are local nationals being used to the maximum extent practicable?
   b. Are training and development programs adequate?
   c. Are all governmental requirements being properly complied with?

4. Finance
   a. Are local financing sources being adequately utilized?
   b. Are accounting activities in conformance with home-office requirements?
   c. Do accounting activities at the same time properly provide for conformance with local governmental requirements?
   d. Are basic financial control activities effective? If not, what can be done to achieve proper control?
   e. Evaluate the adequacy of financial planning activities.
   f. What specific problems of profitability exist, and how can they be dealt with?
5. Admistration
   a. Does the local operational organization have adequate organizational status and related authority? If not, what modifications seem to be needed?
   b. Are relations with headquarters and key domestic activities adequate?
   c. Is the local operational unit developing the best possible relations with the people and government of the host country?

V. Audit Reivew Approach
The normally greater detachment of the overseas activity from home country management, combined with the special operational problems of the activity being reviewed, provide the internal auditor with especially great management service potentials. Some of the areas of special service include:

A. Identifying types of action that can provide embarrassment to the total company reputation.
B. Helping to provide better protection against laxity or special interests of local personnel.
C. Appraising individual performance of personnel at all levels.
D. Finding means for making the company presence in the particular overseas setting more acceptable to local government and public opinion.
E. Providing information and training to personnel.
F. Doing everything possible to demonstrate to company personnel, both at home and abroad, that the internal auditing work can be directly useful to company management at all levels.

VI–IX. Not used.

X. Overall Appraisal of the International Activities
A. See standard Audit Guides, Chapter 13.
B. The overall appraisal is applicable to the international activities as a whole and to the particular activity or group of activities being reviewed.

ILLUSTRATIVE AUDIT FINDINGS: INTERNATIONAL OPERATIONS

Duplicating Services Available

A review by the internal auditor of administrative functions performed in overseas divisions indicated that computer and accounting services available at the home office were not being utilized. Savings of $50,000 a year could be achieved by relying on available services.

Need for Finding Additional Suppliers

An overseas division was making continued purchases from the same suppliers without adequate justification, resulting in excessive prices for materials. Division personnel stated that they were not following company policy requiring competitive bids because of the difficulties in finding suppliers for overseas operations. The internal auditor recommended that the division develop alternative sources of supply with the assistance of the home office. In addition, adequate documentation should be included in the files when competitive bids are not obtained.

Idle Time

During his visit to an overseas plant the internal auditor observed significant idle time of employees, mostly local nationals. This was caused by ineffective work scheduling and lack of supervision of untrained personnel.

Need for More Effective Monitoring

Excessive monitoring trips were made to some foreign offices while insufficient monitoring was made to other offices. The internal auditor found a need for improved scheduling and approval of foreign visits to assure that attention was given those foreign offices with priority needs.

Action on Deficiencies Noted

The foreign subsidiary was not taking corrective action on prior audit findings and recommendations made by supervisory personnel in overseas visits. The internal auditor recommended a reporting system to the home office to assure that prompt action was taken on conditions noted.

CHAPTER TWENTY-FOUR

Social Responsibilities and Business Ethics

Social responsibility and business ethics activities are areas of total managerial performance that are relatively unique. This uniqueness lies in the fact that we have relatively intangible areas that combine certain values, existing in their own right, with other values that have a direct relationship to corporate self-interest and profitability. That is, corporations, and in turn corporate managers, see their social responsibilities and standards of business ethics as qualities that are directly rewarding in terms of being good citizens, while being necessary components of corporate welfare. In this connection social responsibilities and business ethics have common roots and relationships, but involve differing problems and objectives. Together, however, they represent an increasingly important concern of corporate managers. The related problems and opportunities that exist in this modern age must somehow be dealt with. Because they are concerns of managers, they are also the concerns of internal auditors as a part of a dedicated professional effort to serve management. It is appropriate, therefore, that we devote a chapter to these increasingly important areas.[1]

Our desire in this chapters is to achieve three key purposes. The first of these purposes is to provide better understanding of the nature and scope of the problems of social responsibility and business ethics—both individually and in combination. The second purpose is to build on the foregoing understanding and to identify typical action programs by managers for coping with the related problems and opportunities. Third, our purpose is to identify and describe the various ways in which internal auditors can provide useful assistance to managers in carrying out the total program to achieve effective results. The understanding of the new problems relating to social responsibility and business ethics, and helping managers deal with these problems, clearly represent a new higher-level challenge and opportunity for internal auditors.

---

[1]The material in this chapter is based in part on Chapter 14, "The Impact of New Expectations," in *Understanding Management Policy and Making It Work* by Victor Z. Brink (New York: AMACOM, 1978).

Although the problems of social responsibility and business ethics are in many respects closely related, and to a considerable extent overlap, it will be more convenient to deal first with the broader social responsibilities, then with the more definitive problems of business ethics, and then to look at the combined areas in final perspective.

SOCIAL RESPONSIBILITY ACTIVITIES

"Social responsibility" is a general term that for us covers the obligation of corporations and their corporate managers to serve the broader needs of society. These broader needs include the needs of the corporation and its members individually, but go further to include the needs of the total society. "Business ethics," in turn, refers to the standards of corporate conduct in terms of established social values. Although these established social values again are a part of the broader social needs, they typically involve a narrower and more definitive sector. However, social needs and social values constitute a common base for social responsibilities and business ethics.

Relationship of Social Responsibilities to Social Expectations

The needs of the society cover a wide range of physical and intangible considerations regarding which there is no common agreement. All of us have different views as to the nature and scope of social needs. We also have different priorities for their satisfaction. In general terms these social needs involve, however, such issues as physical safety, living standards, freedom of choice, opportunities for self-expression and development, and love of our fellow human beings. These needs, as individually and collectively expressed, define the kinds of responsibilities of all participants—again both individually and collectively—to help satisfy those needs. The evaluation of these needs and responsibilities are also directly related to the nature and scope of social expectations. We know also that for many reasons these social expectations have rapidly accelerated in recent years in terms of both range and intensity. People now have a broader variety and higher level of needs, and at the same time want those needs to be satisfied more quickly. The particular concerns cover a wide range, but typically include the following:

1. *Undue Neglect of Various Aspects of the Physical Environment.* In this area the environmentalists point to increasing air pollution, contaminated bodies of water, commercialization of the countryside, inadequate sanitation, and the like. An example is pumping industrial waste into a river or lake, making that lake unfit for drinking, bathing, and fishing.

2. *Waste and Destruction of Natural Resources.* The concerns here center around the destruction of wildlife, the loss of natural areas supporting that wildlife, the defilement of land surfaces, leveling of mountains, destruction of forests, dissipation of energy resources, and the like. Examples include strip mining and the Alaska pipeline.

3. *Below-Subsistence Level of Much of the World Population*. The concern here is both for large groups of people who are literally starving to death and for other groups with submarginal standards of life and health. Examples include the starvation conditions in Asia for large numbers of people and the needy in our slum cities.

4. *Lack of Physical Security*. At issue here is the rising crime and violence and the insecurity of people both in their homes and on the street. An example is the typical large city, where mugging, vandalism, burglary, and murder flourish.

5. *Protection of Human Rights*. The concern here is for minority groups that directly or indirectly have been denied legal and social rights believed to be the dues of all human beings. The plight of the blacks and other minority groups is illustrative.

6. *Freedom of Opportunity and Self-Development*. At this higher level there are the concerns for the total fulfilment of self-expression and for healthy economic and spiritual growth. Here too, the plight of the blacks and other minority groups is illustrative.

Accelerating Levels of Social Expectations

The foregoing social expectations have always existed as long as there has been human life. What is new, and at the same time of major significance, is that in recent years these expectations have been dramatically accelerated. In some cases the initial steps of independence for existing colonies have sparked the demand for total and more immediate action. In some cases the correction of long-existing social problems has led to exaggerated demands and related threats of violence. In some cases the recipients of the new privileges have also misued their new rights. In total the mood is extremism instead of planned and orderly transition over longer periods of time. Why this has come to pass raises questions to which there is no common agreement. What is important, however, is to recognize the existing fact of that dramatic acceleration and the necessity of somehow finding appropriate solutions whereby the transition can be made in a way that will avoid a major collapse of needed stability. It is in this environment that the business corporation finds itself as it seeks through its managers to maintain needed profitability and sound growth for business corporations. As managers, and as internal auditors serving those managers, we therefore must somehow find the needed solutions if there is to continue to be an environment in which business corporations can survive and continue to need internal auditing services.

Impact on Business

The basic concern of the business corporation is how it can effectively function, or even survive, in this new environment. These are the typical concerns of all responsible members of the society. The problem for the business corporation, however, is further compounded by the varying way in which the total society views the business corporation. Normally, the thrust for correcting the problems of society should come from the people themselves through its established government. This is especially true in the Western countries, where the government is what the people determine it should be through the free election of the persons who carry on the governmental function. But many citizens are not satisfied with this traditional process. Instead, they see the business corporation as a more convenient way of achieving faster social action. As a result they seek by every available means to influence the business corporation to take actions for solving perceived social problems. These methods in some cases involve new laws and related governmental regulation. But additionally, they involve appealing to the emotions of the public. In still other cases there is an effort to infiltrate and bring pressure on boards of directors. The problem of the corporation is then the extent to which it should yield to or resist these varied pressures. The answer to that question also raises questions as to what the proper role of the business corporation should be in a free society.

Conflicting Views about Responsibility of Business. An evaluation of the social responsibility of the modern business corporation needs to begin with the recognition that there are two basically different viewpoints. At one extreme is the view that in a free enterprise system the proper role of the corporation is to make a profit. With corporations competing for consumers of its products, the society thereby is able to vote on how all the resources of society should best be utilized to satisfy the needs of that society. If the corporation tries to take on the governmental role of administering to social needs, it not only takes on a role for which it is not properly qualified, but also impairs its capability to carry on its aforementioned basic role. According to this view, the business corporation should concentrate on achieving profitability and leave to government the job of responding to broader social needs.

The opposing view is that the business corporation was created by the society to serve the needs of the society. Therefore, the business corporation has a direct responsibility to help deal with all social needs. Put another way, the business corporation is a citizen and as such has the same responsibilities as every other citizen. Indeed, it is reasoned that, because the modern business corporation controls so many assets and people, its responsibility as a citizen is all the more sound. This view does not necessarily relieve government of its responsibilities, but it does attribute a major responsibility to the corporation itself. Indeed, according to this view, responding to social needs often comes as a higher priority than profitability. There is the apparent belief also that profitability is somehow sufficiently automatic to assure corporate survival.

Need for Enlightened Self-Interest. What, then, is the business corporation to do in the face of such conflicting views? On the one hand, the corporate manager knows that he operates under the grace of a charter granted by the society. He knows therefore that the charter can be modified directly or indirectly by that same society. As a result he has a primary responsibility to satisfy the society in return for the corporation's continuing existence. At the same time the corporate manager knows that unless the corporation is profitable, he will have failed in his responsibilities to the investors and creditors who have provided the corporate resources. Moreover, corporate managers who do not achieve profitability are displaced with other corporate managers who *can* achieve the needed profitability. Corporations must also be profitable to survive and to avoid liquidation. Somehow, therefore, his job is to satisfy both types of needs. That is, he must be sufficiently responsible to public pressures to protect his corporate existence and at the same time be profitable enough to assure the health and survival of the corporation for which he is responsible. It is therefore the special challenge of the corporate manager to reconcile the too often conflicting forces by finding the proper middle ground. This longer-range reconciliation capability can conveniently be called "enlightened self-interest." Within that framework the modern corporation and its management are committed to at least partial involvement in developing action programs for satisfying a varying range of social responsibilities.

Problems of Satisfying Social Responsibilities

A policy decision for satisfying social responsibilities, sound as it is, calls for a good understanding of the difficulties involved. These difficulties spring from the special problems that exist. These problems include:

1. *Question of Right Priorities.* Individuals, and in turn the groups those individuals work through, have widely differing views as to the merits and relative priorities of the various social needs. Any decision in this area is therefore always bound to be controversial—applauded by some, and condemned by others. In this connection there are indeed both questions of propriety and feasibility.

2. *High Emotional Content.* The foregoing varying views tend to have exceptionally high emotional content, coupled with correspondingly decreasing objectivity. Individual social needs are frequently viewed with missionary zeal and lead to demands that are both unsound and impractical.

3. *Limited Capacity for Impact.* Frequently, the particular social problems involved are so great that the capacity of an individual corporation to deal with it is unavoidably miniscule. This is inevitably true irrespective of the large resources of the particular corporation.

4. *Susceptibility to Manipulation.* Because social causes have such high emotional content it is always tempting to use them in a manipulative sense to achieve other personal goals and objectives. In this way social causes become political footballs or covers for more sinister objectives. Some groups see the pressures as an opportunity to discredit both the corporation and the free enterprise system.

5. *Difficulties of Implementation.* Decisions to satisfy social responsibilities, even though often theoretically sound and appealing, are typically hard to implement in terms of corrective action. Here also the choice of methods for that implementation are usually exceedingly controversial—and again typically emotional.

6. *Difficulties of Measurement.* The difficulties of implementation just indicated are compounded by the fact that the results achieved in the way of corrective action are usually very hard to measure and evaluate. Again the evaluation of what has been accomplished in the way of corrective action is exceedingly controversial and subject to further emotional manipulation. The difficulties here apply to both input and output.

7. *Special Problems of Cost/Benefit.* The difficulties of measurement are further compounded by the complicated interrelationships of the various costs and benefits. For example, the lower costs for a pollutive factory are offset by other economic and social costs. A decision to close a plant because of desired lesser pollution may achieve that particular objective but at the same time deprive workers of needed employment. Equating all of these varying costs and benefits thus becomes almost impossible—and again always very controversial.

8. *Problems of Credibility.* In many cases well-intentioned efforts to discharge social responsibilities are challenged by hostile groups as misguided or improper commercialism—often for the sole purpose of discrediting corporate management or the corporate system itself. Corporate managers are therefore often disillusioned and demotivated to continue really meritorious programs. Also, even when they do persevere, they face special problems in demonstrating that their efforts are sincere and credible.

9. *Removing Pressures on Government.* A more fundamental problem is that the corporate efforts may somehow remove the pressures on government to take needed corrective action. Such developments thus undermine the working of the democratic system as basically intended. To that extent, then, the needs of society are not as properly served as they should be.

The explanations of these special problems of satisfying social responsibilities should not be viewed as unduly pessimistic or to discourage definitive action to satisfy social responsibilities. Such definitive action *must* be taken within the framework of enlightened self-interest. It is necessary, however, that corporate management fully understand the special problems so that those problems may be given appropriate consideration when developing definitive action programs.

Action Programs Available to Management

The development of an action program for a particular corporation to deal with its social responsibilities, within the framework of enlightened self-interest, is its own distinctive problem. The controlling considerations include the types of relationships existing between the various social needs and its own corporate goals and objectives. A second consideration is the level of resources of the corporation. The proper response will then need to be evaluated by the particular corporate management in terms of its own management approach. We can, however, identify the types of programs typically available. These programs can conveniently be grouped as between those that are internal in nature and those that are external—recognizing always, however, that there is unavoidable overlap.

Internal Programs. A corporate management that is seeking to properly discharge its social responsibilities will have a number of ways in which this can be done within the corporation itself. These include:

1. *Consideration in All Ongoing Managerial Decisions.* All business decisions, both in the areas of policy and implementing action, have components that involve various types of social responsibility. What is needed therefore is to provide continuing consideration of those components in the decision process. Especially illustrative would be decisions relating to new facilities where consideration is needed of possibilities of reducing socially undesirable features such as noise, pollution, and accidents.

2. *Special Research for New Approaches.* Back of ongoing day-to-day decisions just described are also the possibilities of special research efforts to minimize or eliminate undesirable features. Illustrative would be the research efforts of the automotive industry to reduce the impact of engine exhausts. Here there are both the possible direct benefits and the better demonstration to the public of the sincerity of efforts being made.

3. *Special Training.* Many opportunities exist whereby corporations can train needed workers and at the same time reduce the social impact of the numbers of the disadvantaged that cannot otherwise qualify. Illustrative programs would be for drug addicts, alcoholics, and other persons lacking basic needed skills.

4. *Incorporation in Management Policies.* To a major extent a business corporation can augment its social role by incorporating such intentions in its public statements and internal policies and procedures. Social-responsibility-oriented plans can also be incorporated in the determination of desired managerial objectives at all lower organizational levels. This coverage then needs to be actively supported by all levels of management and to be made visible to the general public.

5. *Assignment as a Specific Organizational Responsibility.* Another way in which the corporation can better ensure the needed action relating to social responsibility is to set up a special department or responsible officer to devote full time to studying and providing direction in this area. This officer would be charged with the responsibility of constantly reviewing all pertinent outside developments, maintaining liaison with people active

in this area, preparing plans for effectively dealing with the existing problems, and working with those people charged with the responsibilities of actual implementation. This approach better assures proper attention to social responsibility developments.

External Programs.   The second group of action programs focus more directly on people outside the corporation itself. These types of action include:

1. *Giving Money.* Perhaps the easiest way of supporting social causes and needs is to contribute funds directly to groups that are, directly or indirectly, serving various social needs. Such financial support can be on a one-time basis or as part of a continuing program. The fact remains, however, that the decisions as to the cause to be supported, the amounts, and the timing of contributions should be based on informed judgments.

2. *Assistance and Counsel.* In many situations business corporations can make officers and employees available in various ways to provide advice and counsel to worthy social causes and to the organizations directly involved. In some cases the corporation can provide individuals to directly manage such socially oriented activities for limited periods of time. Employees can also be encouraged to engage in such activities in a private capacity.

3. *Profit-Based Involvement.* To an increasing extent there are opportunities for business corporations to become involved in socially oriented actvities on a profit basis. In this way the corporation takes on particular jobs and uses its own managerial skills as a substitute for a governmental or institutional group that would otherwise do that job. Examples include, building public facilities, running training programs, and actually operating institutional units. Although profit margins may be fixed at below-normal levels, tbere is still presumably compensation to the business corporation that includes a reasonable profit.

4. *Working with Government.* An especially potentially rewarding type of action is to work directly with government. The assistance here can pertain to the shaping of particular legislation and related regulations. It can also pertain to the ongoing administration of those laws and regulations. To a considerable extent the relationship with government has been that of an adversary. A more enlightened view, however, is to better understand the problems faced by government and to help so that resulting legislation and regulatory efforts will be more sound and effective. What is needed here is a better appreciation on the part of both government and business of their underlying common interests and a more vigorous effort to work together as partners to achieve those common interests.

5. *Effective Communication to Outsiders.* In the last analysis it is the outside public that in various ways is discharging the multiple role of being corporate customers, investors, sources of legislation, and participants in all existing social problems. It follows therefore that there is a major need

for the business corporation to help that outside public to better discharge
its multiple responsibilities. Especially important to the business corporation is to help the public to better understand the impact on business—and in turn thereby on the society itself—of various types of actions
in response to asserted social needs. The challenge here is to make the
voice of business heard and to do it in a way that is both sound and
credible to the public. In part this is the problem of having an effective
public relations department, but it is also the problem of all corporate
managers.

Special Problems of Implementing Social Responsibility Programs

Earlier in this chapter we reviewed the range of problems associated with
satisfying social responsibilities. These problems are again directly applicable
to the total process of implementing social programs. This coverage of problems
needs, however, to be further extended for application to the implementation
area:

1. *Internal Resistance*. We have previously noted the wide range of values
   and views relating to the various social responsibilities—including much
   emotional content. It is inevitable therefore that subordinates will often
   feel quite differently about decisions made by higher-level managers in
   this area. In many cases the socially oriented actions will be seen as being
   directly at odds with their own views. Although this resistance can never
   be fully overcome, the understanding of its existence will result in a
   better effort to administer the implementation in the proper manner.
2. *Lack of True Management Support*. A related aspect of the problem is
   that higher-level managers—even those at the very top—may give official
   support to the legitimacy of social responsibility policies and procedures,
   but then not really support them. When their subordinates—already
   often at odds with the policies involved—detect that lack of real dedication, the forces for effective implementation are immediately undermined. The need here is for better understanding at all levels, coupled
   with better communication.
3. *Confusion with Regular Reward System*. The traditional reward system
   in the corporation has been based on elements of volume, cost, revenue,
   and profitability. Typically, however, the injection of social responsibility
   considerations conflicts to some extent with those long-accepted standards. What we then have is a combination of differing measures of
   performance, and under conditions where the impact of the social responsibility aspects is unavoidably very intangible. Under these circumstances the evaluation of performance and the determination of related
   rewards becomes more and more difficult. This is especially true when
   the merits of the social responsibility objectives were already controversial. In total this difficulty can often significantly undermine an effective
   implementation of social responsibility programs.

Role of the Internal Auditor

The existence of a major concern of management sets the stage for a similar concern on the part of the internal auditor. In more practical terms, what can the internal auditor do specifically to assist management with this major problem? The available types of assistance include:

1. *Basic Operational Auditing Activities.* Since, as we have seen, the basic objectives of managerial efficiency are also a way to provide better services to society, it follows that the total operational auditing activity of the internal auditor is similarly directly beneficial. The identification of every possible opportunity to expand sources of revenue and to reduce costs are specifically applicable. At the same time the internal auditor can expand his audit program to cover specifically appropriate operational aspects relating to significant social responsibility programs.

2. *Reporting on Consumer Interests.* Similarly, the normal range of operational auditing activities provides the opportunity to identify problem areas in protecting customer/consumer interests. Illustrative would be the observation of promotional programs in action, the review of sales activities, the exposure to customer responses (as in the case of receivable confirmations) and the review of warranty programs. In many other instances the operational auditing will include customer contact surveys. In all these situations the internal auditor can be alert to the levels of customer satisfaction, and be able to report on them.

3. *Legal Compliance.* Compliance with legal requirements has always been a part of the internal auditor's interests. These legal requirements now also include compliance with socially oriented legislation such as fair employment practices, minimum pollution standards, and the like. The compliance evaluation can also in all cases be expanded to cover the broader spirit of effective compliance.

4. *Reporting on Public Opinion.* The internal auditor while carrying out his normal operational auditing activities can learn much about existing public opinion, and its indicated trends. In some cases also the internal auditor can take on direct assignments in this area.

5. *Citizen Responsibilities.* The internal auditor has a number of excellent opportunities in the area of citizenship responsibilities. In many cases internal auditing services can be made available directly to local philanthropic or public groups. Thus an operational audit of the community hospital can be a positive expression of direct citizenship service by the company. The internal auditor himself as an individual can also do a great deal in his own private life.

6. *Direct Review of Organized Efforts.* Where a corporation has set up a special department or office to deal with social-type problems, the review of the operations of that organizational component can be a normal extension of the regular internal auditing effort. Similarly, the internal auditor can review the progress and/or final results of particular programs.

7. *Social Audit*. A social audit can be made in the form of a complete evaluation of the organization's various social responsibilities and what has been done toward dealing with those responsibilities.

In summary, the internal auditor has the opportunity to serve management in the various areas pertaining to social responsibility first, by doing his regular internal auditing in an effective manner; second, by being alert to special aspects that pertain to the particular dimension of social responsibility; and third, by making specific reviews of activities and programs of a social responsibility nature. The independence of the internal auditor, combined with his special analytical skills, provide a major opportunity to render important assistance in this new critical area of management concern. Hopefully also, the internal auditor can make some contribution in the development of the newer approaches such as social accounting and the social audit.

AUDIT GUIDES

Social Responsibility Activities

I. Introductory

   A. Reference should be made to the general discussion of audit guides, Chapter 13.

   B. The nature and scope of audit programs relating to social responsibility activities will necessarily depend on the type of assignment. These assignments will be generally of the following type:
   1. A special assignment.
   2. The review of the operations of an office set up for social responsibility purposes.
   3. The review of a particular social action project.
   4. The coverage of social responsibility issues in other audit assignments.

II. Preparatory Activities

   A. See standard Audit Guides, Chapter 13.

   B. The preparatory activities will depend directly on the scope of the assignment. The standard guides will be most applicable when a social responsibility office and its related program are being reviewed.

III. Organizational Factors

   A. See standard Audit Guides, Chapter 13.

   B. Because of the relative newness of a definitive social responsibility program, the definition of the mission and the related organizational status will normally not be clear. Hence a special effort may be needed to probe for further clarification.

IV. Operational Aspects

   A. The Social Responsibility Office

1. What are the current plans? How comprehensive are they?
2. What has been accomplished to date? How effective have been the results? What has been learned?
3. What provision has been made for keeping informed as to developments on the outside—legislation, specific critics, organizational action groups, and general public opinion?
4. How adequate is the internal coordination?
   a. With top management?
   b. With other company activities?
5. Is there adequate qualified staff?
6. How adequate is the budget?
7. Is there a satisfactory reporting program?
8. How sound is the total program?
   a. What major problems exist, and what can be done about them?
   b. What major opportunities exist, and how can these opportunities best be exploited?

B. Specific Social Responsibility Projects
   1. How did the project originate?
   2. Appraise the adequacy of the planning.
   3. Was an adequate budget provided?
   4. What has been accomplished thus far? Are these results satisfactory? If not, why not?
   5. What can be expected in the way of costs to complete the project? How sound are these estimates?
   6. Is management receiving proper information and being given the opportunity to evaluate future action?
   7. What is the overall appraisal of the project?
      a. As to concept?
      b. As to performance?

C. Coverage in Other Reviews
   1. The major approach will be that the internal auditor is continuously alert to how all aspects of the operational activities being reviewed relate to the previously mentioned social responsibility issues. These include:
      a. Impact on customer.
      b. Legal compliance.
      c. Standards and practices that will not bear public scrutiny.
      d. Opportunities for more positive contribution.
   2. The second approach can be through a specific overall appraisal of the previously mentioned social responsibility issues as a part of the completion of each review.

V–IX. Not used.

X. Overall Appraisal of Social Responsibility Activities
   A. See standard Audit Guides, Chapter 13.

BUSINESS ETHICS ACTIVITIES

Nature and Scope of Business Ethics[2]

The term "business ethics," like the broader "social needs and responsibilities," covers matters for which again there is no common agreement. It starts, however, with the implicit assumption that there are sufficiently identifiable sound ethics for human conduct that can serve as standards. Therefore, ethical action by corporations and corporate managers can, to that extent, be measured and evaluated. Although that ethical action is directly rewarding to corporate people as good and desirable in its own right, there has been at the same time increasing social pressures on corporations for higher-level ethical action. These pressures focus typically on such aspects as honesty, fairness, integrity, reliability, and legality. The Foreign Corrupt Practices Act of 1977, discussed in Chapters 1 and 6, was itself a direct response to the widespread pressures for higher levels of business ethics. The more directly focused ethical considerations therefore merge into the broader framework of social needs and social responsibilities. Business ethics, however, does have a more definitive and directly operational character in terms of corporate welfare, and therefore deserves more definitive recognition and further elaboration.

Sources of Business Ethics Standards

The common bond between all aspects of business ethics is that it is the "right" thing to do. In part the measure of that rightness is the law and in part basic morality. Its roots are in broader social ethics but it has particular application in business and must be compatible with the long-range interests of the effective business operations. This total rightness in a business environment applies to all types of business activities, all of which are closely interrelated. It will be convenient, however, to focus more directly on the two major areas that involve especially significant problems.

Compliance with Law.   In the various sectors—federal, state, and municipalities—the people, through their directly or indirectly elected representatives, have defined how various types of business activities should be conducted. It is therefore appropriate that compliance with that existing law—and as further supplemented by the responsible regulatory agencies and interpreted by the courts—should be a major standard for the evaluation of business ethics. The law as here defined includes first, the specific requirements of that law. The obligation goes further, however, to include the intentions of the legislators, as far as those intentions can be reasonably interpreted. This broader coverage is often referred to as involving both *the letter and the spirit* of the legal enactments.

[2]This section draws heavily upon the "Statement of Business Ethics" prepared by J.C. Penney Company, Inc.

As a practical matter it must be recognized that laws represent a judgment of the people through its representatives. It is inevitable, therefore, that the soundness of specific laws will be viewed differently by different people—and in turn by different corporate managers. In that connection there may well also be continuing efforts to amend existing law. In the meantime, however, there is an obligation to conform to existing law. That existing law is the basis therefore for judging ethical business practice.

An excellent treatment of compliance with law, contained in a Statement of Business Ethics by the J.C. Penney Company to its officers and employees, and indirectly to all outsiders who deal with or are interested in the corporation, is shown in Exhibit 24.1.

Compliance with Other Criteria. Although the aforementioned law covers a large portion of business activities, it does not go far enough. Further coverage and input is provided from such sources as religion, philosophy, and the experience of many people over long periods of time. In the Western world, to a considerable extent, there are also the principles of Christianity as interpreted and tempered by the business environment. Similarly, there are the principles from other religions. As a result we have many basic concepts and guidelines as to what is right and wrong. Again there can be much variation as to how different individuals will make such determinations, especially as to how we evaluate supporting actions in particular situations. The fact remains, however, that such guidelines do exist to a major extent and that there is much common agreement about them. In this connection the J.C. Penney statement begins appropriately with a reference to the foundation of morality—the Golden Rule—that individuals should "do unto others as you would have them do unto you." Although we cannot be specific in this area as we would like to be, these other nonlegal standards provide a major basis for guiding us in the area of business ethics. These guidelines need to be made visible and interpreted for all corporate managers and employees.

Equating Personal and Organizational Interests

The compliance with law and with other criteria just discussed are component sources of business ethics standards by which ethical behavior is evaluated, and at the same time problem areas in terms of administering the total business ethics effort. A further problem area has to do with the operational application of all business ethics standards. What is now involved is how individuals in the corporation balance their own personal interests in relation to the broader interests of the total organization of which they are a part. This balancing and reconciliation is at the heart of all operational actions and for all related conduct. It has two major subcomponents, the first of which involves so-called questions of conflict of interest and the second, which involves the closely related determination of when corporate resources are improperly diverted for personal advantage. We look first at the area of conflict of interest.

EXHIBIT 24.1. Types of Legal Compliance

1. Maintenance of Books, Records and Accounts

The results of operations of our Company must be recorded in accordance with the requirement of law and generally accepted accounting principles. It is Company policy, as well as a requirement of law, to maintain books, records and accounts which, in reasonable detail, accurately and fairly reflect the business transactions and disposition of assets of the Company. In order to carry out this policy and assure compliance with applicable laws, no Associate should take, or permit to be taken, any action in a manner whereby the Company's books, records and accounts would not accurately, fairly and completely reflect the action taken. No false or misleading entries should be made in any books or records of the Company for any reason, and no fund, asset or account of the Company may be established or acquired for any purpose unless such fund, asset or account is accurately reflected in the books and records of the Company. No corporate funds or assets should be used for any unlawful purpose.

2. Antitrust

Broadly speaking, the antitrust laws regulate the competitive conduct and dealings of business. Penalties for violation can lead to extremely serious consequences for both the Company and the individuals involved. A complete description of the antitrust laws is beyond the scope of this document. However, it should be noted that any activity with a competitor or supplier in restraint of trade, such as price fixing, is illegal. Such activities with suppliers as discriminatory pricing, terms, promotional allowances, services and facilities may violate the antitrust laws. This does not mean, of course, that we cannot and should not negotiate hard in all areas with our suppliers.

3. Product Safety

Products sold by the Company must not only meet all applicable safety standards set by law, they must also meet our often more stringent Company standards. It is Company policy not to handle knowingly any defective product and to minimize as much as possible hazards from products which inherently entail some risks. The reputation and success of our Company has been built upon the performance of our products. Our customers have a right to expect that our products will not endanger their health or safety in any way.

4. Advertising

Advertising used by the Company is legally required to be true and not deceptive in any manner. All product claims must be substantiated by supporting data before they are made. We must be careful to assure that the Penney customer is not disappointed by claims for our products which are not supported by performance. The purpose of our advertising has always been to emphasize the quality of our products and the fairness of our prices. We believe that a properly informed customer will be a loyal Penney customer.

5. Political Activities

The impact of government on business in our society continues to grow. The Company and its Associates have a legitimate interest in the composition of our state, local and federal governments and in the laws which prescribe the ways in which business should be conducted. This is, however, an extremely sensitive area. There are laws on the

EXHIBIT 24.1. *(Continued)*

federal, state and local levels which govern the involvement of the Company and its Associates in political activities. Corporate payments of cash, merchandise or service in connection with political activities are generally either illegal or strictly regulated by law. Examples of political activities include the support of, or opposition to, candidates for public office; contributions in support of, or opposition to, initiatives or referenda; and contributions, gifts or honoraria to government officials. All proposed payments or donations or services must be reviewed in advance and approved in writing by the designated representatives of the Government Relations Department and the Legal Department. Failure to obtain the requisite approvals can lead to serious embarrassment and problems for the Company and its Associates.

6. Securities Laws

The securities laws and the rules of the securities exchanges affect a wide variety of the Company's activities. No Associate may engage in, or permit any other Associate to engage in, any activity on behalf of the Company which he or she knows, or reasonably should know, is prohibited by the securities laws. Examples include the following: No false, misleading or deceptive statements may be made in connection with the purchase or sale of any security or in any report filed with the Securities and Exchange Commission, or distributed to any financial analyst or stockholder. Improper or premature disclosure of confidential information to outsiders or Associates who do not require the information to perform their jobs must be avoided. In addition, no Associate may trade in securities of the Company when he or she has knowledge of material events affecting the Company which have not been made public.

7. Personnel Related Laws

The Company's business operations, as they relate to Penney Associates (their wages, hours, working conditions and other terms and conditions of employment) will reflect the importance the Company places on fair and equitable treatment of all Associates and will conform in every respect to federal, state and local laws.

The employment relationship is increasingly controlled and regulated by legal requirements. For example, laws such as the Age Discrimination Act, the Civil Rights Act, the Equal Pay Act, the Fair Credit Reporting Act, the Fair Labor Standards Act (Wage/Hour), the National Labor Relations Act and a variety of similar state acts cover all or nearly all aspects of the employment relationship. Violations of these laws can result in corporate and individual liability. It's not possible in this statement to list all the laws which apply, or to furnish specific guidance. Such guidance is provided in the Digest of Personnel laws which should be supplemented, as required, by the Regional Personnel Relations Attorneys, Division Personnel Relations Attorneys or Corporate Personnel Relations in the New York Office, as apropriate.

Conflict of Interest.   At the heart of all situations involving conflict of interest is the fact or possibility that decisions and actions in behalf of the organization are somehow influenced by considerations of serving personal self-interest. For example, if the officer responsible for purchasing in his corporation awards a contract to a firm in which he has an ownership interest, there is the fact or possibility that this procurement decision was influenced by his own self-interest. In such a situation the existence of the appearance of dual interest—and hence conflict of interest between the corporate and his own personal interests—is enough to condemn the arrangement. In this kind of a situation it is the *possibility* as well as the fact that is wrong. That is, the contractual award may well have been the best available alternative for the corporation, but the existence of the possibility of the compromising of corporate interest is again enough to condemn the particular relationship. In this situation the lack of propriety goes still deeper, to condemn the purchasing agent for even having a personal interest in a company that produces or controls products normally procured by either his employer or competitive companies.[3]

The coverage of conflict of interest in the J.C. Penney statement is again illustrative, as shown in Exhibit 24.2.

Preservation of Company Assets. The problems of equating personal and organizational interests also include a related but somewhat different type of situation. What is involved here is the fact that assets of the organization exist for the benefit of the organization and should therefore not be used in any way for the unauthorized personal enrichment of the individual. The principle thus stated sounds very clear. In practice, however, the problem is more complicated. The use of the company asset may in fact affect the corporate interest very slightly, or perhaps not at all. Or the use by the individual may somehow also be in the longer-range company interest. The problem is further complicated by the effect that the improper, or at least questionable, use may have on other persons—including fellow employees, suppliers, customers, and other outsiders. In all these connections there are two basic requirements. The first of these requirements is that the organization clearly define its intentions in policies and procedures. The second is that the employee acquaint himself with those guidelines and requirements and exercise careful judgment in their application.

A good example of this problem is an individual's use of an assigned company car. In such a situation there is first, the need for clarification by the company of the extent of the privilege and the conditions of the use of the company vehicle. This clarification is needed not only for the actual user of the vehicle, but for all other parties who are either legitimately interested or who will otherwise be aware of the situation and be evaluating it. The individual is then obligated to conform to the established rules and guidelines. The obligation here also extends to aspects not technically covered but reasonably implicit—as, for example, care of the vehicle as if it were his own or by the reasonable standards with which he should be caring for his own property.

---

[3]Admittedly, the extent of that interest could be so small that as a practical manner it did not generate real conflict of interest. However, defining that "extent" is itself controversial and hence it is better to avoid any conflicting interest of any kind.

EXHIBIT 24.2. Types of Conflict of Interest

1. Gifts, Loans, Entertainment

Commercial bribery is illegal and the payment or receipt of any business-related bribe is prohibited. An Associate should not, directly or indirectly, accept gifts of cash or anything else of value from anyone having or seeking business with the Company, other than non-cash gifts of nominal value generally used for promotional purposes by the donor.

Participation in business related functions, including the acceptance of lunches or other meals on occasion, is a normal and permissible business practice. However, care must be exercised to ensure that they are necessary and that their value and frequency are not excessive under all the applicable circumstances.

Other forms of entertainment or "outings" such as dinners, theatre tickets, golf dates, fishing or hunting trips, may be accepted only if it is practicable for the Associate to reciprocate at an appropriate time. In those cases where reciprocation does not seem possible, but the Associate believes it is in the Company's interest to attend, he should get the agreement of appropriate supervisory personnel such as a unit manager or department head.

Associates should not accept loans from any persons or entities having or seeking business with the Company except recognized financial institutions at normal interest rates prevailing at the time of borrowing. In discussing personal financing with banks, no Associate should state or imply that the bank's response will in any way affect its relationship with the Company. The Company's business relationships with financial institutions are not to be considered to influence in any way personal loans to Company Associates.

In summary, nothing should be accepted which could impair, or appear to impair, an Associate's ability to perform his or her Company duties or to exercise his or her judgment in a fair and unbiased manner. A divided loyalty will invariably create serious problems for the Company and its Associates.

Examples of situations that might be encountered by Penney Associates are presented here to help clarify the Conflicts of Interest Statement and its applications.*

2. Interest in Other Businesses and Organizations

An Associate should not have any direct or indirect interest in, or relationship to, any transaction to which the Company is or will be a party if such interest or relationship might influence, or appear to influence, that Associate in the performance of Company duties. Associates should not have any interest, financial or otherwise, in any competitor or supplier of the Company, which could influence the Associate's objectivity or independence of judgment in performing his or her duties or could otherwise create a conflict of interest.

2A. Interest in Competitors

A competitor of the Company is any organization which sells goods or services similar to any of those offered for sale by the Company. An Associate should not have any direct or indirect interest in, or relationship with, any competitor of the Company if such interest or relationship might influence, or appear to influence, that person in the performance of his or her Company duties.

*The examples are not reproduced in this book.

EXHIBIT 24.2. *(Continued)*

2B. Interest in Suppliers

A supplier is one who furnishes or offers to furnish goods or services of any kind to the Company. It is Company policy to select a supplier solely on the basis of price, quality and performance. An Associate must avoid financial or other involvement with a supplier with whom he or she does or is likely to do business. Such involvement might appear to cause the Associate to select a supplier for reasons other than price, quality and performance.

3. Indirect Interests and Relationships

Direct interests and relationships of Associates have been described and illustrated in the preceding pages. With respect to indirect interests and relationships, there are three general rules to follow. First, an Associate should not be in a position to make or influence a decision relating to the Company's engaging in business with a relative of the Associate. Second, an Associate should not be in a position to derive an indirect benefit from a Company transaction involving a relative. Third, an Associate should disclose any situation in which a relative has an interest in a competitor or in any Company transaction. For these purposes, "relative" should be construed to include the Associate's spouse and any relative who resides with the Associate. When other relatives are involved—including sons and daughters and their spouses; parents; brothers and sisters and their spouses; and other "in-laws"—Associates should protect themselves against the appearance of a conflict by reporting the situation to their supervisors.

4. Use of Company Information

An Associate should not use for personal benefit information concerning any aspect of the Company's business or information acquired as a result of his or her relationship with the Company. Moreover, such information should not be disclosed to any other person or entity except as required in the performance of Company duties or as expressly authorized by the Company. An Associate can be held liable to the Company for any benefit gained from improper use of such information or any damages·sustained by the Company as a result of improper disclosure of such information.

5. Diversion of Corporate Opportunity

An Associate should not appropriate to him or herself, nor divert to any other person or entity, a business or financial opportunity which the Associate knows, or reasonably could anticipate, the Company would have an interest in pursuing.

6. Holding Public Office

The Company encourages Associates to become involved in the political process. However, in the case of an Associate holding public office, whether elective or appointive, the potential for conflict of interest, or the appearance of conflict, must be taken into account as in the following examples.

Implementing the Business Ethics Program

With a better understanding now of the nature and scope of sound and comprehensive business ethics, it will be useful to review the components of an effective implementation program. We suggest the following:

1. The starting point is clearly the understanding of the business ethics problem by top management and the dedication by top management to achieving high-level standards.

2. This commitment then needs to be expressed in comprehensive and clearly stated policies, including adequate explanations of the underlying rationale for corporate welfare.

3. These policies then need to be properly supplemented by procedures covering the application of the policies to the operations of the particular company.

4. In developing the aforementioned policies and procedures, everyone should be involved to the extent practicable so that all problems can be given fair consideration and that all persons directly or indirectly involved have an opportunity to present their views.

5. Provision should be made for dealing with the many problems and questions that arise in the ongoing day-to-day operations. Such questions should be invited and dealt with promptly.

6. Every means should be utilized by top management both initially and during the ongoing operations to demonstrate the importance attached to the program by top management and the dedication to high standards. In turn, each corporate manager has the responsibility to demonstrate that support to his subordinates.

7. There should be a periodic systematic sign-off by all parties involved as to the adequacy of compliance with the program. (Exhibit 24.3 from the J.C. Penney program is illustrative.)

8. Appropriate audit coverage should be sought by top management and provided by the internal auditors.

Special Problems of an Effective Business Ethics Program

Although the principles of sound business ethics and the components of effective implementation can be stated with reasonable clarity, the fact remains that there are especially difficult obstacles to achieving the total desired results. Many of these obstacles have their common roots in the way different individuals view business ethics. The problem here is essentially the varying way different individuals view their own self-interest in relation to the interests of others—including the organization of which they are a part. These views are ingrained in each individual depending on overall character and levels of morals, but at all times are subject to changing influences and to ever-existing human frailties. Often also, these individual determinations are viewed as being per-

EXHIBIT 24.3. Certificate of Compliance

Certificate
of Compliance

All JCPenney management associates (and those non-management associates designated by their unit managers or department heads as being in sensitive positions) are required to fill out and sign this Certificate of Compliance. In the event you are not now in compliance, or are not certain, you should discuss the matter with your unit manager or department head and attach a memorandum to your certificate explaining the situation.

I certify that I have received and read the booklet setting forth the Statement of Business Ethics of JCPenney Company, Inc. and that as of this date I am in compliance, and will continue to comply, with the policies set forth in the booklet, except to the extent described in the attached memorandum of exceptions.

Signature: _____ Date: _____

Please print or type name, department or other area of responsibility, and unit number.

Name: _____

Department: _____

Unit Number: _____

Social Security Number: _____

☐ I have attached a memorandum of exceptions to this Certificate.

sonal and private. There is therefore often conscious and unconscious resistance to accepting rules and guidelines imposed by the organization. The fact that the concepts imposed are themselves often soft and intangible makes the problem even more difficult. We do not know how all of these problems should always be best dealt with, but we can be conscious of the existing problems and therefore use special care in dealing with them.

There is, in addition, however, another type of difficulty in achieving the desired corporate results. The difficulties here—much like we found when discussing social responsibilities—have to do with the conflict often inherent with the established corporate reward system. Typically in the organization, the rewards for individuals are based on well-identified measures such as number and quality of products produced, markets developed, sales, profitability, and the like. On the other hand, business ethics objectives are more often difficult to measure and at times in direct conflict. Illustrative is the offering of a payment or other gratuity to a foreign government official to obtain a needed regulatory approval—a course of action all the more attractive when there is no available alternative in terms of local practice and where competitive companies from other countries have no legal or higher-level policy constraints. This conflict is also all the more difficult when officers at higher intermediate levels give lip service to compliance with business ethics standards but in reality, in their own self-interest, press for the related operational results. Again these problems are manageable, but they do present continuing special difficulties and we need to be eternally alert to their possibilities.

Internal Auditor's Business Ethics Role

Again, as in the case of social responsibilities, the existence of this major concern of management sets the stage for a similar concern on the part of the internal auditor. The opportunities in the business ethics area are, however, still greater because of the fact that sound business ethics are to a major extent at the heart of all operational activities. The range of the services that can be rendered by the internal auditor can be outlined, as follows:

1. *Basic Operational Auditing Activities.* Since the standards of sound business ethics are a part of all operational activities, it follows that these same standards are properly a part of every review and appraisal activity of internal auditors. That business ethics oriented coverage, however, needs continuously to be kept specifically in mind. Specific coverage can also be included in individual audit programs to the extent appropriate.

2. *Legal Compliance.* In many instances the business ethics requirements have been covered by specific legislation. In these cases there is a further responsibility to review and appraise compliance with such legal requirements.

3. *Direct Review of Business Ethics Programs.* In those situations when the organization has set up a special organizational arrangement to develop and administer a business ethics program, such an organizational arrangement needs to be periodically directly reviewed and appraised like any other organizational activity. In some cases—as it also is in the J.C. Penney program—the head of the internal auditing department is himself directly named in the assigned organizational responsibility and is a participant in its overall administration.

4. *Spearheading Business Ethics Consciousness.* In addition to all of the foregoing types of service, the lack of existence in an organization of a definitive business ethics program provides an excellent opportunity for

the internal auditor to help initiate the development of an adequate program. Typically, the action will take the form of discussing the need with top management and obtaining their agreement and support for a more formal and extensive organizational study effort.

5. *Review of Status of Business Ethics.* The internal auditor may be directly assigned the responsibility of making a complete review of the organization's problems in the business ethics area and an evaluation of what has been done in the way of dealing with those problems.

AUDIT GUIDES

BUSINESS ETHICS ACTIVITIES

I. Introductory

   A. Reference should be made to the general discussion of audit guides, Chapter 13.

   B. The nature and scope of audit programs relating to business ethics activities will generally be of the following type:

      1. A special assignment.

      2. The review of the organizational activities being carried out pursuant to a specially assigned organizational activity—as, for example, a particular office, committee, or individual.

      3. The review of a particular activity relating to business ethics compliance.

      4. The coverage of business ethics considerations in other audit arrangements.

II. Preparatory Activities

   A. See standard Audit Guides, Chapter 13.

   B. The preparatory activities will depend directly on the scope of the assignment. The standard guides will be most applicable when a business ethics office and its related program are being reviewed.

III. Organizational Factors

   A. See standard Audit Guides, Chapter 13.

   B. Because of the all-inclusive character of business ethics responsibilities, the definition of mission and the related organizational status will normally not be clear. Hence a special effort may be needed to probe for such further clarification.

IV. Operational Aspects

   A. Business Ethics Organizational Assignment

      1. What are the current plans? How comprehensive are they?

      2. What has been accomplished to date? How effective are the results? What has been learned?

3. What provision has been made for keeping informed as to developments on the outside—legislation, special critics, organizational
   action groups, and general public opinion?
4. How adequate is the internal coordination?
   a. With top management?
   b. With other company activities?
5. Is there adequate qualified staff?
6. How adequate is the budget?
7. Is there a satisfactory reporting program?
8. How sound is the total program?
   a. What major problems exist, and what can be done about them?
   b. What major opportunities exist, and how can these opportunities
      be best exploited?

B. Coverage in Other Reviews
   1. The major approach will be that the internal auditor is continuously
      alert to how all aspects of the operational activities being reviewed
      relate to previously mentioned business ethics issues. These include:
      a. Impact on the customer.
      b. Legal compliance.
      c. Standards and practices that will not bear public scrutiny.
      d. Opportunities for more positive contribution.
   2. The second approach can be through a specific overall appraisal of
      the previously mentioned business ethics issues as a part of the
      completion of each review.

V–IX. Not used.

X. Overall appraisal of Business Ethics Activities
   A. See standard Audit Guides, Chapter 13.

Social Responsibility and Business Ethics in Perspective

At the beginning of this chapter we recognized that social responsibility and
business ethics issues had common roots in social values and that the problems
were closely interrelated. We saw that in both cases they involved objectives
that were both directly rewarding and increasingly a needed part in achieving
corporate welfare. The more detailed coverage of each area we believe has
confirmed that total common character and the increasingly high level of corporate interest. Because of that higher level of corporate interest, the internal
auditor must have a better understanding of the combined problems and provide internal auditing services that adequately serve the needs of management.
Moreover, the predictions for the future indicate the further intensification of
all of those needs. What this means is that social responsibility and business
ethics activities represent a new challenge to the internal auditor and a new
high potential for organizational service.

ILLUSTRATIVE AUDIT FINDINGS: SOCIAL RESPONSIBILITIES AND BUSINESS ETHICS

Impact of Waste Disposal Practice

A divisional manufacturing plan was disposing of chemical waste in a nearby open pond area. The internal auditor noticed the concerns of the community as reported in the local press and alerted central office management to the need for both finding a waste deposal alternative and for recognizing the importance of reducing existing community hostility.

Conflicting Minority-Group Training Policies

Through a series of different field audits the auditor became aware of the wide range of company approaches to minority-group training programs—ranging from very effective to complete failures. Management was alerted to the need for a more consistent corporate effort and the resulting opportunity for building goodwill through informing the public of that effort.

Lower-Level Organizational Compliance

The corporation had developed comprehensive policies as to company participation in community social programs. However, in a divisional audit it was found that lower-level management was pressing for work efforts and profitability levels that precluded such participation. The central headquarters was alerted to the inadequate downward communication through the organization, and as a result the basis was laid for effective corrective action.

Needed Consolidation of Social Responsibility Activities

Through a series of divisional audits it was found that a number of major policies were being developed independently that involved considerable duplication of effort and potential conflict. As a result central headquarters was alerted to the need to provide better control direction. Action was subsequently taken to set up a new office to develop and monitor all corporate policies in the social responsibility areas.

Uncontrolled Use of Company Cars

It was found in an important divisional audit review that company cars were being used to a major extent for personal purposes—including vacations, school transportation for children, and shopping by wives—whereas company policies restricted such use to business purposes. Coverage in the audit laid the basis for needed reinforcement of management intent and more intensive compliance efforts.

Conflicting Procurement Interests

In an audit of purchasing, including review of procurement sources, it was found that the purchasing agent had a significant investment interest in one of the supplier firms. As a result of the disclosure the purchasing agent disposed of his investment interest and top management made clear its determination to eliminate all similar types of situations.

Improper Payments

The audit of disbursements disclosed significant payments that were not adequately explained. There was also considerable reluctance on the part of auditee personnel to produce supplementary information as to the propriety of those payments. As a result of the continuing probing it was ascertained that local officials were being paid to give preference treatment for needed governmental approvals relating to required quality standards. Appropriate corrective action was then taken by top management.

Excessive Gifts from Suppliers

The internal auditor was alerted by disgruntled employees to the fact that large and expensive gifts were periodically being received by certain personnel controlling various subcontracting and procurement decisions. As a result of the audit disclosure the corporate headquarters established a company-wide policy prohibiting such actions and disseminated that policy statement both to corporate employees and affected third parties.

CHAPTER TWENTY-FIVE

Integrated Operational Components and Mergers and Acquisitions

INTEGRATED OPERATIONAL AUDIT

Scope of Audit Reviews

The scope of the individual audit review can vary widely. At one end of the spectrum it can deal with a single question raised by management or initiated by the internal audit group. Such a single question might be relatively simple—as, for example, ascertaining the validity of a particular document—or more complex, as would be the case of probing the origin of a fraud development. In other cases the review can deal with a functional activity such as purchasing, or perhaps a particular type of purchasing activity. In such a situation the review might deal with the activity on a company-wide basis, or only with a particular part of the total company function. In still other cases the review will deal with the total activities of a given organizational component, or group of components. Here the operational activities of that organizational component might involve a number of functional responsibilities. This involvement could in some cases be so broad as to represent an integrated situation like a relatively independent operating division or subsidiary company. This is also the kind of situation that exists when a new company is being examined as a possible candidate for acquisition or merger.

Nature of the Integrated Audit

Since the integrated audit in its most complete sense deals with the complete span of operational activities of a self-sufficient company or other broadly based operational unit, the review is a composite of everything that has been said in the preceding discussion of the various operational areas. Whatever may be said here will, therefore, tend to be repetitive of our other discussions. At the same time, however, the integrated audit provides a good opportunity to view the total operations as a whole and to pull together the key operational issues.

The resulting integration also identifies more clearly the total management interest that has been a part of our necessarily more fragmented coverage of individual operational activities. All of this suggests that the development of some separate audit guides for the integrated audit will be useful. The development of such audit guides also provides an opportunity to provide some additional coverage of the historical background of the operational entity being reviewed. It also provides a good opportunity to focus in a more definitive manner on the entity's future prospects.

AUDIT GUIDES

INTEGRATED OPERATIONAL AUDIT

I. Introductory
   A. Reference should be made to the general discussion of audit guides, Chapter 13.
   B. The scope of the operational activities will determine the extent to which the audit guides subsequently outlined can be used.

II. Preparatory Activities
   A. See standard Audit Guides, Chapter 13.
   B. Preparatory activities will be tailored to the size, importance, and scope of operational activities carried on by the entity to be reviewed.

III. Organizational Factors
   A. See standard Audit Guides, Chapter 13.
   B. Organizational factors will again depend directly on the nature and scope of the operational entity to be reviewed.

IV. Historical Background
   A. When was the company[1] first created, and under what conditions?
   B. What corporate changes have subsequently taken place in the way of major acquisitions, mergers, spin-offs, and the like?
   C. What has been the financial record of the company, in terms of profits and asset management, as reflected in the annual profit and loss statements and balance sheets?
   D. What have been the major sources of outside capital?
   E. What major changes in management have taken place over the historical life span?
   F. What have been the major types of capital expenditures, including types of plants, locations, and the like?

---

[1] For convenience the operational entity being reviewed will be referred to as "the company."

G. Describe the major product lines produced or handled.
   1. Types of products.
   2. Sources of supply.
   3. Major markets.
   4. Manner of distribution.
   5. Sales of individual product lines.
   6. Profits of product lines.

H. Who are the major competitors in the various product-line activities in such areas as:
   1. Size?
   2. Location?
   3. Nature of competition, in the following areas:
      a. Product features?
      b. Geographical areas?
      c. Types of customers?
      d. Service?

I. What is the nature and scope of governmental relationships:
   1. As a supplier to government?
   2. As to regulatory relationships?

J. What has been the experience with unions as to:
   1. History of unionization of company operations?
   2. Record of success in union relationships?

K. What have been the major organizational arrangements, as to:
   1. Organizational approaches?
   2. Major organizational changes?

V. Current Situation

   A. Scope of the Management System
      1. Planning
         a. Goals and objectives
            (1) Are they defined and expressed in writing?
            (2) Are they reasonably quantified? (For example, in terms of market penetrations, sales volume, profits, return on investment, and the like.)
            (3) Are they supported by adequate backup data?
            (4) Do subordinate levels of management participate adequately in their development?
            (5) Do they seem to be reasonable in terms of the company's resources, the competition, and other environmental factors?
            (6) Do they provide for reasonable task incentives?
            (7) Is there provision for periodic reappraisal?
         b. Major policies and strategies
            (1) Is the master strategy reasonable in relation to resources, environmental factors, and established goals and objectives?

  (2) Are functional policies and strategies supportive of the master strategy? Apply this test in the major functional areas:

   (a) Marketing?

   (b) Production?

   (c) Personnel?

   (d) Organizational?

   (e) Finance?

  (3) Are policies and strategies periodically reviewed and reappraised?

 c. Supporting operational plans

  (1) What is the scope of supporting plans—budgets and longer-range profit plans?

  (2) What is the manner of development:

   (a) As to established time schedule?

   (b) Participation of lower-level managers?

   (c) Adequacy of review?

   (d) Final resolution on a basis mutually acceptable to those charged with performance and their superiors?

  (3) How adequate are the supporting project plans:

   (a) As to backup detail?

   (b) As to timing of accomplishment?

  (4) How adequate is the provision for periodic review and modification?

 d. Supporting manuals and procedures

  (1) Are they sufficiently detailed?

  (2) What is the level of clarity?

  (3) How adequate is the dissemination and availability?

  (4) What provision has been made for continuing study?

  (5) Are there adequate provisions for updating and revision?

2. Organizing

 a. Development of organization charts

  (1) Are they based on a reasonable total approach?

  (2) With grouping of activities that need to be integrated?

  (3) In adequate detail?

  (4) With adequate dissemination to parties who need to be informed?

  (5) With proper provision for updating?

 b. Adequacy of treatment of particular organizational issues, as to:

  (1) Whether organizational status is sufficiently high in relation to importance of the individual activities?

  (2) Adequacy of balance between various internal activities?

  (3) Standardization of job titles?

  (4) Size and location of staff activities?

  (5) Size and location of service units?

(6) Avoiding confusion in reporting responsibilities and clarity
as to who is the superior of a particular subordinate?

(7) Use of committees to the extent helpful for coordinating but
without excessive dilution of individual responsibilities or
dilution of time?

(8) Effective use of project teams?

c. How adequate are the operational features relating to:

(1) Continuing study of needed organizational changes?

(2) Delegation in terms of clarity of job assignments, providing
of needed authority, and obtaining acceptance of obligations?

(3) Supervision that is reasonable without being excessive?

(4) Cooperative line–staff relationships, without undue domi-
nance by either party?

(5) Backup job descriptions which clearly define responsibilities
without confusion or overlapping with other organizational
assignments?

(6) Reasonable cross communication and coordination between
individuals at the various organizational levels without going
through formal organizational channels?

(7) Avoidance of shortcutting organizational levels, except in
emergency situations, and then in such circumstances to
advise all intervening parties as quickly as possible?

3. Staffing

a. How adequate is the organizational setup as to:

(1) Placement in the total organizational structure?

(2) Scope of responsibilities?

(3) Size and qualifications of staff?

b. How effective is the planning of company personnel needs, as
to:

(1) Projection of company personnel needs in relation to total
company operational plans?

(2) Compilation of current inventory of personnel?

(3) Identification of the gap between (a) and (b) above, and in
the development of plans to cover the deficiency?

c. Is there an adequate development of supporting personnel programs in such areas as:

(1) Recruitment policies and plans?

(2) Training programs for personnel development?

(3) Periodic personnel reviews as a basis for measuring development progress, and for assistance in resolving individual
problems?

(4) Review of eligible candidates at time job opportunities develop?

(5) Proper job ratings and salary ranges?

        (6) Sound compensation programs?

        (7) Competitive fringe benefit programs?

        (8) Provision for responding to grievance and counseling needs?

   d. Consideration of human factors

      (1) Is reasonable consideration being given to the needs of individuals:

        (a) In job assignments?

        (b) In administering subsequent relationships?

      (2) Are group needs adequately considered in such areas as:

        (a) Communication?

        (b) Working conditions?

        (c) Social needs?

4. Directing

   a. How adequate are the means of providing instructions to individuals with respect to:

      (1) Clarity?

      (2) Completeness?

      (3) Backup information?

   b. As to continuing coordination

      (1) How adequate is the formal reporting system with respect to:

        (a) Coverage of reports?

        (b) Proper distribution?

        (c) Availability of information when needed?

      (2) Is formal coordination adequate:

        (a) From boss to subordinate?

        (b) From subordinate to boss?

        (c) Lateral coordination?

   c. Excellence of leadership

      (1) Is a good "climate" being provided:

        (a) For free expression of views?

        (b) Avoiding undue fear of error?

        (c) In inducing mutual respect?

      (2) Is a good example being set by superiors for their subordinate (at all levels and especially at higher levels) as to:

        (a) Competence?

        (b) Objectivity?

        (c) Integrity?

5. Controlling

   a. As to standards

      (1) Extent to which standards are developed in all operational areas?

      (2) Care in development of standards as to:

        (a) Participation?

          (b) Fairness of task level in relation to knowledge of past and consideration of future expectations?

          (c) Measurability?

    b. How adequate is the measurement of performance against the standards with respect to:

      (1) Measurement in same terms as the standards?

      (2) Prompt and accurate reporting?

      (3) Dissemination of results first to those who are responsible?

    c. Is the analysis of performance deviations satisfactory with respect to:

      (1) Being on a timely basis?

      (2) Being done carefully and in a thorough manner?

      (3) Communication and understanding between boss and subordinate (versus mechanical type of follow-up)?

      (4) Care in formulation of comparable situation conclusions?

    d. Is the determination of appropriate action:

      (1) Sufficiently prompt?

      (2) Use of good judgment in evaluating causal factors?

      (3) Possible reappraisal of fairness of standards being used?

    e. In taking action:

      (1) Importance of being sure action is initiated?

      (2) Adequacy of follow-up to assure completed action?

    f. Miscellaneous

      (1) Completeness and adequacy of authorizations for approval role?

      (2) Adequacy of summary reporting controls?

      (3) Extent to which benefits derived from particular controls are sufficiently great to justify costs?

      (4) Extent of systematic feedback from persons who are users of company services?

B. Appraisal of Current Operational Results

  1. Is the level of profitability satisfactory in terms of:

    a. Adequacy of current profit performance in relation to industry experience:

      (1) As a percentage of return on investment?

      (2) As a percentage of sales?

    b. As to profit trends?

    c. Level of cost performance?

    d. Size of backlog of orders?

    e. Impact of forward contracts for sales and/or procurement?

    f. Competitive position?

  2. How satisfactory is the asset management in respect to:

    a. Adequacy of liquidity?

    b. The levels of asset commitments and efficiency in relation to comparable industry experience with respect to:

      (1) Cash?
      (2) Inventories?
      (3) Receivables?
      (4) Plant and equipment?
      (5) Research?
      (6) Capital costs?

3. How effective is the marketing effort with respect to:
   a. Whether current products are sufficiently competitive?
   b. Adequacy of product line coverage?
   c. Extent of market penetration being achieved?
   d. Strength of distributors?
   e. Effectiveness of advertising program?
   f. Consumer loyalty and acceptance?
   g. Product development status?
   h. Packaging appeal and related cost?
   i. Effectiveness of sales organization?

4. How should the company personnel be appraised in the three key areas?
   a. The management group
      (1) Number?
      (2) Depth backup?
      (3) Competence?
      (4) Age distribution?
      (5) Leadership qualities?
   b. Supporting white-collar personnel
      (1) Adequacy of numbers?
      (2) General competence?
      (3) Morale?
      (4) Adequacy of supply?
      (5) Extent of unionization, and if so, the existing degree of good relations?
   c. Production and service labor
      (1) Adequacy of numbers?
      (2) Coverage of needed skills?
      (3) Morale?
      (4) Extent of good union relationships?

5. How adequate is the research and development effort as to:
   a. Quality of personnel?
   b. Adequacy of overall effort?
   c. Worth of projects in process?

6. How should the various types of facilities be appraised:
   a. Production facilities
      (1) General adequacy?
      (2) Operating condition?
      (3) Levels of quality performance?

    b. Office facilities
        (1) General adequacy?
        (2) General appearance?
    7. How satisfactory is performance in other areas
        a. Adequacy of financial control system?
        b. Adequacy of scheduling controls?
        c. Overall order and efficiency?
        d. Indicated public relations image?
        e. Any special problems?

VI. Appraisal of Future Prospects
    This appraisal builds on the previous analysis but focuses on betterment
opportunities that potentially would be available if additional management
counsel and resource assistance were provided. The latter will include synergistic relationships with the reviewing company (if the operational unit is not
owned) or other components of the company (where already a part of the
company).

    A. Can the levels of investment in individual assets be reduced?
        1. Cash?
        2. Receivables?
        3. Inventories?
        4. Plant?
    B. Can resources be better utilized?
        1. Plant?
        2. Research organization?
        3. Other
    C. What are the expansion possibilities if capital is provided?
        1. Wider use of credit?
        2. Increased production capacity?
        3. More modern equipment?
        4. Expanded product development?
    D. Can personnel be improved?
        1. Better training and development?
        2. Recruitment of more qualified people?
        3. More up-to-date compensation plans?
        4. Better leadership?
    E. How can better general management be provided?
        1. A more capable top management group?
        2. Outside policy assistance and direction?
    F. What competitive potentials exist?
        1. Potential product opportunities existing in present and projected
            markets?
        2. Possibilities of new types of business activities that may spring from
            present capabilities?

G. What are the overall future prospects?
1. Special opportunities that deserve company top management interest?

MERGERS AND ACQUISITIONS

Basis of Increasing Interest

In recent years there has been a continuing acceleration in the number of acquisitions and mergers in the business community. From the standpoint of the company being acquired or merged, the reasons will range from the one extreme of a desperate need of help to the other extreme of a very attractive price. The company may have lost its top management, be extremely unprofitable, be in need of new capital, or be facing some other major crisis. On the other hand, the decision to sell or merge may be dictated more by the opportunities for present profit, or by the greater potentials of future profits. From the standpoint of the buyer the immediate objective may be stock market gains, tax benefits, or other short run benefits. Or the major benefits may be in the way the new company fits into the longer run strategic plans of the acquiring company. In some cases the gain may be synergistic in nature, that is, where the combined union results in strengths and efficiencies greater than can be achieved as separate companies. An example of the latter would be where an additional product can be handled by the presently existing sales distribution system.

Meaning of Terms

The terms "acquisition" or "merger" generally describe a situation where two companies are joined in some manner. The term "acquisition" tends to suggest a more direct purchase with cash and/or securities. The term "merger" suggests more of a continuing partnership. Usually, however, there is a dominant partner and when this is the case the so-called merger is really not significantly different than the so-called acquisition. In the more unusual situation the two firms may merge through the creation of an entirely new firm. Even here the result may be in fact the continuing dominant role of the one company.

Relationship to the Internal Auditor

The acquisition and merger process involves a series of managerial decisions and operational actions that are both difficult and important. This is especially true when the acquisition is a large one in relation to the size of the acquiring company, and when there is considerable uncertainty as to how advantageous the combined operations will be. It is logical, therefore, that the internal auditor's services should be utilized to the extent practicable in dealing with these problems. The services may take the form of providing better bases for the acquisition decision, for the actual negotiation of the acquisition arrangements, or in effecting the later integration of the new company into the ongoing company operations. Although most of what the internal auditor does in these connections is along the lines of his usual operational and financial auditing, there are some special aspects of the acquisition–merger process that need to be understood and dealt with in the proper manner.

Organizational Approach to Mergers and Acquisitions

Because of the very great potentials of acquisitions and mergers, the chief executive officer of the company will normally take a very active role in this process at all stages. Frequently also, some special aide is given this critical assignment. Such a special aide might then have a small staff of his own, and to a varying extent, draw on the resources of the regular company staffs. In other cases the responsibility may be assigned directly to one of the established staffs like finance or corporate planning, again with varying degrees of self-sufficiency. In any event there must be considerable flexibility because of the varying work demands and the frequent need to move under major time pressures, as when decisions must be made promptly to avoid loss of opportunity. There is also the special need for a team effort of many types of expertise as the individual acquisition moves through its various stages. And there is always the special need for easy access to the top management group, including the chief executive officer, where the final decisions must ultimately be made.

Nature and Scope of the Merger/Acquisition Process

The acquisition/merger process from the standpoint of the acquiring company typically includes the following:

1. Determination of acquisition needs.
2. Identifying the acquisition candidate.
3. Investigation and determination of extent of interest.
4. Negotiating the acquisition.
5. Initial contractual actions.
6. Backup operational integration.
7. Appraisal of results.

We discuss next each of these steps in some detail.

Determination of Acquisition Needs. Some acquisition actions in practice may in fact be unplanned. An opportunity to acquire a company develops, and the company responds in one way or another to that opportunity. In the more orderly situation, however, a company assesses its strengths and opportunities in relation to the present and projected environment, and develops its definitive goals and objectives. At this point the determination of desired growth will then normally include consideration of how this may be accomplished in part by the acquisition of, or merger with, other companies. In a more sophisticated approach this determination of need will also cover such definitive specifications as product lines, size, location, market position, technical know-how, management competence, and the like. When this is done, the search for acquisition candidates can then be carried out in the most intelligent manner, obviously an approach that is very much more productive. Needless to say, the establishment of these criteria does not preclude the consideration of an unusually attractive opportunity that may come along, even though it may not exactly fit the search specifications.

Identifying the Acquisition Candidate.   The first part of an organized effort to identify desirable acquisition candidates will normally consist of a detailed examination of generally available published data. This will include annual reports, evaluations by stock brokers and investment services, credit reports, filings with regulatory agencies, and the like. In some cases feelers will come directly from companies seeking merger. In other cases the inquiries will come from middlemen who specialize in bringing buyers and sellers together. In still other cases investment bankers will function in this capacity. What is critical in these latter cases is the extent to which the company incurs an obligation for remuneration in the event an acquisition is later consummated. For example, candidates may be submitted by different persons, and each of them claim to be the "finder," and hence entitled to the fee. This means that relationships with such middlemen must be clearly defined at all stages, including both whether an obligation is contemplated for a completed deal and in what amount.

Investigation and Determination of Interest.   When an eligible candidate has been identified, the next step is logically to obtain further information about that candidate. The problems at this stage revolve mostly around the degree of secrecy required and the extent of the cooperation from the candidate. In some cases secrecy may be desired both from the candidate and from others who might also desire to acquire that same candidate. Quite apart from the secrecy issue is whether the candidate is friendly or hostile to the acquisition possibilities. In some cases the attitude of the candidate may simply be a lack of interest in a sale or merger. In other cases it may be definitely hostile to such a development. The latter state of affairs exists in its most extreme form when an unwanted takeover is threatened by the acquiring company via a direct offer to the candidate's stockholders. Obviously, a friendly relationship with the candidate can provide a basis for a more informed appraisal of the desirability of the candidate by the acquiring company. In some cases it may even be possible to carry out definitive field reviews at this stage.

Negotiating the Acquisition.   If a takeover is involved, the acquisition is via the direct purchase of stock and the subsequent election of members of the governing board of directors of the candidate company. In other situations there will be a direct determination of mutual interest in the possible acquisition or merger, and the actual negotiation of mutually agreeable terms. At this stage the negotiations may be completed quite quickly, or they can drag on for a much longer time, ending in agreement or coming to a determination to cut off continuing negotiations. At this stage, however, it frequently happens that the company being acquired will agree to supply further detailed information that may be desired by the acquiring company. In some cases also the acquiring company may be permitted to make actual field reviews.

Initial Contract Actions.   The terms as actually negotiated will now specify the timing of the transfer of ownership and also the basis of the transfer of particular assets and liabilities. For example, the transfer of inventories on the specified date might be subject to count, and perhaps also to valuation by independent appraisers. In other cases warranties may be made as to value—as, for example, in the case of accounts receivable—and amounts of money withheld pending the determination of the actual degree of collectibility. In still other cases specific assets will be excluded from the acquisition and retained by the former owners. These arrangements can in fact be whatever the parties of interest wish to negotiate as the terms of purchase or merger. The supporting action is then to carry out that agreement in a manner that accomplishes the agreed-upon objectives. Similarly, the continuing role of the former management will also have been determined, and provision then made for necessary replacements. It is especially important to assure the rank and file personnel of the acquired company that their interests will be protected, thus avoiding a panic type of effort to seek other employment.

Backup Operational Integration.   The initial contract actions are now followed by the period during which the company must learn how to function efficiently under the new arrangements. For all practical purposes it will be necessary to rely on the old personnel to carry on the operations after the date of acquisition. The determination of the extent of replacement applies, therefore, only to a limited number of managerial personnel. In the normal situation the acquisition agreement will have provided that the old managers will continue indefinitely, or for a given period of time. Thus continuity on a reasonable basis is assured, even though some personnel may elect to leave the operation.

But the backup operational integration is much more complicated. There is now a new management that is responsible for results, and there is the power to make such changes as it may deem to be desirable. Even when the declared policy is to leave the acquired company completely alone, there is still the possibility of intervention. And a more reasonable view is that the acquiring company will want over time to do what is needed to exploit the basic purposes of the acquisition. The normal approach is first to get well acquainted with the operational problems and with the operating people. Then as the types of needed moves are determined, there is the greater assurance that those moves will be sound, and that they will be carried out in an effective manner. An additional important advantage of the deferral of major change is greater opportunity to win the cooperation and support of the people who really are needed on a continuing basis.

Appraisal of Results.   In a very real sense the backup operational integration is never complete. However, after a reasonable period of transition there needs to be an appraisal of the accomplishments resulting from the earlier acquisition decision. Have the original benefits really been achieved, and if not, why not? Has the new acquisition been adequately integrated into the total company operation? What remains to be done and how will we proceed? It may well be that original expectations were unrealistic. Or it may be that new conditions have developed that have changed the possibilities. Also, hopefully, lessons can be learned that can be utilized in subsequent acquisition actions.

Role of the Internal Auditor

As previously noted, the role of the internal auditor is to assist management in its effort to carry out the acquisition–merger process in an effective manner. The scope of this assistance will depend directly on the way the particular acquisition is accomplished and the specific desires of the company management. It will be useful, however, to discuss in some further detail the major types of assistance that can normally be rendered.

Services Relating to the Decision Basis.   As we have seen, the acquisition decision may be made on the basis of very limited information. In other cases, however, the relations with the acquisition candidate are such that actual field reviews are possible. In the latter situations the internal auditor can be asked to make the agreed-upon type of review. These reviews normally have the special character that they are done on a much more limited time basis than regular reviews. Consequently, the reviews must concentrate on the larger issues, and utilize the allowable time in a manner that will best contribute to the ultimate acquisition decision and its terms. In this connection at least three types of coverage can be identified:

1. *Review of Financial Statements.* The central objective here is that the financial statements of the candidate company are reasonably reliable and meaningful. To the extent that the financial statements have been re-viewed by independent public accountants, there will be that particular type of assurance. In addition, however, the internal auditor will seek to determine basic financial policies, practices, and methods that might not be disclosed in a conventional financial audit. He will also provide supplementary analysis which can be very useful. With respect to the balance sheet this could, for example, include more information about the composition and value of inventories. In the case of the income statement it could, for example, include information as to the source of profits by major product lines. In some cases also forecasts can be de-veloped for both types of financial statements.

2. *Operational Reviews*. The internal auditor will also be concerned with operational reviews covering all parts of the internal activities of the candidate company. The review here will be along the lines of the preceding chapters covering operational auditing. There will be special focus, however, on the condition of facilities and equipment, the degree of efficiency being achieved, and the qualifications of people. We are concerned whether the particular company, as it is now operating, is a sound base on which to build, when integrated into the larger company operation. The review is at the same time a kind of inventory of all important matters pertaining to the operations, for use as a later reference when questions may arise on the part of top management. Obviously, a high level of experience and judgmental ability is required on the part of the internal auditor.[2]

3. *Direct Information Relating to Specific Management Requests*. Supplementing the two previous types of reviews are the special concerns of management which have been identified by them as having a specific bearing on the acquisition decision. Illustrative would be the status and progress of a particular research project. Or there might be a special concern with the extent to which an adjoining lake or river is being polluted. In these cases the internal auditor acts as the direct arm of top management in attempting to evaluate the various factors pertaining to the acquisition decision.

Services Relating to the Initial Contract Actions. A second type of service rendered by the internal auditor comes at the time the acquisition becomes effective. At that time specific bases of accountability must be established and transferred. Such verifications and transfers may be carried out in conjunction with the personnel of the purchased company, or in some cases together with the independent public accountant. The objective is to see that the acquiring company's interests are being fully protected. At the same time there may be other actions necessary to carry out the terms of the contract. Illustrative would be check-signing authorizations, notifications to employees, and the like. In other cases a program must be established for subsequent action—as, for example, the collection of accounts receivable belonging to the prior owners.

Backup Operational Integration. Although the scope and timing of the actual integration of the acquired company into the total company operation will vary, it is at best a difficult transitional period. There will be new requirements for information on the part of the various line and staff organizational components. There will be a variety of existing policies and procedures that ultimately need to be changed to conform to overall company practice. There will also be the possibility of more definitive moves—as, for example, the supplying of man-

---

[2]The material on the integrated operational audit earlier in this chapter will also be useful.

ufacturing materials from presently available internal company sources. Coupled with all these problems is the fact of new people relationships, and the natural apprehension that present freedom of action will now be restricted.

During this entire difficult period the internal auditor can usually make an important contribution. This can come about in a number of important ways. The first of these is helping to inform local personnel as to the meaning of various policies and procedures. His broad knowledge in all operational areas can be especially helpful. A second contribution can come through providing assurance to management that operational controls are working effectively, and that management need not rush prematurely to other moves that it may have under consideration. A third contribution has to do with the appraisal of people. Quite naturally the management in all key areas is anxious to determine which people have real ability and potential. They are desirous of getting all possible help in making that determination. In summary, the internal auditor can smooth the transition phase, act as a stabilizing force, and keep top management informed of progress and new developments.

AUDIT GUIDES

ACQUISITIONS AND MERGERS

Specific audit programs will depend directly on the particular type of assignment. In preparing such audit programs full use should be made of the following:

1. Audit guides previously proposed for the various operational areas.
2. Audit guides proposed for integrated audits, as presented earlier in this chapter.

Reviews and other types of assistance rendered by internal auditors will very often be less formally structured, and instead involve a more intimate relationship with management. Such relationships, of course, provide special opportunities for the internal auditor to strengthen his standing with top management.

ILLUSTRATIVE AUDIT FINDINGS: INTEGRATED OPERATIONAL COMPONENTS AND MERGERS AND ACQUISITIONS

Additional Standards Needed

An audit of selected operations at a plant indicated that standards had not been adequately developed for some production items. Significant numbers of electronic equipment shipped to customers were returned for defects. These defects would have been noted prior to shipment if there had been better standards. In addition, standards had not been developed for many administrative areas, such as time for processing requisitions, because the plant manager did not believe that standards were necessary.

Interpreting Financial Statements prior to Acquisition

In reviewing the financial statements of two companies being considered for acquisition, the internal auditor noted differing methods of accounting that affected the basis for comparison. One company expensed all research and development expenses at the time they were incurred, used LIFO for valuing inventories, and used accelerated depreciation to minimize income taxes. The other company's assets were stated on a higher basis because research and development costs were capitalized, the FIFO method was used for inventories, and regular depreciation was used. The internal auditor provided analyses of the effect of these different methods on the financial statements in assisting management in making the acquisition decision.

Improved Controls Needed in New Division

At the request of management the internal auditor reviewed the overall operations of a newly acquired company to determine the effectiveness of controls. He found a need for obtaining additional competition in awarding purchase contracts, increased maintenance of equipment, and improved cash management. In addition, he recommended that the internal audit staff of the company be expanded and trained to provide more extensive audits of operations.

Combining Functions after Merger

Significant savings could have been achieved after the merger of two companies if certain functions were combined or eliminated. The companies continued to maintain separate computer facilities, although there was available capacity to combine the two operations. In addition, legal and advertising departments from each company continued intact after the merger and some functions were duplicated. The internal auditor recommended a more extensive analysis of operational and administrative functions to achieve cost savings.

CHAPTER TWENTY-SIX

Fraud and Investigations

ROLES AND RESPONSIBILITIES

Fraud and the Internal Auditor

Fraud is an ever-present threat to the effective utilization of resources, and hence will always be an important concern of management and other parties of interest of all organizations. Existing fraud needs to be detected and potential fraud prevented to the extent practicable. The primary responsibility in these areas is that of management—including its line and accounting personnel. However, management needs assistance and quite properly looks to auditors—especially to its internal auditors—for all possible assistance.

The question is then the extent to which the internal auditor is directly or indirectly responsible for fraud. It is impossible to prevent all fraud. Even if the internal auditor performed very detailed checking, there could be unrecorded transactions, forgeries, and collusion which might not be discovered. It is also too costly to go beyond reasonable levels of fraud prevention. As we have seen in earlier chapters, it is possible to overcontrol. Judgment therefore becomes a basic ingredient in determining the nature and scope of fraud control efforts. It is a challenge to the internal auditor to give fraud the balanced attention it deserves, while achieving the total range of internal auditing services. This challenge also includes helping all parties of interest to understand the desirability of properly balanced fraud control efforts. We have consistently taken that position in all editions of *Modern Internal Auditing*.

Changing Concern for Fraud

In earlier days the internal auditing profession was more directly concerned with fraud. As discussed in our opening chapter, this concern was part of the internal auditor's then existing major orientation to protective-type services —including compliance, accuracy, and preservation of physical assets. This orientation reflected the fact that management depended to a greater extent on internal auditors for fraud-type services, especially as to the detection of existing fraud. This situation began to change as the nature and scope of internal auditing services broadened. This change involved first a greater emphasis on fraud prevention versus fraud detection. It was wisely perceived that it was more beneficial to the organization to develop good systems and managerial capabilities that would reduce the possibilities of fraud.

The shift away from fraud detection through better systems then—among other factors—helped to make it possible for internal auditors to provide more constructive service to the organization via the new operational auditing. The fraud-oriented services then became proportionately a smaller part of the total work of the internal auditor. However, good internal auditors were always conscious of their very real responsibilities in the way of helping to prevent and detect fraud.

The pendulum has recently swung back to a greater interest in fraud prevention and detection by internal auditors. Management itself has been held increasingly accountable for various white-collar crimes, such as embezzlement using the computer. The Foreign Corrupt Practices Act, with its related penalties, has added incentive to having better systems of internal control. In attempting to have a strong fraud prevention and detection program, management has called on finance personnel, internal auditors, investigators, and external auditors for assistance. The internal auditor thus often finds that an increased amount of his resources is presently being devoted to this area.

The current emphasis on fraud is reflected in the standards published by The Institute of Internal Auditors. In the 1978 "Standards for the Professional Practice of Internal Auditing," Section 280, it is stated:

> . . . In exercising due professional care, internal auditors should be alert to the possibility of intentional wrongdoing, errors and omissions, inefficiency, waste, ineffectiveness, and conflicts of interest. They should also be alert to those conditions and activities where irregularities are most likely to occur. . . .

> . . . the internal auditor cannot give absolute assurance that noncompliance or irregularities do not exist. Nevertheless, the possibility of material irregularities or noncompliance should be considered whenever the internal auditor undertakes an internal auditing assignment.

The Standards thus do not state that the internal auditor is responsible for the detection of fraud. They do require, however, that he be alert for it, know that it can exist, and consider it when carrying out an audit. As the Standards point out also, the auditor cannot give absolute assurance that there are not irregularities.

Approach of the External Auditor

The American Institute of Certified Public Accountants (AICPA) has similarly changed its approach to fraud, resulting in changes in public accounting standards. In the early 1900s there was strong emphasis by external auditors on the detection of fraud because audits were primarily involved with cash records. Auditing textbooks indicated that the detection and prevention of fraud errors were among the main objectives of an audit. This gradually changed over the next three decades, until the accounting literature emphasized that the external auditor did not assume any direct responsibility for fraud.

There were many reasons for the change in approach. The growth of business entities in size and complexity meant that the auditor had to use testing techniques rather than a detailed review of all transactions. This made it especially difficult to detect irregularities. In addition, the inability of the auditor to detect fraud involving unrecorded transactions, theft, and other matters made the profession more cautious. This became more important as lawsuits were filed against accounting firms holding them responsible for losses resulting from frauds. At the same time, there was a growing trend toward strengthening systems of internal accounting control, which could then prevent fraud and related deficiencies.

This led the AICPA to adopt a position on fraud, set forth in the codification of statements on auditing procedure published in 1951, which read:

> The ordinary examination incident to the issuance of an opinion respecting financial statements is not designed and cannot be relied upon to disclose defalcations and other similar irregularities, although their discovery frequently results.
> . . . If an auditor were to attempt to discover defalcations and similar irregularities he would have to extend his work to a point where its costs would be prohibitive. It is generally recognized that good internal control and surety bonds provide protection much more cheaply. . . .

This position was criticized by some for attempting to relieve the external auditor of the responsibility for the detection of fraud. In recognition of this, the AICPA issued Statement on Auditing Procedures No. 30 in 1960. This statement was incorporated in Statement on Auditing Standards (SAS) No. 1, along with all other statements on auditing procedure in November 1972. Section 110.05 of this Statement says:

> The responsibility of the independent auditor for failure to detect fraud (which responsibility differs as to clients and others) arises only when such failure clearly results from non-compliance with generally accepted auditing standards.

In light of increased litigation against accountants, and the concern of external auditors that there may be material misstatements as a result of fraud, the profession developed SAS 16. This superseded SAS 1, as it dealt with the auditors' responsibility for fraud. This states:

> . . . Consequently, under generally accepted auditing standards, the independent auditor has the responsibility, with the inherent limitations of the auditing process, to plan his examination to search for errors or irregularities that would have a material effect on the financial statements, and to exercise due skill and care in the conduct of that examination.

This Statement thus requires the auditor to look specifically for irregularities which may have a material effect on the financial statements.

The foregoing change of emphasis by the external auditors has in turn helped to relieve the internal auditor of direct responsibility for fraud in organizations.

Impact of Management Pressure

Regardless of differing opinions on whether or not internal auditors and external auditors have a responsibility to detect fraud, management tends to look to them in fraud matters. When a fraudulent act is committed, the question is invariably asked: "Where were the auditors?" or "When was the last audit?" The burden is thus placed on the auditors as to why their last examination did not reveal the fraud, or at least disclose the internal control weakness that led to the fraud. The auditors' responsibility is thus seen as doing their work in such a professional manner that, if fraud exists, the chances are that it will be exposed. In addition, management expects the auditors to perceive opportunities to provide more prevention, since prevention is preferable to detection where frauds are concerned.

There are, of course, limits to the ability of any organization to prevent fraud. No internal control plan can prevent an employee from stealing cash that he handles, and no controls can prevent a purchasing agent from colluding with a supplier. Also, no control can be expected to disclose a fraud the instant it is committed. However, management looks to the auditors to be imaginative in the application of comprehensive and well-thought-out audit programs so that, if fraud exists, there is a reasonable assurance that it will be discovered. Moreover, they look to the internal auditors, especially because of the latter's deeper involvement in the total activities of the organization.

Responsibilities of the Internal Auditor for Fraud

The internal auditor's responsibilities in the area of fraud control in principle can thus be summarized, as follows:

1. In the review of systems to help evaluate the extent to which fraud prevention and detection are given fair consideration along with other operational objectives.

2. To be alert to the possibilities of fraud in the review of operating activities carried out by organizational personnel—including the constructive evaluation of managerial capabilities.

3. To assist and cooperate with organizational and other personnel that have been assigned responsibilities in connection with the investigation of actual or suspected fraud.

4. To carry out such special assignments relating to fraud as may be requested by responsible members of the organization.

5. In all of the foregoing to seek directly and indirectly to achieve the balanced fraud oriented efforts that will assure maximum achievement of all other types of needed organizational services.

Priorities for Fraud Work

With the current increased emphasis on preventing, detecting, and investigating fraud, the internal auditor is often faced with the problem of resources to perform his other audit work load. Normal coverage of areas on a recurring basis may be disrupted by fraud efforts. In some instances internal auditors have had to curtail operational auditing and the resultant recommendations for cost savings. This may be especially frustrating when it has taken many years to develop an operational auditing capability with demonstrated results.

In order to accomplish overall audit objectives with available resources, it is necessary to set priorities carefully in coordination with management. Based on previous experience an estimated amount of time should be budgeted for fraud work. In some cases the functions performed by the internal auditor may be handled by others: for example, work by investigators, law officials, departmental personnel, and external auditors. In addition, to make time available for operational audits it may be necessary to lengthen the cycle for other coverage which may not be so productive. Overall, the internal auditor has to weigh the benefits of various audit efforts to arrive at the best utilization of audit time. The objective is that there will be time available both to perform operational audits and to carry out fraud responsibilities.

EFFECT OF FOREIGN CORRUPT PRACTICES ACT

In 1976 the Securities and Exchange Commission (SEC) submitted to Senator Proxmire's Committee on Banking, Housing and Urban Affairs a report on its investigations into questionable and illegal corporate payments and practices. The report recommended legislation to correct bribes and other illegal payments. In response to the recommendation, the Foreign Corrupt Practices Act (FCPA) was enacted on December 19, 1977. Excerpts from the act are included as Exhibit 26.1. The act contains provisions as to books and records, internal accounting control, and bribery prohibitions. We discussed in Chapter 4 the provisions of the act as they pertained to basic control concepts. Our focus here is the effect of the act on possible fraud and other types of corrupt practices.

Books and Records Required

This provision applies to issuers that have securities registered under Section 12 of the Securities Exchange Act of 1934 and does not apply to nonpublic companies. It was adopted as a result of SEC comments that illegal payments disclosed in SEC filings were often hidden by either falsification of records or maintenance of incomplete records. The provision requires that issuers keep, in reasonable detail, books, records and accounts which are accurate and fairly reflect transactions. The phrase "in reasonable detail" was added by the conference committee to give effect to concerns by the accounting profession that no accounting system could achieve freedom from error. However, there is no definition as to the exact meaning of "in reasonable detail." Basically, the intent of the rule is to cause the company to keep records to reflect transactions in conformity with accepted methods of recording economic events, preventing off-the-books slush funds and payments of bribes.

EXHIBIT 26.1.   Public Law 95-213, 95th Congress

91 STAT. 1494   PUBLIC LAW 95-213—DEC. 19, 1977

An Act

Dec. 19, 1977
[S. 305]

To amend the Securities Exchange Act of 1934 to make it unlawful for an issuer of securities registered pursuant to section 12 of such Act or an issuer required to file reports pursuant to section 15 (d) of such Act to make certain payments to foreign officials and other foreign persons, to require such issuers to maintain accurate records, and for other purposes.

Securities Exchange Act of 1934, amendment.
Foreign Corrupt Practices Act of 1977.
15 USC 78a note.

Be it enacted by the Senate and House of Representatives of the United States of America in Congress assembled,

TITLE I—FOREIGN CORRUPT PRACTICES

SHORT TITLE

SEC. 101. This title may be cited as the "Foreign Corrupt Practices Act of 1977".

ACCOUNTING STANDARDS

Assets, transactions and dispositions.
15 USC 78m.

15 USC 78l.
Post, p. 1500.
Records, maintenance.

SEC. 102. Section 13 (b) of the Securities Exchange Act of 1934 (15 U.S.C. 78q(b)) is amended by inserting "(1)" after "(b)" and by adding at the end thereof the following:

"(2) Every issuer which has a class of securities registered pursuant to section 12 of this title and every issuer which is required to file reports pursuant to section 15(d) of this title shall—

"(A) make and keep books, records, and accounts, which, in reasonable detail, accurately and fairly reflect the transactions and dispositions of the assets of the issuer; and

Internal accounting controls, establishment.

"(B) devise and maintain a system of internal accounting controls sufficient to provide reasonable assurances that—

"(i) transactions are executed in accordance with management's general or specific authorization;

"(ii) transactions are recorded as necessary (I) to permit preparation of financial statements in conformity with generally accepted accounting principles or any other criteria applicable too such statements, and (II) to maintain accountability for assets;

"(iii) access to assets is permitted only in accordance with management's general or specific authorization; and

"(iv) the recorded accountability for assets is compared with the existing assets at reasonable intervals and appropriate action is taken with respect to any differences.

Exemption directive, issuance and expiration.

"(3) (A) With respect to matters concerning the national security of the United States, no duty or liability under paragraph (2) of this subsection shall be imposed upon any person acting

712

EXHIBIT 26.1. *(Continued)*

in cooperation with the head of any Federal department or agency responsible for such matters if such act in cooperation with such head of a department or agency was done upon the specific, written directive of the head of such department or agency pursuant to Presidential authority to issue such directives. Each directive issued under this paragraph shall set forth the specific facts and circumstances with respect to which the provisions of this paragraph are to be invoked. Each such directive shall, unless renewed in writing, expire one year after the date of issuance.

"(B) Each head of a Federal department or agency of the United States who issues a directive pursuant to this paragraph shall maintain a complete file of all such directives and shall, on October 1 of each year, transmit a summary of matters covered by such directives in force at any time during the previous year to the Permanent Select Committee on Intelligence of the House of Representatives and the Select Committee on Intelligence of the Senate.".

File maintenance. Annual summary, transmittal to congressional committees.

FOREIGN CORRUPT PRACTICES BY ISSUERS

SEC. 103. (a) The Securities Exchange Act of 1934 is amended by inserting after section 30 the following new section:

"FOREIGN CORRUPT PRACTICES BY ISSUERS

"SEC. 30A. (a) It shall be unlawful for any issuer which has a class of securities registered pursuant to section 12 of this title or which is required to file reports under section 15(d) of this title, or for any officer, director, employee, or agent of such issuer or any stockholder thereof acting on behalf of such issuer, to make use of the mails or any means or instrumentality of interstate commerce corruptly in furtherance of an offer, payment, promise to pay, or authorization of the payment of any money, or offer, gift, promise to give, or authorization of the giving of anything of value to—

15 USC 78dd-1. 15 USC 78l. Post, p. 1500.

"(1) any foreign official for purposes of—

"(A) influencing any act or decision of such foreign official in his official capacity, including a decision to fail to perform his official functions; or

"(B) inducing such foreign official to use his influence with a foreign government or instrumentality thereof to affect or influence any act or decision of such government or instrumentality,

in order to assist such issuer in obtaining or retaining business for or with, or directing business to, any person;

"(2) any foreign political party or official thereof or any candidate for foreign political office for purposes of—

EXHIBIT 26.1   (Continued)

"(A) influencing any act or decision of such party, official, or candidate in its or his official capacity, including a decision to fail to perform its or his official functins; or

"(B) inducing such party, official, or candidate to use its or his influence with a foreign government or instrumentality thereof to affect or influence any act or decision of such government or instrumentality,

in order to assist such issuer in obtaining or retaining business for or with, or directing business to, any person; or

"(3) any person, while knowing or having reason to know that all or a portion of such money or thing of value will be offered, given, or promised, directly or indirectly, to any foreign official, to any foreign political party or official thereof, or to any candidate for foreign political office, for purposes of—

"(A) influencing any act or decision of such foreign official, political party, party official, or candidate in his or its official capacity, including a decision to fail to perform his or its official functions; or

"(B) inducing such foreign official, political party, party official, or candidate to use his or its influence with a foreign government or instrumentality thereof to affect or influence any act or decision of such government or instrumentality,

in order to assist such issuer in obtaining or retaining business for or with, or directing business to, any person."

Internal Accounting Control Requirements

The act requires that companies with registered securities maintain a system of internal accounting controls. These controls should be sufficient to provide reasonable assurances that transactions are authorized and recorded to permit preparation of financial statements in conformity with generally accepted accounting principles. In addition, accountability is to be maintained for assets and access to the assets permitted only as authorized. Also, recorded assets are to be physically inventoried periodically and differences analyzed.

The cost of fully controlling each transaction in the face of existing risk would not be justified, and thus the term "reasonable assurances" is used. Management must therefore estimate and evaluate the cost/benefit relationships, exercising judgment as to the steps to be taken. Although a discussion of cost/benefit decisions is not mentioned in the act, it is included in the conference committee's minutes. Thus it is apparent that Congress intended that management have the right to make cost/benefit decisions as to controls

Bribery Prohibitions

The bribery provisions, which are applicable to both issuers of securities and all other U.S. domestic concerns, prohibit bribes to a foreign official. The maximum penalty for violation of the bribery prohibitions by a company is $1,000,000, and for individuals who participate in bribes the punishment is a fine of not more than $10,000, or imprisonment not more than five years, or both.

The purpose of the payment must be to influence a foreign official to assist a company in obtaining business. The offer or gift must be intended to induce the recipient to misuse his official position, such as to direct business to the payer or his client. Excluded from the definition of foreign official are government employees whose functions are clerical or ministerial in nature. Thus so-called "grease payments" to minor officials are permissible

Role of the Internal Auditor

There are various groups involved in determining compliance with FCPA standards. The controller or vice president of finance is responsible for the financial control system of the company. The external auditor is involved through reviewing management's representations of its control system. Legal counsel is interested because of the interpretations of compliance with the act. The internal auditor is involved because of his responsibilities for the evaluation of internal control. Also, in some companies the board of directors and the audit committee have taken an active part in directing reviews of internal controls to assure compliance with the act.

The internal auditor is in a unique position to work with these groups to accomplish the objectives of the act. The approaches described in this chapter for detecting fraudulent practices can be adapted to the company needs. In addition, the internal auditor's current reviews of internal control can play a strong role in preventing bribery and other acts.

Specifically with respect to bribes, the internal auditor would examine certain accounts for disguising the payment as a legitimate business expense. These may include entertainment, travel, advertising, consulting services, engineering services, selling costs, legal fees, and individual expense accounts. The examination of documents may give an indication of a bribe, such as the name of the bribe recipient appearing on copies of airline tickets or delivery tickets. This information may be compared with endorsements on checks. Loans made to individuals may in reality be bribes. Items such as automobiles and boats may be purchased by a company to be used as bribes. Significant events and transactions related to obtaining large sales contracts with foreign governments should be examined. Through these and other audit steps, the internal auditor attempts to determine compliance with the act pertaining to bribe prohibitions.

WARNING SIGNALS FOR FRAUD

Although on occasion internal auditors carry out direct assignments in the investigation of suspected or actual fraud, the greater part of his fraud-oriented efforts are an integral part of a broader audit assignment. These fraud efforts may take the form of specific procedures included in a broader audit program. They also include all of the general alertness of the internal auditor as he carries out all parts of this audit assignment. This general alertness, in turn, includes various areas, conditions, and developments which provide warning signals.

Sensitive Areas

The internal auditor must be aware of the overall organizational climate and its potentialities for fraud. He should be especially alert for sensitive areas for review which may, in some instances, disclose wrongdoing. The following are examples.

Insufficient Working Capital. This may indicate such problems as overexpansion, decreases in revenues, transfer of funds to other companies, insufficient credit, and excessive expenditures. The auditor should be on the lookout for diversions of funds to personal use through such methods as unrecorded sales and falsified expenditures.

Rapid Turnover in Financial Positions. Loss of key accounting and other financial personnel may signify inadequate performance and result in weaknesses in internal control. Accountability for funds and other resources should be determined upon termination of employment.

Use of Sole-Source Procurement. Good procurement practices encourage competition to assure that the organization is obtaining the required materials or equipment at the best price. Sole-source procurement, if not adequately justified, indicates potential favoritism or kickbacks.

Excessive Travel Costs. In reviewing travel the auditor is on the lookout for unauthorized or personal trips, entertainment, costs in excess of those allowed by the organization, and unsupported travel and other expenses.

Transfers of Funds between Affiliated Companies or Divisions. A pattern of transfer of funds between companies or divisions may indicate unauthorized borrowings, coverup of shortages, or inadequate controls over funds.

Change in Outside Auditors. In some instances the change in outside auditors may indicate differences of opinion as to the appropriate method of handling certain transactions. There may be a reluctance on the part of management to disclose problems or events that are significant.

Excessive Consultant Costs or Legal Fees. These may be indicative of abuses in having services performed on the outside, favoritism, and undisclosed problems within the organization which require extensive legal work.

Downward Trends in Key Financial Figures and Ratios. The use of ratio, change, and trend analysis may indicate problems in certain areas which require follow-up. Downward trends may be symptomatic of significant losses, diversion of funds and resources, and inadequate controls over operations.

Reported Conflicts of Interest. The auditor should be aware of any rumors or allegations of conflicts of interest pertaining to outside employment, vendor arrangements, and relationships between employees. Company transactions with officers or employees should be carefully scrutinized.

Unexplained Shortages in Physical Assets. Inadequate physical storage may lead to pilfering or other diversion of assets. Shortages in assets should be analyzed carefully to determine their cause.

Decreases in Performance. One division of a company may be performing less adequately than other divisions. In addition, there may be a decrease in performance from prior experience. The reasons should be determined for indications of poor management or possible wrongdoing.

Management Control by Few Individuals. Domination of an organization by one or a few individuals may provide the opportunity for diversion of assets or other manipulations.

Collection Difficulties. Problems in collecting on receivables should be analyzed to determine whether there are fictitous sales or diversion of funds received from collections.

Many Bank Accounts. The use of a large number of bank accounts, in excess of what is normally needed, indicates possible diversions of funds or cover-up of illegal transactions. Transfers among these accounts, and to personal bank accounts, should be reviewed carefully.

Late Reports. Reports may be consistently delayed so that the preparer can manipulate data to cover up fraudulent actions.

Copies Used for Payments to Creditors. Rather than making payments based on original invoices, copies may be used to hide duplicate payments and kickbacks.

Shortages, Overages and Out-of-Balance Conditions. These may be symptoms of a larger problem, and explanation should be obtained as to the variances.

Checks or Other Documents Written in Even Amounts. For example, a check might read $10,000 or $3,500 when it might normally be expected to be in odd amounts, such as $10,261.34 or $3,532.28.

Exhibit 26.2 (pages 718–719) is a list prepared by the American Institute of Certified Public Accountants of conditions or events that may signal the existence of fraud.

Personal Characteristics

There is no specific profile of the white-collar criminal that would identify him to the auditor. Although a prior criminal record would indicate the need for observation, many white-collar criminals have had no prior record of criminal activity. In many instances they are members of the middle-class, well-educated families with status in the community.

There are, however, certain early warning signals of personal behavior which require close watching. Some of these are listed on page 719.

EXHIBIT 26.2. AICPA List of Fraud Signals

1. Highly domineering senior management and one or more of the following, or similar, conditions are present:
   ☐ An ineffective board of directors and/or audit committee.
   ☐ Indications of management override of significant internal accounting controls.
   ☐ Compensation or significant stock options tied to reported performance or to a specific transaction over which senior management has actual or implied control.
   ☐ Indications of personal financial difficulties of senior management.
   ☐ Proxy contests involving control of the company or senior management's continuance, compensation or status.

2. Deterioration of quality of earnings evidenced by:
   ☐ Decline in the volume or quality of sales (for example, increased credit risk or sales at or below cost).
   ☐ Significant changes in business practices.
   ☐ Excessive interest by senior management in the earnings per share effect of accounting alternatives.

3. Business conditions that may create unusual pressures:
   ☐ Inadequate working capital.
   ☐ Little flexibility in debt restrictions such as working capital ratios and limitations on additional borrowings.
   ☐ Rapid expansion of a product or business line markedly in excess of industry averages.
   ☐ A major investment of the company's resources in an industry noted for rapid change, such as a high technology industry.

4. A complex corporate structure where the complexity does not appear to be warranted by the company's operations or size.

5. Widely dispersed business locations accompanied by highly decentralized management with inadequate responsibility reporting system.

6. Understaffing which appears to require certain employees to work unusual hours, to forgo vacations and/or to put in substantial overtime.

7. High turnover rate in key financial positions such as treasurer or controller.

8. Frequent change of auditors or legal counsel.

9. Known material weaknesses in internal control which could practically be corrected but remain uncorrected, such as:
   ☐ Access to computer equipment or electronic data entry devices is not adequately controlled.
   ☐ Incompatible duties remain combined.

10. Material transactions with related parties exist or there are transactions that may involve conflicts of interest.

11. Premature announcements of operating results or future (positive) expectations.

12. Analytical review procedures disclosing significant fluctuations which cannot be reasonably explained, for example:
    ☐ Material account balances.
    ☐ Financial or operational interrelationships.
    ☐ Physical inventory variances.
    ☐ Inventory turnover rates.

13. Large or unusual transactions, particularly at year-end, with material effect on earnings.

EXHIBIT 26.2.   (*Continued*)

14. Unusually large payments in relation to services provided in the ordinary course of business by lawyers, consultants, agents and others (including employees).
15. Difficulty in obtaining audit evidence with respect to:
    ☐ Unusual or unexplained entries.
    ☐ Incomplete or missing documentation and/or authorization.
    ☐ Alterations in documentation or accounts.
16. In the performance of an examination of financial statements unforeseen problems are encountered, for instance:
    ☐ Client pressures to complete audit in an unusually short time or under difficult conditions.
    ☐ Sudden delay situations.
    ☐ Evasive or unreasonable responses of management to audit inquiries.

Source: Reprinted from March 12, 1979 CPA Letter. Copyright © 1979, American Institute of Certified Public Accountants, Inc.

Early warning signals of personal behavior:

High personal debts or financial losses.

Expensive life-style.

Extensive gambling.

Heavy investments.

Excessive use of alcohol or drugs.

Significant personal or family problems.

Extensive overtime and skipping vacations.

Questionable background and references.

Excessive sick leave.

Domination of specific activities.

Regular borrowing of small amounts from fellow employees.

Refusing to leave the custody of records during the day.

Common Fraudulent Practices

Fraud is so directly a product of the individual operational situation that it is impossible to cover all possibilities. Any list must also recognize that a particular type of fraud can perhaps be possible in one situation and not in another. However, it may be useful to enumerate some common types of fraud.

1. *Nonrecording of Revenues.* When an employee has control over both the sale and collection of cash, it is relatively easy to pocket the cash without recording the sale. This can also occur when the employee handles receipts of cash and also does the record keeping.
2. *Withholding Receivable Collections.* There may be a temporary withholding of collections on account, or keeping the amount received and later writing off the account as a bad debt. In some cases shortages are

made up by using new cash receipts, and the latter shortage then covered by still later receipts. This type of action is known as "lapping."

3. *Theft of Materials.* Sensitive items of materials and equipment with high resale value may be especially susceptible to pilferage, especially if not adequately secured. Theft losses may be covered up by arbitrary write-offs, transfers between departments, and inadequate inventory-taking procedures. In some cases release passes are forged, or there may be collusion of security guards with individuals.

4. *Diversion of Securities.* This could occur in a situation where there was unauthorized access, or where the custodian was able to remove the securities without being detected.

5. *Padding Payrolls.* In some situations a payroll clerk or supervisor has been able to carry nonexistent or terminated people on the payroll, and then later get the cash or check used for payment. In other instances the payroll clerk may overstate an employee's wages in return for a share of the excess.

6. *Misuse of Credit Cards.* Credit cards may be used to make personal purchases, or may be lent to others in return for favors. Also, expenses paid for by company credit cards may be simultaneously claimed and reimbursed by check.

7. *Falsification of Disbursement Documents.* Cash disbursements may be supported by documents that are false or improperly altered. Warehouse receipts may be forged, or receiving reports may be falsified. Copies of invoices or receipts may be submitted for duplicate payments.

8. *Payment of Personal Expenses.* Miscellaneous expenses of a personal nature may be submitted which are not authorized by the company. These may include entertainment, expenses of spouse, equipment bought for personal use, and unauthorized travel expense.

9. *Purchase Kickbacks.* Arrangements may be made with vendors to purchase from them in return for special favors or money. In some cases vendors will specifically offer bribes to members of the purchasing department.

10. *Misuse of Petty Cash Funds.* Funds may be used for personal or other unauthorized purposes. In some cases supporting documents may be forged or falsified to cover the shortage.

11. *Transfers of Assets.* In some cases there may be transfers of funds between bank accounts in various divisions or affiliated companies. These transfers may be used to camouflage unauthorized expenditures or use of funds.

12. *Excessive Allowances to Customers.* In some instances sales allowances or discounts may be overstated. Also, preferred customers may be charged less in return for favors.

13. *Conflict of Interest.* This may occur in various parts of a company,

involving relatives, employees with an outside interest, or dealings with related companies.

14. *Bribes and Other Corruption*. Payments to obtain business may be made to a foreign officials, in prohibition of the antibribery provisions of the Foreign Corrupt Practices Act, as discussed earlier in this chapter.

15. *Misappropriation of Receipts*. Through having incoming customer checks made payable to an employee rather than the company, the employee can cash the checks and have company funds available.

PROCEDURES FOR HANDLING FRAUD

Obtaining Leads

Fraudulent acts may be disclosed in various ways. The internal auditor may discover them during the course of his reviews. Documents may contain questionable items which when followed up disclose irregularities. Employees or outsiders may make allegations or bring up items of a suspicious nature during discussions. In some instances an employee who has committed or participated in a fraud may come forth and make a confession. In addition, management may specifically request auditors to review sensitive areas for possible wrongdoing, for example, conflict of interest. Also, there may be general warning signs which require close attention by the internal auditor as indicators of potential fraud. The internal auditor needs to be on the alert for any leads that indicate irregularities, assuring that staff members recognize and identify the leads when found. This often takes curiosity and imagination to separate the normal from the abnormal. Being independent from day-to-day operations and personnel, the internal auditor is in a good position to recognize irregularities.

Informing Management

As soon as fraud is suspected, it should be reported to the proper company officials. Generally, management is interested in obtaining information about fraud anywhere in the organization. This is important for alerting management at an early stage before there is unfavorable publicity. In addition, this provides top officials an opportunity to provide input as to how the investigation will be conducted, and to make key decisions as to the disposition of the case. Normally, cases are not dropped without the concurrence of management. Also, management becomes aware of control deficiencies that enabled the irregularities to occur. Employees should be informed that all frauds must be reported to management immediately. The official to whom reports are provided may be the president, vice president, treasurer, controller, or other designated executives.

Usually, a report is also made to the bonding company. This may be a requirement under the provisions of surety bonds. In addition, the bonding company may be of assistance in the investigation and determination of action to be taken based on evidence available. A report is also made to the legal counsel and to any special investigators in the company. The director of internal auditing should of course also be informed of all frauds.

In some instances the immediate supervisor of the employee for whom there is a complaint should be informed. The employee may be relieved of his duties to aid in the investigation or to prevent further manipulation. The employee may be assigned to other work or suspended. It may be necessary to take immediate control over the employee's records to prevent him from altering or destroying them.

Initiating Action

As soon as the preliminary facts are reviewed, a plan of action should be developed, and an auditor or investigator is designated to be in charge. It is especially important to start the investigation as soon as possible to prevent the destruction or alteration of records, obtain confessions, and gather evidence that can be used for interviewing witnesses.

The internal auditor should determine the types of records and supporting documents that should be reviewed. To prevent the need for detailed checking, it may be preferable to interview key personnel and witnesses prior to performing the review. The type of evidence necessary to prove the case should be discussed to assure that the data obtained are pertinent.

Resources needed should be carefully reviewed. In some cases the work may require professional investigators because of the questioning involved or other factors. Discussions with law enforcement officials may be necessary. The role of the internal auditor should carefully be defined, both in performing the investigatory work and writing the report.

In planning the work information should be gathered as to the number of persons involved and their positions. Personnel files should be reviewed to determine if background checks had been performed and whether there is any indication of personal problems.

Conducting the Investigation

Coordinating Efforts. In conducting the investigation it is first necessary to coordinate the efforts of all parties involved. In an individual case this may involve the internal auditor who carries out various audit tests, including following the paper trails; the investigator, who conducts interviews, interrogates witnesses, and gathers other evidence; the legal counsel, who provides technical advice and support; and prosecuting attorneys, who perform early case review and provide guidance on evidence needed. Close communication should be encouraged among the internal auditor, investigator, legal counsel, and prosecutor during the investigation.

Selecting Audit Procedures. There are no audit procedures that are unique to fraud situations—each case is different and requires study and analysis to determine the best approach. In a case involving lapping in accounts receivable, in which the employee diverted collections to his own use during the early months of a year, confirmation of accounts was performed. In another case involving theft of sensitive equipment, a physical inventory was taken which the auditor observed. In both cases the auditor made inquiries of selected employees to obtain explanations of circumstances surrounding the irregularity. The internal auditor relies on his judgment in selecting the best procedures for gathering evidence. He must also be imaginative to detect such items as falsification of documents, forged signatures and collusion. It should be emphasized that as soon as an internal auditor begins investigating fraud, his role changes. His normal cooperative role of reviewing controls as part of routine auditing is changed. He now assumes duties more like a detective, gathering evidence to determine whether there is a fraud, to ascertain who committed the fraud, to determine the extent of loss, and to find out how the fraud was perpetrated. He must investigate all discrepancies, believing no explanations until they can be proved. He must suspect transactions, and consider possible collusion. Speed is essential in the investigation to prevent destruction of records and obtain evidence for interviewing witnesses and the defaulter.

Determining Personal Gain. The internal auditor is on the lookout for diversion of funds to personal use. Although certain practices followed by an employee may be wasteful or not in the best interests of the company, the individual may not benefit personally, and it may be difficult to prosecute him. Transfers of funds between accounts and divisions of the company are examined closely, as are personal withdrawals in various forms.

Isolating Specific Areas. The internal auditor attempts to concentrate his efforts on those areas that will provide specific evidence as to fraud. To conserve time and resources, his test checks should be limited as to detail and should emphasize areas of concern. Once fraud is uncovered, other activities of the employee may have to be examined to detect possible fraudulent actions. As the investigation proceeds, information obtained by interviews with employees is used to help determine audit emphasis. The auditor begins to develop answers to the following questions and plan his work accordingly.

Have cash, securities, or other assets been stolen?

Can the defalcation be easily determined, or does it require extensive tracing of transactions through the records?

What documents and other evidence are needed to prove both shortages and intent?

How far back does the shortage go?

Do records indicate that there have been prior shortages which have not been thoroughly investigated or have been covered up?

Has management been aware of any wrongdoing and taken any action?

How many persons are involved?

What is known or can be learned about their habits and finances?

Do personal files indicate employment verification?

Interviewing Techniques.   Interviewing and making inquiries of employees and outsiders become especially important procedures in conducting investigations. Information made available by a complainant, by employees and other witnesses, and by the suspected defrauder is often the key to the investigation. The internal auditor thus has to plan his interviews carefully to obtain the maximum evidence and benefit for the investigative effort.

Information from Complainant.   The original complainant should be interviewed in depth as soon as possible. If the complainant desires secrecy, he should be informed that his identity and confidentiality of information will be protected. If the complainant has documentary support for this allegation, this should be requested at the time of the interview. If the allegation is general in nature, the complainant may be able to refer the investigator to other personnel or records for more information. In some cases the allegation should be put in writing. Any evaluation should be made as soon as possible of the merits of the complaint. During the interview and preliminary survey of evidence, the internal auditor should attempt to determine action to be taken as follows:

Action dropped because allegation unsupported.

Turned over to management for administrative action, because there was no intent to defraud.

Full-scale investigation recommended and possible prosecutory action.

Considered abuse or wasteful management action rather than fraud; recommendation made for improvement in procedures.

Timing of Interview.   The auditor should make a determination as to whether interviews will be conducted early in the examination to enable him to pinpoint his approach and limit the extent of review of books and records. In some instances he may wish to perform preliminary auditing of the records in order to obtain information for conducting meaningful interviews. Generally, it is preferable to conduct the interview with the suspect early in the audit, while he is still on the job and available to answer questions as the audit progresses. In some cases, however, it may be necessary to remove a suspected employee from his position because his duties involved handling assets or controlling records where there is a possibility of hiding the fraud or misappropriating assets.

Rights of Employee.   Legal precedent supports the authority of the internal auditor to question individuals about company-related duties and actions while they are employed. This procedure is based on the employee's stewardship responsibility to the company. If an official investigation is begun to gather evidence for prosecution, however, the requirements for informing a suspect of his rights should be observed. When there are any questions on this, prosecuting officials or the legal staff should be consulted.

Conduct of Interview. The internal auditor should prepare an outline of the questions he wishes to ask. He should be prepared for both affirmative and negative responses to key questions. The auditor should avoid creating the impression that he is seeking a confession or conviction. It is preferable to appear in the role of one merely seeking the truth. The interviewer should be tactful when replies to questions do not agree with the facts obtained. He should point out the inconsistencies and ask for additional explanations. He should listen carefully to whatever the interviewee has to say, and relate questions to specific transactions and documents of interest. The skill of the interviewer is often a determining factor in obtaining information to use in the investigation. He must use one or more techniques, relying on his ability to size up the suspect and determine the approach that will work best.

There are various types of questions that can be asked, as listed below.

Open-Ended. This type of question is broad and unstructured, letting the interviewer give the answer as he sees it. Open-ended questions are intended to establish good communications and obtain the viewpoints of the interviewee. An example is: "Tell me about the internal control system."

Restatement. The purpose of restatement is to check the listener's understanding of what was said and to encourage the speaker to continue. An example is: "You say that the mail clerk sometimes hands envelopes to the accounting clerk without checking for receipts of cash?"

Probes. The purpose of probes is to obtain more specific information. The speaker is asked to explain in more detail when the responses are not sufficient. An example is: "Do you have any other information that would explain how this happened?"

Closed. This type of question is used when it is desired to lead the interviewee to express himself one way or another. An example is: "Do you record transactions daily or wait until near the end of the month?" The use of closed questions requires the interviewer to have background knowledge of the subject. This method is useful when it is desired to have the interviewee think through several alternatives and arrive at a conclusion.

Yes–no. This is a form of closed question which allows the interviewer to answer "yes," "no," and "I don't know." This type of question does not elicit much information, and should generally be replaced by questions that require more detailed answers.

Confession Statements. The employer has a right to ask a suspect to prepare a written statement explaining his actions, whether or not he confesses. A confession statement will be useful as evidence for prosecution and/or recovery. If there has been no confession, the suspect should be willing to explain his version of the facts. The confession, if made, must be voluntary and not under threat. The interrogation and subsequent confession may provide leads to additional fraudulent activities or to other individuals involved. If the confessed embezzler does not raise the question of restitution, the auditor should ask him when and how he proposes to make restitution.

Reappraisal of Internal Controls

At the conclusion of the investigation the internal auditor should make a careful analysis of the related internal controls. He should be concerned with the following:

Was the cause of the problem ineffective internal control, or controls not functioning?

Could the type of fraud committed occur elsewhere in the company?

Are additional preventive controls economically justifiable?

Would any proposed expansion fit into the normal pattern of the business and be accepted by employees, or would they be unworkable?

How could the audit program be revised to detect fraud of this nature?

Action against Employee

Based on the facts in the case, decisions have to be made on whether the employee will be dismissed, whether he will be prosecuted, and whether management will ask restitution. In addition, if the employee is prosecuted and found innocent, management must decide what his later position in the organization will be.

The internal auditor must be aware that it is very difficult in some cases to get a district attorney to prosecute. Decisions as to whether or not to prosecute may depend on the amount of the fraud, the type of crime, the type of evidence gathered, and in some cases the work load of the district attorney and current political considerations. It is especially frustrating for the internal auditor to complete an investigation, provide the evidence to the district attorney, and then have him decline to prosecute.

The surety company should be consulted regarding restitution. This is generally desired to reduce the amount of the loss. Since any restitution may affect the criminal prosecution, the district attorney's office and the surety company should be closely informed.

Writing the Report

The final report of investigation presents the evidence gathered and conclusions reached. It provides management with a summary of action taken as a result of leads and serves as a basis for decisions on how to handle the employee. A description is included of the process followed in committing the fraud. The amounts and dates of each item involved should also be included for submission to the surety company. Evidence should be retained for use in the prosecution, if needed. The report should attempt to identify the cause for the irregularity.

If there are weaknesses in control that need correction, recommendations should be made for remedial action. Exhibit 26.3 contains an example of an investigation of purchasing fraud conducted by an internal auditor.

Generally, the written report should include the following.

1. Source of discovery (regular audit, complaint, confession).

EXHIBIT 26.3   Fraud in Purchasing

During a test of purchasing transactions the internal auditor noted that purchases of off-the-shelf items were being made without competitive bids. Further analysis of these transactions indicated that most were justified based on competitive bids obtained or technical and emergency needs. However, about $500,000 of purchases with one source, XYZ Company, which were handled by purchasing agent John Weston, did not have justification for sole-source procurement. The prices paid for these items were 10% above the going market prices based on quotes obtained by the auditor and prices paid by other divisions of the company. Examination of the files indicated that there was no review required of justification used for sole-source procurement.

Although it appeared that this was an example of waste and the internal auditor could make a recommendation in his report that would save in excess of $45,000 a year, he decided to go a step further and check for possible fraud. He therefore (1) reviewed the file for a history of purchases of the material, (2) checked for relationships of the purchasing agent with the company, and (3) questioned other employees about the life-style of the purchasing agent. He found that purchases of the material had been made from another company at a lesser cost until two years ago, shortly after the purchasing agent had been hired. During the past two years, the purchasing agent's expense vouchers showed periodic instances of mileage claimed in connection with luncheon meetings with the sales manager of the XYZ Company. When asked about the life-style of Mr. Weston, three employees commented that he had recently gone through a divorce, was making frequent trips to resort areas, and seemed to be spending a great deal.

The auditor then checked the employee's personal files for references. He found that references had been checked only for the last employer. When Mr. Weston's previous employers were contacted by telephone, it was found that he had been allowed to resign a previous job when questions were raised about his dealings with suppliers.

The internal auditor discussed the matter with the legal counsel, who recommended that Mr. Weston be questioned. After discussion of the facts obtained by the auditor, Mr. Weston confessed that he had received kickbacks from XYZ Company of $30,000 in the past two years. Since the purchases of material were made for use under a contract funded by the state, the matter was turned over to the State Attorney General's office for prosecution.

A review of internal controls over purchasing indicated that there was the need for more segregation of duties among the staff, including the review of all sole-source procurement by an independent official. In addition, there was a large backlog of unfilled purchase requisitions, requiring extensive emergency purchasing and bypassing existing procedures to expedite the work effort. Management had previously been made aware of the problems but had not taken corrective action. The internal auditor's report included recommendations to management for strengthening controls to correct the above.

2. What was discovered (theft, misappropriation of funds).

3. Who was the defrauder (employee, manager, outside accomplice, collusion).

4. How much (audited amount, suspected amount, admitted amount).

5. How concealed (lapping, forgeries).

6. Length of thefts (when first started).

7. Effect on financial statements (how will loss or potential loss be reported).

8. Method of prevention (control deficiency, recommendations for future).

9. Prosecution (waived, pending, sentence, restitution).

FRAUD IN PERSPECTIVE

The need to assist management in the prevention and detection of fraud presents a real challenge to the internal auditor. To meet the need there must be sufficient time planned in the budget to provide this service. Because of its importance to management the prevention and detection of fraud often take precedence over other work. As such, careful planning and assessment of priorities are needed to assure that the broad responsibilities of internal auditing are met. For the short term it may be necessary to do fewer operational audits to handle investigations. It may also be necessary to devote significant resources to study the risk of fraud in a company and devise preventive measures. For the long term, however, the amount of time needed to be devoted to fraud measures should decrease. Also, the internal auditor should coordinate closely with management to assure that there are sufficient resources and time available to perform meaningful operational auditing. Demonstration to management of competence and beneficial findings in all areas of internal auditing will help in accomplishing this objective. It is thus important that the internal auditor and management work together to achieve the proper balance between fraud-oriented objectives and other broader needs and services. The internal auditor must then always be alert to the prevention and detection of fraud.

ILLUSTRATIVE AUDIT FINDINGS: FRAUD AND INVESTIGATIONS

Double Reimbursement of Expenses

Expenses for meals and other services were being billed twice because an employee submitted original bills for items that had been charged to a company credit card. The company did not require support for the credit card purchases, and did not review travel and expense vouchers of employees with credit cards for possible duplication. As a result, one employee received excess reimbursement of $3,400 in a two-year period.

Accepting Entertainment from Vendor

A company computer specialist was terminated for accepting more than 200 dinners for himself and his wife from a computer firm that received a $12 million contract from the company. Since these dinners were not in connection with regular business meetings of the company, and the computer specialist was in a position to influence the award of the contract, the dinners were considered in the nature of kickbacks.

Stealing Company Pension Checks

A review of company pension checks issued to retired employees indicated inadequate control over returned checks. Through further analysis it was found that an employee who had access to the returned checks (returned primarily because of death) was forging the checks and cashing them.

Sale of Company-Developed Material

At one leading research organization a scientist was asked to resign after the internal auditor found that he had sold human cell cultures developed with company funds to other groups at a personal profit of $67,000. The scientist agreed to make restitution of the money.

Theft of Receipts

As a result of inadequate control over refunds from vendors an employee was forging refund checks and cashing them. During a one-year period he misappropriated $75,000 in cash. In addition, unauthorized returns of goods were made, thus slowing the receipt of materials and equipment.

CHAPTER TWENTY-SEVEN

Auditing in Government and Other Nonprofit Organizations

GOVERNMENT CLIMATE

Taxpayers have increasingly raised questions concerning the operations of government at all levels. In recent years this had led to the rejection of proposed school bond and other issues on the basis that the benefits did not appear to justify the increased costs. There has also been greater emphasis on accountability. However, in spite of the questions raised, there has been a continuing increase in the size and complexity of government. Between the mid-1960s and the mid-1970s, the size of receipts and disbursements at all levels of government has more than doubled, and the range of their activities has widened.

Recently, taxpayers have taken a stronger stand on attempting to reduce the cost of government. The passage of Proposition 13 in California is one example of this. At the federal level, there have been increased attempts to balance the budget through reductions in spending. In some cases the attempt to reduce costs has led to the abolishment of programs and the lowering of service levels. In other cases decisions have been made without sufficient analysis of priorities and justification. This has sometimes resulted in discontinuing services without a substitute source for performing the service.

Accountability

By their nature public organizations are accountable in some sense. Police departments are accountable for keeping law and order, and the public works departments are responsible for keeping streets paved. Government officials and employees, as persons, are also considered accountable. The public organizations may be accountable to other government entities as well as to taxpayers at large.

Accountability means being responsible for constructive results and acts, including effective use of resources available. In a private business management is primarily judged by its ability to generate profits. A government organization, however, is responsible for delivering the best possible services and goods with the resources available.

On the surface, it may seem that it is much easier to hold businesses accountable since there is a better yardstick for performance. There are complications, however, caused by such factors as inflation, long-term versus short-term considerations, technology development, and environmental and energy problems. In the public sector, it may even be more difficult to evaluate performance because of the lack of definitive measures.

In determining accountability there is first the need to define exactly what the entity is accountable for. Agreement has to be reached as to what is expected, and policy has to be clarified. Next there has to be a measurement of performance, a gathering of evidence of accomplishments. This information has to be verified to determine reliability. Finally, there must be an evaluation or appraisal of performance data. There may be valid reasons for shortcomings in light of conditions. Judgments thus have to be made on accomplishments as to the extent they are good or bad.

Management of Resources

As applied to government the management of resources first involves identifying public needs and establishing priorities. Once needs are identified, specific objectives are developed for programs to meet the needs, and available resources are allocated to the programs.

The required resources should be obtained in the desired quantities, at the least cost, and in a timely manner. These resources include personnel, facilities, equipment, materials and supplies, and contractual services. Effective management of these resources results in increased utilization and output, decreased costs, and improved capability. These results are not obtained without effort, however, requiring specific programs and the use of sophisticated management techniques.

Another approach for reducing the cost of government has been the emphasis on cost-saving techniques. Attempts are made to improve the management of resources through improved government processes and methods, based on comprehensive cost–benefit analysis.

Financial Controls

The problems of large metropolitan cities have demonstrated the need for stronger financial controls over government operations. As part of controls, managers need valid financial information on a current basis for making decisions. There has thus been an increasing public awareness of the importance of effective financial administration.

This has been heightened by reports of fraud, abuse, and waste in government. In an attempt to improve the situation various levels of government have set priorities on eliminating such fraud, waste, and inefficiency. Single officials have been designated as accountable directly to agency heads to oversee their agencies' efforts to eliminate fraud and error.

In addition, the federal government has launched a Financial Priorities Program to resolve the major financial issues facing government. The program is designed to direct top management attention to needed improvements in agency financial systems. The priorities are worked out by the Office of Management and Budget, Congress, the Comptroller General, and the agencies. Some of the priorities agreed to by this group are upgrading internal control, improving accounting systems, taking more timely action on audit findings, encouraging prompt debt collection, and improving grant financing and accountability.

Government Activities

Government organizations at various levels perform many diverse and complex functions. Social programs are administered federally by such organizations as the Department of Health and Human Services, the Department of Labor, the Department of Education, and the Department of Housing and Urban Development. Special agencies such as the Veterans Administration also contribute to the social programs. The Department of Defense and its components carry out the military mission. Other organizations are regulatory in nature or have other functions, such as the Department of Commerce, the Department of Energy, and the Department of Justice. Above this level there is the Office of the President as well as Congress and the judiciary. At the state level there is the governor's office, the legislature, and various operating departments. At the county and city level, similar operating entities carry out local functions. In addition, there may be special districts, such as school districts and sanitation districts, for carrying out specialized functions. Exhibits 27.1 and 27.2 show the interrelationships of the various federal departments and state organizations as they bear on programs within one county, as presented in a survey report of the Office of State Controller, California.

Because of the number and complexity of the programs and size of the budget, auditing in government presents a challenge to the auditing profession. Internal auditing is continuing to expand in these various levels of government as officials recognize the need for periodic reviews of administration. The internal audit concepts and approaches developed in this book are similarly applicable to the reviews of governmental administration. There are, however, differences that present unique problems for the internal auditor.

Impact of Public Interest.   Government units are ultimately answerable to taxpayers, rather than to stockholders as in the private company (see Exhibit 27.3). There are no ownership accounts in government, but only surplus accounts or their equivalent, which represent the excess of fund assets over liabilities and reserves. Pressures are put on the public organization, however, by various interest groups, and the resultant policies may or may not be best for the individual taxpayer.

Lack of Public Yardsticks.   Public organizations do not have the profit yardsticks that the private sector has. As discussed in Chapter 24, private companies

EXHIBIT 27.1. Types of Grants Received in Alameda County

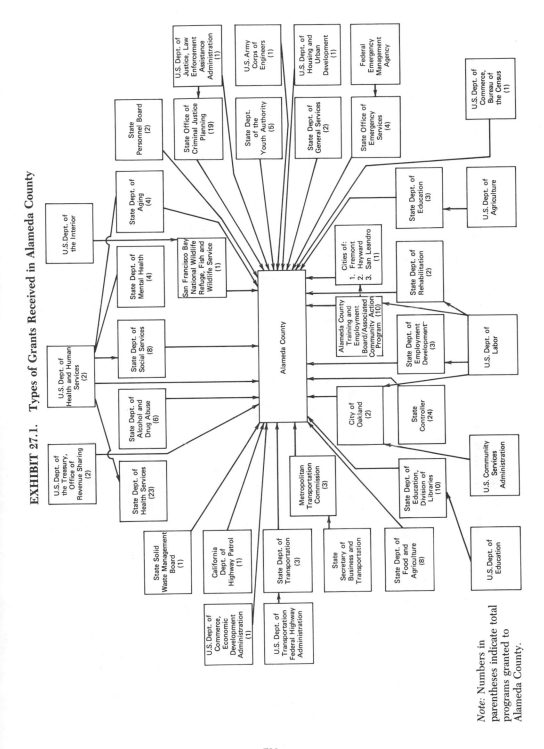

Note: Numbers in parentheses indicate total programs granted to Alameda County.

733

EXHIBIT 27.2. Alameda County Single Audit Concept:

Summary of Grantor Agencies Awarding Grants to Alameda County for the Period 1978–1979 Fiscal Year and 7/1/79 through 3/31/80

Grantor Agency	Revenues Received by Alameda County for the Period		Number of	
	1978–1979 Fiscal Year	7/1/79–3/31/80	Programs	Grants
1. State Department of Health Services	$ 33,674,793	$ 46,159,529	23	39
2. State Department of Alcohol and Drug Abuse	3,225,518	2,036,474	6	15
3. State Office of Criminal Justice Planning	1,845,470	841,862	19	38
4. State Controller	55,855,837	23,912,117	24	24
5. State Department of Education, Division of Libraries	318,289	284,832	10	14
6. Alameda County Training and Employment Board/Associated Community Action Program	7,498,135	4,398,910	10	21
7. City of Fremont; City of Hayward; City of San Leandro	16,392	9,706	3	4
8. State Department of Food and Agriculture	134,744	106,765	8	11
9. State Department of Social Services	140,674,932	108,934,727	8	10
10. State Department of the Youth Authority	428,964	1,000	5	5
11. State Department of Mental Health	8,498,808	5,289,525	4	4
12. State Department of Education	335,302	279,282	3	7
13. State Department of Transportation	213,623	502,153	3	4
14. State Department of Employment Development	230,529	46,321	3	4
15. U.S. Department of Health and Human Services	976,539	574,684	2	5
16. State Personnel Board	50,073	3,330	2	2
17. State Department of Rehabilitation	17,432	9,734	2	3
18. U.S. Department of Commerce, Economic Development Administration	7,402,933	256	1	2
19. Metropolitan Transportation Commission	140,485	213,740	3	7
20. City of Oakland	42,000	30,549	2	2
21. U.S. Department of Justice, Law Enforcement Assistance Administration	756,822	329,194	1	1
22. State Department of General Services	287,100	78,968	2	2
23. U.S. Department of Housing and Urban Development	2,090,174	2,100,962	1	1
24. State Office of Emergency Services	68,070	78,280	4	9
25. U.S. Army Corps of Engineers	87,342	63,528	1	1
26. San Francisco Bay National Wildlife Refuge, Fish and Wildlife Service	10,244	-0-	1	1
27. State Department of Aging	740,003	789,214	4	7
28. California Department of Highway Patrol	9,630	5,217	1	2
29. State Solid Waste Management Board	-0-	35,849	1	1
30. U.S. Department of Commerce, Bureau of Census	28,477	-0-	1	1
31. U.S. Department of Treasury, Office of Revenue Sharing	12,409,473	6,243,814	2	2
Total	$278,068,133	$203,360,522	160	249

734

EXHIBIT 27.3.   Private versus Government Organization

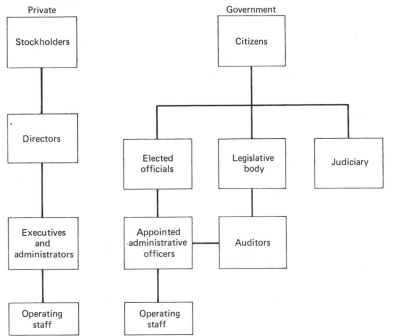

may have many objectives not directly related to profit, such as community betterment. The underlying objective, however, is the making of profit—the company with a significant increase in earnings is generally considered to have performed well. Without the profit yardstick in public organizations there has to be clear definition of the objectives of the programs. Measurement of how well these objectives are achieved, such as services rendered, is often very difficult.

Budgets.   Governmental entities operate on the basis of budgets, with constraints placed on spending in accordance with funds available during the fiscal year or other period. If an agency has spent all funds allotted, it cannot operate unless supplementary funds are appropriated or otherwise made available. On the other hand, if the agency has spent less than the funds available during the period, it must return the funds. Thus there is a tendency to use up all available funds, with expenditures sometimes made late in the year. There may also be restrictions on spending funds within classifications; that is, funds budgeted for salaries cannot be used for travel.

Financial Statements.   Emphasis in governmental entities is on reports prepared for individual funds, rather than on the overall balance sheet and income statement as in private companies. For grants and contracts received from other governmental or private resources, expenditure reports need to be submitted for reimbursement.

Type of Audits.   Government organizations may be audited annually, biennially, or for some other period, depending on the circumstances. Also, whereas audits of private companies are financial and operational in nature, audits of government organizations include more specialized financial and compliance auditing, reviews for efficiency and economy, and program results audits, as described later in the chapter.

Legal and Regulatory Requirements.   Programs of government organizations are often prescribed by legislation. Implementing regulations and grant and contract provisions add other constraints to performance. These may include such requirements as eligibility for services and cost sharing.

SCOPE OF GOVERNMENTAL AUDITS

In the discussion of objectives of internal audits we have emphasized the importance of decisions as to audit coverage. Because of the diversity of audit objectives there has been an attempt on the part of the profession to define the government auditor's general responsibilities as part of auditing standards.

The 1981 publication of General Accounting Office (GAO) Standards for Audit of Governmental Organizations, Programs, Activities and Functions defines the elements of an audit as follows:

1. *Financial and Compliance.* Determines (a) whether the financial statements of an audited entity present fairly the financial position and the results of financial operations in accordance with generally accepted accounting principles and (b) whether the entity has complied with laws and regulations that may have a material effect upon the financial statements.

2. *Economy and Efficiency.* Determines (a) whether the entity is managing and utilizing its resources (such as personnel, property, space) economically and efficiently, (b) the causes of inefficiencies or uneconomical practices, and (c) whether the entity has complied with laws and regulations concerning matters of economy and efficiency.

3. *Program Results.* Determines (a) whether the desired results or benefits established by the legislature or other authorizing body are being achieved and (b) whether the agency has considered alternatives that might yield desired results at a lower cost.

Similar requirements for audit coverage were included in the "Standards for the Professional Practice of Internal Auditing" published by The Institute of

Internal Auditors in 1978. Under Scope of Work, Section 300,[1] the following are required:

Internal auditors should review the reliability and integrity of financial and operating information and the means used to identify, measure, classify, and report such information.

Internal auditors should review the systems established to ensure compliance with those policies, plans, procedures, laws, and regulations which could have a significant impact on operations and reports, and should determine whether the organization is in compliance.

Internal auditors should review the means of safeguarding assets and, as appropriate, verify the existence of such assets.

Internal auditors should appraise the economy and efficiency with which resources are employed.

Internal auditors should review operations or programs to ascertain whether results are consistent with established objectives and goals and whether the operations or programs are being carried out as planned.

In Chapter 2 the scope of The Institute's Standards was also interpreted to include the internal auditor's concern with helping the organization to achieve the best possible utilization of organizational resources—thus seeking *maximum effectiveness* in developing and implementing all organizational objectives. There were also other interpretations of possible extensions of practice that the authors considered to be constructive. With those additional interpretations, we believe that The Institute Standards combine well with the GAO Standards to be a sound basis for all internal auditing activities in governmental organizations. We believe also that the entire book *Modern Internal Auditing* —despite its greater emphasis on business practice—can be very useful in all governmental internal auditing practice. To a considerable extent government representatives and officers have less control over governmental objectives and policies than do the manager and board of directors of business organizations. Nevertheless, a great deal can still be done, and it follows that internal auditors in government should do all possible to assist in the greatest possible achievement of those improvement potentials.

Types of Government Audits

In Exhibit 27.4 the various types of government audits are classified. However, it should be recognized that these types of audits are not mutually exclusive, but often overlap. For example, a financial review may disclose the overstatement of costs in a grant through misclassification, resulting in less funds available for the project. This, in turn, may affect the program results obtained. Also, in compliance audits the program results may be specifically defined as part of

---

[1]See also Chapter 2.

EXHIBIT 27.4. Scope of Government Audits

	Financial and Compliance	Economy and Efficiency	Program Results
Criteria	Generally accepted accounting principles, laws, regulations	Policies, procedures, standards, budgets	Goals, objectives, performance standards
Effect	Accuracy of reports, use of funds	Cost savings or waste	Accomplishment of objectives or progress made
Audit emphasis	Financial statements	Acquisition and utilization of materials, facilities, and personnel	Programs or departmental operations
Period	Historical	Historical, present and future	Historical, present and future
Audit report	Opinion on fairness of presentation and compliance	Conclusions and recommendations to obtain corrective action	Conclusions and recommendations to obtain corrective action

the requirements. Efficiency and economy factors may relate to financial and compliance audits and to reviews of program results. Thus the auditor should be aware of the expanded scope of auditing when performing his work, and extend his scope as needed to achieve the objectives of the assignment.

Financial and Compliance Audits

In the early days of internal auditing in government the major emphasis was on financial and accounting matters. Many internal auditors were thus recruited from the ranks of external auditors. Similarly, the emphasis of government auditors was on financial reviews of billings to the government, together with reviews of compliance with laws, regulations, and contract and grant provisions.

Although there has been a trend toward audits of efficiency and economy and results, the need for financial reviews remains. When annual audits are performed by external auditors and efforts are coordinated, the need may be reduced. The GAO Standards, as they relate to financial audits, endorse the generally accepted standards of the American Institute of Certified Public Accountants. Unqualified audits performed by the external auditors should thus meet those requirements.

In some nonprofit entities, however, there may be a lack of financial controls as indicated by any of the following:

Records not posted currently.

Monthly financial statements not prepared.

External audits not performed annually or reports qualified.

Inequitable allocations of indirect costs.

Budgets not prepared.

Overruns on projects.

Budgeted figures used for salary charges.

Working capital position weak.

Nonsegregation of costs by projects.

Unauthorized use of restricted funds.

Under these circumstances, the government auditor may have to give increased attention to financial matters.

Compliance auditing may be considered as separate from financial auditing in many instances. However, noncompliance with certain program requirements may create real liabilities or loss contingencies that must be reported. Specific compliance requirements for governmental grants and programs are included in audit guides prepared by some departments. When guides are not available, the auditor should review applicable statutes, regulations, instructions, and copies of grant or contract documents.

The GAO has listed six general compliance requirements of governmental programs: recipient eligibility, coverage of services, matching requirements, maintenance of effort, indirect cost rate determination and allocation, and cost principles.[2]

In practice the auditor may encounter difficulty in obtaining all the data needed to perform a compliance audit. The statutes and regulations may be unclear in some areas, and changes in regulations may not be readily available. In some cases audit guides may not be prepared, or if prepared, may be in draft form without approval. In other cases the audit guides may not be updated to reflect current requirements and revised approaches based on experience in prior audits. It is thus incumbent on the auditor to obtain up-to-date information from a variety of sources during the survey phase.

Efficiency and Economy Audits

The purpose of an efficiency and economy audit is to determine whether an entity is managing or utilizing its resources (personnel, facilities, materials, etc.) in an effective manner. Managers are interested in obtaining cost savings, and thus look for ways to improve the management of resources. The term "economy audit" means the appraisal of performance at least costs; the "efficiency audit" involves a review of benefits obtained in relation to costs incurred.

This type of auditing was often an outgrowth of financial and compliance

[2]United States General Accounting Office, "Guidelines for Financial and Compliance Audits of Federally Assisted Programs," Supt. of Documents, Washington, D.C., February 1980, p. 9.

auditing. In addition to reviewing the transactions for proper support, auditors began asking such questions as whether an expenditure was necessary and whether the service could be obtained at less cost. Findings with significant cost savings tended to receive the immediate attention of management. With the increased emphasis on operational auditing, internal auditors revised their traditional approaches to look specifically for areas for achieving economy throughout all the entity's activities. This has been increasingly important to government organizations with inflation and the emphasis on reducing taxes.

Audit Approach.   The auditor should begin by reviewing the entity's system and operations to identify areas where efficiency and economy might be improved. Meetings should be held with officials to discuss sensitive areas and to obtain information as to problems. Budgets and actual expenses are reviewed for significant deviations and to determine material items for emphasis.

The auditor searches for efficiency inhibitors (such as problems in organizational structuring and responsibilities), operational breakdowns, and substandard results. He also looks for the continuation of projects that have outlived their usefulness.

The auditor then reviews specific functions, or operations, to determine potential cost savings. Some of these are procurement, personnel, cash management, facilities acquisition and utilization, research activities, and maintenance. He looks for noncompliance with the organization's policies and procedures, and also determines whether efficiency can be improved by good management practices. He looks for variances between planned and actual performance. He also analyzes operations for various cost improvement opportunities.

The auditor's ability to determine potential cost savings quickly depends on his experience and knowledge of sensitive areas. He reviews past audits for various leads. He studies publications of various professional organizations, both within and outside government, for the experiences of other auditors. Through this background he knows what to look for in audits, and can shorten the time needed to arrive at conclusions. For example, in his review of purchases the auditor looks into the following areas for potential cost savings:

Insufficient competitive bids.

Feasibility of using more economical purchasing systems, such as blanket purchase orders and use of charge accounts.

Lack of adequate review of cost data for sole-source procurement (possible inflated quantities or prices).

Excessive or unwarranted prices paid for change orders.

Delays in filling requisitions.

Unjustified use of emergency purchases.

Uneconomical quantity purchases.

Unjustified buy, lease, or make decisions.

Lack of follow-up on defects caused by warranties.

Program Results

Program results or effectiveness is goal attainment, or the extent that a program or activity achieves its objectives. Basically, it is the answer to the question: What is management or the taxpayer getting for money spent? The emphasis is thus on "outputs" rather than on "inputs."

Audits of program results have sometimes been performed on an experimental basis because of the state of the art. Often there has been no precedent for this type of audit, and specific guidelines have not been prepared. In addition, measurement criteria may not be available for some programs.

Although the General Accounting Office Standards require a coverage of program results, those Standards do not expect auditors to render an opinion on effectiveness. Instead, they require the auditor to state conclusions and recommendations based on his work.

The following are some suggested approaches for performing an effectiveness audit. In general the auditor first determines the specific goals, reviews the measurement system of the auditee (if there is a system), develops data independently when not otherwise available, and arrives at conclusions as to results obtained.

Determining Goals.   The auditor begins by obtaining an understanding of the program and determining its goals. In some cases goals and objectives may be clearly defined, whereas in others they may be obscure. For government programs the auditor first reviews legislation and legislative intent by studying background data. He also reviews regulations and instructions issued to implement the program. Finally, he examines specific proposals and contract and grant requirements. In some cases he may determine goals by review of correspondence and reports or interviews with operating officials.

Review of Measurement System.   The auditor should first determine whether the organization has a system to measure effectiveness. After setting goals, managers attempt to chart progress toward achieving the goals. The data generated by this system can be used by the internal auditor in reviewing program results. Exhibit 27.5 shows the elements of an effectiveness measurement system. This system includes performance indicators, standards for achievement, and the collection of data for comparing performance with that expected.

In some instances the program objective may be the performance indicator. However, generally, performance indicators need to be developed. Often, multiple performance indicators and measurable surrogates need to be developed, such as in the program to improve highway safety. Although safety is not directly measurable, several measurable surrogates exist, such as number of accidents, number of injuries, and extent of property damage.

The performance standard may be difficult to select because objectives are often stated in terms of providing or increasing services. It is management's responsibility to set the desired level of attainment, and this should be part of

EXHIBIT 27.5.   Elements of an Effectiveness Measurement System
_____

I.   Structural Components

A.   Performance indicators:
        quantifiable expressions of program objectives
B.   Data source:
        base from which information about performance indicators can be obtained
C.   Performance standards:
        desired level of achievement for a performance indicator

II.   Process Activities

A.   Data collection process:
        collecting performance indicator data from the data source
B.   Comparison process:
        comparing the actual status of a performance indicator with the appropriate
        performance standard to determine the extent of program effectiveness
_____

Source: U.S. General Accounting Office, Draft, "Comprehensive Approach for Planning
and Conducting a Program Results Review," 1978, p.16.

the measurement system. Generally, the performance standard is set at a level
that is reasonable and compatible with program objectives and legislative intent.

Development of System.   When management does not have an effectiveness
measurement system, the auditor should attempt to develop a method for
reviewing effectiveness. This will involve working closely with management or
program officials to develop mutually acceptable criteria for the assessment of
performance. Without such agreement, the auditor would have the burden of
defending the criteria used. In some cases he can obtain reasonable criteria
based on knowledge of the subject being audited. In Chapter 12 we discussed
the use of various criteria in audits when there are no identifiable performance
indicators.

   In general, the auditor attempts to develop a system (sometimes called an
"ad hoc" system) that would obtain similar results to a management system.
In some cases this means the separate identification and gathering of data to
document results. Although the results may not be as precise as a management
system, the auditor may be able to pinpoint significant problems in obtaining
program results.

Conclusions.   Once data as to performance are obtained, the auditor compares
performance with standards. Deviations are then analyzed as to their significance, and whether there is the need for improvement. In some cases, the
standards may have been unrealistic. The deviations should be discussed carefully with management to determine cause, for example, diversion of resources,
insufficient direction and monitoring, faulty standards, and changed conditions.

AUDIT COORDINATION

Government organizations have recently extended their efforts to coordinate the audits of various government programs. This is especially important because of the overlapping interest in various programs. Often, federal grants are made to a state, which in turn grants funds to counties, cities, or special districts. In addition, grants may be made directly to local entities by the federal, state, and county, or city governments. Each of these entities may share in the costs of the grant. In addition, more than one federal department may be providing grants to a state or local entity. In other instances, grants may be made directly to private organizations with joint funding by the various government entities as well as private means. This grant process results in audit interest in a particular entity by various audit groups. The relationships illustrated in Exhibit 27.1 are diagrammed by flow in Exhibit 27.6.

Need for Coordination

The growth of federal, state, and local expenditures has placed increasing burdens on the audit function. In fiscal year 1980 federal aid amounted to about $90 billion, of which about $84 billion went to state and local governments. The magnitude of the audit work loads, coupled with the limited availability of staff and the need for timely audits, requires the implementation of approaches that provide audit coverage with a minimum of effort. At the same time, the audit effort must be of sufficient scope to provide reasonable assurance that programs are being operated in an efficient and effective manner. There has therefore been the need to develop programs of coordination that would maximize the

EXHIBIT 27.6.   Flow of Grant Funds—Federal, State, and Local Governments

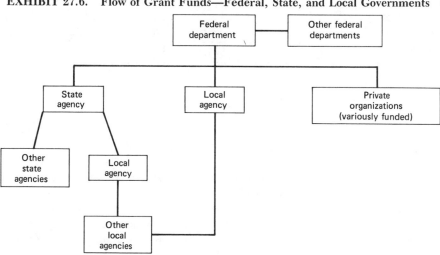

use of resources of various audit groups which have a common interest in an auditee's operations.

This need has been intensified by the objections of grantees that they are audited by too many different audit groups. This results in some instances in duplicate auditing, inordinate use of time of auditee personnel, and disruptions in operations. In addition, piecemeal auditing of specific departmental grants does not provide the assurances that an overall review provides. The various governmental audit groups have thus experimented with different methods of coordination to avoid some of these problems.

Joint Audits

One approach has been to staff audits jointly when audit groups have a common interest in programs. This assures that both audit groups provide input as to how the audits are conducted. In addition, training can be provided where an auditor is unfamiliar with a particular problem. Upon completion of the audit a joint report is prepared which is signed by the head of each audit group.

Cooperative Approach

In some cases one audit group will perform an audit at the request of another group, using that organization's guidelines and technical assistance. This is especially helpful where one audit group has developed expertise in the review of a program and can thus be of assistance in a cooperative audit. Reliance on audits of others may be desirable when audit resources are insufficient for the one organization to perform the audits, and the other organization is willing to perform a review of various programs of the auditee.

The extent of coordination and planning and monitoring needed is, of course, dependent on such factors as the complexity of the program, adequacy of guides, capabilities of staff, and familiarity with the programs. Exhibit 27.7 contains a guide used by one governmental audit organization for providing technical assistance and monitoring the audit work of another. This guide also can be very useful by individual government audit groups to evaluate the effectiveness of their own audit activities.

Single Audit

Under the single-audit approach one agency performs the audit of all government contracts and grants at a specific entity. This is illustrated in the audit of most of the universities, at which the Department of Health and Human Services, the cognizant audit agency, audits all grants and contracts for the government on a reimbursable basis under cross-servicing agreements. The use of cross servicing was encouraged by the issuance in September 1973 of a circular, now called OMB Circular A-73, which required the federal agency with the principal financial interest in a multifunded grantee to study the feasibility of conducting audits for the other grantor agencies.

EXHIBIT 27.7. Guide for Coordinated Audits

I. Background Data

Once it has been determined that another audit group will perform the audit, it is our responsibility to assure that all pertinent data relating to the program to be audited are available to those concerned.

1. To help assure the timely promulgation of information required by outside audit groups, preparations of informational packages might be advisable. This package should include the following:

   a. Audit Guides
   b. Copies of significant findings or reports.
   c. A synopsis of known or suspected problem areas. Remarks or suggestions by program personnel should be solicited and included.
   d. Comments on suggested audit approaches or specific program steps.
   e. When possible, an inventory of contracts, grants, or appropriation amounts which will be audited by the outside group.
   f. Related reviews or audits completed, planned, or in progress (GAO, CPA firm, state or local audit groups, etc.).
   g. Summary information from program representatives' correspondence file and trip reports.
   h. Summaries of findings from reports on similar entities from other States and Regions.
   i. Applicable acts, laws, regulations, state plans, and general counsel decisions.
   j. All other information deemed appropriate.

2. Current information on the status of all audits in process or planned by outside groups should be maintained. This would enable immediate dissemination of any new data received.

3. Names and location of program representatives should be provided in case technical matters need to be discussed during the audit. In some instances it may be desirable for our office to provide the liaison.

II. Discussing Audit

The necessity and advisability of periodic meetings during the course of an audit should be determined. All possible questions cannot be covered in background information which is disseminated to the audit group. Therefore, we should inform the group that we will make personnel available to answer additional questions. These meetings could be on a planned or as needed basis.

1. The frequency of these discussions should be based on several factors, such as past experience under the cooperative audit concept, complexity of assignment, etc. For example, for the first audit performed under this concept, pertinent discussions could be held after the survey, during the field work, and before the report is finalized.

2. During the course of the audits, we will probably be approached several times to answer specific questions. Although we should provide answers to questions, care must be exercised to prevent giving the impression that we are managing the audit.

EXHIBIT 27.7. (*Continued*)

3. At the conclusion of each discussion, a memorandum should be prepared covering points discussed and areas for follow-up.

III. Evaluating Completed Audits

The final procedure to be considered under this concept is to provide a method of evaluating the audits completed by other audit groups. Depending on the adequacy of the audit, we can either accept the audit fully or in part. Normally, evaluations will be performed after completion of the audit. However, interim evaluations including reviews of approach or scope may be performed.

1. Determine whether planning was performed. Did the outside auditor obtain sufficient background information on the audit prior to the initiation of field work?

2. Determine the adequacy of audit programs prepared. Did the programs specifically identify the objectives of the audit? Determine whether the audit program used substantially agrees with the recommended audit steps contained in the guides.

3. Compare the outside auditor's objectives to our objectives for the audit.

4. Determine whether the experience and qualifications of the outside auditors meet our minimum standards.

5. Determine the extent of supervision exercised during the course of the audit and evaluate whether it was adequate.

6. Determine if the working papers define the scope of audit such as:
    a. Amount subject to audit.
    b. Whether or not random sampling was used.
    c. Description of how items were selected for test.
    d. Specific list of documents tested and the audit techniques applied.

7. Ascertain whether conclusions and discrepancies are identified on workpapers where testing occurred. Are all open discrepancies carried forward to a summary for resolution? If not, determine what other procedures were used to control exceptions. Secure, if necessary, copies of exception control schedules.

8. Determine whether discrepancies were discussed and fully investigated during the resolution process.

9. Determine whether working papers generally showed the scope, source, conclusion, and purpose of preparation.

10. Determine whether the effect of findings was quantified and recommendations made for recovery of funds in accordance with our procedures.

11. Determine the sampling plan used, and if random sampling was not used, determine whether there was any adverse effect.

12. Ascertain the amount of audit time expended and determine whether this time appears reasonably close to our estimate of requirements.

13. Determine whether a copy of the audit report was referenced to the applicable working papers.

14. Determine whether the period of audit was reasonably close to the period in which we are interested.

EXHIBIT 27.7.   (*Continued*)

---

15.   Determine whether the audit group prepared its report in such form and included such information for review to reasonably meet the requirements of the granting agency.

16.   If the report was prepared in our behalf, determine if the required format was followed. Where material deviations are noted, determine the circumstances and evaluate their effect on our responsibilities.

In October 1978 the General Accounting Office issued "Guidelines for Financial and Compliance Audits of Federally Assisted Programs" (updated February 1980) to serve as a guide for ensuring a uniform audit approach for audits of organizations receiving funds under several federally assisted programs. In October 1979 the Office of Management and Budget issued attachment P to Circular A-102, which directed federal departments and agencies to improve audit coordination by requiring the use of these guidelines and to increase their reliance on audits by state or local governments. Under this attachment audits of federally assisted programs are to be made on an organization-wide basis rather than on a grant-by-grant basis, and a single audit is to be performed.

Several barriers inhibit additional use of cross servicing. These will include (1) lack of definitive guidelines for audit of various programs, (2) lack of direct reimbursement policies, (3) large number and complexity of government programs, (4) individual service desired by program representatives of each department, (5) unwillingness of auditors to accept the work of others, (6) limited government audit staff and inflexibility in adjusting the number of positions, (7) lack of independence of auditors under GAO Standards, (8) lack of agreement on use of statistical sampling to project exceptions, (9) need for uniform interpretation of materiality in determining whether adjustments are needed in specific programs, and (10) extent of problems disclosed in quality of audits performed by other audit groups. Currently the various federal, state, and local auditors are working together to solve some of these problems through the Intergovernmental Audit Forums.

In addition, Appendix P to the Guidelines requires that quality assessment reviews be made of the work of nonfederal audit organizations. A study is being made of methods of performing peer reviews to determine the acceptability of work of others. As efforts are made to expand the use of single auditing, it is expected that peer reviews will be a useful device to ascertain capabilities and determine the need for improvements.

Need for Additional Guides

As coordination efforts increase and auditors are faced with reviewing programs of other departments, the need for guides increases. In addition, the increases in the number and complexity of social programs require that more attention be devoted to effective audit guides.

Audit guides serve to:

Standardize approach.

Assure that objectives of the audit are met.

Provide guidance on special technical and compliance matters.

Select audit procedures most appropriate.

Decrease audit time required.

Audit guides for government programs usually show background, audit objectives, audit program, method of report presentation, and details as to entrance and exit conferences. Where there is the need to report on specific compliance matters, detailed instructions should be given relating to the program. In addition, audits of program results require information as to program objectives, performance indicators, and performance standards.

The General Accounting Office has developed three sets of guidelines for the performance of financial and compliance (as previously noted), efficiency and economy, and program results audits. These guidelines attempt to provide the auditor with overall guidance for review of various programs.

Because of the changes in programs the applicable audit guides must be revised periodically. Often, revisions are made informally as auditors gain experience with the programs. All revisions should be defined as soon as possible and disseminated to other interested auditors. This is especially important because of the various groups performing the audits.

TRENDS IN GOVERNMENT AUDITING

The demand for auditing in government continues to increase with the growth in government activities and emphasis on cost effectiveness. This trend exists at the various levels of government: federal, state, and local. Along with this growth there has been increasing emphasis on professionalism. Government auditors are interested in attaining excellence, attempting to improve their skills commensurate with the auditing profession as a whole and the standards of both the General Accounting Office and The Institute of Internal Auditors. At the same time, they have developed special auditing procedures and techniques to solve problems unique to the public sector.

Use of Advanced Audit Techniques

The size and nature of government operations have stimulated the development of advanced audit techniques. Government auditors have pioneered in the use of statistical sampling to review large populations of data. Findings projected based in statistical sampling have been increasingly translated into money terms. This has enabled the auditors to review voluminous data with a minimum of resources, both for taking dollar exceptions and for quantifying the magnitude of potential cost-saving opportunities. As an example of advanced sampling techniques, one audit group used stratified multistage sampling to project state-wide results of activities that were performed at 58 counties within the state.

The use of computer software packages in auditing data has also become widespread. As an example, one department reviewed the acceptability of all physician and pharmacy bills for one year in every state using a special program which compared bills for services to predetermined standards. Significant exceptions were then printed and used by the auditor in reviewing individual physicians' practices.

Reliance on Other Auditors

There has been a trend toward accepting the work of others in determining the extent of government auditing to be done. This has resulted from new demands on the auditors' time which limit resources, complaints from auditees as to duplication of effort and disruptions of personnel, and a growing acceptance of the capabilities of others. Public accountants and internal auditors are more and more being asked to perform reviews of public grants and contracts. Federal, state, and local auditors undertake cooperative efforts and rely on others' work. Pilot studies are being made to refine the cooperative efforts, in some cases using a single audit that will suffice for all interested groups. Guidelines are being developed for peer reviews, with some consideration given to determining the overall capability, and possible accreditation, of audit groups. The overall trend is based on a realization that professional auditors, regardless of their employer, can do the job of auditing the large and often complex activities of government.

Reporting Levels

Similar to the internal audit profession as a whole, there has been increasing emphasis on reporting to higher levels of government. This trend is to assure the independence of the government auditor and to obtain better actions on audit recommendations. The need for a higher level of reporting has been intensified by the expanded scope of auditing in government beyond the financial areas.

This trend is exemplified by the statutory requirement for an Inspector General in various federal departments. Under this change the audit function is part of the Office of Inspector General, who reports directly to the Secretary and to Congress.

Timely Corrective Action

The role of the government auditor has tended to go beyond the development and reporting of audit findings to the corrective action stage. This includes providing technical assistance to management in implementing the findings, clarifying questions raised, and performing follow-up reviews to assure that corrective action is taken.

On-Line Auditing

Experiments have been made in auditing systems and operations on a more current basis. This approach, called on-line auditing or concurrent auditing, makes it possible to detect weaknesses in control at an early stage and recommend more timely corrective action. Because of the large volume of government transactions, it is often difficult to audit two or three years after the fact and question large amounts. Some audit groups are experimenting with concurrent auditing to prevent questionable spending of government funds over extended periods. In total government administrators are enabled to improve operational approaches in time to minimize ongoing deficiencies.

Training and Professionalism

Increasing demands on government auditors has led to a growth in training provided, both within government organizations and on the outside. Professional organizations, for example, The Institute of Internal Auditors, the American Institute of Certified Public Accountants, and the Association of Government Accountants, have sponsored special courses in government auditing. These have covered a wide spectrum, from operational auditing and advanced audit techniques to requirements for auditing specialized programs. Also, government auditors have increased their membership in professional associations as they develop capabilities and wish to enhance their professional growth. They have also expanded their numbers of staff who are certified under various programs, and have attempted to gain increased recognition of governmental experience.

OTHER NONPROFIT ORGANIZATIONS

Many of the audit approaches used in reviews of governmental organizations also pertain to other nonprofit organizations. The sources of the funds for these entities may be from various levels of government, as well as from individual persons, foundations, or business corporations. Gifts and donations received from private foundations and others may have restrictions in the use of funds similar to those placed on government grants. Being nonprofit, these organizations have management objectives and responsibilities similar to those in government. From an audit viewpoint, therefore, the review of these organizations may not be essentially different from that of government grantees. However, operational activities of these organizations will vary greatly.

For many nonprofit organizations—especially when those organizations are new—there may be problems in management. These problems may also occur when an organization obtains new grants or gifts, expanding its conventional operations. Under these circumstances special audit approaches may be necessary in light of the problems faced.

Types of Organizations

The types of other nonprofit organizations cover a wide range. They include such organizations as hospitals, churches, universities, foundations, libraries, associations, professional groups, youth groups, cultural groups, and miscellaneous service organizations. They may be funded in part by private corporations and individuals, grants from the government and foundations, and donations. They may also receive revenue from services performed or goods sold. Some are relatively small in size, whereas others are large corporations with many divisions and employees. In many cases individual organizations, such as hospitals and universities, may also have extremely large numbers of personnel and resources, and involve many types of specialized activities. Some of the older organizations, such as the Boy Scouts or American National Red Cross, have established systems of internal control. Other entities, organized to meet the need for special services, may have limited resources and management expertise.

Nature of Problems

The problems of nonprofit organizations can be described in general terms as the failure to apply sound business standards of the quality practiced in typical profit-based organizations. In many situations personnel serve without compensation or at levels below those in the business world. In many situations also there is a concentration on the human aspects of the activities that conflicts with the more business-oriented approach that is the requirement for efficiency and survival in profit organizations. This typical character of nonprofit organizations varies widely, depending on the particular type of organization, but may include the following more specific deficiencies.

Money Management.   Managers often face problems of cash levels becoming dangerously low because of inadequate financing, unexpected expenditures, and ineffective collections. Often there is the need for more careful cash budgeting and control over acquisitions and expenditures.

Financial Records.   Ineffective record keeping often leads to inadequate financial information for managers to make decisions. This may be caused in part by the failure of a professional accountant to develop a system and assure that it is operating effectively. In addition, management must understand the accounting system and the information that it provides.

Revenue Fluctuations.   Often there is the problem of developing a strong revenue base that will make it possible to stabilize operations. For new, developing organizations it may be especially difficult to prevent wide variations in revenues. A marketing strategy may also be needed to determine additional sources of revenue and keep the entity going.

Management Abilities. In smaller organizations management may be relatively unsophisticated. Before starting a new organization, the top people may not have the time to familiarize themselves with all aspects of operations —personnel, budgeting, purchasing, accounting, and proposal preparation. Also, management may change frequently in a new or growing entity. Under these circumstances problems may be encountered in developing effective controls and running the organization.

Internal Control. Management may be turned over to a few individuals in the organization. Under these circumstances there may be no separation of duties and other elements of an effective system of internal control. Within the limitations of staff and other resources, internal controls may need strengthening to help the organization achieve its purposes. Exhibit 27.8 is an example of audit program steps used by an audit department to identify problem areas in a private nonprofit organization.

INTERNAL AUDITING IN GOVERNMENT AND OTHER NONPROFIT ORGANIZATIONS IN PERSPECTIVE

Internal auditors in government and other nonprofit organizations have unique problems as they seek to provide the best possible assistance to those not-for-profit areas. It is desirable, however, that internal auditors there understand and make use of the professional resources of the total internal auditing profession. At the same time internal auditors in the business sector have an interest in the effectiveness with which all of the governmental and nonprofit activities are conducted—and in turn the level of effectiveness of the internal auditing activities. There are thus important common interests which set the stage for a closer relationship between the internal auditors of both the profit and nonprofit groups. As is true for *all* internal auditing, we achieve progress through sharing, and in this case there are especially major rewards from working together in a partnership relationship.

ILLUSTRATIVE AUDIT FINDINGS: GOVERNMENT AND NONPROFIT ORGANIZATIONS

Claiming Costs for Equipment Not Used

A review of expenditures made under a cost-type contract indicated that capital equipment of $17,500 was acquired two weeks before the end of the contract. Since this equipment could not be used on government work, the auditor recommended that the contractor refund the $17,500 to the government.

EXHIBIT 27.8. Audit Guide:
Review of Private Nonprofit Organization

1. Review and analyze current balance sheets and income statements to determine major fluctuations and financial capability.

2. Ascertain whether an annual audit is performed by a public accountant.

3. Determine whether property and supplies are acquired through a competitive bid system.

4. Determine whether there is excess cash on hand representing premature withdrawals under letter of credit (excess advances) received from government agencies.

5. Ascertain whether books are posted currently and monthly financial statements are prepared.

6. Examine the payroll system to assure that payroll charges are based on actual work performed rather than budgeted.

7. Review the methods of accumulating costs in overhead and methods of distribution to assure consistency of charges and equitable allocation methods.

8. Review the bid proposal system to determine that proposals reflect current costs and projected increases.

9. Determine whether compliance provisions of grants and contracts are being met, such as eligibility and cost sharing.

10. Ascertain whether there are significant cost transfers between programs substantially after completion of work.

11. Analyze overruns and underruns experienced under projects.

12. Review the personnel system for controls over hiring and setting pay levels.

13. Determine whether there is unused capacity (space, equipment).

14. Examine lease agreements and other contracts to determine possible cost savings.

15. Review consultants' agreements to determine whether the services were needed and performed.

16. Ascertain that all revenues are properly accounted for and distributed to appropriate programs.

17. Review the budgeting system for revenues and expenditures.

18. Review the reporting system to management, granting and donor agencies, and the board of directors.

19. Review controls over donations and determine that revenues from donations are used for purposes intended.

Spending Funds for All Students Rather than for Group Authorized

In a review of the ESEA Title I program at a school district the auditor found that the school district had spent $97,000 for a closed-circuit TV system which was used for all students at the schools rather than solely for the educationally disadvantaged. This was contrary to the legislative requirements, since it deprived the educationally disadvantaged of special programs for their benefit. A refund of $97,000 was recommended.

Credit Not Given for Checks Uncashed

The grantee was not giving the government credit for checks that were out-standing for long periods of time. Some checks were outstanding for as long as five years. It was recommended that the grantee give the government credit for $1,200,500, representing all grant checks outstanding over six months.

Earning Interest on Excess Government Funds

The university was drawing excess funds from the federal government under the letter of credit and investing the excess funds along with other cash at the university. During the past year the internal auditors calculated that the university earned $42,000 on the excess government funds. It was recommended that the university give the $42,000 to the federal government and withdraw funds only when needed.

Unacceptable Financial System for Performing Government Work

Significant improvements were needed in financial systems of a community health center applying for a grant. Monthly or quarterly financial statements were not prepared, books were not posted to date, year-end statements were not audited by public accountants, and budgets were not being prepared. The internal auditor recommended in a pre-award report that the financial systems be strengthened to provide better control over costs and provide more accurate reports to management and the government.

PART FOUR

Special Relationships and Evaluation

CHAPTER TWENTY-EIGHT

Serving the Audit Committee
of the Board of Directors

ROLE OF THE AUDIT COMMITTEE

In Chapters 1 and 2 the expanding use of audit committees of the board of directors was discussed. It is now appropriate to focus on the audit committee in greater depth and to consider more specifically how the internal auditor can provide needed services to it. Because audit committees are still relatively new in many business organizations, their roles and responsibilities are very much in a state of evolution. It follows directly that the activities of the internal auditor in serving those needs must likewise be flexible and subject to change. We need, however, to understand the general directions better and to determine how the services of internal auditors can best be provided. In addition, the internal auditor should be able to play an important role in helping audit committees to find the best way to respond to the evolving committee roles and responsibilities. This is consistent with the operational approach of the internal auditor—that he should always lead as well as follow in serving the organization.

Changing Responsibilities of the Board of Directors

An understanding of the expanding role of the audit committee depends importantly on a better understanding of the changing role of the larger board of directors of which the committee is a part. As outlined earlier in Chapter 24, there has been an acceleration of social expectations of the entire society. One result of these accelerating expectations has been to put pressure on corporate management for higher standards of corporate responsibility. At the same time there has been more of an effort on the part of the public to achieve control over corporations through strengthening the role of both the stockholders and the board of directors. The latter pressures have expressed themselves in such forms as having the majority of the board members be individuals who are not regular corporate officers and in defining a more demanding commitment of ability and time from those outside directors. These higher social expectations have also been expressed in legislation, such as the Foreign Cor-

757

rupt Practice Act of 1977 and the related regulations issued by the Securities and Exchange Commission. At the same time corporate boards themselves, spurred on by their now greater social and legal responsibilities, have taken their appointments much more seriously than previously. The total result is that the boards of directors are recognizing they have greater responsibilities and hence are becoming increasingly active in the way of discharging those responsibilities.

Expanding Role of Audit Committees

The recognition of greater responsibilities on the part of boards of directors has unavoidably involved various areas where special levels of expertise are needed. This was especially true with respect to the completeness and reliability of the financial statements and the adequacy of the auditing activities relating to those financial statements. This area of responsibility was then further expanded when the Foreign Corrupt Practices Act established the requirements that management should devise and maintain a system of internal accounting control that could provide reasonable assurance of specified underlying activities.[1] To cope effectively with such more specialized types of responsibility, the board of directors has typically looked to a small committee that is composed of outside individuals especially qualified in the areas of finance and auditing. At the same time, groups such as the New York Stock Exchange and the Securities and Exchange Commission have strongly supported and more specifically required the creation and use of audit committees. All of this means that audit committees are now needed which are better able to assure the entire board of directors both that their auditing and financial record responsibilities are being given adequate study and that appropriate action is being taken.

Impact on Internal Auditors

The assumption of these greater and more specialized responsibilities of the board of directors by its audit committee has posed new problems for the audit committee members. Typically, these individuals are devoting only a portion of their time to the individual audit committee and are functioning without special staff assistance. The places where they can go for help include typically the officers of the organization, the external auditor, and the internal auditing department. The corporate officers alternative, however, has the disadvantage that these officers are the very individuals who are being evaluated as part of the committee's broader responsibilities. The external auditor in turn has limitations in that the regular annual audit activities do not require the depth of internal review that fully satisfies the broader responsibilities of the audit committee.

But in the case of the internal auditing department, this group already has as its major mission the review and appraisal of the system of internal control

[1]See Chapters 1 and 6.

of the organization—including the internal accounting control. Typically also, that group is in day-to-day contact with the entire range of operational activities of the organization. A limitation, however, is that traditionally the internal auditing group is responsible to the operational management and is serving primarily the needs of that management group.

Although the audit committee does not, and should not, limit its utilization of any one of the aforementioned sources of assistance, it does follow that the internal auditor emerges as the source that can be most valuable. It follows also that the audit committee becomes directly interested in the competency and independence of the internal auditing department, together with the arrangements by which the services of that internal auditing group are utilized. At the same time the internal auditor should also be studying the nature and scope of the new needs of the audit committee and be developing better ways of satisfying those needs. The purpose of this chapter, therefore, is to examine in greater depth how these particular service potentials can be more effectively utilized. In doing this we first consider the needs of audit committees and the manner in which those needs can be best satisfied—including the utilization of the internal auditor. We also look both at the underlying concepts and the supporting actual practice. The objective is to provide the basis for achieving the best possible productive interrelationship between the internal auditor and the audit committee.

Auditing Committee Responsibilities and Internal Auditor Service

The starting point in developing effective internal audit service to audit committees is to understand the needs of audit committees. These needs are an extension of the broader needs of the board of directors, of which the audit committee is a part. Hence the needs are related directly to the philosophy of the roles and responsibilities of the board of directors. Although such needs will necessarily vary greatly depending on the size and type of the business involved, a major issue is the extent to which a particular board becomes involved in the management operations of the organization. Stated in other terms, the question is where the line should be drawn between the broader responsibilities of the board and the operational responsibilities of management. Although views differ greatly, the more commonly held view—with which we also agree—is that the primary operational responsibilities should remain with the corporate management group under the chief executive officer, and that the board should have a more limited, higher-level policy and procedural role. Under that approach a majority of the board members are individuals who are not management officers of the organization, these outside individuals serve on a part-time basis, and the board relies almost entirely on staff support from the operational group. The role of the audit committee is then to help the board discharge those more limited and higher-level responsibilities that pertain to their area of special expertise.

Under the kind of approach just described there can still be substantial variations in the amount of involvement of audit committees in the ongoing corporate operations. As always, that involvement depends on the personalities

of individual audit committee members—especially on the chairman of the
audit committee—who typically sets the tone of the involvement in each individual situation. Moreover, as previously indicated, the internal and external
environment of the organization is continuously evolving. Our own treatment
will, however, focus on what we believe to be the most progressive and most
effective practice.

Building on this conceptual foundation, we are ready to look more precisely
at the major basic areas of responsibility of the audit committee. For each basic
area we will at the same time consider the kind and extent of services which
potentially can be provided by a well-managed internal auditing department.
The individual areas unavoidably overlap but together represent the most significant directions of the audit committee interests and the related utilization
of internal auditing activities.

Financial Reports and Related Public Reporting

Organizations of all types must ultimately express the results of their operations
and the status of their resources and obligations in financial terms. This includes
in particular the annual financial reports which are prepared by management,
typically reviewed by independent public accountants, and used for all types
of reporting to government and the outside public. They reflect the results of
management's stewardship and are used to satisfy the requirements of a wide
range of users—including stockholders, investors, creditors, governmental
agencies, and other special interest groups. Although management has the
primary responsibility for the financial statements—including the accounting
principles applied, the accuracy of the data, and the manner of presentation—the board of directors unavoidably also has a major responsibility for
them to its stockholders. In discharging this responsibility the board quite
naturally turns to the audit committee for special expertise in the many technical
aspects that relate to those statements. The audit committee receives important
assistance from the external auditor, who is engaged to express his independent
opinion, but it must additionally seek all other assistance that may be available.
The sources of this further assistance also importantly include the internal
auditor.

Customarily, the internal auditor in the organization does not formally take
any direct responsibility for the financial statements. To do so would in fact
tend to dilute the responsibility of the chief financial officer and the accounting
arm of that officer. To do enough work to be able to express a formal opinion
with respect to those financial statements would also tend to duplicate unduly
the role of the independent public accountant, who for other necessary reasons
must function primarily in this area. Notwithstanding the foregoing, however,
the internal auditor has been directly involved in the review of many aspects
of the ingredients of those financial statements and he does, therefore, indirectly
contribute importantly to the content and reliability of those statements. The
internal auditor, therefore, has a certain degree of responsibility for them.
Additionally, the internal auditor's contribution and responsibility emerge through

his role in connection with other related responsibilities of the audit committee, as discussed below. Thus to a considerable extent the internal auditor has an underlying partnership interest in the financial statements of the organization and to that extent helps the audit committee discharge that particular responsibility.[2]

Adequacy of the Internal Accounting Control

The responsibilities of the board of directors, and in turn of the audit committee, also extend to the underlying internal accounting control—the foundation upon which the financial reporting importantly depends. In addition, the adequacy of the internal accounting control pertains to financial propriety and integrity, issues next to be discussed. That adequacy also pertains to the specific statutory requirements of the Foreign Corrupt Practices Act of 1977 and the regulations of the Securities and Exchange Commission, which are supportive of that legislation. The specific requirements established by the act are that reporting companies make and keep books, records, and accounts which, in reasonable detail, accurately and fully reflect the transactions and disposition of the assets of the issuer. Reporting companies are also required to devise and maintain a system of internal accounting controls sufficient to provide reasonable assurance that specifically designated objectives are achieved.[3] The Securities and Exchange Commission is also presently considering requirements for management to report formally on the adequacy of the previously described system of internal accounting controls.

For all the reasons outlined above, the audit committee has special responsibilities in this area. It must therefore look for further assistance from corporate management (including especially the financial and accounting group) and the internal auditor. To some extent also the audit committee can look to the independent public accountant—at least to the extent to which that external auditor reviewed the internal accounting control as a partial basis for the opinion expressed relative to the financial statements prepared by the particular organization. Typically, however, the external auditor would expect that an informed view as to the soundness of the internal accounting control be a separate special assignment.

As described in Chapters 1, 2, and 6, the work of the internal auditor relates primarily to the adequacy and effectiveness of the *total* internal control activities of the organization. The internal accounting control is, however, a major part of the larger internal control activities and is therefore also an important concern of the internal auditor. It follows logically therefore that the internal auditor is in an especially advantageous position to render assistance to the audit com-

---

[2]The interests of internal auditors and other key parties in the reliability of the financial statements are also confirmed in *Research Report 24*, "Evaluating Internal/External Audit Services and Relationships" (Altamonte Springs, Fla.: Institute of Internal Auditors, 1980); see Tables 4 and 13.
[3]See Chapter 4.

mittee in this particular area of responsibility. In providing this service, the internal auditor works closely with the financial and accounting personnel who have direct line responsibility for the system of internal accounting control, and also with the external auditor, who is making some review of that system as a part of his outside audit.

Standards of Financial Conduct

Related to financial statements, the system of internal accounting control, and the larger internal control is the possibility of financial conduct by the organization as a whole, or by individual members of that organization, which is contrary to established legal or other broader social standards. Although essentially a part of the previously discussed responsibilities of the board of directors—and in turn of the audit committee—this individual impact can potentially be of such significance as to merit separate consideration. In particular instances the improper conduct of corporate officers can be so significant that the impact on the public image of an organization is extremely serious. As has been recently demonstrated, they can also set the stage for further legislation to curb apparent deficiencies. An especially difficult problem exists in the case of fraud, where there are both the fact of loss and great public interest. The prevention and detection of fraud is also an onerous responsibility because the conduct involved may be at very high levels in an organization and be most difficult to control through conventional procedures.

Internal auditors, like external auditors, have consistently taken the position that their own efforts can provide no absolute guarantee of preventing or detecting the various unacceptable actions. In all cases the point is reached where expenditures for controls are not justified in terms of cost benefits. Necessary delegations of authority to corporate officers also carry with them the unavoidable risk of occasional violations. Additionally the authority of high-level corporate officials can sometimes be improperly used by them to hamper the depth of the internal auditor's probing. Nevertheless, the fact remains that all auditors cannot escape having a certain amount of responsibility for such deficiencies. It is therefore to be expected that audit committees will look for and expect to get all possible assistance from all available sources. Since the internal auditor is so closely in touch with all phases of the corporate operations, there is all the greater expectancy of assistance from him on the part of the audit committee.

Auditing Activities

The effective operations of the organization—including its financial activities, records, and reports—carry with them the need of auditing to provide proper assurance of various desired aspects. In the financial reporting areas these desired aspects include accuracy, compliance, reliability, efficiency, and effectiveness. In some cases, the audit assurances are required—as, for example, by the New York Stock Exchange or the Securities and Exchange Commission—but in other cases the extent of provision is based on judgment of the resulting benefits. Although a number of individuals can participate in rendering these audit services, the principal sources are the internal and external auditors. It therefore becomes the responsibility of the board of directors—and, in turn, its audit committee—to procure and administer the usage of audit services in a manner deemed to be most beneficial to the organization. In the case of the external audit services, this includes typically the selection of the independent public accountant, the negotiation of the terms of the engagement, the review of audit results, and the disposition of findings and recommendations. In the case of the internal audit services, it typically includes the overall monitoring of a total planning and action program—irrespective of the primary reporting responsibility of the internal audit group—and the ultimate disposition of the audit results. It follows also that the audit committee needs to plan and coordinate the two audit efforts in a manner that best assures the total effectiveness of the combined audit effort.

The merits of alternative reporting responsibilities of the internal auditor have been discussed in Chapters 1 and 2. We also discuss below the more specific operational components of providing internal audit services to the audit committee. At this point, therefore, we need only to confirm the fact that the internal auditor should be able to satisfy most[4] auditing needs of the audit committee other than those obtained from the external auditor. This recognizes that independent opinions are required of the independent public accountant for public acceptance. This is true irrespective of whether other auditing or nonauditing services may be procured from that same source, if deemed to be in the interest of the organization. At the same time the internal auditor may provide other auditing services desired by management, even though not required by the audit committee. The internal auditor should also work in a cooperative manner with the independent public accountant as the latter provides authorized external audit services.[5] But in all cases the internal auditor should be providing his services as an integral part of a total audit program that is coordinated by the audit committee.

Audit Committee Role in Perspective

The responsibilities of the audit committee and its related role can now be viewed in perspective. The audit committee is a committee of the board of directors and hence to some extent is guided by the full range of board responsibilities. But its particular responsibilities cluster around the financial functions of the organization. These financial functions include the basic accounting and procedural systems and activities, but in addition they include the managerial and public implications of all financial activities. The audit committee then stands as the specially qualified group of directors who can

---

[4]Some auditing services are also rendered by governmental agencies, although such audits are primarily to serve the particular interests of such agencies.
[5]These relationships are discussed in greater detail in Chapter 29.

better understand, monitor, coordinate, and interpret all of those financial activities for the entire board.

The responsibilities just described can also be best understood if we recognize both the protective and constructive aspects. There is first the very necessary service to the board of protecting its members from developments that are either illegal or otherwise so damaging that they threaten the public standing of the corporation and its operational welfare. There is also the need to protect all individual board members from personal legal liability and other types of personal embarrassment. The typical board member is extremely apprehensive of such developments and needs to have all reasonable protection, including that provided by his more technically qualified colleagues—the members of the audit committee. The members of the audit committee thus have the dual responsibility of protecting both themselves and their other fellow board members.

But at the same time totally protective-oriented responsibilities cannot properly serve the total interests of the organization of which the board and its audit committee are a part. The corporation must effectively utilize its resources and be healthy and profitable. Although those broader profitability objectives are basically the responsibilities of the total board, the audit committee shares them. What this means is that the audit committee must administer its protective role in such a way that it does not unduly inhibit the capability of the organization for profitability. This requires a sensitive blending and balancing of the protective services with the broader constructive objectives. It is in this area where the relationships with the internal auditors can be especially helpful.

Exhibit 28.1 shows an actual board resolution of a major corporation for establishing an audit committee.

OPERATIONAL COMPONENTS OF INTERNAL AUDIT SERVICES TO THE AUDIT COMMITTEE

The preceding coverage of the needs of the audit committee and the kinds of related services provided by internal auditors provides the basis for a more detailed coverage of the operational components of the actual service program.

Importance of an Adequate Charter

The need of an adequate charter as a basis for every effective internal audit program has been discussed in Chapter 2. Such an adequate charter is all the more important as an operational component if an internal audit group is to serve the audit committee properly. It is here that the mission of the internal auditor must clearly provide for service to the audit committee as well as to corporate management. It is here also that the nature and scope of the specific service responsibilities of the internal auditor to the audit committee need to be outlined. These responsibilities should include periodic written reports, regularly scheduled meetings with the audit committee, and both the right and

The XYZ Corporation
Board of Directors Resolution
Restating the Responsibility and Authority
of the Audit Committee

RESOLVED, that there is hereby continued an Audit Committee of the Board of Directors, whose members shall consist of the directors of this Corporation herein or hereafter designated by the Board of Directors, none of whom may be an officer or employee of this Corporation or any of its subsidiaries and all of whom shall, in the opinion of the Board of Directors, be free from any relationship which would interfere with the exercise of their independent judgment as a member of the Audit Committee. The Audit Committee shall have no alternate members. Each member shall serve until the Board of directors shall choose his successor. No member of the Audit Committee may be removed except by the vote of a majority of the non-management directors of the Corporation. The Board of Directors shall fill any vacancies occurring among the members of the Audit Committee.

The Audit Committee is authorized:

(a) to review and make recommendations to the Board of Directors with respect to the following matters as they relate to the Corporation and all of its subsidiaries:

1. The engagement or re-engagement of one of more independent accounting firms to audit the financial statements for the then current fiscal year and to provide such other audit-related services as the Audit Committee believes desirable, including the terms of the engagements and the cost thereof,

2. The engagement of an independent accounting firm to provide non-audit services, including the terms of the engagement, the cost thereof and, if such firm has been retained to provide audit services, whether such non-audit services will, in the opinion of the Audit Committee, adversely affect the independence of the firm in carrying out its audit assignments as included in 1. above,

3. The accounting policies, procedures and principles adopted or continued by the operating management of the Corporation which, in the opinion of operating management, will conform to the standards required:

    (a) for the purpose of maintaining or establishing the books, records, accounts and internal accounting controls of the Corporation in compliance with Section 102 of the Foreign Corrupt Practices Act of 1977, as codified in Section 13(b)(2) of the Securities Exchange Act of 1934, and

    (b) for the purposes of preventing or detecting

    (i) any improper or illegal disbursement of corporate funds or property of value, or

    (ii) the making of any arrangement on behalf of the Corporation which may provide for or result in the improper or illegal disbursement of funds or property of value, in order that the Corporation shall be in compliance with Section 103(a) of the Foreign Corrupt Practices Act of 1977, as codified in Section 30A of the Securities Exchange Act of 1934,

4. The adequacy and implementation of the internal audit function and the adequacy and competence of the key personnel engaged in such function,

EXHIBIT 28.1. (*Continued*)

---

5. The procedures to provide and encourage access to the Audit Committee, and to require that there be access, by a duly authorized representative of an independent accounting firm retained as provided in 1. and 2. above, the General Auditor of the Corporation, or any principal financial officer of the Corporation or any of its subsidiaries, when, in the judgment of such representative or General Auditor or principal financial officer, information or questions relating to the adoption, continuance or maintenance of principles, policies or procedures referred to in 3. above, or any other matter believed to fall within the oversight responsibility of the Audit Committee, should be brought to the attention of the Audit Committee or the Board of Directors,

6. The procedures to provide access by the Audit Committee to a duly authorized representative of an independent accounting firm retained as provided in 1. or 2. above, to the General Auditor of the Corporation and to the principal financial officers of the Corporation or any of its subsidiaries in order to review any matters which the Committee in its discretion deems appropriate, and

7. The conduct of such investigations relating to financial affairs, records, accounts and reports as the Audit Committee may in its own discretion deem desirable or as the Board of Directors may from time to time request, and

(b) to employ such experts, personnel and legal counsel, including those who are already employed or engaged by this Corporation and all of its subsidiaries, as the Audit Committee may in its collective judgment deem in the best interest of this Corporation and its subsidiaries to be reasonably necessary to enable the Audit Committee ably to perform its duties and satisfy its responsibilities.

---

obligation of direct access on the part of the internal auditor to the audit committee. The importance of the aforementioned coverage is to inform the audit committee what it can expect from the internal auditor. It also puts corporate management on notice as to the supplementary definitive responsibility to the audit committee. The acceptance of these provisions by all parties of interest then means that the internal auditor is freed from barriers that might otherwise prevent him from making needed disclosures to the audit committee, even though of a very sensitive nature. Instead, there is the specific obligation to make such disclosures. This clarification of supplemental responsibilities is especially important when the internal auditor's primary reporting responsibility is to corporate management—the arrangement most often in effect.

The need for an adequate charter is sometime discounted by corporate management on the grounds that no restrictions actually exist on the internal auditor's independence in that company. Similarly, the need for a provision establishing separate periodic meetings of the internal auditor director with the audit committee is denied on the grounds that the internal auditor can have such a meeting if he really wants it. But that is not enough. The internal auditor needs to have the propriety of his freedom of action more formally confirmed. Also, even if the present freedom of action in fact exists, it is important, in terms of long-run corporate interests, to protect that freedom from successive managements who might not be that liberally inclined. The audit committee therefore needs to recognize the importance of an adequate charter for the proper protection of its existing responsibilities.

Participation in Naming Director of Auditing

In the more commonly existing situation where the head of the internal auditing department—the Director of Internal Auditing—reports administratively to corporate management, it is also important that the audit committee participate in some reasonable manner in the hiring and/or dismissal of that director. The objective here is not to deny corporate management the right to name the person who will administer the internal auditing department in serving the combined needs of corporate management and the audit committee. Rather, the significance of this participation is to involve the audit committee so that there can be better assurance that there will be good continuing service of its own needs by the internal auditing department. At the same time this participation better assures the independence of the internal auditor when he needs to speak out in his review and appraisal of corporate activities. The actual participation can take a number of forms but typically would be a formal written concurrence. Its minimal form would be an advice of the intended action with enough opportunity to comment before a personnel change is actually made.

The provision for participation in the naming of the director of internal auditing goes far beyond the protective features just covered. The kind of qualifications that the modern internal auditor must possess to be able to serve both management and the board of directors effectively makes it particularly essential that the audit committee have an adequate opportunity to assure itself that the proper levels of qualifications are being provided by the individual given the director assignment. Agreement on the adequacy of the qualifications to serve the needs of both management and the board of directors is an essential condition of an ongoing effective relationship between the senior management group and the audit committee. It is an aspect of that ongoing relationship which, therefore, warrants the most careful kind of joint review and discussion.

The participative role at the same time should also extend to the action involving the outgoing director of internal auditing. In many cases the present incumbent may be receiving a promotion or being given a planned exposure to other corporate responsibilities as a part of a management development program. But in other cases he may be transferred or terminated because of the unwillingness of management to accept the impact of a really sound internal auditing approach. In such a situation it is all the more important to the audit committee that it be able to review the particular personnel action. In this way an opportunity is also provided to the particular director of internal auditing to have a fair hearing for the issues involved. The audit committee is thus better protected from higher-level corporate deficiencies.

Review of Plans and Program

As previously covered in our discussions, the audit committee will ideally have developed an overall appraisal of the total audit needs of the organization. Such an overall appraisal then enables the audit committee to appraise more effectively the portion of those audit needs that will be carried out by the internal and external auditors. This action by the audit committee is consistent with its role as the ultimate coordinator of the total audit effort. At the same time corporate management will have its own ideas about the total audit effort and how it should be carried out. Also an effective director of internal auditing will properly have his views as to what needs to be done. It is therefore essential that the varying views of the key parties of interest be jointly considered and appropriately reconciled. Normally also, that overall reconciliation will include the decisions as to the scope of the external review and the related fees.

The foregoing review of all forward audit plans is of course essential if the policies and plans for the future are to be most effectively determined. Of equal importance, however, is the fact that all parties of interest better understand the nature of the total audit plan so that they have a proper basis for their later involvement in the actual implementation of those plans. Corporate management, the internal auditor, and the external auditor alike then have a sound basis for knowing what is to be expected from the two suppliers of audit services. The audit committee also then has the necessary basis for assuming its highest-level coordinator role. Although there are practical limitations as to how actively the audit committee can become involved, its involvement is steadily deepening and increasingly demonstrating its high value. Typically, it is the chairman of the audit committee who is the most active, but even this person is subject to major time limitations.

Participation in Budgetary Authorization

With the kind of broad planning just discussed, the basis is laid for the presentation and approval of the annual budget for the internal auditing department. Normally, that budget will be a part of the total corporate budgetary process and administered under the same rules as for all corporate components. This budget phase is very important, however, because now the levels of spending for personnel and related auditing and other service activities are more precisely established. The audit committee therefore needs to be sufficiently involved to be able to satisfy itself that resources actually committed by management are consistent with the previously agreed upon policies and plans. The budgetary process is also important because it establishes the format within which the audit activities during the year are to be reported and controlled. The involvement of the audit committee in the budgetary process thus establishes the basis for a meaningful monitoring and audit coordination role. It also provides a further means by which the audit committee and the director of internal auditing and his staff can come to better understand each other's needs and to thus be able to relate effectively to each other.

Reporting to Audit Committee during the Year

The extent of the formal reporting during the year to the audit committee by the internal audit group can vary considerably. In some cases, the audit committee will wish to receive a copy of all reports covering completed audits. In other cases only executive summaries of those reports will be distributed to the audit committee. In still other cases, summary reports on a quarterly, semiannual, or annual basis will be distributed. Such summary reports can cover both activity statistics and highlights of audit findings and recommendations. It is desirable in any event to keep the audit committee informed as to the extent to which the audit plan is being achieved, and the reasons for any significant variance from that plan. Normally, these reports are for information only and the audit committee would expect the internal auditor to bring to its specific attention anything requiring special consideration and/or action on the part of the audit committee or its chairman. However, they do enable the audit committee to raise questions of any kind relative to the audit developments, and an alert audit committee will do just that.

The total reporting of the internal auditing group to the audit committee of course needs to be a combination of written and oral presentations and in such depth as will keep the audit committee properly informed. Such ongoing communication becomes all the more important as a basis for more critical situations when the support of the audit committee is specifically needed. All this means that a relationship with the audit committee needs to be developed and consistently maintained both to satisfy current needs and as a foundation for more serious developments. The head of the internal auditing department needs to recognize his responsibility for protecting an adequate foundation relationship with the audit committee.

Special Assignments from Audit Committee

It can generally be assumed that the regular internal program being carried out by the internal auditing group for management at the same time fully serves the interests of the audit committee. However, situations may well arise when the audit committee initiates audit assignments particularly desired by that committee. The fact that the audit committee has no staff of its own means that the audit committee must, in situations such as those indicated, look either to the external or internal auditor for such further audit service, or to the two sources jointly. The coverage of such supplementary work by the internal auditing department is in no sense inconsistent with the fact that the primary responsibility of the audit group runs to corporate management. Typically also, the fact of the supplementary audit assignments would be known to all parties of interest. Also, such assignments would generally not be of such magnitude that they would seriously handicap the internal auditing group in carrying out its regular program. In any event, it is the responsibility of the head of the internal audit group to demonstrate continually his willingness to satisfy these supplementary needs of the audit committee. It is at the same time another important way in which the relationship with the audit committee is established so that it can be utilized when there are more urgent and critical needs for support.

Scheduled Meetings between the Audit Committee and the Director of Internal Auditing

Normally, the audit committee will hold a number of scheduled meetings during the year. In some cases the director of internal auditing may attend all such meetings and in other cases only specific meetings. In some cases, also, the director of internal auditing is the secretary of those meetings—an arrangement that assures a close tie between the audit committee and the internal audit group. Ideally, the director of internal auditing should attend all meetings, but there will always be portions of individual meetings when the audit committee will wish to excuse all and/or specific parties. It is important also, as previously discussed, that at least once a year the director of internal auditing be alone with the audit committee for a portion of the time.

Because the internal and external auditors have so much common interest and potential overlap, it is especially desirable that there be meetings in which the two audit groups participate jointly. In some cases these joint meetings will be initiated by the audit committee as a part of its basic auditing integration responsibility. In other cases the initiative may come from the chief executive officer or the chief financial officer. In still other cases the initiative will come from the internal and external auditors themselves. As we will see in more depth in Chapter 29, an effective coordination between the internal and external auditors leads in many instances to joint reviews and presentations by the two audit groups.

Other Communication between the Audit Committee and Internal Auditor

An important aspect of the internal auditing services rendered to the audit committee is the understanding on both sides between the chairman of the audit committee and the director of internal auditing that either party is available to the other whenever there are questions that need to be answered or significant information to be communicated. This continuing availability is basic to an effective utilization of internal auditing services by the audit committee. What is needed is that the chairman of the audit committee clearly declare his desire for this kind of relationship and then that he demonstrate his support of it by calling the director of internal auditing from time to time. The director then feels an obligation to keep the chairman properly informed and has no hesitancy in doing so. At the same time, the audit committee must demonstrate to the management group that this kind of continuing contact is being invited from the internal auditing group. In this connection, the internal auditing group should not unduly burden the audit committee with matters that should properly be resolved with management. What is important, however, is establishing an atmosphere where all parties of interest understand that the internal auditor is expected by the audit committee to keep it informed and to communicate with the chairman whenever the total organizational welfare can be best served by such communication.

Evaluation of Internal Audit Service

The year-end reports and meetings provide an appropriate time for the audit committee to look back over the year and to make summary judgments as to the overall effectiveness of the internal auditing services being provided. In making these judgments the members of the audit committee—especially its chairman—can utilize other corporate experiences to which they have been exposed. There can also be useful input from corporate management and from the independent public accountant. A more recently emerging input can be the external reviews of the internal auditing department now a part of the Standards for the Professional Practice of Internal Auditing, as described in Chapter 2. These evaluations then also become important input for determining optimum budgetary levels, as previously discussed. They also quite properly become input for the determinations relating to rank and compensation of the director of internal auditing—a matter in which the audit committee and its chairman should also participate. It is especially important that the internal auditor recognize the need on the part of the audit committee for this kind of in-depth evaluation and that he welcome all types of useful input generated by the audit committee. Indeed, when the internal auditor has adequate confidence in the quality of his performance he will all the more welcome every possible opportunity for encouraging the various types of cross evaluation. At the same time the internal auditor will better achieve all possible improvement in his services.

Guidance Responsibilities of Internal Auditors

As we have continuously emphasized, rendering effective internal auditing services always combines both responding to needs expressed by responsible members of the organization and initiating service to cover other perceived needs of those same individuals. This dual approach is especially important in the case of the audit committee. The committee members typically are busy with their own organizations or other professional careers and often have other audit committee or board responsibilities. There is also the previously mentioned evolving character of audit committee roles. These problems are also further compounded by the fact that many audit committee members are new to the job. It is all the more important therefore that internal auditors take the initiative in expanding and refining the nature and scope of their service roles to audit committees. Admittedly, there may be various types of barriers to developing such effective service roles. However, all available sources should be utilized. In some cases the problem is one of the adequacy of the basic charter, whereas in other cases it is one of better implementation of an existing charter. But in all cases the internal auditor—especially the head of the internal auditing department—needs to be aware of his own responsibility to make the service relationship effective with the audit committee, and with the board of which that committee is a part.

Illustrative Corporate Policies and Procedures

Many of the operational components just covered are dealt with in the excellent policies and procedures of a major corporation, as shown in Exhibit 28.2.

ACHIEVING EFFECTIVE AUDIT COMMITTEE RELATIONSHIPS

The understanding of the underlying needs of the audit committee and the related internal auditing services, together with a review of the operational components of those services, are not in themselves enough. To make it all work in an effective manner requires something else. This something else is a combination of understanding, competence, and attitudes which applies—at least to some extent—to all of the major parties of interest.

In the chief executive officer (CEO) there needs to be a statesmanlike recognition that his own interests are being best served when the internal auditing group fully serves the audit committee needs, even though the primary reporting responsibility of the internal auditor is to himself (or perhaps to the chief financial officer). Total organizational welfare then becomes the standard by which to judge all internal auditing services, as opposed to lower-level or more provincial views that the interests of management and the audit committee are to any extent conflicting.

For the chief financial officer (CFO) the same considerations apply, but they go on to include the subordination of possible provincial interests of that CFO versus his CEO superior. This is sometimes difficult because the CFO has traditionally thought of the internal auditing effort as part of his own domain.

In the case of the audit committee—which we may conveniently view through the eyes of its chairman—there is also the similar need to view the total auditing activity in terms of total company interest. This means that the audit committee must be properly understanding of management's operational needs and not be unduly motivated by its own often narrower protective needs. It is this statesmanlike approach which avoids excessive control over the internal auditing service, including any belief that the primary reporting role of that group should run to the audit committee.

In the case of the independent public accountant, a somewhat different situation exists. However, here too this external auditor needs to see his own self-interest as being best achieved through total organization welfare. Quite clearly the independent public accountant must protect his own primary responsibilities, the adequacy of his fees, and the integrity of his independent opinion. But he needs at the same time to understand the other organizational objectives fully and to work cooperatively toward their maximum achievement. He must also at times take a statesmanlike view of his own professional interests and resist shorter-range revenue potentials that might not be properly justified over the long run.

Finally, internal auditors—and in this case especially the director of internal

General Scope

Internal auditing activities conducted internally focus on assuring the adequacy of accounting, financial, administrative, and operating controls and procedures, compliance with such controls and procedures, and their proper application in support of overall management control. Internal auditing shall evaluate the company's procedures to protect its assets and to insure the preparation of fair and reliable reports to management, *members of the board of directors,*[a] stockholders, government agencies and legislative bodies, creditors and the general public.

Authority

Internal auditing will have full, free, and unrestricted access to all company activities, records, property, and personnel. After an audit or investigation is undertaken by Internal Auditing, only the Director of Internal Auditing may terminate it prior to its completion, and the reasons to terminate it will be reviewed by senior management, when deemed appropriate by the Director of Internal Auditing. Any action by company associates which is designed to impede the conduct of an audit or investigation undertaken by Internal Auditing or which results in the termination of such audit or investigation prior to its completion will be reported by the Director of Internal Auditing to senior management as soon as practicable. If a course of action acceptable to both senior management and the Director of Internal Auditing cannot be agreed upon, the matter will be reported to the *Audit Committee of the Board of Directors*.

Frequency of Audits

All facilities and activities will be scheduled periodically, based on a frequency schedule maintained by the Director of Internal Auditing and approved by the *Chairman of the Board and the Audit Committee of the Board of Directors*. More frequent review of activities will be conducted when considered necessary by the Director of Internal Auditing.

Types of Reports

The Director of Internal Auditing should provide copies or extracts of those copies of individual reports as are deemed to be necessary to properly inform the *audit committee*. In addition, summary type reports should be provided at least quarterly, together with a comparison of audit coverage versus originally approved plans, and explanations of significant variances.

Distribution of Audit Reports

Audit reports will be distributed in a controlled manner, on the basis or organizational relationships and "need to know" primarily to those activities and levels of management which have functional responsibility for acting on the findings and recommendations reported. Copies of all reports will be provided to the company's external auditors. Reports and audit findings will be reported to the *Chairman of the Board and/or the Audit Committee of the Board of Directors* in such detail, or in such form, as deemed appropriate by the Director of Internal Auditing.

EXHIBIT 28.2. *(Continued)*

Corrective Action

Management shall develop a written Corrective Action Report (with copy to the Director of Internal Auditing) of the action on audit findings and related recommendations. In instances where management indicates that no action will be taken, the audited entity will state the reasons for non-action. If the Director of Internal Auditing is not fully satisfied with the foregoing disposition of the finding or recommendation, the matter will be reported to senior management, and if no agreement can then be reached, to the *Audit Committee of the Board of Directors*.

[a]Underlining here and in remainder of excerpt is for author's emphasis.

auditing—must have both the technical competence and the broader capabilities to work effectively with all parties of interest at all levels. In these relationships he especially needs the capacity to demonstrate his own dedication to total company welfare as opposed to the lower-level special interests of his own internal auditing group or any of the particular parties of interest. It is important also that he keep all parties of interest informed as to the impact on them of particular activities that he is pursuing in connection with his individual audit efforts. This means that rights established by charters and supporting policy statements are used with care and made more acceptable through adequate coordination. The internal auditor is certainly entitled to the kind of independence which will enable him to carry out his full range of auditing services in accordance with the highest professional standards. He must, however, continuously recognize the truth that such power improperly used endangers the substance of that power and instead generates hostility and resistance. Most important, such a misuse of authority and power gets in the way of accomplishing the needed corporate action results and thus deprives the organization of the valuable benefits. It is the special challenge to the internal auditor to keep his eye on the right priorities and to administer his relationships with all parties of interest in a manner that will continue to command their respect and cooperation.

SERVING AUDIT COMMITTEES IN PERSPECTIVE

The broad acceleration of social expectations, the resulting impact on the areas of corporate responsibility, and the related growth of audit committees has generated new and expanded needs for the organization. As a result there are new and expanding needs for internal auditing services that constitute new challenges and opportunities for internal auditors. There is especially the greater emphasis on the protective services generated by the Foreign Corrupt Practices Act and the related challenge of blending these high-level protective needs with the traditional management service role. There is the overall challenge to internal auditors to understand the new needs and to develop the composite capabilities of dealing with them effectively. It is because of these new opportunities and challenges that understanding audit committee needs and how to provide effective services to them becomes so important. Hopefully, internal auditors can both respond to those existing service needs and at the same time help shape the roles of audit committees as part of their overall objective to provide maximum service to the organization.

CHAPTER TWENTY-NINE

Coordination with External Auditors

WHY COORDINATION?

The fact that the organization receives its major auditing services from two different sources—the internal auditor and the external auditor—provides a normal expectation that there are interrelationships which are a basis for desirable coordination. Although one audit service comes from the independent public accountant and the other from the organization's own internal auditing department, both audit efforts work with the same company records and personnel. There is thus inevitably the possibility of unnecessary duplication of effort or avoidable excessive demands on company personnel. There is always also the potential possibility that the total auditing effort can somehow be integrated in such a way that it will more effectively serve the larger goals and objectives of the organization. We need, therefore, to know more about the primary objectives of each audit group and how the achievement of these primary objectives might involve, directly or indirectly, common interests which could justify productive coordination. We need also to know more about those common interests and how they can be best served through particular types of coordination.

Our approach is through the internal auditor as he serves the organization—including both management and the board of directors (via its audit committee). We cannot, of course, speak directly for the external auditor, but we must, however, endeavor to understand and give consideration to his concerns if we are to achieve an effective coordinated effort.

Official Support for Coordination

As we saw in Chapter 28, the responsibilities of the auditing committee typically include the coordination of the total audit effort, thus carrying with it the need to interface with both the internal auditing department and the firm of independent public accountants engaged to carry out the annual external audit. The overall responsibility for the total auditing effort thus unavoidably carries with it the further responsibility of coordinating and integrating the two audit efforts.

At the same time the official announcements of the professional associations representing the two audit groups provide additional official support for coordination. The American Institute of Certified Public Accountants' major pronouncement in this area is its Statement on Auditing Standards 9, "The Effect of the Internal Audit Function on the Scope of the Independent Auditor's Examination." The opening sentence in this pronouncement states: "The work of internal auditors cannot be substituted for the work of the independent auditor; however, the independent auditor should consider the procedures, if any, performed by internal auditors in determining the nature, timing, and extent of his own auditing procedures." The second sentence then goes on to say that this Statement provides guidance on the factors that affect an independent auditor's consideration of the work of internal auditors in an examination made in accordance with generally accepted auditing standards.

The foregoing Statement (usually referred to as SAS 9) by the American Institute of Certified Public Accountants has been criticized by many practitioners, including both leading internal and external auditors. Most of the criticism focuses on its very general nature—as opposed to providing definitive guidance to external auditors—and on its failure to recognize adequately the proper high-level partnership relationship that exists between the internal and external auditor in the typical large corporate situation. A reasonable explanation of this asserted inadequacy of the Statement is the understandable reluctance of certified public accountants to make public statements which may be subject to misinterpretation and which then may become the basis of serious legal liability. Certainly, it is the experience of the authors that best practice goes far beyond the relatively general and cautious language expressed in SAS 9.

The coverage of the coordination process by The Institute of Internal Auditors in the "Standards for the Professional Practice of Internal Auditing" has been discussed in Chapter 2. The essence of that coverage is that the director of internal auditing should coordinate internal and external audit efforts, and that the purpose of the coordination is both to ensure adequate audit coverage and to minimize duplicate efforts. A supporting substandard then goes on to list four types of coordination. As stated in Chapter 2, this coverage is good as far as it goes but is, in many respects, incomplete. A more illuminating coverage by The Institute is contained in its research report covering the relations of the internal and external auditor.[1] In this chapter we draw on both the findings of that research report and our own experience and contacts.

Historical Perspective

We can better understand the current environment for coordinating the internal and external auditing efforts if we consider what has happened over the past 40 years. At the time the first edition of this book was published in 1941,

---

[1]*Research Report 24*, "Evaluating Internal/External Audit Services and Relationships" (Altamonte Springs, Fla.: The Institute of Internal Auditors, 1980).

internal auditing departments had most often been linked closely to the work of the external auditor. Typically, it was the concern of the external auditor about the growing magnitude of his own responsibilities and the cost of the needed external audit effort that caused him to recommend to his client the creation of an internal auditing department. Under such circumstances the internal auditing activities tended to be viewed by all parties of interest as being directly supportive of the external auditor's audit objectives. Additionally, the internal auditing departments were often largely staffed by personnel drawn from public practice. The net result was typically an unusually close coordinated effort between the internal and external auditors.

In 1941 The Institute of Internal Auditors was founded and the internal auditing profession moved to a much greater extent into modern operational auditing, with its stronger emphasis on management service. The related diversion from the earlier "financial statement oriented" internal auditing was bound to some extent to weaken the linkage to the external auditor and, in turn, the closeness of their coordination. In some cases indeed, the two audit groups seemed to go pretty much their own way. The changing atmosphere of the 1970s and 1980s, however, coupled with the enactment of the Foreign Corrupt Practices Act of 1977, have again generated a much stronger emphasis on the adequacy of a company's system of internal accounting control. These developments have once more swung back the pendulum toward a much closer coordination effort between the internal and external auditors. Although internal and external auditors have quite different primary missions, there are still important common interests, and we must now view coordination between the internal and external auditors in a much more serious manner.

Plan of the Chapter

We propose in this chapter to view coordination first in terms of the broader views and conditions which so importantly set the stage for the actual coordination effort. This portion of the chapter therefore covers essential background prerequisites, the broader range of motivating factors, and the typical constraints. In the portion of the chapter that follows we deal more directly with the more definitive components of the actual coordination practice. Together it will be the objective to provide both depth of understanding of the conceptual factors and guidance in developing an effective program of coordination in all organizations.

FOUNDATIONS FOR EFFECTIVE COORDINATION

Understanding Primary and Secondary Interests

It needs to be emphasized that effective coordination of the internal and external auditor starts with an understanding of the primary and secondary interests of each type of auditor. This understanding then makes possible the identification of common interests. These common interests, in turn, generate the kinds of coordinative efforts that are supportive of the needs of the two audit groups.

Primary Interests of the Internal Auditor.   As described in Chapter 1, internal auditing is an independent appraisal function established within an organization to examine and evelute its activities as a service to the organization. The objective is to assist members of the organization in the effective discharge of their responsibilities. We saw also in Chapter 2 that the internal auditor achieves his objectives predominantly by reviewing and appraising the system of internal control. In doing so, the internal auditor seeks to protect the organization in such areas as the reliability and integrity of information; compliance with policies, plans, procedures, laws, and regulations; and the safeguarding of assets. At the same time he seeks to assist the organization in achieving a more productive utilization of its resources. These broader interests are linked to the total system of internal control, but they include and build on the portion of the internal control that pertains to the recording of transactions and preparation of the financial statements. This more limited portion of the larger whole is the system of internal accounting control previously described in Chapter 6. Thus, although the internal auditor's total interests go far beyond the system of internal accounting control, they do specifically involve these more financially oriented basic building blocks.

Primary Interests of the External Auditor.   As we know, the organization operates in an environment in which it must interrelate in various ways with stockholders, investors, creditors, governmental agencies, other organizations, and various individuals. In these interrelationships the organization must provide information and representations which center to a major extent around its financial statements—especially the showing of financial status as expressed in the balance sheet and the results of its operations as expressed in its income statement. These financial statements are the responsibility of the organization preparing them but they need to be reviewed by someone who is outside the organization and who, through his independence and special expertise, can better assure greater reliability. Although the external auditor may also provide a number of other services, his primary mission in connection with the financial statements is to provide the aforementioned needed independent opinion as to the fairness of the presentation of those statements. The external auditor's primary concern must therefore quite properly be with the professional soundness of that independent opinion.

As we have seen, however, the financial statements of the organization are based directly on the underlying procedures and records, which reflect the results of the ongoing operations of the organization. This is again the system of internal accounting control previously identified as being a part of the broader concerns of the internal auditor. Thus, although both the internal and external auditors have different higher-level primary missions, they find a secondary common interest in the adequacy of the system of internal accounting control of the organization. It is that common interest which provides the major rationale for an effective coordination effort between the two audit groups.

Other Secondary Common Interests.   The fact of the major common interest in the system of internal accounting control in no sense denies other secondary common interests. The internal auditor, for example, is interested, in terms of overall company welfare, in the organization procuring the external auditing service in a manner that provides good value for the fees charged and that minimizes interference with other ongoing organizational activities. The internal auditor here has the same basic interest in the external auditor as he does in any other vendor, with the special capability in this case of better understanding the manner in which this particular vendor product is provided. The external auditor, on the other hand, is also interested in the welfare of the company, especially in the sense that a healthy and prosperous client becomes a more important factor in the prestige and revenues of the individual external audit firm. The external auditor also knows that management will, to some extent, look to him for counsel in evaluating the effectiveness of the internal audit group, including the range and quality of its various services. The external auditor knows also that management will normally be expecting—if not insisting—that the external auditor give all possible consideration to the work of the internal auditor while carrying out his own external audit. All of these interlocking secondary interests of the two audit groups therefore have the effect of further strengthening the already strong common interest in effective coordination efforts.

The Right Attitude by Each Audit Group

Although the foregoing primary and secondary interests of the internal and external audit provide an ample basis for generating an effective coordination effort, there is the further need of a right attitude on the part of each audit group. This right attitude goes beyond an understanding of the common interests just described and pertains to the sincerity and cordiality with which each of the two audit groups view each other. Audit professionals in the last analysis are human beings just like any other individuals. They can therefore be subject to the same problems of pride, jealousy, distorted self-interest, inertia, lack of self-confidence, and other counterproductive forces. Such possibilities are often not viewed objectively and become unconsciously the basis for the assertion of more substantive excuses for resisting an effective coordination effort. Too often these problems unduly prevent a really effective coordination effort. The value of identifying them here in this chapter is therefore to help alert both parties to the danger and to encourage a more substantive approach to the problem. A healthy and friendly attitude is unavoidably a necessary basis for the kind of cooperative interface that is essential for a really effective coordination effort.

Collaborative Understanding at Higher Organization Levels

Still another major foundation factor for effective coordination of the two audit efforts is the understanding of the related factors that exist at the higher organizational levels. Although the identity of these individuals at higher organizational levels will vary in different organizations, three individuals are typically importantly involved—the chief financial officer, the chief executive officer, and the chairman of the audit committee of the board of directors.

Role of the Chief Financial Officer.   The first of these individuals—the chief financial officer (CFO)—is usually the person who has the most direct interface with the external audit firm partner who is in charge of the particular auditing engagement. This is true because the CFO most often has the line responsibility for the accounting and financial control activities that make up the system of internal accounting control, and that also include the range of activities culminating in the financial statements being reviewed by the external auditor. It is the CFO typically who first works with the external auditor in coming to agreement as to the nature and scope of the external auditor's review.

It thus follows that the extent to which the CFO stresses the importance of the internal auditing input and the possibilities of greater utilization of it through effective coordination becomes a major determinant of how much consideration is given to that coordinated effort by the external auditor. This does not ignore the fact that the internal and external auditors have their own roles in generating the coordination effort. It does recognize, however, that the CFO may press for that coordination with varying degrees of conviction and intensity, and that the strength of that effort is a major determinant of the scope and depth of the coordination actually achieved. This influence is of course all the more powerful when the CFO plays a dominant role in the negotiation of the external auditor's fees.

Role of the Chief Executive Officer.   Traditionally, the chief executive officer (CEO) has delegated to the CFO the responsibility for activities pertaining to the accounting and financial control activities—including the preparation of the financial statements and the arrangements with the external auditor for the customary annual audit. The enactment of the Foreign Corrupt Practices Act in 1977 has now, however, tended to more deeply involve the CEO in these areas. This has especially been the result of proposed regulations by the Securities and Exchange Commission requiring the CEO to sign a management report that includes coverage of the adequacy of the system of internal accounting control. All of this has tended to more deeply involve the CEO in the interface with the external auditor, and in turn the coordination of the work of the internal and external auditors. Needless to say, the deeper involvement of the CEO in the coordination effort makes a very important contribution in the way of inducing a more serious approach to the coordination process.

Role of the Audit Committee. The expanding role of the audit committee in the area of total audit services has been described in Chapter 28. As a result, the audit committee, under the leadership of the chairman of the audit committee (CAC), has more and more taken over the responsibility of engaging and approving the terms of the engagement of the external auditor. The audit committee in turn has also taken a more active role in coordinating the internal and external audit efforts. This does not mean that the contributions of the other key parties of interest are not extremely important. Effective coordination starts at the previously mentioned lower levels—including especially the head of the internal auditing department, the external auditor, and the CFO. But the involvement of the especially prestigious audit committee—particularly the CAC—and the deeper concern with effective coordination adds a very important force for achieving the best possible coordination arrangements.

Importance of Proper Understanding. In all of the coordination activities of the key higher-level officials of the organization described above, proper understanding by all these individuals becomes increasingly important. Especially needed is an understanding of the primary and secondary interests of each audit group and the need to blend the coordinated audit effort in a manner that will make possible the proper achievement of *all* major objectives. It is especially important also that these key parties of interest recognize the need for high-level professionalism of each audit group and the need for the same high-level professional partner relationship between the two partners—the internal and external auditor. This includes the further recognition both that the internal audit group does not function primarily to assist the external auditor achieve his audit objectives and that the group's resources must be protected so that the services to management for achieving operational objectives can be properly provided. The earlier major emphasis previously described on assisting the external auditor is definitely a thing of the past in corporate organizations that are operating in accordance with the best practice.

Range of Motivating Factors

The discussion of background factors bearing on effective coordination between the internal and external auditors has unavoidably touched on a number of key motivating factors. It is apparent, however, that various motivating factors tend to overlap. It needs to be recognized also that they range from relatively low level factors to those of high-level importance. Coordination at a low level may, for example, be as basic as preventing representatives of the two audit groups from arriving at a given field location simultaneously and then seeking to examine the same records or interrogate the same company employees. Coordination can also be so narrow as to involve doing low-level work directly under the supervision of a representative of the external auditing firm. In the latter case the motivation appears essentially to save the time of a staff person of the external audit group and thus to reduce the cost of the external audit. On the other hand, the motivating factors can be higher-level cooperative assistance. This would include the coverage of defined portions of the audit work by the internal audit group with a later relatively limited review of that work on the part of the external audit staff. It could include also the exchange of findings and related information together with joint discussions and agreement as to further follow-up and correction of indicated deficiencies. Motivation at such higher levels does not ignore the more elementary types of benefits, but it goes much further and focuses on the deeper common interests of achieving an effective system of internal accounting control. The deeper interest then also is in the benefits to the organization of each audit group achieving its own primary mission in an effective and economical manner.

Who Is Responsible for Motivation?

The preceding discussions have stressed the benefits of having each of the participants and key individuals in the organization assuming certain responsibilities for motivating an effective coordination effort. It thus becomes increasingly evident that motivation is something in which all parties of interest need to be involved. Having said this, however, the special responsibility of the internal auditor needs to be emphasized. The reasons for this conclusion stem from the special opportunities that the internal auditor has to provide leadership in inducing the best possible coordination effort.

The internal auditor's special advantages for effective motivation include his continuing greater "in-depth" involvement with the total span of corporate operations. This puts the internal auditor in an especially advantageous position to know what the audit problems are and how they can be better dealt with. A further advantage is the internal auditor's good professional understanding of the work of the external auditor. He can, therefore, then take the initiative in proposing and helping to work out the arrangements that are most likely to satisfy the external audit needs.

The internal auditor's responsibilities also extend to exerting reasonable pressure on higher-level individuals, such as the key parties discussed above, relating to the importance of their support in working at their respective levels for adequate coordination. This broad motivating responsibility of the internal auditor is, we believe, one of the unique ways in which the internal auditor can maximize the welfare of the organization.

Range of Constraints

In the previous discussion we have also touched on many of the constraints that stand in the way of an effective coordination effort. Again also, like the motivating factors just considered, these constraints can range from very low level factors to very significant barriers. They can range also from the deficiencies of individual internal or external auditors to higher-level actions or pressures which prevent the effective coordination that would otherwise develop at the working level. In combination they constitute barriers to effective coordination. In this total range of constraints, we are, however, concerned with anything that directly or indirectly weakens the entire effort on the part of the external auditor to give fair consideration in determining the nature and scope of his external audit effort to the work of the internal auditor. In this connection we need to reemphasize several key types of constraints that especially warrant continuing attention.

Adequacy of Internal Audit Standards.   Basic to the proper coordination relationship is the necessity that the internal audit work relied upon be done by the kind of people and in a manner that adequately meets standards acceptable to the external auditor. In all fairness to the external auditor, his professional reputation is always on the line and it is only reasonable that he be properly satisfied that the work of the internal auditor meets the same professional standards as his own. A real constraint can exist, however, when the internal auditor is not sufficiently objective as to recognize his own need for proper standards and where, therefore, he expects reliance on his own audit work beyond that properly justified. In many situations, however, the internal audit personnel have themselves been in public practice and are fully cognizant of the need for proper standards. In other situations also, internal auditors have developed this cognizance in other ways. But we identify this need as a potential constraint because adequate professional standards for the internal auditor are the initial and absolute foundation requirement for all aspects of effective coordination between the internal and external auditor.

Although typically the problem of achieving proper standards relates more to the internal auditor, the problem can also exist in reverse. For various reasons the work of the external auditor does not always meet the desired standards. In such situations the internal auditor may look with considerable skepticism on effective coordination—especially when he believes that his own competence and standards are superior.

Possible Organizational Deficiencies of the External Auditor.   We have already spoken of the personal factors and broader understanding required by the external auditor—especially the partners in charge. We focus at this point on the potential higher-level organizational deficiencies which can exist within the external auditing firm. One significant type of deficiency pertains to the extent to which high-level policies are disseminated, both downward through a number of organizational levels and to various offices of the firm or cooperating firms, all often widely geographically scattered. In this respect, the modern large external auditing firm is an exceedingly complex organization in which effective communication becomes increasingly more difficult. As a result the condition can sometimes exist when top-level partners express strong policy support for effective coordination but where that message never properly reaches lower-level personnel and other professional associates at different locations—all of whom in one way or another participate in the total audit process. Major problems can also often exist in the form of overly rigid budg-

etary controls, where pressures for budgetary performance do not allow sufficient time for proper planning or do not provide adequate time for developing
adequate coordinative arrangements with the internal auditor. Again these are
the practical problems that can emerge as significant barriers to an effective
coordination effort.

Potential Legal Liability of the External Auditor.   Still another potentially
significant constraint to effective coordination is the fact that external auditors
are increasingly being charged with responsibilities pertaining to losses sustained by various individuals dealing with the organization. A frequent assertion
is that the injured party relied on the opinion of the external auditor and that
deficiencies disclosed later in the financial statements of that organization could
have been identified if there had been a proper external audit effort. In this
connection, undue reliance by the external auditor on internal audit work may
be asserted or believed to be one of the bases for the failure to discover the
now evident corporate deficiency.

The result of all these developments is quite understandably to make external
auditors extremely cautious in entering into many aspects of a coordination
effort that would otherwise be sound and reasonable. The solution here includes
better education of the public as to what can and what cannot be fairly expected
from the external audit effort. It includes also needed objectivity on the part
of the judges who administer the cases. Finally, it includes a high degree of
courage on the part of external audit firms to take the attendant risks when
good professional judgment supports the propriety of effective coordinative
arrangements with the internal auditor.

Research Findings Relating to Foundation Factors

In the previously mentioned research carried out by The Institute of Internal
Auditors, the views of the two direct participants—the internal auditor (IA) and
external auditor (EA)—were queried. Respondents in this case included a substantial questionnaire group and a number of selected field situations where
especially sophisticated coordination efforts were known to be in effect. In
addition, inquiries were made of chief financial officers (CFOs), chief executive
officers (CEOs), and chairmen of audit committees (CACs)—to the extent possible—in the same organizations. Where applicable, the queries also covered
information about current practice and views as to optimal practice. Findings
and related conclusions from this research bearing on the foregoing discussion
included the following:

1. All four of the selected key participants served by the internal auditor
   rank very highly the contribution of the internal auditor pertaining to the
   assurance of a sound system of internal financial control.[2] The IAs also

---

[2] The term "system of internal financial control" used in the research is essentially the same as the
term "system of internal accounting control."

rank very highly this same type of contribution being made both by themselves and by the EAs. There is thus major agreement by all five of the selected parties of interest in the importance of the adequacy of the system of internal financial control.

2. There is remarkable agreement between IAs and EAs—except for the understandably higher-level concern of the IAs for helping management achieve operational objectives as compared to the EAs' higher-level concern with achieving their own audit objectives and the desire to receive assistance from IAs for that purpose.

3. There is significant agreement by the CFOs, CEOs, and CACs on all issues, thus demonstrating their very similar common concerns.

4. CFOs, CEOs, and CACs rank more highly than do the IAs the services of the IA in assisting the EA achieve the latter's audit objectives. The IAs, on the other hand, rate higher than the three key recipients the former's services in helping managers achieve their operational objectives. All this indicates significant gaps between the views of the IA and the three key recipients.

5. The IAs and EAs both see themselves as the leading motivator of effective coordination, although each of them believes that the other is the next most important motivator. The contradiction here is probably reasonably understandable.

6. The CACs rate highest their belief in the effectiveness of the total coordination effort between the IA and EA, with lower ratings coming in turn from the CEOs, CFOs, EAs, and IAs. It is interesting that there is this correlation between the increasing level of belief and the distance from direct involvement.

COMPONENTS OF EFFECTIVE COORDINATION

We come now to the identification and evaluation of the specific components or types of coordination practices. In doing this it needs to be recognized that any classification of individual types will not satisfactorily measure the varying complexity of low- and high-level usage in different-size organizations. What this means is that particular coordination activities can take place in the most simple forms between the two audit groups in the most unsophisticated situations while each audit group pursues its own mission. On the other hand, the same particular coordination activity can become a major part of a very comprehensive coordination effort in one of the largest and most sophisticated corporate situations. The possibilities of this multiple applicability need to be kept in mind at all points in the following analysis. But notwithstanding the foregoing variables, we will endeavor to develop a classification of coordination activities that will make for an orderly understanding of the various major components of an effective coordination program. Our own plan is to group coordination activities in 11 categories for more detailed discussions, as follows:

1. Exchange of audit documentation.
2. Face-to-face sharing of information.
3. Use of common methodology.
4. Collaborative work assistance.
5. Cooperation in training personnel.
6. Supportive follow-up of audit findings.
7. Joint planning.
8. Segmented audit work.
9. Integrated audit records.
10. Joint reporting to higher organizational levels.
11. Cross evaluation.

Exchange of Audit Documentation

A basic type of coordination centers about the exchange of audit documentation. The two major types of such documentation are working papers and reports, and the flow of those documents can be from both the internal auditor and external auditor to the other.

Exchange of Working Papers. In the case of working papers, the availability of those of the internal auditor to the external auditor is the least controversial and consequently the most common in practice. The logic here is that the external auditor must examine those working papers as part of his determination of the extent to which he can rely on the work of the internal auditor. Moreover, it is normally viewed as the sensible thing to do to make information available to the external auditor that the latter would otherwise have to spend extra time getting in other ways. In some cases an internal auditor might be reluctant to expose working papers that are not of the desired professional quality, but that would be a problem which needs basic correction on its own merits. Certainly, no really good reason can exist for the internal auditor withholding his working papers from the external auditor.

The reverse type of action—making the working papers of the external auditor available to the internal auditor—is a slightly different problem. Some external auditors may feel in principle that such availability is not compatible with their independent status and broader responsibilities to the outside world. Also, in some cases the external auditor may not be too proud of the quality of all of his working papers. In still other cases it may be the inconvenience involved. Generally, however, such availability is extended by the external auditor, except in the possible case of a specially confidential nature. Freer availability seems to be an increasingly accepted practice.

Exchange of Reports. The exchange of reports between the internal and external auditors seems also to be reasonable, and is typically general practice.

The flow of reports from the internal auditor involves the same principles covered under working papers. Reports of the internal auditor are therefore normally distributed automatically to the external auditor, and they constitute an important means of keeping the external auditor properly informed. However, in some cases the particular reports of the internal auditor may be confidential or not really concern the external auditor. However, this would be a more unusual situation.

In the case of the external auditor it needs to be recognized that narrative-type reports in addition to the regular opinion are less common, and that they vary with the terms of the individual audit engagement. Also, particular reports of the external auditor may be confidential. Otherwise, there should be no reason why the reports should not be available to the internal auditor. Therefore, normally it is standard practice to make that distribution.

Face-to-Face Sharing of Information

In every corporate situation it would normally be desirable for the internal and external auditor to cooperate to the extent of responding to day-to-day questions from each other. Especially would that be true when needed information is thus available with relatively little effort. More extended needs might of course require extra work efforts to provide responses and at that point other factors of cost and effort required need more careful consideration.

The face-to-face sharing of information reaches a more sophisticated level when there is an ongoing *offering* of information from one audit group to the other. Typically, the internal auditor is more likely to run into matters during his more detailed and broader coverage of operational activities that would be important for the external auditor. Typically also, the external auditor depends very much on such a flow of useful information and it is generally understood by both parties to be part of the overall cooperation between the two audit groups. In this connection the internal audit group can be viewed as an effective sensing group, alerting the external auditor on a timely basis to developments that bear importantly on that external auditor's total audit effort. In some cases other corporate personnel may be sensitive to this kind of disclosure, but its propriety is generally accepted in best practice.

Although the external auditor is less likely to develop information that is useful to the internal auditor, there is the same need and the same mutual benefit in that reciprocal action. A particularly important input source here is discussions that the external auditor typically has with high-level corporate officers, and which can then be made properly available to the internal auditor.

Use of Common Methodology

In many situations it is believed by the two audit groups to be desirable that the internal audit group follow technical procedures similar to those followed by the external auditor. The most common examples of this are the auditing procedures followed in individual portions of the total audit effort and the format of the related working papers. The rationale here is that all this makes it easier for the external auditor to review and utilize the work of internal auditors.

Other practitioners, however, view such common procedures as relatively unimportant and rely more on basic professional competence. In any event, it must be recognized that the internal auditor's objectives are broader than those of the external auditor and that at some point there need to be different approaches to the specific audit tasks. Probably the best approach is to recognize that such common methodology may be useful to some extent in different corporate situations, but that judgment needs to be exercised in the actual application. Certainly, this approach should not be carried to such an extreme that it gets in the way of individual efforts for developing meaningful and useful audit results. In short, common methodology is a tool to be used with reasonable care and caution.

Collaborative Work Assistance

In some instances personnel of the internal auditing department may be assigned to the external auditor and work directly under the supervision of the external auditor, essentially as one of the latter's employees. As previously noted, this was more common practice in earlier years when the emphasis on the coordination effort was primarily to reduce external auditor audit hours and fees. In its lowest-level form the internal auditor assigned might function as a junior helper. In its most sophisticated form, however, the two audit groups work together under a single administrative head on something like an inventory count only because of the need for tight coordination and control. The same situation may also exist in the case of a fraud investigation.

Under conditions of current practice any of such collaborative work arrangements must be handled with extreme care. Internal auditors generally resist direct assignment as implying a second-class work status that is not in keeping with their own professional competence. This resentment exists especially when the internal auditor person thus assigned is actually older and more experienced than the external auditor staff person who directs the work efforts. But in other cases, the problem can be solved by having the internal audit person function as an assigned consultant, or with the clear understanding that the arrangement involves co-equals working in this manner on a temporary basis to meet a clearly recognized need. Still another solution is to put the best qualified person in charge of the joint work effort, regardless of whether he is an external or internal auditor, and regardless of who is to ultimately be in possession of the working papers involved.

Cooperation in Training Personnel

A quite commonly existing situation is when either the internal or external audit group has training capabilities that are useful for both audit groups. The external auditor who serves many clients is especially likely to have the resources to develop training programs of various types which can be useful to the internal auditors in the client companies. In other instances, however, the internal auditor may be conducting training sessions, or developing other training materials, which are unique to the particular client company. There may be a need on the part of the external auditor to utilize such materials for his own staff—especially for those individuals working on that particular audit. Good examples here may be when the training relates to special production processes of the particular company or where the EDP program of the company needs to be used by the external auditor. In actual practice, however, the fact that the internal and external auditors have different primary missions means that it is usually more advantageous for each audit group to develop and administer its own training programs.

Normally, when training materials of one audit group are used by the other audit group, such usage is provided without extra charge because of the common interests thus served. In recent years, however, external auditing firms have developed training programs for internal auditors as a separate business venture and to provide a supplementary source of professional income. Such training programs are less directly linked to the more definitive coordination program.

Supportive Follow-Up of Audit Findings

Both the external and internal audit groups will be developing findings and recommendations affecting the activities of the corporation's operational organization. Although the line organization personnel individually and collectively have the basic responsibility for the ultimate consideration of such recommendations and the related corrective action, both audit groups have a common interest in the nature and scope of all reported deficiencies and in the later correction of these deficiencies. It is quite understandable therefore that they will both be alert to all developments in this area and work in a coordinated manner to achieve the desired level of effectiveness in the underlying operational procedures. The two audit groups will therefore both try to be alert to the status of all recommendations and work in a cooperative manner. In both cases they will also be very much interested in the overall monitoring system and how effectively it is being administered.

As we have previously seen, the external auditor's primary interest is in the fairness of the presentation of the financial statements and he will not be involved with the underlying operational procedures in the same depth as the internal auditor. Hence the external auditor will normally have fewer audit findings and recommendations pertaining to those operational procedures. It also follows that the external auditor will be less involved in the follow-up than will the internal auditor. However, the particular findings and recommendations by the external auditor normally have very great visibility with corporate management. As a result, the initiation and subsequent follow-up by the external auditor is viewed with special concern by all parties of interest.

What is important is that the external and internal auditors cooperate in every possible way to share information as to anything bearing on the current and evolving effectiveness of the corporate operational procedures, especially in the areas pertaining to the system of internal accounting control. By working together they best assure needed corrective action. At the same time also, they are both better able to shape their own ongoing audit efforts to serve their common interests best and in turn their own primary interests.

Joint Planning

When the internal and external auditors work cooperatively to achieve effective audit coordination, they will find increasingly that they need to sit down together to plan their respective audit programs in advance of the actual audit efforts. As discussed in Chapter 28, the planning process involving the audit committee and the two audit groups typically covers a number of years and has been expressed partially in the budget approved for the upcoming year. Although the external auditor will normally participate to some extent in that long-range planning process, his own plans focus more sharply on his need each year to develop his proposal for reengagement by the board of directors. Typically, that proposal is made just following the completion of the annual audit.

We have here a continuing planning process whereby new years are added and upcoming years further refined, but always to the extent practicable preceding the performance of actual audit work. Through that joint planning the needs of each audit group are reconciled. On the one hand, the internal auditor determines what he should be doing in the way of audit work but with appropriate flexibility to best accommodate to external next-year audit needs. The external auditor, on the other hand, makes his judgment of what he needs to do to satisfy his audit responsibilities, giving consideration of what he can expect from the internal audit group. In making that judgment, proper weight is given to the size of the internal audit staff, its demonstrated capabilities, and the extent to which it can be available for audit work.

The benefits derived from the foregoing coordination are essentially the same as those obtained from any kind of advance planning. Auditors, like any other kind of managers, need to determine in advance what they want to accomplish and how they will make that desired future become reality. This is true irrespective of the fact that such agreed-upon plans can and should be modified when changing conditions so require. The application of these high-level management tools to the achievement of overall audit objectives thus provides the most essential foundation for an effective coordinated audit effort, and is standard practice in the typical well-managed large organization.

Segmented Audit Work

While the advance planning between the internal and external auditor provides the essential foundation for an effective coordination effort, its benefits are, however, best achieved when the planned audit work involved is divided in a fashion that is most suited to the needs of two qualified professional groups. The need here is to divide the planned audit work in such a way that each audit group can deal with substantial segments of that audit work in an independent manner. This segmentation is achieved by assigning to each audit group the primary audit responsibilities for individual manufacturing plants, departments, divisions, companies, or procedural areas. The audit group with the primary responsibility then goes on to plan in greater detail the required audit effort and to carry out that plan with his own staff under its own supervision. At the same time, working papers, reports, findings, and recommendations are shared in the manner previously discussed. At the same time also, the audit work of the internal auditor is subject to such further review as is necessary to satisfy the external auditor of its adequacy, as part of the backup for the external auditor's ultimate evaluation of the fairness of the corporation's final statements.

The advance planning previously discussed, together with the application of this segmentation, now becomes the most sophisticated and most effective type of coordination between the two professional audit groups. It provides the best possible basis for an ongoing coordination while the two audit groups, as respected professional partners, proceed with their work, respond to new developments, and work together under the overall leadership of an audit committee to achieve the best possible total audit effort. It is this professional partnership that again typically exists in the best managed large organizations.

Integrated Audit Records

The accessibility by one audit group to the other in such areas as auditing procedures, working papers, and reports has already been discussed. The extent of the accessibility and the manner in which that accessibility is achieved become major factors in every coordinated effort between internal and external auditors. We refer to integrated audit records at this point to provide some additional insight into the potential scope of the accessibility. In one situation known to the authors the internal auditing department has so well demonstrated its professional capabilities that the working papers of that audit group have become the major working paper files for both audit groups. In this situation, the external auditor still has some working papers of his own but they are very limited in scope. These separate working papers have to do primarily with the external auditor's review of the internal auditor's working papers plus such further limited tests of the internal auditor's work back of those papers. In principle, this is no different from the relationships previously described, but the relatively low amounts expended for external audit services in this situation, compared with the amount expended for internal audit work, testifies to the greater major reliance by the external group on the internal audit group. This situation is especially likely to prevail in banking institutions but can also be applicable in other industry situations.

Joint Reporting to Higher Organization Levels

An especially significant aspect of an effective coordination effort is the trend toward joint reporting to higher-level organizational levels. These higher levels are typically corporate executives, corporate committees, or boards of directors (including its audit committee). This joint reporting can cover a wide range. It can, for example, take the form of joint discussion at the higher organizational level of separate reports from the two audit groups. In other situations it may come about through a joint assignment to the two audit groups of a query in which both audit groups have a substantive interest. The two audit groups may then present a single joint report or coordinated individual reports. What has actually happened here is that the recipient group—as, for example, the audit committee—has not wished to assign the query to either audit group alone or to be able to assign particular portions of that query individually. Instead, the audit committee chooses to leave to the two audit groups the manner in which they will divide the audit work involved and how they will jointly respond. Needless to say, this assumes that the cooperative collaboration between the internal auditor and external auditor has been demonstrated previously. In total, however, we then have a very advanced and sophisticated type of audit coordination between the internal and external auditor.

Cross Evaluation

The fact that the two audit groups have professional backgrounds that are very similar in particular areas, together with the fact that they see a great deal of each other's work, provide a considerable basis for effective cross evaluation. From the standpoint of the external auditor there is the further truth that his reliance on the work of the internal auditor automatically involves extended evaluation of the internal audit effort. All parties of interest need to recognize that proper and inevitable evaluation activity. Moreover, the external auditor's self-interest in having good internal auditing, combined with his good access to high-level organizational levels, has helped to get better organizational status and resources for the internal auditor. The internal auditor should therefore encourage cross evaluation by the external auditor and make full use of it.

Evaluation of the external audit effort by the internal auditor is also inevitable and useful, although subject to traditional differences. In some situations the external auditor may be unduly disdainful of the possibility or propriety of constructive counsel from outsiders and not really welcome evaluation by the internal audit group. A more healthy attitude, however, is to recognize that there is always room for improvement and that very often the internal auditor can make a good contribution. Moreover, the acceptance of constructive cross evaluation is more consistent with the professional partnership approach we have previously described. It can therefore be expected that there will be more of the two-way cross evaluation. This too has been accepted practice in many large organizations, and with the more active audit committee role, we believe that it will become increasingly standard procedure.

Research Findings Relating to Components of Coordination

In the research by The Institute of Internal Auditors mentioned previously there were many interesting and significant findings and conclusions that bear

EXHIBIT 29.1. Summary of Internal/External Auditing Coordination Activities

	IA Evaluation				EA Evaluation			
	Current[a]	R[b]	Optimal[a]	R[b]	Current[a]	R[b]	Optimal[a]	R[b]
1. IA sends copies of future plans to EA	3.4	8	4.1	6	3.5	4	4.7	1
2. EA sends copies of future plans to IA	2.2	17	3.9	9	2.8	14	3.8	8
3. IA and EA develop future plans together	2.7	12	4.0	8	3.3	7	4.4	4
4. IA sends copies of his reports to EA	4.1	2	4.4	3	4.1	2	4.7	3
5. EA sends copies of his reports to IA	3.5	5	4.4	2	3.2	8	3.7	9
6. IA work papers are available to EA	4.7	1	4.8	1	4.5	1	4.7	2
7. EA work papers are available to IA	3.4	7	4.3	4	3.3	6	3.6	12
8. IA personnel assigned work under direction of EA	2.7	13	2.7	21	3.3	5	3.9	6
9. EA personnel assigned to work under direction of IA	1.4	25	1.8	26	1.5	25	1.8	25
10. IA and EA work together on specific tasks	3.0	9	3.6	12	3.2	9	3.8	7
11. IA takes primary responsibility for specifically agreed-upon portions of audit work	3.6	4	4.1	7	3.1	10	3.6	10
12. IA participates in training meetings and programs of EA	1.8	21	3.3	14	2.2	20	3.3	18
13. EA participates in training meetings and programs of IA	1.5	23	2.4	24	1.7	23	2.9	22
14. IA and EA develop joint-training meetings and programs	1.4	24	2.6	23	1.5	24	2.7	23

15. IA uses same audit procedures as EA	2.6	15	2.9	19	2.6	18	3.1	19
16. IA prepares work papers in manner of EA	2.9	10	3.2	15	2.7	17	3.6	13
17. EA calls upon IA for miscellaneous information about company	3.4	6	3.9	10	3.0	11	3.6	14
18. EA requests breakdown or analysis from IA	2.7	13	3.0	17	2.7	15	3.5	17
19. IA follows up on EA recommendations	3.7	3	4.2	5	3.5	3	4.2	5
20. EA follows up on IA recommendations	2.4	16	3.3	13	2.9	12	3.6	11
21. EA is assigned job of making appraisal of IA effectiveness	2.8	11	3.6	11	2.8	13	3.5	16
22. IA is assigned job of making appraisal of EA effectiveness	1.8	20	2.9	20	2.2	19	2.7	24
23. EA provides substantive periodic counsel to IA	2.1	18	3.0	16	2.7	16	3.5	15
24. IA and EA make joint presentations to company officers	1.8	19	2.7	18	2.0	22	3.0	21
25. IA and EA make joint presentations to board of directors	1.9	22	2.9	21	1.8	21	3.0	20
26. IA personnel take leaves of absence with EA for meeting state's EA experience requirements	1.3	26	1.9	25	N/A		N/A	

[a] Arithmetic means based on scale of 1 (lowest) to 5 (highest) for current and optimal practice.

[b] Ranking of arithmetic means for the 26 types of coordination.

Based on The Institute of Internal Auditors, *Research Report 24*, "Evaluating Internal Audit Services and Relationships" (Altamonte Springs, Fla.: The Institute of Internal Auditors, Inc., 1980).

on the effectiveness of the coordination effort between the internal and external auditor. These findings include:

1. The remarkable extent of agreement between internal and external auditors, subject only to the reasonable differences between the two audit groups that would be expected because of their varying primary missions. This agreement was especially strong in the selected field group.

2. The significant gap in the views of both internal and external auditors of the questionnaire group between actual and optimal coordination practice, thus confirming the potential range of further improvement beyond current practice.

3. The lesser but still considerable gap in certain areas between the views of optimality in the more broadly constituted questionnaire group, compared to the current practice in very highly selected field group—thus confirming the feasibility of the partnership-oriented practice in most of the selected field visit situations.

4. The inquiries to the questionnaire group, covering 26 types of coordination practice, provided the basis for findings as to the extent of the use of various specific types of coordination practice. These findings are shown in Exhibit 29.1. Especially interesting findings include:

    a. The lesser current availability of the external auditor's working papers to the internal auditor, as compared to the reverse process; also, that the views by the external auditor as to optimal practice in that area were relatively restrictive.

    b. The not fully understandable greater reluctance on the part of the external auditor that copies of his reports be sent to the internal auditor.

    c. The low ratings as to the extent of current practice with respect to the internal auditor and external auditor developing audit plans together. Also, although both audit groups rated optimal practice higher, the internal auditors' rating was surprisingly lower than the rating of the external auditors.

    d. The uniformly low ratings as to cross evaluation by both audit groups—both for current and optimal practice.

    e. The low ratings for current and optimal practice of internal auditors being assigned to work under the supervision of the external auditor—although ratings by the external auditors as to that practice were significantly higher.

COORDINATION IN PERSPECTIVE

The indicated common interests of internal and external auditors in the adequacy of the system of internal accounting control, as a basis for achieving their respective primary missions, provide substantial motivation for exerting every reasonable effort by each audit group to achieve an effective coordination effort. Clearly, effective coordination makes good sense for all parties of interest. Clearly also, effective coordination importantly serves the overall interests of the organization. The challenge for all is to perceive and support those factors that contribute to the achievement of effective coordination. Especially important is it to understand the primary missions of each audit group while building on the strong common interests as foundations for the achievement of those primary missions. Especially important also is the need for internal auditors to demonstrate their compliance with standards of professional excellence to provide the needed basis for effective coordination between two mutually respected professional partners. Only then can the coordination effort best support the achievement of an integrated audit process for maximum organizational welfare. There is the need for an effort by all parties of interest—especially of the internal and external auditors themselves—to foster effective coordination. It needs also to be recognized that effective coordination must be *continuously* sought after. The potential rewards, however, clearly warrant the efforts that may be expended.

CHAPTER THIRTY

Evaluating Internal
Auditing Services

THE NEED FOR EVALUATION

The entire book has dealt with the ways in which an internal auditing department in a large business or nonbusiness organization can make its services of more value to the organization. The direction and thrust of that increased value has been expressed in terms of the professional objectives of the internal auditor as applied to the various areas of operational activity and other organization components. The test of effectiveness in all cases has been the extent to which value is provided. But this still leaves the question of how one does actually *measure* the value of the various services provided. This is a question that is faced each time a budget is approved for the internal auditing department. One part of this question centers on the determination of how much money the organization should be spending on internal auditing. The other and related part of the question is whether the organization is getting the maximum value from the amounts that are actually being expended. The responsible head of the internal auditing department must provide the best possible answers to these questions. In more precise terms he must be able to present his proposed budget with adequate backup and to be able to defend it. It is our first purpose in this chapter to consider more specifically the ways in which this evaluation problem can be handled.[1]

Closely related to the evaluation problem just outlined is the need for quality assurance, as discussed in Chapter 2. The purpose of quality assurance is to see that audit work conforms to proper standards for the professional practice of internal auditing. The specific elements identified in the Standards developed by The Institute of Internal Auditors are supervision, internal reviews, and external reviews. The first element was dealt with in some depth in Chapter 11. The second element has to do with the special evaluations carried out by members of the internal auditing staff—the self-audit activity discussed later in this chapter. The third element is the external review which we also discuss

---

[1]This part of the chapter should be of special interest to management and the audit committee as background for the evaluation decisions which are periodically being made about internal auditing.

later in this chapter, together with a consideration of the alternative ways of making it. That discussion will also consider reviews of the internal auditing activities made by other components of the same organization.

EVALUATING THE WORTH OF INTERNAL AUDITING SERVICES

Profitability as a Sound Basis of Evaluation[2]

We know that a business can have a number of goals and objectives. We know also that some of these goals and objectives can be of a noneconomic nature. Illustrative would be goals of social responsibility, being a good citizen, or leadership in technological research. But at the same time consideration must be given to profitability. In some companies profitability may be the primary goal. In other companies it may be an objective on par with the other non-economic objectives. But at least profitability must be a subgoal, which exists as a necessary basis for both survival and the capacity to achieve other types of goals. Thus no matter how ranked or specifically identified, the goal of profitability is a cornerstone of every business operation. The profitability core means that all company activities must be viewed in terms of what costs are incurred and what benefits are obtained. In more simple terms each activity must pay its way and contribute to the overall profitability objective. In this respect the internal auditing department must be viewed in exactly the same manner as any other company activity.

In applying the profitability yardstick to internal auditing it is, of course, necessary to recognize the special nature of internal auditing services, and the consequent difficulties of applying the approach in the conventional profit-and-loss sense. One of these problems is that the benefits received are often of a qualitative nature that make definitive measurement very difficult, and often impossible. A related problem is that benefits obtained frequently extend over long periods of time, thus requiring the decision maker to appraise the profitability in a much longer time frame than just the year ahead. On the cost side the same kinds of difficulties also exist. Costs in a complete sense go beyond the dollars expended to the costs that the organization sustains because of inadequate internal auditing services. Another type of problem exists in the fact that good company conditions, which may be attributable to effective internal auditing, show reverse cost results. That is, the better the internal auditing program is in certain kinds of areas, the less there is in the way of hard evidence of current internal auditing findings. But despite all these problems of measurement, there is the final truth that internal auditing activities deserve support only to the extent that they represent a profitable investment of company funds. Our task is to find the best possible way to measure the various factors that together determine that profitability.

---

[2]While the focus on profitability is directly applicable to a business organization, the same principles are also applicable to all types of governmental and not-for-profit types of organizations. Indeed, profitability becomes generally synonymous with effectiveness of the utilization of resources.

Application of Profitability Concept to Service Areas

In earlier chapters the value of internal auditing has been discussed in terms of various protective and improvement services. Value has also been discussed in relation to specific areas of the operational activities of the company. However, for the present purposes of measuring profitability it will be more useful to consider the internal auditing services in terms of the following broader categories:

1. *Basic System of Financial Controls.*[3] We know first, that the basic and underlying system of financial control must be maintained at a satisfactory level of efficiency. Revenues must be collected, cash properly handled, disbursements made as authorized, and basic accounting records prepared. The benefits are the avoidance of the errors, delays, and losses of resources that would otherwise result. A portion of the direct costs to assure this required level of protection is the utilization of internal auditing services. A second aspect of the basic financial control system is that extra benefits can be obtained through various types of improvement. These improvements can come through either better design of the system or through higher levels of operational efficiency. At this level there is a direct test of profitability through the value of these extra benefits in relation to the cost of the internal auditing services that made them possible.

   The desirability of applying the profitability test to the basic system of financial control as a specially defined operational area is that management frequently associates the internal auditing activity with this area. The evaluation of the worth of the internal auditing group can, therefore, be best established by first demonstrating the contribution there in terms of both protection and improvement.

2. *Broader Operational Areas.* This category includes all the other line and staff operations of the company that do not directly pertain to the basic accounting and financial control activities. These would normally be the types of operations that are not under the direct jurisdiction of the finance department. In these areas also there will be the dimensions of assessing the costs and benefits of maintaining the current operations under the presently existing policies and procedures. This will again involve a focus on whether the efficiency of operators is being maintained at required levels. The second dimension will again also have to do with the improvement of these operations. This improvement can be made possible as a result of different policies and procedures, or through higher levels of operational efficiency on the part of the people doing the job. It is in this improvement of operations that the profit potentials are more likely to be both substantial and impressive.

---

[3]The coverage of financial controls is slightly broader than internal accounting controls but can be conveniently viewed as being substantially the same.

The broader operational areas are especially important as a measure of the profitability of internal auditing services because they represent new areas with which the internal auditor has not always been associated. Hence the nature and scope of the contribution are more clearly identifiable. Moreover, improvements in these broader areas are more likely to be of greater monetary value and, hence, to make a more definitive impact on management.

3. *Line Activities*. As we have seen, the internal auditor is sometimes given current operational assignments of the type that in strict theory should be handled by other line accounting and operational personnel. The profitability of these assignments in most respects can be clearly and separately evaluated in terms of the specific needs of the company for that particular work versus the costs of the internal auditing people assigned. The evaluation here is essentially the same as would be made of any other regular operating activity. The extra benefit is presumably the more independent and more competent way in which the work is accomplished. The extra costs are the impact on the image and operational effectiveness of the larger internal auditing effort.

4. *Special Projects*. A final type of internal auditing service has to do with special projects to which the department is specifically assigned. Although the range of these special projects will vary widely, there is a common characteristic in the sense that they can be more satisfactorily evaluated. In these cases the mission is established, the costs of servicing the request can be determined with reasonable accuracy, and the results achieved are usually subject to specific evaluation. The possible extra cost is, of course, the extent to which the regular internal auditing program may have been delayed or otherwise affected.

Measuring Profitability

In view of the fact that the line activities and the special projects of the internal order involve more conventional types of evaluation, the major problems of measuring profitability center around the review work carried on in connection with the first two types of areas discussed above—the basic system of financial control and the broader operational activities. Although these two areas need to be separately identified, the problems of measuring profitability are similar and can be discussed together. For discussion purposes it will be convenient to group the measures into four categories. These are:

1. Negative guides.
2. Positive guides.
3. General guides.
4. The savings relating to coordination with the external auditor.

All these categories lack precision to some extent, and all involve intangible factors. Nevertheless, each group has some special characteristics that make the particular category worthy of separate attention.

Negative Guides. The nature of negative guides is that some unfavorable development or deficiency discovered provides some greater insight on what the company has lost by not giving adequate attention to the soundness of its internal procedures and practices. This inadequate attention directly involves the internal auditing department, since it can be presumed to some extent that the conditions that gave rise to the unfavorable development could have been perceived and corrected if there had been an adequate internal auditing program. What happens in a case like this is that the loss sustained focuses everybody's attention on its causes and what can be done to prevent future losses of the same kind. In many respects, this locking of the door after the horse is stolen is very inefficient, but such incidents sometimes seem to be the only way that a management can come to appreciate properly the value of effective control measures. Typical situations of this type that provide significant negative type guides include:

1. *Defalcations*. We know that the detection of defalcations is not a primary objective of the internal auditor. However, the discovery of individual defalcations attracts management attention and immediately raises questions of why they occurred. In addition, the amount of the defalcation is determinable within reasonable limits, so that the impact of the loss on management thinking is all the more dramatic. This is true even if the loss is recoverable under existing insurance coverage. There is also the human cost for the individuals affected, a matter of special concern if lax conditions somehow provided undue temptation. There is also the injured pride of a management that the internal procedures can be so manipulated. All of these factors combine to demonstrate the need for better internal control, including more comprehensive internal auditing.

2. *Other Financial Losses*. Many situations can arise where individual assets are subjected to losses. In the area of cash it might be theft or losses through inadequate control and accountability. In the case of receivables it might be misappropriations, imprudent extensions of credit, ineffective collection procedures, or faulty records. In the inventory sector it might be imprudent purchases, excessive stocks, inadequate protection from theft, failure to protect from weather, lack of control over accountability, poor fire safeguards, faulty insurance coverage, and the like. In the case of fixed assets and equipment the possibilities would be similar to those listed for inventories. In connection with liabilities the problem might well be a lack of control over the commitment of the company for various types of obligations. The common character of all of these types of developments is that a definitive loss is likely to point up certain deficiencies in the company's internal control procedures, suggesting the worth of a more comprehensive review effort by the internal auditors.

3. *Government Penalties*. A particular type of negative guide exists when a company is subjected to penalties because of its failure to comply with existing laws and regulations. These requirements may be imposed by

federal agencies, or by state, county, or municipal bodies. Illustrative would be requirements as to the hiring practices, compensation of labor, or pricing standards. The costs involved are first, the penalties imposed by the particular governmental body, but they also include the impact of the developments on the reputation of the company—both to the outside public and its own employees. Again the questions are: What was wrong with the internal procedures and operational practices that made the violation possible? What can be done to prevent the recurrence of such developments?

4. *Lost Improvement Opportunities*. Even when a profit opportunity is identified, either by the internal auditors or in other ways, the question can also be raised as to why that profit improvement opportunity had not previously been discovered. Especially when the identification comes about from other sources than the internal auditor, the negative guide exists as to what it may have been worth to have a better and more comprehensive internal auditing effort.

Positive Guides.   The nature of positive guides for the measurement of the profitability of the internal auditing program is that the internal auditor's review leads to the identification of a specific way in which costs can be reduced, revenues increased, or the two combined in some way for greater profitability. Since the measures of this type are quantified, they are especially convincing. Hence they are eagerly sought after by all internal auditors. Here is more specific proof that the internal auditing department is paying its way, and also that it can be an increasingly profitable way for the company to spend its money. In some companies, in fact, the reporting of specific profit improvement accomplishments by the internal auditing department is part of the regular system—the reporting typically being on a quarterly, semiannual, or annual basis.

The use of such positive guides, appealing as it may appear to be, is not without problems. First, the estimates themselves are frequently both difficult and hard to support on a basis that meets the other operational standards of the internal auditor. Second, the credit for the various types of profit improvement normally involves a number of other people. This involvement includes both the actual discovery of the specific way to improve profit, and then the necessary subsequent actions by which the increased profit will be achieved. Under these circumstances it is usually questionable whether the internal auditor can claim all or part of the credit. Moreover, many internal auditors feel that claims of this type tend to antagonize the company personnel with whom the internal auditor must have a continuing close relationship. For these reasons they may prefer not to cover such items in a regular reporting system, but to use them in some other manner. Nevertheless, positive guides are a very important basis for the evaluation process, and it will therefore be useful to identify some representative types of these positive guides.

1. *Cost Savings*. The most common type of positive guide is undoubtedly the development of a conclusion that operating costs can be reduced if

certain recommended actions are taken in a specific area of the operations. The savings expected may depend on the change of various procedures, methods, or policies. Perhaps the basis for the savings is different materials, changes in equipment, or modified working conditions. In other cases the problem may be organizational arrangements, or the below-standard performance of specific individuals. In any event, the changes proposed are identified, and the relationship of these changes to the expected cost savings explained. The amount of the savings is then projected over a specific future period, typically over a year. In some cases the estimate can be made with reasonable accuracy, but in most cases there will be important variables, and hence care must be exercised not to be unduly optimistic.

2. *Better Value for Current Costs.* A related type of positive guide exists when the increased benefit comes, not from the reduction of costs, but from the increased level of value that is received. For the same money we may, for example, get a paint that will stand up better. Or with different equipment we may provide a higher quality of service. Or perhaps the work of a particular employee can in some way be made more productive. Benefits achieved in this manner are, of course, often interwoven with pure cost savings, and may in many situations be reported as a combined type of item.

3. *Contractual Findings.* In many situations there are various types of contracts with suppliers, joint operators, and customers. The contracts may be simple or extremely complicated. They may be for relatively small dollar amounts or of very significant scope. The review of contracts deals principally with ascertaining whether rights are being properly recognized and obligations properly complied with. Frequently, it will be found that payments being made by the company are excessive, or that benefits received are too low. Findings of this nature represent important gains to the company either in the way of savings in expenditures or through increased revenue. These findings, therefore, provide a very specific measure of the value of the work of the internal auditor.

4. *Eliminating Deficiencies in Reporting of Revenue.* Another type of finding of a positive nature is the situation where controls over various types of revenue are inadequate, with the result that all of the revenue is not being reported. Typical situations of this kind are cash sales, service fees, admission charges, items erroneously omitted from billings, unauthorized price reductions, and the like. The deficiencies in these cases are normally due to a lack of proper control over the various stages of the revenue transaction. Findings of this kind are relatively precise, and very impressive to management.

5. *New Sources of Revenue.* A higher-level type of finding that can have very substantial dollar implications occurs when a new source of revenue is discovered. Illustrative would be the determination that waste products could be used for other purposes, or sold. Or it may be that better

realization values can be obtained by better preparation of waste or scrap, or perhaps by a wiser selection of buyers. In other cases, there may be the possibility of charging for services now provided free. In still other cases, extra revenue may come from higher prices or different pricing relationships within a product line. The findings of this kind usually involve a number of other collaborators. Additionally, the idea may have to be further tested to ascertain its real merits. But to the extent that the internal auditor can contribute to such a development, we have one of the most impressive types of positive guides by which management can judge the internal audit effort.

6. *Combined Profitability.* In other situations the finding combines various expense and revenue dimensions and is expressed in combined measures of total profitability. This is true especially in operational reviews of profit-center units where more comprehensive evaluations are made, and programs developed to eliminate operating losses or to increase profits. Management reviews of this type represent some of the highest-level assignments for the internal auditing group, and present substantial opportunities for positive evaluation.

General Guides. The negative-type guides are at the one end of the spectrum of the ways to measure profitability, whereas the positive guides are at the other end. In between is a group of measures that do not have the specific character of either of these two, but that at the same time include important means by which management evaluates the worth of the internal auditing services. The basic nature of these general guides is that they support the worth of the internal auditing program without specific monetary determinations. The worth includes both protective and profit improvement types of services. What we have is the general belief that the internal auditing program is useful and needed, and that the company cannot afford to be without it. The basis upon which management reaches this kind of a judgment will include the following kinds of guides:

1. *Quality of Reports.* To a major extent the company management evaluates the worth of the internal auditing program on the basis of the perceived quality of its reports. "Quality" is used in a broad sense here to include the scope of the issues dealt with, the priorities assigned to these issues, the depth of the supporting analysis, the soundness of the interpretations, and the logic of the conclusions and recommendations. In addition to these items relating to the substance of the report, quality also includes the manner in which the report is organized and presented. Is it readable, and does it have a professional tone and appearance? In short, does it create confidence as a basis for serious study and possible action?

2. *Acceptance by Auditees.* A second way in which top management judges the worth of the internal auditing program is by what it hears from lower-

level executives and other personnel whose activities have been reviewed by the internal auditor. In some cases there may be adverse criticism that stems primarily from the inadequacies of the critic. But often the comment is more soundly based. When these comments emphasize the value of the contribution made by the internal audit personnel to the effectiveness of particular operational activities, these supporting endorsements are a most important means of demonstrating the benefits actually being achieved. Especially is this true when the endorsement is enthusiastic.

3. *Direct Personal Contacts.* From time to time the opportunity usually develops for face-to-face contacts of one kind or another between the top, or other high-level management executives, and the general auditor and his key staff personnel. Most often these contacts occur in connection with special projects, or in the review of especially important findings and recommendations. These contacts provide an important means by which management evaluates the internal auditing effort. They are also a major means by which the management executives size up the general auditor and his staff members as persons. Is the internal auditor well informed about the particular issue and associated company matters? How useful is he in helping the executive to deal properly with the issue? Does he conduct himself in a professional manner? Does he demonstrate his capacity to be persuasive? As we know, we live in a world of people relationships, and the internal auditor, like any other person in the organization, will be measured by his ability to operate effectively on a face-to-face basis.

4. *Timeliness of Reporting and Other Responses.* A further measure of importance has to do with how efficiently the internal auditing department meets its various commitments from the standpoint of timing. In the case of reports, one basis of evaluation is how promptly reports are finalized and released after findings have been developed in the field. The concern here on the part of management is that it can act on significant issues in time to protect and enlarge company interests. Similarly, the internal auditing department will be judged by how promptly it responds to supplementary inquiries. Included here also will be requests for budgets, profit plans, and other company-wide programs.

5. *Source of Company Managers.* A final general measure of the worth of the internal auditing department is the extent to which the department is developing people and making them available for other company needs. When this is being done there is the greater conviction that the internal auditing department is making a major contribution to the total company operations. In addition, there is the logical conclusion that the personnel still in the internal auditing group are people of the same high caliber. In total there is the greater confidence in supporting proper budget levels for the department.

Savings Relating to Coordination with External Auditor. A fourth type of measuring the profitability of the internal auditing activity can in some situations be the extent to which a more coordinated effort is achieved with the external auditor, thus resulting in a lower cost of the external audit. Such a contribution is most likely to be significant when an internal auditing program is first initiated and where the new program then makes possible the contraction or stabilization of an overly extensive external audit effort. But in other cases there can be further savings. A good example is where company operations are expanding but increases in the external audit cost are tempered as a result of a more effective program of coordination. The relationships here do, however, become very difficult to appraise accurately, and we propose in the next section of this chapter to cover some special aspects of this problem.

Cost Standards Based on Comparative Studies

A comprehensive effort to find a sound basis for evaluating the worth of an internal auditing program in a given company inevitably leads us to the possibilities of developing standards that can be linked to the size and operational scope of the particular company. These operational dimensions might, for example, include total sales, number of employees, or geographical dispersion. The theory here is that the magnitude of these dimensions can be useful guides as to the nature and scope of the internal auditing effort, and that within reasonable limits we would expect to find a definite correlation. At the same time it must be recognized that specific management decisions within a given company will have its special impact on any of the aforementioned operational dimensions. One company may, for example, use agents rather than directly controlled company operations and still have as much of an internal control problem as the company that went the other way. Also, different kinds of business will have entirely different degrees of risk exposure.

What this means, first, is that standards based on operational dimensions will have less value when used for companies in different industries. Also, we must be cautious even within the same industry since each company is still different from the others in many important respects. It means also that reliance on a single operational dimension would have to be more limited. Nevertheless, when used with care and used as a group of standards, the prospect is very attractive that we can at least identify wide variances, and thus provide a basis of useful inquiry as to the merits of the causes. Thus, if through the use of these standards it appears that a particular company is spending only half as much for internal auditing as the general average, it may well ask itself whether it is adequately exploiting the potential value of a modern internal auditing department.

Number of Audit Personnel. One measure of the fairness of the size of an internal auditing department is the number of audit personnel compared with the total size of the organization expressed in various ways. Although such measures ignore the qualifications of the staff members, comparative data may still provide a guideline of some value.

In one survey recently carried out by a large international corporation, comparative data were obtained from 16 other large corporations in different industries. The results obtained were as follows:

Internal Audit Personnel in Relation to Size of Corporation	Number of Internal Auditors		
	Low	High	Weighted Average
Per billion dollars of sales	3.4	35.3	13.6
Per billion dollars of gross assets	4.5	42.9	17.1
Per 1000 total employees	0.2	4.1	1.0

An examination of these findings immediately discloses the extreme range between the low and high use of internal audit personnel. This of course reflects an unidentified combination of organizational needs—in terms of the nature and scope of audit problems—and the propriety of the response to those needs. Nevertheless, the use of the weighted average figures may provide a useful starting point for self-examination of the problem in a particular organizational situation.

Internal Audit Costs.   Three other similar research studies recently made by corporate groups covered the total cost of the internal auditing department in relation to the same measures of the total size of the corporation. These surveys yielded the following results:

Internal Audit Costs in Relation to Size of Corporation	Cost (dollars)		
	Low	High	Weighted Average
Per $1000 of sales			
Study 1	0.33	1.59	0.75
Study 2	0.28	1.19	0.70
Study 3	0.20	1.76	0.66
Per $1000 of gross assets			
Study 1	0.53	2.87	1.39
Study 2	—	—	—
Study 3	0.26	1.92	0.79
Per 1000 employees			
Study 1	20.00	130.00	60.00
Study 2	11.00	74.00	29.00
Study 3	17.00	196.00	45.00

Again, there is extreme variation between the lows and highs in each of the studies, and between the three studies. But again, however, the averages can be some basis for initial self-appraisal in individual corporate situations.

Relations of Internal Auditing and External Auditing Costs.   Another intriguing question is what internal auditing costs in a given organization should be in comparison with the external audit costs. In this case we have all of the previously discussed variables to contend with, plus the further variables of both the scope of the external audit desired by the organization (as, for example, the desired extent of supplementary internal review beyond that required for only an opinion) and the level of the fees for whatever work is done. But again it will be useful to examine the results obtained in the three studies just described.

	Internal Audit Costs as a Percent of Total Audit Costs		
	Low	High	Weighted Average
Study 1	33	80	51
Study 2	20	90	55
Study 3	27	93	65

Although the range between the lows and highs in the three individual studies shows extreme variability—thus confirming the complexity of the resulting multiple impact of the aforementioned variables—the weighted averages are more similar. Again these averages may provide an initial starting point for self-appraisal in individual corporate situations. In such a self-appraisal one can hardly resist the question of why in the mix of internal and external auditing activities in a particular organization there should not be at least as much of an expenditure for the internal as for the external portion. Put another way, if the complexity of a particular business is such that a given amount is expended for the external audit, it would seem that the needs and opportunities for internal auditing services would exist in *at least* a similar amount.

Overall Conclusions as to Evaluation

The efforts to find satisfactory measures for the evaluation of the worth of internal auditing services are essentially a response to the fact of the necessity for the evaluation. Somehow and in some way that judgment must be made. Management will in fact make it as it grants organizational status and budgetary support to the internal auditing department. Quite clearly, it is in the internal auditor's direct interest that these evaluation judgments be made in a manner that is sound and fair. It is important, therefore, that we continue to refine the means by which this evaluation process can be carried out most effectively. As we have seen, the development of good measures is extremely difficult and in the last analysis there will always be a major dependence upon judgment. Nevertheless, the search must go on in every way possible. In this connection more extended research appears to be a potentially rewarding approach. If we can learn more about what companies of various types and sizes are doing in the way of work done and results achieved, we can perhaps have better guide-lines for application in the individual company situation. The term "results," as used here, includes, of course, the view from the standpoint of company management as well as from that of the internal auditor himself. Hopefully, such broader research can be forthcoming.

Internal Reviews of the Internal Auditing Department

As indicated at the beginning of this chapter, one of the ways of providing quality assurance is to have internal reviews performed periodically by members of the internal auditing staff. The Institute's Standards also stipulate that such reviews should be performed in the same manner as any other internal audit.

As to the format of internal reviews, one approach is to follow the general structure of the audit guides presented in this book and to draw on such audit guides to the extent deemed to be appropriate for the purposes of an overall review. Another approach is to use the guidelines for external reviews given later in this chapter.

Any evaluation of the merits of internal reviews by members of the particular internal auditing department must recognize that such reviews can never have the level of objectivity of an external review by someone outside the depart-ment. This is because the reviewer can never quite forget that he is evaluating the very associates with whom he is going to have a continuing relationship. The problem is also further magnified by the fact that other associates will tend to have less objectivity with any conclusion in which they themselves have a personal stake. This is not to say that internal reviews cannot be useful—at least up to a certain point—but they can never fully substitute for needed external reviews.

A special situation does exist when the internal auditing group in a corporate headquarters reviews the effectiveness of the internal auditing work of an internal auditing group in a fully decentralized corporate subsidiary. In such a situation the directors of the two audit groups have different organizational missions and report to different corporate officers. However, there is still the closer bond of the total corporate family that prevents total objectivity, even though that relationship comes much closer to the external review standard.

INDEPENDENT REVIEWS OF THE INTERNAL AUDITING DEPARTMENT

Nature of Independent Reviews

A major premise of the internal auditor is that there will be benefits if every internal component or activity in the organization is subjected to an indepen-dent review by the internal auditing department. This independent review is over and above the review and evaluation by higher-level management as made from day to day or during the budgetary process. It is also over and above the internal reviews made within the internal auditing group, as discussed previously. Its essential characteristic is that it is a formally structured review made by individuals or groups of individuals who are not a part of the organizational component being reviewed. The use of the independent review concept for the internal auditing department itself is therefore both logical and sound. What is really at issue therefore is the manner in which such independent reviews can be made and the considerations that are involved as particular alternatives are utilized. We need to know what alternatives are available and how they compare in terms of the professional expertise of the reviewer and the extent of that reviewer's independence.

Independent Reviews by Other Organizational Components

The first possibility of a review by someone not a part of the internal auditing department itself is another organizational component. This is a type of review that falls between the internal and external reviews covered in the IIA Standards. It is a review that is done by individuals outside the internal audit group, but not outside the organization. The other organizational component might be another organizational review group or some other high-level corporate group. In many respects it is the application of the approach of the internal auditing department where, as one organizational component, it reviews and appraises the effectiveness of another organizational component. The value of such an independent review of the internal auditing activities by another organizational component of course depends on the criteria mentioned earlier. Critical here is the professional expertise of the reviewing group and the degree of independence as measured by the organizational status and the extent of absence of conflict of interest. In the typical situation these limitations can be very substantial. However, if these limitations are not excessive, and if the limitations are understood by all parties of interest, such independent reviews can be very useful. In actual practice they are, therefore, frequently authorized by top management.

External Reviews of the Internal Auditing Department

As noted at the beginning of this chapter, the Standards for the Professional Practice of Internal Auditing provide that external reviews should be performed to appraise the quality of the department's operations. These external reviews are then further defined as being performed by qualified persons who are independent of the organization and who do not have a real or an apparent conflict of interest. This is a type of review that is over and above the type of in-house review just discussed. The Standards further stipulate that such reviews should be conducted at least once every three years, and that upon completion there should be a formal written report. A final stipulation of those Standards is then that there should be an opinion expressed as to the department's compliance with the Standards, and that the report, as appropriate, should include recommendations for improvement. The fact that reviews of this kind are both professionally sound and specifically mandated by the Standards is the basis for our search for the best available alternatives by which such reviews can be made and the merits of the various related considerations.

Peer Reviews by Other Internal Auditing Departments

In casting about for reviewers who have the requisite expertise and independence one possibility is that of having the required independent review made by a highly regarded internal auditing department of another organization. To follow this direction would in fact be a similar approach to that followed by the external auditors when another external auditing firm has been engaged to make the needed peer review. In theory this alternative would indeed be very logical. It would also have the very important advantage of two-way training benefits. One objection frequently expressed is that one company might be reluctant to expose its internal auditing activities to another company, believing that there is the need to preserve privacy. This reluctance would probably be all the greater if the reviewing group came from a competitive organization. We are not fully impressed, however, with this objection. It would seem that internal auditors, as professionals, should be viewed as being capable of respecting confidentiality. The fact that external audit firms make peer reviews of each other also demonstrates that the professionalism of the reviewing group is rated higher than the competitive threat. Moreover, the internal auditing group selected could certainly be selected from another company that was not directly competitive.

A perhaps more substantive problem is that companies may not be willing or able to free up their own personnel for such peer review assignments. That is to say that the pressures of regular work would too often be an unsurmountable barrier, as viewed both by the internal auditing department itself and by the higher-level management or audit committee of the organization involved. This problem, we believe, is a very real one, and may well prevent this practice from being sufficiently feasible.

External Auditor as the Independent Reviewer

Another possible alternative is that an external auditing firm could be engaged to make the independent review. In that event it is possible that the independent review might be made by the organization's regular external auditors or by still another external auditing firm. In both cases some questions might be raised as to the adequacy of the qualifications. Because external auditors interface to a major extent with internal auditors, the external auditor group would normally assert that they did possess the proper level of competence. As viewed by internal auditors, however, the judgment is not that clear. Internal auditors in many instances complain of the lack of real understanding of internal auditing practice by external auditors—especially in the areas of the more managerial-oriented operational auditing.

There is, in addition, the question of independence. When the external auditor is doing the review in a company where he also makes the regular annual audit, the relationships already established and still continuing with the internal auditing department in that organization make for more complicated cross interests. On the other hand, if the reviewer is a different external audit firm, there may be reasons why the regular external auditor might be opposed to having a second firm of external auditors involved. Certainly, these problems are not necessarily controlling and when the external auditor is in many cases the only available alternative, there is no question but that the problem will be handled in that way in many situations. We are also in no position to assert that the level of competence and independence of the external auditor as an external reviewer may not be adequate.

Internal Auditors as Public Practitioners

A third possibility is that qualified, experienced internal auditors may become public practitioners and provide an additional alternative for the required external reviews. One source of such individuals could in fact be retired internal auditors who have both the proper qualifications and time for such professional reviews. It is also possible that internal auditors now employed by organizations would see opportunities in this area of such magnitude that they could elect to move into public practice. All in all, it would seem that there should be considerable motivation for the development of new firms by qualified internal auditors. Another alternative would then be available to organizations for complying with the Standards. Thus far there have been only a few instances of this new type of development. We believe, however, with the more formally established requirement for such external reviews, that there will be a more active pursuit by internal auditors of the obviously available professional rewards. The ever-increasing dependence by government and society on the internal auditing function will also, we believe, contribute importantly to the desirability of this new professional opportunity for internal auditors.

Continuing Search for Value and Excellence

The basic thrust of this chapter has been to develop better tools and approaches for determining the extent to which proper value is being received for expenditures made for internal auditing services. This is a complicated question because value is measured by both intangible and tangible considerations. Closely allied also is the fact that a major component of value is the quality of the internal audit being provided. This then leads us to a consideration of the ways in which quality can be best assured. In the latter connection we find ourselves utilizing the approaches both the internal and external auditor use in serving others, but this time applying those approaches to the assurance of our own quality. All of this is a major challenge. As our own professional competence grows, the expectations of those we serve increase proportionately. Meanwhile there is always the threat of our own complacence and inertia. This chapter therefore has dealt with some very serious issues, and for that reason deserves our most careful attention. But even more basic is the realization that the pursuit of value and excellence is one that is never ending. That pursuit is a continuing part of our total professional responsibility in internal auditing.

REVIEW GUIDES

When the third edition of this book was published in 1973, it included a set of audit guides for the review of the effectiveness of an internal auditing department. Since that time, however, the "Standards for the Professional Practice of Internal Auditing" has been released by The Institute of Internal Auditors (1978). Later also, in 1980, the Foundation for Auditability Research and Education—the research arm of The Institute of Internal Auditors—released "A Framework for Evaluating an Internal Audit Function."[4] The Framework was based directly on the above-mentioned IIA Standards. Because of the broad distribution of the Framework it has been deemed best to use that Framework as a reference for review guides in this book, instead of trying to update our old version. However, one needs to understand that the Framework is a pioneer effort and that it will be modified further after there has been more experience. That expectation has been fully expressed in Chapter 5 of the Framework. Meanwhile it will be useful to express our own views as to the approach used in the Framework and to consider how that Framework can best be utilized in its present form.

Approach Followed in the Framework

In the Framework the belief is expressed that the external review can best be made if one first compares the scope of work stated in the third section of the Standards with that authorized by the management and board of the particular organization. Then second, the performance of the internal auditing department in the other four sections of the Standards is to be *compared with the scope of work authorized by management and the board*. To accomplish the foregoing the Framework provides the following documents: (1) Profile of the Internal Auditing Department, (2) Policies and Procedures Questionnaire, (3) Suggested Review and Program Steps, (4) Summary of Questions for Interviews, and (5) Checklist for Review of Individual Audits. The first two documents are to be completed by the director of internal auditing prior to the review, and the other three documents by the evaluation team during the field visit. The second and third documents are both structured to correspond to the Standards and presented together in a facing format.

---

[4]Copies can be obtained from The Institute of Internal Auditors, 249 Maitland Avenue, Altamonte Springs, Florida 32701.

Evaluation of Framework Approach

An understanding of the proper review process begins with the recognition that review issues relate either to "design" or "implementation," even though those two phases are closely interrelated. In the area of design there are at least four conceptual approaches to the very necessary determination of standards. The major available versions of standards are:

1. Those presently defined in the Standards for the Professional Practice of Internal Auditing.
2. The foregoing Standards as further interpreted and expanded in Chapter 2 of this book.
3. The evaluator's own views as to what those standards ought to be.
4. The scope of work and related standards authorized by management and the board in the particular organization being reviewed.

In the Framework there is the requirement to evaluate the implementation of the particular program asserted by the organizational spokesman to be in effect. However, we believe that a better approach would be to determine what the actual performance of the particular internal auditing department is and then to evaluate that performance in terms of *all* four of the above-mentioned standards. That total evaluation would also apply to both the design and actual implementation of the internal auditing program in the given situation.

We prefer the composite review because the significance of individual standards and their impact in a particular organization vary greatly, and to be able to evaluate the particular elements of the performance in terms of all standards provides necessary and useful flexibility. The ultimate composite evaluation then can recognize all pertinent dimensions of existing problems and provide the best possible basis for the desired final evaluations and recommendations. This is especially true when management in a particular organization is not providing the foundation for an adequate internal auditing program, and when therefore there is the need to provide all possible sound guidance. That evaluation of course also needs to give recognition to perceived trends in the internal audit performance and to existing forward plans by both the internal auditing department and the larger organization.

We are in greater agreement with respect to the detailed coverage developed in the Framework, and believe that it constitutes a very useful first effort. We do, however, agree with the statement in the Framework that the guides provided are to be modified in individual situations based on different needs and with sound professional judgment. That professional judgment comes from many sources, including experience and intensive study. In the latter area this entire book also becomes useful input for effective external reviews of internal auditing performance.

CHAPTER THIRTY-ONE

Conclusions and
Future Prospects

RESOURCES AND OPPORTUNITIES

Manner of Assessment

The closing chapter of this book on modern internal auditing provides an appropriate opportunity to assess the health and future of the profession. Such an assessment involves first, a kind of inventory of the progress made to date. This is the base of resources from which we can move to new levels of achievement. At the same time we need to look at the environment in which internal auditing departments operate and to understand how the various environmental factors are changing, and may further change, over the future. We also need to look at our resources in relation to the changing environment and to evaluate the alternative possibilities of dealing with the existing constraints and the potential opportunities. This will include the identification of certain major problems that are involved as we seek to find the best fit of our resources to the environment. Out of this analysis and evaluation comes then the determination of proper goals and objectives. These goals and objectives need to be challenging in the sense of reflecting the best possible utilization of our own resources, but at the same time realistic in terms of achievability. Involved here also is the evaluation of the available strategies and major policies that should be followed to achieve the established goals. Last, but not least, there must be adequate plans, programs, and administration to assure effective implementation of strategy and policy. The purpose of this final chapter is to look at the foregoing issues, and to provide the basis for a more intelligent projection of what can be ahead for internal auditors.

Where Internal Auditing Stands Today

Without question the most important development of internal auditing practice has been the major changes that have taken place in the nature and scope of basic internal auditing activities. Whereas originally internal auditing came into being in organizations as a response to the need to assure basic accuracy of records, compliance with procedures, and control of fraud and dishonesty, the focus has now over time come to be on broader service to the organization in all areas. Internal auditing has thus achieved a new character in terms of its basic philosophy and approach. It now has a broadly gauged approach that comprehends service in every area of organizational needs.

The second development is closely related. This is the extent to which the broader type of service has been recognized by individual organizations. This recognition has included higher-level organizational status, larger operational budgets, endorsement of broader review objectives, and greater utilization for various types of special assistance. In most companies the general auditor and staff are now viewed as important partners in the total organizational endeavor. All of this acceptance and recognition directly reflects the broader and more substantive scope of the services provided by internal auditors.

A third important development is the progress that internal auditing has made as a profession. Although there had been associations of internal auditors in a few industries at an earlier time, as, for example, in banking and public utilities, the first industry-wide professional effort was the creation in 1941 of The Institute of Internal Auditors. At the time of incorporation there was one chapter and some 25 members. This professional body has since grown to the point where it now has some 150 chapters and some 25,000 members in various countries throughout the world. Over this same period a practically nonexistent literature has grown to include a professional journal, and a wide range of books, reports, and articles. Especially significant has been the broadened and extensive program of research covering all phases of internal auditing practice. Significant also has been a program of educational conferences and seminars for the better training of internal auditors. Included also has been a program for the formal certification of individual internal auditors.

Thus, in total, there has been a remarkable record of growth and achievement of internal auditing over the last four decades. Whereas previously internal auditing had been known only as a relatively minor and low-level type of activity, and in most cases existing as an integral aspect of the accounting functions, internal auditing has emerged as an established professional activity. Today it is a profession rendering a distinguishable and significant type of organizational service with the more fully developed attributes of that professional worth.

Public Recognition and Responsibilities

Closely related to the foregoing developments have been the dramatic emergence of the internal auditor in terms of public recognition and the related responsibilities of responding in a substantive fashion to higher-level social and governmental expectations. The search by society and government for greater corporate accountability has led to the identification of the internal auditor as an important ally. Internal auditors are being increasingly recognized as having the special capabilities for furthering the achievement of these desired corporate responsibility objectives. Especially noteworthy has been the new interest of the Securities and Exchange Commission in the internal auditor as a major partner in the governmental effort to achieve an effective administration of the Foreign Corrupt Practices Act of 1977. These governmental pressures have affected the internal auditor directly through SEC discussions with The Institute of Internal Auditors. At the same time the governmental pressures on the organization—especially through boards of directors (including its audit committees), chief executive officers, and chief financial officers—have motivated those higher-level organizational leaders to put the internal auditor in a position to respond adequately to the newly expressed governmental expectations.

The foregoing developments have resulted in expanded opportunities for the internal auditor but at the same time new responsibilities. These new responsibilities have also involved new problems of major dimensions. These problems have centered mainly around the feasibility of properly serving the newly imposed public responsibilities, while continuing to satisfy fully the needs of management for effective internal operations. In this connection there has been some fear that the internal auditor would be either directed or persuaded to serve these new needs with such intensity that he would unduly dilute or even abandon the traditional management service role. The internal auditor's thus far demonstrated capacity to serve the now more widely expanded range of user needs has been a major achievement for the internal auditing profession.

Other Resources of Internal Auditing

The record of achievement just described in itself is a major resource of the internal auditing profession as it faces the future. In the individual situation this resource takes the form primarily of the extent of the specific accomplishments in that particular organization. But the total accomplishments of the profession indirectly also add an extra dimension to the individual record of achievement. The resources of internal auditing also include certain other powerful forces. These are the two major types of management needs, the universality of those needs, and the advantageous organizational position of the internal auditor. We will look briefly at these important supplementary resource factors in relation to the protective and constructive needs of the organization.

Protective Needs of the Organization. From the beginning of time the organization has been faced with a range of protective needs. Organizational activities unavoidably involve the handling of resources, transactions with outside parties, delegations to people, and administration of internal relationships. There is always the need that these activities be carried out in accordance with designated policies and procedures, and in a manner that reflects appropriate standards of care and integrity. These protective needs exist both in the area of basic financial control activities and broader operations. With the expansion of the size and scope of operations of all organizations, these needs of a protective nature become all the more important. What this means is that the continuing and growing need for protection insures a growth market for basic internal auditing services. The existence of that continuing market need is by its very nature a resource of internal auditors, in that internal auditors have the capacity to satisfy this type of need.

In more recent times the aforementioned pressures of government and society for increased corporate responsibility have further emphasized the importance of the protective needs of management. In addition, there is now a new level of protective needs which focuses first on the boards of directors and then spills over onto the more directly responsible corporate management. What we then have is an expanded range of protective needs that results in a still greater resource of the internal auditor as he demonstrates his capacity to satisfy the greater range of protective needs for the total organization.

Improvement Needs of the Organization.   The other type of organizational need has to do with finding better ways to utilize the organization's total resources. This is a need that springs from the necessity of surviving in the face of environmental constraints, including intensive competition of all kinds. It is a need also that comes from pressures of owners, investors, or other groups to which there is a major responsibility. Finally, it is a need that springs from the normal objectives of professional managers to achieve maximum excellence. There is thus a continuing pressure to obtain all possible assistance in providing the means for achieving the best possible utilization of resources. Here also the same factors of growth and increasing complexity of the organization's operations make these needs for assistance all the more urgent. Again from the standpoint of the internal auditor the existence of this increasing need provides a further market for internal auditing services. Again also the ultimate interest of the board of directors in operational improvement and adequate profitability (over and above the newly emphasized protective needs) results in the improvement needs of the organization as a whole.

Universality of Need for Internal Auditing Services.   It is perhaps sufficiently clear that there is a universal need for internal auditing services, but the point deserves special emphasis and some elaboration. The first important aspect of the universal need for internal auditing is that it exists for all types of organizations irrespective of the purpose of the particular type of organization. What this means is that every organization that has management responsibilities also has internal auditing needs. The purpose here may be to make a profit, to administer a philanthropic organization, or to carry out the mission of a governmental entity. In all cases the organization has both protective and improvement types of needs, and in turn needs the related internal auditing services.

The second aspect of this universal need is that it exists at all levels of each organization. A particular organization may carry out its total operations by decentralizing portions of those operations to subsidiaries, divisions, departments, or other internal components. In each case the management of the individual organizational component has assigned resources and related managerial responsibilities. That management, therefore, at the same time has a legitimate need for internal auditing services. There is, of course, the practical problem of whether these needs can be most efficiently satisfied by a local internal auditing group, or whether they should be provided by a higher-level organizational component. But in any event the need is there and ought to be properly satisfied. Here again this universal need constitutes an important resource for the internal auditor.

Situational Vantage Point of the Internal Auditor.   Another somewhat different type of resource of the internal auditor has to do with his advantageous organizational position in the company. When the internal auditing activity has been properly established, in terms of organizational status and detachment from day-to-day operational activities, the internal auditor is in an especially good position to provide all types of service. First, the separation from current operating responsibilities gives the internal auditor the time to make substantive reviews and appraisals of regular operational activities. Second, the internal auditor is provided with the independence and objectivity to look at these various operational activities in the light of total company welfare, and without the bias of specific operational interests. Important also is the familiarity with the accounting activities, where the transactions relating to all company activities are ultimately reflected. These accounting activities provide a supplementary means of access to all the other operational activities. In a similar manner the contacts with the computer activities, including the systems there developed and implemented, provide an additional useful means of access to all other operational activities involved in the computer applications. In all cases also the protective-type activities provide a major opportunity for convenient access to operational activities. In summary, the internal auditor has a built-in position in the company that normally cannot be matched by any other line or staff group.

Changing Environment of the Firm

With some understanding of the resources possessed by internal auditing groups, the next step is to examine the environment to which the internal auditing function must effectively relate. Our interest in the environment is at two levels. One of these levels is the total external environment in which the organization operates. This is the environment with which the management and its board of directors must contend as they establish organizational goals and supporting strategies. As discussed in more detail in Chapter 3, this environment has basic dimensions of an economic, technological, competitive, social, and political nature, operating to some extent on the total industry, and to a further extent on the company within a given industry. All of these dimensions involve dynamic change at increasingly greater rates of change. Especially illustrative is the impact on the organization of the accelerating social expectations and related social responsibilities discussed in Chapter 24.

   In all of these areas responsible organizational personnel must try to achieve a better understanding of these environmental factors, and try as effectively as possible to predict the nature, scope, and timing of evolving change. It needs to do this so that it can most intelligently plan the commitment and utilization of organizational resources to the various possible courses of action. The internal auditor's interest in these environmental changes, and how the organization is relating to them, is based on the fact that this is the way the internal auditor can determine how he can best serve that organization. It is basic that if the internal auditor is to serve the organization effectively he must understand that organization's problems and needs.

The second level of the internal auditor's concern with environmental factors now centers on the situation within the firm. What is the nature and scope of the company's operations, and what changes are taking place? What does the company management and board of directors want in the way of specific assistance, and with what priorities? The internal auditor will presumably be doing everything possible to use his resources in a manner that will provide the most effective response possible to the defined needs. At the same time he should be considering what he can do to ascertain needs not presently perceived. He should also be taking all possible actions to change the environmental factors in any way that would enable him to render higher-level and more complete service. Thus the internal auditor also seeks both to respond to the environmental factors and to take innovative action to effect modifications in the factors themselves.

In a very real sense the internal auditing group is competing with other organizational activities, especially those of a staff nature, to render useful service to the organization. On the one hand, voids in providing organizational service provide the impetus to other organizational groups to move in to render the needed service. In other cases also a more aggressive staff group may come to provide a better kind of service than that presently being rendered by the internal auditing group. This threat exists especially in the case of the improvement-type services to the organization. Every company staff group likes to feel that by using its own special expertise as a base, it can expand into broader areas of organizational service. All of this means that the internal auditor must be extremely alert and sensitive to all of the internal environmental factors and the various changes in them. We must remember also that change can include a spectrum from the very sudden and abrupt, to the more evolutionary types that are extremely subtle and difficult to identify.

PROBLEMS OF UTILIZING RESOURCES

The basic job of the internal auditor, like any other manager, is to utilize his resources most productively. The foundation analysis for this effort is to consider carefully how particular strengths and limitations match the problems and opportunities that exist in the current and changing environment. This is essentially the process of identifying and evaluating the expertise and general

capabilities of existing personnel, the amount of funds provided, and the time
available, and then relating these factors to the priorities of both identified
requirements and potential opportunities for improvements. The analysis also
leads us to the recognition of certain key problems that exist in achieving
effective utilization of resources. We will identify a number of these problems
that we believe are especially significant to the internal auditor both now and
in the foreseeable future.

Keeping Up to Date about Organizational Needs

We have previously emphasized the basic necessity of understanding organizational needs so that the internal auditor can most effectively render service.
To a considerable extent this needed understanding can come through reading
current magazines and periodicals of both a general and industry nature. The
internal auditor can also be alert to operational changes and internal announcements of new developments. But there still remains the practical problem of
how the internal auditor can know of planning and developments within the
company quickly enough that he can most intelligently do his own planning
in an effective manner. The most ideal means of knowing what is going on in
a timely manner is based on the general auditor or key members of his staff
being sought out at the planning stage for information and counsel. This kind
of relationship is not a common one, but it does exist in individual situations.
The next best type of arrangement is one in which a regular liaison relationship
is established with informed individuals. This then enables the internal auditor
to make the moves that are most consistent with changing managerial approaches. Still another deliberate approach is to establish a reporting relationship within the internal auditing department whereby all staff members will
be alert to cues relating to planned operational changes, and then will report
them promptly to the general auditor. Subsequently, the information can then
be confirmed directly by the general auditor and disseminated to other staff
personnel, as appropriate.

It is also important to recognize that keeping up to date with management
needs is something that should take place at all levels of operations. Thus the
internal auditor in charge of the review of a given operational activity should
be in direct touch with the manager who is responsible for that particular
operational activity. Moreover, proper preparatory work, as we have seen,
normally involves contact with managers who are at least one level above the
"in charge" manager. In the case of larger reviews, as, for example, of the total
purchasing function, or for a major subsidiary, these contacts could on occasion
involve the chief executive officer himself. All of these contacts provide a further
opportunity for keeping up to date with organizational problems and needs.

Right Blend of Financial and Operational Auditing

A second key problem confronting the internal auditor is how he should fit
together the emphasis on financial and operating auditing. Included here also

is the problem of how the newly emphasized protective services to the board of directors can best be combined with all services being rendered to the management group. It is recognized that to some extent this blend or mix may be specifically determined by management or the audit committee. That is, a given organization may be chiefly concerned with the review of basic financial activities. In other cases the situation will exist where the organization sees the internal auditing effort primarily in relation to the external audit. In still other cases, however, the internal auditor may have wide latitude as to how he directs his internal auditing effort. In the latter cases the problem that must be resolved is the extent to which one type of auditing will be subordinated to the other. We have previously stated our belief that the review of basic financial control activities is an essential part of the total service rendered, and that these activities can provide an important stepping stone for other types of operational auditing. At the same time it is believed that the greater emphasis needs to be given to the broader operational auditing, with its larger opportunities for profit improvement. The problem still remains as to how the internal auditor adequately covers the basic financial control responsibility, and still effectively exploits the higher-level and more professional areas of management service. One aspect of this problem is whether different people will be used for the two types of activity, and whether there should be different review assignments. In our own view such a separation loses the direct benefit of the financial activity becoming the foundation base for the higher-level extension. However, there is no absolute answer as to how the two types of work shall be combined.

Resolving Dual Client Relationships

As we know, conflict often comes to exist between the responsibilities of the internal auditor to higher-level management, and to the management directly responsible for the activity being reviewed. The responsibility in both cases is to provide the protective and improvement services that we have discussed throughout the book. But to the higher-level management the work of the internal auditor is viewed also as a part of the control system by which that upper-level management is apprised of deficiencies and problems. To the organizational component being reviewed there is, on the other hand, the desire to deal with the internal auditor as a partner and with a kind of private confidential relationship. The dilemma is that it is this latter type of relationship that best induces cooperation between the auditor and auditee, and that is more likely to achieve meaningful results for local improvement, whereas the former relationship is more likely to be the basis for evaluating the performance and career rewards for the internal auditor.

The problem for the internal auditor is how he can reconcile the two different kinds of desires and satisfy both parties. We do see the trend in the direction of adjusting more to the needs of local management. In fact, many higher-level managements are encouraging this approach, both because it provides more substantive operational results and because it relieves them of burdensome control activities. It also fits more neatly into a concept of modern decentralization, where the performance results are based more on results achieved than on how the job is done. But on the other hand, there are certain minimum needs on the part of higher-level management in controlling adherence to given company policies. There is also a certain minimum need for the higher-level management to have a basis for evaluating the worth of the internal auditing effort. There must, therefore, be some kind of a compromise. The ongoing problem then for the internal auditor is to understand the partial conflict and to handle everything in a manner that will best command the respect and support of both groups.

This same kind of potential conflict exists at a higher level between the management of the organization and the board of directors (including its audit committee). Although both parties here are concerned with the overall welfare of the organization, it is sometimes true that each party will evaluate that overall welfare in a different manner. In such cases the board may be more concerned relatively with compliance with governmental pressures and with assuming a good corporate image. The management may, on the other hand, be motivated by longer-term operational considerations and be more prepared to bend legal requirements. Again, the internal auditor must somehow achieve a proper balance and satisfy the needs of both parties. This is the problem of resolving dual client relationships where the challenges and rewards are at their highest level.

Adjusting to the New Computer World

The development of computer technology and its application to all kinds of problems of our contemporary life has been one of the most significant forces ever experienced by society. In the business and governmental area it has come to be the major means of processing clerical-type data, and has in more recent years moved into the area of operational systems. It has also provided a new capability for a wide range of management science applications. These developments have at the same time created both opportunities and problems for management. Here also, the internal auditor's objective of organizational service has required that he understand these opportunities and problems, and assist all parties in achieving effective utilization. In addition, the widespread utilization of computers has had a more direct impact on the work of the internal auditor. A number of these matters have been previously discussed in this book, but we summarize the key dimensions of this impact as part of a clearer recognition of the significance of the total continuing problem of computers in relation to the work of the internal auditor.

1. *Review of Operational Data That Are Now Computerized.* Prior to the advent of computers the internal auditor dealt with documents and related data that were either manually prepared, or developed through the use

of mechanical devices where the human dimension was fairly clearly identifiable. Today these underlying data are printed out by computers in accordance with a wide range of complicated programs and processes. The review of those data necessarily takes the internal auditor back into the programs and controls on which the output data are based. The internal auditor's review thus necessarily centers upon the underlying computer processes.

2. *Computer as an Audit Tool.* The aforementioned examination of computer processes leads naturally into an independent use of the computer. The usage here is to test the accuracy with which basic data are being produced through the programs, and also to test the validity of the original data prior to its injection into the computer process. An illustration of this latter type of testing is the statistical sampling previously discussed in Chapter 8.

3. *Review of Computer Operations.* As we saw in Chapter 22, the operations pertaining to the acceptance, processing, and release of computerized data involve a completely new kind of operational activity that must be reviewed and evaluated just like any other part of the company operations. The magnitude of these operations, the special technical aspects, and the changing nature of the activities all combine to make this type of review a continuing challenge to the internal auditor.

4. *Participation in Development of Computer Systems.* The actual processing of data by the computer is based on previously determined instructions known as programs. When programs are of significant scope and involve the interrelationship of several operational activities they are referred to as systems. The development of systems is carried out over a considerable period of time, at great cost, and once finalized the systems are difficult to change. The result has been that if the internal auditor is to be a constructive force for the development of good internal control and efficient internal procedure, he must make his views known while the systems are being developed. This requires that the internal auditor have sufficient technical expertise to be able to work with the systems development personnel. It also means that he must establish and maintain his liaison on a timely basis. Doing all of this effectively is a continuing challenge to the internal auditor.

5. *Staffing Requirements.* From the foregoing it becomes apparent that all internal auditors at all levels of responsibility need to have some minimum understanding of computer processing. In addition, there will be the need for some individuals to have special computer expertise. These latter individuals can serve as counselors and trainers of the other internal auditing personnel, and can also function as liaison people in systems development. The continuing problem is that the internal auditing department works out this staffing problem in a satisfactory manner.

6. *Relationship with Management Information System Department.* The more extensive utilization of computers has led in many companies to a high-level centralization of computer processing, systems development, and operations research. These combined activities frequently carry an organizational title of Management Information Systems (MIS) Department. The carrying out of these combined functions by its very nature involves the analysis of operational activities and related management problems. Moreover, the control of both the current processing and the development of new applications generates a major influence over the way information is created and disseminated. As a consequence, MIS departments have tended to emerge as a new and powerful force in determining company welfare. To this extent the MIS department can be regarded as a new contender for special management service. The challenge to the internal auditor is that he is not unduly isolated while this is going on. The need is to work with this new group in a way that maintains and further enhances the service role of the internal auditor.

Blending Pre-Audit and Post-Audit

In the early days of internal auditing one of the major concerns was that internal auditors separate themselves from day-to-day activities that were essentially a part of the regular operations. A related concern was to avoid having a responsibility for the development of procedures, and then later be subjecting those same procedures to an audit review. In recent years this philosophy has been modified in the case of computers to recognize the need for liaison participation in the development of computerized systems. There is also emerging in a number of companies the view that internal auditors can render better organizational service by participating more actively in the development of both company plans and major policy decisions. The rationale is that the internal auditor has the experience and overview of broader operations, which makes his counsel very valuable to all parties. The internal auditor in this way also has a means of keeping up to date as to organizational developments, as a base for the planning and administration of his own department. Admittedly, this participation as a consultant is a possible threat to the internal auditor's later independence in the review of the subsequent operational actions. If, therefore, it is done, the internal auditor must handle himself in such a manner that the later independence is not undermined. The internal auditor must also avoid an excessive diversion of his time away from regular internal audit service needs. We believe, however, that on balance there are important potential benefits to be achieved and we list it as one of the continuing problems with which modern internal auditors should be concerned. It could well be that the internal auditing profession has now matured to the point where it could render this new type of service, and still go on providing the now existing range of organizational services, perhaps on an even more efficient basis.

Education

The continuing vitality of any profession lies to a major extent in its attention to matters of education. One important question has to do with what the minimum educational requirements should be for acceptable professional standing. This objective has been dealt with by The Institute of Internal Auditors by defining the desired levels of knowledge in the various major functional areas. The baccalaureate degree from an accredited college-level institution has also been established as a future educational requirement. The preparation for the CIA examinations also involves extending study. The Institute also now requires certain minimum hours of continuing education to cover new developments with which practicing internal auditors should be familiar. Some of this education can be achieved on an individual basis, some through the use of already established educational institutions, and some through the organized work of The Institute of Internal Auditors. There is especially the need to cover new types of knowledge currently being developed for possible application in a practical manner. Important also is the need to keep raising the educational level over time. The continuing problem is to find the means of adequately dealing with these basic educational needs.

Utilization of The Institute of Internal Auditors

A final key problem for the profession is how it can best utilize its professional association—The Institute of Internal Auditors. An initial type of benefit is providing a means by which individual practitioners can more easily meet other practitioners and learn from each other. A second type of benefit is the more organized impact on the general public, especially on those groups with which the internal auditors have contact, as they carry out their professional activities. A third type of benefit is in providing the financial capability to conduct useful research pertaining to the work of the internal auditor, and then to make this research available to the total profession and other interested parties. A related benefit here is the capability to publish a journal that contains material covering matters of current professional interest. A fourth type of benefit pertains to the role in providing opportunities for continuing education, as already discussed. Finally, there are the benefits that can flow from direct membership service. This is perhaps the area least possible to define accurately but it would cover all of the specific needs of individual members. Illustrative would be a request to obtain a particular type of publication, to determine what other members might be consulted on a given problem, or to get direct counsel. In total, the continuing problem is how a professional association can be most productive and be best utilized. In the last analysis the success will be determined by what the members want and what they set out to get. In the shorter run, however, the degree of successful achievement depends more on the efforts of the headquarters staff of the association itself.

THE CONTINUING CHALLENGE

Determining Goals and Objectives

The previous discussion of internal auditing resources, the environmental factors, and the key problems of relating resources to the environmental factors now provides the proper basis for a determination of what the goals and objectives of the internal auditor should be. The highest-level goal should presumably be to provide meaningful and comprehensive service to the organization, both of a protective and an improvement nature. In the individual organization these protective and improvement goals need to be specifically identified and to be quantified to the extent practicable. Subsidiary goals would include the desired numbers and qualifications of staff personnel, an operating budget of a given size or proportion, achieving a needed level of organizational status, agreement to particular salary grades for staff personnel, and even more adequate compensation for the general auditor himself. All of these goals need to reflect specific dimensions of magnitude, and the length of time allowed for accomplishment. In all cases they represent the evaluation of resources in relation to the environmental factors with a realistic but challenging level of task, and with some consideration of the definitive strategies and major policies to support the goal effort. Each internal auditing department must work out this determination of goals and objectives in its own way, but in as definitive form as possible.

Strategy Formulation

The determination of goals and objectives has already, as we have seen, involved some consideration of the strategies to be used. At the strategy level, however, the internal auditor, and especially the general auditor, who has the top responsibility, must determine in a more definitive manner the strategies to be followed. Strategy at its highest level has to do with the way the internal auditing department will go about it to provide service to the auditees and higher-level management and the board of directors. This will include the determination of the character of the auditing service to be rendered and how the internal auditor will go about it to demonstrate the worth of the service to the organization. At a lower level the strategy will deal with specific key issues of the type previously outlined in this chapter, to the extent not previously covered. It can also include, for example, the way the internal auditor should relate to the external auditor. It can also include a particular organizational approach, or a special type of reporting. In all cases we are dealing with specific concepts as to the way particular aspects of the internal auditor's activities will be carried out. The common bond of all these strategies is how they best utilize internal auditing resources in the face of environmental factors to achieve the previously established goals.

Strategy Implementation

Once strategies have been formulated the final need is for definitive action programs whereby the selected strategies will be implemented. People are hired, training is carried out, reviews are made, reports are released, and contacts are made in a manner consistent with the chosen strategies. The actual work done thus has direction and purpose in terms of those strategies. This implementation includes also backup planning, organizing, staffing, administering (directing, coordinating, and leading), and control at lower levels as lower-level objectives are established and administered in the light of higher-level departmental strategies. Strategy formulation and implementation are like twins, in that one without the other is not enough.

Periodic Reevaluation

All of the resources and environmental factors are subject to continuous change. Also, as strategies are tested in actuality there is a continuing learning process that presents new problems and opportunities. What is needed, therefore, is a periodic reevaluation of the relationships between resources and the environment, the realism of established goals, the soundness of strategy concepts, and the effectiveness of implementation. Out of this reevaluation should come then appropriate modifications of goals, strategy concepts, and implementing actions. This total reevaluation is necessary both at the organization level and at the level of the total profession. It is a natural consequence of the fact that we are living in a dynamic world. Such a periodic reevaluation needs to take place at least once a year. The preparation of the annual budget indeed provides a very convenient opportunity to do this.

FINAL PERSPECTIVE

As we now view the total scene, what seems to be most significant is that there is an increasing complexity of the organization and its activities and hence an increasing range of opportunities for the internal auditor. This means that there is a rich growth market for internal auditing services. The next most significant conclusion is that the internal auditor is remarkably well positioned to exploit advantageously these opportunities. His position in the normal organization is unique, his credentials are excellent, and his prestige we believe is at the highest levels yet achieved. Admittedly, things can change and there is always the danger that internal auditing will become unduly complacent, and thus lose ground in relation to other company groups. But the total prospects on balance are most excellent for further progress.

The progress of internal auditing has come about for the most part through the performance of individual internal auditing departments in business and governmental organizations. This performance has been the basis for success in the individual organizations involved. In addition, that success has spilled over to other organizations through writing and speaking, especially through the medium of The Institute of Internal Auditors. The future progress of internal auditing will also be achieved in large part through these broader professional efforts. In the main, however, the progress of internal auditing has its basic roots in the achievements in the particular organizational situations. Individual internal auditors will thus, we think, continue to be the key figures in developing new concepts, methods, and approaches to effective practice. It will also be the leaders in practice who provide the impetus for broader professional efforts such as The Institute of Internal Auditors. Fortunately, the profession has been unusually blessed by having a large number of leaders who have provided both substance and inspiration.

But in a broader sense the professional progress depends on the accomplishments of *every* internal auditor. The objective is, therefore, to increase the level of performance of each individual and department in every organizational situation. The total objectives of the profession must, therefore, be to provide that individual help, and thus to add to the aggregate contributions to the needs of business, government, and society as a whole. At the same time each of us must do our part both in our own organizations and in the larger professional effort. By working together the further progress of internal auditing can thus be assured. Indeed, the accomplishments to date and the vigor of the current outreach indicate that internal auditors can face the future with high expectations.

APPENDICES

APPENDIX A

Statement of Responsibilities of Internal Auditing

STATEMENT OF RESPONSIBILITIES
OF INTERNAL AUDITING

The purpose of this statement is to provide in summary form a general understanding of the role and responsibilities of internal auditing. For more specific guidance, readers should refer to the *Standards for the Professional Practice of Internal Auditing*.

NATURE

Internal auditing is an independent appraisal activity established within an organization as a service to the organization. It is a control which functions by examining and evaluating the adequacy and effectiveness of other controls.

OBJECTIVE AND SCOPE

The objective of internal auditing is to assist members of the organization in the effective discharge of their responsibilities. To this end, internal auditing furnishes them with analyses, appraisals, recommendations, counsel, and information concerning the activities reviewed. The audit objective includes promoting effective control at reasonable cost.

The scope of internal auditing encompasses the examination and evaluation of the adequacy and effectiveness of the organization's system of internal control and the quality of performance in carrying out assigned responsibilities. The scope of internal auditing includes:

- Reviewing the reliability and integrity of financial and operating information and the means used to identify, measure, classify, and report such information.
- Reviewing the systems established to ensure compliance with those policies, plans, procedures, laws, and regulations which could have a significant impact on operations and reports, and determining whether the organization is in compliance.
- Reviewing the means of safeguarding assets and, as appropriate, verifying the existence of such assets.
- Appraising the economy and efficiency with which resources are employed.
- Reviewing operations or programs to ascertain whether results are consistent with established objectives and goals and whether the operations or programs are being carried out as planned.

RESPONSIBILITY AND AUTHORITY

Internal auditing functions under the policies established by management and the board. The purpose, authority and responsibility of the internal auditing department should be defined in a formal written document (charter), approved by management, and accepted by the board. The charter should make clear the purposes of the internal auditing department, specify the unrestricted scope of its work, and declare that auditors are to have no authority or responsibility for the activities they audit.

The responsibility of internal auditing is to serve the organization in a manner that is consistent with the *Standards for the Professional Practice of Internal Auditing* and with professional standards of conduct such as the *Code of Ethics* of The Institute of Internal Auditors, Inc. This responsibility includes coordinating internal audit activities with others so as to best achieve the audit objectives and the objectives of the organization.

INDEPENDENCE

Internal auditors should be independent of the activities they audit. Internal auditors are independent when they can carry out their work freely and objectively. Independence permits internal auditors to render the impartial and unbiased judgments essential to the proper conduct of audits. It is achieved through organizational status and objectivity.

Organizational status should be sufficient to assure a broad range of audit coverage, and adequate consideration of and effective action on audit findings and recommendations.

Objectivity requires that internal auditors have an independent mental attitude, and an honest belief in their work product. Drafting procedures, designing, installing, and operating systems, are not audit functions. Performing such activities is presumed to impair audit objectivity.

The *Statement of Responsibilities of Internal Auditors* was originally issued by The Institute of Internal Auditors in 1947. The current *Statement*, revised in 1981, embodies the concepts previously established and includes such changes as are deemed advisable in light of the present status of the profession.

Code of Ethics of
The Institute of Internal
Auditors

THE INSTITUTE OF INTERNAL AUDITORS, INC.
CODE OF ETHICS

INTRODUCTION: Recognizing that ethics are an important consideration in the practice of internal auditing and that the moral principles followed by members of *The Institute of Internal Auditors, Inc.*, should be formalized, the Board of Directors at its regular meeting in New Orleans on December 13, 1968, received and adopted the following resolution:

WHEREAS the members of *The Institute of Internal Auditors, Inc.*, represent the profession of internal auditing; and

WHEREAS managements rely on the profession of internal auditing to assist in the fulfillment of their management stewardship; and

WHEREAS said members must maintain high standards of conduct, honor and character in order to carry on proper and meaningful internal auditing practice;

THEREFORE BE IT RESOLVED that a Code of Ethics be now set forth, outlining the standards of professional behavior for the guidance of each member of *The Institute of Internal Auditors, Inc.*

In accordance with this resolution, the Board of Directors further approved of the principles set forth.

INTERPRETATION OF PRINCIPLES: The provisions of this Code of Ethics cover basic principles in the various disciplines of internal auditing practice. Members shall realize that individual judgment is required in the application of these principles. They have a responsibility to conduct themselves so that their good faith and integrity should not be open to question. While having due regard for the limit of their technical skills, they will promote the highest possible internal auditing standards to the end of advancing the interest of their company or organization.

ARTICLES:

I. Members shall have an obligation to exercise honesty, objectivity, and diligence in the performance of their duties and responsibilities.

II. Members, in holding the trust of their employers, shall exhibit loyalty in all matters pertaining to the affairs of the employer or to whomever they may be rendering a service. However, members shall not knowingly be a part to any illegal or improper activity.

III. Members shall refrain from entering into any activity which may be in conflict with the interest of their employers or which would prejudice their ability to carry out objectively their duties and responsibilities.

IV. Members shall not accept a fee or a gift from an employee, a client, a customer, or a business associate of their employer without the knowledge and consent of their senior management.

V. Members shall be prudent in the use of information acquired in the course of their duties. They shall not use confidential information for any personal gain nor in a manner which would be detrimental to the welfare of their employer.

VI. Members, in expressing an opinion, shall use all reasonable care to obtain sufficient factual evidence to warrant such expression. In their reporting, members shall reveal such material facts known to them, which, if not revealed, could either distort the report of the results of operations under review or conceal unlawful practice.

VII. Members shall continually strive for improvement in the proficiency and effectiveness of their service.

VIII. Members shall abide by the bylaws and uphold the objectives of *The Institute of Internal Auditors, Inc.* In the practice of their profession, they shall be ever mindful of their obligation to maintain the high standard of competence, morality, and dignity which *The Institute of Internal Auditors, Inc.*, and its members have established.

APPENDIX C

Standards for the Professional Practice of Internal Auditing

Standards for the Professional Practice of Internal Auditing [1]

The Institute of Internal Auditors, Inc.
Altamonte Springs, Florida

ISBN 0-89413-073-9

IIA79040 Mar79

First printing, August 1978
Second printing, October 1978
Third printing, March 1979

Copies of the *Standards* may be purchased from The Institute of Internal Auditors, Inc., International Headquarters, 249 Maitland Avenue, Altamonte Springs, Florida 32701. The price is $2.50 for a single copy and $1.00 for each additional copy. Payment must accompany order. **Order No. 462**.

Foreword

In 1941, The Institute of Internal Auditors, Inc. (IIA) was created by and for internal auditors. Today, IIA is the only international organization dedicated solely to the advancement of the individual internal auditor and the internal auditing profession. Since 1941, IIA has been instrumental in helping its members meet the generally accepted criteria of a profession by:

- adopting a *Code of Ethics*
- approving a *Statement of Responsibilities of Internal Auditors*
- establishing a program of continuing education
- developing a *Common Body of Knowledge*
- instituting a certification program

Adopting professional standards is another vital step in the development of internal auditing. To accomplish this, IIA formed the Professional Standards and Responsibilities Committee in 1974.

The *Standards for the Professional Practice of Internal Auditing* are the result of nearly three years of effort by that committee. These *Standards* are meant to serve the entire profession in all types of business, in various levels of government, and in all other organizations where internal auditors are found.

The term "standards," as used in this document, means the criteria by which the operations of an internal auditing department are evaluated and measured. They are intended to represent the practice of internal auditing as it should be, as judged and adopted by the Board of Directors of The Institute.

As internal auditing adapts to the continuous changes taking place in business and in society, our *Standards* will be modified from time to time to meet the changing needs of auditors everywhere.

The Institute of Internal Auditors is grateful to those governmental agencies, professional associations, internal and external auditors, and members of management, audit committees, and academe who provided guidance and assistance in the development of these *Standards*. It is deeply indebted to the following individuals and members of the IIA Practice Standards Subcommittee and their employers for their dedicated services:

Roger N. Carolus, CIA, CPA, Chairman
Northwest Bancorporation

Michael J. Barrett, DBA, Vice Chairman
University of Minnesota

R. Glen Berryman, PhD, CPA
Consultant, University of Minnesota

LaVonne Carpenter
  Northwest Bancorporation

M. A. Dittenhofer, PhD, CIA
  Association of Government Accountants

Donald E. Friedlander, CIA
  Honeywell, Inc.

Robert E. Gobeil, CIA, CA
  Alcan Smelters & Chemicals Ltd.

Robert E. Rivers, CIA
  IIA staff liaison

Lawrence B. Sawyer, JD, CIA
  Consultant

John F. Stucke, CIA
  The First National Bank of Boston

R. Scott Vaughan
  Aluminum Company of America

H. C. Warner, CIA
  IIA staff liaison

Organizations which already have established an internal audit function or are planning to establish one, are urged to adopt and support the *Standards for the Professional Practice of Internal Auditing* as a basis for guiding and measuring the function.

James R. Kelly, CIA, CPA
International President
1977-1978

W. J. Harmeyer, CIA, CPA
International President
1978-1979

The Institute of Internal Auditors, Inc.
International Professional Standards and Responsibilities Committee
1977-78

Roger N. Carolus, CIA, CPA, *Chairman* — Northwest Bancorporation, Minneapolis, Minnesota
Ernest W. Brindle, Standard Oil Co. (Indiana), Chicago, Illinois
Charles J. Doerner, CIA, The Penn Mutual Life Insurance Co., Philadelphia, Pennsylvania
William J. Duane, Jr., CPA, Manufacturers Hanover Trust Co., New York, New York
Charles L. Duly, MBE, CIA, FCCA, Standard Telephones & Cables, Cockfosters, Barnet, Hertfordshire, England
Donald E. Friedlander, CIA, Honeywell, Inc., Minneapolis, Minnesota
Clyde F. Haggard, Jr., CIA, CPA, El Paso Natural Gas Co., El Paso, Texas
Robert L. Jones, CIA, CA, Chartered Accountant, Calgary, Alberta, Canada
J. Cyrille Lavigne, CA, Department of National Revenue Taxation, Ottawa, Ontario, Canada
Robert P. Ness, CIA, Gamble & Associates, Pty. Ltd., Melbourne, Victoria, Australia
Stanley E. Petrie, CIA, CPA, Badger Meter, Inc., Milwaukee, Wisconsin
Charles E. Petry, CIA, Northwest Bancorporation, Minneapolis, Minnesota
Victor Phillips, CIA, FCA, Government of Canada, Ottawa, Ontario, Canada
Wilfred A. Ronck, CIA, Sun Oil Co., Dallas, Texas
John F. Stucke, CIA, The First National Bank of Boston, Boston, Massachusetts
Gordon A. Trew, CIA, John Swire & Sons (HK) Ltd., Hong Kong
R. Scott Vaughan, CIA, Aluminum Company of America, Pittsburgh, Pennsylvania

Board of Regents Representative
Robert E. Gobeil, CIA, CA, Alcan Smelters & Chemicals Ltd., Montreal, Quebec, Canada

IIA Staff
William E. Perry, CIA, CPA, Director of Professional Practice, The Institute of Internal Auditors, Inc.
Robert E. Rivers, CIA, Director of Certification, The Institute of Internal Auditors, Inc.
H. C. Warner, CIA, Manager of Professional Standards, The Institute of Internal Auditors, Inc.

Practice Standards Subcommittee — 1977-78
Roger N. Carolus, CIA, CPA, *Chairman,* Northwest Bancorporation, Minneapolis, Minnesota
Michael J. Barrett, DBA, *Vice Chairman,* University of Minnesota, Minneapolis, Minnesota
R. Glen Berryman, PhD, CPA, University of Minnesota, Minneapolis, Minnesota
Mortimer A. Dittenhofer, PhD, CIA, Association of Government Accountants, Gaithersburg, Maryland
Donald E. Friedlander, CIA, Honeywell, Inc., Minneapolis, Minnesota
Robert E. Gobeil, CIA, CA, Alcan Smelters & Chemicals Ltd., Montreal, Quebec, Canada
Lawrence B. Sawyer, JD, CIA, Consultant, Camarillo, California
John F. Stucke, CIA, The First National Bank of Boston, Boston, Massachusetts
R. Scott Vaughan, Aluminum Company of America, Pittsburgh, Pennsylvania

Administrative Assistant
LaVonne Carpenter, Northwest Bancorporation, Minneapolis, Minnesota

Staff Liaison
Robert E. Rivers, CIA, Director of Certification, The Institute of Internal Auditors, Inc.
H. C. Warner, CIA, Manager of Professional Standards, The Institute of Internal Auditors, Inc.

iii

Contents

Introduction

Internal auditing is an independent appraisal function established within an organization to examine and evaluate its activities as a service to the organization. The objective of internal auditing is to assist members of the organization in the effective discharge of their responsibilities. To this end, internal auditing furnishes them with analyses, appraisals, recommendations, counsel, and information concerning the activities reviewed.

The members of the organization assisted by internal auditing include those in management and the board of directors. Internal auditors owe a responsibility to both, providing them with information about the adequacy and effectiveness of the organization's system of internal control and the quality of performance. The information furnished to each may differ in format and detail, depending upon the requirements and requests of management and the board.

The internal auditing department is an integral part of the organization and functions under the policies established by management and the board. The statement of purpose, authority, and responsibility (charter) for the internal auditing department, approved by management and accepted by the board, should be consistent with these *Standards for the Professional Practice of Internal Auditing.*

The charter should make clear the purposes of the internal auditing department, specify the unrestricted scope of its work, and declare that auditors are to have no authority or responsibility for the activities they audit.

Throughout the world internal auditing is performed in diverse environments and within organizations which vary in purpose, size, and structure. In addition, the laws and customs within various countries differ from one another. These differences may affect the practice of internal auditing in each environment. The implementation of these *Standards*, therefore, will be governed by the environment in which the internal auditing department carries out its assigned responsibilities. But compliance with the concepts enunciated by these *Standards* is essential before the responsibilities of internal auditors can be met.

"Independence," as used in these *Standards*, requires clarification. Internal auditors must be independent of the activities they audit. Such independence permits internal auditors to perform their work freely and objectively. Without independence, the desired results of internal auditing cannot be realized.

In setting these *Standards*, the following developments were considered:

1. Boards of directors are being held increasingly accountable for the adequacy and effectiveness of their organizations' systems of internal control and quality of performance.

2. Members of management are demonstrating increased acceptance of internal auditing as a means of supplying objective analyses, appraisals, recommendations, counsel, and information on the organization's controls and performance.

3. External auditors are using the results of internal audits to complement their own work where the internal auditors have provided suitable evidence of independence and adequate, professional audit work.

In the light of such developments, the purposes of these *Standards* are to:

1

1. Impart an understanding of the role and responsibilities of internal auditing to all levels of management, boards of directors, public bodies, external auditors, and related professional organizations
2. Establish the basis for the guidance and measurement of internal auditing performance
3. Improve the practice of internal auditing

The *Standards* differentiate among the varied responsibilities of the organization, the internal auditing department, the director of internal auditing, and internal auditors.

The five general *Standards* are expressed in italicized statements in upper case. Following each of these general *Standards* are specific standards expressed in italicized statements in lower case. Accompanying each specific standard are guidelines describing suitable means of meeting that standard. The *Standards* encompass:

1. The independence of the internal auditing department from the activities audited and the objectivity of internal auditors
2. The proficiency of internal auditors and the professional care they should exercise
3. The scope of internal auditing work
4. The performance of internal auditing assignments
5. The management of the internal auditing department

The *Standards* and the accompanying guidelines employ three terms which have been given specific meanings. These are as follows:

The term *board* includes boards of directors, audit committees of such boards, heads of agencies or legislative bodies to whom internal auditors report, boards of governors or trustees of nonprofit organizations, and any other designated governing bodies of organizations.

The terms *director of internal auditing* and *director* identify the top position in an internal auditing department.

The term *internal auditing department* includes any unit or activity within an organization which performs internal auditing functions.

2

SUMMARY OF GENERAL AND SPECIFIC STANDARDS
FOR THE PROFESSIONAL PRACTICE OF INTERNAL AUDITING

100 **INDEPENDENCE** — *INTERNAL AUDITORS SHOULD BE INDEPENDENT OF THE ACTIVITIES THEY AUDIT.*

    110 **Organizational Status** — *The organizational status of the internal auditing department should be sufficient to permit the accomplishment of its audit responsibilities.*

    120 **Objectivity** — *Internal auditors should be objective in performing audits.*

200 **PROFESSIONAL PROFICIENCY** — *INTERNAL AUDITS SHOULD BE PERFORMED WITH PROFICIENCY AND DUE PROFESSIONAL CARE.*

    The Internal Auditing Department

    210 **Staffing** — *The internal auditing department should provide assurance that the technical proficiency and educational background of internal auditors are appropriate for the audits to be performed.*

    220 **Knowledge, Skills, and Disciplines** — *The internal auditing department should possess or should obtain the knowledge, skills, and disciplines needed to carry out its audit responsibilities.*

    230 **Supervision** — *The internal auditing department should provide assurance that internal audits are properly supervised.*

    The Internal Auditor

    240 **Compliance with Standards of Conduct** — *Internal auditors should comply with professional standards of conduct.*

    250 **Knowledge, Skills, and Disciplines** — *Internal auditors should possess the knowledge, skills, and disciplines essential to the performance of internal audits.*

    260 **Human Relations and Communications** — *Internal auditors should be skilled in dealing with people and in communicating effectively.*

    270 **Continuing Education** — *Internal auditors should maintain their technical competence through continuing education.*

    280 **Due Professional Care** — *Internal auditors should exercise due professional care in performing internal audits.*

300 **SCOPE OF WORK** — *THE SCOPE OF THE INTERNAL AUDIT SHOULD ENCOMPASS THE EXAMINATION AND EVALUATION OF THE ADEQUACY AND EFFECTIVENESS OF THE ORGANIZATION'S SYSTEM OF INTERNAL CONTROL AND THE QUALITY OF PERFORMANCE IN CARRYING OUT ASSIGNED RESPONSIBILITIES.*

    310 **Reliability and Integrity of Information** — *Internal auditors should review the reliability and integrity of financial and operating information and the means used to identify, measure, classify, and report such information.*

3

320 **Compliance with Policies, Plans, Procedures, Laws, and Regulations** — *Internal auditors should review the systems established to ensure compliance with those policies, plans, procedures, laws, and regulations which could have a significant impact on operations and reports and should determine whether the organization is in compliance.*

330 **Safeguarding of Assets** — *Internal auditors should review the means of safeguarding assets and, as appropriate, verify the existence of such assets.*

340 **Economical and Efficient Use of Resources** — *Internal auditors should appraise the economy and efficiency with which resources are employed.*

350 **Accomplishment of Established Objectives and Goals for Operations or Programs** — *Internal auditors should review operations or programs to ascertain whether results are consistent with established objectives and goals and whether the operations or programs are being carried out as planned.*

400 **PERFORMANCE OF AUDIT WORK** — *AUDIT WORK SHOULD INCLUDE PLANNING THE AUDIT, EXAMINING AND EVALUATING INFORMATION, COMMUNICATING RESULTS, AND FOLLOWING UP.*

410 **Planning the Audit** — *Internal auditors should plan each audit.*

420 **Examining and Evaluating Information** — *Internal auditors should collect, analyze, interpret, and document information to support audit results.*

430 **Communicating Results** — *Internal auditors should report the results of their audit work.*

440 **Following Up** — *Internal auditors should follow up to ascertain that appropriate action is taken on reported audit findings.*

500 **MANAGEMENT OF THE INTERNAL AUDITING DEPARTMENT** — *THE DIRECTOR OF INTERNAL AUDITING SHOULD PROPERLY MANAGE THE INTERNAL AUDITING DEPARTMENT.*

510 **Purpose, Authority, and Responsibility** — *The director of internal auditing should have a statement of purpose, authority, and responsibility for the internal auditing department.*

520 **Planning** — *The director of internal auditing should establish plans to carry out the responsibilities of the internal auditing department.*

530 **Policies and Procedures** — *The director of internal auditing should provide written policies and procedures to guide the audit staff.*

540 **Personnel Management and Development** — *The director of internal auditing should establish a program for selecting and developing the human resources of the internal auditing department.*

550 **External Auditors** — *The director of internal auditing should coordinate internal and external audit efforts.*

560 **Quality Assurance** — *The director of internal auditing should establish and maintain a quality assurance program to evaluate the operations of the internal auditing department.*

100   **INDEPENDENCE**

                INTERNAL AUDITORS SHOULD BE INDEPENDENT
                    OF THE ACTIVITIES THEY AUDIT.

.01   Internal auditors are independent when they can carry out their work freely and objectively. Independence permits internal auditors to render the impartial and unbiased judgments essential to the proper conduct of audits. It is achieved through organizational status and objectivity.

110   **Organizational Status**

The organizational status of the internal auditing department should be sufficient to permit the accomplishment of its audit responsibilities.

.01   Internal auditors should have the support of management and of the board of directors so that they can gain the cooperation of auditees and perform their work free from interference.

.1   The director of the internal auditing department should be responsible to an individual in the organization with sufficient authority to promote independence and to ensure broad audit coverage, adequate consideration of audit reports, and appropriate action on audit recommendations.

.2   The director should have direct communication with the board. Regular communication with the board helps assure independence and provides a means for the board and the director to keep each other informed on matters of mutual interest.

.3   Independence is enhanced when the board concurs in the appointment or removal of the director of the internal auditing department.

.4   The purpose, authority, and responsibility of the internal auditing department should be defined in a formal written document (charter). The director should seek approval of the charter by management as well as acceptance by the board. The charter should (a) establish the department's position within the organization; (b) authorize access to records, personnel, and physical properties relevant to the performance of audits; and (c) define the scope of internal auditing activities.

.5   The director of internal auditing should submit annually to management for approval and to the board for its information a summary of the department's audit work schedule, staffing plan, and financial budget. The director should also submit all significant interim changes for approval and information. Audit work schedules, staffing plans, and financial budgets should inform management and the board of the scope of internal auditing work and of any limitations placed on that scope.

.6   The director of internal auditing should submit activity reports to management and to the board annually or more frequently as necessary. Activity reports should highlight significant audit findings and recommendations and should inform management and the board of any significant deviations from approved audit work schedules, staffing plans, and financial budgets, and the reasons for them.

120 Objectivity

Internal auditors should be objective in performing audits.

.01   Objectivity is an independent mental attitude which internal auditors should maintain in performing audits. Internal auditors are not to subordinate their judgment on audit matters to that of others.

.02   Objectivity requires internal auditors to perform audits in such a manner that they have an honest belief in their work product and that no significant quality compromises are made. Internal auditors are not to be placed in situations in which they feel unable to make objective professional judgments.

.1   Staff assignments should be made so that potential and actual conflicts of interest and bias are avoided. The director should periodically obtain from the audit staff information concerning potential conflicts of interest and bias.

.2   Internal auditors should report to the director any situations in which a conflict of interest or bias is present or may reasonably be inferred. The director should then reassign such auditors.

.3   Staff assignments of internal auditors should be rotated periodically whenever it is practicable to do so.

.4   Internal auditors should not assume operating responsibilities. But if on occasion management directs internal auditors to perform nonaudit work, it should be understood that they are not functioning as internal auditors. Moreover, objectivity is presumed to be impaired when internal auditors audit any activity for which they had authority or responsibility. This impairment should be considered when reporting audit results.

.5   Persons transferred to or temporarily engaged by the internal auditing department should not be assigned to audit those activities they previously performed until a reasonable period of time has elapsed. Such assignments are presumed to impair objectivity and should be considered when supervising the audit work and reporting audit results.

.6   The results of internal auditing work should be reviewed before the related audit report is released to provide reasonable assurance that the work was performed objectively.

.03   The internal auditor's objectivity is not adversely affected when the auditor recommends standards of control for systems or reviews procedures before they are implemented. Designing, installing, and operating systems are not audit functions. Also, the drafting of procedures for systems is not an audit function. Performing such activities is presumed to impair audit objectivity.

200   **PROFESSIONAL PROFICIENCY**
                    INTERNAL AUDITS SHOULD BE PERFORMED WITH
                    PROFICIENCY AND DUE PROFESSIONAL CARE.

.01   Professional proficiency is the responsibility of the internal auditing department and each internal auditor. The department should assign to each audit those persons who collectively possess the necessary knowledge, skills, and disciplines to conduct the audit properly.

The Internal Auditing Department
210   **Staffing**
The internal auditing department should provide assurance that the technical proficiency and educational background of internal auditors are appropriate for the audits to be performed.
.01   The director of internal auditing should establish suitable criteria of education and experience for filling internal auditing positions, giving due consideration to scope of work and level of responsibility.
.02   Reasonable assurance should be obtained as to each prospective auditor's qualifications and proficiency.

220   **Knowledge, Skills, and Disciplines**
The internal auditing department should possess or should obtain the knowledge, skills, and disciplines needed to carry out its audit responsibilities.
.01   The internal auditing staff should collectively possess the knowledge and skills essential to the practice of the profession within the organization. These attributes include proficiency in applying internal auditing standards, procedures, and techniques.
.02   The internal auditing department should have employees or use consultants who are qualified in such disciplines as accounting, economics, finance, statistics, electronic data processing, engineering, taxation, and law as needed to meet audit responsibilities. Each member of the department, however, need not be qualified in all of these disciplines.

230   **Supervision**
The internal auditing department should provide assurance that internal audits are properly supervised.
.01   The director of internal auditing is responsible for providing appropriate audit supervision. Supervision is a continuing process, beginning with planning and ending with the conclusion of the audit assignment.
.02   Supervision includes:
    .1   Providing suitable instructions to subordinates at the outset of the audit and approving the audit program
    .2   Seeing that the approved audit program is carried out unless deviations are both justified and authorized
    .3   Determining that audit working papers adequately support the audit findings, conclusions, and reports
    .4   Making sure that audit reports are accurate, objective, clear, concise, constructive, and timely
    .5   Determining that audit objectives are being met

.03 Appropriate evidence of supervision should be documented and retained.

.04 The extent of supervision required will depend on the proficiency of the internal auditors and the difficulty of the audit assignment.

.05 All internal auditing assignments, whether performed by or for the internal auditing department, remain the responsibility of its director.

The Internal Auditor

240   Compliance with Standards of Conduct

Internal auditors should comply with professional standards of conduct.

.01 The *Code of Ethics* of The Institute of Internal Auditors sets forth standards of conduct and provides a basis for enforcement among its members. The *Code* calls for high standards of honesty, objectivity, diligence, and loyalty to which internal auditors should conform.

250   Knowledge, Skills, and Disciplines

Internal auditors should possess the knowledge, skills, and disciplines essential to the performance of internal audits.

.01 Each internal auditor should possess certain knowledge and skills as follows:

.1 Proficiency in applying internal auditing standards, procedures, and techniques is required in performing internal audits. Proficiency means the ability to apply knowledge to situations likely to be encountered and to deal with them without extensive recourse to technical research and assistance.

.2 Proficiency in accounting principles and techniques is required of auditors who work extensively with financial records and reports.

.3 An understanding of management principles is required to recognize and evaluate the materiality and significance of deviations from good business practice. An understanding means the ability to apply broad knowledge to situations likely to be encountered, to recognize significant deviations, and to be able to carry out the research necessary to arrive at reasonable solutions.

.4 An appreciation is required of the fundamentals of such subjects as accounting, economics, commercial law, taxation, finance, quantitative methods, and computerized information systems. An appreciation means the ability to recognize the existence of problems or potential problems and to determine the further research to be undertaken or the assistance to be obtained.

260   Human Relations and Communications

Internal auditors should be skilled in dealing with people and in communicating effectively.

.01 Internal auditors should understand human relations and maintain satisfactory relationships with auditees.

.02 Internal auditors should be skilled in oral and written communications so that they can clearly and effectively convey such matters

as audit objectives, evaluations, conclusions, and recommendations.

270 **Continuing Education**

Internal auditors should maintain their technical competence through continuing education.

.01 Internal auditors are responsible for continuing their education in order to maintain their proficiency. They should keep informed about improvements and current developments in internal auditing standards, procedures, and techniques. Continuing education may be obtained through membership and participation in professional societies; attendance at conferences, seminars, college courses, and in-house training programs; and participation in research projects.

280 **Due Professional Care**

Internal Auditors should exercise due professional care in performing internal audits.

.01 Due professional care calls for the application of the care and skill expected of a reasonably prudent and competent internal auditor in the same or similar circumstances. Professional care should, therefore, be appropriate to the complexities of the audit being performed. In exercising due professional care, internal auditors should be alert to the possibility of intentional wrongdoing, errors and omissions, inefficiency, waste, ineffectiveness, and conflicts of interest. They should also be alert to those conditions and activities where irregularities are most likely to occur. In addition, they should identify inadequate controls and recommend improvements to promote compliance with acceptable procedures and practices.

.02 Due care implies reasonable care and competence, not infallibility or extraordinary performance. Due care requires the auditor to conduct examinations and verifications to a reasonable extent, but does not require detailed audits of all transactions. Accordingly, the internal auditor cannot give absolute assurance that noncompliance or irregularities do not exist. Nevertheless, the possibility of material irregularities or noncompliance should be considered whenever the internal auditor undertakes an internal auditing assignment.

.03 When an internal auditor suspects wrongdoing, the appropriate authorities within the organization should be informed. The internal auditor may recommend whatever investigation is considered necessary in the circumstances. Thereafter, the auditor should follow up to see that the internal auditing department's responsibilities have been met.

.04 Exercising due professional care means using reasonable audit skill and judgment in performing the audit. To this end, the internal auditor should consider:

.1 The extent of audit work needed to achieve audit objectives
.2 The relative materiality or significance of matters to which audit procedures are applied
.3 The adequacy and effectiveness of internal controls
.4 The cost of auditing in relation to potential benefits

.05 Due professional care includes evaluating established operating standards and determining whether those standards are acceptable and are being met. When such standards are vague, authoritative interpretations should be sought. If internal auditors are required to interpret or select operating standards, they should seek agreement with auditees as to the standards needed to measure operating performance.

300   **SCOPE OF WORK**

*THE SCOPE OF THE INTERNAL AUDIT SHOULD ENCOMPASS
THE EXAMINATION AND EVALUATION OF THE ADEQUACY
AND EFFECTIVENESS OF THE ORGANIZATION'S SYSTEM OF
INTERNAL CONTROL AND THE QUALITY OF PERFORMANCE
IN CARRYING OUT ASSIGNED RESPONSIBILITIES.*

.01 The scope of internal auditing work, as specified in this standard, encompasses what audit work should be performed. It is recognized, however, that management and the board of directors provide general direction as to the scope of work and the activities to be audited.

.02 The purpose of the review for adequacy of the system of internal control is to ascertain whether the system established provides reasonable assurance that the organization's objectives and goals will be met efficiently and economically.

.03 The purpose of the review for effectiveness of the system of internal control is to ascertain whether the system is functioning as intended.

.04 The purpose of the review for quality of performance is to ascertain whether the organization's objectives and goals have been achieved.

.05 The primary objectives of internal control are to ensure:

.1 The reliability and integrity of information

.2 Compliance with policies, plans, procedures, laws, and regulations

.3 The safeguarding of assets

.4 The economical and efficient use of resources

.5 The accomplishment of established objectives and goals for operations or programs

310 **Reliability and Integrity of Information**

Internal auditors should review the reliability and integrity of financial and operating information and the means used to identify, measure, classify, and report such information.

.01 Information systems provide data for decision making, control, and compliance with external requirements. Therefore, internal auditors should examine information systems and, as appropriate, ascertain whether:

.1 Financial and operating records and reports contain accurate, reliable, timely, complete, and useful information.

.2 Controls over record keeping and reporting are adequate and effective.

320 **Compliance with Policies, Plans, Procedures, Laws and Regulations**

Internal auditors should review the systems established to ensure compliance with those policies, plans, procedures, laws, and regulations which could have a significant impact on operations and reports, and should determine whether the organization is in compliance.

.01 Management is responsible for establishing the systems designed to ensure compliance with such requirements as policies, plans, procedures, and applicable laws and regulations. Internal auditors are responsible for

determining whether the systems are adequate and effective and whether the activities audited are complying with the appropriate requirements.

330 Safeguarding of Assets

Internal auditors should review the means of safeguarding assets and, as appropriate, verify the existence of such assets.

.01 Internal auditors should review the means used to safeguard assets from various types of losses such as those resulting from theft, fire, improper or illegal activities, and exposure to the elements.

.02 Internal auditors, when verifying the existence of assets, should use appropriate audit procedures.

340 Economical and Efficient Use of Resources

Internal auditors should appraise the economy and efficiency with which resources are employed.

.01 Management is responsible for setting operating standards to measure an activity's economical and efficient use of resources. Internal auditors are responsible for determining whether:

   .1 Operating standards have been established for measuring economy and efficiency.

   .2 Established operating standards are understood and are being met.

   .3 Deviations from operating standards are identified, analyzed, and communicated to those responsible for corrective action.

   .4 Corrective action has been taken.

.02 Audits related to the economical and efficient use of resources should identify such conditions as:

   .1 Underutilized facilities

   .2 Nonproductive work

   .3 Procedures which are not cost justified

   .4 Overstaffing or understaffing

350 Accomplishment of Established Objectives and Goals for Operations or Programs

Internal auditors should review operations or programs to ascertain whether results are consistent with established objectives and goals and whether the operations or programs are being carried out as planned.

.01 Management is responsible for establishing operating or program objectives and goals, developing and implementing control procedures, and accomplishing desired operating or program results. Internal auditors should ascertain whether such objectives and goals conform with those of the organization and whether they are being met.

.02 Internal auditors can provide assistance to managers who are developing objectives, goals, and systems by determining whether the underlying assumptions are appropriate; whether accurate, current, and relevant information is being used; and whether suitable controls have been incorporated into the operations or programs.

400   **PERFORMANCE OF AUDIT WORK**

AUDIT WORK SHOULD INCLUDE PLANNING THE AUDIT,
EXAMINING AND EVALUATING INFORMATION,
COMMUNICATING RESULTS, AND FOLLOWING UP.

.01   The internal auditor is responsible for planning and conducting the audit assignment, subject to supervisory review and approval.

410 **Planning the Audit**
Internal auditors should plan each audit.
.01   Planning should be documented and should include:
   .1 Establishing audit objectives and scope of work
   .2 Obtaining background information about the activities to be audited
   .3 Determining the resources necessary to perform the audit
   .4 Communicating with all who need to know about the audit
   .5 Performing, as appropriate, an on-site survey to become familiar with the activities and controls to be audited, to identify areas for audit emphasis, and to invite auditee comments and suggestions
   .6 Writing the audit program
   .7 Determining how, when, and to whom audit results will be communicated
   .8 Obtaining approval of the audit work plan

420 **Examining and Evaluating Information**
Internal auditors should collect, analyze, interpret, and document information to support audit results.
.01   The process of examining and evaluating information is as follows:
   .1 Information should be collected on all matters related to the audit objectives and scope of work.
   .2 Information should be sufficient, competent, relevant, and useful to provide a sound basis for audit findings and recommendations.

   Sufficient information is factual, adequate, and convincing so that a prudent, informed person would reach the same conclusions as the auditor.
   Competent information is reliable and the best attainable through the use of appropriate audit techniques.
   Relevant information supports audit findings and recommendations and is consistent with the objectives for the audit.
   Useful information helps the organization meet its goals.
   .3 Audit procedures, including the testing and sampling techniques employed, should be selected in advance, where practicable, and expanded or altered if circumstances warrant.
   .4 The process of collecting, analyzing, interpreting, and documenting information should be supervised to provide

400-1

reasonable assurance that the auditor's objectivity is maintained and that audit goals are met.

.5 Working papers that document the audit should be prepared by the auditor and reviewed by management of the internal auditing department. These papers should record the information obtained and the analyses made and should support the bases for the findings and recommendations to be reported.

430 **Communicating Results**

Internal auditors should report the results of their audit work.

.1 A signed, written report should be issued after the audit examination is completed. Interim reports may be written or oral and may be transmitted formally or informally.

.2 The internal auditor should discuss conclusions and recommendations at appropriate levels of management before issuing final written reports.

.3 Reports should be objective, clear, concise, constructive, and timely.

.4 Reports should present the purpose, scope, and results of the audit; and, where appropriate, reports should contain an expression of the auditor's opinion.

.5 Reports may include recommendations for potential improvements and acknowledge satisfactory performance and corrective action.

.6 The auditee's views about audit conclusions or recommendations may be included in the audit report.

.7 The director of internal auditing or designee should review and approve the final audit report before issuance and should decide to whom the report will be distributed.

440 **Following Up**

Internal auditors should follow up to ascertain that appropriate action is taken on reported audit findings.

.01 Internal auditing should determine that corrective action was taken and is achieving the desired results, or that management or the board has assumed the risk of not taking corrective action on reported findings.

500 **MANAGEMENT OF THE INTERNAL AUDITING DEPARTMENT**

THE DIRECTOR OF INTERNAL AUDITING SHOULD
PROPERLY MANAGE THE INTERNAL AUDITING DEPARTMENT.

.01 The director of internal auditing is responsible for properly managing the department so that:

    .1 Audit work fulfills the general purposes and responsibilities approved by management and accepted by the board.

    .2 Resources of the internal auditing department are efficiently and effectively employed.

    .3 Audit work conforms to the *Standards for the Professional Practice of Internal Auditing.*

510 **Purpose, Authority, and Responsibility**

The director of internal auditing should have a statement of purpose, authority, and responsibility for the internal auditing department.

.01 The director of internal auditing is responsible for seeking the approval of management and the acceptance by the board of a formal written document (charter) for the internal auditing department.

520 **Planning**

The director of internal auditing should establish plans to carry out the responsibilities of the internal auditing department.

.01 These plans should be consistent with the internal auditing department's charter and with the goals of the organization.

.02 The planning process involves establishing:

    .1 Goals

    .2 Audit work schedules

    .3 Staffing plans and financial budgets

    .4 Activity reports

.03 The *goals* of the internal auditing department should be capable of being accomplished within specified operating plans and budgets and, to the extent possible, should be measurable. They should be accompanied by measurement criteria and targeted dates of accomplishment.

.04 *Audit work schedules* should include (a) what activities are to be audited; (b) when they will be audited; and (c) the estimated time required, taking into account the scope of the audit work planned and the nature and extent of audit work performed by others. Matters to be considered in establishing audit work schedule priorities should include (a) the date and results of the last audit; (b) financial exposure; (c) potential loss and risk; (d) requests by management; (e) major changes in operations, programs, systems, and controls; (f) opportunities to achieve operating benefits; and (g) changes to and capabilities of the audit staff. The work schedules should be sufficiently flexible to cover unanticipated demands on the internal auditing department.

.05 *Staffing plans and financial budgets*, including the number of auditors and the knowledge, skills, and disciplines required to perform their work, should be determined from audit work schedules, administrative

activities, education and training requirements, and audit research and development efforts.

.06 *Activity reports* should be submitted periodically to management and to the board. These reports should compare (a) performance with the department's goals and audit work schedules and (b) expenditures with financial budgets. They should explain the reasons for major variances and indicate any action taken or needed.

530 Policies and Procedures

The director of internal auditing should provide written policies and procedures to guide the audit staff.

.01 The form and content of written policies and procedures should be appropriate to the size and structure of the internal auditing department and the complexity of its work. Formal administrative and technical audit manuals may not be needed by all internal auditing departments. A small internal auditing department may be managed informally. Its audit staff may be directed and controlled through daily, close supervision and written memoranda. In a large internal auditing department, more formal and comprehensive policies and procedures are essential to guide the audit staff in the consistent compliance with the department's standards of performance.

540 Personnel Management and Development

The director of internal auditing should establish a program for selecting and developing the human resources of the internal auditing department.

.01 The program should provide for:

.1 Developing written job descriptions for each level of the audit staff

.2 Selecting qualified and competent individuals

.3 Training and providing continuing educational opportunities for each internal auditor

.4 Appraising each internal auditor's performance at least annually

.5 Providing counsel to internal auditors on their performance and professional development

550 External Auditors

The director of internal auditing should coordinate internal and external audit efforts.

.01 The internal and external audit work should be coordinated to ensure adequate audit coverage and to minimize duplicate efforts.

.02 Coordination of audit efforts involves:

.1 Periodic meetings to discuss matters of mutual interest

.2 Access to each other's audit programs and working papers

.3 Exchange of audit reports and management letters

.4 Common understanding of audit techniques, methods, and terminology

560 Quality Assurance

The director of internal auditing should establish and maintain a quality

assurance program to evaluate the operations of the internal auditing department.

.01   The purpose of this program is to provide reasonable assurance that audit work conforms with these *Standards*, the internal auditing department's charter, and other applicable standards. A quality assurance program should include the following elements:

.1   Supervision

.2   Internal reviews

.3   External reviews

.02   *Supervision* of the work of the internal auditors should be carried out continually to assure conformance with internal auditing standards, departmental policies, and audit programs.

.03   *Internal reviews* should be performed periodically by members of the internal auditing staff to appraise the quality of the audit work performed. These reviews should be performed in the same manner as any other internal audit.

.04   *External reviews* of the internal auditing department should be performed to appraise the quality of the department's operations. These reviews should be performed by qualified persons who are independent of the organization and who do not have either a real or an apparent conflict of interest. Such reviews should be conducted at least once every three years. On completion of the review, a formal, written report should be issued. The report should express an opinion as to the department's compliance with the *Standards for the Professional Practice of Internal Auditing* and, as appropriate, should include recommendations for improvement.

APPENDIX D

Manual Supplement

Department of the Treasury
Internal Revenue Service

September 27, 1978

STATISTICAL SAMPLING PROCEDURES IN THE EXAMINATION OF ACCOUNTING RECORDS

Section 1. Purpose

This Supplement provides general guidelines and procedures to be followed whenever statistical sampling techniques are employed in an examination.

Section 2. Background

.01 For some time, the Service has been exploring the use of statistical (probability) sampling techniques in tax examinations, where effective use of resources make it uneconomical to audit voluminous accounting data. Statistical sampling techniques are permitted under the generally accepted auditing standards of the accounting profession. Also, several Revenue Procedures have been published which specifically allow its use by taxpayers in certain situations (e.g., trading stamps and revolving credit plans); however, the Service has not, up to now, made general use of scientific statistical sampling techniques in its examinations.

.02 The Office of the Chief Counsel and the Department of Justice have jointly analyzed the legal ramifications of utilizing probability sampling techniques in the examination of large accounts, and have concluded that substantial authority exists for the determination of tax deficiencies based on statistical samples.

.03 The application of statistical sampling audit techniques should be confined to those revenue agents who have received training in the principles and use of statistical sampling. The application of these principles to tax examinations holds the potential of substantially increasing both the efficiency and quality of IRS examinations.

Section 3. Scope

.01   The instructions contained herein are designed to:

1.   Ensure that estimates of adjustments to tax liabilities resulting from statistical samples are statistically sound and legally defensible; and

2.   Ensure the fair and equitable treatment of taxpayers examined by using statistical sampling techniques.

.02   A comprehensive discussion of statistical methods and procedures is beyond the intent and scope of this document. Such information is presented in Training Course 3172, Statistical Sampling for Audit Personnel, and Course 3174, Advanced Statistical Sampling for Audit Personnel. As problems arise in the area of statistics which are beyond the knowledge and expertise of field personnel, they should be referred to the Director, Examination Division, National Office, Attention CP:E:E:C

Section 4. General Instructions

.01   Projections obtained from examination of statistical (probability) samples of accounting records may be used as the basis for proposing adjustments to items reported on a tax return.

.02   Statistical sampling should be considered whenever a group of accounting entries or transactions has sufficient adjustment potential to warrant examination, but the examination of the totality of all such transactions is prohibitive in terms of time and resources. In any audit situation where it is reasonable to examine 100% of the items under consideration, statistical sampling techniques should not be used.

.03   In most sampling situations, it is possible to estimate, with some degree of reliability, the incremental beneficial effect of increasing the sample size. This may be obtained by determining the variability of the items in question. The decision on sample precision and thus on sample size is to be made after performing such an analysis.

Section 5. Determination of Proposed Population Adjustment

.01   As a general rule, the proposed population adjustment will be determined, such that, 95% of the time, it will not be greater than the actual adjustment obtainable by a 100% examination of the population. This applies regardless of whether the adjustment favors the government or the taxpayer.

.02   The above result will be attained by using the lower limit of the estimated population adjustment at the 95% confidence level. (The estimated population adjustment is also referred to as the point estimate.) This lower limit will generally be computed by subtracting the sampling error (the standard error of the estimated population adjustment multiplied by 1.65) from the population adjustment. (The population adjustment is derived by multiplying the average adjustment for the sample by the number of items in the population.) In making the computation, the following specific rules should be applied; in applying these rules, an adjustment which reduces an expense or increases income is considered positive in sign.

1.   If the point estimate is positive and greater than the sampling error, the proposed population adjustment is obtained by subtracting the sampling error from the point estimate.

2.   If the point estimate is positive and is less than the sampling error, either select additional sampling units to attempt to reduce the sampling error or abandon the sampling plan and propose only those adjustments specifically identified.

3.   If the point estimate is negative, and the sampling error is less than the absolute value of this adjustment, the proposed population adjustment is obtained by adding the sampling error to the point estimate.

4.   If the point estimate is negative, and the sampling error is greater than the absolute value of this adjustment, either select additional sampling units to attempt to reduce the sampling error or abandon the sampling plan and propose only those adjustments specifically identified.

.04   An exception to the general rule, stated in .01 above, occurs whenever both of the following occur:

1.   The Code or Regulations provide for determination of portions of a tax liability on what may of necessity be an estimated value (e.g., certain determinations of fair market value or inventory values), and

2.   The sampling error at the 95% confidence level is less than 10% of the point estimate.

.05   Under such circumstances as stated in 1 and 2 above, it is appropriate to use the point estimate as the basis for the proposed population adjustment.

.06   Whenever two or more accounting populations for a particular tax return are examined, a stratified sampling situation exists, and statistically the sample result and sampling errors can be combined according to the rules for a stratified sample. However, combining strata which cross natural account categories will cause difficulties for Revenue Agent Report (RAR) and Notice of Deficiency purposes. Therefore, examiners are restricted to the combination of strata within a line item category on the tax return. For example, if a travel and entertainment account, and a repair and maintenance account are sampled, separate projections of the population adjustment for each type of account must be made. (These projections cannot be combined.) But if the travel and entertainment accounts in a number of separate divisions are independently sampled, the results from each division should be combined to arrive at an overall adjustment to the total travel and entertainment expense claimed on the tax return. (The word "projection" as used in this Supplement is synonymous with the proposed population adjustment applied only to the sampled population.)

Section 6. Sampling Procedures

.01   Sampling units should be selected for the sample based on random number selection techniques. Systematic (nth item) selection methods should not be used.

.02   Any unusually large transactions should be grouped into a separate stratum and examined in their entirety. Transactions should only be considered unusually large in terms of magnitude.

.03   In stratified sampling situations, a stratum could be deleted or added to the population without affecting the validity of the sample; however, there should be sound reasons for doing so.

.04   The examiner must come to a conclusion as to the correctness of each item in the sample. It is never valid to replace a sample item that is included in the sampling design with another sample item which is not included in the sampling design, merely because documentation is unavailable or difficult to obtain.

.05   The decision reached as to the validity of any sample item must be the same as the conclusion which would be reached if that item were encountered in a 100% examination.

Section 7. Related Entries Originating from a Sampled Transaction

.01   All business transactions generate a minimum of two accounting entries. Frequently, multiple entries are generated. The correctness of a particular entry, whether sampling is used or not, can only be determined by reviewing the transaction in its entirety.

.02   In analyzing individual entries generated by a transaction, the examiner must deal with two types of problems: determining the validity of an entry, and determining the associated adjustments to other accounts when errors are encountered. These problems must be properly dealt with in any audit; however, if sampling techniques are being used, special care must be taken. The following principles should be observed when using sampling methods.

1.   Adjustments with Sampled Accounts:

a.   The examiner should review the basic documents supporting a sample entry in order to determine how the taxpayer handled the entire transaction. If the examiner feels the transaction was handled improperly, it must be decided how it should have been handled.

b.   The way the examiner allocates adjustments among the various entries must not be influenced by which entries are drawn in the sample and which are not.

c.   If, within a population which is to be sampled, errors in specific entries are known to exist beforehand, these entries, if substantial, should be separated into a separate stratum and examined in their entirety. However, if after the sample is drawn, specific adjustments to items not part of the sample are discovered, projections must be based only on items selected in the sample. This does not preclude making adjustments to related entries in other accounts that are not subjected to sampling; nor does it preclude the option of abandoning the sample and proposing only those adjustments specifically identified.

d.   No adjustment to a sample entry should be made unless that particular entry can be shown to be in error. The amount of the adjustment to a sample entry should not include any adjustment that properly belongs to some other entry.

e.   In those instances where an adjustment applies not to a specific entry, but to a group of related entries, it is appropriate to allocate the total error in the group over all involved entries in proportion to the reported value of each entry.

f.   A sample entry that has been totally offset by a reversing entry anywhere in the same account is considered to be correct and is not to be adjusted.

2.   Associated Adjustments to Other Accounts:

a.   When adjustments are made to sample entries in an expense account, the normal procedure for making associated adjustments to asset accounts, depreciation, investment credit, etc., cannot be followed. As the adjustment to the sample items will be projected to a larger total, so must the associated adjustments be projected to a corresponding level.

b.   When an examination of sample items results in the capitalization of amounts for which the taxpayer is entitled to an allowance for depreciation, two separate projections must be made—one for adjustments resulting from the capitalization of items for which depreciation is allowable and one for all other adjustments. The sampling errors must be computed independently and separate adjustments determined as described in Section 5 above.

c.   Since the projected adjustment from capitalized items will generally be based on the lower confidence limit of the estimated population adjustment, the ratio of the lower confidence limit to the amount of adjustment in the sample (before projection) is to be used to derive the projected value of the associated adjustment characteristic. It must be remembered, however, that these projected adjustments represent aggregate values rather than specific identifiable assets.

d.   Projected depreciation write-offs in subsequent years can be determined by first computing the depreciation which would be allowable on the items in the sample (without projection) and then applying a multiplier to project the write-off to the total amount actually capitalized. The multiplier is derived by computing the ratio described in Section 7.022c above for the amount capitalized; i.e., the total projected adjustment for items capitalized (lower confidence limit) divided by the actual amount of capital items in the sample (before projection).

Section 8. Coordination with Appeals Division

Upon receipt of cases containing issues which involve statistical sampling techniques, the regional Appeals offices should notify the Director, Appeals Division, Attention: CP:AP:SS, so that appropriate coordination can be maintained.

Section 9. Effect on Other Documents

.01   This supplements IRM 42(13)0.

.02   This also supplements IRM 8240, and this "effect" should be annotated by pen and ink, beside the text cited, with a reference to this Supplement.

/s/ John L. Wedick, Jr.
Director, Examination Division

Index